$50.00

THE BOOK OF
BUSINESS
KNOWLEDGE

By the Editors and Experts
of Boardroom Reports

BOARDROOM® BOOKS

330 West 42nd Street, New York, New York 10036

Second Revised Edition
Second Printing

Library of Congress Cataloging in Publication Data
Main entry under title:
The Book of Business Knowledge.

    Includes index.
    1. Business—Addresses, essays, lectures.
2. Industrial management—Addresses, essays, lectures.
I. Boardroom reports.
HF5351.B652   1983   658   83-11754
ISBN 0-932648-44-4

Printed in United States of America

CONTENTS

CONTENTS

CONTENTS

CONTENTS

CONTENTS

ADVERTISING

STRATEGIES

HOW TO APPLY 'POSITIONING'

Successful advertising should hinge on *the unique selling proposition*, i.e., the particular merit that distinguishes a product and makes it meaningful to consumers.

WELL-KNOWN NAME TRAP. Millions of dollars have been lost by corporations because of one very simple mistake: They failed to understand that trade names stand for something specific in the consumer's mind.

Singer stands for sewing machines. So when Singer bought Friden, the business machine maker, and put the Singer name on the Friden machines, consumers got confused. Singer's years of advertising positioned it with the consumer as the maker of top-notch sewing machines—not business machines. The massive write-off of Singer's business machine losses was one of the biggest in U.S. history.

Other examples abound: Bic (the manufacturer of inexpensive ball-point pens) unsuccessfully tried such trade name extension with panty hose. Coke came out with Tab as its diet cola, and Pepsi came out with Diet Pepsi, which, to no one's surprise, trailed Tab by wide margins.

This is called the *well-known name trap:* After all, the logic goes, if our name is so important and well known, it should rub off on any new product, **even if it's in a different field. But it** leaves the wrong image, the incorrect *position*, in the consumer's mind. And consumers don't like to be confused.

The great exception: When you're No. 1. *Example:* Where does the 800-pound gorilla sleep? Wherever he damn pleases—because no one is going to tell *him* what to do. So it is with the No. 1 firm. Having been there first with the most leaves it in the position of the 800-pound gorilla.

Warning: If the product is No. 2, it's suicide to try to position it as No. 1. The consumer knows it's not and won't believe anything else the company says.

Hence: 7-Up fights Coke by positioning itself as, "When you're ready for a change of pace—the Uncola."

MARKETING AND WAR STRATEGY. The best book on marketing is a war strategy book by Carl von Clausewitz, a Prussian general of the early 19th Century. Its title: *On War* (Pelican Classics, (625 Madison Ave., NY 10022). Its major point, as interpreted to relate to marketing:

• *An army of superior force will nearly always beat an army with an inferior force.* So don't try to butt a $100,000 ad budget against a product that has a million-dollar ad budget. For the smaller ad budget to have any effect, it must find a new *position*.

• *The army with a superior defense (it dug in first) will always be in a stronger position.* Thus, there are times when testing might be cut short, to keep the time advantage over the competition as wide as possible.

• *The value of strategic reserves.* The urgent need is to mobilize as much focused force as possible at the moment of battle, or product introduction. The company that halfheartedly spends on a product will likely get halfhearted results. That's not to say that the marketing budget should be spent in one big surge—but strategic funds should be available whenever needed.

Source: Al Reis, chairman, Reis Cappiello Coldwell. For more information, send for *The Positioning Era*, free from Reis Cappiello Coldwell, 1212 Ave. of the Americas, New York 10020.

HOW TO BUDGET ADVERTISING

A company's advertising budget is probably too often the result of "intuitive judgments" and sloppy reasoning.

Marketing, financial, and accounting personnel should *all* work on the budget. *Do not* use one of the most popular "automatic" formulas: *percentage of sales.* Advertising is supposed to *produce* sales, not vice versa. Try using a *sales objective* approach if the market research is reliable. Calculate the advertising necessary to reach the sales level set for *each* product. That total is the advertising budget.

Another flexible approach is to set an amount per unit cost. The unit can be defined by tons, by product group, or by customer group. And the advertising budget per unit can be set by market population or by determining the level of market penetration.

Also, consider the company's com-

petitive situation. Since it's not possible to accurately forecast what the competition will spend on advertising, concentrate heavily on what your advertising should be doing independent of what your competitors are doing.

THREE WAYS TO PICK AN ADVERTISING AGENCY

Ask these questions:
• *Will the people who do the day-to-day work on my account—copy, account work, etc.—talk to my potential customers on a regular basis? Will they personally interview consumers, buyers, and purchasing agents to learn my business first-hand?*

Most agencies have able people. The difference is often the firsthand insight gained in personal interviews.
• *Will the agency take on a single problem-solving assignment for a fee?*

Many agencies do interesting work, but aren't geared to problem-solving. Before awarding one agency your business, it's wise to try them on a single assignment. How do they attack it? Do they deliver all that they promise? Do you work well together? A single assignment first can save you a lot of serious problems later.
• *Are their present clients happy?*

In one afternoon you can talk to five or six of their clients, learn the agency's strengths and weaknesses firsthand, quickly discover whether or not they are right for you.

Source: Gerald Schoenfeld, Gerald Schoenfeld, Inc., 341 Madison Ave., New York 10017

AUDIT FINANCIAL CONDITION OF YOUR ADVERTISING AGENCY

There are sound reasons for checking on how your ad agency handles your company's payments:

• More and more, media are holding clients responsible for payment when agencies default on ad bills.

• When ad agencies get into trouble — as several of them have — it's tempting for them to use funds received from quick-paying clients to pay older bills. If the roof caves in, the client can be hurt.

HOW TO DO IT. The audit can be accomplished with a simple form that the agency completes and returns to you.

It should list several media purchases (selected on a spot-check basis), the date the supplier mailed his invoice to the agency, the date the agency received it, and the date the agency paid the bill.

Along with the completed form, request the agency to check numbers and photocopies of invoices and statements. Be sure to ask for the completed audit package *back within three days.*

RESULTS. The results should tell you how your agency is handling your cash. If you have any doubts, you can go directly to the suppliers to confirm information.

Source: Roy A. Heckenbach, Action Communicators Inc., Wauwatosa, Wis.

THE WEAK LINK IN MOST AD PROGRAMS IS RESEARCH

Far too weak emphasis on asking consumers at *focus group sessions* which of three or four mediocre ideas is the least mediocre. Far too little emphasis on using consumers to *actually generate ideas*. Three ways to get the most out of the consumer research team you've commissioned:

• Attend sessions and insist on being able to inject your own questions. Listening to a group of your potential customers talk freely about their needs will stimulate you to have scores of ideas. If you listen closely you'll hear consumers tell you exactly what they want and need.

• Don't approach consumers with a "tell me all you know" attitude. They will need to be *stimulated* to express their ideas. Use even the mediocre ideas developed in your office to stimulate consumers' thinking. In telling you why your ideas are bad, they'll come up with many good ones.

Present your competition's ideas to consumers *before* you present your own. That way you avoid the danger of letting a bruised ego affect your judgment. It's easy. Simply take the selling copy from the competition's product and make a little ad out of it with your product name on it. You'll be amazed at how much you'll learn about your competition's strengths and weaknesses as well as those of your own product.

Source: Gerald Schoenfeld.

CARRYING THROUGH

WHICH OF THESE WORDS IS THE BEST WAY TO START AN AD HEADLINE?

"New."

"Amazing."

"Suddenly."

"Which."

The answer is: "Which." It's almost impossible to write a bad headline starting with the word "Which," because you invite the reader's immediate participation:

"*Which* twin has the Toni?"

"*Which* of these investment benefits would you like for yourself?"

"*Which* of these common mistakes in English do you make?"

It's also smart selling. A good clothing salesperson never asks, "Will you take this one?" Better question: "Which color would you like?"

HOW'S YOUR HEADLINE?

In the booming '60s, advertising went through a period of irreverence and superficiality that fit the mood of the times. But the last recession spawned a return to *hard sell.*

Hard sell is really *clear sell.* And the *king of clear sell* is the *headline.*

Don't let your adman tell you that "the picture's the thing," or "overall impact is what counts." The first impact is the word or words that capture the imagination *and* convince. The more specific, the more *convincing.* Specifics are built on facts, not superlatives. "Big Sale" isn't as convincing as "4,568 Items on Sale." "5 Times Better" is a hundred times better than "Better."

Beware of generalities. They are indicators of a weak writer, a weak agency, a weak advertiser, and a weak product. Try "I was a weakling" against "I was a 97-pound weakling" or compare "Pure" with "99 and 44/100% Pure."

TURNING OFF PROPOSALS

It's natural for small advertisers to mimic the biggest ones, but some of the biggest are fatally misjudging their markets. Here are strategies that should *not* be imitated by anyone:

• *Male "authority figures" pitching a house cleanser.* Not only ineffective but insulting. The best rule is older than TV or women's lib, and still works: To sell a woman, show a picture of a woman. Resist anything else your agency gives you.

• *Selling women's products only on daytime TV.* The set may be on, but most housewives are too busy to watch and you miss working women altogether. *Best bet:* Evening hours, when the woman is relaxed. Costs more but worth it.

• Youth market strategies can boomerang, too. *Bad for business:* Trying to sound hip; using fad words like "groovy."

• *Tip for print advertisers with low budgets:* Stick to full-page ads. Only the biggies can afford to fritter their money away on small space. Shoot the works on an ad everybody will see, count up your sales, and use some of the profit to finance the next full page.

Source: *Advertising Pure and Simple*, by Hank Seiden (AMACOM, American Management Associations, 135 W. 50 St., New York 10020).

HOW TO WRITE A SUCCESSFUL AD

What's the news? Before you do anything else, write down the news you wish to convey. People read newspapers, magazines, and books to learn, to find out things they didn't know before. *Most ads merely try to persuade.* Put the news about your product or service in the headline. Potential customers will then read on.

What's the story? Make a list of all the points you'd like prospects to know. Then write a story.

Subject? The news that's in the headline.

How to begin? Start with something close to the headline. If people are reading at all, they're reading because they're interested in the headline.

Hook them with copy in the same vein.

As you tell your story, think of it as a coatrack. You can put lots of pegs into a coatrack, and you can make lots of points in a copy story. But if the central post isn't there, the coats all fall down. And if all your copy points aren't pegged into the story so that they hang upon the single piece of news you want to communicate, the whole ad will fall apart.

Too many ads are a buckshot load of scattered copy thoughts. A successful ad tells a single copy story upon which all the copy points are tied in.

Who's the customer? As you write your ad, keep your prime prospect in mind. Read your first draft aloud to a typical prospect. As he raises questions and reacts to your copy, you'll be able to improve the ad as you respond.

What's the action? Few ads tell the reader what action to take. If he's sold by your copy, whom should he see? Are his phone calls welcome? How does he get more information? Wherever possible, include a coupon in your ad. Offer literature, a free trial, dealer information—whatever you can put in.

Pictures are not mere ornaments to ads. They are basic to their communication. The right picture deepens the meaning of the ad and helps in the communication. Ask yourself, "Is it a different ad with this picture in it?"

What's the caption? What's the sign-off? Like a P.S. in a letter, a picture caption is always well read. In captioning your picture you build the news value of your ad.

The sign-off—the final line in an ad (like Parliament cigarettes' "more than just a low-tar number," or Pan American's "America's airline to the world") —gives you an invaluable chance to summarize the story in a handful of words.

What's the follow-up? Don't think of an ad by itself. Think of a campaign, *i.e.*, a series of ads all based on the same theme, all telling the same story.

Once you've run two or three ads telling the same story, try even harder, the way Avis did. First they announced a piece of news: Avis is only No. 2 in auto rentals, so Avis will try harder. (At that time, few people knew there was a No. 2 in rent-a-cars.)

Then Avis told the same story ad after ad: We're only No. 2, we have to try harder. They didn't stop there. They put it on their letterhead. They wore it on buttons. And they sang it in jingles.

Once *you* find a story worth telling, it pays to try harder.

Source: Gerald Schoenfeld, Gerald Schoenfeld, Inc., 341 Madison Ave., New York 10017.

HOW TO TEST AD'S EFFECTIVENESS

Nabisco, a solid company with slow-growth products, planned to boost sales by concentrated advertising in selected markets requiring smaller expenditures. Nabisco discovered that products were not advertised enough and that increased ad expenditures brought considerable sales gains. One very slow product was revived and grew sharply. The company could then confidently increase its national ad budget because it knew that its advertising worked.

CUT SIZE, EXPAND AUDIENCE

Most marketers recognize the immediate sales value of a good newspaper ad. Unfortunately, estimates are that over 33% of adults don't read newspapers. And, of those who do, only 29% of women readers and 25% of men readers note the average ad. Is the answer to make ads bigger? Usually not. One four-city study (by Daniel Starch & Staff, Inc.) showed cutting full-page ad size 25% reduced recognition only 9%. Cutting half-page ad size 50% cut it 36%, and an additional 50% cut in size didn't decrease it any more.

Consider cutting newspaper ad size and, with dollars saved, supporting your product or store message with a *radio supplement* to your newspaper program.

Either broad-spectrum radio or selective radio can reach a target audience not well covered by newspaper: men 18 to 24, women 18 to 34, lower-income and lower-education group, blacks, Hispanics, other ethnic groups. A dual media buy often accelerates the sense of importance of your message. And radio gives you a special opportunity to talk beyond price or today's offering.

USING THE COMPETITOR'S NAME

Unless you're particularly savvy about TV advertising, you might well be wondering whatever happened to the infamous Brand X. In fact, it's been replaced by real names—product names that consumers know and trust (or distrust).

The government now *prefers* the advertiser of a product having a significant superior feature over competitive products to inform the consumer of that feature and of the specific brands which its product has *proven* (through actual testing) to surpass. *Rationale:* If the advertiser is specific about the competition, the consumer is less likely to be misled into generalizing the inferiority of all other products.

The real-names approach isn't necessarily a sign of more aggressive advertising. It *is* an example of more *factual* advertising. Perhaps it's time for you to start coming up with more facts in your ads. But if you do, be prepared to back them up, for your competitors will be watching very carefully.
Source: Jack Byrne.

TELLING PEOPLE WHAT THEY WANT TO HEAR

Tab's doing it. Geritol's doing it. L'Oreal's doing it. Picking up on the theme, "Be good to yourself."

It all started with the book, *How To Be Your Own Best Friend*, a record-setting best seller. Advertisers figured, "If people need to read a book to discover how to be a friend to themselves, we'll show them how to do it *with our product*."

Does it all seem too facile?

Well, each of those campaigns is doing well. More advertisers are getting on the "Be good to yourself" bandwagon every day. The approach leads to personal advertising devoid of annoying gimmicks and inflated claims.

It's unselfish in tone and has the ring of psychological validity.

The only question is, when these commercials tell us how to be good to ourselves, our figures, our hair and our blood, are they really saying, "Quit worrying about your floors, your wash, and the percentage of meat in your dog's food"? If that's the message, it's a timely one.

Source: Gerald Schoenfeld.

DEMYSTIFYING SALES CLAIMS

Sell your product more convincingly by toning down, cutting out exaggerations like "magic" and "miraculous." They turn off today's consumers. Replace exaggeration with moderation in claims. If your competitors are making lots of noise, your company will be heard by being a little quieter, offering a constructive contrast to your competitors' noise.

MANAGING TV/RADIO DOLLARS

Get the most for your spot TV or radio dollar by giving the media buyer time and room to maneuver. Spots for a 25- to 50-market campaign take about

ADVERTISING

five weeks to find and negotiate *effectively*. Lesser purchases take two to three weeks.

If you give your buyer less time, he can purchase the first spots immediately, show you a prospective schedule for the entire campaign and buy the balance of the spots later. If he is less conscientious, he'll merely buy what's easy to get and you'll be stuck with it.

Rigid specifications for time slots, types of program and the like, can lock the buyer out of alternatives that could deliver the audience you want to reach at lower cost-per-thousand exposures.

Inflexible rules about station selection—leading two in a market, for example, or network stations only—inevitably increase your costs. When broadcasters know the buyer has nowhere else to go, they price their time accordingly.

Source: Ed Papazion, vice-president, Batten, Barton, Durstine & Osborn, New York.

WRITING BETTER RADIO COMMERCIALS

• Message should be absolutely clear. Leave no doubt about what's being offered and why people should want it.
• Get down to business fast. Start selling with the first word.
• Mention the product at least twice.
• Be sure every word is easy to pronounce and understand.
• Tape the commercial and listen to it at each stage of development.

Source: *Brainstorms*, 1280 Saw Mill River Rd., Yonkers, N.Y. 10710.

SMALL AD BUDGET DOESN'T PRECLUDE TV SPOTS

A small advertising budget doesn't mean that TV spots can't be used. An effective television commercial can be produced for $1,000 or less if it's done the right way. *Cost savers to keep in mind:*
• Use prerecorded music (if already in the public domain), available at a low price through music libraries.
• Use either 16mm film or video tape. (The latter is a bargain if you use local TV station crews during breaks.) Or consider cheap, portable minicameras.
• Get extra mileage from your advertising artwork. Reuse it for TV work on a camera stand.
• Don't edit. Shoot commercials straight through from beginning to end.

CO-OP TV ADS

Idea for co-op TV advertising: Do-it-yourself campaigns that let retailers concoct their own low-cost commercials, book local media spots when and as they think they'll be most effective.
Basic equipment: Standard TV kit containing promotional films, slides, and scripts for retailers and their local TV station people to devise a variety of original spots, add pertinent local themes, and capitalize on individual store reputation with goodwill.

Result: Well-timed, noncanned commercials with zing. Makes for fast-close presentations that outperform uniform national tie-in campaigns.

The satisfied pioneer: Lees Carpets sells the kit to retailers below cost at $175, splits time costs 50-50, makes program available to all the dealers that also participate in strong point-of-purchase programs.

Big advantage: Outstanding retailer participation and cooperation, elimination of the slip-ups that characterize standard national campaigns, big benefits from strong local theme and identification.

CHANGING AUDIENCES FOR ADVERTISERS

Magazines that focus on women and the home have a sizable percentage of *male* readers and no longer try to hide this fact. Even the traditional women's page in the newspaper—which is less often called the "women's" page—has a growing percentage of male readers. And the female readers of, if not subscribers to, some traditionally male publications are increasing: Important consideration in new ad and publicity plans.

• When the divorced male takes over the children for weekends, he is compelled to shop for products he seldom purchased before without being overseen by a woman. Toy stores report that the divorced father represents a rapidly growing segment of the year-round toy/game business.

• Do-it-yourself for women will spread into almost all aspects of male do-it-yourself. Currently, a large percentage of ready-to-assemble furniture, which has become a fast seller due to its price appeal, is being assembled by women. A rising percentage of floor tiles (soft and hard) is now installed by women. The paint industry's roller (recently redesigned for female use) was one of the first major marketing thrusts directly related to growing involvement of women in what has traditionally been male activity. Some small power tools, too, are now being bought —and used—by women.

IT CAN PAY TO BE A PUBLIC-TV SPONSOR

By supporting public TV, a company can gain prestige with consumers and create goodwill with local opinion leaders. Most local stations welcome corporate contributions and acknowledge them on the air when they cover all or part of the costs of acquiring or producing a program. *Example:* WNET, New York's public-TV station, lists its corporate contributors on the air and in its monthly magazine and program guide. For $125 a year a company can be included in the stations weekly on-the-air credits that list corporate supporters. A $250 contribution buys a place among those listed annually in the program guide.

Far more visible are the firms that receive on-the-air credit for their contribution each time the program is aired. Costs of this support vary widely, depending on the expense of either producing or acquiring a show and whether the firm provides all or part of

ADVERTISING

the funding. Actual production costs for successful national series are usually assumed by a corporate giant, but local stations need local funding to air the show and offset its acquisition costs. Before the series theme sounds, stations carrying the program show logos of the local supporters and provide a brief description of the underwriters. Credits appear at the end of each program as well.

ample is the use of TV for sufferers from hemorrhoids (note also that women are being used to deliver these commercials!). Marketing executives for products that had been barred from TV try again—and again. Many using cable TV for openers. That outlet is still "hungry." They get a toehold there, then move to weak local stations and, with research proving the public doesn't mind, "crash the gate" of bigger stations and national television.

BETTER BUSINESS BUREAU HIT FOR DEFAMATION

Not long ago, a Louisiana Better Business Bureau got hit with a $1-million verdict that a Better Business Bureau bulletin defamed the accuracy and information in a manufacturer's advertising. This is believed to be the first time BBB has been beaten in a consumer advertising protection case.

In this particular case the successful manufacturer engaged in a public campaign denouncing the Better Business Bureau.

TV LESS SQUEAMISH ABOUT ADS

As a more highly educated public loses some of its squeamishness, traditional barriers to the use of TV for "forbidden" products are now tumbling with increasing rapidity. A current ex-

WITH NEWSPAPER ADS, THE KEY WORD IS 'NEWS'

That's not as obvious as it sounds. Unlike magazines, newspapers have a single day's life span.

To succeed, a newspaper ad must tell readers some piece of news that is true today, right now, this minute.

Build your ad around a sudden blizzard or heat wave. Tie in to a sporting event or a strike.

You can't redo your TV commercial overnight, and with radio it will take weeks to reach a large number of potential customers and by then the news might be cold. But with a single *timely* newspaper ad, you can capture everyone's attention at once.

Retailers have long understood the need to be newsy and up-to-the-minute in their newspaper ads.

Today's ad has today's price and today's special. Yesterday's newspaper is just something to wrap the fish in. So make your ad newsy and you'll be amazed at the results.

Source: Gerald Schoenfeld.

CUTTING COSTS

RECHECK NEWSPAPER AD BUDGET

Newspapers are *not* about to disappear from the advertising scene, but bear these developments in mind when planning your ad media breakdown:

The trend toward broadening television and radio news coverage will be continuing over the next several years. There are more two-hour television news broadcasts than ever, with talk of expanding national coverage. Newspaper ad revenue continues to climb—but not by much more than increased rates. Total gain in newspaper circulation barely equals population growth. Reading time for newspapers has probably dropped, especially among the young, but also among women who work. However, suburban newspapers continue to outperform city newspapers.

ADVERTISING EXPENSES AREN'T ALWAYS DEDUCTIBLE

Advertising is such an ordinary and necessary business expense, it's easy to believe that all such spending is tax-deductible. Not always the case. *When the deduction may be denied:*
• Costs are excessive in terms of expected benefit.

• The advertiser isn't actually soliciting orders, because he has nothing to sell. *Examples:* (1) All of the company's capacity is committed to government contracts. (2) No inventory is available because of strikes, lack of raw materials, etc.
• The advertiser isn't yet in the business that he is advertising. Deductions for pre-business expenses must be spread out over the first five years a firm is in business.
• The advertising is in the nature of a penalty. *Example:* A governmental regulatory agency orders a manufacturer to run advertisements that correct misstatements in previous advertising.
• Advertising that attempts to influence legislation.
• Advertising expenditures of another corporation. *Example:* The parent company pays for ads of products that actually are sold only by subsidiary companies.

CELEBRITIES AT A DISCOUNT

Celebrities needn't break an advertising or promotion budget, especially if you find a celebrity who's going to be in town.

Ideas: Follow theater listings, news of benefit performances, schedules of upcoming athletic events.

ADVERTISING

Other good sources: Newspaper and TV station personnel who receive advance publicity about movies on location, authors coming to promote books, etc.; hotels that feature headline entertainers.

In dealing with an agent, state precisely what you have in mind and what you are prepared to pay. They have standard prices for various services and know the star's availability as well as the kinds of things he is willing to do.

Don't be afraid to offer too little: Agency people who specialize in this realize you don't know the going rates. They'll state their usual requirements, *e.g.,* round-trip first-class plane fare for two, full-time use of two limousines, adjoining hotel suites *plus* fee.

If some of these expenses are being picked up by a different sponsor on the same trip, there is room for some negotiation, although the agent may demand equivalent reimbursement from both.

Remember: If a celebrity is in Des Moines to do a seven-minute TV appearance, he may rehearse for a half-hour and that's it. He probably has several hours to kill before the return flight and might gladly put in a brief appearance at your sales meeting for $500. (Breaks the boredom.)

Other ways to use celebrities: Invite other important customers or suppliers for luncheon or dinner, with the star making a talk or short monologue before business session. Ask star to come to company picnic for a treat that employee spouses and children will long remember. Take lots of pictures of celebrity with personnel, customers, product. These can be used in many ways including company publications, publicity releases, sales literature.

For special, big-budget projects such as a long-range commercial tie-in, it's probably wise to enlist the help of middlemen who specialize in mediating between the celebrity agents (who, after all, get 10%—or more—of whatever they negotiate for their star) and advertising agencies (which want a good price for their clients). Best known of these middlemen is Lloyd Kolmer Enterprises, Inc. (65 W. 55 St., New York 10019). That firm's fee may run upward from $2,500, depending on the complexity of the search and the eventual deal. Others who specialize in the talent search game: Marty Ingels, former Hollywood comedian, 7560 Hollywood Blvd., Los Angeles 90046; Mark Korman Management, 250 W. 57 St., New York 10019; Richard Fulton Lecture Bureau, 850 7th Ave., New York 10019.

Major stars who have resisted commercial work("virgins" in the trade) can command six-figure prices for signing on as a corporate "spokesman." But there are many lesser lights, anxious for the extra income provided by commercial work. It pays to first find out who's going to be in town.

Source: Bill Robinson, head of William A. Robinson, Inc. (601 Skokie Blvd., Northbrook, Ill. 60062).

SHOP AROUND FOR TV TIME

The ever-spiraling cost of television time makes it even more important to do some bargain-hunting. Insist that your advertising agency and ad department look not just at network time but also at available time in weaker, more scattered markets around the country. There are bargains around—the trick is to find them.

Source: Walter F. Staab, SFM Media Service, New York.

TRY A HIGHER PRICE ON CONSUMER CATALOGS

Advertisers promoting a consumer catalog are often too timid about increasing its price. Now, some are raising the price of their catalogs and are learning that consumers continue to order the catalog in satisfactory numbers.

Careful testing will show optimum price. It may be possible to make the consumer catalog immune to inflation. (*Often desirable:* Include a purchase discount certificate with catalog that customer can use to offset cost.)

NEW LIFE FOR AGE-OLD BARTER

Simply put, barter is a way of moving *excess* inventory—anything from atlases to zippers. It used to be that *excess* meant goods the manufacturer was stuck with (or thought it was stuck with). Today, that definition is much broader. In fact, a manufacturing firm that wants to produce 10% more goods in an effort to reduce per-unit costs may turn to barter.

Here's how it works: The barter company "buys" the manufacturer's inventory at the usual wholesale price. The trader gives the manufacturer credits toward a wide range of items or services that the barter company has either bought at a reduced price for cash or traded for with other goods.

Examples: Advertising time or space, cars, hotel rooms or meals, trucking, corrugated packaging material, computer time. *Other examples:* Wristwatches, radios, umbrellas, toiletries. (The major *single* "commodity" traded is ads: TV, radio, newspaper, magazine.)

ADVANTAGES TO THE MANUFACTURER. Manufacturer retains its profit margin because it gets the wholesale price for its goods. It would receive much less if it tried to move the merchandise through its regular marketing channels at cut prices or sold it to a closeout company or salvage house.

The merchandise stops depreciating. It goes out of the manufacturer's inventory immediately and, in return, becomes a hard asset—a receivable.

The barter company buys and sells on its own account. It takes possession of the merchandise. Selling, shipping, and warehousing are its problem. If it sells from the manufacturer's warehouse, the barter company can pay for the storage handling.

The manufacturer's goods are not sold in ways that would hurt its other sales.

Some major barter firms: Advertising Agency Associates, 1320 Center St., Newton Center, Mass. 02159; William B Tanner, 2714 Union Extended, Memphis, Tenn. 38112; S.M.Y., 360 North Michigan Ave., Chicago 60601; Media Communications, 660 Madison Ave., New York 10021.

BUYING, SELLING, MERGING A COMPANY

WHY MERGERS BREAK UP

Corporate mergers, like marriages, produce divorces (one of three), as well as wedded bliss. Among the reasons for failures and/or breakups:
• Unfamiliarity with tricks of the trade. Acquiring companies often fail to realize other businesses cannot always be run successfully in the same way as their own.
• Takeover candidates with problems require managerial skills different from those needed to build a business. Executives not specifically dedicated to corporate cures should avoid "sick" situations.
• Acquiring to remedy internal ills is a generally poor practice; odds are improved when both partners are healthy.
• Incompatible operational methods and goals can lead to problems—particularly when the going gets rough, as during a credit crunch.
• Personality conflicts—both individual and corporate, can arise. Managerial styles and industry ethical standards of mergers may be at considerable variance.
• Sloppy investigation of takeover candidates' true circumstances invariably misses risks inherent in get-togethers.
• Great expectations can blind even savviest managers to prospective drawbacks of "living together."
• Heavy-handed attempts at instant operational integration can produce long-lasting resentments.
• The management of acquired concerns, having secured lush contracts and stock positions, plus perhaps options, may ease up on efforts.

Source: Alan Seed, Arthur D. Little, Inc., Cambridge, Mass.

GOING PUBLIC CAN BE A MISTAKE—PERSONALLY, IF NOT FINANCIALLY

That's the opinion of Richard Salomon, formerly the sole owner of the hugely successful Charles of the Ritz cosmetics company. The company went public in 1961, subsequently merged with Lanvin, the perfume company, and finally was merged into the giant pharmaceutical conglomerate, Squibb. Eight months later, Salomon quit. *His advice:*
At the time I was weighing my major decision [to go public], I should have asked:
• Would I, once I had taken the public in as shareholder-partner, be able to resist or disregard their preoccupation with short-term results and/or fluctuations in the price of our shares?
• Am I the type who can ignore the stock market demand for consistent and constant increases in sales earnings?
• Can I accept with grace and equanimity the embarrassing public exposure of mistakes, which in a proprietorship will probably remain hidden?
Salomon says that if he had asked himself these questions before the sale, he would have sold out directly, once he was sure no one in his family was interested in taking over the business, and gotten out.
Source: *Harvard Business Review.*

19

HOW TO GET PROTECTION IN BUYING A SMALL BUSINESS

The federal securities laws can protect the buyer of a small business against false and misleading statements made by the seller of the business. However, these laws can offer protection only if securities are involved in the transaction. If you buy *stock* in an incorporated business, you're buying a security and you're entitled to protection of SEC Rule 10b-5, which makes it unlawful to make a false representation of a material fact, or to omit to make a disclosure of a material fact, in connection with the purchase (or sale) of a security.

But suppose the business is unincorporated. Or, for tax or other reasons, you decide to buy the *assets* of the business and you give the seller a note for part of the purchase price. Can the transaction be viewed as one involving securities?

The answer depends on how those notes are defined. If, for example, they represent investments, and the holder expects profits without any efforts on his part and through the efforts of others, they are considered *securities*.

Comment and recommendations:

• If you're buying an incorporated business, you'll want to structure the deal as a stock purchase unless there are strong contrary tax or legal liability reasons.

• If you're buying assets or an unincorporated business and you have notes, you'll want to have your attorney structure them so that they take on the character of securities. If the deal is set up so that the seller is given some sort of contingent payments based on future profits of the business, that should do the trick. The longer the term of the note, the better the buyer's position. It helps, too, if the note is a negotiable instrument.

C.N.S. Enterprises v. G&G Enterprises, Inc., C.A. 7, CCH Fed. Sec. L. Rep ¶94,938, 1/13/75.

INTERCOMPANY SPINOFFS CAN LOSE A TAX ADVANTAGE

If the corporation is spinning off a subsidiary, setting up a new subsidiary, or realigning the corporation's operations in some other way, be careful how machinery and equipment are transferred. If it isn't done properly an unnecessary tax liability may be created.

Not likely to be a tax problem where assets are transferred at a loss. But there could be a problem when property is sold for a gain, and it is important to sell to the right person. *Where there is a gain, it's important to make the right choice.*

If depreciable business property is sold at a gain after having been held for more than a year, this is treated as a long-term capital gain (*even though the equipment isn't a capital asset*). But the gain will be taxed as *ordinary income* if the transaction is between (1) an individual and a corporation where he and his immediate family own 80% or more of the stock, or (2) between husband and wife. This restrictive rule has been extended by the Tax Reform Act of 1976 to sales or exchanges between two or more corporations which are commonly controlled.

Solution: Sell the used equipment to an unrelated party and let the subsidiary buy its own. Or, alternatively, choose assets where no gain is indicated for the transfer.

HOW TO SELL A COMPANY

The merger and acquisition field is quite different from what it was in the 1960s, when all a broker had to do to bring a buyer and seller together was to pick up a phone. Since the recession, the long bear market, and the collapse experienced by many conglomerates, the market has changed.

For the seller, especially, the situation has gotten difficult: There are far fewer potential buyers. Many buyers feel their own stock is underpriced and so are hesitant to use their stock. (They're equally unhappy about buying for cash.)

Realize that in today's market, *successfully* selling a business is a long shot. Most deals, even after some exploring and negotiation, are never consummated.

The biggest reasons are:
• The potential buyer can't see a high enough return on capital.
• The seller waited too long. Possibly his company's growth curve has flattened and the future looks less exciting. Or, because of advanced age and the lack of backup management, the po-

tential buyer sees no easy or safe way to capitalize on the business potential.

Recommendation: The best time to sell a business is when the entrepreneur is relatively young and the growth curve is at its strongest point.

WHOM TO TALK TO ABOUT SELLING. Conventional wisdom says speak first to your lawyer, accountant, and close associates about an interest in selling. That's often bad advice, for two critical reasons:

• Few accountants or lawyers (even those in major firms) see enough deals to know what is really available (at what terms, etc.).
• There's a serious danger that the news of selling interest may leak out prematurely—hurting relations with staff, customers, vendors, and the potential buyers.

Some merger brokers charge a fee for the early investigative work and also a commission on the consummated deal. Most brokers *will* frankly say when a deal isn't possible—as is the case in more than 99% of those that come up.

If stock prices stay high over the next few years, expect to see fewer and fewer cash transactions, as buyers will tend to use stock, rather than cash, as a form of payment. The situation today is much like that of the 1960s, when most acquisitions (two-thirds) were for stock. By the late 1970s, the majority of transactions were a mixture: stock up front with a cash payout.

In a typical arrangement (especially if the seller is still relatively young), the owner and his key people get employment contracts either to continue working in the firm or just to remain a noncompetitor. Most (80% or more) relationships become very strained in just two or three years.

What that means: If the seller really wants to stay with the business, he should study his new "boss" carefully. The potential seller should explore what *he* really wants and expects from the new relationship. It's likely to turn out that the seller can't have both the cash-in value of the business he built up and the freedom to still be an entrepreneur.

TYPICAL TRAP. A would-be seller decides which firm he'd like to sell out to. His decision is carefully made. That firm understands the seller's business and he knows enough about the potential buyer to feel comfortable about any relationship. So he makes his interest known on his own—without an intermediary.

Frequent reaction: The sought-after suitor is in the driver's seat. He knows there is no competitor. He knows the seller's interest without disclosing his own. The potential buyer can drag his feet. And very likely he will also ask seller to agree not to negotiate with anyone else during their expensive, time-consuming exploration of the proposal.

The request is usually made in good faith but the effect is that there is nothing to prod the negotiations along. The seller may well discover that he has lost a year of selling time that is often critical to making the best deal.

'HOT' AND 'COLD' INDUSTRIES. The "hottest" industries today are energy-related, health services, publishing, printing.

The "cold" industries are toys, furniture, restaurants.

Neutral: Manufacturing.

Source: Victor Niederhoffer, Niederhoffer, Cross & Zeckhauser, Inc., 825 Third Ave., New York 10022.

THE TAX OPPORTUNITIES IN BUYING A BUSINESS

High interest rates are putting more and more companies to the test. But these same conditions provide an opportunity for healthy firms. Now is the time that an aggressive company may be able to *expand* on the most advantageous terms.

Tactic: Buy out the business of a financially shaky supplier, customer or competitor to broaden the business without the strain of starting a new division or subsidiary from scratch. In some cases, the tax savings can pay the *entire* cost of the transaction. The tax implications will depend on whether the business has been making money or losing money.

BUYING A HEALTHY COMPANY. Typically, the seller wants *cash*. And there is cash in the business. But if the seller withdraws the cash *before* selling the company, the withdrawal will be a dividend taxed as ordinary income. *Goal for the purchaser:* Use the cash in the business to make a down payment on the company.

What to do: Suggest to the present owner that the company redeem *some* of the shares he holds, paying him cash directly for those shares. Simultaneously, have the owner transfer the *rest* of the shares to the purchaser. *Result:* Section 302 of the tax code provides the owner with tax-favored long-term capital gains treatment for his profit on the deal. And the seller avoids paying any funds out of pocket.

Tax trap: The purchaser must not commit itself in writing to purchase *all* the seller's stock, and then use funds taken from the company to make payment. *Reason:* The used funds are a taxable dividend to the purchaser, who winds up paying *both* the seller *and* the government.

BUYING AN UNHEALTHY COMPANY. *Tactic:* Before announcing the sale, have the old owner put the company into Chapter 11 bankruptcy proceedings. *Risk saver:* The liabilities of the company are declared and defined, so the purchaser avoids buying unknown debts. *Money saver:* The purchaser appears as a white knight to the business's creditors. They will probably be ready to negotiate a reasonable reduction of their debts, rather than risk losing everything by having the buyer walk away.

It may take some time to turn around a business that has been losing money. But the purchaser gets these *immediate tax benefits:*

• Continuing losses of the company that is bought can be used on a consolidated return to offset the profits of the purchasing company.

• Capital investments made to turn around the acquired business will result in large investment credits and depreciation deductions. Under recent tax law changes these benefits are larger than ever.

• When the acquired business turns profitable, its post-acquisition losses may be used to offset future gains. The losses may be carried forward 15 years and reduce the tax for those years.

Trap: When purchasing a company, it may become necessary to give key managers a stake in the business. *Do not* give these employees more than 20% of the company's stock. Consolidated returns cannot be filed unless the purchasing company owns 80% of the stock of the other. Without consolidated returns, these tax benefits will be lost.

A key tax consideration in buying a business is assigning a cash value to the purchased company's assets.

Points at issue:

• A high value for depreciable assets increases depreciation deductions available in the future.

• A high value for a noncompete agreement signed by the seller increases the business expense deduction available for its cost.

PRICE NEGOTIATION. The seller may want *little* value attached to the noncompete agreement (its price is taxed as ordinary income to him). And want as much as possible attached to the goodwill of the business (to qualify for long-term capital gains).

Solution to the problem: The buyer forms a subsidiary company which purchases the target firm's stock. *After* the purchase, the subsidiary merges the target into itself. *Result:* Under Section 334 of the tax code, the subsidiary then gets to allocate the cost of the acquired firm's stock over its assets in any reasonable manner. The seller is no longer involved, so he cannot object.

REVERSE TWIST. It is possible for a *losing* company to purchase a profitable one, with the government footing part of the bill.

How: After the purchase, the two companies merge in a deal that is *not* structured to be a tax-free reorganization. *Result:* A refund of taxes paid by the profitable company in recent years. *Impact:* The refund itself may cover the down payment on the purchase price. Thereafter, the profits from the purchased company may be used to pay the balance.

Source: Edward Mendlowitz, Siegel & Mendlowitz, 310 Madison Ave., New York 10017.

HOW TO 'CASH IN' WITH MINIMUM TAX BITE

Practical way to transfer a business to the principal's children (or other family members) with a minimum of tax liability: First, arrange to transfer some stock to family. Later, have the corporation redeem the rest of principal's share. *But*, instead of paying a lump sum of cash, have the money paid as a life-time annuity. In that way, the money is distributed in fixed, annual installments. *The advantages:*

The business is removed from the owner's estate immediately, without the imposition of gift or inheritance taxes. It becomes the sole property of the remaining shareholder.

The owner gets a lifetime income, which can meet retirement needs just as well as a lump-sum payment.

The estate isn't swollen with cash or notes that would be received in a lump-sum redemption. The annuity lasts only during the principal's lifetime.

Business isn't saddled with a traumatic outflow of working capital.

The annuity is paid out of profits and is spaced evenly over the lifetime of the former owner of the business.

How to do it: Calculate the fair market value of the shares. Then use Internal Revenue Service actuarial tables to translate the value of those holdings into a monthly lifetime annuity *plus* interest.

Taxes are paid only on the income that's received each year, not on the cash value of the annuity in the year received. For tax purposes, the annuity payments are divided into three layers: (1) return of capital (not taxed); (2) profit on the sale of stock (capital-gain tax); (3) interest on the unpaid balance (taxed as ordinary income).

DIVERSIFICATION INTO MORE PROMISING BUSINESS CAN BRING ACCUMULATED EARNINGS TAX

If management believes that the future of its particular business looks bleak and that some other field looks more promising—and decides to go into it—be careful how that entry is financed. Don't make the mistake of thinking that the government will subsidize a corporation's entry into a different business by bypassing the *accumulated earnings tax*.

A corporation is subject to that tax if earnings are allowed to pile up beyond the reasonable needs of the business. The very fact that earnings have accumulated beyond the reasonable needs of the business sets up a presumption that this had been for the purpose of avoiding taxes which shareholders would have had to pay had dividends been declared.

The question, *What are the reasonable needs of the business?* triggers a second question, *What really is the corporation's business?* Usually that means the regular needs of the corporation in the business in which it is engaged *at the time.*

Typically, corporations with declining profits in their own field are taxed to the extent that earnings accumulated in that field have been retained for the purpose of entering an unrelated new field.

Diversification *within its own particular field* has been held justifiable.

What to do: If it's decided to enter a new field, finance the move with borrowed funds or by raising additional capital.

ALTERNATIVES TO SELLING OR MERGING A BUSINESS

Problem: *Can't raise cash for expansion.*

Alternatives: Issue stock; sell bonds; obtain capital from a venture capital firm or the Small Business Administration; bring in a partner; establish a joint venture with another company.

Problem: *Sales force is ineffective.*

Alternatives: Hire a new sales manager; cut salesmen's salaries and increase commissions; use more wholesale distributors, fewer salesmen; develop or acquire new product lines.

Problem: *Estate settlement would*

threaten liquidity; a merger would provide management with ready cash.

Alternatives: Purchase an insurance policy with the company as a beneficiary and begin training a successor; bring in an experienced executive with money to invest; bring your children into the company's management.

Problem: *You wish to reduce your business activities and enjoy the benefits of the labor and profits you have plowed into the company.*

Alternatives: Increase your salary and perquisites; shift operational responsibilities to others; share ownership with one of your top executives or with an outsider with management experience; sell some of your stock.

THE 'FAILING COMPANY' DOCTRINE MIGHT PERMIT AN ANTICOMPETITIVE ACQUISITION

Antitrust laws may bar the acquisition of another company if the effect may be to substantially lessen competition. But if the target company is in danger of failing, the courts permit the move under the "failing company" doctrine. It's worth investigating.

Failing, in the view of the courts, is a high or grave probability of failure. But the courts have never explicitly defined *failure.* It clearly includes bankruptcy. It also includes inability to meet debts as they become due. But skipping a preferred dividend wouldn't be evidence of failure.

What's *high* or *grave probability* of failure? The courts have never stated that in more explicit terms, either.

Since application of the doctrine isn't simple, get advance clearance from the Justice Department—an informal opinion on the antitrust consequences of a proposal.

BUYING THE DIVISION

A financing technique that eases the way for managers who want to buy a division from a parent company:

Create a new corporation that purchases the division, by borrowing up to the hilt against the division's assets. It might borrow 80% of the value of receivables, 60% of inventory, and 60%-75% of land, buildings, and equipment. If it isn't possible to borrow the full purchase price (plus working capital that the new company may need), the selling company may take back a subordinated note for part of the purchase price.

Many lenders are willing to finance these leveraged buy-outs, even where the new owner-managers don't have much cash to invest, if the division had a good track record and if they believe management is strong.

WHAT TO DEMAND OF JOINT VENTURE

Small, technically oriented companies continue to find joint ventures attractive. *Reason:* The new-issues market has soured. Licensing usually is a less profitable route. Most large companies are cautious about outright acquisition.

Key to success: Finding the right partner. *How to do it:*

• Choose a *big* partner. Companies of equal size magnify each other's weaknesses.

• *Obvious requirement:* Find a company strong where you are weak (finances, marketing). *Not so obvious requirement:* Find one weak where you are strong. This kind of match fosters mutual respect, minimizes second-guessing and sharpshooting by your big new partner.

• Define exactly what joint venture will do, with as much detail as possible, to prevent disagreements later on. Better to focus on market use rather than specific products.

• Define the market exactly—by geography and end use. The small company should *never* give up the entire world market or all of the possible domestic markets to one large company.

• Define specific responsibilities of each company—which will do what. *Purpose:* To keep joint decision-making down to a minimum.

If a third company is set up to market the product, be specific about accounting rules and distribution of profits. (A big company will usually want to plow back profits. A small company usually wants dividends.)

If the agreement is just a partnership where the small company sells its product to the larger company, the small company should have protection in the form of written clauses which specify what kind of activities and how much of them the larger company will perform over a specific period of time.

Require periodic review of the performance of each party by a group of directly involved managers.

The small company should retain parallel marketing rights, so the continuity of its marketing can continue unbroken. The larger company benefits from this by getting early customer feedback during product development.

Either company should be able to break the agreement with notice or at certain time intervals.

Source: *Harvard Business Review:* "The Small Business Technology to Marketing Power" by Prof. James D. Hlavacek, State University of N.Y., Albany; Brian H. Dover, president, Survival Technology Inc.; John J. Biondo, president, Solid State Technology Inc. For full report, write to *Harvard Business Review,* Soldiers Field, Boston, Mass. 02163.

PREPARING A SUCCESSFUL MERGER

In *successful mergers*, the chief executive of the acquired company typically finds himself with the autonomy he needs to manage the business plus increased financial resources for expansion, more clout with suppliers, and even more time to do his job as the parent corporation staff begins providing support.

In *mergers that go sour*, the chief executive is typically suddenly burdened with excessive and inappropriate reporting procedures and controls, and spends too much time at meetings, explaining his decisions. Frequently, the acquiring company imposes ineffective, even destructive, decisions designed to force the new acquisition into its business plan. *Result:* The business suffers and an embittered chief executive departs within a few years.

What goes wrong? In a study of a group of unsuccessful and successful acquisitions, management consultants Robert H. Hayes and Associates* detected two distinct patterns:

1. *Failure:* The chief executive considered selling only price and stock multiples. In some cases, he simply accepted the highest bid. *Other faults:*
• Dealt mostly through intermediaries, failed to get to know the top management of the acquiring company.
• Didn't understand the parent company's motives for the acquisition and made no effort to learn its plans.

2. *Success:* The typical executive in a productive merger went well beyond the evaluation of financial terms.

*20 N. Wacker Dr., Chicago 60606.

BUYING, SELLING A COMPANY

Legal expenses incurred in an unsuccessful attempt to acquire a *specific* business or investment are currently tax deductible, even though no contract has ever been signed, according to an IRS ruling. A prior ruling had indicated that expenses would be deductible only if the taxpayer had actually entered into a transaction for profit (even if the contract was later abandoned). However, expenses incurred in a *general business search* (or in preliminary investigation of businesses or investments, such as expenses for travel or ads) aren't deductible.

Rev. Rul. 77-254, amplifying Rev. Rul 57-418.

COMPENSATION

SETTING POLICY

CURRENT TRENDS

GROWTH OF BONUSES. Bonuses are becoming more important as an incentive device. Years ago, bonuses were generally given only to top executives. Now their use is moving through the organization and becoming a substantial part of total compensation.

Who's getting them: Managers—at *all* levels. In some cases, down as far as the *general* foreman (but not the *shift* foreman).

Developing bonus plans makes management come up with an *employee assessment.* Each level of management requires a totally different bonus plan—linked carefully to the job's true requirements. *That isn't easy to do.* It involves personal, qualitative judgments about people. Managers don't like to be put on the line with such assessments.

Problems:
• Devising a bonus plan when a division or product line does well but the company does poorly.
• A division does poorly but outstanding management in one department does better than would have been expected.

One solution: Set a two-part bonus (one part based on how well the overall company did, and one based on how the particular manager did after subtracting positives or negatives beyond his control).

Important: Avoid rewarding windfall "profits."

THE MINIBONUS. Increasing numbers of companies are setting up small funds to reward workers for special efforts. This would cover employees not generally included in regular bonus plans.

Example: A staff person may receive *immediately* a check for $75 for an excellent report prepared under extreme time pressure.

Such spontaneous minibonuses tend to work well in boosting staff morale—and getting even higher levels of achievement from employees.

Note: The bonuses needn't be very large—just *immediate.*

Best way to administer: Set aside a small fund in each department and let the supervisor have total discretion in dispensing the funds. *Caution:* Monitor to be sure that bonuses aren't given for *standard* work. They're for *exceptional achievements.*

Size of payment: Bonuses can get as high as 30% of total compensation in jobs below top management.

MOTIVATION LEVELS. With the exception of those one-time, immediate minibonuses, a bonus payment must be in excess of 10% of employee's annual salary to be sufficient to motivate him to really improve his behavior. Applies to salesmen and managers.

Danger: If the bonus plan is administered too rigidly, following arbitrary,

31

COMPENSATION

bureaucratic rules, it's possible to convert "turned-on" people into grudging "time-servers." Assessment of achievement must be sensitive to what the employee is actually contributing to the corporation.

COMPENSATING SALESMEN. Even though most sales jobs are very rigid, they are still compensated with commissions. Top management is fixing route, customers, products, etc., with little "salesmanship" by the salesman.

What many companies are doing: Switching to straight salary—with bonuses. The bonus is earned by finding new customers, new uses for the product, getting current customers to boost regular orders. *In short:* An unusual improvement over the standard effort.

Extra: With a bonus system, management can change the objective as often as the business operations require. The salesman working on this system is no longer in business for himself. (He can't easily slack off any more when his quota is reached.)

Source: David Weeks, director of compensation and labor relations research, The Conference Board, 845 Third Ave., New York 10022.

SALARIES FOR BLUE-COLLAR WORKERS?

Companies that have tried it and made it work report these tangible benefits: (1) Simpler benefit plans, simpler personnel records, and reduced administrative costs. (2) Absenteeism, af-

ter an initial spurt, falls below previous levels.

Intangible benefits: Breaking down the walls between production and office workers induces a sense of common goals, increases loyalty to the company, eases relations between workers and supervisors, acts as an additional bulwark against unionization.

Does it always work? No. In some plants, when the time clocks were taken off and personnel policies for blue-collar workers liberalized, workers took advantage of the change and foremen lost some of their leverage. In one case, morale fell because men felt deprived of "the right not to work." They couldn't take a day off to go hunting or fishing without feeling guilty.

AVOID MERIT RAISE TRAPS

Anxious to get out of the merit increase trap? Many companies want to, because of difficulties inherent in performance appraisals. The validity of those appraisals is unproven, and the system is frequently abused.

Consider these alternatives:
• Drop the system entirely and base compensation increases on job evaluations *combined* with such factors as company service, time in grade, internal and external economics, salary range, and peer relationships. This is how most employees view salaries anyway, so no harm will be done to their sense of equity.
• Reduce the damage of questionable appraisals by limiting them to three categories—marginal, competent, and

exceptional—and award increases accordingly. (Typically, about 85% of a company's employees will be classed as competent.)

• Keep the merit system, but reduce the merit pool by sufficient funds to finance an award program, in which 5% of the covered employees receive 5% of their annual salary for exceptional work. This kind of standout performance is easily identified, and the presentation of the award bonus when it is earned (rather than at some future sheduled raise time) increases its effectiveness.

Source: Nathan B. Winstanley, manager, personnel planning, Xerox Corp.

YEAR-END BONUSES

If the extra check, or turkey, or other "gift" is required by a union contract, the practice cannot be discontinued without the union's consent. But what if the union contract doesn't cover that point? Can an employer who is obligated to bargain with a union over working conditions decide not to grant the extracontractual benefit?

Points to remember:
• It doesn't matter whether you called the benefit a *bonus* or a *gratuity.* If the bonus was granted in the past on the basis of a separate decision by management each year and was tied to *company profit,* you have a strong argument for suspending it during a year of losses. On the other hand, if the year-end gift has become automatic, you have probably created what one arbitrator called a "psychological commitment" to continue it.

• If the *amount* of the bonus was keyed to wages—cents per hour, or number of hours worked, for instance—you have made the conclusion more compelling that the bonus was really a form of deferred earnings. But if all bargaining-unit employees received the same amount, you have a point in your favor.

• Although the union contract may be silent on year-end bonuses, the matter may have come up during negotiations. Let us say, for instance, that the union claimed you were paying less than a competitor for the same kind of work, and you replied that you give a bonus at the end of the year and the competitor doesn't. The union will take full advantage of that.

• A voluntary bonus, like any other form of gratuity, is supposed to express appreciation for good work and is intended to boost morale. Unfortunately, it can have the opposite effect when employees have come to depend on it.

ALTERNATIVES TO MERIT RAISES

Alternative ways to compensate employees (who often complain that merit raises are eaten up by higher taxes):
• Overtime pay for normally exempt employees.
• More promotions in job title.
• Incentive awards.
• Special one-time merit awards not built into individual's base salary.
• Geographical pay differentials.
• New incentives (perquisites) tied to performance.

THE BENEFIT PACKAGE

GIVING STOCK TO EMPLOYEES

Think twice about incentive plans based on giving stock to key employees.

Such plans as qualified or nonqualified stock options, stock bonuses, stock-purchase plans, and employee stock ownership plans (ESOPs) may be effective as an incentive to greater performance, but they also contain traps for owner-management. Ownership of stock gives an employee the same rights as any other shareholder to inspect the books and records of the company. And an employee, especially one in a responsible position who may have some grievance against management, real or fancied, may be a special problem because he knows just where to look.

If he attempts to exercise his rights to inspect the books, management may be tempted to fire him (especially if he's without an employment contract). That could be a mistake. It would expose management to a suit for action taken to deny the right of inspection and terminate employment for reasons unrelated to the welfare of the company. Management might be *personally* liable in such a suit.

That suit could be maintained even though the stock was acquired by a purchase in the marketplace. But the employee might be on even firmer ground if his stock was acquired from the company under some form of compensation arrangement. Then the connection between his rights as a shareholder and his rights as an employee would be clear.

OPTION PLAN PLUS

A unique compensation technique which has won Tax Court approval and has advantages for both the employer and employee: The employer adopted a stock-purchase plan which permitted some employees to buy common stock on a deferred-payment plan.

• The stock remained unissued until paid for, and cash dividends as such didn't accrue.

• But the employees received credits against the unpaid purchase price equivalent to the dividend that the company was paying on its regular issued stock.

The court allowed the company a deduction for these phantom dividends, over the objection of the IRS. It ruled that the dividend credits were intended as additional compensation to the employees.

From the employees' point of view, the price at which the stock is bought is a superdiscount: the option price minus the phantom dividends. *Warning:* When the stock is held, the price used to compute the capital gains might be the low, superdiscounted level.

DEFERRED COMPENSATION WITH PREFERRED STOCK

An executive won't voluntarily take deferred compensation unless he feels sure he'll make out better than if he takes current cash, pays taxes on it, and invests what's left in something of his own choosing.

One way to come out ahead with deferred compensation: Say an executive is in the 50% top tax bracket and effectively defers $10,000 in compensation. The company invests the $10,000 in preferred stock yielding 9%. The dividends-received credit of 85% results in an after-tax return of 8.7% for the corporation in the 20% tax bracket and 8.31% for the 46% corporation. If dividends can be reinvested at the same yield, *at the end of 10 years the $10,000 would have grown to over $23,000 for the corporation.*

If the executive remained in the 50% tax bracket at time of pay-out, he'd be left with at least $11,500. *Better still:* In the year of pay-out, the executive retires and drops into a lower tax bracket. *Alternative:* The executive took the $10,000 in current cash, paid tax, and invested the remaining $5,000 at 9%. His after-tax yield on the original $10,000 would be only 4.5%. At the end of *10 years he would have $7,765.*

What the company gets: A tax deduction for $23,000 with the deferred-compensation arrangement, as against $10,000 if it had paid that amount in current cash. To make a true comparison, the present value of the larger deduction 10 years hence would have to be calculated by applying a discount fac-

tor. *Another factor to weigh:* The corporation's tax bracket at the time of the deferral and its anticipated rate at the time of the payout.

The risks: Investing in a limited portfolio (probably only a single issue) of preferred stock, and problems of investment management. But a preferred stock mutual fund is now on the market that could solve both problems. The sales charge would have to be taken into consideration in computing yield.

Note: Deferred compensation is not taxed until actually received, if the rules are followed. *Most important rule:* Payment is on a fixed schedule and can't be accelerated by the choice of the executive. The employer must not be required to make specific, actual investments.

STOCK APPRECIATION RIGHTS

How it works: An executive gets the choice of exercising a nonqualified stock option or taking cash (or stock) in an amount related to *appreciation in price* of stock from the time it was granted to the time of exercise. *Tax treatment:* Executive is taxable at ordinary income rates on value of pay-off. Company gets tax deduction of equivalent amount in year of pay-off.

Advantages over options, qualified and nonqualified: The executive isn't faced with possible "alternative minimum tax." Much more flexibility than with qualified options. Better than both qualified and nonqualified plans, in that *no financing of purchase* is necessary.

From company's standpoint, if pay-

35

off is in cash, there's *no permanent dilution of per-share earnings* and there's never any dilution of voting power. If cash is a problem, pay-off may be made in stock, accepting dilution. Some companies, to help executive's income tax problems, provide pay-off equivalent to more than stock's appeciation, so that he may net after-tax an amount roughly equal to actual appreciation.

Special break for insiders: Officers, directors, and 10%-plus shareholders don't have to worry about the short-swing profit recapture (Sec. 16(b) of Securities and Exchange Act of 1934), if they sell some company stock acquired within six months of being given *appreciation rights.*

Big drawback: No chance for capital gains treatment, as with qualified options. But company tax deduction permits company to be more generous.

HOW TO CUT PENSION CONTRIBUTIONS

In searching for new ways to cut costs, don't overlook several bond-management techniques that can make a substantial dent in yearly corporate pension-fund contributions. Dozens of major US corporations, such as General Motors, GAF, and Firestone, have lopped millions of dollars each off their annual funding of pensions. Smaller pension plans, with as little as several million dollars in bonds, can also generate sizable savings.

The techniques, called *immunization* and *dedication,* are computerized mathematical formulas offered by large banks, investment consultants, and brokers. They enable portfolios to lock in today's high interest rates, giving actuaries a rationale to raise assumptions on the overall return rate on pension investments. When the rate goes up, firms need lower contributions to meet pension liabilities.

IMMUNIZE AND DEDICATE. By immunizing a portion of a portfolio, a corporation hedges against fluctuations in rates at the same time it retains the flexibility to convert to cash. The idea of immunization is to stagger maturities. *Effect:* Declines in rates that adversely affect reinvestment of coupon income and principal of maturing bonds are offset by increases in prices of existing long-term bonds. The formulas include regular selling of longer-term bonds and reinvestment in shorter securities, thereby foreshortening the investment period. As a result, anticipated yields for actuarial periods of up to eight years in length can be met whether rates go up or down. At the end of the period, all securities will have matured and a new pool of cash will be available for reinvestment.

A *dedicated* bond portfolio can pay out interest income and principal from maturing securities along the way, and it can be in existence for a much longer period than an immunized portfolio. That's because it is targeted for a specific purpose, usually the funding of benefits for existing retirees. By segmenting such a group from overall pension liabilities, pension managers are able to structure a portfolio that has corresponding cash-flow characteristics.

THE DRAWBACKS. Locking in yields

by either technique may not provide the most productive use of assets. Common stocks, for example, may provide a higher return. Also, when an immunized portfolio is converted to cash at the end of its tenure, sharply lower interest rates may prevail for reinvestment. It may have been better to have had an actively managed portfolio than continued to lengthen maturities rather than to shorten them.

Set up a pension reinvestment program that makes sense in the long term. It's misguided to start with the sole aim of raising assumptions in order to save on contributions. If one of these techniques is adopted, *designate only a portion of the total bond portfolio.* Only the most troubled companies these days are switching to immunization or dedication on a grand scale. *Important:* That the securities immunized or dedicated are of the highest quality, usually those of the US government or its agencies.

Source: Martin Levenson, senior VP and actuary, Martin E. Segal & Co., 730 Fifth Ave., New York 10019.

WHY PHANTOM STOCK MAY BE BETTER THAN THE REAL THING

A top-level executive who expects to build company profits substantially generally wants something more than a good salary. Frequently, it's some sort of stock deal. But if he's working for a close corporation or a subsidiary whose stock isn't publicly traded, stock presents problems: Need for buy-back arrangement and valuation for *buy-back.*

Case in point: An executive thought he had both problems licked with a straight stock deal. He developed a formula for arriving at a value for the stock and proposed that the company buy it back after a set time, at that price.

The company, while not disputing the validity of the formula, didn't relish the prospect of buying back the stock at an astronomically high price, if all worked out well; especially so, since the buy-back would be without any offsetting tax benefits to the corporation.

Actually, the executive's proposal *didn't* stack up *that* well for him, either. If he really struck it rich, he'd be hit with a huge capital gains tax.

In this perspective, a phantom stock deal proposed by the company stacked up better for both.

• The firm accepted his formula for valuing the stock.

• Starting five years from the date of the agreement, the firm would give him the increase in the value of the stock that would have taken place under his formula. The first time around he'd get five full years of appreciation.

• Thereafter, he'd be paid the phantom appreciation annually.

• Payments were conditioned on his staying with the company, which was no problem.

This meant that the payments would be eligible for the earned income ceiling rate of 50%. It's true that that is higher than the 20% maximum rate on long term gains. But actually, he was better off in the sense that under his original plan, he was to buy company stock at the then prevailing value. With this deal, he didn't have to put up any money to acquire the stock. And from the company's standpoint, it was also a much better deal. It was able to get a full income tax deduction for whatever payments it made under the phantom agreement. For the company in a 46% tax bracket, the after-tax cost would be 54 cents on the dollar.

CORPORATION'S REACQUISITION OF SHARES NO BUSINESS EXPENSE

When a corporation buys back stock from a shareholder, the transaction is a nondeductible capital expenditure. *Exception:* When the corporation's survival depends on getting back its stock, because the shareholder was in a position to hurt the company and intended to do so.

One corporation hired an executive and transferred 11% of its stock to him, subject to agreement that the shares be redeemed at a formula price when his employment terminated. Later, management realized it had made a bad bargain. The executive would get a higher price under this formula than was justified by the value of his services. To get rid of him and his ability to cash in on an unjustifiably profitable stock deal, the company fired him and bought back his stock before the value could go up too far. The court noted that the price paid was *not* deductible as an expense to secure the company's survival. The expenditure had *not* been dictated by outside forces directly threatening the company's

business but by desire to correct a bad bargain.

WARRANTS ISSUED TO EXECUTIVES MAY PRODUCE FULLY TAXABLE INCOME

A publicly owned corporation adopted a *Key Personnel and Employees' Stock Warrant and Restricted Stock Option Plan*, under which the corporation sold to designated executives warrants to purchase company stock. The stated purpose of the plan was to provide additional incentives to promote the success of the business.

An officer-stockholder bought the warrants and subsequently sold them at a substantial profit. (He used none to get additional stock.) He claimed a *capital gain*, alleging that the warrants had been issued to the management group to allow them to acquire enough stock in the corporation to retain effective control should they ever be challenged by outside shareholders. He also argued that the warrants had been purchased as an investment and hence were capital assets.

Decision: The court disagreed on both counts. Where assets are transferred to an employee to secure better services, that represents *ordinary* income in the form of compensation.

The plan itself said the warrants had been issued as an incentive, that is, compensation. And since the warrants had no readily ascertainable fair market value at the time they were issued, it couldn't be said that originally they had been intended as an investment rather than compensation.

USING BOOK VALUE AS AN INCENTIVE MARKER

Many executives in public companies have become disenchanted with stock purchases and options geared to stock market prices. Of course, those in nonpublic companies don't have the opportunity to become disenchanted. But what both public and closely held companies can do—and what they're doing with increasing frequency—is adopting stock purchase plans not geared to stock market price or some other external yardstick, but to *book value* (as measured by the balance sheet).

Book value generally increases steadily over the years. Most of the time it's not subject to the sharp fluctuations of the stock market. Occasionally, of course, a company's stock sells below its book value. You can never sell stock to company employees at book under those conditions, but that's a relatively rare case. Usually book value will be substantially below the current market, in good times and bad, so sales at book value are an obvious incentive.

The incentive is provided, however, at the expense of diluting the equity of existing shareholders to a higher degree than with an equivalent amount of qualified stock options (exercisable at market price at time of grant). Hence, the shareholders may offer greater resistance to the book-value plan.

One way to lower their resistance: Require the resale of stock to the company at the *then* book value on termination of the employee's services at retirement or otherwise. Properly structured, this type of arrangement gives the executive capital gains treatment on the difference between his purchase and the resale price. While he holds the stock, any dividends paid to him are, of course, taxable as ordinary income.

Caveat: Book value may increase even with mediocre earnings. Hence, a book-value plan, unless somehow geared to earnings, may simply reward longevity without regard to company or individual performance.

What to do: Structure a book-value plan so that the right to purchase is only available in years in which targeted earnings levels are achieved, and limit the participation to employees achieving targeted individual performance levels.

Book values obviously depend to a large extent on the accounting techniques and principles applied in computing them. These may change over time and the plan must make provision for appropriate adjustments to avoid possible windfall benefits to participants. If a company were to switch from cost-basis accounting to current value at some time in the future, assuming inflation continues apace, a sizable windfall would result.

DEFERRED PLANS

Hold on to, or attract, key executives by setting up a deferred compen-

COMPENSATION

	CASH	PHANTOM STOCK	PERFORMANCE UNITS
EXECUTIVE BENEFITS	• Taxed at maximum rate of 50%. • No danger of forfeiture. • Easy to understand. • Market performance of company stock not a factor.	• Option award accompanied by a like number of "phantom share" awards, so when executive exercises options he receives an additional payment equal to gains in phantom shares. Less need to raise cash to exercise options.	• Usually awarded together with nonqualified options, the performance units take on value later in time and the value is based on predetermined goals for executive (or for function or division of the company). Units are paid in cash or additional stock.
DISADVANTAGE	• No direct participation in growth of the company.	• Still must have enough cash to exercise options.	• Might have to raise cash to exercise options.
COMPANY BENEFIT	• Straight, current tax deduction.	• Better cash flow than with SAR, because executive actually exercises the option.	• Cash flow is better than with SAR, because executive exercises options. • If performance unit structure is well done, system can be effective incentive.
DISADVANTAGE	• Talented executive may be lost to company that offers more cash, plus chance to participate in ownership, growth.	• Gain for executive tied to market performance of stock rather than his own performance.	• Setting up performance goal for award of units is difficult.

sation arrangement that provides the company with both *current* and *deferred tax deductions.* *(Under the usual arrangement, the corporation only gets deferred* tax deductions.) With this plan, the corporation can select exexutives *and* dollar amounts in a discriminatory way, since the plan is nonqualified, *i.e.,* no IRS approval is needed.

How it works: Under a written agreement, the corporation invests a specified amount of dollars (say $10,000 each year for 10 years) in a mutual fund or other investment, in the name and ownership of the corporation. The investment becomes a corporate asset on the balance sheet.

The corporation borrows 40%, or $4,000, each year against the collateral of this investment to buy a cash-value life insurance policy (over $100,000) on the life of, and owned by, the executive.

Upon retirement, the executive or his beneficiary receives an annual percentage of the *net* investment value of the investment at the time of retirement.

What the corporation gets: A *current tax deduction* each year for the life insurance premium and for interest on the loan. *Future tax deductions* when the annual compensation payments are made to the executive after retirement.

What's more, if the investment

growth is good, then the entire plan might cost the company nothing or even return a profit.

What the executive gets: Additional *current compensation*, a substantial life insurance policy. He has to pay annual income tax on the premium, but since he owns the policy, he can borrow against the cash value, which far exceeds his income-tax liability.

He also gets *deferred compensation* at retirement—an annual percentage of the net value of the investment.

PAYING EXECUTIVE'S TAXES: A TRICKY FRINGE

Even if the corporation assumes the tax, or reimburses the executive for his higher taxes, the executive must report the company's tax payment as personal, taxable income. Then the corporation will have to offer to pay taxes on *this* taxable income.

	NONQUALIFIED STOCK OPTION	STOCK APPRECIATION RIGHTS
EXECUTIVE BENEFIT	• Employee has the choice of having value of the option (difference between price he pays and the market price) taxed to him, *at ordinary income tax rates,* either at the time of the grant *or* at the time he exercises the option. Subsequent appreciation, when stock is sold, taxable at lower capital-gains rates.	• Usually granted at the same time as nonqualified options, the SAR gives the executive the choice of either exercising the options in a conventional manner or receiving payment either in stock or cash, of an amount equal to the spread between the option price and the current market price of the optioned stock. • Executive needs cash only to pay for increased ordinary income-tax obligation if he elects simply to cash in SAR, as most do.
DISADVANTAGE	• Size of gain is related to market performance of stock. • Must have cash to exercise option.	• No extra remuneration if stock doesn't go up in value.
COMPANY BENEFIT	• Tax deduction for the company is equal to the amount of ordinary income realized by the executive at the time the option is granted or exercised.	• No need for insiders to sell company shares in order to raise cash to realize options.
DISADVANTAGE	• Best tax saving for company would be if executive elects to be taxed at the time option is exercised. *But* the executive will probably prefer to be taxed at time of grant. Conflict would have to be resolved.	• Less cash flow than with simple nonqualified option if executive simply cashes in SAR because of the loss of cash that would have been generated by purchase of option and the failure to realize Federal income deduction the company could take if the executive exercises option (as above).

COMPENSATION

INTEREST-FREE LOANS

The Tax Reform Act of 1984 effectively eliminated interest-free loans as a *family* tax-saving device by making them subject to income tax. Loans from an employer to an employee are also subject to income tax under the new law. But the way the new rules work, employer-employee interest-free demand loans remain a viable and attractive way to provide a fringe benefit to an employee.

Employer-employee demand loans under $10,000 are not covered by the new rules unless their purpose is tax avoidance.

The tax impact of loans above $10,000 amounts to a double wash. The loan is first taxed as though the employer paid and the employee received *wages* in the amount of the interest that was not charged on the loan. Then it is taxed as though the employee paid and the employer received *interest* on that amount. The deal is a wash for both —there's no net tax liability for either employer or employee. The employer lists imputed interest income but deducts the imputed wages. The employee reports the wages and deducts interest expenses of the same amount.

Interest deduction problems: An interest deduction could be denied if the employee is subject to:
• The alternative minimum tax on tax preferences.
• The limitation on the deduction of interest on investment indebtedness.
• The denial of a deduction for interest incurred to earn tax-exempt income.

Caution: Below-market-rate-loans to a shareholder are subject to different rules than employer-employee loans.

PROPER HANDLING OF EXECUTIVE DEATH BENEFITS

Many executive employment contracts provide for death benefits to be paid to the executive's beneficiary if the executive dies before retirement. If the benefit is included in his taxable estate, a sizable portion of it will be lost to federal taxes.

To keep the benefit out of an executive's estate, the employment contract should:
• Name both primary and contingent beneficiaries to keep down the value (to 5% or less) of any reversionary interest, *i.e.*, any amount that might revert to the executive's estate because named beneficiaries die before he does. IRS tables are used to calculate the value of the reversionary benefit.

Use language making it clear that the beneficiary is getting a present interest, *not* a future interest.
• Make clear that the executive has absolutely no right to change the beneficiaries nor any other right over the payment under the contract.
• Provide that no amounts are to be paid to the executive during his lifetime or to his estate on his death, either directly or indirectly.

To exclude *qualified* plan benefits, make sure that beneficiaries *other than the estate* are named and that they aren't paid in a lump sum. The executive may retain the right to change the beneficiary without qualified benefits being included in his estate.

HEALTH PROGRAMS

MEDICAL REIMBURSEMENT PLANS FOR EXECUTIVES

Two ways for executives, owners, or partners to pay large medical and dental bills incurred by their families but not covered by insurance:

1. The individual pays. (Assume the sum to be $5,000.) If he is in the 50% tax bracket none of his expenses are deductible unless his adjusted gross income (AGI) is $100,000 or more. (An individual can deduct only those medical expenses that exceed 5% of AGI.)

2. His company has a qualified medical reimbursement plan. It reimburses him for the *full amount* of the bill. He doesn't pay tax on this reimbursement. If the company is in the 46% tax bracket, its after-tax cost would be only $2,700.

Conclusion: Tax benefits of this kind of plan for executives are clear. *Best candidates:* Companies with a small number of employees eligible for benefits.

Discrimination in favor of highly compensated employees is not allowed. These are (a) the 5 highest paid officers of the company, or (b) a shareholder who owns more than 10% of the company's stock, or (c) the highest paid 25% of all employees. If the IRS rules that the benefit program is discriminatory, the executives will be taxed on the amounts that they were reimbursed on the same basis as though they had been paid dividends.

The plan should spell out: (1) Which employees are covered, by level of employee; (2) whether or not their spouses and dependents are covered; (3) the benefits that are provided; (4) the maximum dollar amounts allowed; (5) how bills will be substantiated; (6) when the plan is effective; and (7) when coverage is terminated.

It is *not* easy to limit the medical reimbursement plan to a specified group of employees. The Revenue Act of 1978 requires that plans be *non-discriminatory* beginning in 1980, unless they are funded through insurance carriers, or the restrictions on some employees (i.e., short-term workers) are "reasonable."

MEDICAL REIMBURSEMENT PLANS

Smaller companies shouldn't consider providing a medical reimbursement plan without first taking two steps:

1. Combine it with an existing health care plan to reduce costs overall.

2. Purchase stop-loss insurance to limit what the company has to pay over the amount covered by the basic medical plan.

Reason: Costs are so high that a serious illness could impose a disastrous and untimely expense, namely, higher insurance premiums the next year.

43

DESIGNING A DENTAL PLAN

Dental insurance plans, as well as other medical plans, assume increased importance as employee benefits today as dental costs continue to outpace the general inflation. Key factors to consider in structuring a dental plan, which add nothing to the cost but which make most employees happier with the plan:

- Employees should be allowed to select their own dentists and decide what dental procedures are to be followed.
- If the company has a large number of employees in the area, it will want to try to line up as many dentists as possible to participate in the plan and accept assignments of benefits in payment of their fees. But many dentists won't participate, and employees *shouldn't* be limited to participating dentists.
- The employee is expected to pick up a percentage of the cost, but the percentage shouldn't be higher for the employee who receives services from a nonparticipating dentist.
- Keep the administrative procedures simple. The average claim can be expected to be about $65 and can be handled on a cash basis. More extensive work may be performed on an installment basis.
- Costs are reasonably predictable. Second-year costs can normally be expected to be *less* than those of the first year. Where the group of employees is of sufficient size and diversity in age to assure maintenance of average costs, *self-insurance* should be seriously considered.

Predetermination of claims. The dentist is asked to send the company or insurance carrier a description of the dental work to be performed. In this way, all concerned will understand what costs are to be reimbursed.

OPTIONS IN DENTAL CARE PLANS

Consider all the options before settling on an employee dental plan benefit. Set priorities for who should be covered, and how much employees can be expected to contribute toward care. A minimum benefit plan will cost approximately $75 annually for each employee and costs can go up to five times that amount. A checklist of options:

- Cover only employees or employees *and* their dependents.
- Pay for all dental costs or a stated amount for each standard procedure. (Will help hold the lid down on premiums and claims.) The schedule might also exclude cosmetic orthodonture or other specialized coverage; or that type of coverage can be taken care of in a schedule where employees share more of the cost.
- *Another alternative:* Provide dental care from a dental service corporation or a group dental practice. Or include a contractual arrangement with several dentists to provide care.
- Use deductibles to reduce the number of smaller claims and cut the amount of optional dental care. But some care (emergency or preventive) may not have deductibles at all. Major procedures may use one deductible and general basic procedures another.

• Maximum benefits can be included in the plan, with either an annual limit or a lifetime limit. Special limits may be included for orthodontics.

• Dental coverage shouldn't begin until an employee has worked for a specified time, thus eliminating those who only take a job for the dental benefits.

Heavy use of plan in first year will slow down after a while—after employees have made up for neglected dental care.

Plans that pay expenses can be set up using insurance companies or Blue Shield or a 501(c)(9) trust can be established and self-insurance provided.

CHOOSING CORPORATE DENTAL PLAN

Best to avoid the type of dental plan that combines dental and medical insurance. Medical plans are designed to *discourage* use, while dental plans are tailored to *encourage* use. In dentistry, early treatment is always cheaper.

Better: A separate plan, based either on a schedule of fees or on reasonable fees prevalent in the region.

Big advantage of the fee schedule system is that costs are predictable, especially during the first three years of the plan. The problem is that it's difficult to adjust fee schedules from region to region in a way that's equitable to employees.

Five items to avoid in any kind of dental plan:

• High coinsurance levels.
• High annual maximums.
• Large deductibles. They tend to dis-

courage use of preventive services.

• Incentive plans. They encourage employees to postpone major services until maximum coverage is available.

• Block benefits. Potential bad experience when blocks are added.

SHIFTING TO A HEALTH MAINTENANCE ORGANIZATION

If your company provides health insurance benefits to more than 25 employees, you are required by law to give them the option of membership in a local health maintenance organization (if there is one in your area) instead of renewing coverage with a conventional carrier. And if there is a health maintenance organization available, you may be missing a good bet for the company *and* your employees if you don't *push* for the shift.

Reasons:

• Superior benefits. Comprehensive health care, including many services conventional policies don't cover (regular checkups, emergency care, certain laboratory, diagnostic, and treatment procedures if they're performed outside the hospital).

• Emphasis on *preventive* medicine pays big dividends in reduced absenteeism, fewer long leaves for serious illness, less frequent charges for rapidly escalating hospitalization and related costs. HMO coverage encourages tests and exams often postponed for lack of coverage under conventional plans.

• Effective cost control, eliminating

unnecessary services, duplicate exams, ineffective treatments prevalent under employee-chosen medical service plans. (Operating under a fixed prepayment plan, the HMO *makes* money when the patient stays well, loses if he needs frequent treatment or hospitalization.)

More important, HMOs offer companies an ideal vehicle for reducing workmen's compensation premiums and Occupational Safety and Health Administration compliance costs.

Of special interest: Tie-in arrangements with HMOs for low-cost rehiring and executive physical exams (screening out persons with defects or conditions predisposing them to occupational illness); regular physicals required by OSHA (soon reaching the point where company medical staff must otherwise be expanded); analyzing medical data on company employees exposed to specific hazards.

IN WHAT FORM TO ACCEPT DISABILITY PAYMENTS

An employee can exclude from gross income any illness or accident payment from his employer or its insurance company if the payment is for *permanent loss* of use of a member or function of the body. But for the exclusion to apply for tax purposes, the payments must be attributable to a *period of absence from work*.

The case: A 50-year-old employee was permanently and totally disabled. In lieu of making monthly payments to

him until he became 65, the insurance company offered to make him a lump-sum payment, and he accepted. *Too bad.* What he received had to be included in his gross income, for *prospective* payments aren't "for a period during which the employee is absent from work," but are for a period during which he *may* be absent. Rev. Rul. 74-603, 12/23/74.

In screening candidates for top positions, it is vital to test the psychological fit of the person. One top corporate executive makes it a practice to take a candidate out for a night on the town, dining, drinking. *Purpose:* To see how the candidate wears over a period of several hours of intense social activity and talk.

INSURANCE VS. LABOR CONTRACT

Make sure the benefit booklet furnished by your insurance carrier for distribution to your employees is entirely consistent with your union contract. If it isn't, you may find yourself picking up the tab for sums the insurer refuses to pay.

Case in point: An unmarried woman was hospitalized for a miscarriage. Blue Cross refused to pay the cost because (1) she hadn't signed up for family coverage, and (2) the medical attention she received wasn't what the booklet referred to as "usual, reasonable, and customary" benefits under a policy for *single* people.

But an arbitrator's reading of the *union contract* turned up no language putting the employee on notice that maternity benefits would *not* be covered in her case. So the company had to pay.

An opposite conclusion would have been reached if the contract had said it would only cover items the Blue Cross contract covered. In that event, there would have been no question or ambiguity about the insurance coverage, and the company would not have had to assume the cost of the woman's hospital bill.

PENSIONS & PROFIT SHARING

MANAGEMENT LIABILITIES UNDER THE PENSION LAW

Anyone who participates in any significant way in the administration of an employee benefit plan may become personally liable to make good any resulting losses if he fails to act with a very high degree of skill. That's the essential message of fiduciary standards provisions of the Pension Reform Act of 1974.

Who's liable: Anyone who's involved in running the plan or its investments. What's more, anyone with the power to appoint these fiduciaries (the board of directors, for example) may also be liable for resulting losses.

How to measure skill: The "prudent man" standard (under which a person is expected to act with the same degree of skill and care that a prudent man would exercise in the management of his own affairs) no longer applies. The 1974 law requires that fiduciaries act as *prudent experts.*

Investment hazards: Anyone not qualified as an investment expert shouldn't be involved, at least in common stock investments. Remember, even investments in debt instruments involve risks; long-term debt securities can fluctuate greatly. If the rule of a recent New York case were to be applied to the federal law, then each security in the fund must meet the "prudent expert" test and an overall increase in total fund value wouldn't excuse a single *im*prudent investment.

Important: A professional should be listed for the job—either as trustee or as investment manager. The directors or committee who select the professional won't be liable for his acts or omissions, provided they act prudently in making the choice and in overseeing him on the job. The investment manager, if not a trustee or named fiduciary under the plan, must be a bank, insurance company, or registered investment adviser and must acknowledge in writing that he is a fiduciary before those who select him will be relieved of liability.

Diversification: The law requires diversification of investments. Ordinarily, it won't be considered prudent to invest the entire fund or a large part in one type of security or even in different securities if all are dependent on conditions in one locality or industry. This doesn't mean, however, that you can't put all of the funds into a single pooled investment fund, mutual fund, or insurance or annuity contracts.

Prohibitions: The law sets out a number of transactions that are prohibited between the plan and a so-called *party in interest.* The transactions include sales, exchanges, or leases of property, lending of money and extensions of credit, furnishing of goods, services, or facilities. *Caution:* The law prohibits the acquisition of the company's own securities or real estate, except within narrowly defined limits.

Liability for cofiduciaries: One fiduciary may be held liable for the defaults of a cofiduciary if he conceals an improper act or if he fails to make reasonable efforts to remedy it. The same applies to trustees.

Insurance: The law permits the fiduciary to buy insurance for himself. Or the company can buy the insurance, but only if the policy permits recourse by the insurer against the fiduciary if he's committed a breach of duty. The insurance in this case would protect only the plan and not the fiduciary himself. It is well to bear in mind that fiduciary or company-purchased insurance will very likely protect the fiduciary only against what may be deemed negligent breaches of duty. If a fiduciary, for example, were to knowingly engage in a prohibited transaction, it's doubtful he'd be protected.

Excise taxes: If you run afoul of the investment rules or the prohibited transactions rules, and ignore an IRS notice calling for correction, you may be hit with an excise tax of up to *100%*

of the amount involved.

Minimizing the risks: Some things that may be done to reduce risk exposure: (1) Amend plans to reduce the number of fiduciaries. (2) Use a bank as trustee and custodian. (3) Use a qualified, financially sound investment adviser to direct investments. (4) Make very careful investigations before designating in-house or outside fiduciaries. (5) See that fiduciaries are adequately insured. (6) Set up machinery for policing compliance with standards and replace fiduciaries whose performance is questionable. Make sure that reports to IRS, the Secretary of Labor, and employee participants are properly made and are on time.

WEAKNESSES OF 'CAFETERIA' BENEFIT PLANS

Much talk is making the rounds about "cafeteria" benefit plans. Under these plans, each employee can select, at the beginning of the year, the kinds and amounts of fringe benefits that meet his individual needs. The idea sounds great, but don't jump in without considering three drawbacks:

1. Possible unfavorable tax rulings from the IRS if the plan favors highly compensated executives under qualified retirement plans. If the plan discriminates in favor of highly compensated individuals, their benefits will be taxable.

2. Adverse selection insurance. Employees who anticipate heavy medical expenses will favor medical benefits, while older employees will prefer

retirement benefits and the like, loading each category with high risks.

3. Employee resentment. An employee who chooses his benefits imprudently is just as likely to blame the company as himself.

PENSIONS RISING

A top executive can expect a pension of almost half his salary when he retires at age 65.

The following are the actual percentages based on estimated pension benefits for the top three highest paid executives in five different types of businesses.

1. A manufacturing executive can expect a pension that's about 46 percent of his salary.

2. A retailing executive can expect 37 percent of his salary.

3. A commercial bank executive can expect a pension of 49 percent of his salary.

4. An insurance executive can expect a pension of 49 percent of his salary.

5. A gas and electric utility executive can expect a pension of 48 percent of his salary.

Source: *Across the Board*, published by The Conference Board, 845 Third Avenue, New York 10022.

WHY SWITCH TO DEFINED CONTRIBUTION PLAN

Most pension programs are *defined benefit* plans, which spell out *what the plan is to deliver* eventually to the par-

ticipants. But it might be prudent business to switch your pension to a *defined contribution* plan, which spells out *how much will be contributed* to the pension fund annually. The participant effectively collects what's in his pot at the time he is ready to retire or opt out in any other way.

Reasons for the shift: The minimum vesting (that part of the fund which is unequivocally the employee's) requirements of the 1974 Pension Reform Act figure to add from 10% to 20% to the cost of *defined benefit* plans. Either the company must come up with more money or benefits must be cut.

With a *defined contribution*, however, minimum vesting is no problem so long as the plan isn't top heavy—there are no fixed costs.

In the past, the funding of *defined benefit plans* could be geared to economic conditions. Now level funding (equal annual payments) is required. Further, in valuing the assets of the trust for funding purposes, you must take into account market values. Hence, a drop in market values during a period of recession will call for increased funding.

The stiff rules that come into play should you terminate a defined benefit plan don't apply to a *defined contribution plan*. And the federal guarantor of the funds, the Pension Benefit Guaranty Corp., may look to the terminated company for up to 30% of the company's net worth for *each* plan. A company with two plans could have a lien on 60% of its net worth.

Converting a defined benefit plan into a defined contribution plan won't be easy. It will call for expert guidance. Certainly, no new defined benefit plans should be started without weighing the factors mentioned. There may still be situations in closely held corporations where a defined benefit plan will better suit the interests of the principals than a defined contribution plan. But again, expert assistance will be required to make that determination.

HOW TO CUT PENSION FUNDING COSTS

The most commonly used insured pension plan around is the so-called split-funded individual policy plan—and that's one of the more expensive ways to provide coverage.

Here's how it works: The trustee of the plan buys an ordinary life insurance policy for each individual in the plan. It's then determined what the cash value of the policy should be at the time of retirement and how much cash must be added to buy an annuity for the retiree for the rest of his life. The life insurance portion will be a level contribution (the *same amount* each year). The other portion is usually calculated each year by the life insurance company, and it is apt to be very conservative in making the necessary calculations—which means you'll likely pay the "high" side of the estimate. Also, the cash values of the life insurance policies accumulate at a low guaranteed rate (3% to 3½%). In addition, the individual policies have high sales commission rates and high processing charges—and no discounts are available.

A better way: It is entirely possible to reduce these costs substantially by moving to a self-administered plan that provides equivalent benefits. The cost savings result from: (1) Removing life insurance from the plan and substituting group term insurance provided by the company. (2) The adoption of cost-saving actuarial methods and assumptions that are more realistic than those used by insurance companies. (3) Shopping for better buys for annuities. (4) Taking the cash surrender values of existing policies and investing them to produce much greater yields than those provided by the insurance policies.

JUST BECAUSE IRS APPROVES PENSION PLAN DOESN'T MEAN EXAMINER WILL ALLOW DEDUCTIONS

Even if a corporation's pension plan has been approved ("qualified") by the IRS for tax purposes, management shouldn't become complacent—it still faces obstacles.

One corporation sent a copy of its plan to the IRS and received written word of its qualification. But when an examination was made of the corporation's tax returns for the next three years, the pension *expense* deductions were disallowed on the ground that the plan shouldn't have been qualified in the first place, and the ruling was withdrawn *retroactively.*

Reason: Impermissible discrimination existed in favor of highly compensated employees, for although all persons on the payroll were eligible for pension coverage, those receiving low salaries all elected to take advantage of an option to receive a current cash bonus instead of long-term pension benefits. It was held that the IRS could retroactively withdraw a ruling which had been given when *the service wasn't in possession, at the time of approval, of all material facts.*

Comment: The corporation's advisers should have foreseen that the plan, as written, might ultimately benefit only those persons in whose favor there cannot be discrimination, that is, officers or other highly compensated employees.

Source: Harwood Associates, Inc., 63 T.C., No. 22, 11/26/74.

IMPACT OF EX-EMPLOYEE'S FORFEITURE OF RIGHTS

What happens to money earmarked for employees' benefits upon retirement under a deferred profit-sharing plan, when some of the employees leave their jobs before they become entitled to vested (non-forfeitable) rights in these amounts?

Such "forfeitures" cannot go back to the employer in a Treasury-approved profit-sharing plan. So, customarily the plan provides for allocation of forfeited money to the accounts of employees still covered by the plan. But the plan must be drafted carefully in this respect. If forfeitures go to the remaining participants under a formula based upon length of service to the company, and they are primarily officers and employee-stockholders and other highly compensated persons, the plan, in actual operation, is considered

discriminatory. *And that's the end of the tax advantages of the plan.*

Source: Quality Brands, Inc. et al., 67 T.C., No. 14, 11/8/76.

SALE/LEASEBACK AIDS PENSION PLAN

Here's a good deal for a company and its profit-sharing or pension plan: Sell the company real estate to the pension plan and rent it back. If handled correctly, the tax advantages benefit both.

The 1974 pension law allows both pension and profit-sharing plans to arrange such sale/leasebacks. In the case of pension funds, the total investment in company real estate *and* securities can't exceed 10% of the value of total assets. But this limitation doesn't apply to profit-sharing plans if they specifically provide for it.

With both types of plans, however, only qualifying real estate may be acquired, that is, the funds can only be invested in a substantial number of parcels that are dispersed geographically and are adaptable to more than one use.

Chain stores, branch headquarters, and warehouses spread over a wide area should qualify. Undeveloped land used for storage or possibly parking, or being held for future expansion, is likely to qualify also.

Reason: Undeveloped land gives the company no depreciation deduction for tax purposes, but reasonable rent paid will be deductible. Neither the pension fund nor profit sharing is concerned with depreciation deductions, since the fund is tax exempt.

These same depreciation considerations come into play in a different way when dealing with improved real estate. In such a situation, the company would be expected to want to utilize the real estate upon which there is not much depreciation left and it will be able to get substantially greater deductions by way of rent payments. In any case, the company will have to consider the capital gains impact, if any, of the sale. If its tax basis is low and the fair market price and selling price is high, timing the transaction so that there will be offsetting losses could be an important consideration.

Warning: Retirement plans, if they are to retain their tax-exempt status, can't be run for the benefit of the employer, but only for the exclusive benefit of the plan participants and beneficiaries. A sale/leaseback that shapes up as a bailout of the employer places the tax-exempt status of the plan in jeopardy and exposes those responsible to personal liability.

Best to have an experienced tax lawyer for guidance every step of the way.

WHEN AND HOW TO ADVISE EMPLOYEES

Many corporations, as a matter of goodwill, permit employees to bring personal tax or retirement problems to the appropriate company department for answers or advice. That can be very dangerous for the corporation. Even when the corporation isn't obliged to furnish answers to such questions, if the company does undertake to give a reply, the answer must not only be accurate, but delivered in a manner that the employee can understand.

One case: A retiring executive asked his firm for advice on which of several settlement options he should choose for his pension, advice he eventually followed. However, because of unique circumstances, his pension payout was much less than the company had estimated as a maximum figure. The executive's estate sued the corporation for the difference and won. No matter that the advice was completely accurate; it hadn't conveyed the risk in a way that the executive could understand.

Under the Pension Reform Act of 1974, employers *must* explain the complexities of their pension plans to employees in language they can understand. That's quite a problem, considering the complex employee mix of poorly schooled persons, recent immigrants, and even brilliant scientists who may not have equipped themselves with a knowledge of financial planning.

SETTING UP A PENSION FOR NONUNION EMPLOYEES

A loophole in the 1974 pension law solves one of the stickiest problems posed by the IRS: The situation where a company wants to set up a retirement plan for *non*union employees and there are one or more unions in the picture.

Formerly, the IRS required *comparability of plans.* The employer and *non*union employees couldn't have a sweeter plan than the union's. The problem became impossible when there were several unions involved—each with a different pension plan. And if a union had no plan, it might have to be offered one before nonunion people could be covered.

Now, a plan can be set up for the owner-employee and other executives without regard to the union's plan—or lack of one, if they turned a plan down in the past (possibly taking cash instead).

You can exclude employees who are covered by a collective bargaining agreement, provided that benefits were bargained for in good faith.

TOP-HEAVY PENSION PLANS: NEW RULES

Starting in 1984, companies will not be able to make tax-deductible contributions to *top-heavy* retirement plans unless certain steps are taken. A plan is top-heavy if more than 60% of the benefits go to *key employees:* Officers of the company, 5% owners, 1% owners who receive more than $150,000 in compensation and the 10 employees with the largest ownership interest. Under new law, no executive earning less than $45,000 a year will be considered a key employee. Also, only top-ten owners earning over $30,000 a year will be considered key employees.

To qualify a top-heavy plan for tax purposes, a company must:
• Vest benefits on an accelerated basis. There must be 100% vesting of benefits after three years of employment, or *graded* vesting over six years (20% after two years, 40% after three

years, 60% after four years, 80% after five years, 100% after six years).
• Limit the amount of compensation on which benefits are calculated to $200,000 a year.
• Provide minimum benefits for *non-key* employees. *Definition of minimum benefits:* 2% of pay × number of years of service, or 20% of compensation, for a defined-benefit plan. And 3% of compensation for a defined-contribution plan.

PENSIONS FOR PART-TIME HELP

Try to keep part-timers' attendance less than 1,000 hours per year. *Reason:* Under the 1974 pension reform act, you must include in your corporate pension plan any employees working at least 1,000 hours a year (if they have been employed for a year).

Then, the company must contribute the same percentage as it puts in for the principals. Corporate plans, of course, may require even greater contributions.

IDEAS FOR GETTING EMPLOYEES READY FOR RETIREMENT

Best way to prepare employees for retirement: Workshop meetings throughout the year to answer questions, hand out material.

Alternative: A series of face-to-face interviews with a well-informed benefits manager. *Topics:* Company pension plan benefits; life/health insurance information and options; policy on unused sick days, vacation time; Social Security,

53

Medicare, Medicaid; local benefit programs, tax planning, housing, travel, volunteer work. *Also:* Discounts available for senior citizen associations' travel and entertainment.

Source: Otto Kramer, consultant, Massapequa Park, N.Y.

SETTING UP A RETIREMENT PLAN

A corporation set up an employee benefit plan, which the Internal Revenue Service *qualified.* Two years later, when the corporate income tax return was audited, the IRS determined that the plan was discriminatory because rank-and-file employees weren't covered. The company offered to amend the plan to provide retroactive coverage. *No way,* ruled the court. It might seem harsh to deny the plan qualification retroactively. But *any failure* to provide nondiscriminatory coverage is fatal to qualifying a plan. No basis exists in the current tax law to correct an employee benefit plan retroactively.
Myron v. U.S., 9th Cir., 2/23/77.

MANAGEMENT MUST CONTINUALLY CHECK VALIDITY OF ITS PROFIT-SHARING PLAN

A corporation adopted a deferred profit-sharing plan which had been approved by the Internal Revenue Service. Two years later, when the plan

was amended in certain respects, approval was again granted.

Seven years later, an IRS Revenue Ruling held that, with similar facts, a plan could not be approved because it was discriminatory in favor of the corporate elite.

When the corporation's tax deductions or contributions to its profit-sharing plan were disallowed on a return for a subsequent year, the corporation argued that its deduction had been protected by the Service ruling specifically addressed to the company (and none of the factors on which the ruling was based had been misrepresented or had changed).

Tax Court's view: A private ruling to a taxpayer is automatically revoked by a subsequent published ruling.

What to do: Alert your accountant (or some other knowledgeable person who keeps abreast of current tax matters) to what the court warned here: *"A taxpayer must keep informed about subsequert published rulings of the IRS which may affect his private ruling."*

Wisconsin Nipple & Fabricating, 67 T.C., No. 36, 12/16/76.

SOME TOUGH PENSION RULES APPLY TO PROFIT-SHARING PLANS

Many companies switched from pension plans to deferred profit-sharing plans as a result of the Pension Reform Act of 1974. But a later Treasury ruling made it clear that it's dangerous to think that a corporation can completely avoid the law's strict requirements by changing to a profit-sharing deal.

The trap: In crucial areas, both types of plans are treated in the same manner. For instance, by law, a retiring employee who has been married for at least a year has to be given the option of a joint and survivor annuity instead of a single-life contract. That is, a surviving spouse is entitled to *not less than half* of what otherwise would be payable to the employee. The employee's benefit is correspondingly pared to finance this. This protection is automatic *unless the employee files an election to keep the full annuity for himself.*

Company responsibilities: The company has the responsibility of writing this into the retirement plan. It must also explain the complexities of the joint and survivor provisions, with individualized dollar illustrations, "in layman's language," which can be quite difficult to do. The Internal Revenue Service has just ruled that this applies to profit-sharing plans as well as to pension plans.

KEEPING THE BOOKS CONFIDENTIAL

Executives of a closely held company might feel that a profit-sharing plan is a good idea but they may be unwilling to give a union, either present or potential, the right to look at the company books.

Solution: A deferred profit-sharing plan with profits defined as net income as listed on the company's federal income tax return.

The union cannot question the accuracy of the computation of profit, because book income is not being used for the purpose. The employees and their union are assured that the corporation isn't doctoring the income figures in order to cut down on the shareable profit. And the IRS is probably better equipped than the union accountants to find out whether income has been understated.

NO FORFEIT OF VESTED PENSION BY NONCOMPETE CLAUSE

Every state places some limit on the extent to which management can enforce an agreement that an employee won't work for a competitor when he leaves.

Courts don't like restrictions that broadly prevent someone from plying his trade anywhere. But if the noncompete restriction is limited to not working for competitors in the nearby area for a year or two (and especially if the employee has been exposed to key information), the restriction will probably be upheld under a rule of reasonableness.

Many profit and pension plans provide that a participant *forfeits* his benefits *if* he goes to work for a competitor. Is such a limitation subject to the same rule of reasonableness or not? One case considered the problem both in terms of the recent federal legislation and state law.

The case: For 17 years an executive worked for a Charleston, South Carolina, bank. He was a vice president when he left to go to work for a Greenville bank—miles away. The Charleston bank refused to pay the executive his share of its profit-sharing plan. It argued that the forfeiture provisions of the plan were reasonable. They didn't prevent the executive from working for a bank in another town. They simply provided that he lose his benefits. The choice was his.

The federal Pension Reform Act of 1974 provides that vested benefits may not be forfeited "because the employee later went to work for a competitor or in some other way was considered 'disloyal' to the employer." Although the executive changed jobs *before the effective date* of the 1974 Act, the South Carolina Supreme Court was impressed by the congressional determination that it is in the public interest to have a mobile working population, unimpeded by forfeiture provisions, and so ruled *in his favor.*

Almers v. S.C. Natl. Bank of Charleston, S.C. Sup. Ct., 1975.

ESOPS MUST BE RUN FOR EMPLOYEES' BENEFIT

Employee stock ownership plans (ESOPs) may provide incidental benefits to *owner*-shareholders. *But* they must be operated for the primary benefit of *employee participants.* If shareholders are to serve as trustees, their dealings on behalf of the plan must meet the standards of fairness and pru-

dence imposed on them by the Employee Retirement Income Security Act (ERISA).

The Department of Labor has shown concern about the use of ESOPs to benefit the owners at the expense of employees. In a recent suit, the first of its kind brought thus far, the Labor Department succeeded in having a purchase of closely held stock set aside and the trustee-owners ousted on the basis of their having failed to act prudently.

PROFIT SHARING FOR REHIRED WORKERS

If you have a profit-sharing plan, you may have to "unscramble the eggs" if you allocate money forfeited by employees who are laid off or quit in one year, then are rehired and work the next year.

Forfeitures of terminating employees sweeten the profit-sharing pot of those remaining. But the 1974 pension law spells the new ground rules for covered employees, breaks in service, and nonforfeitable benefits.

Example of the danger: An employee has worked 1,000 hours minimum in a year for employee to be defined as a full-time for a company in a calendar-year plan; he's laid off in September, then rehired in March, and works more than 1,000 hours in that year. It is likely, under the 1974 rules, that this employee, having more than 1,000 hours both in the year laid off and the year rehired, didn't incur a one-year break in service and is entitled to at least a partial benefit for both years. And if the employer had forfeited the employee's account, say in

January, and allocated it to the remaining employees, the money would have to be broken out.

The same sort of problem could come up in a *pension plan*, although no unscrambling is required—only a possible actuarial loss.

INSURANCE

ONE WAY TO CONTINUE GROUP TERM INSURANCE COVERAGE FOR RETIRED EMPLOYEE

There is a way to continue an employee's group term life insurance coverage even after he has retired. *Benefit:* It can be very attractive to both the company and the employees.

The plan works for companies that currently provide group term life coverage in excess of $50,000—the level where the premium for the coverage becomes taxable to the employee.

How it works: Funds are set aside, either through a trust or directly with an insurance company. These funds are to be used at a *future* date to provide a form of paid-up life insurance for an employee after he retires. Thus, the employee is able to maintain the same level of protection after retirement that he had while he was working—and he will not be burdened with any income-tax consequences.

The dollars that are used to fund this retirement benefit can be deducted currently by the employer. *Attractive feature:* It doesn't cost the company anything extra to provide the insurance after the employee retires.

During his lifetime, the employee pays taxes on that portion of the cost of his company-paid insurance, which provides more than $50,000 in coverage.

DON'T BE QUICK TO OFFER MASS-MERCHANDISED INSURANCE TO EMPLOYEES

Be wary of the growing trend toward arranging with an insurance carrier to offer your employees cut-rate home-owner, automobile, and even term life insurance coverage. The benefits to the employees are major because the insurance company can sell a lot of policies with little or no sales and administrative cost.

Be aware: Many of the direct and direct administrative costs fall in your company's lap. You become the "broker." Complaints end up going through your personnel office. If the employee is unhappy with the insurance company's handling of his case, you carry the burden of his ill will.

Probably best to *avoid* the arrangement. But if you decide the benefits to the employees are worth the trouble, consider, at the very least, arranging to work the plan through a local insurance broker. Let him handle the paperwork. (He'll be delighted to gain the business.)

COVERING EMPLOYEES' SPOUSES

Now spouses of employees covered under *group* insurance plans can get low-cost life insurance up to $50,000 with liberal underwriting (just a health statement up to age 55, medical exam after 55). The amount of insurance on a spouse was *previously* limited to $5,000, never exceeding 50% of the insurance on the *employee*.

Is this coverage necessary? Many families today are two-income households. In the event of the death of a spouse, the surviving employee suffers considerable losses; in addition to the loss of wages, other losses include no joint income tax return, estate taxes, loss of marital deduction, loss of joint gifts.

Premiums are paid *by the spouse* through payroll deduction. Thus this low-cost coverage can be provided by the employer at no cost to the company.

TAX TRAPS

PROMISE TO PAY ISN'T DEDUCTIBLE AS A PAYMENT

Not long ago, the United States Supreme Court spoke on a question about which other courts disagreed among themselves for years. At last we have the answer.

An accrual-basis corporation is allowed a deduction for stipulated amounts paid into a Treasury-approved employee benefit plan by the filing time of the federal income tax return for the year.

One corporation, which apparently was cash-poor at the moment, made the required contribution to the trusees of its deferred profit-sharing plan in the form of an interest-bearing promissory note. It was secured by collateral and personally guaranteed by three officers as individuals. The value of the collateral, plus the net worth of one of the guarantors, greatly exceeded the face value of the note. It was therefore as good as gold, better in fact. But *no tax deduction was permitted.* Deduction of the employee benefit plan contribution depended upon *payment* on time, and a note, however amply secured, is only a *promise to pay.*

What to do: If cash isn't available to make payment into the profit-sharing plan by the specified date, borrow from a bank. Here there could have been that very same collateral for a bank loan which had been used to secure the note.

Don E. Williams Co. v. Comm'r., U.S.S.C., 2/22/77.

CONSOLATION PAYMENTS MAY BE TAXED

The services of the president of a merged company no longer were required, although admittedly he had contributed to the success of the company that was being scrubbed.

The directors of his old corporation got permission from the new owners to appropriate part of the company's surplus for payments to him and other officers who couldn't be absorbed.

Since the payments were made in recognition of past services and had not been thought of as *gifts*, they were treated as taxable compensation. The fact that there was no *legal obligation* to make payments to the dispensable president or other officers didn't mean that the payments were not *in recognition of services*, thus taxable as compensation.

INCLUDE PERKS' 'REASONABLENESS'

A corporation's payment for executive or other salaries is deductible only to the extent that it is "reasonable." If the Internal Revenue Service determines that the amount paid an executive is "unreasonably" high, the excess won't be deductible from the corporation's income tax and it *will* be taxable to the individual.

Reminder in a decision: Salary is only the starting point. Bonuses and corporate contributions to the company pension plan for the benefit of a particular employee also count. So do group insurance, expense accounts that don't have to be justified to the company, advice to an individual from outside consultants whose fees are paid by the company, and all the other perks that are now being built into executive compensation packages.

Edwin's, Inc. v. U.S., D.C., W.D. Wis., 2/24/77.

UNREASONABLE COMPENSATION CAN BE COSTLY

In the past, the Internal Revenue Service took the position that compensation to an executive that might appear to be "reasonable" (and therefore deductible) might still be treated as a nondeductible dividend if the corporation had distributed little or no dividends to its shareholders. But the IRS has advised informally that it will *no longer* use this so-called *McCandless rule.** Whether or not compensation is reasonable will no longer involve the company's dividend policy. It will be reckoned *only* by assessing the executive's contribution to the company's operation.

*From a case in the Court of Claims.

59

COMPENSATION

USE OF COMPANY CAR SOLELY TO GET TO WORK IS TAXABLE INCOME

As everyone knows, the cost of getting to and from work is not deductible—even when there is a good excuse.

Case in point: A busy corporate executive was supplied with a company car to use exclusively for travel between his home and the office. "That's not commuting," he argued, "for I'm required by the conditions of my job to do so much work at home that my trips between my house and the office really amount to travel between one place of employment and another, which is deductible."

Not so, the Tax Court ruled. It's still commuting if the travel is for an individual's benefit rather than the corporation's. And there was nothing to show that any corporate purpose was served by allowing him to use a company car.

C.A. White Trucking Co., Inc. et al., T.C. Memo. 1977-6, 1/13/77.

HOW TO PROTECT A COMPANY AGAINST IRS SALARY CHALLENGE

When the Internal Revenue Service disallows part of a corporate deduction for executive salaries as unreasonable, the company has to pay a tax deficiency with interest and the executive is in an embarrassing position because the Service says he's overpaid.

Solution: An agreement that requires the executive to repay any amount disallowed the corporation because it was excessive. He can then be paid a very generous salary without fear of tax loss to the corporation. But it can't be retroactive.

In one case, the president agreed on December 14, of a certain year, to repay his corporation any portion of his salary disallowed as unreasonable. Sure enough, part of his pay package for that year was disallowed, and he repaid it all. IRS wouldn't allow him a deduction for that part of the repayment representing compensation before the December 14 agreement. Those payments were made without restrictions, conditions, or liability for repayment.

The repayment was *not necessary.*

John G. Pahl et al., 67 T.C., No. 23, 11/22/76.

HOW EXECUTIVE'S USE OF A COMPANY CAR MAY BE TAXED TO HIM

Here's a very common situation, with an unsuspected trap.

Case in point: A company-owned car was used totally by the company president. In cases of this sort, the Internal Revenue Service often treats the fair market value of the *personal use* of the car as taxable income to the user. It's treated as a dividend if he's a stockholder or as compensation if he's not.

The remaining problem is what part of the value represents business use (nontaxable) and what part personal use. Here the president, a shareholder, argued that his personal use of the car was merely incidental to business use. But when asked the make of his own automobile, he admitted that he owned none.

The court ruled that the full value was a taxable *dividend* to him. Since dividends aren't deductible by the corporation, the president claimed that the value of the car, if anything, represented *compensation*. That argument misfired too, for there was no proof (like a reference in corporate minutes) that the use of the car had been *intended* to be compensation. A dividend, on the other hand, can be *assumed*, even if none was declared or intended.

Personal ownership of a car, any car, would have been helpful.

William D. Gardner et al., T.C. Memo. 1976-349, 11/6/76.

CONTINGENT COMPENSATION ARRANGEMENTS

Some closely held corporations make *sizable* year-end salary adjustments for *officer-stockholders* after a highly profitable year. *Problem:* The Internal Revenue Service, predictably, will rule that these generous pay-outs really represent nondeductible dividends, for in fact they are a splitting of corporate profits.

There is a far greater chance of justifying the payments as deductible compensation if the arrangement is made early in the year—before that year's profits are known (or even suspected). *For example:* Bonuses of x% if profits exceed a figure which is completely unknown, are apt to be acceptable to the IRS. Handled this way, the ultimate pay-outs weren't based on any knowledge of what profits would be available for sharing.

According to Treasury regulations, if *contingent compensation* is paid as a result of free bargaining between corporation and individual *before* the services are rendered, the deduction may be allowed. That applies "even though in actual working out of the contract it may prove to be greater than the amount which would ordinarily be paid."

EXPECT IRS TO DELVE INTO THE COMPANY'S RECEIVABLES

IRS examiners have been instructed to look into corporation receivables for loans to stockholders and "any nonbusiness-connected loans."

What the IRS will try to do: (1) Tax stockholder loans as dividends if there were corporate earnings and there are neither interest-bearing notes nor any corporate authorization for the loans. (2) Impose accumulated earnings tax if they can demonstrate that earnings were retained, not for *corporate* purposes, but to benefit the stockholders by transmitting funds to them other than in the form of dividends, which are taxable.

Action: Have all such "loans" formalized by signed obligations to repay, with adequate interest. And be sure that each "loan" is liquidated periodically. Otherwise, both corporation and stockholders are vulnerable.

Audit Techniques Handbook for Internal Revenue Agents, IRM 4231, Section 643(11).

CREDIT UNIONS A BETTER-THAN-EVER FRINGE

Credit unions have long offered members (usually employees of a company) loans at low-interest. Recent changes in banking regulations make them a more attractive benefit than ever. *What they can do:*

- Make 30-year conventional mortgage loans.
- Make secured or unsecured loans for 12 years (or less).
- Offer different interest rates for *long-* and *short-*term money.
- Provide revolving lines of credit that function like credit cards (at a far lower interest charge).
- Provide members with "share drafts," much like checks—but interest is paid on the money on deposit until the draft is drawn.

Credit unions can cover all employees, or some segment(s). For information on how to get one started: Credit Union Natl. Assn., Box 431, Madison, Wis. 53701.

THE EXTRA FRINGES

HOW A COMPANY CAN BAIL EMPLOYEE OUT OF FINANCIAL CRISIS

A salesman contemplated bankruptcy for himself because of his financial difficulties. The company president felt straight bankruptcy would hurt the company's reputation, and he persuaded his employee to file a Chapter XI petition instead—offering the salesman an advance of enough money to provide his creditors with 20% of the amount due them.

The salesman agreed. And the company advance was set up on its books *as a debt payable from future com-* *missions.*

When the IRS sought to attach those funds as property owned by the salesman, in order to satisfy a federal tax lien against his property for unpaid taxes, the court blocked the move.

Reason: Had the Service attended the meeting at which creditors agreed to accept 20% of the amounts due them, the source of the funds used to pay them would have become known, for it was no secret. (As a result of Chapter XI proceedings, the IRS even got $143.27, 20% of what was owed. *All* taxes would have been discharged had the salesman gone through *regular bankruptcy proceedings.*)

The money advanced by the corporation couldn't be regarded as the salesman's, subject to claims against him.

The funds belonged to the company, "whose sensitivity to the good repute of its salesmen," commented the court, "together with the debtor's willingness, brought about the success of this proceeding to the benefit of all the debtor's creditors." And that included the U.S.

Comment: Had the books not clearly reflected the money as a loan of corporate funds, the money might well have been gobbled up by the Service as the salesman's property.

In the Matter of Marshall Gefke, Debtor, D.C., W.D., Wis., 9/5/74.

EMPLOYEE WELLNESS PROGRAMS MAKE BIG MONEY

In these days of still-increasing costs of medical benefits, more companies are adopting employee *wellness* programs.

The most prevalent are programs to stop smoking, control hypertension and promote fitness and nutrition. There are also programs for stress reduction, time management and cholesterol reduction. No conclusive evidence presently exists showing that in the long run these offerings will reduce employee medical costs. *But in the short run they:* Improve morale. Cut absenteeism.

Cost: About $10 per employee per year. Companies that offer many options will find costs running as high as $150 per employee. *Comparison:* $3,000 —$4,000 is typically spent per employee in traditional *rehabilitative* programs for employees who suffer strokes and heart attacks.

Find out from employees which programs they value most. Get the union involved from the start. Pilot test a program at one plant or office location.

Make sure a wellness plan is *voluntary.* Some companies offer a regimen that's the pet of the chief executive. *The word goes out:* Participate or else. Also, the program must be *confidential.* If, for example, someone is determined a "health risk" and the news gets around, it will discourage other employees from making use of the program.

Source: Dr. Andrew J.J. Brennan, Center for Health Help, 1 Madison Ave., New York 10010.

FUNERAL LEAVES

It's common for companies to pay for up to three days of leave to attend funerals or make funeral arrangements when an employee's close relative dies. But if the union contract clause or personnel policy statement hasn't been phrased carefully, this benefit may cost more than the employer intended. Some questions that arise:

• Is an employee entitled to three days' pay when the funeral interrupts a paid vacation or when he is on layoff for lack of work?

• What rate of pay does a worker receive for funeral leave on an overtime day?

• Are employees entitled to pay for three days of "mourning" on learning of a death in the family in a place too distant for them to attend the funeral?

• The death of a friend or a distant relative may have a greater emotional impact on a person than that of a parent or an immediate relative. Does the funeral leave provision obligate the company to pay for time off when such circumstances are alleged?

COMPENSATION

No policy statement can hope to cover every contingency. But one company put an end to most uncertainty (and wasteful arbitration cases) with this contract clause:

An employee having a death in the immediate family (father, mother, brother, sister, father-in-law, mother-in-law) shall be granted a leave to attend or arrange the funeral, and for travel incidental to such activity. Such employee shall be given 8 hours pay at his regular straight hourly rate, for up to three days so taken. This allowance will not be paid for any day for which the employee is otherwise compensated, or for any day for which the employee would otherwise not have been at work.

CUTTING OUT EXTRA FRINGES

When management agrees to a benefit (time off or some other extra) to compensate employees for some inconvenience, does the benefit have to continue even after the inconvenience has been eliminated? Foresight can save lots of money. *Some examples:*

• Because it was unsafe to smoke at work, a printing company in an old building permitted employees to take a third smoke break each day, although the union contract called for only two. Years later the company moved to a building where smoking could be permitted at the machines. Management tried to eliminate the third break, but the union objected.

The company won this case. The arbitrator said the "past practice" didn't outweigh the specific contract language calling for two 10-minute breaks. The problem could have been avoided if the employer had had the foresight to make it clear *at the beginning* that the extracontractual benefit applied *only* if smoking couldn't be permitted at work.

• A distributor customarily ran overtime on Fridays and Saturdays to meet demands for quick deliveries. But then he put new clerks on the night shift, eliminating the need for overtime. The union didn't object to the change as such, for management's right to a second shift was clearly spelled out in the contract. But it insisted that day shift employees had to be given overtime anyway.

The union won. *Critical point:* The employer had cited average *overtime earnings* as a reason for keeping hourly rates down during the most recent contract talks. Although the plans for a night shift were already under way, the company's negotiators didn't mention it.

• Several years ago, when few women worked in a plastic products manufacturing plant, they were permitted to stop work ten minutes ahead of the men. The reason wasn't clear. Recently, more women were added, and they constituted just about a third of the workforce. Fearing that such discrimination might be illegal, and that the men might begin demanding longer wash-up periods, the wash-up time for women was reduced to that of men. An arbitrator upheld this action.

Advice: Once your company bargains collectively with a union, it is hazardous to grant benefits in excess of those in the collective agreement. If extra benefits *are* granted for special

64

reasons, the union should be placed on notice that those benefits may be withdrawn when circumstances change.

COST OF MOVING

What happens if an employer transfers an employee and takes his home off his hands? To make the deal more palatable, the company agrees to buy his existing home at fair market value, as set by independent appraisers. If this is done privately, there are no broker commissions to be paid by the employee.

He must pay tax on any gain he makes, should he be paid more than his adjusted basis for the home. But although an employee customarily must report as taxable compensation any economic benefit which he had received because he is an employee, he won't be taxed upon the value of the real estate commission which this deal saved him. Source: Revenue Ruling 72-339.

OVERTIME: PAY OR TIME OFF

Some legal interpretations of amendments to Fair Labor Standards Act indicate there's some room for interpreting "compensatory time." You must pay *non*exempt employees for work *in excess of* 40 hours per week at a minimum of time-and-a-half. However, previous ruling prohibiting compensatory time now gives way to interpreta-

tion that compensatory time *within the pay period* is acceptable.

Example: Given a two-week pay period at $200 salary for work of 40 hours, employee works 50 hours during first week. He then only has to work 25 hours during second week to get his regular $400 for the two weeks (40 hours less time-and-a-half for 10 hours accrued overtime). Lunch periods don't count as hours worked; breaks, short rest periods, however, do.

Warning: Employer's failure to provide adequate compensation entitles employee to unpaid overtime compensation *plus* an additional equal amount as damages and payment of "reasonable" attorney's fee.

CAUTION ON SALARY 'ADVANCES'

Think twice before you bail your employees out of financial emergencies with loans or salary advances. A recent Circuit Court of Appeals ruling forbids payroll deductions you might have to make to recoup the advance—even if the employee's willing.

Case involved sums advanced to cover fines and vehicle damage in a drunken-driving accident. *The off-setting payroll deductions brought the driver's wage below the legal minimum.* Court ruling upheld a Fair Labor Standards Act regulation that permits a deduction to be made at the direction of an employee for payment to third parties. But the wage deduction cannot be paid to an employer, who would ostensibly "benefit."

COMPUTERS

STARTING OUT RIGHT

HOW TO COMPUTERIZE

Virtually any company probably has considered or should be considering computerization of its business systems. With minicomputers now costing $3,000, the obstacle of high price has disappeared.

Key problems: (1) Pain of the conversion, and (2) fear of what will happen if it doesn't work.

Computers, it's important to understand, *won't reduce accounting payroll costs.*

WHAT A COMPUTER CAN DO. Handle paperwork faster. Give management a clearer view of the business. Move invoices out faster (thereby improving cash flow). A computer gives management an easy way to study each customer—with a view toward assessing how profitable a customer is (or isn't). And more.

It will take time: The switchover won't be made overnight or even in a few months. Minimum turnaround is about three months for a simple system. It may be a year for a complex one. There's no way to do the job faster, even if a prepackaged computer program is acquired that seems to fit your company's operations perfectly. *Reason:* No two companies operate alike. Even proven programs need changes, adaptations, and careful debugging checkouts.

WHEN DOES A COMPANY NEED A COMPUTER? Accounting bogs down. Bills go out later and later. Receivables begin to accumulate. Discounts for prompt payment are lost. More clerical help must be hired. Part-timers are brought in to try to catch up on paperwork.

The presence of one or more of these symptoms does not mean that a pro-computer decision is essential. *One possibility:* Improving procedures may solve the problems without buying a computer.

How to find out: It's nearly impossible to make the assessment yourself. Never ask a computer salesperson to make the decision—no matter how honest he is (and most are), there's no way that he will recommend *against* a computer.

The assessment must be made by an outsider with no direct vested interest. The outsider could be an accounting firm (if it has experience in this area) or a computer consultant (CPA can help you find one).

Important: We find that of all the assessments we run, 25% indicate that a computer *is not* called for—an improvement in the accounting procedures is all that is needed.

Potential for a massive mistake: Proceeding with a computer plan just to satisfy the ego of the top person in the company, who may equate "computer" with "having made it in business." Often, those horror stories (of systems that don't work, cost 10 times the estimate) are the result of such a rationale.

COMPUTERS

COMPUTER CONVERSION SUGGESTION. Plan to phase one small part of the business into the computer at a time. Don't close down the manual procedures. Continue to run them parallel to the computer.

In a typical situation, the switchover of, say, the accounting system may take about six weeks. Four more weeks should be spent on testing. Then run the manual and computer systems simultaneously for another two weeks. After that, consider dropping the manual system.

Resist any effort to shorten these times. If anything, you may want to extend them for safety.

Remember: There will be problems. No switchover is error-free. At best, you can minimize the problems, but not eliminate them.

Source: Kenneth O. Cole, Seidman & Seidman, accountants, 15 Columbus Circle, New York 10023.

WHY COMPUTER SYSTEMS DISAPPOINT MANAGERS

Problems plague computer users because of the lack of involvement of management (at all levels). As a result, systems are put together which really don't fulfill management needs.

In part, it's a communication problem. Data processing has its own jargon, and the typical "expert" enjoys befuddling his clients. This leaves management in awe of the technical complexity of computers—unable to cope with the system as well as *unable to improve it.*

Eventually this problem will disappear. Managers climbing the ranks of the organizations are becoming more familiar with—hence less awed by—the technology. In addition, most current business college graduates have a working familiarity with computer technology.

In the meantime, organizations using or contemplating the use of computers should set up a training program for management.

Caution: Although all computer vendors offer "free" top management courses, these inherently have drawbacks:

Much of it is sales-oriented—toward the vendor's equipment.

Too little attention is given to the costs of planning and preparation.

The applications discussed or proposed are usually far too advanced for first-time users.

The complexities of computer use are oversimplified.

Source: Dick H. Brandon, Brandon Consulting Group, Inc., 1775 Broadway, New York 10019.

HIDDEN COSTS COMPUTER SALESPEOPLE FAIL TO DISCLOSE

When buying or renting a computer for the first time, be especially wary of any computer salesperson who quotes the rental cost of the computer as the *principal* cost involved in computer use. It just isn't true!

Rental cost is probably only one-fifth of the *total* cost, which includes:

Hidden but necessary staff:

At least one *programmer* to maintain vendor-supplied hardware.

Systems and program *maintenance* staff (can be a major expense). Many computer installations have as many people in maintenance of applications as in development.

User staff: Whenever you are developing a new application, at least as much user time is required as data processing staff time. Though not directly measurable, it will be significant and may result in temporary expansion of user staff.

Hidden supply costs:

Perhaps the most significant and surprising supply cost is *paper.* A line printer with a rated speed of 1,100 lines per minute can produce some 700,000 pages of information per month, in six copies if necessary. A paper bill of $5,000-$10,000 per month is possible if system is running at full capacity.

Magnetic tapes, disk packs, cassettes, diskettes also build up quickly in inventory. A library of 5,000 tape reels and 200 disk packs isn't unusual; it could cost $100,000!

The cost of copying becomes surprisingly heavy.

Other costs to recognize:

• Rental charges for *software.* A variety of software may be needed for your installation. Some of it is free, but more and more vendors are charging a licensing or rental fee.

• Power prices are increasing also. Electricity to run a typical computer might add between $1,000 and $2,400 to the monthly bill. And the cost of power for air conditioning the installation (a must) can double that.

• Taxes can be surprising, too: sales taxes on computers, supplies, certain software, computer services, maintenance, etc.; property taxes on the hardware (often passed through in leases) and sometimes on software as well.

• Physical installation costs. Buyer usually pays for shipping, power, and air conditioning hook-ups, uncrating and installation. Site preparation costs still more for false flooring, security, fire protection, etc.

• Initial cost of *data conversion* and input can be high. And if the data in its present form can't be read by machine, someone is going to have to convert it into machine-readable form. These tasks can be very expensive—costing up to $2.50 per 1,000 *characters.*

• Costs of running a new system *with the old.* A cautious management may wish to operate on a parallel basis for two to three months—which can double staff requirements for that period.

Source: Dick H. Brandon.

COMPUTER NEGOTIATIONS —GET THE BEST PRICE

Goal: To get the minimum *total price.*

What to avoid: Being swayed by the vendor's flattery so that you accept the quoted price as the best price.

Solution: A "most favored user" clause in a written contract that states the product is being sold at the lowest possible price, *and* that if it is later discovered that the unit was sold to someone else for less, the customer will get a retroactive discount amounting to the difference.

What to expect from the vendor:
- Inclusion of the clause.
- Refusal to provide the clause either because he has a policy preventing this, or because the price really was *not* the lowest that the product had been sold at.
- Inclusion of the clause but with modifications that result in confusing the terms of the discount, or provide him with a way to protect himself in dealing with other favored users.

Source: *CN Report*, International Computer Negotiations, Inc., P.O. Box 364, Winter Park, Fla. 32790.

ELUSIVE MANAGEMENT INFORMATION SYSTEMS

The concept of a *management information system* (MIS) is an exciting one. But, more important, despite much publicity, a *true* management information system isn't attainable—not today, and not until management itself is highly structured and clearly defined.

As long as management is an individualistic process, it is difficult to see how a management information system can be built. Each time a manager of an organizational element is changed, the information system would have to change to accommodate the requirements of the new manager. If an organization has 2,000 managers, with 25% turnover, promotion, or transfer, it would mean changes in 500 management positions a year, or two a day. Clearly, it's impossible to achieve the infinite flexibility of a complete infor-

mation system required to meet the demands and whims of such a changing population. The limit here isn't technology, but human capacity for designing and programming this huge amount of flexibility into an inherently rigorous discipline—that of the moronic computer.

OTHER RESTRAINTS. The aggregate cost of producing a single computer instruction (from design to installation) has about doubled since 1960. Just a payroll system, for example, requires some 20,000 unique instructions. A total, all-encompassing *management information system* for a typical company could run from $50 million to $100 million, with an annual maintenance cost of 30%-40% of that original cost.

WHAT TO DO IN THE INTERIM. An intermediate type of information system is achievable—focusing on *common data bases*. It isn't possible today to build an all-encompassing corporate data base, with an infinitely flexible access system; it is possible, however, to build *several* data base systems concentrating on single-purpose data bases, thereby reducing the complexity.

Here are some suggestions for getting started, in an *evolutionary* rather than *revolutionary* way:

1. Isolate the typical, functional data base components your organization needs. It will include data bases on:
- *Employees:* Salaries. Benefits. History. Performance. Skills. Etc.
- *Products:* How made. Pricing. Costs.
- *Materials or manufacturing resources:* Production facilities. Time standards. Etc.
- *Money:* Accounts receivable and

payable. Budget. Etc.

- *External contacts:* Customers. Vendors. Regulatory agencies. Etc.

2. Identify the logical components of the organization, such as production, marketing, finance, etc., to find out who needs what data.

3. This will provide a two-dimensional matrix (data base vs. who needs data) of the overall systems components you need.

4. Then develop what appears to be close to a *10-year information system plan*—it will take that long to develop, mature, and get a payback from this type of system. Thus, you need:

- A corporate long-range plan, so you don't design an information system for today's needs that's obsolete before it is operational.
- An assessment of the impact of the corporate plan on information system's resource needs.
- An information system plan.
- Resources.

5. The key resource requirement is systems analysis and management analysis skill. This is the one that will take the longest to develop and implement, and this is probably where to start. Needed in this case is a businessman with a high degree of analytical skill—a top-flight manager capable of and willing to undertake the design of a complex information system.

6. Typically, it is best to work with a small number of high-powered analytical talents, a task force of full-time senior management staff, highly trained in management science, reporting directly to top management, *with significant authority*, where necessary, to alter corporate organization and *information flow channels*.

Today, in most organizations, information systems are developed randomly, to meet the day-to-day requirements identified by today's managers. This random growth will never build into an orderly, evolutionary corporate information system. This can only be done to a careful *plan*, after which a building block approach is feasible. The building blocks will include data bases and functional information systems keyed to growth and flexibility, with a certain amount of open-endedness for ultimate interconnection.

Source: Dick H. Brandon.

USING CONSULTANTS

Computer consultants can be useful, provided they are selected extremely carefully. Principal effective uses: Those areas where it is *not* necessary for a company to develop permanent expertise.

Do not use data processing consultants for regularly recurring activities in your organization, or you run the risk of becoming overly dependent on them.

Key areas which are typically nonrecurring:

- Feasibility analyses (although most subsequent projects will also require some form of feasibility analysis).
- Personnel selection, in first-time installations.
- Equipment selection, in first-time installations.
- Acquisition method determination.
- Vendor contract negotiation.
- Standards development.
- Staff training, in special skills.
- Installation and project audits.

• Performance measurement (on a one-shot basis).

In selecting a consultant or consulting firm, remember that it is easy for an unemployed technician to use the title "consultant." Make sure that the people who are going to do the consulting for your organization (and who may not be the people to sell you on the concept) have explicit, specific experience at the task you need performed. Best to check references by calling the last company or, preferably, last three companies for which these individuals performed similar work.

Consultants normally charge on a per-day basis, often at high rates. It is wise to incorporate a detailed *scope statement* in the contract. That would include a description (table of contents, in the case of a report or study) of the product to be created. This, coupled with some form of upper limit on costs and expenses (be especially cautious about markups of expenses, and charges for unsubstantiated typing, telephone, etc., which should be covered in the basic overheads) will provide some qualitative and quantitative protection.

Source: Dick H. Brandon.

SELECTING A DATA PROCESSING MANAGER

The key to a *successful* new data processing installation is the person chosen to manage it. Too often, the manager of accounting or his deputy is promoted to the slot by default. It is usually far better to look inside the organization, since the management and technical expertise required in a new installation are usually significantly higher than in an ongoing or replacement installation.

Computer manufacturers sometimes offer assistance in recruitment on an "unofficial" basis. *This is very risky.* The candidates of vendors are likely to be one-vendor-oriented and relatively easy to manipulate. Since the success of the installation is highly dependent on *proper vendor performance*, this is the time for a tough manager who will hold the vendor to its commitments.

Evaluating the experience of computer candidates is tricky. *Recent instance:* Management recruited a person with apparently comparable installation experience and a record of two successful installations. Unfortunately, the experience was *not* truly comparable. The manager had no explicit experience in one key facet of the job, data base design, the importance of which was not recognized by the company. *Results:* (1) The installation schedule underestimated the time and effort by 50%; (2) a crisis occurred at installation time; and (3) ultimately the whole data processing effort had to be aborted.

Technical experience counts more in an *initial installation* than in an *ongoing* one. After successful operations, the principal skills required are managerial: planning, control, top management communication and liaison, and profit orientation. Two sets of characteristics must be present in someone who can successfully perform as a DP manager: ability to set up an installation and then run it.

Source: Dick H. Brandon.

BUYING OR LEASING A COMPUTER

Acquiring a computer generates many of the same tax questions as acquiring any major asset. But *software* adds to the complications. Important tax savings are possible because software can often be treated differently (and more favorably) than hardware. It is therefore wise to consult qualified counsel before the contract is signed. Considerations:

Federal income tax.

• The purchase price of the computer *and* any simultaneously purchased software can be depreciated in five years, without residual value.

• The software can be *expensed. Caution:* The price must be separately stated (or otherwise provable for tax purposes). Most software "purchases" are single-payment, perpetual license fees, which can be treated either way.

Guideline: Purchased software must be treated for tax purposes identically to software developed in-house: Either deduct entirely in one year as a current expense, or depreciate as a capital investment. If there is no in-house software development to serve as a precedent, the tax treatment of the initial purchase will generally govern.

• The 10% federal investment tax credit is applicable to purchases of software. The credit (a dollar-for-dollar reduction in taxes owed) is allowed no matter what the company's previous treatment of software for tax purposes. That applies if the software is purchased as a package with the hardware. The credit is also applicable to any sales taxes paid. *If the credit is taken, software must be depreciated along with the hardware.* It cannot be deducted in one year as a current expense.

• Used computers: An investment credit is allowed on used-equipment purchases.

Local taxes.

• Sales taxes are generally applicable only to the hardware. If software is included in the package price for investment tax credit purposes, have the vendor provide a *separate statement* of the hardware and software price.

• Property taxes are only applicable to that portion of the hardware price which relates to the actual components. If the "hardware" price includes any software (such as operating system) or vendor service and advice, installation, education, documentation, etc., that portion of the hardware price is *not* subject to property tax.

What to do: Check rulings in the local tax jurisdiction and others to determine what percentage of the hardware list price should be subject to property tax. Tax counsel can obtain this information.

Leasing or renting a computer has similar tax consequences.

• A company that rents its equipment to another firm pays property tax only on its manufacturing cost (typically 18% to 25% of the purchase price).

According to computer consultant Robert London, computer courses are not necessary for executives. Desk-top terminals are not difficult to master, and can easily be explained by sales reps. From there, the instruction manuals that accompany software packages explain adequately how to perform specific tasks. Few executives ever have to develop their own software.

• Most vendors will pass through the investment tax credit, or reduce lease payments accordingly. *This is negotiable.*

• Lease payments are generally deductible as a current expense, unless the lease is structured as an *installment purchase.* Many complex deals can be made with a computer purchase, such as through a *leveraged lease.* In any of these, it requires a qualified professional to optimize the benefits.

Recommended: Include a provision in the lease giving the firm the right to legitimately dispute any property or sales tax that might be levied.

Source: Dick H. Brandon

TIME TO JUMP INTO WORD PROCESSING

Companies that have held off on word-processing equipment because of the cost or for fear of new technology should *now* jump in. Although in the future technology will improve and prices will come down, there's so much good hardware and software now that even small offices should use the equipment. The investment will justify itself *immediately* by reducing costly paperwork.

What has tipped the scales: The explosion in personal computers and the development of increasingly sophisticated and user-friendly software. Personal computers can be used as word-processors, and they're now adequate to meet the needs of all but the most paper-intensive operations.

In constrast are stand-alone *dedicated* word processors (so called because they're dedicated only to word processing). A personal computer can be used as a data processor and as a word processor. *Dedicated word processors* can cost up to $20,000, and make sense for law firms, government offices, insurance companies, medical and health groups, banks, and others that have heavy volumes of mail.

For the average office, *personal computers* are best suited. On ease of operation and quality of output they still fall short of dedicated word processors, but are about a third to a half as costly, including necessary software.

Training and service support are growing in importance. Proper initial training and ongoing support greatly enhance productivity of any word-processing system. Be sure to have clearly written manuals and a number to call in case of operating problems.

Source: Patricia B. Seybold, editor in chief, *The Seybold Report on Office Systems,* and *The Seybold Report on Professional Computing,* Box 644, Media, PA 19063.

PAYROLL PACKAGES

One alternative to the high cost of program development and maintenance is, of course, to purchase a software package. Payroll is again the outstanding example, because the general uniformity of product (dictated by the U.S. government, banks, and labor unions) makes payroll systems very comparable across different organizations. Yet a recent survey has shown that the 45,000 computer-using organizations in the U.S. have developed some 55,000 payroll systems! They have fallen victim to the NIH ("not invented here") syndrome.

STAYING EFFICIENT

TRAINING AN INSIDE AUDITOR

In this computerized age you need a computer auditor—someone to evaluate control problems associated with your data processing. How to find one: Don't take a data processor and train him to be an auditor; instead, take an auditor and send him to computer school.

TRIMMING THE DATA PROCESSING BUDGET

Data processing costs are often regarded as fixed—except in an upward direction. The tradition of an annual 10% budget increase is so strong that most financial officers are delighted to just reduce the *increase*, considering a real cut impossible. The budget, however, *can* be cut.

HOW TO DO IT.
Break down data processing costs into *functional* areas and expense each.
Separate *maintenance* costs from *development* costs,
Assess return on investment in two ways: When it will occur and how much.
Postpone projects where the return on investment is projected to start more than two years forward, or the ROI falls

below 25%.

TO REDUCE EQUIPMENT COSTS.
• Eliminate all *emulation* (a special program whose function it is to make an old program, designed for an older machine, work on a new machine—albeit less efficiently) by converting or discarding old programs.
• Do an immediate *report-distribution analysis*. The easiest way to do this is *not* to send out various reports when they are due. If no one screams, *those* particular reports may not be required, or a lesser frequency may be acceptable.
• Reduce the number of disk and tape drives attached to your machine. *Rule of thumb:* You have two drives too many or you can reduce the number by 15%, but don't reduce below four.
• You probably also can reduce the core size of your machine by 10% to 20%.
• Consider using off-branded peripherals for a 10% saving.
• Stop all purchases of tape reels and disk packs. Examine and revise the recycling procedures.
• Reconsider the possibility of purchase or leasing.

TO REDUCE SUPPLY COSTS.
• Stock forms may replace custom forms.
• Reduce carbons in pre-printed sets.
• Print reports eight lines to the inch rather than the traditional six lines.
• For program tests and listings, reuse paper on the second side.

COMPUTERS

PEOPLE COSTS. The reduction of people costs can be accomplished only by an examination of the company's functional and expense category model. The numbers in the following model represent typical cuts that will give you nearly a 10% net budget reduction:

Computer Expense Categories

	% Typical EDP Budget	% Net Gain Possible on Total Budget
A. Equipment		
Main frame...............	10	1.0
Peripheral storage devices.	12	1.8
Printers/card readers......	5	0.5
Communications	3	0.15
Total	30	3.45
B. Supplies		
Paper	4	0.8
Cards, tapes, disks, ribbons	1	0.4
Total	5	1.2
C. Operating Costs		
Operating personnel.......	10	0.5
Data entry personnel......	8	0.8
Library – scheduling	3	0.0
Total	21	1.3
D. Development Costs		
Analysis	9	1.3
Programing	8	1.6
Research.................	1	0.1
Standards/control	2	0.2
Maintenance prog.........	16	0.0
Total	36	3.2
E. Management		
General overhead.........	5	0.5
Direct management.......	3	0.0
Total	8	0.5
Grand Total	100	9.7

• A 5% reduction in operating personnel is possible by eliminating overtime. If it's further possible to eliminate an entire shift or reorganize the operation through three- or four-day work weeks, you may save both operating personnel and equipment overtime.

• Data entry personnel should be analyzed functionally, by user. Since sales may be down, data entry volume should be down proportionately, making savings possible on a 10% basis.

SURROUNDING OPERATIONS.

• Reduce the air conditioning load by increasing the computer room temperature by up to five degrees without damage, *if the humidity is controlled.*

• Reexamine the data communication telephone costs. It is possible that a change of service may be warranted.

• Consider centralizing functions. Use batch terminals and lower-cost data communications.

• Terminals are status symbols, some are undoubtedly unnecessary.

Source: Dick H. Brandon.

SUPPLIES FOR COMPUTERS

Computer users have found there are few bargains in supplies.

Cheap continuous forms may have operators stopping every few pages to realign the printer. Magnetic tape and disks must be high-quality; imperfections or weakness in the coating can produce read/write errors or, worse, data loss if the processor slows down. Any variations in tab cards' length, width, or thickness may foul punches and card readers. Ribbons, though less critical, should nonetheless be logged for the print volume they can produce before replacement; settle on brands that perform best on your system.

Storage tips: Invest a few extra dollars in data binders that will speed search for information in bulky printouts. Punched cards should be in a file drawer with movable back plate, which can be tightened to keep them flat. Forms should be retained in atmospheres with controlled (40%-60%) humidity. Dampness causes registration problems, while dry environment can lead to buildups of static electricity that impair handling. Store tapes and disks well away from sources of electromagnetic radiation. Tapes should not be stacked, since the edges can be damaged. Instead, use racks that allow reels to stand or hang vertically.

SECURITY RECOMMENDATIONS

THEFT BY COMPUTER

Computer security continues to be a hot topic these days, and has been responsible for the employment of many guards, the installation of thousands of sophisticated locking systems, and the sale of a fair number of tranquilizers to concerned executives. But physical aspects of computer security have been overemphasized, resulting in deemphasis of a far greater threat: thefts by computer-wise employees.

More such thefts have been found than any other form of security breach, because they're easier to perform and far harder to detect.

IDENTIFICATION. Step one in stopping such theft is identifying those employees with the opportunity or the ability to steal. Characteristics:
● Must have access to actual programs used in actual operation.
● Must be capable of making a program change in such a way that the added or altered instructions are not obvious to the normal user.

● Must be capable of accessing the *data*.
● Must have an understanding of systems and program controls, so they can be bypassed.
● Must have access to system and program documentation.

In most installations, *all* managers, *all* project managers, *most* analysts, and a fair number of programmers fit this picture. In some installations, even senior operators could qualify.

HOW TO STEAL. The best way to catch a thief, or to prevent a theft, is to have a clear understanding of how to steal. You can try to cover all bases in a realistic audit and prevention program. Major steps in stealing with a computer:
● Identify where the corporation's cash is dispensed—payroll, accounts payable, claims processing (insurance), and dividend payments.
● Alternately, identify where cash for a large number of outside users, with a wide range of amounts, is controlled—deposit systems and mutual fund share purchases.

Depending on the system, cash need and patience of the perpetrator, these are the thieving possibilities. Note that risk rises as greed increases.

● *The truncation game.* Usable in payroll, mutual fund share purchases and sometimes in a dividend system. *Here is how it works:* In payroll, for example, the gross pay calculation may result in an uneven amount, such as \$132.435. The normal approach is to round upward amounts ending in 5 and over, while those with 4 and under are truncated. On average, this creates the ability to balance, in total. The game is played by eliminating the rounding and adding the $2/3$ cent saved. Total gross pay for the company is the same. A variation of this is to take, say, 3 cents from each employee—programmed to take effect whenever an employee is given a raise (to avoid comparisons by the employee). Payroll truncation, by the way, should be started at the beginning of the year—preferably one in which the FICA rates have changed, for the same reason.

In mutual fund share purchases, an amount paid by the purchaser is divided by the current share price. This always results in fractions and it depends on company policy to what decimal the purchaser is given credit. The rest can always be credited to an employee account.

Note that in the truncation game there is no *external* input or output—only the program is changed, and no trace of the activity is available for audit.

● *The phony activity game.* The most common and least imaginative approach is to generate phony activity—for example, to submit a phony bill for services or goods for payment to an accounts payable system, bypassing the authorization cycle, and entering approvals for payment directly into the system. Payments, of course, are made to phony companies or accounts owned by the employee-thief.

● *The product disbursement game.* Used where a company has a product that is readily marketable, or has a high value-to-volume ratio (*e.g.,* airline tickets, watches). Legitimate orders are entered and the product is shipped to the employee-purchaser. What is suppressed, however, is an invoice, which is simply never issued.

AVOIDING DETECTION. Standard techniques:

● Modify the programs used in operation with a correction (called a *patch*) in machine language. Include in the correction a series of instructions that eliminate the correction whenever the program is printed out.

● Establish any external procedures required to escape detection—systems for cashing checks, disposing of products and the like.

● Obtain responsibility for the maintenance of the programs in question.

● Do not go on long vacations.

Source: Dick H. Brandon.

HIRING & FIRING FOR SECURITY

Theft, fraud or sabotage by employees or ex-employees is the most difficult risk to guard against.
Some suggestions:

● When hiring, be sure to check *all* references carefully. Since recent legislation makes unauthorized disclosure of unfavorable information subject to control, make your request in writing — and state the items to be confirmed (employment dates, title, salary, duties, etc.). *Any discrepancy* points to someone willing to overstate or misstate, or possibly to someone who may be tempted to steal.

After firing employees, don't allow them unsupervised access to the computer facility.

NINE WAYS TO PREVENT PROGRAMMER THEFTS

• Never allow a programmer access to data files.
• Scrupulously separate operating from development activities.
• Always separate program and systems development from program and systems maintenance.
• Lock data file and program libraries and control access and release of material on a sign-out basis.
• Always make a copy of each operating program when it is placed into production. Seal the copy, give it to the auditors, and let them compare it and its results at random times with the actual program in use.
• Force compulsory vacations of at least two contiguous weeks for personnel working in sensitive areas.
• Spot-check your payments to vendors, employees, shareholders. Calculate a few by hand (to catch truncation). Statistically analyze frequency and amount of payments to vendors and look at list of names of significant cases of either for recognition.
• Establish audit trails in all systems with multiple checkpoints.

• Follow basic audit principles in all activities. For example, maintain a carbon of the console typewriter output, sequentially number pages of output records, and the like.
• In general, audit the computer department with the same precision that other cash-handling activities are audited. This assumes EDP expertise within the audit organization. And that assumption is vital.
• Limit copies of all programs. Provide any program changes to the audit department (or to outside auditors). The implication, that the audit department can check programs, can be a sufficient deterrent to discourage anyone from tampering with the program.

Source: Dick H. Brandon.

THE AWFUL TRUTH

Most cases of computer fraud are uncovered by accident rather than by design.

The plain fact is that no amount of controls or audits can outsmart a really determined computer embezzler, says Computer Consultant Dick H. Brandon, who offers plenty of sound advice on discouraging computer fraud.

No reason to give up efforts though, he says. The best defense is to keep changing controls at odd times. And keep people in computer department aware that quick changes are in the offing at irregular intervals. Do the same with audits. And change the personnel who conduct the audit to avoid collusion.

CREDIT MANAGEMENT

COLLECTION DOS AND DON'TS

As a general rule, a creditor has the right to urge payment of a *just* debt and to threaten *proper legal procedure* to collect the debt. The conduct of the collector must be extreme and outrageous before legal liability will be incurred.

THE DON'TS. Don't bring suit with a purpose other than collecting. A suit combining revenge and punishment with collecting is an abuse of the legal process and is illegal.

• Don't even think of filing criminal charges if the debt is in dispute.

• Don't use "hotheads" as collectors. Hotheads may get into an argument with the debtor, leading to troubles for which the creditor may be held responsible.

• Don't use force in repossessions. It may be a breach of the peace.

• Don't file bankruptcy, receivership, or insolvency proceedings against a debtor except as a last resort.

• Don't invade the debtor's right to privacy by tricks or deception, or expose him to public contempt or ridicule.

• Don't say anything but the truth about the debtor, and then only if for a justifiable end.

• Don't use threats (other than a threat to bring civil suit to collect a just debt). Threats may be deemed technical extortion or blackmail.

THE DO'S. Do check with your attorney before undertaking to use bad-check laws and criminal statutes to collect. Get a written opinion of counsel if possible.

• Get the approval of top management for any course of action beyond the routine.

• Do have a collector use a friendly approach that impresses on the debtor a purpose to make arrangements for payment which are reasonable and which the debtor will be able to carry out. Do leave the debtor with a friendly feeling toward you.

• If you are on the debtor's premises, do leave, if asked.

CREDIT FRAUDS

Some typical credit fraud ploys that both sales and credit departments should watch out for *before* shipping to seemingly credit-worthy new customers—*or* old ones, for that matter. (If the fraud artist's successful, he'll have resold the goods and disappeared long before you even start pressing for collection.)

• *The unknown company* that places a small sample order and follows through promptly with an enthusiastic mail or phone endorsement and a request for a big shipment that, of course, never gets paid for. (Orders may even be accompanied by faked references.

• *The new customer* who pays for his first, second and third shipments—modest ones—then places a whopping order when he's established himself as a prompt payer.

• *The rush telephone-order artist.* If his firm name *sounds* familiar, his credit standing may not be checked until after the shipment's made.

• *The small COD order-operator.* He "buys" from dozens of suppliers located at least half-way across the country— far enough so that the supplier's willing to buy his hard-up-for-cash story, settle for temporary part-payment. (Return shipment would cost the supplier too much anyway.)

• *The imitator.* His company name's almost identical to that of a well-rated firm, and he opens his office on the same street. Everybody's happy to ship until the bills back up. Then the rated company protests and the shipper finally detects minor differences in name and address.

• *The credit fraud ring*, with the capital to buy a well-known medium-size firm with a top-notch credit rating. One such ring "bought" and resold nearly $1 million in merchandise in less than two months by trading on company reputation, advertising its intention of opening and stocking a chain of general merchandise stores.

LOWER CUSTOMER RISKS

Tightening credit standards isn't always the best way to cut your losses, particularly if it reduces sales to cash-tight customers just when your company needs the volume and they need the goods. *Alternative:* Consignment shipments, with title to the goods remaining in your hands until the customer actually uses and pays for them.

If the customer does go bankrupt, of course, you can recover without sharing with other creditors. And if you ship to a field warehouse, rather than directly to the customer, the warehouse agent can issue warehouse receipts, creating negotiable instruments the customer can use for bank credit to pay for release.

Special advantages: You keep your cash-tight customer in business, maintain your sales and competitive position, limit your inventory-carrying costs and risks of obsolescence, encourage large orders instead of the hand-to-mouth buying that sends your customer service costs soaring.

INFORMATION FROM BANKS

Banks will be more ready to supply you with credit data on their customers if you approach the matter directly and discreetly.

Give pertinent facts of your relationship with the account (size of order, length of the relationship, things you've noticed about the account, etc.).

Don't expect the banker to betray a fiduciary trust by giving you financial specifics, but he will probably answer such questions as whether the company is profitable, whether it exhibits any significant trends, etc.

COLLECTION CAUTIONS

Aggressive debt collection practices should be reviewed carefully in light of current tough regulation by the Federal Trade Commission.

In one landmark FTC consent order, several affiliates of the Diners Club agreed to bar employees or agents from making telephone calls to debtors between 9 p.m. and 7 a.m. on weekdays or at any time Sunday mornings. The affiliates have also agreed to stop other collection practices charged in the FTC's complaint, including:

(1) Threats that debtors would go to jail if they did not pay off their debts immediately;

(2) "abusive and obscene" language when contacting debtors;

(3) urging employers to pressure debtors to pay up;

(4) failing to make credit cost disclosures required under the Truth in Lending Act when arranging for deferred payment plans; and

(5) obtaining credit information illegally from credit data centers.

To stay out of serious trouble, never use deceptive means to attempt to collect debts or to obtain information concerning debtors. Instruct new debt collection employee that he should *not* say:

• That he is simply seeking information in connection with a survey.

• That your company has a prepaid package for the debtor.

• That a sum of money or valuable gift will be sent to the debtor if he furnishes the required informtion.

• That a "credit bureau" or a collection agency is calling (if it is not).

• That the debt has been turned over to an attorney or an independent organization engaged in the business of collecting past-due accounts (when it has not).

• That documents sent to the debtor are legal process forms (when they are not).

Your company and your agents shouldn't use any forms, letters, questionnaires, or other materials which don't clearly disclose that they are being used to collect a debt or to obtain information concerning a debtor. They shouldn't use trade names, addresses, insigniae, pictures, emblems, or anything else that creates a false impression that they are connected with a government agency.

For a free copy of *FTC Guide Against Deceptive Debt Collection*, write FTC, Public Reference, Washington, D.C. 20580.

WARNING!

Don't give customers too much information when they want to know about their credit status. Data beyond what is required by the Truth in Lending Act can be interpreted as unlawful attempts to confuse buyers by obscuring the key figures.

EIGHT RULES FOR CREDIT AND COLLECTION DEPARTMENTS

1. *Communications:* Companies sometimes don't tell customers their terms. Have salesmen explain them when taking orders even if they appear on the invoice form.

2. *Promptness:* Late invoices encourage late payment.

3. *Records:* Are they set up to show each customer's status and payments quickly? If you don't know who owes what and for how long, you may be doing *more* business with slow payers.

4. *Intelligence:* Keep abreast of customer's financial status. Scan the financial and trade press and other information services for items such as strikes, legal actions, annual statements, quarterly reports, industry crises, and other information of a similar sort that may signal that a debtor's resources are strained or threatened.

5. *Consistency:* Don't favor large accounts, unless you have negotiated special credit terms for big orders. Insisting on prompt payment will create respect rather than ill will. Don't ignore small accounts, either. Small debts *do* multiply until they can amount to a substantial portion of your turnover.

6. *Direct action:* Go to the decision-maker when pressing for payment. Your invoice will stay at the bottom of the clerk's pile unless his instructions are changed.

7. *Credibility:* Don't threaten legal action unless you mean it. If you're bluffing, your debtors will find out about it and you'll have *more* difficulty collecting.

8. *Surveillance:* Monitor efficiency. *One way:* Divide total outstanding receivables by average day's sales to determine the average day's receivables outstanding. If this figure rises over a period of time, an overhaul of your credit and collection procedures may be indicated.

Another guide: Periodically segregate your outstanding invoices into percent of total overdue for one month, two months, three months and six months.

Objective: Keep debts owed for more than one month at a minimum. Keeping these figures over a period of time is the simplest way for your company to know its system is working.

LIENS ON A BANKRUPT CUSTOMER

In dealing with a debtor of dubious credit standing, don't be lulled into feeling secure by acquiring a lien on some or all of his assets. Certainly, under the Uniform Commercial Code, it's easy enough to acquire a lien. And if proper steps are taken to perfect the lien (filing in the appropriate place), that lien will usually be good.

However, the acid test of a lien's validity occurs only if the debtor goes into bankruptcy—either straight bankruptcy or a reorganization proceeding under Chapter X or an arrangement under Chapter XI. In all three bankruptcies, there are weapons to attack certain liens.

Frequent types of vulnerability:
● A lien not perfected until after the bankruptcy petition is filed.
● Those which may be deemed to have been fraudulently created within a year of the filing of the petition.
● So-called preferential liens. Briefly, these are liens created within four months of the bankruptcy petition to secure an antecedent debt, with the creditor having reason to believe that the debtor was insolvent at the time.

Assuming the creditor is able to escape one of these weapons, what then?

● *In straight bankruptcy:* Normally, the creditor has no problem in reclaiming the property unless it's worth more than the claim it secures. In the latter case, a sale of the property will be ordered and the creditor will be paid out of the proceeds. No big problem.

• *Chapter X:* The whole idea of this proceeding is to effect a reorganization of the business so it can continue to operate. Obviously, if creditors were permitted to reclaim their property with liens, reorganization might be impossible. Hence, the law provides an automatic stay.

The creditor can have the stay vacated if he can show that there's *no* reasonable possibility of a successful reorganization, *or* that the reclamation of the property won't materially affect the prospects of reorganization. These aren't easy to prove.

In the meantime, if the property on which the creditor holds a lien is subject to depreciation, the depreciation continues and his security interest becomes worth less and less. That, of course, can amount to an actual taking of the secured creditor's property without compensation.

• *Chapter XI:* There's the same automatic stay of proceedings to enforce the lien, and the secured creditor must ask to have the stay vacated. But the burden is on the debtor or trustee to make a case for the stay, and the courts are less likely to sustain it. If there's *ample* security, however, a stay will usually be upheld.

Practical steps: Both legal and business considerations are involved in credit transactions. Here we list only the *legal* considerations:

• Do everything possible to assure the existence of a valid lien not subject to attack as fraudulent or unperfected.

• Get security sufficient in amount to withstand economic depreciation pending Chapter X or XI proceedings.

• To the extent you have a valid lien on current assets—inventory and accounts, for example—and your debtor gets into Chapter X or XI, recognize the fact that such assets are apt to be highly perishable and much of their value may be lost if the debtor goes out of business.

• Particularly in Chapter XI, it may be to the advantage of a secured creditor to go along with the debtor, for a brief period at least, with the idea of trading off that cooperation for compensation for economic depreciation or a lien on additional assets in the rehabilitated company.

The dangers of computer crime are greatly misunderstood, says one FBI expert on embezzlement. Installing a computer can actually deter financial juggling because few dishonest employees know how to use it. Most computer-related crimes are committed by a team—one employee steals, and another covers up the theft in the accounting system. But most of these crimes would occur with or without a computer. It's just another tool for wrongdoers.

BUILT-IN USURY

Credit agreements often provide that if the creditor is obliged to sue for overdue payment, the debtor becomes liable for the expenses of collection, including attorney's fee. These agreements sometimes give a *fixed percentage* of the amount due as designated *attorney's fee.*

That arbitrary designation has been declared usurious and is no longer acceptable in New York State. It could soon be prohibited elsewhere.

Background: In one case involving a major bank, which enforced agreements of this kind to collect loans in default, the court found it a "misrepresentation" to label as *attorney's fee* a percentage which had no necessary correlation with the amount actually paid. The court went on to advise that when the lawyers aren't paid for the service but receive a flat yearly salary, the bank cannot collect attorney's fees at all. And a State Supreme Court Justice declared that in default judgments against consumer creditors, the attorney will have to show that the fee claimed is both *necessary* and *reasonable*. Unless a fee can be proven to have been earned, it won't be assessed.

Indicated actions:

• Change the wording of company credit agreements to eliminate any reference to an *arbitrary* charge for your attorney's fee in the event that your company must sue to collect.

• Specify that the consumer is liable for a *reasonable* attorney's fee.

• If you often sue consumer creditors, perhaps your attorney (whether salaried or not) should claim his fee by an affidavit filed in court as to the value of services he actually rendered, having the court thereby attest that the fee is reasonable.

AGE AND CREDIT

Re-examine the way your company uses information on age to evaluate credit risks. Federal Reserve rules make it difficult to turn down an applicant because of age. And the Federal Trade Commission may get power to sue companies that consistently discriminate in credit applications. The age of a credit applicant can be one fac-tor in deciding if that person is a good risk. But those over 62 *cannot* be given a lower score than younger customers just because of age. The fact that old-sters cannot get life insurance to cover the debt must not be used as a reason for saying no.

COLLECTION CALLS

Even if your regular collection letter series or get-tough collection techniques are working well enough with past-due accounts, consider this telephone collection technique. It has proven effective and is often cheaper than letters.

On the first round, your collector identifies himself and your firm, explains why he's calling—and pauses, forcing the customer to explain his past-due status. If the customer pleads that he can't pay, your collector offers to work out a plan for taking partial payments over time.

If the customer fails to abide by the payment agreement, the collector calls again, works out another set of terms. (And he calls to say thanks whenever the customer comes through on schedule.)

ONE TOUGH STRATEGY

An almost forgotten way to collect a trade bill that's being used effectively by a few firms:

If your customer has delayed sending you a check, find out where he banks. Then tell your bank that you want to draw a draft against his account. Explain that you're trying to speed up a slow payer. Attach your invoice to the draft your bank then sends to his bank. His bank will call yours to find out what's going on.

Once the customer receives the draft, he has two options: refusing it or paying. If he rejects it, he'll be admitting to his bank that he's not paying his trade bills. And most businessmen aren't anxious to broadcast that fact—especially to a banker that may also be a creditor.

Caveat: Banks aren't going to like doing this—so don't overdo the strategy. Save it only for the right situations.

MONITORING COLLECTION AGENCIES

If your company uses a collection agency, investigate *why* it is being used. In some cases, corporate credit managers were found to be receiving kickbacks from the agencies. In others, the company's legal counsel handled collections for a big, *fat* fee.

Easy to test the relative merits of collection agencies. Give them each a number of accounts. See which performs the best. (It's similarly easy to check on your current agency's performance.)

Commercial agencies can make good on nearly 90% of claims three to four months delinquent. Agency charges vary, but average around 25% of total collected by commercial agencies, up to 50% for retail accounts.

One good bet: Hire a flat-rate company to act as a third-party motivator in getting slow accounts to pay. *Advantages:* The creditor retains control of the account. The fee is low (7% in one instance). Ideally, that collection agency would be able to take cases to court.

LOCATING A DEBTOR WHO MOVED

Post office change-of-address information is confidential, but you can sometimes get it from the postmaster or mail carrier. It's worth a try. Other tactics:

• Send a registered letter to the debtor's last-known address, return receipt requested. Don't address to the debtor, rather to a fictitious person, *c/o the debtor* and marked "Deliver to Addressee Only." It will be forwarded to the new address, which will be marked on the envelope. *But it won't actually be delivered* because of the quoted phrase, and will be returned to you with the debtor's new address marked on the envelope.

• Use third-class mail marked, "If forwarded to new adress notify sender on form 3547, postage for notice guaranteed." This will get you the new address within 20 days.

• If debtor has sold his home, send letter addressed to occupant requesting that he send you the debtor's new address, return post card enclosed.

• If you think you've located the debtor, but you're not sure, a "tantalizer" can be used. Send a note in script on plain paper, *Page 2* (there is no page 1): "I await your immediate reply to this most important matter. Yours truly, etc." Good chance curiosity will work. (Naturally, you can't use a return address the debtor will recognize.)

Unlawful use of the mails: Be sure not to use unlawful prize gimmicks. *Example:* A letter sent to the debtor with a Detroit postmark informing him he has won a car, and will he please fill out his name and address, his employer's name and address, his wife's place of employment, etc.

EFFICIENT COLLECTION FILES

How to flag overdue accounts receivable without having to thumb through hundreds of ledger cards.

Use filing stickers, the kind that can protrude above the ledger card to which they are attached. Use different stickers marked "30 days past due," "60 days past due," etc. Instead of replacing a 30-days' sticker with a 60-days' sticker, attach the new sticker *to the top* of the old one. This makes the *more* overdue accounts stand higher than the rest.

KEEP IN CONTACT WITH DEBTORS

Main cause of collection problems is lack of contact with the debtor. Remember, overdue accounts have other creditors, too, and your company is competing with them.

How to keep your line of communi-

cation open:

● Don't lecture, question integrity or threaten. It's counterproductive. Most companies sincerely want to pay their bills.

● Be prepared. Learn whether your debtor is a partnership or a corporation or whatever. Do you have collateral? Have you made a Uniform Commercial Code filing? Is the debt guaranteed by a third party, and is it time to contact that third party?

● Vary written correspondence. The same old dunning letter loses attention. The letter should include a definite schedule for repayment including amounts, dates due and total time required to complete.

● *Last resort:* A collection agent.

SPECIAL DANGER IN INSTALLMENT NOTES

A default on an installment note can make the entire balance, including interest, immediately payable—so long as the usury statutes aren't violated.

The case: A homeowner borrowed $6,600 from a savings bank on a home-improvement loan, signed a 10-year note for $11,428, payable in equal monthly installments, which included interest at the rate of 11.9% per annum. After making only three payments, he defaulted and the bank sued for the entire balance by virtue of an acceleration clause in the note. The court limited the recovery to the unpaid principal, holding that collecting it *all* was illegal under a New York statute limiting interest to 25% per annum—almost $5,000 of the balance was viewed as interest.

Comment: While the borrower came out all right in this case, it serves to underscore the risk to the borrower in situations in which usury might *not* be available as a defense. With a properly drafted acceleration clause, the borrower might have been hit for interest far in excess of the basic rate provided in the note. Also, *the usury defense may not be available at all to corporate borrowers.*

Recommendation: Before committing yourself or your company to an installment obligation carrying interest and providing for acceleration of the entire balance on default, make sure you're not expected to pay interest for the balance of the full term of the loan.

Jamaica Savings Bank v. Mercer, N.Y. Sup. Ct., Bronx County, New York.

IMPORTANCE OF DOCUMENTING LOAN-REPAYMENT DETAILS

A bad debt deduction can't be claimed without a bad debt.

Case in point: An individual and his wife lent money to the wife's brothers to use in a corporation. Neither date of repayment nor interest was discussed, and there was no such formality as a note. Efforts *never* were made to collect the so-called debt. Not until actual bankruptcy was declared did the lenders file a claim. And they got nothing, not even a bad-debt deduction.

Where repayment of a debt is actually contingent upon the success of the borrowing corporation, a court is

likely to conclude that there was no legally enforceable debt and, hence, no allowable deduction.

Caliguri et al. v. Comm'r., 8th Cir., 2/18/77.

THE TIME TO PUSH DEBTORS

A creditor frequently hesitates putting the heat on a debtor, lest the latter become angry and transfer patronage. Patience toward a *slow* payor can pay off if your company's competitors are nasty.

But if shortly after the start of a new year, efforts to collect outstanding debts (or at least to ascertain precisely what the status of each nonpayor is) are made, there is *less* likelihood they will be offended. The efforts at this time can be attributed to accountants, who need to close the books.

WRITING OFF BAD DEBTS OF POLITICAL PARTIES

Used to be that worthless debts of political parties couldn't be written off by creditors other than banks. Now a deduction is allowed for worthless debts owed by political parties or by campaign committees, if the debts arose from *bona fide* sales of goods or services in the ordinary course of business, *and* if substantial efforts had been made to collect the debt.

EXECUTIVE STRATEGIES

DECISION MAKING

HOW MANAGERS SHOULD THINK

Many executives believe their biggest failing as managers may be their inability to think *analytically*. They have trouble working through a problem and logically coming to a truly clear decision.

INTUITION VS. LOGIC. Their biggest failings actually are:

● Their *refusal* to think *intuitively*.

● Their sense that *feeling* a decision is something unacceptable or unprofessional.

These statements don't mean to make a case for fuzzy thinking or shooting from the hip. But it's important that managers learn to reassess their priorities. They must move from *reliance* on logic to an *acceptance* of intuitiveness.

It's the intuitive approach to decision-making that often is the most creative and the most reliable. A person's intuition usually grows out of a huge reservoir of accumulated information (much of it isn't even on a conscious level). Data have been collected over years and fed into decisions with no conscious effort.

Example: A manager interviews a candidate for a job. Without quite knowing it, he gets signals about the person's character that aren't based on specific comments the person made or data on his resume. Yet those intuitive signals often form a much more valid basis for assessing the candidate.

THE BEST WAY TO SOLVE PROBLEMS. There are four distinct stages to creative problem solving:

1. *Immersion:* Let yourself steep in the data. Collect information. Search out symptoms. *Talk to all the people involved.* Learn all you can firsthand. *Avoid coming to any conclusions. Resist formulating any answers.* (It's easy to err at this step by quickly jumping to a conclusion.) *The danger:* You're so relieved to have found an "answer" that you triumphantly give up the search for more symptoms. Now you're likely to invest great faith in that answer. That immediately closes your mind to alternatives.

This occurs frequently with management consultants who offer "prepackaged" solutions to problems. The answer seems so convenient that the manager invests more faith in it than is warranted—and blocks out any other solutions.

2. *Incubation:* After collecting the data and listing the symptoms, step back. Make a conscious decision to stop collecting details. Let the information incubate. Don't actively think about the problem or a solution. There's no telling how long this stage will take. Much depends on how much faith and experience one has in dealing with the intuitive approach.

3. *Eureka:* The exciting moment when a solution springs forth. We've all

97

had the experience: While driving, shaving, relaxing over a cocktail. Usually, the solution or the idea appears full-blown, completely developed.

4. *Verification:* This is the stage in which logic and analysis are especially important. *The danger:* Some managers (usually the entrepreneurial types) skip this stage. They're so excited by the solution, they don't bother to follow up and *assess the consequences,* the real costs, the implications.

STRATEGIC PLANS. It's no secret, managers frequently hate to plan. They resist laying out what they and their company will be doing in five years. Because of that, one of these three things happens:

1. The planning chore is given to a strict analytical person on the staff who abhors the intuitive approach.

2. The manager takes on the job. But instead of letting himself think intuitively, he goes through the *motions* without really thinking. (That's called *number crunching:* Stuffing numbers into their apparently *logical* places.)

3. No planning is done at all.

Fact: In many businesses, strategic planning may not be appropriate—except on the most elementary level.

Reason: In some companies, there is so little change in the business environment that the smartest thing for a successful company to do is to *consciously change nothing.* Change will evolve with no specific planning necessary.

And in other companies, the change is so rapid that planning wouldn't work anyway.

AGONIZING OVER DECISIONS. This *sounds* a bit flippant, but in fact it's very useful to think of it this way:

Many decisions over which one agonizes aren't worth the agony.

Reasons:
• There are insufficient data upon which to make a decision. *The real decision should be:* Can we wait to decide? If not, flipping a coin is often as effective as agonizing.
• Either decision is equally bad (or good), so the choice is best left to a coin throw.

Source: Dr. Henry Mintzberg, professor, McGill University, Montreal. Author of *The Nature of Managerial Work* (Harper & Row, 10 E. 53 St., New York 10022).

FIVE MISTAKES MANAGERS CAN'T AFFORD TO MAKE

1. Stealing credit for the achievements of others.

2. Slandering other workers, either colleagues or subordinates.

3. Spreading rumors.

4. Letting power go to one's head.

5. Ignoring individual differences and treating everyone in the same way.

Source: *Supervisory Management.*

PUBLIC ACCLAIM AND THE EXECUTIVE

It's a rare leader—in business or public life—who doesn't like adulation of the crowd. For the corporate executive, the endless tensions of negotiations and decision making are eased, in part, by the opportunity to see and feel appreciation. It's a heady wine that few can resist. Many executives seek out situations in which they will receive the rewards of status and recognition. While it's not unreasonable that they *should* seek out this kind of psychological reward, they should, at the very least, recognize their motivation.

Another part of an executive's job is to make *himself* available to certain people—bankers, government officials, division heads, key employees—to provide *them* with the message that they, too, are important enough for the executive to make time to see them personally. This is true even with people down the ladder—to give them the feeling that they know the boss personally, that he is interested in them as individuals, and that the organization isn't run by an impersonal "him."

It's important to distinguish between the two roles. The first is designed primarily to lift *his* spirit, while the *second* gives a lift to *both* him and the people he's meeting. That kind of gratification giving serves the needs of the organization.

Source: Leonard R. Sayles, management professor, Columbia University Graduate School of Business.

DELEGATION

Prime offenders when it comes to failure to delegate authority: Executives with small staffs—even *excellent staffs.* Here's how to make your working life easier: Think results, rather than methods. Let your people know what you want, and let *them* figure out

how to accomplish it.

Delegation doesn't mean abdication. You still need to assign tasks, set standards, and monitor results.

Key questions: Why did you bring that to me? and *What is your recommendation?* Train your staff to be ready with an answer to both whenever they bring a problem to your attention.

OBVIOUS CANDIDATES FOR EXECUTIVE STRESS

How do you recognize executive stress? As opposed to normal, *constructive tension,* stress is marked by actual changes in behavior. *Outward signs:* The executive becomes much harder to deal with, frequently exhibiting aggressive, angry reactions. Peers, subordinates, and superiors observe him speaking more loudly and rapidly or shouting, showing impatience and annoyance with others, and interrupting them frequently. Previously smooth or tolerable relationships become stormy or intolerable.

The five most obvious candidates for stress, and what to do if you're one of them:

1. *The executive who is always "fighting" time.* He's unrealistic about how long things will take. So he places unrelieved time pressure on subordinates, assuming that all activities and contacts can be supershort and superefficient. He schedules more appointments than he can handle—ending conversations abruptly—and insists on doing a multitude of things at once. The result, of course, is that nothing

really gets done well: The subordinate doesn't understand the hasty instruction; the slapdash "fix" falls apart; he makes an enemy whom he'll have to take more time to placate tomorrow. And that leads to still more stress.

How to cope: Take one problem at a time. Stop watching the clock. Remember that most managerial tasks can't be timed. Training and influencing people take lots of time.

2. *The manager who expects that all employees share his goals:* He expects all company policies to be directed consistently toward those goals, too. He's likely to experience stress when having to deal with the contradictory instructions and inputs and diverse, irrational people that abound in any organization.

How to cope: Understand that others have different objectives than you, that subordinates are often less motivated, and that there's no such thing as a rational organization.

3. *The manager who expects more responsiveness and acclaim than his particular boss provides:* People differ in what they expect of authority figures (and what they can give to subordinates).

How to cope: Be aware of your own need for praise, and assess your boss' usual responsiveness to subordinates. Don't assume that just because your boss isn't effusive it means you're doing an inadequate job. It's possible you'll have to start getting your approval elsewhere. But don't constantly push for more recognition from him. It'll be interpreted by him as insecurity and defensiveness on your part.

4. *The manager who is trapped in a position he finds unsuitable to his preparation:* The manager without a college degree who works solely with college grads or the one who feels he's ready for a greater degree of responsibility than he's getting.

How to cope: Keep in mind that there are bound to be times in a career when you're under- or over-prepared. And take positive action to change your situation when it becomes intolerable, rather than letting any stressful, negative behavior trap you in it longer.

5. *The manager whose job requires behavior beyond the "limit" of his personality:* His position requires more personal contacts than he finds comfortable, or it surrounds him with people who dominate or repress him.

Although most managers try to shape their jobs to fit their own personalities, doing more of the things they like (*e.g.,* wheeling and dealing) and less they dislike (*e.g.,* isolated, detail work), there are limits to a job's flexibility.

How to cope: If your job puts you in too many situations each day that are discomforting, start looking for a transfer. It's amazing how many times a manager who is unsuccessful in one job will blossom in a different one. All managerial jobs aren't alike. Recognize your own personality and its inflexibilities, and seek a job with the right components for *you.*

Source: Dr. Leonard R. Sayles.

PROBLEM-SOLVING GUIDELINES

• Question an assignment in depth. Find out the true objective before following it exactly as presented. It should be restated so the person with the assignment feels comfortable with it. All those related to the problem should agree with that statement, too.

• Apply common sense, *not* just book knowledge, to the assignment.

• Get to the root of the problem, not just the symptoms.

• The solution should fall within reasonable limits.

• Statistics should be used as guidelines, not as answers.

• Don't work in a vacuum. Remember that communication means involvement. That, in turn, will gain acceptance.

• Take time to spot flaws. Stop and think about the best approach before you jump in.

• Trust gut reactions to lead to an answer.

• Be flexible in approach.

Source: Robert E. Footlik, Footlik & Assoc., Evanston, Ill.

THE EFFICIENT SUPERVISOR

The efficient supervisor is one who is willing to accept *full* responsibility for the performance of the entire work unit. He *acts* responsibly and is *seen* by others as being responsible.

The inefficient supervisor, on the other hand, assumes that someone else is in charge whenever there is the least bit of ambiguity surrounding an issue.

The four key factors to consider when analyzing responsible supervisor behavior are:

1. When dealing with subordinates, an effective one takes charge. He passes along praise and stays on top of major problems. Disciplines and/or terminates inefficient employees without hesitation, when necessary.

2. Accepts criticism for his entire group, acting as a buffer.

3. Ensures that his group meets its objectives (on time and within the budget).

4. When other groups must be reckoned with, he takes on problems that are not expressly his own, making sure that no gaps exist between his area and others'.

EXECUTIVES' BIGGEST WORRIES

Ever wonder if your major worries and big decisions were in line with those of other executives? Check yourself against this profile of major company presidents.

Chief concerns (in descending order):

• Availability or lack of capital.

• Government restrictions or intervention.

• Inflation.

Less pressing problems:

• Sluggish sales.

• Energy availability and price.

• Profitability.

• Productivity.

• Raw materials. (These worries bothered 25% or less of the presidents surveyed.)

Source: A survey sponsored by four executive search firms: Thomas A. Buffum Assoc., Boston; Oliver & Rozner Assoc., and Hunt Co., New York; Rambert & Co., Chicago.

HOW MEN TEST WOMEN MANAGERS

A woman who becomes a manager and joins an all-male group of managers alters the identity of the group. Usually, the men respond subconsciously, setting up three types of tests for her: Social, overtly sexual, and intellectual. If she gets upset or angry or emotional when the men try these tests, she will have lost.

- *Social:* They may try to get her to be the group's secretary, writing down the minutes of a meeting, making copies, setting up a conference room, serving coffee. The woman shouldn't let the men make these things into tests. Instead, she should *take the initiative* and do one thing while suggesting that someone else do another and that someone else do the third. If she does serve coffee, she should maneuver to have someone else serve it next time.

- *Sexual:* The best way to deal with a sexual overture is to *not* respond, to act as if it did not occur. *One way:* Answer a question related to the work being done as if nothing happened at all. A woman should not encourage a man, flirt, enjoy sexual jokes, or tease a man along. *Problem:* The man's ego. When the "game" stops, he isn't likely to react pleasantly. (When the woman acts as if nothing happened, the man's ego isn't so involved, and the man recovers quickly.)

If the man *persists* and he's the boss and suggests career advancement for the woman if she goes along (while implying career termination if she doesn't), the woman should list the details of the overtures (times, places, conditions, etc.). She might tell another male supervisor who is trustworthy, without mentioning any names.

In a large company, she should meet with the Equal Employment Opportunity officer and cite all the details (except the name). She should record all the details, including promises and threats, and ask that the record be placed in her personnel file. And she should request a job transfer.

To sue, the evidence must be clear and overwhelming.

- *Intellectual:* Again, the answer is to stick to the task at hand. Respond only to that element of any statement a man may make, ignoring all the other elements which may suggest that he is smarter, more experienced, more influential, or knows more.

Source: Margaret Hennig and Anne Jardim, *The Managerial Woman* (Anchor Press/Doubleday, 501 Franklin Ave., Garden City, N.Y. 11530).

SUBORDINATES

- Do not trust your opinions about subordinates in areas which are not related to their work.
- Do not try to be in on company gossip.
- Do not try to be a different person to different people.
- Interactions and exchanges between you and a subordinate mean much more to the subordinate than they do to you because he or she has much more to lose or gain.
- Communication between you and a subordinate is decreased when it occurs in the presence of *any* third party.

TIME PLANNING

BRING VISITORS TO THE POINT QUICKLY

- Rise, walk around your desk, and meet caller halfway. Keep standing during talk.
- Simplify your office decor. Mobiles, tropical fish, paintings, and the like invite comment. Spartan austerity can cut meeting time.
- Ask questions, or even suggest to the speaker what's on his mind. If you're right, he'll come to the point faster. If you're wrong, he'll correct you—with the same result.
- Bunch up your appointments and phone calls so each visitor feels the pressure of a full waiting list and flashing telephone lights. These also provide ways to terminate the conversation.
- Use a timer or alarm watch. Set it for a few minutes before it's time to end conference. The buzzer alerts your caller so he can close the meeting.

STRETCHING EXECUTIVE TIME

- Make time for yourself and subordinates by abandoning strategies and activities obsoleted by new developments or overshadowed by new demands and priorities.

- Schedule your work load to achieve the *sequence* of activities that will best bring big projects to early completion, implement new policies most effectively.
- *Never* try to get all the little jobs out of the way before you start a big one. Many small tasks take care of themselves if you leave them alone. *Remember:* Phone calls, mail, and visits can take up whole day—if you let them.

Make time for getting *big* tasks done every day. Plan your daily work load in advance. Single out the relatively few small jobs that absolutely *must* be done immediately in the morning. Then go directly to the big tasks, try to pursue them to completion. (If you procrastinate on big jobs, it can be forever; if you start, you'll feel compelled to finish.)

- Tackle tasks that interest you least when your energy's at its peak. They're usually harder, and often more fruitful, than the ones that interest you most.
- If you can't find a solution to a problem, don't continue to waste time on it. Drop it; come back to it later.
- Avoid getting immersed and involved in what subordinates or associates are doing, particularly if you're a professional-turned-manager with a passionate interest in research, engineering, or the like.
- Delegate *anything* that someone else can do *well enough*. Extra time spent achieving optimal quality is usually wasted, particularly if it's *your* time.
- Never delegate anything you really

can do far better and faster than anyone else—anything that absolutely requires your authority and judgment or that takes more time to explain than to do yourself.

• Merge smaller problems and issues into larger ones to save time, broaden your thinking. *Example:* Review reports on turnover, absenteeism, productivity *at the same time.* Read, think, analyze in terms of the larger task: Improving employee motivation.

CAPTURED MINUTE PLAN

Use the *Captured Minute Plan* to make wasted time productive, stave off stress and anger when you're waiting in line at the bank, airport, etc.

What to do: Update your expense record. Plan tomorrow's activities. Jot down notes about work, a new project, or colleagues. Read something. Look around, and see what's happening.

Source: Rob Rutherford, time training specialist, Pasadena, Calif.

TIME CONSERVER: BENIGN NEGLECT

Compulsive punctuality can be the thief of time—yours *and* the company's. Tips on the art of *personal* discreet procrastination:

• *Committee meetings:* Ever notice that half the key participants are usually late? Skip the preliminaries and reading of the minutes. Prescreen the agenda, arrive in time for the action on matters for which you're really needed.

• *Phone messages:* Don't return all the calls the minute you get back to the office. Spot the crucial ones. Half the rest will be from people who've already solved their problems; the rest will be back to you soon enough.

• *Memos and correspondence:* Stop straining for snap, same-day responses when tomorrow's events could change your answer. Review last month's correspondence file. How many weighty missives did you dictate needlessly on "problems" that resolved themselves?

AMPLE WORK SPACE IMPORTANT TO EXECUTIVE TIME MANAGEMENT

• Use an L-shaped desk, plus a back table.
• Keep only the most pressing, current work on the desk. Put away all else.
• Keep the front desk area clear for visitors and shorter jobs. (Put them into folders or desk files when visitors come.)

ROI TIME MANAGEMENT

Executives who are naturally well organized may be able to use this Return on Investment (ROI) approach to manage their time even *more* effectively.

• List all the tasks ahead of you by day or by week (whichever fits your personal and business requirements).

• Estimate the relative value of each task on a scale of 1 to 100 (task value). Estimate the *time available* for each task; then divide the *task value* by the *time available*. This gives the "return on investment" values. The higher the number, the higher the rate of return.

• Using the ROI values, put the tasks into priority. Group together tasks that can be done together or that can be done more efficiently if done in sequence.

Whether you're organized or not: Develop tactics to disengage politely from people who encroach upon your time. Try a Memo-time pocket/desk reminder unit, an alarm watch, a ship bell clock that rings every half hour, or any inanimate device that signals the passing of time and seems to be a factor outside your control. This relieves you of blame for cutting short the chitchat and helps keep break time within reasonable limits.

TIME WASTERS

Most executives feel guilty about time they *waste*. They believe they should, and could, be more effective managing their own time. Many have tried the conventional methods of boosting efficiency—making lists of priorities, keeping diaries, etc.—only to find that nothing has changed. They're *still* wasting time—and still feeling guilty about it.

Their problem, says Rutherford, is that they fail to attack the sources of the problem: *Why* time is wasted and *how* time is wasted.

An example that will make the point:

Mr. A's desk is cluttered with piles of papers, memos, reports. His briefcase is equally cluttered. When someone suggests a new project or responsibility, he points to the clutter, which is a clear message: How busy he is, how overwhelmed he already is with responsibility, how it might be better to look to someone else to take on that task.

The clutter is also another kind of *crutch:* It tells the world how really important he is, since so much is *pending* on his desk.

And if the executive complains to his peers, subordinates, or the boss about the overwhelming paper work, he's also providing for himself a perfect opportunity to play the martyr: "Look what the world has dumped on me!"

(For the example of a cluttered desk, you can substitute an executive who complains about the number of intrusions during the day, the lack of time to explain to a subordinate how to do something, the lack of opportunity to *think*, the inability to work out a corporate plan, etc.)

The key: The first step in becoming more time-efficient is to identify how you *waste* time. Then puzzle out what your *payoff* is for using that particular time waster. *Example:* If, in fact, the cluttered desk really fills your need to avoid more work, then you just may not want to give up the defense. You need it—and shouldn't feel bad about it.

Naturally, once you come to grips with that insight, *why* the desk is cluttered, you've taken a big step in attacking that problem.

Here's an exercise that gives a good understanding of time wasting: Make a list of the things that give you the greatest satisfaction (*high payoffs*). Don't worry about whether they are work-related or not—just be sure they leave you satisfied. The idea is to get the high payoffs down on paper.

Now scan the list: You'll probably find that none of the things are particularly time-related. They are all fairly open-ended.

Scan it again: There's a good chance that most of them require some difficult step. The outcome isn't at all certain. *Examples:* Starting a new business venture; reorganizing an operation to make it more efficient; selling an idea to someone, and the idea may alter your operation; getting closer to your children or spouse; getting your business plans down on paper so your subordinates know in what direction you want the business to move.

Each goal could have a high payoff—yet each is at least a bit difficult and scary to undertake, and so each requires a reason not to do it.

And that's where the time wasters come in. Each time waster is an excuse for putting off the *high payoffs.*

Source: Robert Rutherford, who conducts time-management seminars for executives and administrative assistants.

TICKLER FILE

A tickler file is a simple way to organize work, save time, and eliminate desk clutter. It is merely a set of manila folders numbered for each day of the month—and a set labeled with each month of the year.

Place the folders in your desk or in a file cabinet nearby. Any piece of paper that can't be acted on immediately should be placed in a "future" folder. Beyond the day folders, put it in the one for the appropriate month.

Each day, go through the current file. Anything that can't be disposed of on that day goes into a future slot in the file. When the current day's file is empty, move it to the back of the row, so the next day's file is in front.

Idea: Do certain kinds of work on specific days. Just drop the relevant material into the appropriate folder as it arrives at your desk. (Good, too, for allocating materials to regularly scheduled meetings.)

Source: *Chronolog*, Box 456, Orinda, Cal. 94563.

SHOULD YOU BUY OR LEASE A BEEPER?

A beeper, or a small pocket pager, allows an executive to stay in touch with his office when he's out. When something important happens or he gets a crucial phone call, his secretary calls a special phone number which has been assigned to the beeper. That number rings in a computerized switchboard, which then automatically causes a radio signal to be sent out, which is received by the beeper, signaling the need to call the office. Some beepers also allow a voice message to be transmitted, giving a secretary up to 15 seconds to relay a message.

Other available features on beepers include: (1) A memory which will store a beep, allowing it to be shut off until the user is ready for it; (2) a vibrating silent signal which alerts the user, instead of the noisy beep; (3) and a second signal, which allows the user to receive messages from a second source who is identified by a shorter beep.

If you aren't certain whether you will get much use from a beeper, it's best to rent or lease one for a while to see what it might do for you and what features you might need. Monthly rentals vary, depending on the features. If you want to buy one, look in the *Yellow Pages* under "Paging and Signaling Service," and compare costs.

MANAGING THE STAFF

A QUICK COURSE IN MANAGING PEOPLE

Most managers find managing people the most frustrating, least rewarding part of their job. It's inherently difficult. And the advice and jargon are both overwhelming and contradictory. *Typical ways of coping:* Apply common sense, rules of thumb, or simply avoid the problem.

In an effort to simplify and provide straightforward counsel, here is a list of what we think are the most critical components of decision making by any self-aware manager:

• If you're a line manager, you'll find yourself spending from 75% to 95% of your time with people or dealing with people problems—like it or not. Many times, people problems will be mixed with technical questions. Don't be frustrated by all this talking and listening.

• The essence of managerial skill is to "keep moving." Learn to tolerate short, but frequent interactions, to tolerate not finishing a subject, to tolerate having to go back to individuals again and again. People problems are rarely solved forever. *Objective:* Keep them within limits. Keep making contact. Easy give-and-take is the only guarantee of reasonably good interpersonal relationships. You can't have that without constant listening and talking.

• **Find good people, and support them** with backup and encouragement. The right person, well motivated, will perform significantly better than the average person.

• Satisfaction with earnings is almost entirely related to *what other relevant people are earning.* Comparisons, not absolute amounts, count.

• Job relationships are more predictable and less upsetting than many family or community relations. Earning one's way and having a job are the sources of great personal satisfaction. Grousing is *not* a measure of discontent. Often the most committed are the most critical, and the least committed are often the most indifferent.

• Boundaries are the most important elements of a job. How does performance fit into the needs of other jobs? In selecting and appraising people, consider their capacity for relating to the other people upon whom their jobs impinge. *Technical knowledge is secondary.*

• Organizational productivity results, not from speed and sweat, but from jobs smoothly intermeshing one with the other, a minimum of argument over who should do what and how. Continuity and regularity comprise the only reliable source of cost saving.

• You and your subordinate will almost *never* see a problem the same way. Your experiences and perspectives are different. Stop before you delegate or discipline. Find out by good interviewing how the other person perceives an issue before you do anything about it.

• Before you get progress or agreement on an issue involving another person, there must be agreement that there is a problem. Spend your time getting agreement on the nature of the problem. Then it's relatively easy to agree on a solution that meets conflicting needs.

• Feedback on performance and positive encouragement are the sources of improved motivation. Ignorance of results and/or a climate of criticism are the two most common sources of apathy and lack of motivation.

TACTIC AGAINST TIME WASTERS

Bothered by subordinates (or peers) who come for assistance or advice and then systematically shoot down all the suggestions? Actually, they're playing a little "game" that inflates their egos by "proving" (to themselves) that they're better than you. *Tactic:* When you recognize that he's "playing" again, *turn the tables.* Say you're flattered that he has come for advice but feel he's in a better position (because of his experience) to come up with ideas. You, of course, will be more than willing to critique them for him.

WHEN A SUBORDINATE COMES TO YOU WITH A PERSONAL PROBLEM

Listen. Many times, this is all that is necessary to be helpful. A survey of employees by behavioral scientists at York University in Toronto, Canada, found that only 3% wanted the manager to take over the problem. One in seven just wanted the supervisor to listen. But 13% of the *managers* thought they (the managers) should take some action.

Remember that the problem is the subordinate's, not yours. Don't take it over. Don't get sucked into emotional involvement with the other person's personal problem. Don't impetuously offer to help.

Instead: Question the person who comes to you before you start to make declarations. By *questioning* instead of *declaring,* you give the other person a chance to define the problem and explore options without being sidetracked by *your* point of view.

Wait until you hear a direct request for action. Then, if you must do something, state what you will and won't do.

This will avoid misunderstandings later. Some problems, though, need time to solve.

THREE WAYS TO WORK SMOOTHLY WITH YOUR SECRETARY

1. Give each assignment a priority. #1 means urgent, need now; #2 means need by end of day; #3 means low priority (but add a deadline).

2. Have your secretary circle most important or interesting portion of each piece of incoming mail. Almost anyone can learn quickly to make these evaluations, and even if she misses some, you'll pick it up anyway when you scan the material. When key sections are marked, rest falls quickly into place in your mind.

3. Have correspondence to be signed given to you in odd-size, conspicuously colored folder so it isn't misplaced under other work on your desk.

CONFIDENCES TO THE SECRETARY

Because of the potential opportunity for blackmail, some states have enacted laws providing that a secretary *cannot* divulge confidential information imparted to her while on the job. When the Internal Revenue Service sought to compel a secretary to describe matters of possible tax significance that had been dictated to her, she replied that under state (Oregon) law, her lips were sealed. *The court ordered her to talk.*

A *federal* tax was involved, and for federal purposes there is no employer-secretary privilege despite what the *state* law provides.

U.S. et al. v. Schoenheinz, 9th Cir., 3/1/77.

REMEMBERING NAMES

Managers of up to 80 or so employees can usually remember each employee's name *and* something about them. With 500 or so employees, one can only expect to recognize them. *More than that:* Recognition problems.

USEFUL PERSONAL ASSISTANTS

• Personal assistants to the top executive can be useful, but often create problems in the executive ranks. *Best advice:* Assistant should not be expected to report to anybody but the top manager, but he should *never* have authority over an operating manager.

• Office staff of top executives must be capable of screening letters and phone calls, referring calls to proper lower-level executives, handling routine correspondence on own initiative. Having competent assistants costs far less than having executives do those chores.

MEETINGS

GROUP DECISION-MAKING DOs AND DON'Ts

• Don't bother with it unless all members of the group know each other well, trust each other, and have faith in each other's abilities. If these factors don't exist, there will be more jockeying for position than intelligent discussion, and the results won't be trustworthy.
• Don't use it for analytical problems. *Individuals* are better at this.
• Do use it for solving controversial, complicated problems. Group discussion tends to generate more solutions than individuals can, and allows for better scrutiny of solutions.
• Don't use it if the time available for working on a problem is very short. A harried group is more likely to generate bad feelings and sloppy thinking.

Source: Corwin King, in *S.A.M. Advanced Management Journal.*

BETTER THAN A BRIEFING

Department manager had to increase control while his company was undergoing extensive organizational change.

He set up a formal weekly meeting at which each of his subordinates briefed him and left a written report.
Problem: Too much time spent at meetings, too many reports to read.
Solution: The executive canceled the formal meeting. Instead he reserved a two-hour period each Friday, during which every subordinate manager had to visit him, even if only to say he had nothing to report. The subordinates could drop in without an appointment or could reserve a block of time. And the subordinates themselves decided whether they should see the executive singly or in groups.
Result: No subordinate spent *unnecessary* time at meetings. The executive had a better chance of limiting discussion to what was relevant, and since the only records were his own notes, nothing irrelevant got in the file.
Source: *Behavioral Science Newsletter.*

POINTERS ON MEETINGS

• Tape-record meetings with consultants and review the material between sessions to increase understanding of their advice. Taping is much less intrusive and distracting than taking notes.
• Brief meetings among managers from different departments (such as the purchasing, manufacturing, and marketing departments) allow for consultations between people who otherwise work separately. Try to limit the ses-

sions to 10 minutes. The more frequently they are held (weekly might be best), the less socializing and wasted time there will be at each one.

MEETING LOTTERY ENCOURAGES QUESTIONS FROM AUDIENCE

Issue numbered question cards with matching numbered stubs. When a member of the audience has a question, he writes it on a card, passes the card to the moderator, and keeps the stub. The moderator asks the question and places the card in a box. At the end of the meeting, cards are drawn and prizes awarded.

WHEN MEETINGS LOSE STEAM

Voices fall in volume; inflection diminishes; monotones prevail. In addition, as meetings get duller, participants betray their withdrawal from the group by slouching, sitting farther back from the table, facing sideways rather than forward. Internally, you have an uncomfortable feeling that something has gone awry.

Action: First, the direct approach. Try, "The meeting seems to have gotten off the track in the last few minutes. Does anyone else feel the same way?" The response should tell whe-

ther the cause is something said during the discussion or whether it's simply fatigue and stretched attention spans.

Only remedy for fatigue is a break. They are more effective if they are taken when needed rather than on a fixed schedule. *Critical time:* After lunch, when frequent breaks are required to combat the post-meal lassitude that affects many people.

Other techniques:

• *Play for a while:* Five minutes of joking and light conversation will stimulate more vigorous discussion afterward.

• *Change the scene:* Have people form smaller groups and move briefly to some other site—the lawn, a lounge, chairs in the hall.

• Break the main group up into subgroups for more specialized discussion.

Source: Richard J. Dunsing, professor, University of Richmond.

TO KEEP EXECUTIVE UP TO DATE

• Has the company's market potential for the current year been thoughtfully estimated?

• What share of each market segment is your firm getting?

• How many commercial accounts have been gained or lost this year? Why?

• What are the current and future needs of your firm's top 25 accounts?

• How have customers reacted to any newly introduced products (or services)?

• Does management consider change an opportunity or a threat?

QUESTION CARDS ENCOURAGE ATTENTIVENESS

Involvement of participants at large (and small) business meetings can be improved by distributing cards (and pencils) for questions. At the start of the meeting, everyone in the audience is asked to prepare questions as they arise. As the cards are collected, aides sort them, eliminate duplicates, and have them ready in a logical sequence by the time the speaker is finished.

Variation: Break up the large audience into smaller groups, and have each group consult among its members and write out questions.

Advantages: Speed, a more attentive audience, elimination of duplicate questions, avoidance of wasteful silences.

PHYSICAL SETTING SHOULD BOLSTER SIZE AND PURPOSE OF MEETING

• For a meeting of a small group (10-15) in which participation is encouraged, use a conference table.

• For a slightly larger meeting (about two dozen), a horseshoe table with participants seated on the outside will work best. This setup will also work for a meeting in which a presentation will be given or training will be presented.

• A classroom-style meeting room with narrow tables will accommodate about four dozen people, and participation is much easier than if those attending were seated in rows.

• For larger meetings, speeches, or talks, use an auditorium format, with rows of chairs. Questions can still be asked. This style of meeting isn't conducive to participation.

Source: *Sales Meetings* magazine.

WHAT A CONFERENCE ROOM NEEDS TO FUNCTION EFFECTIVELY

Square shape to bring participants together. (If this isn't possible, make sure the length isn't more than 50% greater than the width.)

• At least 36 sq. ft. of space per person for a U-shaped setup; six to eight sq. ft. for an auditorium layout.

• Lighting should be fluorescent, supplemented by incandescent, and recessed into the ceiling. Use spotlights on strips to highlight blackboards and the like. (Avoid windows—they're distracting. Or cover them with drapes to control light.)

• Avoid low ceilings. *Best heights:* 10 ft. for a room holding fewer than 25 people; 11 ft. for 25-50 people.

• Use dividers that really divide groups by creating a seal with floor and ceiling. Avoid freestanding partitions.

• Bright colors (orange, yellow, blue, green) encourage alertness. Dark colors reduce attention spans and create fatigue.

• Keep decorations and accessories plain and functional so they're not distracting—bright, solid-color carpets;

plain walls (no pictures, bookcases, or clocks permitted).

● Watch out for reflective surfaces—they can "hypnotize" participants and reduce awareness.

● Select a conference table with a modesty panel so shifting feet do not become a distraction, and be sure all chairs are comfortable—but that the leader's chair is higher than the others so he is dominant.

Source: James L. Davis, National Conference Center, East Union, N.J., writing in *Training* magazine.

HOW TO GET THE BEST SERVICE FROM CONVENTION HOTELS

● Insist on meeting *every key* person, from the manager down to the porter. Prepare a gratuities list, and let the staff know you have one. Include every employee's name, as well as spaces for filling in good and bad ratings and dollar amounts.

● Give each person at your meeting three chits to award to hotel employees for exceptional service. Use the exceptional service chits as lottery tickets for prizes awarded at the end of the convention.

● Tip some key people heavily on the first day, and then let the word spread throughout the hotel. One top convention executive gives the bellboy who carries his bags when he checks in $25.

● *Don't tip management personnel:* Their reward is a return visit and increased business. If managers seem to be looking for tips, best to take your business elsewhere in the future. If a

hotel has, in fact, done a particularly good job, it is appropriate to send a letter of appreciation.

Source: *Successful Meetings.*

SPEAKERS

Hassle-free way to deal with speakers for a company (or association) that conducts many meetings: Develop a standard kit containing a speaker's agreement, tips for the speaker on how to meet audience needs, and space for recording nitty-gritty details, such as travel and hotel arrangements, need for audio-visual aids, and the like.

RUN A SUCCESSFUL SALES MEETING

Advice from a leading sales consultant:

● Don't hold a sales meeting just because the schedule calls for one. The meeting must have a specific objective in mind.

● Meeting should cover only that part of the information load that cannot be put across in other ways (manuals, bulletins, direct contact with supervisors, etc.). *Common mistake:* Trying to cover more ground than time will permit.

● Give salespeople real information, not just a pep talk to "get out there and fight."

● Find out what they need to know by sending them a questionnaire *before the meeting.* Build at least part of your meeting around responses.

• *Elementary but often overlooked:* When introducing a new product, don't just show it and talk about it; *explain how to sell it.*

• Inspect the meeting room when you rent it. Check lighting and ventilation. Try out the chairs. (The more comfortable they are, the fewer times you'll have to break for standing and stretching.) Sit at the back of the room, and see if you can read the flip chart up front.

Source: J. Porter Henry, 103 Park Ave., New York 10017.

SERIOUS MEETING? USE A CONFERENCE CENTER

A conference center conveys the message that the session will be serious and intensive, businesslike, without interruptions—with no place for spouses.

Conference centers have professional staffs to provide needed equipment or services. They are good places to try new or different ideas for meetings, such as a shirt-sleeve session around a table with pitchers of beer or reorganizing the setting of your meeting room several times a day. The facilities of conference centers are most conducive to holding meetings. Outside interruptions are almost nonexistent.

Source: Ann Wold, meeting planning consultant, Gallagher-Wold, Inc., 420 Lexington Ave., New York 10017.

Informal meetings of suppliers' management and company management are worth the time invested. A free exchange of problems and plans can pave the way for more efficient operation on the other levels.

COMMUNICATIONS

HOW TO WRITE UNSTUFFY BUSINESS LETTERS

• Avoid dictating a letter if you can phone, wire, cable, or use handwritten memos (but keep copies).

• When dictating, try to use the same style you use on the phone: Short, modern, crisp, efficient. No Victorianisms ("I am in receipt of your letter and wish to inform you...").

• If you have to include details, put them on a formal second sheet; attach them to your short original letter. (The receiver can have them duplicated and send them on to a subordinate for action.)

• In letters abroad, skip the business jargon; use basic, sixth-grade English. (Just imagine the trouble a businessman or translator will have with terms like "low profile.")

• Be friendly, sincere, informal. Adding a handwritten P.S. helps. So does just signing the letter without having your name typed under it. (Use title if necessary.)

• Never put personal letters or thank-you notes to business acquaintances on company stationery. Get some small, private stationery with just your first and last name on it. No initials. No address (type it in, if necessary, over the date). No pretentiousness. No typed-out signature. And no secretary's initials at the left. *For handwritten notes:* 4 × 5 cards with your name embossed at the top or printed on miniature-size legal pads.

• For extra-special occasions, send a night letter. No telegraphese. Enthuse, use all 25 words. (Mailgram is cheaper —with strong impact, too.)

Source: John Weitz, *Man in Charge* (Macmillan, 866 Third Ave., New York 10022).

SAVING WORDS

Verbosity wastes time and diminishes comprehension. Check your reports, memos, and letters for these common business phrases, and substitute the shorter version for the more wordy one.

• Enclosed, please find—*here's.*
• According to our records—*We find.*
• At an early date/At your earliest convenience—*Soon/Now.*
• In the event of—*If.*
• In the amount of—*For.*
• In accordance with—*By/Under.*
• Inasmuch as—*Since/Because.*
• In our opinion—*We believe.*
• It is obvious that/It goes without saying—*Clearly/Obviously.*
• Finalized our decision—*Decided.*
• For the purpose of—*For.*
• Reflects a balance of—*Shows.*
• With regard to—*Re:.*
• With the result that—*So that.*

SPEEDING CORRESPONDENCE

• *For immediate reply:* Ask the recipient to respond right on your original memo and return it. (The person you're writing to can make a copy if one is needed.)

• *Delayed answers:* Keep an extra copy of your original letter; send it out as a follow-up with a written note if you don't get a reply within reasonable time. Gets attention; saves your correspondent from looking for "lost" incoming letters.

Source: *Chronolog.*

SEVEN WAYS TO IMPROVE YOUR BUSINESS WRITING

1. Use an outline to organize your thoughts.

2. Write a rough draft, and then rewrite it.

3. Dictate. Even if it seems awkward, it's faster and it will help you write as you speak.

4. Keep the absent reader in mind. You won't be there to explain pas-

sages he can't understand.

5. Avoid clichés.

6. Be generous with headings, sub-headings, charts, and diagrams. They invite attention and make your thoughts easier to follow.

7. Edit your own work, and invite comments from a close colleague.

USE DICTATING MACHINE FOR BETTER REPORTS AND MEMOS

Technique is everything when it comes to using dictating machines effectively. Here are some simple steps to follow in using a recorder to compose first drafts of nondetailed material.

• Make a "laundry-list" outline of basic ideas.

• Deliberately become *uninhibited;* record whatever comes to mind concerning those ideas—don't edit.

• Have the material typed triple-spaced; this provides plenty of editing room.

• Edit by hand.

• Dictate again only those pages that are too heavily edited for the secretary to decipher.

TIMESAVERS

• Order an extra copy for each letter you have typed. Collect the extra copies chronologically in a three-ring loose-leaf binder, and keep it on your desk. You'll find yourself using them fre-

quently as an instant reference for names, addresses, reminders of past decisions.

• Do the same for telephone messages, having your secretary type each on a sheet of loose-leaf paper. Use the sheets for call-backs. The large amount of blank paper on each sheet can be used for notes.

• Time needed to prepare for meetings can be reduced markedly if you keep a portfolio on your desk with a slot for each manager you supervise. When meeting minutes, memos, and the like arrive, drop each into the appropriate slot. That way, much of the agenda of each future meeting compiles itself automatically. When meeting time comes, just pick up the proper folder—you're ready to go.

HOW TO PREPARE A SPEECH

Decide exactly and precisely what your subject is. Then logically think through your subject. Make a list of the ideas and conclusions you wish to stress. Become thoroughly familiar with the important books, speeches, and other literature on the subject.

Prepare an outline of the speech: Introduction, main body (usually divided up into two to four sections), and the conclusion.

Start by *writing* the speech. Be complete.

Prepare a brief introduction. Various ways in which you can introduce your speech: (1) Attack the topic head-on by simply announcing it. (2) Begin with a human-interest story, an illustration, or a funny anecdote relevant to the topic. (3) Startle the audience by beginning with an exciting question or an arousing statement. (4) Use a quote or an idea from somebody else. (5) Explain in factual terms why the topic is important to your audience.

The main body of the speech should make it apparent to your audience that you have a thorough knowledge of the topic. Back up your points with facts, numbers, examples. If you want to convince your audience of the wisdom of your views on the topic, begin with material that agrees with those views. Don't argue. Just explain your points. Those points should be clearly defined either at the beginning or the end of the speech, or as they develop within the speech, or any combination of those three.

Conclude: Briefly go over the points you've made. Use a quote. Strive for a big climax. You can compliment the audience. Or end by being encouraging and optimistic or by detailing a particularly dramatic story, a historical anecdote, or with a joke. You can also recommend that your audience take some action. Another ending would be to suggest that they change their views to yours.

Source: H. V. Prochnow, *The Public Speaker's Treasure Chest* (Harper & Row, 10 E. 53 St., New York 10022).

NO BORING SPEECHES

Business speeches can be a bore. Good idea if you're called upon to give one is to take a point of view that is fresh or causes debate or is vital and constructive. If that's impossible, ask to have the topic changed, but reserve the right to decline should the speech committee insist that you stick to their topic.

Reasonable rule of thumb to follow: If *you* can't get enthusiastic about the topic yourself, don't give the speech. If you're naturally gung ho for the subject, chances are you'll be more spontaneous, more constructive, and less of a bore.

SPEECH WRITING FOR THE BOSS

When asking a subordinate to write a speech for you or another top executive, give him this advice:

• Get hold of the group that's inviting the boss to speak, and find out what topic is *really* wanted. Learn the nature of the speaking occasion, the dignitaries expected, the knowledge and attitude of the audience toward the boss, and whether the news media will be present. Include these data on a separate fact sheet for the boss' use.

• Sit down with the boss to discuss what he'd like to talk about, and then interview him on that topic. Take copious notes, and use a tape recorder if possible. The writer will want to give him back his own ideas couched in his own words.

• Conduct additional research to supplement the boss' general ideas. This should include any previous speeches he has made.

• Write the first draft, and write it simply. Use short sentences and short words. Stick to the topic. Keep the overall length to about 10 pages, double-spaced and typewritten. That's a 20-minute speech.

• Read the finished draft aloud, and polish it up.

• Give the corrected copy to the boss for his suggestions.

• Incorporate them into the final draft.

• Listen to him deliver it a few times, and help him make the necessary adjustments.

• Be there when he delivers the speech. Make notes on strong points, problems and on how to do it better next time.

Source: Dr. Douglas P. Starr, associate professor, North Texas State University.

THE RIGHT JOB

THE MARKET

Executive demand is expected to continue strong in the 80's. Organizations continue to seek superior performers to fill newly created posts and replacement positions. Functional demand will be highest for general management, financial and marketing executives, continuing the 1970s' pattern, when demand in these functions outpaced that in engineering, manufacturing and personnel.

GETTING AHEAD

Lucky breaks, good connections, and education aren't always the only reasons that others of equal ability get further ahead on the job. Fact is, people who advance most usually work harder, longer, and more thoughtfully. And without imperiling their health. Don't confuse hard strivers with compulsive "workaholics." Long-hour per-

formers usually enjoy their work; add 100 days more per year to production; do more reading, thinking, and self-improvement than 9-to-5 groups. It figures they'll merit promotions. Studies show their work to be a positive factor. Stress (the *real* danger) is highest among underachievers.

WHY SOME JOBS CAN'T SUCCEED

Status and power in an organization are usually associated with relative autonomy. That autonomy applies to activities that are perceived as nonroutinizable, problematical, and challenging. These are the functions that get visibility, budgets, and "their way in the organization." Management draws most of the "promotables" from these functions, too.

In other words, if *finance* is seen as the difficult, challenging area (*and marketing the opposite*), the bright "comers" will be attracted to the finance

118

function because they know their ideas will get more support and promotion will be more rapid. Contrariwise, marketing becomes a poor second choice for a career line.

So what? The problem for the organization is that this becomes a vicious spiral. While at some period in its life the organization may have been "hurting most" in finance, which was the big problem and deserving of the most attention, this may not always be the case. But over time, with good, ambitious people being attracted to finance and repelled by some of the other functions, they ossify. Everyone sees marketing, for example, as a routinized function, no challenge, no need for new breakthroughs or accomplishment. Organizational perceptions and people's "self-selection" in career lines then predetermine that marketing will be poorly handled. Management's impression that few good people in marketing are worthy of promotion will be confirmed by marketing's performance. And this, in turn, makes it even more difficult to get innovative work out of marketing.

After a while, management wakes up and tears the place apart. Management replaces most of the marketing people because "it's a lousy marketing department." They don't realize it became mundane and unimaginative because the management-controlled status system (where promotions and deference are given) decreed that its work should be of low quality.

Management needs to exercise care that it doesn't force key functions to become second rate by biased distributions of rewards and cues.

Source: Dr. Leonard R. Sayles, Columbia University, Graduate School of Business.

HIGH SALARIES FOR SWITCHING

● The jobs that command the highest salary increases when the employee moves from one company to another company: Design engineer, tax accountant, systems manager, controller, process engineer, systems analyst, research and development engineer, maintenance engineer, computer programmer, and plant manager.

Source: National Personnel Associates, 6 E. 45 St., New York 10017.

THE NEW TOP MANAGER'S HONEYMOON PERIOD

A new top manager must choose to use his "honeymoon" period in one of two ways:

1. Do little but learn about the job.
2. Innovate new policies and style.

What he should do depends on the type of succession situation he enters—and whether the new manager is an *insider* or an *outsider*.

● *Outsider who takes over from a weak predecessor:* Situation: Very favorable. He should take time to learn as much as he can about the job and the organization.

● *Insider who follows a strong manager:* Situation: Not favorable. He should take time to learn as much as he can about the job and the organization.

● *Insider who follows a weak manager:* Outlook for success: Very bad.

He should innovate as much as possible during the "honeymoon," emphasize policy changes, not changes in style.

● *Outsider who takes over from a strong predecessor.* Outlook for success: Moderate. He should get his authority established right away. But he should emphasize changes in *style*, not policy, and selectively dismiss a few potential opponents.

Source: *How to Run Any Organization*, by Theodore Caplow (Holt, Rinehart and Winston, 383 Madison Ave., New York 10017).

HOW TO ANSWER A BLIND EMPLOYMENT AD

Omit your name and address from your resume and covering letter and use a friend as an intermediary. *Another way:* Rent a post office box, or check classified newspaper ads or the Yellow Pages for telephone answering services and office space.

KEEPING MEDICAL RECORDS CONFIDENTIAL

The medical information release you sign for an insurance company could open the door to indiscriminate access to your personal history. Protect yourself these four ways:

1. Don't sign a blank authorization form.

2. Limit the period, medical facilities, and physicians in the authorization to those necessary to verify the data in your application.

3. Keep the option to determine which additional doctors and treatment facilities may be queried about your insurability.

4. Advise your physician when you have signed an authorization and whether it is blanket or specific.

BEST BUSINESS SCHOOL

According to 85 business school deans answering a survey, Stanford leads by a fairly good margin. Just about tied for second place were Harvard and Chicago, followed by Sloan (MIT), then Wharton.

EXECUTIVE RELOCATION

In addition to paying moving expenses, most companies offer one or more of the following payments:

● Closing costs for the sale of an old house and the purchase of a new one.

● Reimbursement for loss on the sale of a house.

● Cost of house-hunting trips.

● Mortgage interest rate differential. Many pay the difference in interest costs between the cheaper old mortgage and the more expensive one for one to three years.

Another benefit: Guaranteed sale of the old house. Many companies make the guarantee through special relocation services advertised in the *Yellow Pages* under "Real Estate."

IF YOU'RE FIRED

Executive layoffs are becoming more commonplace. What you must do if you get axed:

First, develop an emergency plan. Too many white-collar workers have the attitude that *it can't happen to me;* they can't cope when it does. The plan should call for the *immediate filing for unemployment compensation.* Then evaluate your skills and where you should market them, size of firm, industry, etc.

Warnings:

• Don't try to change career fields too quickly. It looks bad on your resumé. Changing fields isn't generally wise unless your field is in permanent decline.

• Don't seize the layoff as an opportunity to open your own business. If you were laid off because of the economy, there is little chance that the same economy will support your new venture.

Strategies:

• Determine a realistic salary range and think of what trade-offs you'd permit if offered an attractive position *below* your range. Decide what aspects of a job are most important to you, and consider what your attitudes are toward bonuses, compensation, advancement, challenges, and location. Don't demand more than you're offered. Don't play hard to get.

• Work up a good resume that lists information clearly and concisely. Put information in chronological order, listing your accomplishments and responsibilities in each business situation. Don't go over two pages, and *don't* include references. Include all data that will set you apart from others and that will sell you, like a good ad. Also have a printer run off your resumé. Mail resumes on a Friday so they will be there Monday morning.

• When you are being interviewed, talk money last. Don't knock your former employer. After the interview write notes to the people you talked with, thanking them for their time. *Continue notes to prime prospects.*

• While you're waiting, keep up with latest business news. Take nothing for granted, and don't give up until you've received a written employment offer. Tell everyone you can think of you're in the market. Don't ask them for a job—just to keep their eyes open for you.

MORE IDEAS

• Moving from one corporation to another doesn't provide a faster track to the top for high-level executives. *Exception:* A move into one of the top 100 industrial corporations. *Reason:* Job-hopping is less common among executives in these companies, so the newcomer gets special treatment and strong support from the management that selected him.

Source: Dr. W.B. Werther, Jr., consultant and management professor at Arizona State University.

• *Directory of Executive Recruiters* lists more than 1,100 executive search firms and employment agencies that operate on a fee-paid basis. Cross-indexes them by industry specialty, management function.

Write: *Consultants News*, 17 Templeton Rd., Fitzwilliam, N.H. 03447.

PERSONAL STYLE

VERY PERSONAL ADVICE FROM JOHN WEITZ

MARRIAGE AND THE BUSINESSMAN. Many businessmen eventually reach the point where they find they've "outgrown" their wives. In a typical situation, the husband is deeply involved in a career and business, and the wife is often raising children and keeping house—two functions that don't naturally lead to personal growth. How does one bridge the gap?

There's only one way: Involve her! Involve her! Involve her!

If she's intelligent enough to raise children and run a home, she's intelligent enough to help you with your business. So make her privy to everything you do—all your decisions, your worries. Keep her completely briefed on all your plans and dealings with colleagues. Ask her advice. You'd be amazed to find how good her judgment is—that is, if you've regularly kept her up on what's going on.

She has the "distance" on the one hand, and involvement in your affairs, on the other, to provide well-balanced judgments. Don't forget, she has *your* best interest (and *hers*) at heart.

BRINGING A WIFE INTO THE BUSINESS. *In one word:* Don't. No one should (or could, for that matter) spend 24 hours a day with one person. It strains the best relationships.

VACATIONS. I hate what vacations stand for—turning off, unzipping the mind. I've constructed my life around a simple idea: Work is fun, and work is part of my life. So when I vacation, I really take my work with me. All I do, really, is change the atmosphere. That's why I resist the idea of long vacations—one loses touch.

To be sure, my vacation ideas are a bit difficult for my children and my wife. But we manage to piece together many three- and four-day vacations to offset the lack of a long one.

SKIN CARE. It's nice for a man to have wrinkles and that weathered look. Don't try to hide it.

Don't shave against the grain of the beard. It's easier to replace a blade every few days than to change your skin. Five o'clock shadow? Don't worry about it.

In cold weather, use odorless moisturizer to avoid skin flaking.

HAIR GROOMING. Fancy styling? Forget it! Get a good barber, and avoid those stylists. No matter how hard the stylists try to give you the "natural" look, you come out looking foppish. And no one really trusts a foppish man. (One wonders how little really goes on inside him.)

Beau Brummell once said: "Dress and groom carefully at the start of a day—and then forget it."

Source: John Weitz, president, John Weitz Designs, Inc., 600 Madison Ave., New York 10022.

BODY TALK MYTHS

Too easy to misread *body language* signals. Recent popularization of the field has made everyone an "expert." Tips from a real expert:

Don't place too much meaning on isolated tics, idiosyncrasies—or even normal body movements.

Just because someone crosses his arms, don't assume that he's being defensive or is cutting himself off from you.

Avoid making assumptions based on appearances. *Example:* Just because a person appears direct and straightforward, don't assume his character is the same. Similarly, if a person moves in a twisting manner, don't assume a sly personality. Many of those movements are culture-oriented. Relying too heavily on those "obvious" tip-offs will blur other, more meaningful, observations.

Source: Dr. Lynn R. Cohen, psychologist, New York City.

NERVOUS TICS

Unconscious personal mannerisms distract and frequently offend sales prospects or other business contacts. *Watch out for:* Picking or inspecting fingernails. Clicking ballpoint pens. Constant tugging at or readjustment of clothing. Picking teeth. Scratching. Smoothing hair.

Also a good idea to forgo smoking in conference. An increasing number of individuals find it offensive.

EXECUTIVE PORTRAITS

Trend in executive photo portraiture is to natural, casual look; away from traditional, stiff-backed semi-smile-into-the-camera shots. Best to wear what you feel most comfortable in, what is "you," instead of dressing for the camera. Also, choose the location you think will show up your personality best: In the boardroom, behind your desk, in the lobby, etc.

Professional tip: Bring a few *recent* photographs of yourself (including candids) to the portrait session so the photographer can get an idea of how you photograph.

SIGNATURES

• For important papers, sign your name in ink with an *italic* pen. It's very hard to forge. The Osmiroid pen adds much more distinctiveness to your handwriting than even a felt-tip pen. To avoid smearing wet ink, buy one of those special blotter books in any stationery store. Your secretary puts the to-be-signed papers between the leaves; you can sign and turn the blotter pages without delay—the ink will be blotted automatically.

• Use your corporate title when signing documents creating corporate liability, especially checks, notes, and other negotiable paper. *Important legal reason:* Under certain circumstances, using the corporate title can avoid *personal* liability.

NEGOTIATING TACTICS

REASONS NEGOTIATIONS STALL

Sometimes negotiators don't want to make a deal. They're bargaining for other reasons. *Here are some of them:*
• Setting the stage for real talks later.
• Setting the stage for someone else to bargain.
• Tying up production time or inventory.
• Fishing for information.
• Talking while looking for alternatives.
• Stalling for time to get other parties involved.
• Forcing conflict into arbitration after testing your resolution.
• Diverting attention.

Source: Dr. Chester L. Karrass, director, Center for Effective Negotiating, writing in *Purchasing World.*

THE BOGEY TACTIC CAN MAKE BUYER AND SELLER HAPPIER

A negotiating technique that usually works to quickly bring buyer and seller closer together (without a hassle) and with each feeling he's getting what's due him:

The ploy—called the *Bogey Tactic:* Buyer wants a product or service and finally, after seeking formal or informal bids, decides that seller is the most responsive in terms of cost, reliability, and ability. Buyer knows how much he wants to spend. He calls in seller, tells him he's been selected for the purchase but that buyer has only X dollars (the Bogey) to spend on the job. Seller is now in a position either to reject the job or, more likely, to try to seek some substitutions in the order, timing, etc.—all in an effort to get the job within the budget.

The Bogey Tactic is actually best when the purchase is very complex. Through such open negotiations, buyer learns a lot more about what is available (after all, he's directly involved in the cost-saving alternatives). And seller also is more aware of the real needs of buyer. ("He asked for one kind of plating—but really some other will do.")

Source: Dr. Chester L. Karrass, director, Center for Effective Negotiating, in *Purchasing World.*

TELEPHONE NEGOTIATIONS

Don't negotiate on the telephone unless absolutely necessary. If it's unavoidable, use these pointers:
The dos:
• If called, listen. Get the full story. Then call back.
• Talk less and let the other party talk more. He'll probably end up saying

more than originally planned.
- Make a checklist before calling to avoid omissions.
- Have a calculator on desk.
- Lay out papers on desk.
- Take notes.
- Confirm agreements promptly in your own words.
- Have an excuse ready to end conversation.

The don'ts:
- Don't get into a phone conversation while in the middle of a staff meeting.
- Don't negotiate to a conclusion unless issues are understood.
- Don't make a quick decision because phone charges are mounting.
- Don't hesitate to call back if a computation error is made.
- Don't be afraid to reopen an important issue.

Source: *Give & Take: The Complete Guide to Negotiating Strategies and Tactics,* by Chester Karrass (T.Y. Crowell, 10 E 53 St., New York 10022).

ARBITRATION CLAUSES

When drafting a contract, or when confronted with the signing of one, be aware of the pressures at work to include or exclude a clause that requires arbitration of disputes.

If a dispute is moved through a *court* environment, the big company has a clear advantage. It can muster the best legal minds and devote more attention and money to litigation. The small firm is almost always outweighed.

In an *arbitration* environment, the reverse is true. Strict rules of procedure, evidence, etc., no longer apply.

It's harder and rarer for a judgment to turn on a legal technicality. Further, there may even be some bias by the arbitrator against the power of the big company.

For firms of equal size, arbitration is clearly in order. *Big pluses:* (1) speed in getting a decision—just a few months with arbitration (while the facts are being gathered by both sides) rather than years in the courts; (2) dramatic reduction in legal fees; (3) a decision that's often more equitable for both sides of the dispute, rather than a clear-cut win-lose judgment.

Source: Dick H. Brandon, president, The Brandon Consulting Group, Inc., 505 Park Ave., New York 10022.

HOW TO HANDLE A FINAL OFFER

First, listen very carefully to your counterpart across the negotiating table for hedges and face-savers to determine just how "final" the offer really is. Then, choose among any of these reactions:
- In your reply, interpret the offer in the way that is most favorable to you.
- Give the other party a face-saving way to retreat from his position.
- Get angry if it suits your purpose.
- Tell your opponent what he stands to lose by a deadlock.
- Consider making a test of the finality of the offer by walking out.
- Change the subject.
- Introduce new alternatives and possible solutions.

Source: Dr. Chester L. Karrass.

FINANCIAL MANAGEMENT

THE ESSENTIAL TOOLS

BIG BASICS: WHERE THE MOST SIZABLE SAVINGS ARE

• *Inventory reduction:* Even a well-managed company can usually squeeze another 20%-30% savings out of inventory operations. *Important determination:* whether old guidelines of inventory turnover are still valid. Examine business posture. If it has switched from a super-*service* to a higher *profit-margin* operation, inventory can probably turn more quickly than before.

• *Accounts receivable:* Amazing to see how many companies stop pushing late payers. Speed-up of just a *few days* in receivables can make major difference in cash flow. (Often it's *months* that can be picked up.) That's not to say that debtors should be pressed beyond prudence. But don't leave collection schedule to chance.

• *Packaging:* Carefully assess current technology. New developments in shrink materials can produce big savings over old-fashioned boxes.

• *Freight:* Many companies are still shipping by the fastest and easiest route. Important to weigh speed against cost. Speed is often a secondary consideration.

• *Warehousing:* Trend, in general, is toward fewer warehouses; consolidating freight shipments; even establishing inhouse trucking.

Product lines: Continuing assessment of profit lines—which product should be eliminated, which expanded, which amended? Those assessments are not to be made a one-time affair; they must be updated.

• *R&D:* Is your research and development activity moving in the right direction? Are you still working on yesterday's product? What's the cash drain and profit potential? Should you be doing risky research?

• *Personnel:* Maintain tight control. Hold on to advantages of the recession cutback. Use attrition to keep paring away deadwood. Add to staff only with the greatest reluctance—and then consider part-timers first.

Source: Allen H. Seed 3rd, management counselor, Arthur D. Little, Inc., Cambridge, Mass.

OPERATING RATIOS

Businessmen have been conditioned to believe that they should strive to attain some fixed goal for each operating ratio, such as *liabilities to assets or* bad *debt level.* In fact, those ratios should be flexible—adjusted to different economies, different phases of a business, changing corporate aims. They should be in such a form that a business can see how the changing ratio signals not only a dangerous situation, but also a call for a change in operating procedure.

Two examples:

• *Liquidity:* Traditionally, the accountant or financial staff provides a number that relates current liabilities to current assets (liquidity ratio). But what does that tell you about *future* operation (which is what you really want to know)? To what extent is that number window dressing and the result of random variations? *Better:* Data on what real dollar payout liabilities are in the future compared with real liquid assets.

To measure *liabilities:* Include projected labor costs (on a cash-flow basis), raw material costs (adjusted to level of operations), bills coming due, etc. To measure *assets:* Include cash on hand, accounts receivable, etc.

That kind of data reveals what real cash needs are (on a cash-flow basis). It answers the question: How many days' liquid assets do we have on hand? This is the *liquid interval.* It also tells whether *cash cushion* is too high. Could an extra ten days' dollars be put to work in some other way?

The *liquid interval* is easy to generate. Once your accountant sets up the formula, a bookkeeper can tally it monthly. Any drop or rise in the number signals possible dangers or opportunities.

• *Credit policy:* Too frequently, credit policy is calculated from *bad-debt ratio.* Any rise in that number becomes a warning to tighten policy. Any drop suggests loosening up. But the ratio, by itself, fails to tell whether it would be more profitable to boost or lower the ratio.

Better: Add the *incremental cost* of keeping plant/office running closer to 100% capacity. It's that *variable* cost which should be the key to making a decision about whether to adjust credit policies (and revise acceptance of a riskier business).

If the business is operating far *below* capacity, the incremental cost of boosting it may be minimal. Thus, it *may* be prudent to ease credit standards to gain business, even at the risk of incurring bad debts.

ZERO-BASED BUDGETING

The zero-based budgeting (ZBB) system was first developed by Texas Instruments in the late 1960s to provide better budgeting for their *non*-manufacturing operations. Since then, ZBB has been adopted by a number of businesses and governmental organizations to aid in the allocation of funds to competing projects—both operational and capital.

HOW ZBB WORKS. In a conventional system, the budgeting is usually done on an *incremental basis* (that is, a certain percentage increase over the budget in use the previous year). In a ZBB system, all activities are evaluated yearly from a zero-base. For example, if a department had a $50,000 budget in one year, and in the next year the corporation budgets an 8% increase in expenses, the conventional budget would then be $54,000 for that department that next year. Under ZBB, the department's budget is started at $0. A *decision package* is prepared. It explains the operation of the department and lists *various levels of operation,* with a cost applied to each level. Management reviews the budget and determines the level of priority for each item.

THE DECISION PACKAGE. The decision package, the basic element of ZBB, contains all information necessary for management to reach a decision. The package usually contains:

- *Identification:* Name of department and function.
- *Objectives:* How the funds would be spent.
- *Program:* How the objectives are to be realized.
- *Rewards:* What benefits accrue if objectives are realized.
- *Penalty:* What the effect would be of not funding the department.
- *Incremental programs:* What additions could be made to the basic plan to improve the department's operations.
- *Alternatives:* Whether the objectives could be realized in any other manner.
- *Funding:* The cost of the programs, both the basic and incremental programs and alternatives.

A separate decision package is prepared for each identifiable non-volume-related segment of the business: Usually, each cost center or, in the case of capital budgeting, each capital project.

At this point, in large organizations, the individual decision packages go to the first level of management above the department where they were prepared. That manager then ranks the individual decision packages in order. First are those necessary for the operation of business. Then he ranks the incremental projects, in descending order of priority. That manager also reviews and evaluates alternative proposals, as well as new proposals for his area. When he has completed his review, he presents his decision packages, ranked by priority levels, to senior management.

At the senior management level, these packages are consolidated into that which is necessary to maintain "business as usual" and the incremental packages, ranked by priority.

When all decision packages and their incremental packages have been evaluated and ranked, management then decides on a total funding level. Projects whose ranks permit them to fall within the funding limit are funded. The others are dropped.

THE VIRTUES OF ZBB. The advantage of ZBB over conventional budgeting is that a project (or department) doesn't continue at its current funding level just because it was funded in the prior year. With ZBB, old projects or staff groupings that contribute little to the company's new goals are given low priority levels. New projects with high profit or savings potential are able to compete favorably for available funds.

PROBLEMS. ZBB does make the budgeting process much more detailed and complex, requiring additional management time and staff to evaluate and rank each decision package.

ZBB isn't designed for manufacturing or other volume-cost sensitive areas. It is used mainly in nonvariable cost centers (such as personnel, R&D), with relatively fixed costs.

The application of ZBB to capital expenditures follows the same format.

Source: Merwin Leven, director of pension investments and investor relations, Flintkote Co., Stamford, Conn.

FINANCIAL MANAGEMENT

FOR GREATER CONTROL: UNIFIED BUDGETING SYSTEM

A budgeting system based on simple profit-and-loss statements can lead to inaccurate assumptions, which will then be used for future plans. *What's needed:* A budgeting system with checks and controls built in.

The answer: Unified budgeting.

Unified budgeting uses double-entry accounting (where every entry has an equal offsetting entry) as a means of control. Three budgeting accounts are necessary: (1) A balance sheet, (2) a sources and uses-of-funds statement, and (3) a profit-and-loss statement. These statements guarantee a check on the reasonableness of the budget. They also provide management with *additional* information.

Example: A sources and uses-of-funds statement makes it possible to develop a cash plan that allows management to anticipate the need for short-term borrowing or the investment of short-term funds. That cash plan then affects both the balance sheet and the profit-and-loss statement.

How unified budgeting works: Alternative budgets are prepared—with and without a specific expenditure or new product. Management can then see the total effect on the company of a specific decision.

Example: The cash purchase of a delivery truck would be traced through each of the reports in this way:

• *Profit-and-loss statement:* The depreciation expense is increased to reflect the depreciation on the new truck. Net income is also decreased by the after-tax amount of the effect of the depreciation.

• *Balance sheet:* Gross assets are increased by the cost of the truck. Depreciation is increased by the first period's depreciation. Cash is reduced. So are retained earnings.

• *Sources and uses-of-funds:* Capital expenditures show an increase for the purchase. Funds from operations are increased by the *after-tax* effect of the depreciation expense.

• *The cash plan:* Cash is reduced by the amount of the capital expenditure. Cash generated from operations shows an increase to allow for the tax advantage of the depreciation on the truck.

Detailed budgeting such as this not only provides management with valid budgets for the future, it is also a valuable planning tool to evaluate capital expenditures.

RATIO ANALYSIS. A key technique used to measure the validity of budget assumptions in a unified system is ratio analysis. *How it works:* Certain key ratios in the projected budget are compared with *actual* historical data to determine whether or not a certain budget assumption is realistic. *Key ratios:*

• *Day's receivables outstanding* [(accounts receivable/sales) × 365]: This ratio shows how long the average receivable remains outstanding. Significant variance from historical data indicates a change in the company's collection policy.

• *Day's inventory on hand* [(inventory/sales) × 365]: A change in this ratio indicates that the company is experiencing a significant change in inventory levels. *Signal:* Increasing chance to lose sales from being out of stock. Or (if the amount has increased) need for additional warehouse space for the larger inventory.

• *Sales/plant:* Extremely important ratio to remember. It shows management if sales projections from existing facilities are realistic. If the company is running near capacity, and the budget shows that the ratio has increased, then the probability is that it wouldn't be possible to produce the quantity of goods projected to be sold.

The use of a unified system also provides the data for meaningful variance analysis, once the actual results are known. Instead of just sales and profit variance, it will now be possible to analyze the *causes* for changes in both the balance sheet and funds statements.

To install a system: For the medium-size business, a number of budgeting systems similar to the one described are available from time-sharing computer firms or any number of major banks. These systems produce all the statements and provide a complete set of ratios and the data to compare actual results with budget.

HOW TO USE RETURN ON INVESTMENT

Return on Investment (ROI) is an analytic tool which enables the manager not only to monitor closely his own operations, but also to evaluate alternative investments and operations on a comparative basis.

The basic relationships affecting ROI are best illustrated by the following chart, which was developed by Du-Pont:

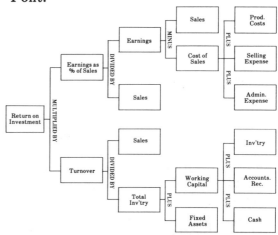

The above chart identifies all factors that affect the ROI of a given operation.

• *Top section:* Identifies all the items that are related to the income produced by the operation or the investment. In the case of a capital expenditure, it contains all the incremental income and expense items that are related to the expenditure.

• *Bottom section:* The denominator of the example contains all the balance sheet items that are related to the operation or expenditure. This includes the expenditure for permanent investment, such as a new machine or plant, or, in the case of an existing operation, the in-place investment. It also includes the funds that are invested in inventories and other working capital items.

To illustrate the use of the ROI technique, take two divisions: one manufacturing and the other distribution. Both have sales of $1,000,000 per year; however, the manufacturing operation has earnings of $100,000 while the distribution division earned only $30,000. The working capital of both is the same: $300,000, but the fixed assets

133

FINANCIAL MANAGEMENT

are $3,000,000 for the manufacturing division, and only $300,000 for the distribution division.

	Manufacturing	Distribution
Earnings as % of Sales	$\frac{\$100,000}{\$1,000,000} = 10\%$	$\frac{\$30,000}{\$1,000,000} = 3\%$
Turnover of Assets	$\frac{\$1,000,000}{\$3,300,000} = .303$ times	$\frac{\$1,000,000}{\$600,000} = 1.67$
ROI	$10\% \times .303 = 3.03\%$	$3\% \times 1.67 = 5.01\%$

In evaluating the performance of the manufacturing division against that of the distribution division, a comparison based strictly on profit produced wouldn't be meaningful.

But using a ROI analysis, it can be seen that the manufacturing operation, while having a high level of earnings, has a correspondingly high investment in fixed assets, resulting in a low asset turnover and low ROI. The distribution operation, while not generating as high a level of earnings, has a relatively low investment in fixed assets, causing a high asset turnover and a higher return on investment.

The use of ROI can also be beneficial in evaluating the results of the investment of new capital into an operation.

Example: If, instead of using the actual income statement and balance sheet figures for the ROI equation, we use only the difference between the period before the new investment was made and the latest figure, we can determine what the investment has produced in terms of an *incremental* ROI.

If earnings increased an average of $50,000 per year over the period, but the investment in new funds was $1,000,000, then the ROI for that investment was 5%. Comparing this figure with other investments made by the company may indicate that further investment may not be warranted, or

that the management of that particular division may not be as effective as a management team that earned a 10% ROI over the same period.

This same concept can be used in the evaluation of *your* operation against that of another company or in the evaluation of the operating efficiencies of two diverse companies against each other.

IT PAYS TO BREAK DOWN COSTS FOR FIGURING ROI

Interested in a new major equipment installation but turned off because the *return on investment* is too slow?

Solution: Have the vendors *itemize* the total cost. Without such "unbundling," accountants too often put the entire cost, or too much of the cost, on the capital budget. Then, when they figure out the time value of the money tied up (it could be earning, say 6% a year), they wind up with an investment return that looks unattractive. But with an itemized bid from the vendor, the accountant can tell what portion of the cost to treat as current expense (software for computer controls, project management, etc.). Then the return may look a lot better.

Vendors will probably hesitate to unbundle bids too early in negotiations. They suspect (often rightly) that you might try to use the itemized list as a shopping guide to work out a better deal with the competition. But most suppliers can give you a good idea of what the ratio between expensed and capital costs will be. And they should agree to give you a detailed breakdown when you are close to making a deal.

DIRECT COSTING USEFUL WHEN PRODUCTION VARIES

In a conventional accounting system, if production varies significantly from budget, the profit for the period will also show a significant variance. These variances can cause misleading profit and loss statements. However, with a direct costing system, these swings can be eliminated.

• *Direct Costing* is an accounting technique which divides manufacturing costs into two segments: *Fixed* and *Variable. Variable costs:* Direct materials, direct labor, etc., are the only costs which are used to value inventory. *Fixed costs:* Supervision, depreciation, etc., are charged against income in the period in which they are incurred.

• *Conventional* (or *Absorption*) *Accounting* charges all manufacturing costs to inventory. Therefore, the cost of goods in inventory contains both fixed and variable manufacturing costs. These costs are entered into inventory on a *per unit basis.* That is derived by taking the total *budgeted manufacturing costs* for the year and dividing by the *budgeted production volume.* In months where the actual volume exceeds budget, the excess is known as *over-absorbed burden*, and deferred to a future period. However, in a case

where production volume estimates are consistently higher than actual, it is often necessary to absorb a large expense item in the final period, since the budgeted per unit charge was not high enough to absorb all costs into inventory.

The effect of these two systems on the income statement can be seen in the following example, using the same assumptions* for both the *Conventional* and *Direct Costing* methods.

Statement of Income and Expenses

	Period I		Period II	
	Conventional	Direct	Conventional	Direct
Gross sales	$50,000	$50,000	$50,000	50,000
Cost of goods sold:				
Opening inventory	0	0	21,000	9,000
Cost of mfd. goods	56,000	24,000	14,000	6,000
Closing inventory	21,000	9,000	0	0
Cost of goods sold	35,000	15,000	35,000	15,000
Gross profits	15,000	35,000	15,000	35,000
Selling, admin. expenses	2,500	2,500	2,500	2,500
(Over) Underabsorbed burden	(12,000)	—	12,000	—
Fixed mfg. expenses	—	20,000	—	20,000
Net operating income	$ 500	$12,500	$24,500	$12,500

In the above example, the variances between budgeted and actual production volume caused a significant swing in net income.

The *Direct Cost* system is more sensitive to swings in sales volume.

The *Conventional (Absorption) Accounting* system shows more sensitivity to production.

*The assumptions used in this table are as follows:

Assumptions

	Period I	Period II
Actual production	8,000 units	2,000 units
Budgeted production	5,000 units	5,000 units
Sales volume	5,000 units	5,000 units
Inventory	3,000 units	0 units

Sales price—$10/unit.
Variable manufacturing costs—$3/unit.
Fixed manufacturing costs—$4/unit, $20,000/period.
Selling and administrative costs—$2,500/period.

In a company where both actual sales and production volume don't vary significantly from budget, the two systems produce the same profit figures.

Direct Costing also provides management with a very useful analytic tool. Since the books of the company segregate fixed and variable costs, the use of such techniques as breakeven analysis, flexible budgeting, and responsible accounting become much easier. The accounting information necessary for these techniques is part of the records of the company, and, therefore, no special preparation is required.

MARGINAL INCOME ANALYSIS. *A Direct Cost* income statement can provide management with "marginal income" data. These figures, which represent sales dollars less all direct costs, are necessary for fixing incremental profitability of product or territory.

When marginal income data by product is available, sales campaigns or salesmen's bonuses can be designed to provide maximum sales effort for those products which produce the highest income. Also, marginal income data readily identifies those products or territories that are operating at a loss on a *Direct Cost*-only basis. Management can therefore take the necessary corrective action much more rapidly than if the company were on an *Absorption Accounting* system, in which case special study would be necessary in order to isolate these costs.

PROBLEMS WITH DIRECT COSTING. There are some difficulties in installing and using a *Direct Costing* system. Since product costs show variable costs only, allocation of fixed expenses must be made before selling prices are determined or bids submitted.

The change from full cost to variable cost in accounting for a company's inventory for income tax purposes is complex and should not be undertaken without the advice of a qualified tax accountant.

For further information on *Direct Costing*, consult *Accountants' Handbook* (Third Edition, Ronald Press, 79 Madison Ave., New York 10016, pp. 6-60); *The Financial Manager*, Gerome Bernard Cohen and Sidney M. Robbins (published by Harper & Row, 1966—out of print but should be in good libraries—pp. 184-191).

MANAGING THE BUSINESS' MONEY

The *Profit & Loss Statement* indicates that your company has record earnings, but the checkbook shows a very severe cash shortfall—why?

Esentially, it's a practical demonstration of the differences between *cash* basis and *accrual* basis method; expenses are charged over a time period, rather than in the month in which they are paid. If, for example, an insurance policy premium is paid in January, and the insurance covers a 12-month period, accrual accounting charges one-twelfth of the premium to expense each month.

Cash basis accounting, on the other hand, expenses (debits) an item when it is paid, regardless of the time period involved. Using the example, we would see the entire insurance premium item charged off in January, when it was paid.

While accrual basis accounting presents more realistic financial information for earnings budgeting and management, it is usually inadequate for cash management. The result is reports that are often misleading. They do not present management with the data necessary to manage the firm's cash need efficiently. The Sources & Uses of Funds Statement presents the firm's operations on a cash-oriented basis. But it isn't designed specifically to aid in the development of an effective operating cash management system.

Accrual accounting reports can be used to develop a modified cash reporting system. That information can provide management with the data necessary to manage effectively and efficiently the day-to-day cash operations of the business.

In accrual reporting, when a payment is made of an expense that encompasses more than one period, the amount that applies to future periods becomes a prepaid expense. By adding or subtracting the change in prepaid items to the expenses for the month, you can determine the cash payments for expenses in that month.

The same technique can be used in determining cash generated by sales. When a credit sale is made, the accounts receivable account is increased. But cash isn't generated until the account is paid.

Applying this concept to operating budgets makes it possible to forecast cash surpluses or short-falls in future periods. When used in conjunction with the Sources & Uses of Funds Statement, cash-oriented accounting can give management better information to use in managing the firm's cash position—on both a short-term and long-term basis.

EVALUATION OF CAPITAL PROJECTS

How is it possible to evaluate a capital project or to choose between two or more alternative projects and select the most advantageous?

A number of methods are available without computers or sophisticated mathematical techniques.

Simplest are the *Pay-Back* and *Return on Investment* methods. *Discounted Cash Flow*, which takes timing of income and expenditures into consideration, can also be used, although it is slightly more complex.

The first step in the evaluation of any capital project is the identification of *all* expenses associated with the project. In nearly all cases, the actual price of the item is only one factor in the total cost of the project. If the project increases sales, then costly working capital would have to be increased to support additional inventory and accounts receivable. The project may also involve additional costs in operating supplies, power, insurance, taxes, interest, finance charges, etc.

The freight and installation on a piece of heavy machinery may add a substantial percentage to the cost of the machinery itself. The purchase of a motor vehicle involves license fees, and possibly increased insurance costs.

When *all* costs have been pinned down, it is time for step two: Determining the benefits to be derived from the project. This benefit may take the form of cost reductions, product improvement, faster service, etc.

Step three is important in a large

FINANCIAL MANAGEMENT

project that requires a long time to complete. This is the timing of the cash flow. If the discounted cash-flow technique is to be used, this data is mandatory.

PAY-BACK METHOD. Once all the above data is collected, evaluation can begin. The simplest evaluation is via the *Pay-Back Method*. It takes the total cost of the project and measures the number of years' profits necessary to "pay back" its cost. If we have a machine that costs $100,000 and gives a profit of $20,000 in the first year and $40,000 in each successive year, then the pay-back period is three years— $20,000 + $40,000 + $40,000. This method doesn't measure return on investment or the total profits to be generated by the investment. It shows only how long it will take to recoup the total cost. This method is usually used only on relatively small projects, where the pay-back period is short enough (1 to 3 years) to make more complex calculations unnecessary.

RETURN ON INVESTMENT METHOD. *The Return on Investment Method* determines what yield management receives on its original investment:

$$\text{Return on Investment} = \frac{\text{Average Return}}{\text{Cost of Asset}}$$

If a capital item costs $20,000 and earns an average of $5,000 per year over the asset's 10-year useful life, then the return on investment would be: $5,000/$20,000 = 25%. A modification of this method uses the average investment, rather than the total investment. In the above example, if the capital is depreciated on a straight-line basis over its 10-year life, the average investment would be $10,000 ($20,000), and the return on investment would be 50% ($5,000/$10,000). The weakness in the *Return on Investment Method* is that it doesn't take into account differences in the time factor in the flow of funds.

DISCOUNTED CASH FLOW METHOD. The *Discounted Cash Flow Method* (DCF) does take into account the time value of money, *i.e.*, a dollar of earnings today is worth more than a dollar next year. In order to use the DCF method, a table giving present values of factors is needed. These tables are arranged by interest rates and period (number of years).† The interest rate used is usually the company's cost of capital or a rate that management coniders to be a break-even rate of return on capital projects.

Assuming a 10% rate. the DCF evaluation of a $200,000 capital project would be as follows:

PRESENT VALUE

Year	Cash Flow	Factor	Present Value
0	($200,000)	1.0000-	($200,000)
1	10,000	.9098	9,091
2	10,000	.8264	8,264
3	20,000	.7513	15,260
4	20,000	.6830	13,660
5	20,000	.6209	12,418
6 to 10	40,000*	2.3538*	95,152*
Total	($ 80,000)		($ 57,155)

*Sum of years 6 to 10

†Book of tables: *Financial Analysis to Guide Capital Expenditures Decisions*, Natl. Assn. of Accountants, 919 3rd Ave., N.Y. 10022.

Since the total present value flow of funds is negative, the project doesn't meet the 10% return requirement, even though it does return more than was invested over 10 years.

COMPARISON. If the above project were evaluated on a *Pay-Back Method*, it would show eight years needed to pay back the original investment. The *Return on Investment Method* would yield 14%, while the average *Return on Investment* would be 28%

If projects are being compared, and the cash flows are similar over time, the *Return on Investment Method* is valid. But if the cash flow varies over time, the *Discounted Cash Flow Method* should be used for a valid comparison.

These methods are easy to use. They permit evaluation of a proposed capital project or comparison of competing projects.

CASH DISCOUNTS: HOW TO USE THEM AND WHAT THEY REALLY COST

Given the uncertainty of interest rates, the question of cash discounts given to purchasers as an incentive for prompt payment becomes very important to both the purchaser and the seller.

"Cash discount" can mean one of two things:

1. A premium paid by the seller to the buyer who pays during the discount period.

2. A penalty paid by the buyer who doesn't pay during the discount period. (Not the typical practice.)

If one knows the terms of discount, it is then possible to calculate the annual rate of interest by the use of the following formula:

$$I = \frac{D}{(G - D)(T/365)}$$

I = Annual rate of interest.
D = Amount of discount.
G = Gross amount of the invoice.
T = The discount period in days.

If we take, as an example, an invoice for $500.00, with terms of 2% 10 days, net 30 days:

D = 2% of the gross value of the invoice.
G = The gross value of the invoice ($500.00).
T = The time difference between the discount and net payment dates (20 days).

The formula then becomes:

$$I = \frac{\$10.00}{(\$500.00 - 10.00)(20/365)}$$

I = 37.24% per annum.

In this example, if only financial considerations are involved, the seller shouldn't offer such terms if he can obtain the funds at a lower interest rate, and the buyer should discount the invoice only if he can borrow for less than a 37% annual interest rate. However, cash discounts involve a number of factors other than financial considerations.

FROM THE SELLER'S POINT OF VIEW. A basic consideration is: What does the competition offer? A number of industries have cash discounts dictated by trade practices. Any variance from these terms could cause a major pricing adjustment within the industry. This is especially important in an industry where a number of sellers have similar merchandise. A seller who changes his discount rate could find that he has caused the entire industry to change, and, in effect, has accomplished nothing.

Advantage of cash discounts: They speed up the collection of receivables, reducing working capital requirements. Early payment of receivables also tends to reduce the amount of receivables that finally end up in the bad debt category. Lending institutions usually consider lower receivable balances a positive sign in credit evaluation.

In some cases, cash discounts are used as a sales promotion device. In these situations, the discount rate obviously isn't strictly an inducement for prompt payment, but is also an inducement to purchase. The problem with this type of promotion is that it may be difficult to change back to the original terms after the promotion is over. The terms could become a permanent reduction in selling price.

FROM THE BUYER'S POINT OF VIEW. If the buyer's competition takes advantage of the cash discount, and he (buyer) doesn't, he is in the position of having a higher cost of goods. To retain a competitive price position, he would have to settle for a lower mark-up.

In a number of high-turnover, low-margin businesses, the savings on cash discounts is the difference between profit and loss.

The buyer can also find himself in a situation where suppliers of scarce items or items in great demand aren't interested in selling to customers who don't pay promptly (*and take the discount*).

The most obvious reason for the buyer to take advantage of cash discounts is the return that he is receiving on the funds that he has used to take

advantage of the discount terms. As was shown earlier here, the discount terms can translate into a very high annual interest rate.

USING THE PRICE INDEX

When a supplier or customer insists on "indexing" the price of an item—that is, raising it proportionally to some price index—resist using the Consumer Price Index. It's much too volatile. For a more realistic index, use the *Gross National Product Implicit Price Deflator*, issued every month (and reported regularly in *The Wall Street Journal*).

WHAT OUTSIDE AUDITORS WILL SEEK

If your company needs an outside auditor's certification for a bank loan, credit extension or any other purpose, be prepared to meet the tough standards of the American Institute of Certified Public Accountants. They'll be digging deeper if they find:
● A discrepancy within accounting records, such as a difference between a control account and supporting subsidiary records.
● Significantly fewer confirming responses come back than should be expected.
● Unusual transactions are completed at or near the year's end.
● Failure to correct material weaknesses in internal accounting control

that are easy to correct.

• High turnover in key financial positions, such as controller.

• Not enough accounting and financial personnel, so there is a constant crisis situation and control failure.

VARIANCE ANALYSIS CAN MAKE MONTHLY OPERATING REPORTS MORE USEFUL

The monthly figures are in. The amounts of variance from the budgeted sales and costs have been calculated. Now, analyze those variances so that the company's reporting system provides information that is useful and timely enough to spot problems (and opportunities) as early as possible.

The technique of *variance analysis* permits the manager to quantify the major factors responsible for variance from the budget and to assess the dollar impact of each variance item.

ANALYZING SALES RESULTS. In the following example, sales went up, but so did the unit selling price. *Problem:* How much of the net sales variance was due to change in unit volume, and how much was due to change in unit price?

	Actual	Budget	Variance
Net Sales	$10,000	$7,000	+ $3,000
Units	1,250	1,000	+ 250
$/Unit	8	7	+ 1

INCREASED SALES DUE TO INCREAS-ED VOLUME. Volume was 250 units higher than budget. This amount, times the budgeted price per unit ($7), gives the dollars of net sales ($1,750) by the *increase in volume.*

INCREASED SALES DUE TO INCREASED PRICES. The increase in price per unit ($1) applies to the entire actual monthly volume. So, total number of units sold (1,250) times change in price per unit ($1) gives the dollars of net sales ($1,250) created by a *price increase.* The complete variance analysis of net sales in this example is:

Variance due to more units sold	+ $1,750
Variance due to higher sales price	+ 1,250
Total variance in net sales	+ $3,000

The sales report could be even more useful if the budget is prepared in more detail—identifying sales by product, package size, and other such variables that can affect sales. Using the same technique, it would then be possible to quantify the effect of *each of those variables.*

When a budget system is designed, a manager should keep in mind the type of variance information that is necessary for the efficient operation of the firm. Such data should be included in the budget, and in the reporting structure for operations.

ANALYZING DIRECT LABOR COSTS. By analyzing direct labor costs, it is possible to break out the amounts due to regular work schedules, and overtime, as well as the effect of hours worked, and of the rate per hour.

	Actual	Budget	Variance
Total Labor Costs	$3,055.00	$2,500.00	+ $555.00
Hours, Regular	1,100.00	1,000.00	+ 100.00
Hours, Overtime	100.00	10.00	+ 90.00
Rate/Hr., Regular	2.30	2.35	– .05
Rate/Hr., Overtime	5.25	15.00	– 9.75

FINANCIAL MANAGEMENT

The variance analysis would be:

Variance due to hours, regular	
100 hrs. × $2.35/hr.	+ $235
Variance due to rate/hr., regular	
1,100 Hrs. × – $0.05	– 55
Total variance, regular time labor	+ $180
Variance due to hours, overtime	
90 hours × $15.00/hr.	+ $1,350
Variance due to rate/hour, overtime	
100 hours × – $9.75/hr.	– 975
Total variance, overtime labor	+ $375
Total variance, direct labor	+ $555

The analysis of labor costs can be extended to include a shift differential, job classification rates, and productivity per man-hour, if that data is required in the budget.

The same technique can be used to analyze the use of raw materials. It is possible to measure the effect of changes in such items as price, usage, shrinkage, formula, or any other variable which management considers to be important.

If the budget is developed by product, sales territory, or any other similar breakout, the manager can then prepare a separate variance report on each of these individual entities. The key to the success of this, or any type of system, is that management understands its needs, and isolates the variables inherent in its business, so that the reporting system becomes an effective management tool.

RAISING MONEY

FINANCIAL RESOURCES

Keep an up-to-date file of commercial banks and other sources of loans, even if your company isn't contemplating borrowing *now*. Include on the list:

• All local banks with headquarters or branch offices in the immediate area.

• Major regional banks that lend locally. Find them by locating the five largest cities within 50 or 100 miles. Get the names of the banks from a banking directory, the various Yellow Pages, or the Chambers of Commerce in each city. Telephone each bank and ask if it lends in your area.

• Major banks that market loans nationally—usually for $1-million or more. Most of the 50 biggest banks in the U.S. maintain loan offices around the country.

• Also, data on savings banks and savings and loan associations, commercial loan companies, insurance companies, private investors, investment bankers and government sources of loans and loan guarantees.

Each entry should include the chief lending officer's name and direct-dial phone number, bank's loan policies (as you find them out), annual and quarterly reports, newspaper and magazine clippings. Keep information picked up in conversations with fellow businessmen. Do a written evaluation of each loan source.

Source: *The Business Borrower*, Suite 500, 1529 Walnut St., Philadephia, Pa. 19102.

> Best time to take banker to lunch is when things are going well. Keep lenders informed about business and problems. *Uninformed lender tends to overreact in times of surprise or crisis.* The better he understands your business, the stronger the case he can make for your company. It's harder to say no to someone you know.

BEST TIMES AND WORST TIMES TO BORROW FROM A BANK

The best times to borrow are when:
- The bank is new. It is looking for customers. Open an account so the bank becomes familiar with the company. A business may do better at a small bank because it may be a major customer and the bank will extend itself.
- The economy is in an upswing and/or interest rates are low.
- There is substantial competition among banks in a given area.
- Banks are expanding their business. It happened during the 1960s and it may happen again with the increasing use of electronic teller machines.
- A bank is conducting a special program to make high-risk or moral obligation loans to minorities, veterans, small businesses, etc.

The worst times to borrow are when:
- The bank has decided to cut down on loans to build up deposits.
- The economy is suffering from a recession and/or interest rates are high.
- There isn't much competition among banks. A town with only one bank is bad news for the borrower.
- There is trouble in the parent bank —losses, bad loans, etc.

Source: *Business Loans*, by Rick Stephan Hayes (Cahners Books International, Inc., 221 Columbus Ave., Boston 02116).

AUTOMATED SERVICE FROM BANKS

Automated *current balance reporting system* that can help companies fine-tune their cash flow. Most are new, even experimental.

Customers of Manufacturers Hanover Trust (New York City) can get summary book balance reports over the phone or summaries of all transactions on a terminal. *Fee:* $5 to $80 monthly. The fees can usually be paid for, if desirable, with a compensating bank balance.

Another bank in New York City is testing a *computerized cash flow model* to be used with its cash reporting system. The model requires four kinds of input: (1) Planning period; (2) borrowing limits; (3) source and use of funds favored by customer, and (4) interest rate projections. The model will generate the most favorable borrowing and investment alternatives. *Other features:* International wire transfer of funds, intra-day debit and credit information and month-to-date and year-to-date collective balances. Variances and target values are computed, whereupon corrective action is then recommended.

WHEN A 'NOTE' IS A SECURITY

Short-term notes (nine months or less) generally aren't subject to the stiff federal securities laws—but don't count on that exclusion to hold up in court if certain conditions are met. *Example:* If the note is being used for business purposes and has stock-like characteristics, such as exposure of the loan proceeds to the risks of the business, control of the borrower by the lender, and interest payments tied to profits.

Once the security label applies, you're involved with the SEC registration requirements and the tough anti-fraud rules, principally SEC Rule 10b-5.

Zabriskie v. Lewis, C.A. 10, 507 F. 2d 546, 1974.

STANDARDS FOR PRIVATE PLACEMENTS MAY PUT DAMPER ON INVESTORS

Rule 146, which gives certain private investors exemptions from some Securities and Exchange Commission requirements may, in fact, actually put a damper on private investment.

Reason: Under the rule, the private investor must answer so many questions —to be sure he's both *wealthy* and *financially sophisticated*—that he may not consider the exchange of loss of privacy worth the exemption.

Some examples of the many questions that the SEC wants you to answer:

What was your income last year? What is your anticipated income for the next three years? What is your net worth at the present time? Break down that figure, indicating by percentage what part of it represents home, tax shelters, and other assets.

BANKS MOVE INTO INVESTMENT BANKING

Time for capital-short companies to take a closer look at corporate financial services being offered increasingly by key commercial banks. More of the bank leaders reach out beyond conventional short- and medium-term lending and into (one-time) preserves of investment bankers. Advantages:

- Superb international connections through far-flung foreign branches for mergers and acquisitions.
- Arranging private placements here and abroad, often with fewer strings attached than those made via insurance companies, which are usually reluctant to get involved in foreign credits.
- Financial counseling, often at fees well below what a typical investment banking firm would charge.

Available services vary. Citibank, for example, offers a full range, including leasing, real estate and management consultant groups, domestic and international assistance to corporations in all areas. Morgan Guaranty, also strong on tapping foreign capital sources, offers well-staffed services in the merger and acquisition, corporate finance and financial consulting areas. Also has a strong record of fixed-rate, medium-term private loans to companies via its Interfunding Group. Other top-flight banks with breadth of services: Chase Manhattan, First National of Chicago, Irving Trust, Bankers Trust, in addition to smaller regional banks, including Northern Trust, Citizens & Southern, Crocker, and Girard Trust.

THE VALUE OF A REVOLVING CREDIT

Why pay banks a fee to get a revolving credit? Most companies that do—and pay anywhere from 1/2% to 1% of the untapped loan balance—claim it's prudent to "keep their powder dry." That means they can be *assured* they'll get the loan quickly when they need it.

But how much *assurance* is there in a revolving credit? Most bankers say the assurance is considerable, but many experienced businessmen *know that's true only if you're just as healthy when you take down the loan as you were when you got the revolving credit approved.* In other words, many feel the annual fee for revolving credit really isn't buying very much, because "if we're still good customers, and we're still profitable, the bank will grant us a loan whether we have a revolving credit or not."

Background: In a typical revolving credit agreement, the bank says it'll lend, *based on its discretion,* up to a certain amount. But to get the commitment, you're also expected to agree that if your business situation falls below some preset level (and that's nego-

tiable) the bank is free to overturn the agreement (and the courts are full of such cases).

Practical view: Banks are under great pressure now to earn a profit on each customer; in fact, if a bank fails to show a minimum profit, it'll seek ways to raise its fees to you—but if it can't, it could ask you to take your business elsewhere.

So paying for revolving credit could make your account more attractive to the bank.

Review with your banker *his* profitability with your account. If it's sufficient and you see the soundness of your business holding level through the period when you might need a loan, consider the revolving credit as nothing more than your "psychological" crutch —an *additional* assurance that the money will be there when you want it.

RAISING CASH IN A TIGHT MARKET

Many companies don't think of it, but they may have a ready source of cash at hand: Their own buildings.

If the facility is relatively modern, they can easily sell it to an investor for some premium over depreciated book value, and then rent it back in a sale/leaseback arrangement. Thus they can take a *fixed asset* off their balance sheet and turn it into a *cash asset.* The profit would be considerable—because good buildings in good locations—with good long-term tenants—hold up well. *Reason:* The sources of cash—insurance companies, pension funds, etc.— are anxious for safe, high-yield investments. The yield in a deal like this can give them better than 10% *over the long run.*

Likely buildings: factories, warehouses, offices. Older facilities or multistory factories, however, are of little or no interest now.

CORPORATIONS SHOULD CONSIDER CONVERTIBLE PREFERREDS

If your corporation has cash available for investment in the equity or bond markets, you might consider placing the funds in convertible preferred securities.

These securities offer many of the advantages of both common shares and bonds, with one important tax plus when compared to a similar vehicle, convertible bonds:

Corporations are exempt from income taxation on 85% of the dividend yield derived from most domestic corporations. But yields accruing from bond interests are fully taxable.

Convertible preferred shares can be exchanged for shares of the underlying company. If the common of that company rises, so will the value of the convertible preferred shares into which they are exchangeable. In this regard, the convertible preferred is similar to convertible bonds. Some convertible preferred shares even guarantee redemption at a fixed price within a specified time, similar to convertible bond redemption at maturity.

The dividend yields from convertible preferred are secure and generally higher than the yields from com-

mon. Companies are obligated to pay preferred dividends before they pay dividends on common. However, preferred dividends aren't as secure as bond interest, which takes precedence.

ESOP FINANCING

A way to raise capital inexpensively—while at the same time making your company stock available to employees: ESOP (Employee Stock Ownership Plan). Available to any corporation, either privately or publicly held.

Here's how it works: Your company sets up an employee share-ownership trust, which, in turn, borrows the required money from a bank. The bank loan is repaid by the company—both principal and interest—in *pre-tax* dollars through stock dividends and annual payments to the trust on behalf of the employees covered.

Incentive for banks: The Tax Reform Act of 1984 allows a bank to exclude from income 50% of the interest received on loans to an ESOP which is used to acquire employer securities.

If the ESOP is leveraged, the annual contribution limit is generally 25 percent of each employee's compensation plus any amount required for interest payments—not to exceed $30,000. An employer, however, may have to reduce the amount of the contributions allocated to some individuals if it provides other qualified retirement benefits.

Primary advantage of ESOP: It's the only financing technique that permits principal as well as interest to be paid off in pre-tax dollars. So a company in the 46% tax bracket can finance its growth at half-price.

Other important ESOP benefits:

• Employees acquire company stock at zero cost to themselves—no cash outlay, no deduction from take-home pay or fringe benefits—so loyalty and motivation are enhanced.

• Management is in a position to raise employee income without hiking costs of doing business.

• The company can meet its capital needs and also employee-retirement requirements *simultaneously*—with positive impact on after-tax cash flow per share.

Companies that install Tax Credit ESOPs (or TRASOPs) qualify for a special tax credit of ½ of 1% of compensation of participating employees (¾ of 1% for 1985 through 1987). The amount of income tax liability that can be offset by the credit is limited by the Tax Code. But unused credits can be carried forward for 15 years.

While this tax-saving bonus is of special immediate interest to big business and big labor, ESOP should be considered by any company that can use low-cost capital to pay for expansion, to acquire new assets, to accomplish divestitures or spinoffs or to finance mergers. Moreover, ESOP can be used for corporate purposes other than capital formation.

DANGER OF INTERCOMPANY LOANS

Companies with two or more corporations under common control fre-quently "borrow" money from each other in times of need. When the borrowing is done at less than arm's length (with no interest payment), the IRS can step in and reallocate income or expense between the parties.

• Companies once could get away without reallocation if they could prove that the loan had generated no profit for the borrower. But a recent court decision may eliminate that out. Not only does it allow the reallocation and the imposition of an interest charge, but it rules that it makes no difference whether or not the borrower used the loan to create income.

The fact is, the court said, the loan freed the borrower's other assets for different business uses.

Fitzgerald Motor Co. v. Comm'r., 5th Cir., 2/28/75.

AVOID INVESTMENT BANKING FEES FOR REGULAR PRIVATE FINANCING

If your company has already established a financing relationship with a big insurance company or pension fund, you may be able to go directly to it with your financing needs. When approaching a *big* lender for the first time, it may also be desirable to go to it *directly*. It probably has sufficient staff to do the work the investment banker would have done.

Most loans to companies in the same industry are pretty much the same, and the specialist lender may be able to show you the terms of similar loans to other companies. The lender may also be able to steer your company toward other potential lenders who might be interested in participating in the financing.

Caution: If your company and its decision-makers and key financial personnel have never negotiated a major loan before, it's best to start with an investment banker.

THE SEPARATE AGREEMENT: TRAP IN EQUIPMENT LEASING

Beware of *separate agreements* when your company leases computer hardware or other big-ticket items.

The lease itself may say that the lessor can assign the lease and that your company *waives any defenses or claims you might have against the assignee.* The lessor also offers you a separate agreement (not included in the lease agreement) that the lease won't become effective unless satisfactory equipment is delivered.

What can happen: Your company takes delivery and begins making rent payments on the equipment. Meanwhile, the lessor has assigned the lease to a bank, giving the bank an "equipment acceptance notice." You decide that the equipment is far from satisfactory, and withhold a regular rent payment. The bank sues for its money. You defend on the basis of the separate agreement, arguing that the lease was ineffective because of unsatisfactory gear.

Decision: Your company loses. The bank had no notice of the separate agreement. And the general law that

governs these situations, the Uniform Commercial Code, *validates the waiver* of claims or defenses against the assignee.

Comment: Your company still has a claim against the bank as lessor-assignee. You're left with unsatisfactory equipment and an obligation to pay the rent. A bad position.

Solution: Don't buy the separate agreement deal. If you do, make sure that you don't waive claims or defenses against assignees.

Exceptions: If consumer goods for personal use are involved (a car, washing machine, etc.), the customer is in a stronger position. The Uniform Commercial Code provision that worked against the company which leased equipment is subject to any "statute or decision which establishes a different rule for buyers or lessees of consumer goods." Federal regulations also give a consumer protection against assignees who claim to be "holders in due course" of installment obligations and who attempt to collect when the buyer or lessee claims the equipment is unsatisfactory.

HOW TO HANDLE CAPITAL BUDGETS

WEYERHAEUSER: 'DEBOTTLENECKING'. When the 1974 recession dawned, Weyerhaeuser found itself with a very optimistic expansion program that clearly was out of line with the immediate economic future, says senior v.p. in charge of finance and planning, Robert L. Schuyler. The $2-billion expansion plan of the capital-intensive pulp and paper company was slowed drastically. But, says Schuyler, the cutback had to be accomplished without hurting the company's future.

How it was done: The first decision was to stretch the budget's timetable (to four years from three years). Each project in the budget was reviewed more often—monthly instead of quarterly—with emphasis on its cash-flow impact.

First projects to be cut: Expansions.

Cost reduction projects required careful selectivity. Those with the highest certainty of achievement and with the highest return on investment were the least vulnerable.

Parallel problem: Develop contingency plans—just in case the cash-flow projections were wrong. Further cuts were identified—even to the point of accepting penalties to stop delivery of equipment that would have to be reordered later.

Next stage: Recovery. By 1976, with recovery beginning, the question was: Should we go back to the old plan? *Decision:* No, for two reasons. (1) Near-term need for major new capacity wasn't there. (2) Cost escalation for "greenfield" projects (bringing new plants out of the ground) was far ahead of other increased business costs. *New emphasis:* "Debottlenecking." Higher capital costs for new facilities provided a new incentive to pursue marginal increases in capacity by eliminating bottlenecks in existing facilities. With this approach, increased capacity is added in small bits rather than in big spurts, as when a whole new plant comes on stream. That slow increase meshes better with Weyerhaeuser's new projections for market growth.

New problems: Expect the unexpected when fixing something old. You're never sure what you'll find inside, once you start to tinker.

MIDAS: TAKE A RISK AT THE BEST TIME. Recession didn't hurt Midas' muffler business, but the oil crisis and the recession struck the company's recreational vehicle business very hard as early as 1974. Plants to make the vehicles were scattered, small, inefficient. In the depths of the recession, says Midas International's chief executive, Ralph Weiger, the company took a big gamble on capital spending. Because of the shakeout, it was able to buy a new plant (built by a company that got into trouble) at 31¢ on the construction dollar. It doubled Midas's square feet of production space for recreational vehicles and quadrupled production. *Result:* It added enough to capacity so that Midas could go at least another two years with no additional expansion.

In 1975, Midas' capital budget was $22-million. Two years later it was about $10 million, mostly for maintenance. Meanwhile, business had doubled and profits were up 500%.

CONTROLS. Be sure all inventory programs are specific and in writing. Require that *sales, manufacturing,* or *purchasing* follow guidelines for inventory levels, safety stock, reordering and other parts of the procedure if they want to boost inventory levels. Otherwise, a clerk, afraid of facing another stock-out, will place a large order for some minor part, unaware that demand is forecast to fall off sharply.

STANDARDIZATION. Establish an on-

FINANCIAL MANAGEMENT

going program to ask: How can we cut down the number of different items in inventory? Unless the program is continuous, many items with only minor differences will build up in inventory, a costly and time-consuming practice. Designers' whims often cause this buildup.

EARLY BUYING. If a purchase was made far in advance of need, check to see why it was done and the procedure used to approve such a purchase. In all likelihood, the procedure is faulty, and it'll be obvious as soon as the purchase decision is examined. If there was no procedure, it's time to establish one.

CONSIDER 'PIPELINING'. An alternative to inventory is "pipelining." Instead of actually *storing* the goods in your company's warehouse, arrange for shipments by the supplier to be made at prearranged intervals—to dovetail with actual needs. *Bonus:* Volume discounts, yet only billed for goods as received.

SALVAGE POLICY. What does your company do with scrap waste material? Don't accept a policy where the material is eliminated once a year. Continuously monitor scrap and see how to sell it, recycle it, etc. Don't let it build up; take advantage of *fluctuating* scrap prices.

CASH FLOW. Don't omit financial people from purchasing planning. It may take only minor buying shifts to boost cash or to reduce the strain. *Also:* Finance department may be able to speed up accounts receivable efforts to offset temporary higher cash needs

for purchasing. So have cash flow determine inventory—not the reverse.

TOLERANCE CONTROL. Determine whether your company's product standards for quality aren't higher than customers'. The reject rate and materials costs may be much higher than necessary. It's a common problem.

MAKE/BUY DECISIONS. As labor and materials costs change, reanalyze make/buy decisions. Last year's decision may already be out of date. Should be an ongoing review.

EXAMINE 'KITS.' In many companies, "kits" of inventory items are put together—all the units of an assembly—to await actual assembly. But sometimes one item is missing and the useless, incomplete kit is kept in inventory. Break apart incomplete kits; use parts in other assemblies or operations.

REWORK. Too often, "reworks" (items that require additional labor to correct a fault or change a spec) are given low priority and accumulate in inventory. Rework it or get rid of it. *Choices:* Modify it, sell it, if necessary, scrap it.

SAFETY STOCKS. Typical situation: Company runs out of an item. The stock-out created such havoc that the purchasing department decided not to let that happen again, and an overzealous clerk over-orders for safety. *What to do:* Run through all the items and label potential stock-outs as: Critical, major, minor, etc.—and then compare items' need with availability. Likely to see wide divergence between the two.

150

TAX TRAPS AND OPPORTUNITIES

MAKING A DEAL WITH THE IRS

...vice has ...chunk of ...a corpor- ...financially ...*o do:* Sub- ...application ...must be ac- ...tatement of ...her Informa- ...go to jail if ...nt. One indi- ...12, "as of" ...igible assets. ...tually had re- ...)0 which went ...tatement. The ...n which he had ...n in taxes owed ...l was scrubbed, ...ead. .../77.

...ISE ...LICITLY

...l income taxes are ...al Revenue Service ...to compromise if the ...inability to pay the

full amount.

One taxpayer received a deficiency notice for $2,896.83 and countered with a check for $500, on which he wrote "Tax Audit Returns Paid in Full."

The IRS notified him that the settlement proposed was unacceptable, but deposited his check, applying it to the unpaid account.

A bill for the balance arrived, and the taxpayer argued that the matter had been settled by compromise and offered his check in evidence.

Pay up, ordered the court.

There is an established procedure for making compromises (Form 656 must be used.) By depositing a check, the IRS isn't bound by words a taxpayer writes on it, even though other creditors may be bound when they accept such a check.

John W. Colebank et al., T.C. Memo. 1977-46, 2/23/77.

EVEN IRS MUST BE CHECKED

Insist that tax counsel check any formal notification from the government that releases you or your company from an obligation. A letter terminating a case may *not* be the final word. The Internal Revenue Service sought to collect from the president of a corporation *personally* the amount of untransmitted taxes his company had failed to turn over to the IRS.

Details: The president convinced the IRS appellate branch office that he wasn't the executive with responsibility in this area and the chief of the branch approved a recommendation that the matter be closed without further action.

Some time later, another IRS employee demanded that the president pay up personally; by now the company was broke and couldn't do so. The president asked the court to dismiss the matter, presenting as evidence the written notice from the IRS that the matter had been closed.

Let the trial proceed, ordered the court. The government should have used a prescribed form (#866) and not a letter to terminate the matter.

Hospitality Services, Inc. v. U.S., D.C. E.D. Mich., 3/7/77.

TO GET PROMPT IRS AUDIT

There are times—such as when a company is being liquidated—when it's desirable to get a prompt audit from the Internal Revenue Service. But to get the IRS to act quickly requires that strict rules be followed.

Ordinarily, the IRS has three years to make an audit. *If a letter requesting a prompt assessment is made, the IRS is allowed only 18 months.*

A recent case shows how minutely the rules are followed. Here the request was deemed improper and wasn't granted, because: (1) The person signing the letter didn't identify himself as a corporate officer. (2) The letter

was sent to the IRS instead of to the district Director of Internal Revenue. (3) The periods covered were not spelled out.

R.B. Griffith Co., T.C. Memo. 1973-50, 2/27/73.

MINUTES OF CORPORATE DIRECTORS' MEETINGS ESSENTIAL

Those detailed minutes should be kept for a variety of reasons, many of which are tax-oriented. There is no better place to show that corporate earnings had been retained in the taxable year for expansion or other business purposes. It's also the place to record that executive compensation was increased for specific compelling reasons which are spelled out. Some courts recognize that in a closely held corporation, informality is the custom and hence directors' meetings aren't required to prove that certain business decisions were based on general business considerations, not just the tax savings. As was noted in one new decision, "Basically, whenever a decision needs to be made, the president makes it. In essence, when the president arrives at work, there is a board of directors' meeting in progress."

Here the court was willing to believe that "for a plan to be specific and definite, it need not be 'memorialized' in the minutes of the corporation's directors or otherwise be as formal as is customary among large publicly held corporations."

But don't count on all courts being so realistic. Even small and other closely held corporations should be prepared to prove what the directors' minute book can best prove.

Smith v. James et al., D.C., N.D. Texas, 10/7/76.

PROTECTIVE LOSS CAN INVOLVE FRAUD

Sometimes there is real doubt about the year in which a deduction should be claimed on the Federal income tax return. Debts are deductible only in the year when they become bad. Casualties other than theft are deductible the year they occur to the extent they are not reimbursed by insurance or otherwise.

If you claim the deduction in one year and subsequently it is ascertained that you should have taken it in an earlier year, *the deduction may be lost.* And that earlier year might now be closed by the statute of limitations.

Often-heard advice: In case of genuine doubt, claim the deduction in *each* year. Then you'll be sure to have it allowed in the proper one. *Caution:* Seeking to evade taxes which you know are owing is *fraud.* You are not entitled to the same deduction twice, so one return involves reducing tax by a deduction you know isn't proper.

What to do: Attach to each tax return a statement that says, because of uncertainty as to the year of deduction, you are claiming it twice only for that purpose and with the expectation of getting it once.

> Living costs may be a deductible expense if business requires prolonged stay away from home, but at most up to one year.

IRS CAN CHALLENGE ANYTHING IF ONLY PURPOSE IS TAX AVOIDANCE

Any transaction can be challenged —and perhaps disallowed—by Internal Revenue Service, even though it follows the letter of the law, if it has *no other purpose* than tax avoidance. That was the basis for an IRS victory that charged "causing the preparation and presentation to the IRS of false or fraudulent documents."

One case: Low-bracket drifter cashed a winning ticket at the races for a wealthy acquaintance and falsely reported the winnings as his own.

U.S. v. McGee, 5th Cir., 5/10/78.

TAXPAYERS NO LONGER CAN BE PUSHED AROUND AT WILL

Two Revenue Agents entered a corporation's supermarket and said they would close down the business unless some $6,000 in back taxes were paid immediately. The chief stockholder asked for more time to pay, saying that if the place stayed open over the week-end, enough cash could be raised to pay what was owed. No way, replied the agents, closing down the business and selling the inventory for tax money.

The corporation and the chief stockholder brought suit against the tax people individually, claiming they had acted unreasonably and in bad faith for the express purpose of destroying the business, an action that amounted to conduct beyond the scope of their legitimate governmental authority.

The IRS agents asked the court to dismiss the suit against them on the ground that they only had been doing their duty. No, decided the judge. Zeal in collecting taxes is not an automatic shield for government employees. He wanted the facts first, to find out whether the agents had acted in good faith and in a reasonable belief that their drastic actions were indeed necessary.

Garner et al. v. Wilson et al., D.C., E.D. Cal., 1/6/77.

TRANSFER OF AUDIT CASE TO DIFFERENT IRS OFFICE REQUIRES GOOD REASON

No self-respecting business office likes to lose your account. And that goes for Internal Revenue Service offices as well. Some IRS offices are now balking at taxpayer requests to move the audit site to a more convenient place. One office recently announced that cases no longer will be transferred unless there are unusual and/or special circumstances which affect the *taxpayer* rather than the taxpayer's accountant or other representative. Requests for transfer that cite a desire to save the taxpayer's representative time and/or to minimize his fee will be denied unless there are unusual circumstances, such as physical handicap, illness, or the availability of pertinent books which cannot be conveniently transported to the audit site.

Director's News Letter, Newark (N.J.) District, IRS, Dec. 1976, Issue Number XXXVIII, page 3.

TAX-WISE WAYS TO HANDLE WINTER DAMAGE

To the taxpayer who suffers losses because of severe winter, relief is available. Needed for handling write-offs:

• Taxpayer can deduct for casualty losses to the extent that they aren't reimbursed by insurance (or otherwise). In the case of nonbusiness property, the loss is deductible to the extent that it exceeds $100 per casualty and to the extent all casualty losses for the year exceed 10% of adjusted gross income.

• *Casualty,* for tax purposes, means an event that is sudden, unexpected, and unusual. It must possess that *suddenness* which is common to fires, auto accidents, and storms. Damage caused by deterioration over time doesn't qualify. *Example:* The collapse of a building due to gradual erosion of the foundation is *not* a casualty.

• A deduction is permitted where property is destroyed or damaged as a result of simple negligence, as in the case of careless handling of a truck on an icy road. But damage as the result of *gross* negligence isn't deductible. *Example of gross negligence:* Drunken driving.

• Deductible winter casualties can arise from excessive icing, freezing conditions, or from bursting pipes. If a boiler bursts, damage to the boiler itself is apt to be deemed nondeductible because *suddenness* can't be proven, for the boiler may have been wearing out for some time. But damage done by water and steam escaping from this boiler is deductible. Suddenness is involved here.

Casualties (other than theft) are deductible in the year they took place. But if the loss took place in what the President of the United States subsequently proclaims a disaster area, the taxpayer may elect to take the deduction for the taxable year immediately preceding the year of loss.

A winter casualty actually can result in taxable gain. If the insurance proceeds or other payments exceed the original cost of the asset as reduced by allowable depreciation, there is taxable gain. But if the proceeds are reinvested in similar replacement property within two years, this money doesn't represent taxable income.

If your company carries *profit insurance*, what you received as the result of a plant shutdown is taxable as ordinary income. Most types of *use and occupancy* insurance really are profit insurance. Unfortunately, there is some confusion. The so-called *valued* form of *use and occupancy* insurance really is a form of property insurance. Proceeds from that are not taxed to the extent they are used in the acquisition of replacement property.

Some questions to ponder:

• Can you *prove* that damage to your property resulted from freezing conditions and not because of original faulty construction?

• Can you establish the actual damage to your property as the result of the casualty, or that loss was total? In order to do this, it may be advisable to make your first call after the casualty to a good photographer. Then call your insurance agent or maintenance people.

GETTING INVESTMENT TAX CREDIT—THE HOWS AND WHYS

If your company has added facilities lately, a tax expert should probably be retained to tour the plant and offices specifically to pick out all the property that qualifies for investment tax credit. Many companies overlook a lot.

What can be saved: The investment tax credit is a direct, dollar-for-dollar offset against tax liability. The credit is up to 10% of the price of a property (up to 11½% for a company that makes a contribution to an employee stock ownership plan). For a business that is in the 46% tax bracket, the credit is worth just about twice as much as an income-tax deduction in the equivalent amount. But starting in 1983, half of the investment credit that's claimed is subtracted from the cost of the property before depreciation deductions are computed. A firm that wishes to avoid reducing its depreciation deduction may elect a 2% reduction in the investment credit instead.

Criteria for credit: Tangible personal property and certain other tangible property acquired for use in business and having a useful life of three or more years is entitled to investment credit.

Credit for tangible personal property isn't apt to present any problems. Includes almost anything used in business that moves and has a useful life of three or more years: Office equipment, machinery, automobiles, display racks and shelves, wall-to-wall carpeting, movable partitions, signs, individual air conditioners, bookcases, etc.

"Other tangible property" is the category most often overlooked. This category excludes *"buildings and their components,"* but includes tangible property used as an integral part of manufacturing, production, extraction, transportation, communications, and electrical energy, gas, water, or sewage disposal.

A "building" doesn't include a structure that houses property used as an integral part of a manufacturing or production activity if it's so clearly related to the tangible property it houses that it can be expected to be replaced when the equipment is replaced.

Examples of some property that's included: Air-handling units, refrigeration units, steam boilers, temperature controls and related power outlets; electric power, air and vacuum lines, and duct work installed to provide controlled temperature and humidity in a dust-free environment in special work rooms in a factory.

The Internal Revenue Service has issued a great number of rulings on what property is or isn't eligible for investment credit. If your expert discovers considerable overlooked investment credit opportunities, he may recommend a ruling so you don't claim a credit that may be disallowed.

DEALING WITH INVOLUNTARY CONVERSIONS

If a corporation loses property in an *involuntary conversion* (such as a fire or a government condemnation), the compensatory money received is *not* taxable (even if the payment is more than the *adjusted basis** of the property) to the extent that those proceeds are invested in property similar or related in use.

Recent case: One corporation's real property was condemned by a governmental agency. Efforts were made to reinvest the proceeds. Because of a sewer moratorium prohibiting new construction, the corporation was unable to find replacement property in the area. It couldn't get an extension of the replacement time.

What to do: Buy 80% or more of a corporation which owns qualified replacement property in the area.

*Cost plus improvements less depreciation.
Rev. Rul. 76-488.

DAMAGE CLAIMS FUND IS PRUDENT BUT NOT TAX DEDUCTIBLE

Your company's business experience may suggest that a reserve against future damage claims be set up. But don't expect a Federal income tax deduction for the reserve. Except in the case of depreciation and of bad debts, a reserve isn't deductible. *Reason:* Taxes are based upon completed transactions, and a reserve is only a guess (however well educated) of what's going to happen.

From actual experience, one corporation was able to make a good fix on the amount required to settle claims still outstanding at year-end for missing or damaged shipments. (The reserve was computed by making an item-by-item tally on adding machine tape of each claim's probable cost.) Over a two-year period, the total put into the reserve proved to be within 2.9% of what actually had to be paid out. But the court refused to allow the deduction (even though sound accounting principles prudently dictated provision for claims).

The court's view: "Principles of conservatism and principles of tax accounting" don't always mesh. Liability as to each individual claim isn't determined until that claim is paid.

Gateway Transportation Co. v. U.S., W.D., Wis., 12/13/76.

SALES TAX ON INTERSTATE SALES: DEFENSIVE MEASURES

Every business engaged in mail order sales to customers in a state other than the seller's may face a large liability for failure to collect sales or use taxes. That's the result of a recent U.S. Supreme Court ruling.

The case: National Geographic sold its magazine via mail to California residents. It had no subscription sales offices in California, but it did have two offices that solicited *advertising.* The decision turned on that point—the seller's continuous presence in two offices within the state.

While the California Supreme Court had said that the "slightest" presence within the state would be sufficient for liability, the U.S. Supreme Court didn't go that far.

Many states, hungry for revenue and anxious to protect local merchants, can be expected to exploit the route opened by the Supreme Court. If they are in a position to dig back for past years, huge liabilities may be exposed. Chances are they will apply the "slightest presence" test and leave it to the seller to contest the liability.

Defensive measures: Get trade associations to set up "defense departments" to provide legal aid. Withdraw all unnecessary "continuous presence" in states outside the state where the merchandise is sold. Consult counsel about protection of old files showing past "continuous presence" in the state. Make sure that sales are consummated at home office of seller or where no tax is imposed.

National Geographic Society v. California Board of Equalization, U.S. Sup. Ct., 4/4/77.

DEDUCTING DISALLOWED ITEMS AGAIN

Suppose the IRS disallows a part of the compensation as unreasonable but the corporation continues to pay and deduct the full amount on future tax returns?

Answer: A negligence penalty can

be anticipated.

Where a taxpayer continues to take a deduction for an item that the IRS already has removed as improper, this is regarded as evidence that the taxpayer was careless or otherwise had refused to abide by what he now should have recognized as the requirements.

KICKBACKS— THE TAX ANGLE

Kickbacks—some legal, some illegal —present some difficult dilemmas for business. Let's examine them:

Kickbacks to government employees *aren't* deductible by the payor. Payments to businesspersons *are*—if the payor *hasn't* violated any state law that would subject him to a criminal penalty. In many states, such as New York, there are commercial bribery laws, which forbid the payment of money to an employee of another corporation *unless* the recipient's employer knows about it.

The tax relevance: The payor will lose the tax deduction if the employer of the purchasing agent, executive, loan officer, etc., doesn't know about the kickback. That should discourage the making of such kickbacks, which of course is what the law is trying to do.

But these are unusual times. The payee's employer may be hard put to pay a valuable person what he demands.

The employer doesn't have to increase the salary if the employee is permitted to sweeten his own income satisfactorily in another way. Many employers consider themselves sufficiently

familiar with the product (or service) that their employees are buying to know when shoddy merchandise or inflated prices are involved, and they feel that the employee's acceptance of a commercial bribe won't hurt what the company is getting. For his part the employee is hardly likely to let the kickback distort his judgment if it would result in the loss of his job.

So we have the bizarre situation of both employee and employer benefiting from a kickback, which the payor is permitted to deduct for tax purposes.

PROFIT EXPECTATIONS NECESSARY FOR TAX DEDUCTIONS

Expenses can be deducted in connection with a transaction entered upon for profit, even if the profit never materializes. Where the losses keep recurring, *the problem is to show that you really had a profit-making motive.*

• In one case, a court was favorably impressed by the fact that an individual kept adequate books and records and that she sought the assistance of persons competent to advise her.

• In another case (decided three days earlier) the same court would not recognize a transaction as one entered upon for profit, because the taxpayer consulted nobody except his own friends—and he consistently ignored their advice.

• Another case, decided at just about the same time, involved an enterprise that spent five years and $175,000 feeding and studying cats. But none were sold; they were not used for the production of any marketable product; they could not be established as a breed. The costs could not be deducted as business expense. The court also refused to let the loss be characterized as one arising from a transaction entered upon for profit.

MERCENARY GOAL. To realize a profit on the operation, which presupposes not only future earnings but also sufficient earnings to recoup losses sustained along the way.

PARENT CORPORATION TAXED ON FUNDS ADVANCED BY SUBS

When a parent corporation has its subsidiary advance funds to it, even though the amounts are recorded as loans, the IRS can view them as taxable *dividends* to the parent.

The case: A corporation had 52 subsidiaries, which operated retail stores. Each had to advance to the parent all revenue not needed for *immediate* operating expenses, such as payrolls. There were no interest charges, no set time for repayment, no notes of indebtedness, no legal compulsion to make repayment. Further, there was no particular need of the parent for the advances; they weren't intended to meet a particular business exigency or emergency. The money was used for the parent's own general operating expenses and not for the benefit of the subsidiaries.

Alterman Foods, Inc., v. U.S., 5th Cir., 12/30/74.

SELLING BONDS

A closely held corporation with pre-tax earnings of at least $3 million and a minimum net worth of $5 million is big enough to sell bonds. The size of the debt offering should be at least $12 million to attract sufficient market interest and justify the underwriting costs (usually about $200,000).

Essentials: Three years of audited figures for Securities & Exchange Commission registration, and a *specific* need for the money.

Acid test: An underwriter will closely examine the company's position, history, balance sheet, and management team before agreeing to file the offering. This takes about a month. If snags develop, the company usually is not charged for the evaluation.

Caution: The actual interest rate on the issue isn't set until the day before the offering is made. The underwriter can give a close estimate, but there are no guarantees.

PAYING DEFICIENCIES

Interest on *accumulated-earnings* tax only goes back to the date of *assessment,* in contrast to an income tax deficiency, which generally carries an interest charge all the way back to the time set for the filing of the tax return.

The corporate earnings tax is different. If a corporation pays such a tax within 10 days of the time the IRS issues a formal demand for it, there is no interest charge, even though the return being audited was filed three years ago. Interest, in any event, goes back to the time of this formal demand.

PARENT FIRM'S NEEDS MAY JUSTIFY EARNINGS' RETENTION BY SUBSIDIARY

Treasury regulations provide that, for accumulated earnings tax purposes, a parent corporation is justified in retaining earnings for the needs of a *subsidiary company* if it owns 80% or more of the unit's stock. A district court had held the converse situation an invalid defense against this tax because the regulations fail to mention it. A court of appeals reversed this situation.

Ruling: In assessing the reasonable needs of a wholly owned subsidiary company, it is permissible to consider the reasonable requirements of the *parent.*

Inland Terminals, Inc. v. U.S., 4th Cir., 4/26/73.

SUDDEN OBSOLESCENCE

Government ban on a product creates sudden obsolescence for tax purposes. The proposal to outlaw artificial sweetener should alert other manufacturers to what can happen to them. Manufacturers of cigarettes, hair sprays, babies' sleeping garments, agricultural pesticides, and numerous other products may find themselves in a similar situation. *Tax implications:* Machinery used to produce banned products can be written off as abnormal obsolescence for Federal tax purposes until the final switch is pulled.

WHO'LL BE AROUND TO SIGN THE CORPORATE TAX RETURN?

Will the right corporate officers be around to sign the Federal income tax return of a *calendar year* corporation (due March 15)? *Only officers permitted to sign the return:* President, vice president, treasurer, assistant-treasurer, and chief accounting officer, who isn't necessarily the chief accountant. *Not qualified:* Board chairman, controller, secretary, or assistant-secretary. If there is any doubt the authorized officials will be on hand, make certain the corporate minutes show that another party has power of attorney to sign the tax returns, *before* he or she actually does so.

What not to do: Have an officer sign a blank tax return form before he goes on vacation. That can be equated with fraud.

• A corporate officer who signs his company's Federal income tax return in his official capacity isn't signing as an individual, but it may make him liable as an individual. *Example:* Making false statements to the Internal Revenue Service can result in a $5,000 fine, or imprisonment for not more than three years, or both—and if it is *his*

160

signature that appears under a false or fraudulent statement, he is the one likely to face the penalty.

DEFINING A LOAN LOSS

An officer of a company, who is also a stockholder, lends money to the firm, or guarantees its obligation. The company fails. Is his loss a *business* bad debt? The question is hardly academic, because if it is a business bad debt the loss is fully deductible, not just a capital loss.

The criteria for a business loan follow this reasoning: If the dominant motivation in making the loan is to bolster the company so as to protect his job, then the loan can be written off fully.

When it's *not* a loan: The officer's salary was $12,000 and his stock had cost him $38,900.

• The Supreme Court ruled that, since his after-tax salary was only about a fifth of his investment, his primary motivation in making the loan was not protecting his job, but *protecting his earlier investment*, disallowing the business bad debt.

IRS vs. INDEPENDENT CONTRACTORS

The Internal Revenue Service is screening claimed independent contractor relationships to see whether they are what they purport to be or are really employer-employee relationships.

Control of a person's detailed activities points to an employee relationship. Concern for *results only* is a badge of an independent contractor relationship.

IRS's intent: It collects more from employees (and their employers) than it does from contractors. Also, the IRS collects faster from employees.

CHARITABLE GIFTS WITH BENEFITS FOR BUSINESS

Corporations may not deduct charitable contributions in amounts in excess of 10% of their taxable income. Gifts in excess of that amount are subject to a five-year carryover.

Most effective ways to use charitable giving:

• Set up a scholarship fund in a college or university for a specific purpose related to your business, such as accounting, advertising, marketing, research and development. Helps develop contacts with department heads; useful in recruiting top graduates.

• Give to charities directly related to your company's business. Stimulates use of your products.

• Take advantage of new tax law provision which makes gifts of inventory more attractive.

• Build good will in the community where your plant is situated by specific support of municipal recreational facilities. *Example:* Contribution can pay for keeping the facility open later. Encourage employees to participate in community projects. Open your own facilities to the public.

● Help sponsor local education and public TV programs of quality.

A gift which comes out of company inventory might be the best charitable contribution a company can make.

Problem: How to value it for tax purposes? Prior to the Tax Reform Act of 1976, a corporation couldn't claim a charitable deduction that was more than its *basis* in contributed inventory. Basis usually means cost. That makes it tough on firms where fair market value was far higher, as in pharmaceuticals.

For current contributions, however, a corporation may deduct basis plus one-half of any appreciation in value. The deduction isn't to exceed twice the basis of the contributed property. The donee must be a public charity or a private operating foundation. It must furnish the donor with a statement that the donated inventory will be used for the purpose for which tax-exempt status has been granted.

Also, the charity (specifically limited to care of ill, needy, or infants) must certify that the property will not be sold. (This stepped-up basis for deductions doesn't apply to property which fails to meet the standards of the Federal Food, Drug, and Cosmetics Act.)

Tax Reform Act of 1976, Section 2135.

LIABILITY FOR WITHHOLDING TAXES

Personal liability for a corporation's failure to turn over withholding taxes to the government isn't confined to persons on the payroll.

The case: An attorney was a promoter and developer of various ventures. In order to avoid a possible conflict of interest, he had the stock of one corporation put into the name of an associate and the associate's wife.

As a matter of record, he wasn't a stockholder, officer or director of this corporation. But he exercised complete control. In the court's "unlegalese" language, *he was the boss.* Since he made all decisions (such as which creditors got paid first) the lack of *record* association with the corporation didn't insulate him against personal liability for withholding taxes which weren't turned over to the government.

Bersani v. U.S., D.C., N.D.N.Y., 11/18/74.

WHEN TAXPAYER ASKS LAWYER TO GO INTO MINUTE DETAIL IN WRITING UP BILLS

A corporation might request detailed descriptions of every item for the convenience of the corporation's own accounting department. Then every charge can be assigned to the appropriate division or department. But a carefully described bill can show an alert Revenue Agent that some of the charges represented services for an officer personally, or related to items which are not immediately deductible (fees for negotiating a 15-year lease), or have to do with matters that the corporation doesn't desire the Internal Revenue Service to question. Although matters discussed by client and lawyer are in most instances regarded as *privileged* (so that the Service can't inquire into what was discussed), the attorney's copy of its bill to a client was held not to be protected in a case involving a client of the lawyer's, one Spiro T. Agnew.

U.S. et al. v. Mintz et al., D.C., D.C. 1/31/77.

INVENTORY MANAGEMENT

WAREHOUSE OPERATIONS—MAKING THEM MORE EFFICIENT

Expand upward, where possible. It's cheaper. Build new facilities as high as codes permit. Steel rack flooring can be added later.

• When moving from city to suburb, retain the old building. Shut down two-thirds of it, and use the rest to service old customers until they're used to traveling to the new location. (When part of the building is closed off, be sure to ask for a tax reassessment.)

• Have order-pickers place a card with their name in each order. Improves performance.

• Don't let company personnel do the work that common carrier truck drivers are supposed to do: "Tailgate delivery" means just that (although it's okay if the driver borrows a hand truck).

• Place cartons for pickers on carts and have them packed *right from the shelf.*

• Supply the receiving department with multi-shelf carts, each shelf for a different warehouse section or sub-section.

• Name warehouse areas for their supervisors so that layouts are more easily remembered.

INFLATION TRAPS IN INVENTORY

During an inflationary period it's easy to get carried away and buy more inventory than is needed—in anticipation of higher prices. But it may not be wise to stock up. There are advantages to buying some things ahead. *However:* Capital is being tied up when you do this—and you should take time to figure the *true cost* of that capital and of your inventory. The smart way to look at inventory:

Separate *variable* costs of inventory from *fixed* costs (which should not be charged to inventory). Many costs that are considered *variable* are really *fixed*—or at the most, variable only in incremental steps. Two examples: (1) Two men handling 100,000 boxes annually at the warehouse can take on an additional 20,000 without adding personnel. At some level over 120,000, extra help may be needed.

(2) Inventory carrying costs remain fixed over fairly large fluctuations in volume. Realize that there's no sense building in an increase that doesn't exist.

How to find what is *fixed* and what is *variable* and what to include in your calculation:

• Would insurance be paid regardless of whether your space is occupied by inventory? If so, then consider it a *fixed* cost.

• Are taxes paid on land and buildings whether or not they're occupied by inventory? If so, they're a *fixed* cost. (However, taxes on the inventory itself are a true *variable* cost.)

• If your inventory is reduced, would the space it occupied be used for production or other purposes? If *not*, then it's a *fixed* cost.

• What proportion of material-handling equipment and manpower will vary with inventory size? The figure is probably never very high. A lot of volume must be involved before you can treat this as a *variable* cost.

• Does inventory volume ever have an effect on damage and deterioration? *Answer:* No connection. Security procedures and storage facilities are a bigger factor here.

• *Zero in on opportunity profit.* This is a cost area that really counts. It's a *pure variable. Ask:* Is cash freed through inventory reduction usable elsewhere—for reducing the amount of money borrowed, for example?

Next step: Ignore the *fixed* costs and compare the *variable* costs with anticipated price hikes. If the variables are lower, stock up to beat the increase. (Ignoring *fixed* costs isn't foolish when you're doing it *temporarily* to beat a price increase.)

Why ignoring fixed costs, short-term, works: Many inventory carrying costs are fixed over a 3-6 month—or longer—period. They cost the same whether you have more inventory or not during that period. What you're doing is figuring if increasing normal levels by 2-3 months' supply will let your company spend less additional money on variable costs than by buying the material at anticipated prices.

How to do this: Add the cost of the variables to the price paid for inventory. Then match this against the new (anticipated) price. *Example:* Eliminate all variables except the cost of money. Take the order quantity divided by two, multiplied by the old price, then multiplied by one-twelfth the cost of money. Add the result to the purchase price. Compare this with the anticipated purchase price—and decide if you want to try to beat the increase or take it.

SOME TRAPS. Don't use the comparison with a price-at-time-of-delivery item. Don't use it with low cost-usage items, because true variable costs will run higher than any price hikes on these. Don't try it for anticipated increases more than a year out. Only perform the analysis on high dollar volume items.

Source: Norman Kobert & Assoc., 1611 S. Ocean Drive, Ft. Lauderdale, Fla. 33316.

INVENTORY COUNTING

Not everything in inventory has to be counted. In fact, it's usually a waste of time knowing that a warehouse has

535 widgets—when all management wants to know is whether there are enough in stock, based on lead-times, turnover, etc.

Systems monitoring inventory—without keeping an exact count—are usually called *no-record* systems. The name is misleading, since some records are kept. But the level of record-keeping (and its attendant costs) is minimal. *More important:* No-record systems are designed to signal that a reorder is necessary.

Myth of no-record inventory: Invites internal theft. What invites theft is inadequate theft control. Records inventory only gives you a way to see how much is being stolen, but it will never *stop* the theft. In general, no-record inventory control works best with low-priority, non-critical merchandise.

- *Four-wall inventory:* Assumes that it doesn't matter *where* inventory is kept. Only important to know how many of the items are on hand. Simply keep count of the number delivered and the number shipped out (or rejected, spoiled, etc.). The difference is the inventory. *Assessment:* Requires continuous monitoring but almost no paperwork.

- *Two-bin control:* Used widely for low-value items. It should have wider application, since it could replace many of more complicated inventory methods. *How it works:* Store items in two bins. Don't remove items from second bin until first is exhausted. Place a reorder card at bottom of first bin or top of second bin. *Danger:* Irresponsible clerk may overlook reorder cards. *Solution:* Place second bin where a *responsible* person is in charge.

- *Calendar control:* After some ex-perimenting with the speed that inventory is used, set a calendar interval when a sample physical inventory check is necessary. Can be done by employees or even a supplier—if the level of inventory can be monitored easily by the outsider.

- *Bin/tag control* should be avoided.

Records are kept at the specific inventory location. Entries of withdrawals and additions are made on a tag right at the bin. *Problems:* Low-level employees often make gross errors in arithmetic. Tags can be lost or damaged.

Source: Norman Kobert & Assoc., P.O. Box 21396, Ft. Lauderdale, Fl. 33335

IDEAS TO BOOST THE BOTTOM LINE

INVENTORY RESPONSIBILITY. Managers who make inventory decisions should be held accountable for those decisions. So when the *sales department* pushes *manufacturing* to build 1,000 items to set sales goals, charge any unsold items in inventory to *sales.* Show who is responsible for various inventory items, so that line and staff people become responsible for their inventory actions.

TIMING. Do not calculate inventory in dollars or units. Calculate it in terms of time—"X" weeks of supply is a more useful figure. That gives the manager a better perspective on the magnitude of problems that have resulted in inventory accumulation.

LEADTIMES VS. USAGE. Continually update forecasts. Adjust purchase leadtimes to those *new* forecasts. Too often companies use leadtime figures that are out of date. Inventory should be a hedge against *future* use.

GETTING RID OF USELESS INVENTORY

Go over inventory list and question items suspected of not being useful. Make up a form, identifying items by name and with a photo or drawing. Circulate those forms through all the departments that could use them.

Ask every manager:
- Can item be used?
- Can it be used if modified?
- Is it useless?

Useless items can be:
- Returned to the original vendor (if the vendor will take them).
- Sold to another company that can use them.
- Sold to a surplus materials or parts dealer.
- Bartered.
- Sold as scrap.

CRISIS MANAGEMENT

'CREATIVE' ACCOUNTING DEVICES CAN CONCEAL CORPORATE PROBLEMS

"Creative" accounting devices are not causes, but symptoms, of corporate failure. If you're an employee (or an investor, vendor, or customer) and suspect your company has problems, look for these creative accounting devices as possible warnings of trouble ahead:
- Delaying the publication of financial results as long as legally possible.
- Capitalization of research costs, basing the write-off against existing or expected orders.
- Continuation of dividend payments from *new equity* or *loans.*
- Cuts in routine maintenance until repairs are so overdue that it's necessary to renovate.
- Consider leasing agreements as *capital* rather than as what they are—*loans.*
- Dividend increases from subsidiaries to the parent company and consolidation of more and more subsidiary results, from wholly and partially owned subsidiaries, into the parent company account.
- Retention of the main asset of the business in the owner's name (or that of the owner's spouse) rather than the company name (thereby removing it as a source of payment to creditors).
- The valuation of assets at whatever figure is wanted, since nobody may notice.
- Capitalizing interest charges, training expenses, computer *installation*

costs.

● Using inflation as a cloud to hide asset revaluation.

● Paying company debts out of the proprietor's pocket to improve profits before he sells his shares.

● Inventory valuation at latest market *selling* price rather than at actual cost.

● Deferment of current expense to next year to improve this year's sales and profits.

● Inadequate provision for depreciation by failing to revalue assets.

Source: *Corporate Collapse*, by John Argenti, John Wiley & Sons, 605 Third Ave., New York 10016.

HOW TAX RELIEF CAN BECOME A PENALTY

If you're facing a corporate liquidation, beware of the tax-free features of the IRS Code. Although the tax-free features were meant to provide tax *relief* in specific circumstances, a taxpayer may end up being *penalized* if his reorganization inadvertently falls within the language of the tax-free provision.

How it happens: If a corporation sells property at a gain, this isn't taxed if the sale took place within 12 months after the corporation had adopted a plan of complete liquidation (assuming dissolution actually was completed within that time).

The case: One corporation voted to dissolve, and its property was sold at a loss. But this loss couldn't be recognized for tax purposes, because there had been a complete liquidation within 12 months, *i.e.,* a tax-free liquidation.

And in a tax-free reorganization, there is no recognition of gain *or loss*.

Comment: Actually, it would have been very easy to avoid this mournful result. The liquidation could have been allowed to drag out for *more* than 12 months.

Anchorage Nursing Home, Inc., T.C. Memo. 1974-295, 11/25/74.

BANKRUPTCY STRATEGIES

WHEN YOUR FIRM FACES INSOLVENCY. The first step is to face up to your *financial problems* early enough so you have time to act positively. Be careful not to fool yourself, which isn't hard to do if you're working hard to fool your creditors. You may be able to forestall the whole complex procedure that, once started, is both expensive and may lead inevitably toward bankruptcy.

What to do: Communicate with your creditors. Let them have the full story. Don't bluff. Credibility at this point may be the *only* thing that can save you. It buys you time—and even possibly more credit so you might effect a turnabout.

Danger in laying your problem on the line with creditors: One or more nervous creditors can reject your request for cooperation and rush to court to force you into bankruptcy. But if you can get the major creditors behind you, they'll be able to use their leverage to get cooperation. In my experience, they can be *very* persuasive, so play it straight with these big creditors—you need them.

Even if you can't forestall court action, the same general rule applies: *seek creditor cooperation.* Try to work with the committee of creditors in establishing a practical plan to keep the business operating. Don't wait until you're in court to do it. Emotions may be calmed and the credibility factor is higher *before* you get into court.

It may sound self-serving, but it's vitally important: If you think you're going to face *insolvency*—get yourself in the hands of competent bankruptcy counsel—fast. Your corporate counsel will be the first to admit that this is a very specialized field that shouldn't be handled by general counsel.

FORMS OF BANKRUPTCY. There are three major forms of bankruptcy:
- *Straight bankruptcy*, which is limited to liquidation proceedings.
- *Chapter 11*, a voluntary proceeding in which the debtor seeks court protection while it continues in business as a debtor-in-possession and tries to work out an arrangement with *unsecured* creditors.
- *Chapter 10*, generally for large firms with public shareholders and public debt, and it affects the rights of all classes of creditors, secured and unsecured, and of stockholders. It may be voluntary or involuntary.

What the bankruptcy lawyer does: His first job is to explore the reasons for your problems, possible cures, and to determine how you should act. Whether you should seek court protection, the timing and how and when to confront the creditors with your situation. These are critical decisions that can effect the final outcome of the proceedings and may determine whether the firm can stay in business.

Once those decisions are made, he'll be your key liaison between the court and the creditors' committee in either establishing a financial plan to keep the business operating or in dealing with the intricate steps of insolvency.

HOW LONG. Straight bankruptcy liquidations vary depending on such things as size and nature of the assets involved, potential causes of action to be asserted by the trustee. Chapter 11 proceedings also depend on the complexity and can last anywhere from several months (rare) to a few years. Chapter 10 proceedings are generally involved and go on for years.

YOUR CUSTOMER FACES INSOLVENCY. Speed and good information are vital. If you wait too long, you may end up at the end of the line, holding out your hand with scores of other creditors for a share of a fast-shrinking pie.

If you have even the *slightest* hint your customer is in trouble, *investigate that very day.* Many lawyers advise checking with credit-reporting agencies and trade associations. I'm not so sure you should stop there. *Better:* Go to the firm's customers, suppliers and lenders—and do it personally, or have one of your trusted people do it. It requires a person with knowledge of industry insiders, a person who can deal in confidence and a person who is sensitive to people's reactions. *Reason:* Many executives hesitate, except in the strictest confidence, to report someone's financial plight. That's because such a person could face a defamation of credit suit if he's challenged by the firm he's reporting on.

If you determine your customer, to whom you may have just shipped $100,

000 worth of goods, is in trouble, then you may be in trouble, too. *What to do:* Call your lawyer. Check whether you have liens on the goods. Have the liens properly filed (many aren't, for a multitude of reasons, mostly carelessness). *Types of errors:* Name of firm (using the *trade* instead of the *corporate* name) isn't exact, dealings were actually with a subsidiary or some other affiliate, chief place of business is in another state, etc.

RETAKING SHIPPED GOODS. Determine what the customer's chances of rehabilitation are. If bleak, move fast to get your goods back.

The Uniform Commercial Code gives you certain rights to demand return of goods delivered on credit while customer was insolvent (customer may refuse, but you should pursue anyway). You must make the demand within 10 days of receipt of goods. *Another possibility:* Every purchase agreement should contain the customer's written representation that he's solvent. If you can show he misrepresented his solvency within three months before delivery, you can demand the return of the goods, and you aren't bound by the 10-day limitation. *Warning:* These rights of reclamation may be cut off if not acted upon before a bankruptcy petition is filed. However, if you are able to retake the goods before the filing, you may have an excellent tactical advantage, because there's a serious legal question on how a bankruptcy court can overrule the *de facto* return of your unpaid-for goods.

If, on the other hand, you determine your customer *is* in financial difficulty, that by itself is no reason to stop doing business with him. But be prudent.

Maintain all shipments on a cash basis —or, if you're willing, grant him credit, but demand collateral or some security. Keep checking the customer's condition on a frequent basis and keep the level of credit within control.

Filing proof of claims: If you determine to file a claim, after consulting counsel, do so in time so that your claim isn't barred. The time within which a claim must be filed depends on the type of proceeding. If you aren't independently advised by counsel, you should monitor the proceedings and check with the court or creditors' committee attorney to be sure you are fully aware of all critical deadlines—and do not lose tactical advantage or forfeit your claim.

Warning: Don't be *too* quick to file a claim. Check first to see what, if any, claim the insolvent firm has against you. If it does have such a claim, and you make a filing, you now fall under the full summary jurisdiction of the court. It may end up costing you more than you could possibly get back.

IF YOUR SUPPLIER BECOMES INSOLVENT. You may, for sound business reasons, want to protect your supplier from bankruptcy. You may just want him to stay in production to satisfy your supply needs, or you may want to buy him out. Don't be hasty. If you decide to assist him in remaining in business, first check with the creditors' committee. Get their approval; they *could* give you trouble. But chances are they will support you.

Warning: If one form of your assistance is helping the insolvent supplier cover his payroll so he can keep operating, be sure provision is made for payroll taxes. If tax isn't paid, IRS may hold *you* liable.

FINANCIAL MANAGEMENT

If you wanted to acquire the insolvent firm, your main problem is establishing, to the satisfaction of court, creditors and shareholders, that you're paying fair value. Once again, check with the creditors' committee and preferably try to work out the arrangements under the court's umbrella.

Source: Joel B. Zweibel, partner in the New York law firm Kaye, Scholer, Fierman, Hays & Handler.

BANKRUPTCY DOES NOT ERASE DEBT TO IRS

It's been widely reported that corporate officers are *personally* responsible to the IRS if the corporation fails to pay withholding and Social Security taxes that had been withheld from employees. *One case:* If that officer goes into personal bankruptcy (relieving him of all other debts), the money due the government is still not discharged.

Severance v. U.S., U.S.D.C., N.D. Tex 6/30/76.

LET THE IRS KNOW WHO IS REPRESENTING A DISSOLVED CORPORATION

If a corporation is liquidated and unpaid liabilities to the IRS subsequently turn up (*e.g.*, through a tax audit), the IRS can try to collect from shareholders as transferees if insufficient corporate funds remain.

But if the corporation has gone out of existence and there is no known mailing address, any tax deficiency can pile up years of interest before the stockholders ultimately get their tax bills as transferees of corporate property.

To avoid this, the corporation's liquidating trustees (in many states, the officers automatically become such) or other representative should notify the IRS, through a notice of fiduciary relationship, to whom official mail should be sent. Then tax difficulties can be straightened out quickly.

Great Falls Bonding Agency, Inc., 63 T.C., No. 26, 12/9/74.

OPPORTUNITIES IN CHAPTER 11

Voluntary bankruptcy (more formally known as Chapter 11 of the Federal bankruptcy law), doesn't carry as much of a stigma as many people think. Used correctly, a "Chapter 11 company" can restructure and come out quite healthy. Here are some of the things worth knowing about Chapter 11—from the bankrupt's point of view and the creditors':

Under Chapter 11, a business can continue to operate and doesn't have to pay past unsecured debts until a plan arranging repayment is adopted. Typically, it can take two months to a year before a repayment plan is approved. If the business has no assets or, if liquidated, the unsecured creditors would get very little, the creditors are more likely to allow time for repayment. If there are assets to pay creditors all or most of what's owed, the creditors will try to have a trustee run the business. If there is a likelihood the business will continue once the credit and/or liquidity problems are worked out, the creditors also will be more apt to give the debtor more time. Remember, creditors are business men and one thing they don't want to do is close up a customer.

HOW TO OPERATE UNDER CHAPTER 11. Most creditors will continue selling to the debtor. If the situation looks marginal, creditors might want C.O.D. terms or cash before delivery. If it can be shown that the debtor is receiving new working capital as part of a positive plan to reorganize and will have profitable operations almost from day one, then some creditors will usually go along. After a few months of positive cash flow, most will extend credit again. Any debts incurred in the Chapter 11 period must be paid before any *pre*-Chapter 11 unsecured debt can be paid.

If a plan cannot be arranged, the creditors will move to have the company liquidated by a trustee.

PLANNING A TURNAROUND. An infusion of capital is often critical to saving a company. An investor might purchase stock. A bank might be persuaded to lend money if there are sufficient assets and working capital to ensure the repayment. A bank loan could also be combined with the personal guarantee of the principals, who might have substantial net worth. Arrangements might be made with a commercial finance company for a revolving credit agreement with the accounts receivable and inventory as collateral.

Unsecured property could be collateralized to a new creditor.

These arrangements are generally made before the Chapter 11 filing. When the petition is filed, motions should also be filed to have these new credit arrangements approved. Generally, they will be permitted, because it is merely an exchange of one form of asset for another.

Attorneys for the major creditors should be contacted before the filing. The proceedings usually go more smoothly that way. (The attorneys jockey tremendously to get *the creditors committee* as a client. It becomes a very lucrative piece of business for them.)

COSTS OF CHAPTER 11. For a company with perhaps $600,000 in liabilities, the bankruptcy costs could run to $60,000. The attorney for the debtor could receive up to $20,000. The attorney for the creditors would get $10,000 and the accountant for the debtor would get $5,000. Various other costs (referee fees, court costs, transcribing and photocopying and meeting hall rentals) bring the total cost up to the $60,000 range. So that's $60,000 to settle $600,000 of liabilities at 25 cents on the dollar. *Not an expensive price to pay.* The total cost including the payment of liabilities would be $210,000, about 35% of the total debt ($390,000 "profit" on the Chapter 11 proceedings).

PLANS OF ARRANGEMENT. Plans of arrangement can take many forms. Some debts (about $1,000) could be settled for *cash* at, say, 10 cents on the dollar. Bigger debts could be handled with a series of notes payable over several years, also for 10 cents on the dollar. Capital stock in the corporation could also be issued. It isn't unusual for several different settlement arrangements to be approved by the parties.

TIMING CHAPTER 11. If the Chapter 11 could be planned well in advance, there would be a good chance of success for both the debtor and the creditors. Cash can be generated by having a sale at substantially below normal prices (but not below cost) and liquidating dormant inventory. The cash could be used to operate the business and buy additional supplies. Accounts receivable could be collateralized. The debtor is receiving credit and has opened sources of credit that he did not have prior to the Chapter 11 filing.

Most companies on the brink of Chapter 11 have lawsuits against them and major suppliers threatening to cut off or actually cutting off supplies and pressing for payment arrangements or commitments that generally cannot be met. (It is not as great an advantage to liquidate inventory for firms being pressed by lawsuits and vendors cutting off supplies, as there would be if the company had a clean slate and been able to use the money to generate additional supplies and credit.)

A company losing money on one branch of its operations can use Chapter 11 to provide an equitable way to divest itself of those operations and cancel its commitments and contracts.

> Ask to postpone initial payments when negotiating buying contracts. With interest rates high, you can create substantial savings on the contract over a grace period of up to six months.

RISKS IN THE ABANDONED CORPORATION

Safest course when a corporate shell is no longer useful is to file a *formal dissolution.*

Case in point: A manufacturer wanted to retire but couldn't sell his business. He let it run down and sold the plant, equipment, and other assets. The corporation had no obligations. He took the cash out of the corporation, paid taxes on his gain, and moved to "retirement land." He acted completely in good faith.

Years later, a customer filed a product liability suit against the corporation, simply by filing papers with the secretary of the state where the business was incorporated. The state notified the corporation, but there was no one there to get the message.

Result: The customer won a judgment by default *before the manufacturer even knew his company had been sued.*

Common reaction: So what? The corporation stands between the manufacturer and the plaintiff. *Dead wrong!* The courts consider the manufacturer the *trustee* of the assets he removed from his business. He's obliged to pay the debt. It's possible to attack the judgment, but it's difficult.

Prudent course: If the manufacturer had dissolved his corporation, there would have been no corporation to sue. While still possible to sue him, it would have been more difficult. And the judgment could not have been entered without the individual's knowledge. In addition, dissolving a corporation is evidence of good faith.

Advice: Any company that acquires another corporation's assets must be wary of a variation on the same theme. Suppose the owner of the acquired company merely transfers the corporation's assets to another corporation in return for stock, and then retires and sits back and collects the dividends.

Danger: The receiving corporation may be liable for the abandoned corporation's further obligations. If your company acquires assets in this way, make sure the other corporation is *formally dissolved.*

Hope for creditors: Just because a company has gone out of business, don't assume you can't collect a debt. The corporate shell may still exist—it's illegal for a bankrupt corporation to dissolve. If the amount of money justifies the effort, it may still be possible to collect the debt from the corporation's principals.

Source: Dan Brecher, of Brecher, Moskowitz & Altman, 230 Park Avenue, New York, 10012. 5/5/77

ESCAPES FROM ACCUMULATED EARNINGS TAX

Major reasons IRS will allow cash buildup in a company without assessing tax on accumulated earnings:

The possibility that major installations or even complete plants will have to be scrapped and rebuilt because of strict anti-pollution laws.

The escalating amount of jury awards in product liability suits and vehicle accidents.

Cancellation of liability or other insurance by insurance companies because of excessive claims may require the corporation to become a self-insurer.

Necessary replacement of production or other business equipment because of technical obsolescence brought about by new processes.

Mounting interest rates that lead many companies to accumulate earnings so as to become independent of banks.

Impact of inflation taken into account in computing the funds necessary to meet purchase requirements.

CAUTION IN BUYING A COMPANY FOR TAX LOSS

Be wary about those ads offering to sell a corporation with no assets but a tax-loss carryforward. The Internal Revenue Service is almost certain to challenge use of the carryforward losses to shelter the buying company's earnings. And IRS will win unless there were good reasons for making the acquisition.

Examples: Could be a good business reason if the acquired company has other valuable assets (such as franchises, skilled people under contract) that the acquiring company expects to use.

Caution: If IRS thinks the purpose of the acquisition was tax avoidance, taxpayer has the *burden of proving* it was for a good business purpose.

FOR CLOSELY HELD COMPANIES

HOW IRS FAVORS CORPORATE ENEMIES OVER FRIENDS

If the company is building earnings to buy up the stock of a major shareholder, be ready to prove to the Internal Revenue Service that the purchase is for the *corporation's* benefit. Otherwise the company may be hit by the accumulated earnings tax. A case with the IRS is strongest if the shareholder is hostile, threatens the operation or attempts to sell his stock to dubious outside interests.

Case in point: IRS taxed a corporation that retained earnings to buy the stock of a shareholder who simply wanted to devote her energies to travel rather than to business. Her growing disinterest in company affairs didn't obstruct decision-making or business operations, said the IRS. The accumulation might have been justified as meeting a *corporate* purpose. *How:* If the shareholder had acted nastily by voting against good business decision or threatening legal actions.

John B. Lambert Assoc. et al. v. U.S., Ct. Cl., 11/17/76.
Source: Merwin Leven, Mamaroneck, N.Y.

SAVING CAPITAL GAINS FOR EXECUTIVE WHO SELLS STOCK BACK TO COMPANY

Closely held companies often let executives have stock under an agreement that the company will buy back its shares when they leave or retire.

The big risk: If the corporation buying back the stock is profitable, what the shareholder receives is treated as a fully taxable dividend to him.

There are very few exceptions to this rule. One is that this redemption will be regarded as a *capital gain* if the stockholder disposes of *all* of his shares. That includes stock owned by his spouse, parents, and descendants.

A variation on this rule: The president and board chairman of a corporation sold all of his stock back to the corporation and so did all his close relations. He stayed on as president and board chairman. The sale was treated as a capital gain. This ruling can be helpful where an officer wants to sell his stock but the corporation wants to capitalize on his name, and thinks it will be useful on bank loan applications or for customer relations.

Revenue Ruling 76-524.

TIME FOR A SECOND LOOK AT CORPORATE PENSION PLANS

The 1982 tax law dramatically altered the tax treatment of pension plans. *Big winners:* Self-employed individuals. *Hardest hit by the changes:* Businesses with *top-heavy plans,* where 60% of the benefits are allocated to key employees, *usually the owners themselves.* In some cases, it costs these owner-managers more to provide comparable benefits for other employees.

Potential victims: Rank-and-file em-

ployees covered by these plans, if owners decide to terminate or reduce *all* benefits under the plans. *Also hard hit:*
• Key executives earning more than $90,000 and in a plan that provides for retirement benefits of $90,000 or more.
• High-income professionals who have set up generous plans for themselves.
• Individuals who need to borrow large sums from pension plans.

NEW LIMITS. Congress believes that high-income individuals had been getting excessive tax benefits from their pension plans. *To correct this perceived inequality,* the new law:
• Reduced the maximum tax-deferred contributions an individual could make to a defined-contribution plan to $30,000 (from $45,475). *Effective:* Plan years beginning after December 31, 1982.
• Cut the annual retirement benefits under a defined-benefit plan to $90,000 (from $136,425). *Effective:* Plan years beginning after December 31, 1982.
• Suspended from 1983 to 1986 any automatic cost-of-living adjustments to tax-qualified plans.
• Limited early-retirement benefits to defined-benefit plans. The age at which the maximum annual payout *must* be actuarially reduced was moved down from 62 to 55. *Effective:* Plan years beginning after December 31, 1982.

Pension benefits already earned by any individual as of the effective date of the new law were *not* reduced. Executives who were then entitled to retire with annual benefits of $136,425 did not have those benefits cut back to $90,000. But benefits already earned won't be increased, even for the cost-of-living hikes an executive or owner may have counted on.

LESS NEED TO INCORPORATE. Until now, it has been an advantage for many high-income individuals and professionals to incorporate in order to maximize the amount they could put away, tax-deferred, into a pension plan. But the new law brings self-employed taxpayers close to parity with taxpayers who have incorporated. Rethink any recent decision to incorporate simply for the pension tax benefits.

Taxpayers who have already incorporated for tax benefits should consider liquidating the corporation. The new law lessens some of the adverse tax consequences of liquidation for corporations that have not acquired a lot of capital assets. *Relief is available only for 1983 and 1984.*

MORE FOR THE SELF-EMPLOYED. *The new law:*
• Doubled the maximum contribution that can be made each year tax free to a Keogh plan. *Current limit:* 15% of earned income, not exceeding $15,000. *Limit effective in 1984:* 20% of earned income, not exceeding $30,000. *Result:* The maximum annual Keogh plan contribution equals the maximum corporate contribution in 1984.
• *Removed* many restrictions on Keogh plans. *Major change:* Effective for plan years beginning after 1983, self-employed taxpayers with Keogh plans can act as their own trustees. Prior law required a bank or savings and loan to be the trustee.

BORROWING LIMITS: Borrowing from tax-qualified retirement plans is now severely limited. *New limits:* Loans are restricted to $10,000 or half the employee's vested benefits. No loan may exceed $50,000. Loans must be repaid within 5 years unless they are used to build or rehabilitate the principal residence of an employee or a member of the employee's family.

Borrowing in excess of the new limits is treated as taxable income to the employee, even if the loans do not come due until several years from now.

Employees who have above-the-limit loans coming due soon that they cannot repay and must refinance with the pension fund have some protection, too. If they pay off the refinanced loan entirely before August 14, 1983, they won't be taxed on the excess.

BIGGER PENSIONS FOR OLDER INSIDERS IN CLOSELY HELD CORPORATIONS

A provision in ERISA (the 1974 pension law) makes it possible for a small, closely held corporation to provide its older insiders, in a relatively short time, with pension benefits substantially larger than their compensation—and with the cost fully deductible by the corporation.

Example: A Mr. Smith, having elected early retirement from a major corporation, starts up his own consulting corporation. He brings his wife into the business as an assistant and has two part-time employees to help her with various chores. He puts his wife on the books for $6,000 a year, although she's worth more. Even though he considers increasing her pay, he has prudent misgivings, because her earnings will only add to the taxable income on

their joint return.

Taking advantage of ERISA, Smith sets up a defined-benefit pension plan (where benefit payout is fixed) for his corporation. Under the so-called *de minimis* provision of ERISA, he can set his wife's defined benefit upon retirement at $10,000 a year—$4,000 more than her annual salary. She's able to escape the benefit limit of 100% of her annual salary because her salary is under $10,000.

To establish the $10,000 benefit, he must show actuarially what it would cost to provide her with a straight-life annuity of $10,000 a year at age 65. That's easy. All he has to do is ask a life insurance company how much such a policy could cost. *Answer:* $140,000 lump sum. Thus, if you figure an 8% annual interest, compounded, it works out that he must put away $10,000 a year for the 10 years—or a total of $100,000.

What we've done is provide her a benefit worth $140,000, with $100,000 in tax-deductible dollars.

Another plus: If those dollars had been paid to Mrs. Smith as straight compensation (and assuming that Mr. and Mrs. Smith filed joint returns and were in the 50% tax bracket), she would have paid out $50,000 in taxes over the 10 years of employment by the corporation. And that means she'd end up with only $50,000 after 10 years of working—plus any interest.

But by having Mrs. Smith elect a lump-sum distribution of the $140,000 in the pension fund at age 65, tax computed under the special 10-year averaging formula of ERISA would be $32,100, leaving her with $107,900.

Don't fail to investigate annuities. The savings from them could be sizable in the right situation.

179

BUYING OUT MINORITY SHAREHOLDERS

Majority shareholders, in buying out minority shareholders, have a duty to disclose to the minority all material facts they know which would affect the minority's decision to sell right down to the time there's a binding sale.

How the law works: Majority shareholders proposed an agreement to buy the shares of the minority and they conditioned it upon *all* shareholders signing up. The duty of disclosure continued until the last one signed. The majority were under a duty to disclose any negotiations they were conducting leading to a possible merger or acquisition. Their failure to do so gave *all* the minority shareholders a right to recover damages in the amount of the difference between what they'd been paid for their shares and what they would have received if the majority shareholders had made proper disclosures.

Goodman v. Poland, U.S.D.C., Md., CCH Fed. Sec. L.R. ¶ 95, 293.

ONE WAY TO SQUEEZE OUT MINORITY SHAREHOLDERS

There are all sorts of ways majority shareholders may squeeze out minority shareholders. Here's one that's fast and easy—and legal in several states: *The cash merger technique.*

Delaware, for example, permits a parent corporation to merge with another corporation, 90% of whose shares are owned by the parent, simply by filing a certificate of merger, along with a copy of the resolution of the board of directors of the parent. The resolution may provide that the minority shareholders are to get cash for their shares in the subsidiary. In effect, the minority is forced to sell.

A Delaware corporation which did just that was challenged by the minority shareholders of the subsidiary. They claimed that the corporation's failure to notify them in advance of the merger constituted a violation of SEC Rule 10b-5, which makes it unlawful to fail to disclose a materal fact in connection with the purchase or sale of securities. But the court rejected the claim of the minority.

Comment: This may be an effective way of squeezing out minority interests in states where favorable statutes exist *even where there is no existing parent-subsidiary relationship.*

What the majority shareholders must do in such a case is create a new corporation, transfer all their shares in the old corporation to the new one in exchange for its shares, and then have the new corporation effect a merger with the old, paying off the minority shareholders in cash. It's an approach that will require your counsel's careful study before implementation.

ESOPs CAN BENEFIT OWNERS

Employee stock ownership plans (ESOPs) have been attracting a lot of attention as a means of corporate financing. *The essence:* A firm sets up a plan, which borrows money from a bank on a note guaranteed by the corporation. The plan uses this to buy stock from the corporation. The corporation makes contributions annually in cash or stock to the plan, for which it gets tax deductions. The contributions are used to pay off the bank loan. In effect, the corporation raises capital with tax deductible dollars.

The ESOP can be used as a personal financial planning tool for the shareholder-owners of a close corporation who are otherwise locked into the corporation.

If the corporation redeems part of their shares in an ordinary way, they're almost certain to be taxed at ordinary income rates. And that transaction will be treated as a dividend distribution (which the corporation pays taxes on) rather than a sale or exchange taxable at capital gains rates.

The corporation itself faces a major problem on redemptions. It must accumulate the necessary funds. They can be accumulated only out of after-tax dollars.

By interposing an ESOP, the picture changes dramatically. The shareholders have a market for their shares —the ESOP. The plan buys their shares with deductible contributions made with pretax dollars.

What's more, the shareholder isn't taxed at ordinary income rates, but at capital-gains rates on the sale to the ESOP. If there isn't enough money in the ESOP at the time to effect the purchase, then the plan borrows money from a bank in the procedure outlined above.

The same approach may be used by the shareholder's estate as a means of realizing cash on stock held by the estate, without getting dividend treatment.

Insurance angle: The ESOP, as an alternative to borrowing to raise cash to purchase stock from the estate, may, according to current thinking among practitioners, carry life insurance on a key shareholder. If the corporation itself were to carry such insurance to facilitate redemption, the premiums paid wouldn't be tax deductible. By interposing an ESOP, the premiums effectively become tax deductible, since they're paid by the Plan out of tax deductible dollars contributed to it by the company.

OTHER BENEFITS. The shareholder-executive will be able to participate in the plan himself and enjoy its benefits.
● His company will make tax deductible contributions to the plan.
● He won't be taxed until the benefits are made available to him.
● He'll get favorable tax treatment on lump-sum distributions through a special ten-year averaging formula.
● The payout is required to be made in company stock and he won't be taxed on the unrealized appreciation in the stock over the cost to the plan until he sells the stock.
● On a transfer of his plan benefits to his beneficiaries, other than his estate, upon his death, they won't be includible in his estate and will escape estate taxes.

CHIEF PROBLEM. Valuation of shares on a sale to the ESOP. Another is the necessary distribution of corporate information to the employee-shareholders. If corporate progress isn't to the liking of employees, expect worker dissatisfaction.

The concepts are new. But the idea is one well worth exploring.

HOW A FIRM CAN DISCOURAGE STOCK SALE TO OUTSIDERS

One problem that hovers over a closely held corporation is how to prevent shares from getting into the hands of a potentially hostile outside party. One corporate charter provided that the company could redeem at a specified price any shares that were transferred to a third party. This could be tough on a buyer. He might pay one price for the stock, only to have the corporation redeem it at a lower figure.

A number of states have adopted some version of the Uniform Commercial Code that covers such situations. The Florida statute, for instance, declares: "Unless noted conspicuously on the security, a restriction on transfer imposed by the issuer, even though otherwise lawful, is ineffective except against a person with actual knowledge of it."

One case: Court held that the corporation could redeem stock acquired by a third party, for the certificates clearly warned that the redemption price could be enforced upon buyers.

Controlling stockholders should *not* expect any estate tax benefits from tagging a low redemption price on corporation stock. Even though the IRS ordinarily may not value stock for estate tax purposes at a higher figure than its redemption price, in a recent case the IRS was permitted to value the shares of a decedent at a much higher figure that represented its true value. *Reason:* The decedent had such control of the corporation that the corporation he controlled wouldn't have been able to redeem his shares at a lower figure.

Lota Mundy estate, T.C. Memo, 1976, 12/27/76.

WHEN SHAREHOLDERS BORROW FROM THEIR CORPORATION

A shareholder may be tempted to borrow from the corporation in which he own shares. But there are two tax risks:

1. If a Revenue Agent ascertains that such loans haven't been repaid by year-end, or if interest isn't paid and the "loans" aren't covered by notes, the IRS is likely to treat the amounts as *dividends* (if the corporation has earnings and profits large enough to pay dividends).

2. In addition, such loans suggest to the Service that the corporation has retained earnings beyond the reasonable needs of the business. Lending money to a shareholder isn't regarded as a business need of the corporation. That could trigger the accumulated-earnings tax, which is imposed where earnings are retained beyond the reasonable needs of the business for the purpose of avoiding shareholder taxes on dividends.

EXECUTIVES WHO WORK FOR RELATED FIRMS SHOULD BE PAID BY EACH

If an executive works for two or more corporations controlled by the same interests, he should be paid by each of these companies.

Reason: IRS can charge each company with part of his compensation. *But if you wait till the IRS does it, you'll probably not be pleased with the result.* The Service may give most of the compensation deduction to the company which is in the lowest tax bracket, perhaps a corporation which actually is losing money. But if the parties make their own allocation at the outset, it is far less likely to be disturbed *unless it is outlandish.*

Moreover, if part of an executive's compensation is charged to each of the companies under common control, his total compensation won't be pyramided on the books of one company, where a portion of it may be disallowed as unreasonable compensation.

DOCUMENT REASONABLENESS OF AN EXECUTIVE'S SALARY—NO MATTER HOW SMALL

An executive's salary must be *reasonable* (to the IRS's satisfaction) or the Service won't allow it as a business expense—even if the payment is very small.

The case: Two real estate corporations were owned by members of a family. After the death of the head of the family, one of the sons reluctantly assumed the presidency of each corporation out of a sense of responsibility. Cash was tight, and he paid himself a salary in the low $7,000 range by one company and nothing at all by the other. He worked six days a week, kept the corporate books and records, devised sales techniques, supervised the employees, negotiated contracts—but nowhere did he document the reasonableness of his salary. To the IRS, therefore, $1,800 a year was all that could be deducted by the corporation as reasonable compensation. In a move to overturn the IRS ruling, it was noted that janitors in the community (Seattle) were getting such salaries as $7,056 a year during this period (1967-68), so the court was willing to accept the presidential salary as reasonable.

Comment: The problem in the case of corporations which pay low executive salaries is that no one imagines they will be questioned as to reasonableness. Documentation should include what the executive really did or what his opposite numbers elsewhere were being paid. Regardless of how small it is, if a deduction is worth saving, it is worth documenting in the first instance.

Parkside, Inc. et al., T.C. Memo, 1975-14, 1/27/75.

UNEXPECTED DIVIDEND

When a corporation was found to have fraudulently underreported sales,

the Internal Revenue Service was permitted by the courts to increase taxable income by the amount of the underreported sales. A 50% shareholder who had helped to set up that caper was considered to have received a taxable dividend of half that amount. *IRS reasoning:* Had the corporation reported the deliberately overlooked income, the company would have paid that in dividends to the executives.
Joan Dell, T.C. Memo. 1976-356, 11/24/76.

EXPENSES TO MAINTAIN INCOME-PRODUCING PROPERTY ARE DEDUCTIBLE

The chief executive of a closely held corporation arranged to have the most profitable operation spun off to another corporation. And he acquired all that corporation's stock.

The spin-off was termed a fraud, and two other stockholders sued the executive for a restoration to the original corporation of all of its assets and profits. A compromise was worked out.

But the IRS sought to disallow the minority shareholders' legal expenses on the ground that these persons had been trying to perfect title to particular assets, which would have made the expenditure capital.

Decision: Against the IRS. Actually, the minority shareholders were trying only to restore the value of their stock by requiring the corporation to maintain and to conserve income-pro-

ducing properties rightfully a part of its assets.

The litigation had been instituted for a business purpose, and expenses for the conservation and protection of income-producing property are fully deductible.
Brown, Jr. et al. v. U.S., D.C., E.D. Mich., 11/29/74.

SAFEGUARDING LIMITED CORPORATE LIABILITY

A prime reason for incorporating is the limited liability that it offers shareholders. But the limited liability may be lost if the shareholders don't act like persons doing business in corporate form. Then creditors may "pierce the corporate veil" and pin personal liability on the shareholders for what would otherwise be corporate debts and liabilities.

The risk is particularly acute for sole proprietorships and partnerships switching to the corporate form. They're apt to ignore the change and the requirements of corporate operation (board meetings, shareholder meetings, notice of meetings, waiver of notice, motions, resolutions, voting procedures, proxies, election of officers, fixing of compensation, etc.). They may treat the corporate treasury and checking account as their own. At the very beginning of corporate operations, they may neglect to do such simple things as notifying creditors of the change, getting new stationery, listings, and so forth.

Failure to comply with one or more of these corporate requirements won't necessarily be "fatal." Some states now have special laws for closely held corporations, permitting more informal procedures than are allowed publicly traded corporations.

To play safe, have your lawyer supply you with a list of essential "housekeeping" chores to preserve limited liability.

DOING BUSINESS IN CORPORATE FORM HAS ITS RISKS

In most instances, doing business in the corporate form has many more advantages than disadvantages. But not always.

The president and chief stockholder of a closely held corporation suffered a heart attack and had to curtail his normal business activities. The vice-president and the comptroller took over the business. Later, when the president went back to the office, he learned that the two executives had embezzled large amounts of company funds during his absence. In a scheme to cover the fact that they were looting the company, however, they didn't file corporate tax returns.

Penalties were imposed upon the company for willful failure to file its tax returns. The taxpayer argued that the omitted returns were not the result of *corporate* willfulness, but that of the two officers.

Although the president might have felt that as chief stockholder he was be-

ing doubly cheated, first by the looting of the corporation, and then by the penalties for nonfiling, the court concluded: "He chose the corporate form of doing business and therefore must accept the law as it is applied to corporations."

Janice Leather Imports, Ltd., et al. v. U.S., D.C., S.D.N.Y., 7/22/74.

TAX ADVANTAGES IN RECAPITALIZING

Most closely held corporations have only one class of stock—*common.* One reason may be that S Corporation treatment (avoiding taxation at the corporate level) can't be elected if there is more than one class of stock. But S Corporation status isn't available if you have more than 35 shareholders or if one shareholder refuses to consent to the election. Even if available, S Corporation status may not be important if the owners want to use the corporation as a form of tax shelter, taking advantage of the 15% corporate tax rate on the first $25,000 of earnings and building up retirement benefits in excess of those allowed S Corporations. Also, of course, S Corporation status is of no value if there are no corporate profits after payment of "reasonable" compensation to all of the shareholder-employees.

Sub S aside then, there are good personal and estate-planning reasons for recapitalizing a corporation so it has two or more classes of stock.

An often used form is to have the corporation issue preferred stock and distribute this to the holders of common in proportion to their holdings, a

185

step that can be taken tax-free.

Some of the things accomplished by this move:

• The preferred may be kept by the senior member of the family as a continuing source of income.

• It may be given to family members who aren't expected to be active in the business.

• The preferred remaining in the senior member's estate may be made the source of funds to pay estate taxes and administration expenses without affecting control, which remains with the common.

After the issuance of the preferred, the common is often recapitalized tax-free into two classes, one nonvoting, the other voting. *Aim:* Freezing the owner's estate by gifts of nonvoting stock, while the voting common and preferred are retained.

"Freezing" move operates in this way: Both classes of common are intended to carry future appreciation in the value of the business. Many shares of nonvoting common are issued and only a few shares of the voting common. Hence, almost all future appreciation will go to the nonvoting stock. This is then given to family members. It has little value initially because the preferred has a prior claim on earnings. However, there is little or no gift tax liability. At the same time, the gift serves to remove from the donor's estate the great bulk of future appreciation in the value of the company.

IRS doesn't like this type of planning, but so far it has had no success in attacking it and it appears unlikely that it will.

Naturally, in order to implement these ideas, competent professional help will be needed. Also, don't forget

it will be necessary to readjust wills, insurance, retirement plans, buy-sell agreements, and other plans of the principals.

TAX DANGER IN STOCK REDEMPTIONS

If a shareholder's stock is redeemed by the company which issued it at a time when the corporation had earnings and profits large enough to pay him a dividend, the IRS will, in most instances, tax the payment as a dividend. *Exception:* Where all his shares are redeemed.

It doesn't matter that close relatives still own stock, provided he agrees to inform the IRS of any reacquisition within 10 years. (If there *should* be such a reacquisition—unless he inherits stock—his redemption will retroactively be taxed as a dividend.)

What's not well known: If he does inherit the stock and subsequently joins the company as an officer, it's the act of joining the company that triggers the classification of his inherited stock as a reacquisition.

Rev. Rul. 75-2, 1/6/75.

ADROIT CASH MANAGEMENT

Managers dazzled by sophisticated cash management services being offered by banks these days, or by sweep accounts that move excess funds in

186

checking accounts into interest-bearing accounts, are often surprisingly sloppy about moving cash *within* the company.

The goals are simple for in-house float: Keep the level of cash fairly even. Increase velocity. Keep the float as thin as posssible without running out.

SIMPLE GAPS TO FILL. *Small changes can yield big results, as these companies found:*

• Booking and making deposits for a high volume of small cash receipts was such a hassle for clerks at one company that they decided it was "more efficient" to hold the cash in a drawer all week and do the job only on Fridays. A new manager astutely determined that prompt deposits would earn the company far more money than the minor savings in clerical efficiency.

• One office had a regular late mail delivery at 4 PM each day. But it also hired a lot of part-time clerks who worked until only 3 PM. *Past practice:* Checks that arrived in the late mail were held until the next day. *Now:* Several clerks work until 5 PM, and the checks in the late mail are credited to the company's account on the same day they arrive.

• A service company billed clients from its New York headquarters. *Past practice:* Time sheets from professionals in its West Coast office were mailed to New York for billing each day. *Now:* The company sends its time sheets to New York by *overnight delivery service.* Both billing and collecting are substantially speeded up, which saves far more than the additional cost of an overnight delivery.

SETTING PRIORITIES. Basic guidelines for companies with a high volume of small incoming cash items: If cash comes to a single office, make sure that work is organized to credit it to the company *that day.* If cash comes into several locations around the country, work closely with banks to concentrate the cash as quickly as possible. (This is an area in which banks are now actively competing for business.)

Within the company, the managers' priorities are to develop:

• Good cash receipt operations. Quickly identify incoming cash. The information should move swiftly to the department that applies the cash to customer accounts, and the cash should be deposited in the bank immediately.

• Efficient credit and collection.

The priorities for companies that sell fewer high-priced items are simple. They should identify accurately when big checks are due and spend money, if necessary, to speed delivery of the check. It pays some companies to send an employee or a courier service to pick up a large out-of-town check on the day it is ready. And it always pays to walk the check to the bank for deposit.

THE PRICE OF SUCCESS. The biggest in-house float problems surface, ironically enough, when a fast-growing company reaps a high volume of orders from a successful promotion. That is the time when control of incoming cash and order tends to break down—as does the cash-flow situation. Be sure to put money and management time into *controls* at this time. It may seem less exciting than spending resources on sales or production, but the payoff is tremendous.

Source: William Renshaw, cash management specialist, Arthur Young & Co., 277 Park Avenue, New York 10172.

HOW TO INSURE PREFERENTIAL RETURN-OF-CAPITAL TAX TREATMENT

Distributions by a corporation to its shareholders at a time when there are earnings and profits large enough to pay a dividend are taxed as ordinary income, with only a few clearly stated exceptions. One of these is a distribution in partial liquidation of the corporation, such as when it has narrowed its business activities or property holdings and then distributes, as a return of capital, the funds no longer needed in the business.

The case: A corporation discontinued and sold one of its facilities. But in that same year, the corporation spent a far greater amount to purchase other facilities of the same general nature. Thus the business wasn't really contracting, and what the shareholders received wasn't regarded by the IRS or the courts as a return of part of their investment.

Mains et al. v. U.S., 6th Cir., 1/13/75.

HOW ONE OF THE LARGEST PRIVATELY HELD COMPANIES IS RUN

I* don't put too much faith in long-range planning. The simple fact is, there are too many unknowns and un-

*Jervis B. Webb, president and chairman, Jervis B. Webb Co., Detroit.

expecteds in life. And those factors often have a greater impact on future business than the events which can be expected—and thus planned for.

Now that's not to say we don't plan; we do, and we do it very carefully. (Half jokingly, I call it *hindsight planning.*) We also try to stay flexible and keep the planning flexible, so we can shift and adjust quickly as events take shape. What I find is that plans made for one reason often work out—but for an entirely different reason.

BUSINESS RATIOS. This whole field of business ratios (direct vs. indirect labor, debts vs. equity, etc.) is much more complex than most executives think. The important point is, ratios aren't valid for *all time.* They have a place and time when they are valid. In too many cases, myths have been built around them. An example from our business:

We try to sell sophisticated materials-handling equipment, we point out that *direct* labor on an assembly line may get cut by, say, six people. But we may also tell them that now they must add two people to maintain the equipment. Those people are not charged as *direct* labor; they are *indirect* labor. A typical manager reacts quickly to that news: *Can't do,* he says. *That will hoist a warning flag to top management. It'll signal that indirect costs are now out of line with the established ratios.*

It makes no difference that the net reduction is four people; all they see is the out-of-line ratio on *indirect* costs.

Sounds silly? It is. Yet that type of thing comes up repeatedly.

COST ANALYSIS. We take a very close look at many manufacturing operations, for both big and small companies. We have to. That's the way we bid on materials-handling contracts. And what we see over and over again is: Most managers *don't* have a good fix on their costs. That holds true with large and small firms.

That cost analysis should be done by the auditing accountants. We'd certainly never just bring in an outside consultant to do a job like that. It requires close working knowledge of the operation.

Better yet: If you can spare their time, I'd opt for in-house accountants to run such an analysis. In the long run, it's more economical. In fact, where possible, all analysis should be done in-house. The trade-off is always time: How long would it take an expert outsider to learn your business sufficiently to give you a good analysis?

PICKING AN ACCOUNTANT. Years ago, we had a small accounting firm handling us. As we grew, so did our needs. But the accountant couldn't keep pace with our increasingly sophisticated needs. *We had a choice:* Either move to a big firm or (as it turned out) arrange to have our small accountant acquired by a big firm. The result is the same: After the company reaches some critical size, it needs some very sophisticated help. Don't get dragged down by slow-growing advisers.

My attitude is: Don't call us, we'll call you. We invite the accountants to make a presentation periodically on our special consulting-analysis needs. We hear them out and then select the things we think are important to follow through on. Often we opt to handle the special consulting-analysis in-house.

The don't-call-us tactic is important.

Unless you make your position on what you want very clear, you will find the accounting firm coming in more strongly than you anticipated.

HANDLING EXECUTIVES. *Never forget:* Managing a business is really *managing people.* Don't let all the numbers and ratios confuse that point. *It's people!* At least 95% of my time is dealing with people. I have about 25 executives who report directly to me, and they're difficult to keep track of. *My secret:* I keep a little book that lists each person and each conversation I have with them. Each entry contains just a few words—a code to remind me what was going on with that person the last time we talked.

USING TIME EFFECTIVELY. I reserve about 5% of my time to doing what I like to do: *Getting new business,* working out a bid and monitoring it. Some colleagues tell me I shouldn't "waste" my time on that. *I don't agree.* Not only do I enjoy it (and that counts for something), but it's my way of keeping tabs on what's really happening in the business. I use this interest as a check on everything and everyone at the Webb Company.

NEW FINANCING AID

A 1974 SEC rule (Rule 240) permits a company to sell up to $100,000 of its securities within a year without having to go through the arduous and costly process of SEC registration.

Conditions: The securities can't be

offered or sold through general advertising or general solicitation. No commissions may be paid for individual solicitations or sales. The company can't have more than 100 beneficial owners of shares, and the securities sold have the same status as those sold under a so-called private-offering exemption, which in practical terms means they can't be resold until they've been held for at least two years.

This makes it a lot easier for a small corporation to sell securities than to rely on the private-offering exemption provided under SEC Rule 146. There you have to show that the investor is *sophisticated, rich, or both.*

CONVERT CORPORATE PROFITS INTO CAPITAL GAINS

If you're a shareholder in a closely held (not a Sub S) corporation that has, or is likely to have, accumulated earnings and profits, there's a way you can take part of that money out at the lower capital-gains tax rate, instead of the higher dividend-income tax rate. *The technique:*

Details: make gifts of stock to spouse. All gifts are tax-free to a spouse whether made during lifetime or by will.

Next step: After the spouse has held the stock for at least 10 years, she will be able to sell it to the corporation at its fair market value. This price will reflect accumulated earnings and profits, but the gain will be taxable at capital gains rates. (Gain is the difference be-

tween the tax basis of the stock—the donor's cost—when the gift was made and its present value or selling price.)

These conditions must be satisfied:

• The spouse must sell all the stock and have no further interest in the corporation of any kind (including an interest as a director or employee) except that of a creditor.

• For the next 10 years the spouse cannot acquire any interest in the corporation except by inheritance.

The rules must be followed *exactly.* Otherwise the spouse will be taxed as though that portion of the sales proceeds attributable to earnings and profits were dividend income, taxable at a potentially higher rate.

S CORPORATIONS ARE FRAGILE

A company that has elected S Corporation status passes through profits to the shareholders, who are then responsible for the taxes. It allows losses to be deducted on a *pro rata* basis by shareholders up to the extent of their investment.

If a firm's advantageous S Corporation status is terminated for any reason, a new S Corporation election cannot be made within five years (without the very hard-to-get consent of the Commissioner of Internal Revenue). A merger, among other things, automatically terminates the unique tax status of S Corporations.

Recent case: Two years after such a merger, shareholders became disenchanted and undid it with a tax-free reorganization that split the company into two independent corporations once again. A new S Corporation election was submitted to the IRS—and it was *denied.* The Commissioner ruled that the corporation relinquished favorable tax treatment when a merger seemed more desirable. It had to wait the usual five years before making another election.

In another case, stockholders of a company with losses decided to elect S Corporation status so they could deduct their proportionate parts of the loss on their individual tax returns. The corporate secretary reminded one stockholder that he was a member of a *partnership* which owned the company shares. But shares of an S Corporation can be owned *only* by individuals, decedents' estates, bankruptcy estates, and certain kinds of trusts.

The secretary was instructed to reissue the partnership shares in the names of the partners, but failed to do so. *Result:* Loss of S Corporation status.

S Corporation status can also be terminated if a corporation receives more than 20 percent of its gross receipts from *rent* or other *passive income* during a taxable year. *Key question:* What constitutes passive income? A company leased cars and trucks for a fixed rental. The rental rate was not directly related to normal purchase price. The company provided services that included: Routine repairs, installation of special equipment, credit cards to purchase gasoline (which was billed to the corporation and then rebilled to the lessee).

Ruling: S Corporation status continued. The rental income not regarded as passive.

The deduction taken by a shareholder in an S Corporation cannot exceed the sum of his *adjusted basis for his stock* (which usually means what he paid for it) plus the adjusted basis of any indebtedness of the corporation to him.

A shareholder tried to add to his deduction the amount of the corporation's indebtedness he personally had guaranteed. *Court ruling:* Corporate debt which he had guaranteed was not indebtedness *to him.* But if the company defaults, and *he* has to repay the loan, the payment is deductible.

HIRING, PROMOTING & FIRING

HIRING

HOW TO DEAL WITH RECRUITERS

If a company doesn't do regular work with a recruiter in a *special* field, it should seek advice from larger companies in the field. (Include customers or suppliers.) Ask for at least two or three search firms the source has had good experiences with.

Interview a representative of each of the search firms being considered for the assignment. *Meet the person who will head the search effort* rather than the head of the firm or the outside contact person.

Pay careful attention to the kind of questions they ask. If you are looking for a *specialist* rather than a *generalist* to do the search, they should ask sophisticated, detailed questions.

Ask the recruiters the obvious questions: Whom they've worked for in the past, names of people as reference at other client companies, outstanding successes.

Also ask if they have had assignments from management consulting firms that are acting on behalf of corporate clients. That's usually evidence of top performance ability.

Ask about failures, and explanations of them. No firm hits every time. If recruiter claims a 100% success record, forget him.

Have the prospective recruiter describe how the firm would approach this particular assignment. A specialist firm should make every effort, even at this preliminary stage, to get into details of the job.

Inquire about their sources. Do they make use of a "kitchen cabinet"—an informal group of contacts in the particular field that can provide them with leads to the right people for the client? No firm, no matter how expert in a field, can have enough in-house knowledge to handle every assignment.

Important: The recruiter should talk about salary early in the discussions. That's an indication that the recruiter is in close touch with what's going on in the field now.

Source: Herbert Halbrecht, Halbrecht Associates, 695 Summer St., Stamford, Conn. 06901.

WAYS TO INTEREST (AND KEEP) THE MOST TALENTED PEOPLE

Problem: How to attract talented young management from outside to a closely held business.

Solution: Provide *visible* assurance of the company's ability to survive after the owner's retirement or death.

One way: A continuing program to improve the education of company's managers so they share in the problems of the chief executive, gather the knowledge and develop the expertise that will enable them to run the company after his departure.

A chief executive who keeps the operations of his family-owned business a secret only guarantees that business' inability to continue.

First rule in starting an education program: Boss should not go alone to seminars, workshops, and conferences. He should take along the top-level managers.

Benefits:

Next-generation management will be improved.

Current management gains from *team* learning experience.

Don't overlook increasing number of programs offered by concerned manufacturers or sponsored by trade and professional associations—even company suppliers.

Source: Leon A. Danco, president of University Services Institute, P.O. Box 24197, Cleveland 44124, writing in *Restaurant Business.*

NEW WARNING ON AGE DISCRIMINATION

A company can't discriminate against anyone from 40 to 70 even if the one who benefits is over 40.

NASA laid off two 62-year-old employees and later replaced them with men in their early 40s. Since the new recruits were within the protected class, management assumed no charge of age discrimination could be sustained.

The court disagreed. "A 62-year-old is entitled to protection against being replaced by a 42-year-old if the only factor is age," the court said.

Caution: Temptation to "end run" around the requirements of law will become stronger now that the upper age limit is 70.

Polstorff v. Fletcher, U.S.D.C., N. Ala. No. 76-G-0728-NE, 3/10/78.

HIRING—NOT FOREVER

When medium-size and small companies recruit managers, they too frequently lose some highly qualified candidates because they labor under an old prejudice that should be discarded: Don't hire anyone who looks as if he won't stay with the firm forever.

Tenure, by itself, shouldn't be a qualification.

What you want are quality people; even if they do move on after a few years, at the very least you've benefited during those years.

Source: J.K. Lasser & Co. Management Services, 1633 Broadway, New York 10019.

MOST COMMON REASONS APPLICANTS AREN'T HIRED

1. Left too many jobs. Job-hopping is no longer a disability, but employers are suspicious of changes without accompanying career advancement.

2. Applicant or spouse indicates reluctance to relocate if necessary.

3. Wrong personality for the employer.

4. Unrealistic salary requirements.

5. Background inadequate.

6. Poor employment record.

7. Unresponsive, uninterested or unprepared during the interview. (Being "too aggressive" is *not* a serious handicap.)

8. Handled negotiations with employer improperly.

9. Seemed to have little growth potential.

10. "Wrong" personality generally.

11. Long period of unemployment.

12. Applicant was judged to be an ineffective supervisor.

A CASE AGAINST TESTING

There are now so many legal and administrative restrictions on the use of aptitude tests that many employers are wisely concluding that they are better off without tests altogether. If one must prove "validation" and "job-relatedness" according to the exacting standards of the Equal Employment Opportunity Commission and the Labor Department, or risk charges of discrimination, the safest course is to make judgments of employability or suitability for promotion on the basis of interviews alone, or on-the-job trials.

A 1975 decision by the National Labor Relations Board reemphasizes the difficulties. After several senior employees were turned down for a promotion on the ground that they had scored badly on an aptitude test, the union asked to see all the test papers and scores of some 30 other employees who had taken the test. Management refused, asserting the confidentiality of their records. After an arbitrator ruled in favor of management, an unfair labor practice charge was filed with the NLRB. As a compromise, the company offered to turn over the test papers if the union would hire an independent, qualified psychologist to interpret them. The union refused.

NLRB's ruling: The union *had* the right to the information it sought, notwithstanding management's fear that the test's effectiveness would be wasted on future applicants who might be coached by those who saw the answers.

Detroit Edison and Utility Workers, Local 223, July 3, 1975.

QUESTIONS YOU SHOULDN'T ASK JOB APPLICANTS OR EMPLOYEES

Federal law bars *discrimination in employment and hiring practices* on the basis of race, color, religion, national origin, sex, or (within limits) age. Asking job applicants (or employees) questions along these lines is treacherous. *Best policy:* Only ask questions directly and clearly related to the job being sought. *Don't* ask questions about marital status, garnishes and arrests, persons with whom the employee or applicant lives, number and age of children, whether living quarters are owned or rented. These questions are clearly *not* job-related. Asking them may expose the employer to a charge that the applicant or employee was discriminated against because of factors expressly barred and that these unrelated questions were asked merely as a form of cover-up.

Even questions about education and criminal convictions may provoke controversy or litigation. *Examples:*

• Asking an individual applying for a job as a porter a question about his education may be viewed as reflecting prohibited discrimination.

• Questions about criminal convictions may invite charges, especially if the convictions happened a long time ago. A conviction for drunken driving at age 19 shouldn't be used to bar a family man from employment on an assembly line.

THE NEW EMPLOYEE

Probationary period for new employee is wasted by most companies. They overlook the fact that this is the time when the new person is most receptive to training. Here's what to do:

• Provide systematic orientation and follow it up. In addition to the supervisor's follow-up, a higher-level executive should check the worker within the first week to provide additional support.

Performance appraisal: Inform the employee that his work will be evaluated during the probationary period. Rate the employee's performance several times and discuss assessments with him. It can be of great mutual benefit.

• If worker on probation turns out to be a misfit, terminate without delay.

• Once an employee is hired permanently, make a point of it. Post it on the bulletin board. Have someone at a relatively high management level personally welcome him to the staff.

TOO HIGH TURNOVER OF NEW HIRES?

Signal: Company job previews are projecting an unrealistic picture of what working for the firm is like. Even a job visit won't point up long-term problems and frustrations the employees may encounter.

What to do: After the initial screening stages, give the remaining applicants for entry-level positions a *realistic* job interview, which includes important facts about the position and the company as well as typical satisfying and *dissatisfying* employee experiences (job is routine, little praise given, not much freedom to meet others, etc.).

Results reported by some companies: Candidates who wouldn't have been happy with the negative side of the job are screened out before being hired. Those who stay interested have greater job satisfaction and survival.

Caution: Technique won't be effective if applied *after* candidate has made "psychological commitment" to accept possible offer, or in field with high unemployment.

ADVICE ON HIRING MBAs

• Don't paint an unrealistic picture of the job. If you hire an MBA who expects an exciting, challenging position but finds a dull one, he'll just leave. Describe the job in a straightforward manner.

• Don't restrict yourself to hiring graduates from the big-name schools. You can find good candidates at any accredited school, and you'll save the money it costs to pay top dollar to a name school graduate.

• Don't put an MBA into an operations slot immediately. Start him on staff work.

• Don't expect an immediate return from hiring an MBA. Your real return may be 10 years away, when the MBA is in a senior position. Meanwhile, make sure that he moves up steadily in terms of challenge, responsibility, and income, or you'll lose that investment to another firm.

• Don't hire an older MBA in favor of a younger one because you think he's more likely to stay. Switching from job to job is about the same among older and younger MBAs.

Note: There's a case to be made for avoiding hiring *recent* college graduates at all. *That is:* Let them learn to work elsewhere. Their cost after three to four years of work is about where it would be if they started with your organization a comparable time ago.

HIRING OUT OF PRISON

Hiring of convicts can yield profits as well as social good.

In one survey, employers rated *skilled* ex-offenders clearly superior to nonoffenders doing the same work, in these 10 categories: ability to learn, availability, quantity of work, quality of work, industry, initiative, cooperativeness, acceptability by fellow employees and foremen, integrity, and longevity on the job.

Unskilled and *semiskilled* ex-offenders were rated superior to nonoffenders doing the same work in all but longevity.

Caution: The survey results apply only to ex-offenders who have been *prepared* to return to the working population with counseling and training.

Source: Marvin A. Jolson, College of Business and Management, University of Maryland.

MANDATORY RETIREMENT AGE

It does not force large numbers of people to stop working, as commonly thought. Only about 3% would willingly continue. *Other new retirement findings:* Poor health is a factor in nearly half of all retirements. And *early* retirement is used most often by lower-wage employees, probably because even the low retirement benefits more nearly equal their working wages.

Source: National longitudinal surveys by the Census Bureau and Ohio State University, reported in *American Demographics*, Box 68, Ithaca, NY 14850.

RAIDERS' PLOYS

Some headhunters—the unscrupulous ones—actually get company insiders to give them the names of their associates in key positions. *Two ploys:* Asking for a list of employees (engineers, financial executives), with the stated purpose of sending them a free trade-magazine subscription. Or claiming to be a researcher and asking for a list of employees to send a questionnaire to.

FLEXTIME SUCCESS STORY

A small Massachusetts metal spinning company instituted a flexible work week for its 43 employees several years ago in an effort to reduce turnover.

The system requires each employee to average 38 hours weekly over 5 weeks. The plant is open about 12 hours a day, 5½ to 6 days a week.

Results: Tardiness is almost zero—if an employee arrives "late," he simply finishes "late"—and absenteeism is rare. When a worker is out a day, he simply makes it up later. Productivity has increased by the equivalent of one additional full-time employee.

Source: Marcia Greenbaum, consultant, Boston.

PERMANENT PART-TIME CLERICAL HELP

Massachusetts Mutual Life Insurance Co. started using part-timers on a casual basis in the 1950s, found it profitable. Now the company has special "mother's hours"—9:30 a.m. to 2:30 p.m.—attracting a group that is especially stable and productive.

Advantages:
• High productivity: Many scheduled for three-fifths of a day produce a full day's work.
• Part-timers are more likely to accept difficult or unpleasant tasks with a positive attitude.
• Makes available a pool of well-trained women and minority group members to meet its equal opportunity goals for full-time positions.

Disadvantages:
• Some added administrative costs.
• Some pay and work differentials between the full- and part-timers.

MOST EFFECTIVE RECRUITING

Ask current employees for referrals.

One company had packets of special introductory cards mailed to employees' homes. A personal letter suggested that they be given to friends who would be given *special* attention at the company's employment office.

Remember: Employee making a referral should be praised and thanked, even if applicant isn't hired. Maybe a cash payment, too.

Companies that have a well-developed employee referral system report that as many as 40% of their employees are hired from this recruiting method. These employees tend to be higher quality than those who come in from advertising, employment agencies, etc. And the cost of recruiting through referrals, of course, is negligible.

REACHING AN AGREEMENT WITH AN EXECUTIVE YOU WANT TO RECRUIT

These are areas that must be discussed:

• *Chances for advancement.* This is probably the most important consideration for most executives. If you can make it clear that there is room to move up in your company, you may be able to get the person you want.

• *A desirable place to work.* A must. *Other attributes:* (1) Good financial shape. (2) Executives who have been with the company a while and enjoy it. (3) A reputation for product quality and performance. However, if the company's reputation isn't quite that good, industry executives will know that, and your company will have to come up with a better salary offer.

• *Pay.* Expect to offer at least a 20% increase over your candidate's present salary. If he'll have to move into a geographical area which has a high cost of living, you may have to offer more. Salary negotiations should be treated seriously. If you have used a search firm to find your candidate, that firm will be useful to mediate the negotiations and offer advice.

• *The complete package.* Besides salary, an executive earning more than $50,000 will probably want some type of deferred income. Other benefits for almost any executive will be bonuses, stock options, tax shelters, complete medical insurance, and (increasingly) dental insurance, a group life insurance plan, and other perquisites, like a car.

• *Title.* Your candidate will want a title which demonstrates that he has a position of authority which is, at the very least, equal to, or better than his last job.

• *Lines of authority.* He should know exactly where he stands in the organization table, who is above him, whom he will report to, whom he will supervise and receive reports from. He should meet with the people he will be dealing with and talk to them for a while during the negotiations.

• *Write it down.* After everything has been agreed to, it should be written down, in a letter or in a contract, depending on your preference. Writing it down prevents any later misunderstandings.

Source: *Executive Search,* editor: Richard R. Conarroe (Van Nostrand Reinhold Co., 135 W. 50 St., New York 10019).

BEWARE OF THESE EXECUTIVE 'TYPES'

THE USER EXECUTIVE. Will take a job offer to advance his career in his *present* company (possibly one of your competitors). He is easily discernible because his reasons for wanting the job change aren't convincing. He may claim a need for a more stimulating job, despite a recent promotion.

THE PRINCIPLED EXECUTIVE. May very well have left his former job because he simply couldn't get along with his boss. But he won't say so immediately, because that makes him look like a difficult subordinate. He won't criticize his former boss; he will talk instead about differences of policy. If further probing reveals he just didn't get along with his boss, don't downgrade him for not admitting that up front. Few will.

THE EXECUTIVE NOMAD. Has been in many companies, but never in one place long enough to accomplish anything. He doesn't like really hard work and packs his bags when pushed for results.

THE FAME-SEEKING EXECUTIVE. "Drops the names" of his many rich and well known "friends." But his record will be mediocre, since he thinks work is a bore.

THE SYCOPHANT. Will flatter and cajole you into telling him about yourself, while massaging your ego. He has little to tell about himself, since he has no talent.

THE WELL-WORN EXECUTIVE. Has been through many interviews, is relaxed, and will know about your company. He will ask specific questions about the job. He is a solid administrator, not innovative, but competent. He lacks the drive to cope with a crisis-ridden job, but would do well in a stable position.

THE SUPERSTAR EXECUTIVE. Out to be the top man. He will blow in with his attache case full of documents which he will throw out as answers to your questions. His work is his whole life, and his enthusiasm may be grating. Don't hire him unless the job will keep him constantly challenged.

Source: *Industrial Management.*

INTERVIEWING EXECUTIVES

Few in management, including personnel directors, do the interviewing job well. Some guides in candidate interviewing:

• *Job history.* Don't be satisfied with job titles. Dig deeper to learn which tasks he enjoyed the most; the least. What were his outstanding achievements? His specific frustrations? Restrain yourself from jumping from question to question. If you allow him to really think about his answers, you'll be able to see patterns emerging. And you'll find out the answers to crucial questions like: *How does he handle difficulties? Does he rationalize his failures or learn from them?*

• *Goals and aspirations.* When you ask the candidate how he views the job and himself in it—are his answers realistic? Is his ambition backed by demonstrable drive? Is he comfortable saying, "I don't know"?

• *Details of the job opening.* Don't tell the applicant all about the position he's seeking. Let him work to ferret out the details. How well he probes gives you a hint of his interest and managerial ability. The best applicants will help you articulate the job better than before. You'll end up with a clearer image of the position as a result of his questioning.

• *Work Sample.* Under ideal conditions, have the candidate do some work for you on a part-time, consulting, or one-day basis. If that's impractical, invent some problems for him to think about and then discuss with you.

AFFIRMATIVE ACTION

GEOGRAPHY

How big is the geographic area from which you recruit most of your workers? That's an important question when you have to work out a fair set of affirmative action hiring goals with the Justice Department.

Timken Co. said its program was based on availability of minority labor within 15-mile radius of its Bucyrus, Ohio, plant. Justice officials said the plan should take into account more distant Mansfield, Ohio, where 15% of population is black. *Difference:* 13 more black employees. A federal court upheld Timken. Justice appealed, but dropped its action before a decision was handed down. *What is in prospect:* the zeal to pursue cases where difference is negligible may be ebbing at Department of Justice.

'HELP WANTED' GUIDELINES

Be careful not to give an impression that you are violating Equal Employment Opportunity Commission antidiscrimination laws in your "help wanted" ads. Some advice:
• Avoid phrases like "age 25 to 35," "college student," "recent college grad-uate," "retired person," or "supplement your pension."
• If the job is at the beginning level, there is no reason why you can't say that, so long as you don't limit applicants to persons of one sex or below a certain age level. Thus, "beginner," "trainee," "1 to 3 years' experience" are permissible phrases.
• Employers want to show preference to veterans of the Vietnam War. Department of Labor, which monitors want ads, says it is of "doubtful legality" to discriminate in their favor, but it plans no action in this situation.

For a complete list of "dos and don'ts," write to the U.S. Department of Labor, Wage and Hour Division, Constitution Ave. and 14th St. NW, Washington, D.C. 20210, for its *Guidelines on Help Wanted Notices or Advertisements Under the Federal Age Discrimination in Employment Act.*

REVERSE DISCRIMINATION RULINGS KEEP BURDEN ON MANAGEMENT

Decisions by the federal courts (from the U.S. Supreme Court down) now acknowledge that the law doesn't permit discrimination against *anyone* for reasons of race or sex, not even white males. But the decisions don't ease the burden on management. *The approved solution:* Have the employer pay the victims of "seniority override" provisions of affirmative action plans.

One case: In accordance with its well-publicized affirmative action plan, AT&T "overrode" its union contract and promoted a woman to a job which, by virtue of seniority and ability, should have gone to a white male employee. He sued, and his suit was joined by the union.

The U.S. Federal Court for the District of Columbia ruled in favor of the male plaintiff. Three months later, the parties agreed to an out-of-court settlement of $7,500 for him (plus $6,000 for his attorney).

What this means to you: Some companies have been going further than absolutely necessary in their zeal to avoid claims by women and minorities. But unless the bypassed white man was the direct beneficiary of past discrimination, he too has rights that might be asserted in court or in arbitration. In deciding whether to disregard contractual obligations, therefore, management must take into account what it may cost to satisfy the claim of persons who thereby suffer losses.

RECRUITING MINORITIES

Where to find the minority executive talent your company needs to comply with equal employment opportunity rules:

Ordinary sources: Executive recruiters and the like aren't as helpful as they are with other recruiting assignments. Instead, try *non*business sources, where women, blacks, Hispanics, and other minority group members have been accumulating executive skills for some time.

Prime source: Manpower development and community action groups. *Typical:* Leader of one manpower development program manages a staff of 111 persons, a budget of $4 million. In addition to mature executive skills, you'll also find the human relations savvy and political acumen it takes to navigate the swirling tides of community sentiment.

Also look at nonprofit special service organizations for the same kind of talent. *Examples:* NAACP, YMCA, Urban League.

Despite what you've heard about inefficiency in the civil service—federal, state, city—it *is* laced with talented managers, including a disproportionately high number of women and minorities. Many have experience handling large, complex departments and enormous budgets. The military is also a rich source of personnel with technical and executive experience.

The ministry has long been a career path for talented, well-educated blacks, who are often willing to change careers.

The whole field of education is a source of minority biologists, chemists, physicists, mathematicians, as well as administrators. Furthermore, teachers are used to continuing their education and are often amenable to the training necessary to meet corporate goals and skills.

Good bet: Real estate saleswomen. Many are very capable, persuasive, aggressive, and have solid business experience.

KEEPING THE PEACE

INTERNAL ENTERTAINMENT

New idea in employee morale programs: *Half-hour company shows on audio tape*. Pack with skits, inside jokes, company songs, messages from management, training program features and inspirational readings.

One clothing store conducts them every other Saturday morning for their 5,000 employees, and they are working out productively.

EXCEPTIONS TO EQUAL PAY CAN COST YOU MONEY

Federal law calls for equal pay for men and women for essentially equal work.

But that law doesn't always apply—and it isn't always easy to apply. Violations may result in hefty back pay awards, plus a fine of up to $10,000 for each offense, and a possible jail sentence for a second offense.

In making a comparison of a job, consider the actual job functions, the skills, effort, and responsibility required. The latter is most important. Also consider the time spent and the location of the jobs.

Unequal pay may be justified based on seniority or merit systems of performance. Avoid pay differentials based on factors unrelated to job performance, such as a policy of higher pay for those who are heads of household.

Best preventive measure: Grievance procedure (covering more than unequal pay complaints) which employees have confidence in.

DANGER IN SUGGESTION BOX

File suggestions. Retain documents used to evaluate suggestions, and file those with the date of the evaluation.

Use a suggestion form that includes any rules and a place for employee's signature.

Tell an employee why his or her suggestion wasn't used, and be honest.

Don't be too quick to ask suggestions for particular problems; it may be considered as extra work.

Reason for caution: Suggestion boxes can be costly legal traps. Two employees won over $350,000 from their employer because they claimed, in court, that the company had used their suggestion without giving them proper credit for it. A booklet, *Legal Guidelines*, is available for $15 from the National Association of Suggestion Systems, 435 North Michigan Ave., Chicago 60611.

IDENTIFY THE JUNIOR MANAGER'S REAL PROBLEM

When a bright junior manager's performance isn't up to par, there's more to the problem than meets the eye. Instead of dismissing him outright (and losing your investment in recruiting and training), find out what's behind the obvious symptoms.

Some possible troubles to look for:

• He's in over his head. (Determine why—and how—the situation can be changed.)

• He's afraid (of being fired, not being promoted, not being given credit, being criticized, being moved to an unfamiliar job, etc.).

• He's overambitious. (Look for arrogance and abrasiveness.)

• He's underambitious. (Look for apathy and carelessness.)

Once you've discerned the problem, expect a defensive reaction. Be fair, firm, and tough-minded. Emphasize that he must set goals for himself. Get him additional training if necessary, and be accountable for what he decides and does. Stress the advantages and benefits of change, instead of just making threats.

OVERCOMING RELUCTANCE TO MOVE

How to get that executive you want, who isn't eager to relocate, to move:

Include the spouse in the negotiations. If your company is trying to recruit a married woman executive, chances are it would occur to you to make it easy for her spouse to relocate, also. But remember, more wives of top-notch executives now work themselves. These women have their own careers to think about. And their opinions are taken into consideration by their husbands when considering a move. More and more working couples are reluctant to leave *her* good job behind. Even a big salary increase for *him* won't make up for her lost income. Overcome her resistance by going out of your way to help her.

If he is considering your offer, meet informally with both of them, husband and wife. (*Your* wife and wives of your other executives need *not* be present. And *never* delegate the wives to "look after" her.) Find out why she is hesitant to make the move. Offer to help her find a job in her field in your city. Offer your company offices to her to to use as an operating base while she's looking for a new job.

Taking her career seriously may make the difference between getting that executive or losing him.

HOW A LARGE MANUFACTURER CLOSED A COMMUNICATIONS GAP

Norton Co. management felt that it was losing touch with the 4,000 employees in its Worcester, Mass. plant, especially the younger workers.

The problem was aggravated by:

1. Recent changes in the employee benefit program.

2. Transfer of corporate headquarters from the plant to a new facility 15 miles away. The move deprived workers and managers of contact they previously had with each other.

Solution: The company selected a group of 21 hourly and piece workers (about .5% of the personnel) and trained them as employee counselors.

Their functions: Listen to worker complaints, resolve disputes between workers and supervisors when possible, and provide employees with assistance in using company benefit programs.

Results: More effective benefit program and improved morale, as demonstrated by a reduced turnover rate.

Bonus: Employee counselors serve for a term of one year. Period serves as a training ground and as a trial for later promotion to supervisory jobs.

BASIC DECENCY TO EMPLOYEES

The following questions should be asked to be sure your company is preserving employees' self-respect, loyalty, and efficiency:

• Do employees have space where they can keep personal papers and belongings under lock and key? Are supervisors prohibited from rummaging through desks? Is listening in on phone calls permitted? Are calls for "training purposes" monitored without advising the employee?

• Are managers prohibited from asking employees to carry out immoral, unethical, or illegal orders?

• Is there a grievance committee employees can go to when confronted by such problems?

• Are employees solicited for contributions to the boss' favorite causes or charities? Are they drafted to work for organizations? Do top managers (and other employees): (1) Dare to work openly for an opposition party or candidate? (2) Participate in consumer or environmental groups concerned with problems that affect your company? (3) Is there a suspicious attitude toward such activities? Does management capitalize on the opportunity to make contacts, get feedback, or have hearings for its views on specific issues?

• Do professionals and managers who offer persistent constructive criticism of company policies or decisions find themselves passed over for promotion, ostracized, or fired for disloyalty?

It's wise to give careful consideration to dissenters' views. Otherwise the company risks eventual losses, government investigations, product recalls or adverse publicity that might result if the dissenters are right.

WHEN IT'S BETTER TO TELL THE FACTS

Employees can see through obvious lies. The rumor mill will be going, trying to figure out the facts as they really are. Here's a better way to handle it:

Explain what the problem is—exactly. Provide as many facts as possible. (The branch is being closed because its sales potential was over-estimated, or not enough good salespeople could be found, or it was a money-loser.)

Add some interpretation. Your employees want to know what the facts mean. It may not be necessary to conceal facts which one would normally be expected to conceal. If a key executive is leaving, ask if he wants the reasons known. He may, and possibly a joint statement can be issued. If cutting back in one area, ask the manager in charge what he thinks should be said. He may want more known than you expect.

Make an official announcement or public statement *without* any explanation, that is, if there are legal or other reasons for not disclosing all the facts. But brief your top executives and managers on what those facts are and what cannot be disclosed. (*Example:* If somebody is fired for alcoholism or dishonesty, it can't be let out, or there may be legal action.)

Don't make unnecessary assurances. Don't promise *no layoffs* while considering cutting back, because the promise may be broken.

BENEFITS OF RAPPORT

Improve productivity, cut absenteeism, boost plant morale, and cut accidents — simply by getting out there on the floor and establishing a rapport with the workers.

Plant managers who have confronted employee gripes and listened to what their workers have to say, have obtained these results.

A new manager turned a shoddy operation around at one plant by just being with the workers and instilling motivation and pride. He had cigarette butt cans placed around the work areas, restrooms washed, etc. He walked around the floor every morning speaking to the workers, then commenting on whatever he saw into a small tape recorder. Workers sensed a different attitude and responded. Productivity improved. Workers who do outstanding work are now recognized by the manager and by their fellow workers. And the manager is constantly pushing his superiors for quality equipment because the workers have earned it.

Knowing the workers and relating to them also pays off in other ways. Asking them about planned purchases of new equipment and new installations can save significant amounts of money. They know what the job is. When management relates to them honestly, they'll tell what will work and what won't, whether or not to spend thousands of dollars for a particular piece of equipment which management thinks necessary but the workers don't.

PROTECTION AGAINST WHISTLE-BLOWERS

To defuse employees' anger — so they won't report minor wrongdoings to government or consumer groups, establish an internal climate of free speech. Courts are less sympathetic to whistle-blowers who haven't first exhausted internal channels. Improve grievance procedures.

EMPLOYEE INTERVIEWS THAT WORK

Tension often mars the effectiveness of a manager's effort to improve an employee's job performance or attitude. What to do—and not to do—during an interview with the employee:

• Don't talk about the problem standing up. Sitting down reduces the chance of either person getting angry.

• Sit *next* to the employee, not behind a desk. Softens the confrontation.

• Don't start with an accusation. Instead, aim at winning the confidence of the employee by describing the problem that *both* have to work at solving.

• Don't start with irrelevant chit-chat, either. Your aim is to gather information by encouraging the employee to talk.

• Don't deliver a sermon. And don't make any wild promises, either. You want to influence by developing an emotional bond through honest discussion.

• Avoid prejudging the problem from your point of view alone. Consider enlisting the help of an impartial third person to keep the situation from becoming too emotionally charged.

CRITICIZING SENSITIVE PEOPLE

Before meeting with the person, decide precisely what should be said. Writing it out helps.

• Don't allow the person to use the meeting to talk about all his troubles. Some of this may be necessary, but don't let it get out of hand. Constantly bring the discussion back to the main topic, without arguing or being contentious.

• Don't get brought down to the level of the other person's emotions. Stay calm. At the conclusion of the meeting, be sure the person understands what was said. Ask him about the changes he'll make.

WHEN JOB POSTING WORKS

Job posting isn't just for factories. A good program can trim outside recruitment costs, uncover hidden skills in your work force, bolster affirmative action records. *Suggestions:*

• Post only permanent jobs.

• Post vacancies that result from *both* promotions and transfers.

• Monitor posted jobs to make sure they are real. (Supervisors sometimes invent fancy titles, higher pay scale, intending to give job to a favorite.)

• Use bulletin boards, special releases, or the company house organ.

• Require employees to have some length of service, usually six months, before they can apply for posted jobs. Seniority should determine decision between qualified employees.

• Allow employees going on vacation to apply for openings that they think might occur while they're away.

• Use application forms (and retain these forms for Equal Employment Opportunity files).

HOW TO PROMOTE

PROMOTING FROM WITHIN

Every once in a while, a blue collar worker is offered a foreman's job and turns it down. The usual reason: *He is afraid to lose the protection of his union contract.* If the new job doesn't work out for him, he doesn't want to be out in the cold.

But there are ways negotiators of union contracts can minimize the risk. One way is to permit persons promoted out of a bargaining unit to continue accumulating seniority, and to have the right to "bump" back into their old jobs, if necessary.

Unions are reluctant to give that much job security to supervisory employees.

Union-management interests can usually be compromised. Usual way: Permit the promoted worker to *retain* the seniority he had, but not accumulate more. After years of service as a foreman, a worker's unit seniority may no longer be worth much, but by that time he should be secure in his supervisory role.

No suggested contract clause will suit all needs, nor can management expect to get everything it wants. The following clause, taken from a contract at a manufacturing company, shows how these interests were satisfied in one instance:

"An employee promoted to a position in the company over which the union has no jurisdiction shall retain seniority accumulated prior to his promotion and shall continue to accumulate seniority for a period of not more than one year, provided he remains in the employ of the company. Seniority shall cease to accumulate after one year, and the employee shall then retain all seniority rights thus accumulated for as long as he remains in the employ of the company. During the first year after his transfer from the bargaining unit, the employee may assert his seniority to claim any job in the bargaining unit. After the first year, he may return to a job in the unit only if it cannot be filled by the posting and bidding procedure."

TRAPS IN PROMOTING TO LINE SUPERVISOR

Common management error: Promoting the brightest, most responsible or productive worker, engineer or technician to a first-line *supervisory* position or promoting the one who seems to get on best with his fellow employees and assuming he'll simply "grow" into the job.

Danger: He's apt to be the one who *lacks* the leadership qualities, communications and management skills needed for the job.

Worse: He may have difficulty identifying with management, or even dealing with the problems that come with newly found authority.

Recommendation: Careful selection, grooming, continuous contact and training by second-line supervisors, thorough indoctrination in management methods and objectives, and special training (company or outside courses and seminars) in areas in which he's patently inexperienced, needs to grow.

WHITE-COLLAR OVERTIME EXEMPTIONS

Job descriptions, although not required by law, are a prudent investment in time. They can protect you against heavy back-wage settlements that would be incurred if federal inspectors rule against your white-collar exemptions to overtime provisions of the wage and hour regulations.

Keep the description detailed. The best are sequential—what the employee does daily, weekly, and monthly. They should also answer specific questions, *e.g.*, is he in charge of a department, does he supervise, how often he does the same kind of work as the employees he supervises, what kind of decisions he makes.

Danger area: Employees tend to stress the important side of their jobs and omit trivial duties. Have them include all. If an *inspector* finds employee's *lesser tasks take more than 20% of his time*, you may be in for trouble.

How to manage it: Assign one person to familiarize himself with the exemption requirements and give that person final authority to determine whether an employee is exempt.

Helpful publication: *What Every Employer Should Know About the Tough New Wage and Hour Rules*, Research Institute of America, Inc., Mount Kisco, N.Y. 10549.

WHO'S EXEMPT FROM OVERTIME

A bona fide *executive, administrator, professional,* or *outside salesman* is exempt from the wages and hours provisions of federal law, which defines who can get overtime.

• *Executive:* According to Labor Department regulations, an executive is one whose primary duty is management; regularly directs two or more employees; has authority or the right to make recommendations on hiring, firing, promotions; regularly exercises discretionary powers; doesn't spend more than 20% of his time on non-executive functions, and is paid a weekly salary of not less than $155. If his salary isn't less than $250, he's an executive employee if he satisfies only the first two.

• *Administrator:* Defined in terms of doing office work directly related to management policies or general business; exercises discretion; regularly assists an owner or executive; does work requiring special training or knowledge; doesn't spend more than 20% of his time on nonadministrative work, and whose salary isn't less than $155 per week. If his salary isn't less than $250, he is an *administrative* employee if he satisfies only the first two.

• *Professional:* Goes beyond lawyer

and doctor—includes artist, musician; salary level placed at $170 per week. Again, if the salary isn't less than $250, he may still be classified as a professional if his work requires advanced knowledge, discretion, invention, imagination, or artistic talent.

● *Outside salesman:* Defined as salesman regularly and customarily engaged away from employer's place of business. No earnings level.

For further details: Department of Labor, Employment Standards Administration, Washington, D.C. 20210. Ask for publication WH 1281.

FIRING

EXIT INTERVIEWS

Learn more about problems in your company by interviewing those who quit or are fired. Find out what was wrong, why they're leaving or being forced to leave. Were they not getting enough money, or were they in the wrong job? Also, make certain that the supervisor who was responsible for someone getting fired isn't making up the reasons for the firing in order to cover up some problem. Discuss the outcome of the interview with the supervisor soon after it takes place. The supervisor can be brought in to help solve any problems that may exist.

SUPER CRITICAL EMPLOYEES

An employee's *public* downgrading or defaming of company products is a serious enough misconduct to warrant dismissal for cause, arbitrators have ruled. Such disloyalty is deemed *prima facie* evidence of intent to harm corporate economic welfare, and need not be tolerated.

SEVERANCE PAY QUESTIONS THAT CAUSE TROUBLE

Many union contracts provide for some form of lump-sum payment to employees whose jobs are permanently terminated, usually as a result of the sale or discontinuance of a business or because of technological changes. At first glance, this seems to be exclusively an *employee* benefit. But it has big advantages for management as well, because the prospect of a fat check helps maintain employee cooperation during the final months, when it is known that changes are in the offing.

There are questions about severance pay clauses that you ought to be aware of. Here are those that cause difficulties, thus need to be covered in contracts:

- Is a worker who turns down a substitute job entitled to the benefit?
- Does an employee who was eligible for early retirement on pension, and who actually accepted a pension when his job was abolished, also have the right to receive severance pay?
- Are employees who lose their jobs because of poor economic conditions eligible for severance pay just as if their jobs had been abolished due to automation or technological improvements?
- What about the worker who was on an extended leave of absence to serve as a union officer, and who probably wouldn't have returned to the shop?
- Upon the sale of a business: Are employees who accepted jobs with the purchaser and then changed their minds a few weeks later, because they didn't like the new working conditions, *still* eligible for the severance pay they would unquestionably have received if they'd refused the new jobs in the first place?
- Did one company that went out of business because it lost its lease, and another that had to close because of government condemnation proceedings, have to give severance pay? Was there merit to management's contention that the discontinuance of operations wasn't "voluntary" within the meaning of the severance-pay clauses?

Clearly, no standard will suit all companies. These six typical issues should give you an idea of matters to be clarified in advance.

Handy reference: Bulletin No. 1425-2, *Severance Pay and Layoff Benefit Plans*, published by the Bureau of Labor Statistics of the U.S. Department of Labor, Government Printing Office, Washington, D.C. Also available from regional offices of the Department of Labor.

WHEN IS A QUIT NOT A QUIT?

When an employee is insubordinate or refuses to do some work that was assigned and walks off the job in a huff, it's tempting to regard him as having quit. But what happens when the worker, now cooled off, shows up for work the next day? Can you bar him from work? The answer, most arbitrators agree, is that employees are deemed to have quit *only when they expressly say so*, and/or *when a substantial time passes* between the walkout and their reappearance.

Other circumstances where arbitrators have held that employees were wrongfully considered to have resigned:
- Tardy return from layoff or sick leave.
- Other overstayed leave.
- Filing an application for employment with another firm.
- Refusal to accept a transfer to another job within the bargaining unit.

BACK PAY COMPLICATIONS

When the National Labor Relations Board or an arbitrator finds an employee unjustly discharged, customary remedy is reinstatement with back pay. It is also customary to subtract from the employer's back-pay obligations the money the worker earned elsewhere during the period of unjust discharge.

Early in 1977, the NLRB ruled that the financial burden of the employer could be further eased by taking account of the employee's dilatory work habits. In this case, the reinstated worker had obtained other work. But he was often absent without explanation or excuse. His gross back pay was therefore computed on the basis of *what he would have earned* had he been a conscientious worker. *Note:* It's difficult to prove that the reinstated employee was dilatory.

Arbitrators have issued rulings to the same effect as the NLRB decision. In one case, no back pay was awarded, because the discharged employee had a skill that was in great demand. It made him easily employable if he had not chosen to take it easy while awaiting the outcome of arbitration.

DISCIPLINARY INTERVIEWS

It has been established in law, ever since the U.S. Supreme Court decided the Weingarten case, that an employee who is summoned to the personnel office for a discussion about some matter, and who reasonably believes that discipline may result, has the right to be represented by a union steward.

But what if the employee's steward is away (on vacation, for instance)? Does that mean management has to postpone investigation?

Here's the rule, as pronounced by the National Labor Relations Board in a case involving a Coca-Cola bottling company plant in Los Angeles: (1) If the employee asks for substitute representation, he must be given the privilege. (2) If the employee says nothing and shows up for the interview, management has no obligation to remind him of his "rights."

Supervisors aren't required to postpone investigations and interviews which common sense indicates should proceed without delay.

DO'S AND DON'TS WHEN EMPLOYEE IS CAUGHT STEALING

If an employee is caught embezzling or stealing from his company, management sometimes will let him resign and leave quietly. But if the crime isn't reported to the police, or if restitution isn't sought, the IRS will disallow the amount of the theft as a casualty loss deduction. *Reason:* There's no casualty loss if reimbursement wasn't sought and the act won't be regarded as a theft if it went unreported.

● If an employee is discharged for cause so that there should be a waiting period before he is eligible to claim unemployment insurance benefits, but the company "forgets" the incident, the employer's unemployment insurance balance with the state fund will be penalized—affecting its future unemployment insurance tax rates.

● If a corporation is obliged to drop senior employees because of poor business, but they are permitted to apply for early retirement benefits at an age below that specified in the company's pension plan, the actuarial estimates for pay-outs to retirees will be understated and the company will find that the cost of its pension plan has been underfunded, causing problems.

HANDLING PROBLEM EMPLOYEES

An employee is obviously not performing. *Here's how to handle it:*

Talk to him *specifically* about what he's not doing that he should be doing. Concentrate on one area. Try to be helpful. Ask him to suggest ways he could improve his performance.

If no improvement within six or eight weeks, set a deadline to either demonstrate improvement or be let go.

In a well-managed company, most people who aren't doing well know it. All they need is time to find another job. But in many firms, the firing comes *before* they know they aren't doing well (because they've never been told what they should be doing). They only find out after it's too late.

Source: James L. Hayes, president, American Management Associations, New York City.

DISCHARGE FOR IMPRISONMENT

When an employee is convicted of a crime and is sentenced to a term in jail, the company does not necessarily have the right, under union contracts, to fire him for that reason alone.

Bethlehem Steel by one of the country's leading arbitrators, Ralph T. Seward:

A jail sentence of 10 days or more may be a sign that an employee has defaulted in obligations to society. But it is not necessarily a sign that he has defaulted in his obligations to the company. A prolonged jail sentence raises the question of the employee's continued usefulness to the company. A jail sentence (following trial and conviction) cannot be considered 'reasonable excuse' for absence and does not settle the issue. Other things must be considered: the employee's length of service, his prior disciplinary record, and, above all, his record for dependability.

Oddly, companies that rely on strong *leave-of-absence* clauses fare better in getting discharges upheld than those that try to get rid of a worker on moral grounds.

Case: One manufacturing company in Michigan had gotten the union to agree to make leaves of absence entirely discretionary with management (barring personal discrimination). When one of its employees was sent to jail for receiving stolen goods, a leave of absence request was denied by the corporation and termination automatically followed the third day of absence.

If company's labor agreement requires that it consult with union before discharging an employee, don't assume that step can be bypassed because the employee was deserving of discharge beyond dispute.

The safe course is to suspend employee pending further consideration.

INSURANCE

BUYING BETTER

BETTER WAY TO BUY BUSINESS INSURANCE

Premiums on umbrella insurance (a policy that provides coverage over and above primary insurance) are running as much as six times and more over previous umbrella coverage cost. One risk management consultant tells how the sophisticated companies are keeping costs down:

Instead of turning several brokers loose to shop the market, ask each broker which underwriter he feels he has the most clout with. Then assign him to approach that underwriter for a bid on your company's insurance.

Background:
• If an underwriter is approached by more than one broker in your behalf, he'll want to avoid the deal. He won't know which broker to talk to and will want to avoid being in the middle of a quarrel.
• Every underwriter has favored brokers. Once an underwriter makes a quote, he won't reduce it for a favored broker even if he wants to. It just isn't done in the insurance business. That's why it's important to send each of your brokers where he can exert the greatest influence.

What to do if your own broker has already gotten quotes you think are too high: Find out where he's been and assign new brokers to additional sources.

Exception: A very sophisticated broker can go back to an underwriter and get a lower quote. He does it by changing the terms of the policy slightly. It should not have a significant effect on your coverage, but it will give the underwriter an excuse if the original broker complains: The premium is lower because the coverage is different.

Bonus: Your broker will work harder. If he thinks you won't shop around, he'll get complacent.

What about tie-ins? Some brokers won't handle umbrella insurance unless they get your other business, too. But most will. They view it as a door-opener.

Important tip: Make sure your brokers are describing your business accurately. It can make a big difference in rating and, hence, your premium. If annual cost for a policy is $25,000 or more, it often pays to go with your broker to the underwriter to make sure your operations are properly described.

Source: Bernard Salwen, partner, S.B. Ackerman Associates, New York.

GET INTO THE RIGHT RISK CATEGORY

Too many companies simply accept higher insurance premiums—not realizing that there *are* ways to get them under control. *The key:* Most insurance brokers don't really understand a client's business. It's not uncommon for the insurance company to base the premium on the firm's risk category. Such generalizations frequently aren't applicable. If the client's business is really safer, the broker doesn't know it. *Suggestions:* If the premium is sizable, go with the broker to the underwriter and explain why your company has less exposure (e.g., safety procedures). Or, brief the broker on these details so that he can handle it.

Source: Bernard Salwen.

HOW TO NEGOTIATE FOR INSURANCE

The same medical and life insurance coverage can cost your company *less* if the buyer negotiates for one or more of these advantages:

• 90-day (instead of 30-day) grace period, with payment made toward the end of the grace period.

• Insurance company discounts premium rates in advance (say 10%). Employer pays the discounted premium each month, but agrees to make up any deficit at the end of the policy year if premiums don't cover claims, reserve adjustment, other charges. (The *deficit payment* is limited to amount of discount.)

• Insurance company provides service at real cost plus a set charge for profit and overhead. (Obviously, for very large accounts only.)

• Employer self-insures major portion (90% to 95%) of anticipated medical claims. The insurance company covers claims *over* that amount.

SELF-INSURANCE

Look at self-insurance as one way to help ease your company's cash-flow problems. It may not work for all companies, but for some, the savings can be dramatic.

How it works: Typically, self-insurance is easiest to set up in the medical, disability, and death-benefit areas. That's because costs are predictable—relative to casualty coverage, for example. The most popular method is to use a 501c(9) trust fund. The title—501c(9)—refers to that section of the IRS Code which opens the door for such self-insurance trusts.

Why do it? The major advantage is dollar savings—not necessarily on *premium* dollars, although in some cases that is possible, too—but mostly through improved *cash flow. Example:* When you provide health, life, and disability benefits via an insurance company, your premiums are actually funding a reserve for eventual client payments. Each year's premium is based on past performance, and your premium represents an *advance* payment to fund that reserve. That means you lose the benefit of the appreciation of the cash in that reserve during the period it's held by the insurance company. In a small firm, with few employees, the amount isn't significant, but when you reach payrolls of several thousand people, the reserves are in the millions of dollars.

Result: Your "saving," then, is in the appreciation (hopefully) in those reserves—which also works to lower the overall premium. Under a 501c(9) trust, you may put away tax-sheltered funds and invest them (in arm's length transactions, of course) to cover eventual payouts for claims.

Don't expect major savings in other areas—such as administrative costs; there may be some, but small.

Another small saving: Most states levy an insurance premium tax. Although the rates are different from state to state, the average is 2.5% annually; under a self-insurance trust, you eliminate that tax.

Who's eligible: Any firm, but the big savings develop only when thousands of employees are involved. There's no rule of thumb for determining who will save—or how much he will save. Clearly, it requires a survey to work up those numbers. If you've got an experienced insurance department in your company, give the problem to them. They should be able to give you a fairly accurate assessment quickly. Otherwise, turn to an outside consultant. *Cost of such a service:* A few thousand dollars—no matter how large your firm.

INSURANCE ON IMPROVEMENTS

It's a familiar principle of insurance law that you can only insure property in which you hold an "insurable interest" and you can collect on the policy only to the extent of that interest. The idea is that one shouldn't have an incentive to cause damage. But what constitutes an *insurable interest?*

Example: A month-to-month tenant pays for improvements—relying on his landlord's oral, but legally unenforceable, promise to let him stay on for two years. He insures the improvements—and then there's a fire, destroying the improvements. When he goes to his insurance company, he's told, "We're only going to pay you on the basis that your only interest in the improvements is that of a month-to-month tenant."

Decision: For the *insured*. To have an insurable interest, it's enough that a person has a *reasonable expectation of benefit from the property from its continued existence.* Here he had an oral promise of a two-year lease and he should recover on that basis.

Comment: This is another instance showing it pays to formalize business arrangements—*in writing*—even when you're dealing with people whose word may be their bond.

SERVICE CONTRACTS = SELF-INSURANCE

Service contracts are a form of insurance, and insurance is usually cheaper only when there is no likelihood emergency costs will be more than your firm can manage. Be aware:

Contracts seldom cover all costs.

A service contract never guarantees better service—in fact, it limits you to one service source when an alternative may be desirable. (In some operations, service contracts are essential—usually for central air conditioning, heating, or refrigeration.)

Contract can become a complete loss if service firm collapses.

CLAIM STRATEGY

TRAPS TO AVOID WHEN FILING AN INSURANCE CLAIM

Claim-filing and the subsequent negotiations with an insurance company are filled with traps. The following are some smart ways to handle this procedure.

● *Trap 1: Failure to accurately calculate losses.* It's hard to believe, but many businesses can't accurately determine their losses—whether by damage or theft. *Reason:* They fail to maintain effective accounting and record-retention procedures to document the losses. It's not uncommon to hear of a situation where a theft loss amounted to $250,000, but the company could only substantiate $10,000 of it. It's important to plan ahead with your accountant to determine the best procedures for demonstrating what you own, should you have to make a claim.

● *Trap 2: Lack of coordination after the loss.* Following a loss, there tends to be confusion, and the staff is often working at cross purposes. Best to appoint one person (or a team if the company is large enough) to work out a coordination program ahead of time. Then let the team supervise all action stemming from the loss. Part of the team's effort will aim at business continuation. But from the insurance point of view, the team should begin immediately to count up the damage. That means calling in a competent contractor, repair service, or the like, to provide solid, accurate estimates of work. Call in this service immediately. At the same time, start an inventory. Conduct the inventory with a representative of the insurance company; it'll save time and money, since if the rep joins in the checking, you'll save the cost of a full audit.

● *Trap 3: Overstating the loss.* This is a subtle problem. If a claimant purposely overstates the loss to the point where the insurance company could question his integrity, the latter will take a hard line. Generally, if the claimant takes a fair position, the insurer will still bargain over the loss claim but will be more reasonable. The line between accuracy and overstatement is a fine one, often best left to an experienced broker or professional public adjuster.

● *Trap 4: Underestimating the loss.* This sounds like a contradiction of Trap 3, but it's not. Immediately after losses are claimed, the insurance company's adjuster will ask the client for an *estimate* of the damage—*not* an accurate, justified number. The insurer requires such a rough number before taking time to get a reliable estimate. If the adjuster reports a number that's too low and then must go back later to the insurer and restate it much higher, his credibility and yours are hurt. He looks foolish. Those hurt feelings can make future loss negotiations tricky. So tell the adjuster about any problems in coming up with an estimate. During this period, it's best to call in the company's accountants to be sure that most significant items aren't left out.

• *Trap 5: Leaving repairs and spec-writing to the insurer's contractor.* In the long run, it makes no difference to your company which contractor does the repair or rebuilding, as long as the work is done competently. But be sure to get your builder together with the insurer's contractor to work out the specifications. The insured is, indeed, entitled to have its loss repaired or replaced *in like kind and quality.*

Trap 6: Failing to consider a public adjuster. In simple loss situations, a public adjuster is probably not necessary. But if the loss is extensive and complex, it's worth considering.

Examples: (1) When you begin to feel overwhelmed by the details; (2) when your broker/agent clearly isn't competent to handle it; (3) when a large inventory is involved and your staff can't deal with it; (4) when a complex business-interruption claim is involved. Usually an adjuster charges a fee based on the amount the client collects. That's usually between 5% and 12%, depending on the extent of the work involved. The amount is negotiable. *Less common:* A fixed rate based on time and expenses. A good adjuster (and you should turn to someone you trust for this recommendation) is worth the price. (Be aware that your broker or lawyer may get a finder's fee from the adjuster.) The adjuster will bring in his own experts and will prepare the claim in detail. He knows how, and is likely to do it better for you than your own staff.

Source: Louis T. McIntyre, Jr., vice-president, Schiff Terhune International, 100 William St., New York 10038.

TAX TREATMENT OF BUSINESS-INTERRUPTION INSURANCE

A manufacturer had business-interruption insurance policies. After a couple of fires, the corporation collected more than $1 million from its insurance company. This was reported by the corporation on its tax return as capital gain, on the ground that the payments were compensation for loss of use of assets treated as capital for tax purposes.

Decision: No, said the IRS (and a federal court agreed). These payments covered *suspension of the business,* hence were a substitute for earnings. Should be treated as *ordinary income.*

The corporation had *other* policies that covered direct damage to its physical properties, so the use and occupancy insurance indemnity couldn't have been for the loss of investment in the physical assets themselves.

Comment: In the case of a fire, a corporation may consider that it has "sold" its plant or inventory to the insurance company. But that factor didn't exist here. The insurance company hadn't made a payment for assets, but for *profits* resulting from loss of earnings because normal operations had been interrupted by a fire.

Source: Marshall Foods, Inc. v. U.S., D.C., Minn., 12/2/74.

> Always read one important clause in company insurance contracts: The *force majeure* clause. Covers when parties to contract can be released from their obligations.

SETTLING CLAIMS

A technique that often brings rapid settlement of legal claims ordinarily requiring prolonged negotiations or litigation:

Called *Hi-Lo*, it was developed by an insurance company, but can be applied to other kinds of claims, too.

How it works: When negotiations are stuck on dead center, the insurance lawyer calls the claimant's lawyer and offers to guarantee the claimant a minimum payment if the claimant, in return, will guarantee the insurance company a ceiling on the claim.

Example: A claimant wants $50,000 and refuses an offer of $25,000. The company offers to guarantee the claimant a minimum of $20,000 in any ensuing action—no matter what the court rules—if the claimant will agree to accept $40,000, even if the ultimate award is greater. If the award falls between those amounts, then the actual value of the award is paid.

Very often the *Hi-Lo* offer leads to a realistic evaluation of the claim by the claimant and a settlement is reached quickly. If not, the next step is to choose a forum.

Best bet: Arbitration—it's cheaper and much quicker than a trial.

Source: John F. Robinson, vice president, Reliance Insurance Companies.

PRODUCT LIABILITY

BEATING HIGH COST OF LIABILITY INSURANCE

Premiums for liability insurance on some products grew six to tenfold in the early seventies, before leveling off. In some industries, however, it is still hard to get.

For the very large applicants, coverage (at the substantially higher rates) is usually available. Expect difficulty in getting coverage for firms with sales under $50 million. Companies in the $10-million sales range are finding certain kinds of coverage nearly impossible to get—at any price.

The insurance industry, generally, disputes the "unavailability" claim. It told a Congressional committee that, at most, only a "few hundred" firms are unable to get a product-liability coverage. Independent observers in the industry say that number is too low. But they add, more importantly, that the surge in premium prices has made coverage too expensive. Many companies simply can't afford to pay the new premiums and still remain competitive.

Example: A rule of thumb used to be that "expensive" product liability coverage would cost about 1% of sales. Now, some premiums are 10% or more of sales.

Reason for the high cost: The number and size of lawsuits against manufacturers has risen *exponentially* in the past decade. That increase has been caused by the realization, by lawyers and the public, that such suits are winnable.

Another reason: Stupidity of many businesses. *Example:* Before the consumerist movement, when relatively few product-liability suits were filed, the average company handled complaints from customers effectively. Then, when the complaints soared, over-extended customer relations departments often become downright nasty to complainers. Many, they felt, were trying to rip off the company. Some were—but many complaints were valid. In reaction to this unfriendly and uncooperative business response, consumers began to file suits and win awards in record numbers.

Fault, too, corporate reactions to sharply higher costs—and the subsequent attempts to trim costs by cutting quality on their products.

What companies are doing to get around the high premiums and lack of insurance:

• Establishing "captive" insurance companies, which are subsidiaries (typically based in Bermuda or Colorado). These insurance subsidiaries even sell coverage to other industry-related companies. Practically, only the very largest companies can start an insurance subsidiary. *Note:* The IRS frowns on these arrangements, saying that they're the equivalent of setting up a self-insurance reserve. Payments to such a reserve aren't deductible. *Solution:* Substantial business with unrelated firms.

• Forming insurance cooperatives made up of a wide assortment of companies in a single industry. Expect to see many more such cooperatives formed as the problem intensifies. Industry associations will be important in setting up those cooperatives.

• Self-insuring, or "going bare"—which, as one risk manager put it, is like playing Russian roulette. Under the Internal Revenue Service Code, a company cannot put pre-tax earnings aside to build an "insurance" fund. Such funds are *not* considered a business expense. Real premiums *to an insurance company* are business expenses and thus tax deductible.

• Buying insurance with much lower maximums—and then self-insuring the excess. (More Russian roulette.)

• Buying insurance with *huge* deductibles. The deductibles are so high that such coverage is tantamount to "going bare."

LIMITING THE RISK. Bernard Salwen, a partner of S.B. Ackerman Associates, New York risk management firm, outlines this program to deal with problems of high rates and unavailability:

• Develop a thorough quality-control program to cut potential claims.

• Provide an effective defense against potential claims—through legal means and through an intelligent consumer-relations program.

• Show the insurance firm you understand potential liabilities and are doing something concrete about them.

• Develop a "sales" program to educate the insurance broker and underwriter on the real risks your business presents. If your firm has taken important remedial steps, be sure the insurance company is aware of them. Otherwise, it'll place your firm in some standard industrial category that may indicate more potential liability than is present.

Two strategies for making *deductibles* more acceptable to the insurance company:

● *Annual aggregate deductible:* If there is the potential for many *small* claims against your company, it may be cheaper to self-insure—*in a sense.* You can do this by working out an annual aggregate deductible. *Example:* $2,500 deductible for *each* loss, with a $25,000 annual aggregate. Thus you'll be self-insuring for up to $2,500 for each claim —for a total of $25,000 in the year. You'll save on the administrative cost of dealing with the small claims, as well.

● *Disappearing deductible:* Here the deductible applies only to claims that are under, say, $2,500. Over that level, there's no deductible. Again, this is a way of economizing on the small claims.

Another idea: Don't hesitate to use an insurance company's special services. It's usually worth having their loss-prevention experts check your operation to uncover problems. It may involve added costs to eliminate dangerous conditions, but it will also reduce your liabilities—and your insurance premiums.

WORDS TO CHANGE IN PRODUCT LIABILITY INSURANCE POLICY

Consider rewriting company product-liability insurance policy so that limits apply on a "per claim" basis rather than a "per occurrence" basis.

Established insurance law reversed by a decision from the prestigious U.S. Court of Appeals in New York, which could leave manufacturers with a lot less protection than they think they have.

Basic questions: What is an "occurrence"? The court says that *a flaw in the manufacturing process* which results in delivery of defective merchandise to dozens of customers *is a single event.* Insurance company's liability for all the deliveries is limited to the "per occurrence" amount in the policy. Older legal interpretations would have called each accident stemming from the flawed product a separate occurrence. A policy with limits set on a "per claim" basis would have guaranteed the manufacturer multiple pay-offs.

Champion International v. Continental Casualty.

BUILDING THE DEFENSE

One defense against product liability lawsuits: Your salesperson's verification of how, where, when, and why your company equipment and/or supplies are being used.

Alert your sales force to:

Probe for every application the buyer has in mind. Ask which machines the customer will be using your product on. For what purpose the product will be used. Know the places in the customer's plant where the product will be performing.

Look around. See first-hand how the products are being used. The salesperson who tours the plant personally can sometimes notice a misuse of his products and head off problems.

Evaluate the "sales talk" as a company guarantee. A disappointed customer can sue over a salesperson's exaggerated promises.

Find out about the limits and stresses on your product's use. *Example:* Know how fast product will be moving, how often it will be used, how roughly it will be handled. The customer may need a higher-quality product, or a simpler one.

Ask the customer's technical experts if there is any doubt in their minds on the possible use of your product in a particular application. Don't assume the product can be used just because it sounds reasonable. Always double-check.

Correct any past misinformation that may have been given—as soon as it is revealed.

INSURANCE LIABILITY FOR EMPLOYEE VEHICLES

Check the company's insurance liability for a common weak spot—employees who occasionally use their own vehicles on company business. If one has an accident, the company can be liable. *What is needed:* Employer's nonownership liability protection. *Cheapest way:* Include the coverage in the premises operation liability policy or as a rider on the company's insurance. Or the firm can buy it separately. (*Caution:* This insurance does *not* cover employees who use their vehicles full-time for the company.)

INVESTMENT STRATEGIES

THE PSYCHOLOGY OF INVESTING

Many investors are addicted to the stock market as a form of *respectable gambling*. They crave action and must participate in active trading even during periods of market uncertainty.

A number of investors hope to achieve returns for which they don't have to work. Those who receive compensation only in direct proportion to hours worked are particularly prone to seek such income. Naturally, the busy top-level people often have the least time available for the study of the stock market.

The inability to acknowledge mistakes prevents many investors from closing out poor positions quickly (a tactic employed by market professionals). On the other hand, the temptation is strong to confirm good judgment by taking profits too quickly in strong positions that should be held longer.

Some people virtually *gamble away* inheritances because of guilt—they feel that they are financially benefiting from the death, say, of a parent. Their guilt ends only when the inherited funds are lost.

Many investors place too heavy a reliance on authority figures—either their stockbroker or a favorite investment adviser—seeking a magical "parental figure" who knows all the answers—rejecting their own ability.

Conversely, certain investors refuse to allow any input from other persons whatsoever; they insist upon their own infallibility.

Some investors base their actions on fantasy—that a stock will rise because they wish it will, disregarding adverse developments that have occurred since they made their purchase. This is form of "magical thinking" common to many personalities.

The inability to "buck the crowd" keeps large numbers of investors out of the market at market bottoms when stocks are unpopular and lures them in at market tops, when the public becomes stock market-oriented.

The solutions: Stock market investment should be treated in a purely businesslike way. Prospects should be carefully evaluated before action is taken; risk-reward ratios should be considered. It is far better to stay out of the market than to move in unless and until you've clearly established the probability of success.

DIVERSIFICATION AND SAFETY

Most stock portfolios held by individuals aren't well diversified. The average portfolio held only 4.5 dividend-paying stocks. This lack of diversification holds true for virtually all income groups. Portfolios of lower-income persons averaged 3.2 stocks, and it wasn't until an individual income of $100,000 was reached that the average number of issues held surpassed 10.

A study by Wharton professors M. E. Blume, J. Crockett, and I. Friend concluded that individuals tend to concentrate their holdings, probably taking on considerably more risk than necessary. *Also:* "In a major turndown in the stock market, a high proportion of investors will do much worse than the market."

Eight stocks are generally considered minimum needed for adequate diversification. Risk decreases significantly as a portfolio builds to eight. Thereafter, reductions of risk are more moderate.

A CONTRARY REWARDING INVESTMENT SYSTEM

Sidney R. Winters' investment bible *is* the Bible. The semiretired partner in the prestigious investment house of Lehman Brothers, New York, paraphrases lines in Ecclesiastes as his guide: "There's a time for stocks, a time for bonds, a time for both stocks and bonds—and there's a time for none of these." And he adds quickly, "That's the time when it's best to put your money in short-term government-backed securities and wait patiently for the next golden investment opportunity."

Sy Winters, who is over 70, is an unusual investor. After nearly a half century as an investment researcher, he concludes that the stock market is too often mindless, that it's frequently a waste of time trying to predict swings, and that generally the best approach is to avoid the popular investment vehicles.

The alternative, then, is to patiently wait (and that can be frustrating, he concedes) for the right moment and the right investment.

How does one find such golden moments? we asked. "Finding an unusual opportunity requires an unusual search. It's rarely to be found in the popular financial journals. You've got to get below the surface—searching through specialist publications, trade magazines. In annual reports, you've got to read footnotes (they're always more revealing than the president's letter) and 10K reports (which many companies will send to you if requested)."

Most firms have *"their time,"* Winters says. The trick is to catch the signs. *Examples:* The company with flat earnings which just had a shift in management, the firm in bankruptcy proceedings whose parts are clearly worth more than the value Wall Street has put on the stock.

Another element of Winters' investment strategy: Everything is bought to be sold. That's something retailers understand, but not many securities investors do.

"It's corny, but true: Your stock doesn't know you love it," he says. "The smart investor selects his goals (and his downside limits). When those goals are reached, he must contentedly take his profits and not wait for that one more point."

We asked Winters what he thought of such investments as mutual funds, index funds, and other efforts to diversify portfolios for safety.

"They're mostly cop-outs," he says. If an investor waits long enough, he *may re*repeat the *average* 9% annual income plus appreciation that stocks have posted over the past half century or so, averaging the bad years with the good ones. But that may take a great deal of waiting.

"The problem with such diversification," Winters says, "is that you're so often at the mercy of the mindless, swinging stock market. I would prefer having for myself more investment selection and the choice of holding it or selling it."

HAVENS FOR SHORT-TERM MONEY

Questions to consider before making a short-term investment: How long to tie the money up? When will it be needed? It makes a big difference if there's a *chance* that the money might be needed sooner than you believe now or on short notice.

Rates usually are higher the longer money is committed. It always costs something to break the commitment and get money back earlier. That cost might wipe out much of the earlier interest earned.

Some of the best investments require $100,000. But there are places to put amounts from $50,000 down to $1,000. (Less than a few thousand should stay in a bank savings account; it's not worth the trouble to move it around to earn a few dollars more in interest.)

Don't forget, interest rates mentioned here are always *annual* rates. If it's a 12% rate, that means 12% for one year, 6% for six months, and 1% for 30 days.)

SAFEST U.S. TREASURY BILLS. The U.S. Treasury sells three-month and six-month bills (short-term bonds) directly to investors. A new batch of several billion dollars' worth is sold every Monday. Interest earned on those investments is exempt from state and city income taxes.

Disadvantages: The minimum purchase is $10,000 and $5,000 multiples above that. There is no way to cash in before maturity without incurring a penalty.

Advantage: Bills are top-notch as collateral.

How to buy them: Treasury bills are auctioned every Monday by New York Federal Reserve Bank. To avoid fees charged by banks or brokers (rates vary), handle transaction in person at any Federal Reserve Bank (in 37 cities), in person or by mail at Federal Reserve Bank of New York, Securities Department, 33 Liberty St., New York 10045, 212-791-5823.

ALMOST AS SAFE. FINANCE COMPANY COMMERCIAL PAPER. Blue-chip finance companies sell short-term notes called commercial paper. No brokers involved, no fees.

The biggest companies: GM Acceptance, GE Credit, Ford Credit, CIT, Commercial Credit, Sears Roebuck Acceptance.

Most will take money for any period from three to 270 days or a year, including any odd numbers of days. Rates are changed frequently and vary from company to company. Usually they run ¼% to ½% higher than Treasury bills. Sometimes they pay more for 30 days than Treasury does for 90 days.

Disadvantages: Minimum purchase is $25,000 for some companies, $50,000 for others. Can't cash in before maturity. *Slightly more risk:* Blue chips, yes, but still private companies, not the government.

To find rates: Look under the heading "Money Rates" in *The Wall Street Journal.*

How to buy: To avoid bank or brokerage fees (which are negotiable, though), you should deal directly with the finance company. Some require $50,000 minimum, but the following will take $25,000, provided it's for 30 days or more:

- CIT, 650 Madison Ave., New York 10022 (212-572-6500).
- Commercial Credit, 301 North Charles St., Baltimore 21202 (301-332-3850).
- Ford Motor Credit, American Rd., Dearborn, Mich. 48121 (313-322-3000).
- General Electric Credit, 570 Lexington Ave., New York 10022 (212-750-2000).
- General Motors Acceptance, 767 Fifth Ave., New York 10022 (212-486-5000).

IMMEDIATE LIQUIDITY UNDER $10,000. MONEY MARKET MUTUAL FUNDS. Some mutual funds specialize in short-term investing. They buy mostly commercial paper and bank certificates of deposit; few investors can buy that paper of bank certificates directly because it takes at least $100,000. Minimum investment in the mutual funds, though, is as little as $1,000. No sales or cash-in charges, but they do have expenses and management fees, which run about 0.75%. (If they earn 10¼% on their money, investors get about 9½%.) Net yield to investors after expenses often works out about the same as Treasury bills.

Money market funds credit interest every day. And they offer *instant cash-in privilege.* Will even wire funds to your bank within an hour. (One corporation puts money in every Friday,

takes it out every Tuesday.)

Special advantage: Most funds offer *redemption by check.* Withdraw money by writing an ordinary check (usually not less than $500) on the fund's bank account. Collect daily interest until the check clears *their* bank. A few days of extra interest are earned on the float.

Disadvantage: Some risk. But since most funds hold obligations maturing in 60 days or less, the asset value can't drop much. But when short-term interest rates take a sudden jump, as they did in early 1980, asset value can drop. (And, of course, it can go up, too.)

Tax-exempt bond funds are dangerous. The funds buy medium- and long-term bonds. A fund's value could drop *sharply* in a bad bond market. They may be okay for long-term investing, but they are dangerous for the short term.

Which funds to buy: If money now is in a mutual fund or stocks, the easiest move is switching to money market fund of the same mutual fund group. Investment minimums vary from fund to fund (might be $1,000, $2,500, or $5,000).

Brokers aren't very helpful on these no-load funds.

For a free list of addresses of all mutual funds: Investment Company Institute, 1775 K St., N.W., Washington DC.

CONTRARY THINKING

Good rule of thumb in any investment planning: Don't trust the conventional wisdom. In fact, in some situations the prudent investor should do just the opposite of what the conventional wisdom indicates.

Example: When a significantly large majority of investors, financial publications, and advisers turn bullish, it's probably time to sell. *Reason:* By that time, prices have been bid up to about their top. Conversely, when most people turn bearish, it's time to buy because prices have probably ebbed.

Clue: When *Time* or *Newsweek* publishes a story on the bullish market, that is clearly a signal to turn bearish (and vice versa).

The real trick in investing is knowing when to get out and when to get back in. If you do the "right" things — remain diversified, etc. — you'd still do no better than about 90% a year over the long term, and that is because doing the right thing according to the conventional wisdom is essentially staying in the market. Some mutual funds think they're out of the market when only 10% of their funds are in cash.

INVESTMENT VEHICLES. I'd rate bank trust accounts at the bottom. *Their two drawbacks:* They almost always stay in stocks, and they move too slowly, missing good buys and holding bad ones.

Better: No-load mutual funds. They, too, fall into the fully invested trap, but many are flexible and follow the swings. They tend to do better than bank trust.

Better yet: Use mutuals as your investment base, but don't be afraid to sell out when you feel a turn coming and move into cash. By selling out, all you've lost is opportunity — no real dollars. That is important

DEALING WITH A BROKER. Don't believe it when people tell you that you can't bargain with a broker over his commission. You may not be able to

bargain with the giant firms, but medium and small firms are going to be flexible. If you're talking about a trade in the $5,000 range and don't seek special research or any "hand holding," the discount on the commission could be 30%.

Source: Dr. Martin Zweig, editor, *The Zweig Forecast*, investment advisory service.

WHAT MAKES "THE DOW" TICK

The Dow Industrials Average is computed by adding the prices of the 30 stocks that comprise the average and dividing the total by 1.443 (the divisor). The divisor, published every Monday in the Wall St. Journal, changes periodically to reflect stock splits.

As a result of this method of computation, the higher-priced issues in the Dow contribute more to the average than do lower-priced ones. For example, at a recent closing, Westinghouse, one of the lower-priced components at a price of $21\frac{3}{8}$, contributed only about 14.7 points to the Dow when it stood at approximately 1115. If Westinghouse, one of the country's largest corporations, went bankrupt, the Dow would lose only 14.7 points ($21\frac{3}{8}$ divided by 1.443). IBM, one of the highest-priced components, at a price of $103\frac{1}{4}$, contributed by itself 71.5 points to the Dow Industrials ($103\frac{1}{4}$ divided by 1.443).

Were each of the 30 components of the Dow to gain 8 points on average, or 240 points in total, the Dow would rise by approximately 165 points (240 divided by 1.443). If each component lost 8 points, the Dow would go down by 150 points. Of course, this is unlikely, since the higher-priced issues are more likely to show wider fluctuation than the lower-priced issues, on a point-change basis.

A DECEPTIVELY RISING DOW. Very frequently, bull markets end with the Dow rising to new heights, but investors don't make that profit. Such situations come about when one or two influential issues (like DuPont and Kodak) rise to new highs, pulling up the averages significantly because of their weight. However, the rest of the list is faltering, but their troubles are buried in the computation of the Dow Industrials Average. *Result:* A deceptive rise in the Dow, luring in investors, although the bulk of the market is either standing still or falling.

Remedy: Track either the Advance-Decline Line, which shows how many issues on the New York Stock Exchange are actually rising and falling, or check on how many components of the Dow Industrials Average are actually contributing to its rise. The Advance-Decline Line figures are published daily in *The Wall Street Journal.* (A convenient place to review a majority of the Dow components in one place is the American, PBW, or CBOE options listing in the *Journal.*)

Components of the Dow Industrials Average: Allied Corp., Alcoa, American Brands, American Can, American Express, American Telephone, Bethlehem Steel, DuPont, Eastman Kodak, Exxon, General Electric, General Foods, General Motors, Goodyear, IBM, INCO, International Harvester, International Paper, Merck, Minnesota Mining, Owens-Illinois, Procter & Gamble, Sears, Standard Oil (California), Texaco, Union Carbide, U.S. Steel, United Technologies, Westinghouse, Woolworth.

HOW TO BUY STOCK IN AN UP MARKET

Some thoughts on how to approach the timing of stock purchases during an *up* market:

Basic rule (expressed in *exaggerated* form here): There is never a second chance to buy a good stock. However, if the stock is genuinely strong, any downward correction is usually minor, so the longer you wait the more you'll pay. Don't be too concerned about getting in at the lowest price. If it's a good stock (and a steady rise in price confirms that), it will probably be good even if you have to pay a bit more by not jumping in.

How to handle that dilemma of either waiting for a correction or chasing it up:

Consider that a stock has gotten "too far away" if it has already advanced three days in a row or gained 15% in price or both. You should have acted *before* the rise. But if you missed that point, wait.

How long to wait: Since the *normal* retracement is about 50% of the rally (if the stock has gone from 25 to 30, a 50% retracement of that 5-point gain would mean back to about 27⅔). Then "shade" that upward, not only to the next higher round number (in this case 28), but also tack on a small fraction to be first in line ahead of those who more typically use the round number as a convenient place to enter orders. In this example, putting in a limited price order to buy at 28¼ and then waiting to see if the order is executed during the next correction is a sensible approach.

Finally, though, not to miss a stock that is really wanted (one that didn't dip back to the buy-order level), it makes sense to jump on it the moment the stock shoots up past 30 (*its prior high point*) because that usually means the stock you're interested in is on its way again.

WHEN TO SELL A STOCK

It's very difficult to know when to sell a stock. Very little research has been done on the subject, and advice from brokers is usually vague and confusing. *Typical comments:* "Let's watch it one more day." "Can't sell it now, but you should get out on the next rally." "It's not doing well right now, but it's sure to come back over the long haul." If the stock you've bought has gone up, the two conflicting cliches on Wall Street are: "Can't get hurt taking a profit" vs. "Let your profits run."

What to do instead: When it comes to evaluating an individual stock, you should look for one thing—failure. It sounds austere, but what to look for is very specific: A stock that tries to rally and fails to make a new high.

How to identify failure: The stock must sell *below* the price level at which it had held in a previous correction. If you were to look at this sequence visually, on a stock chart, you would see a series of lower highs and lower lows. That type of action establishes failure. It defines the stock's trend as down, not up.

Sell! Put aside all hopes that the stock will stabilize or rally wildly or that it will come back if you hold it long enough. The market is telling you, in no uncertain terms, that something is wrong. You don't have to know what or why. That information frequently doesn't come out until the stock has tumbled a very long distance down. You've made an objective decision. Stick with it.

Source: Justin Mamis, former official in the Floor Department of the New York Stock Exchange, and former editor of *The Professional Tape Reader.*

MARKET PERFORMANCE ON ANY GIVEN DAY GOOD CLUE TO NEXT DAY'S PERFORMANCE

The performance of the stock market on any given day provides an excellent clue to the likelihood that the market will rise or fall on the day following.

Generally speaking, market advances on any given day are likely to be followed by continuing market gains on the subsequent day. Market declines are likely to be followed by declines during the subsequent trading session.

According to a study published in *Stock Market Logic* (by Norman G. Fosback, The Institute for Econometric Research, Ft. Lauderdale, Fla. 33306), the probability that a rising day will be followed by another rising day is 73%. The probability that a falling day will be followed by a rising day is only 38%. About 58% of *all* trading sessions result in a rising stock market, so these disparities are significant.

INVESTMENT STRATEGIES

HIGH-VELOCITY STOCKS CAN INCREASE LEVERAGE

Many investors use either margin accounts or listed call options to increase their leverage in the stock market. Although listed call options do offer high leverage with fixed risk, they lose value with time and lose during flat market periods as premiums erode. Margined positions similarly lose value with time (via margin interest costs) and pose problems with margin calls in the event of declines. High-velocity stocks (those that rise and fall more quickly than the market as a whole) can provide effective leverage with risk-reward characteristics superior to issues of average volatility purchased on margin.

For example, consider the outcome of a $1,000 portfolio of issues of average volatility purchased on full 50% margin and held for three-year periods in rising and falling markets.

AVERAGE VOLATILITY STOCKS DURING RISING PRICES

Net Equity After 2% Commission	Net Equity, Margin Account, Average Volatility Stocks	Pct. Change
$960		
Year 1 — Market rises by 20%	$1,282	+ 28.2%
Year 2 — Market rises by 20%	$1,677	+ 67.7%
Year 3 — Market rises by 20%	$2,161	+ 116.1%

Results reflect assumed 6% interest, but not dividends or possible compounding of gains via the use of additional borrowing power generated by rising prices.

AVERAGE VOLATILITY STOCKS DURING FALLING PRICES

Net Equity After 2% Commission	Net Equity, Margin Account, Average Volatility Stocks	Pct. Change
$960		
Year 1 — Market falls by 20%	$498	− 50.2%
Year 2 — Market falls by 20%	$109	− 89.1%
Year 3 — Market falls by 20%	0	− 100.0%

When you are on 50% margin, a cumulative decline of 50% completely wipes out your starting equity.

By comparison, a portfolio of issues that moves twice as rapidly as the average stock performs better during both rising and falling markets.

HIGH VOLATILITY STOCKS DURING RISING PRICES

Net Equity After 2% Commission	Net Equity, Cash Account— Stocks that Move Twice as Fast as Average	Pct. Change
$980		
Year 1 — Market rises by 20%	$1,372	+ 37.2%
Year 2 — Market rises by 20%	$1,921	+ 92.1%
Year 3 — Market rises by 20%	$2,689	+ 268.9%

Dividends not included.

HIGH VOLATILITY STOCKS DURING FALLING PRICES

Net Equity After 2% Commission	Net Equity, Cash Account— Stocks that Move Twice as Fast as Average	Pct. Change
$980		
Year 1 — Market falls by 20%	$588	− 41.2%
Year 2 — Market falls by 20%	$352	− 64.8%
Year 3 — Market falls by 20%	$212	− 78.8%

Dividends not included.

How to select high-velocity stocks: There are many services that provide rankings of the volatility of different listed and unlisted issues. However, as a general rule, lower-priced stocks will rise and fall by greater percentages than will higher-priced securities. Therefore, aggressive traders who opt for high volatility as an alternative to margin purchases will emphasize lower-priced issues.

Source: Norman Fosback, *Stock Market Logic* (The Institute for Econometric Research, 347 N. Federal Highway, Ft. Lauderdale, Fla. 33306).

HOW TO USE PRICE/EARNINGS RATIOS

Price/earnings ratios* are deceptive. As a forecasting tool, they're mediocre at best. But considered with other information, the ratio can provide the investor with a very sophisticated way of looking at the stock market. Here are some insights using them:

Price/earnings ratios are often deceiving because they are always rela-

*The relationship between a stock's price and its earnings per share. *Example:* If a stock earns $1 per share, and sells at $10, the p/e ratio is 10.

tive. (Is 10 times earnings cheap or too dear?) In the old days, most analysts would have said that 10 was a reasonable level, but in recent bear markets, many stocks sold at three and four times earnings without attracting interest.

Earnings have an effect on price in two ways:

1. If the reported figure is *less* than widely expected on the Street, the stock can get clobbered.

2. If the reported figure is dramatically *different* compared with the year-earlier result.

It's hard to anticipate surprise negative reports; however, if the stock starts to act poorly a few days *before* a report is due, you can make an intelligent guess. *But it is possible, by paying extra attention, to spot those stocks which are likely to report a terrifically exciting earnings statement.*

Example: In the last five quarters, a company reported a deficit of 21 cents a share, a deficit of 34 cents, followed by earnings of 57 cents, 48 cents, and 40 cents. Obviously, the company not only has returned to profitability following two bad quarters, but even more important, you can be reasonably sure the next quarterly report is going to make dramatic reading when compared with that 34-cent deficit.

The basic guideline to keep in mind is that earnings of 40 cents per share compared with a *deficit* of 34 cents a share will have much more favorable impact on a stock's price than 80 cents per share compared with 78 cents.

Another thing to watch for: A stock reported an earning sequence of 27 cents, 18 cents, 30 cents, 80 cents— that big recent jump may be a clue that something exciting is happening. It's obvious that this company has done remarkably well and that its earnings have just moved dramatically to a higher plateau. The comparison of the next-quarter figure with the year-earlier one will be exciting.

Applying simple common sense to these readily available figures is an analytical job you can do. But don't stop there. Now it's time to apply the conventional price/earnings ratio concept to what you've found out. If the stock is still selling at a relatively low p/e, let's say 10 times earnings or less, and you "know" the next report is going to produce a dramatic rise, the odds are good you've spotted a stock with a fine chance to shoot up in price.

Even more important: How many such stocks there are. One or two means the list has been picked over, and the rule is: *When there isn't much to buy, don't buy anything.* But if you find dozens, then you've got a solid clue that stock prices still have a long way to go on the upside.

A child may *earn* up to $3,300 tax-free ($3,430 for 1985) and you may still claim him as a dependent if you furnish over half of the support and he is under 19 or a full-time student for at least five months during the year. (IRS rule: Wedding expenses qualify as *support*.)

Revenue Ruling 76-184.

VIRTUES OF LOW P/E MULTIPLES

Research has repeatedly shown that issues sporting favorable price-earnings multiples (current stock price divided by latest 12-month earnings) consistently outperform issues selling at high price-earnings multiples. No matter how enticing the "story," prudent investors emphasize low p/e issues in their portfolios.

Price-earnings ratios are published for all listed issues every day in the financial newspapers. The Dow Industrials Average, as an aggregate, was recently selling at a price-earnings multiple of 7.6, relatively low by historical standards. An investor's chances of "beating the market" are generally improved if he concentrates on issues selling below that multiple. That's particularly so if the corporations have achieved steady earnings growth.

WHY TO FOLLOW INSIDER STOCK TRADES

Insiders—corporate directors, officers, and very large shareholders—figure to know more regarding the impending fortunes of their corporations than the public at large. Therefore, the trading activity of insiders in shares of their own corporations may be expected to provide advance notice of the direction of movement of those shares.

Dr. Martin E. Zweig, publisher of *The Zweig Security Screen,* has conducted research into this area and has emerged with these significant findings:

• Stocks in which there has been *buying* by at least *three* insiders within a three-month period—*and no sellers*—outperform the market on upswings. They also decline less than most stocks during market downswings.

• Stocks in which there have been *three* insider *sellers* within a three-month period *but no insider buyers* rise less than the market during market advances. They decline by greater amounts during market declines. During the period of the study, "buy" stocks lagged the market by 17.0% compounded. The period studied covered the time span from June 1974 through April 1976, including two rising and two falling market periods.

Investors can secure reports of insider trading by subscribing to the *Official Summary of Insider Transactions and Holdings* (Superintendent of Documents, Government Printing Office, Washington, D.C., 20402, $61.05 per year, issued monthly). This would require the *study and tabulation of many pages of stock* transactions. This material is available, already calculated, from *The Zweig Security Screen* (747 Third Ave., New York 10017).

HOW TRADERS READ SIGNIFICANT NEWS

By the time good news is released, the stock market has usually already risen to reflect it. And by the time bad news is released, the market has already fallen. Bull markets usually end in periods of high corporate profits. Bear markets bottom out in a period of general economic gloom. But these basic rules don't *always* apply.

Timing guidelines used by professional traders:

• When stocks *stop rising* on news of improved earnings, it's time to consider *selling.*

• When stocks *stop falling* on news of declining earnings, it's a good time to consider *buying.*

- Historically, stocks hit their lows immediately after dividend cuts. Prices go up shortly after that.
- Bad political news (*e.g.*, the Arab-Israeli War of 1967, the Kennedy assasination) frequently lead to market sell-offs, which are followed by sharp rallies.
- If bad news is *unexpected* or unexpectedly bad, a sharp sell-off is likely. For example, the stock market didn't discount the effects of the Arab oil embargo in advance in 1973, and sharp declines in oil-sensitive industries resulted.

The reverse is true, too. Unexpected good news can lead to a sharp rise.

- The market will rarely rise during periods of uncertainty if a critical national issue remains unsolved. *Example:* The market couldn't rise while New York's fiscal plight was unresolved.

SIGNAL THAT A LARGE BLOCK OF STOCK IS ABOUT TO BE SOLD

Very frequently, knowledge that a large block of shares of a particular stock is up for sale can influence the decision on whether to buy or to sell those securities. For example, you might postpone or permanently avoid purchasing shares about to come under institutional liquidation. Or you might choose to sell before a competing large *sell* order becomes operative.

While mutual funds and other institutions don't "advertise" that they plan a liquidation prior to actual sale, such information, not infrequently,

manages to "leak out," and this often puts a sizable dent in the stock's price. There usually are hints available to the alert investor that a liquidation of the block is imminent.

TRADING RANGE SHRINKS. The major indication that a block is coming up for sale lies in a sudden shrinkage of the trading range of the issue in question. For example, a stock might usually demonstrate an average trading range of perhaps a full point or point and one-half between its daily high and low in a typical trading day. If, for two or three days, this trading range shrinks to, say, one-tenth to three-eighths of a point, you might anticipate a block is coming up for sale at near current market levels or below.

The shrinkage probably represents awareness on the part of knowledgeable floor and other traders that a large sell order exists and an unwillingness to bid up for the stock until the overhead supply, which is immediately forthcoming, is fully liquidated.

FORECASTING NEAR-TERM TREND OF THE STOCK MARKET FROM THE DAILY PAPER

Investors can often get a good reading of the *near-term trend* of the stock market by monitoring trading statistics carried by daily papers.

For useful information that can be gathered easily:

ADVANCE-DECLINE. To calculate the *Advance-Decline* figures for any day,

241

INVESTMENT STRATEGIES

subtract the number of issues on the New York Stock Exchange that declined from the number that advanced. This gives a reading of the *breadth* of the market. Here's how to read the results:

• When the number of *declines* outnumbers the number of *advances*, odds favor a continuing market decline, whether or not the Dow Industrials is up for the day.

• When the number of *advances* outnumbers the number of *declines*, odds favor a market advance, whether or not the Dow is up for the day.

• If both the Dow and the Advance-Decline are up, the odds are the market will *continue* to rise. If both show negative readings, odds are the market will decline. (If the Dow is up considerably but the Advance-Decline falloff is very slight, treat it as if it were a minus day.)

DOW TRANSPORTATION AVERAGE. When the *Dow Transports* acts more strongly than the Dow Industrials, expect near-term strength in the Industrials. If the Dow Transports acts more weakly than the Industrials, expect the Industrials to turn down.

MOST ACTIVE STOCK. *Here's how to interpret the Most Actives:*

• If most of the 15 *Most Active* stocks are *negative* for the day, anticipate further declines. If most are *positive*, even if the Dow Industrials has declined, anticipate an upside reversal.

• Check the quality of the components of the list. If the list is dominated on the downside by high-priced issues, expect further declines. If it is dominated by low-priced issues on the downside, expect an upside reversal — quality issues are no longer under pressure.

• If the list is dominated by the high-priced issues and the plurality of Most Actives is favorable, then expect further advances. If, however, the list is dominated on the upside by low-quality issues, anticipate a downside reversal. What is happening is low-quality speculation.

COMPARING THE AVERAGES. The Dow Industrials can be biased by gains or losses in just a few high-priced components. To offset this, compare the action of the Dow Industrials with one of the broader averages (Standard & Poor's, New York Stock Exchange Index, *Value Line*).

Hint: For every point gain or loss in the Dow Industrials, the New York Stock Exchange Index should change in a similar direction by approximately 0.06 of a point. Otherwise, the Dow is suspect.

ANTICIPATING REVERSAL AREAS. *Here is how to deal with them:*

• The market rarely rises or falls for more than three days in a row. If the market falls or advances for three days in a row, expect at least one day of reversal. (*Exception:* The most strongly trended markets.)

• If gold stocks begin to pick up strength, anticipate a downside reversal in the rest of the stock market.

• If the market either rises or falls for several sessions in a row and then churns for a session or two, moving neither up nor down by very much, anticipate a market reversal. Reversal odds are even greater if the churning takes place on heavy volume.

Source: *Granville's New Strategy of Daily Stock Market Timing for Maximum Profit* (Prentice-Hall, Englewood Cliffs, N.J. 07632).

TRACKING THE FEDERAL FUNDS RATE

Many investors monitor interest rates for federal funds (overnight interbank loans) as an indication of short-term Federal Reserve policy. They use the policy as a leading stock market indicator. *Example:* Tightening of money supplies usually depresses the stock market; loosening them usually lifts the market.

STOP-LOSS ORDERS: OPPORTUNITIES AND PITFALLS

Many investors employ "stop-loss" or "limit" orders to protect profits if an issue declines below certain levels. For example, if you own an issue which has been trading, say, within a range of 28-33, you might believe that a decline below 28 is a signal for further weakness, since a significant "support" level has been violated.

Stop-loss orders: To forestall serious loss, you may enter an open stop-loss order with your broker to sell the stock at the market should it touch 27. This order will be entered on the specialist's book. It will be executed as a *market order* should the stock decline to the 27 level. You will receive the highest bid price at the time, which may actually be lower than 27 when the order is executed. That is the hazard in placing stop-loss orders.

Limit orders are orders to sell shares at a specified price should they reach and remain salable at the specified level. Should the issue cited above decline to 27, you might prefer to place a limit order to sell at 27. This is, in effect, an order to sell at 27, *but no lower.* You are protected against selling at an artificially low market price because you do not have to accept the first available bid. But you risk the possibility that no buyers will be available at 27. And you risk the possibility that the issue may decline sharply, your shares remaining unsold.

RISKS AND REMEDIES. You may be caught in a rash of stop-loss orders. Chart followers tend to place stop-loss orders at similar points. Since orders are filled in sequence of placement, your market order may be triggered following a succession of stop-loss executions, in which case you may receive a price much lower than you anticipated.

Similarly, the issue may sell down a point or two because of stops placed at popular levels, only to sharply recover after the sell orders are disposed of. *Remedy:* Concede an extra point, and place your order roughly a point beneath estimated support levels. For example, if you anticipate a number of stop-loss orders placed at 27, place yours at 26.

Open stop-loss orders on *odd-lots* are executed *en masse* at the first trade after the attainment of the stop-loss price level. You don't have to wait on line if you place an odd-lot stop-loss order. Therefore, it may be prudent for you to place a sell-stop on 99 shares to ensure that your order isn't executed after a sequence of stop-loss executions. (This regulation may shortly be changed.)

• The Amex will not accept stop-orders on round lots. Rather than place a limit order on 100 shares, consider placing a stop-loss order on the Amex for 99 shares—the type of order that the American Stock Exchange will accept.

• Stop-loss orders may be triggered by sudden political news which will have no long-lasting effect on the stock market. For example, the stock market declined sharply following the assasination of President Kennedy and again following the onset of the 1967 Arab-Israeli War, only to immediately recover. *Remedy:* Do not leave open orders. Give clear instructions to your broker to exercise stop-loss orders with judgment or to immediately contact you should a specified price level be touched. Many traders prefer to enter stop-loss orders on a *daily* basis rather than to enter open orders which could be good until they are canceled.

GENERAL TACTICS. Stop-loss orders are meant to protect profits and/or to protect against serious loss when you open a long or a short position. (To protect a *short sale* against serious loss, you may enter a "buy stop" order to cover your short sale should the issue rise sharply. (A *buy stop* is an order to buy stock at the market should it rise to a specified price, the opposite of a *sell stop*.) Therefore, you should never initiate a position, long or short, unless you can logically place a mental stop-loss order within 10%-12% of the price paid.

For profit protection, stop-loss orders should be raised as the issue advances in price. For example, you purchase some common at 24. It rises to 33 before a normal retracement to 28,

following which it rallies once again to 33. You place a stop-loss order at 27, one point beneath the lowest level of the most recent decline. The issue then advances to, say, 37, trading for a period thereafter within a 33-37 range. You now *raise* your stop-loss level to 32, one point beneath the most recent support level. By operating in this manner, you progressively raise your stop-loss orders to protect accruing profits, remaining, meanwhile, in the situation to benefit from future price gains.

MAXIMIZING PROFITS. Eventually, of course, you will become *stopped out*, probably a few points from the high level reached by your issue. You may be able to sell at higher prices if you can identify market tops near their peaks, but for most investors that's not possible—so the use of progressive stops will maximize profits by minimizing instances in which strong issues are disposed of too rapidly.

GAMBLING ON SMALL COMPANIES

When investors in the stock of a publicly traded company realize a gain, the Internal Revenue Service gets a share of the gain; the higher the investor's tax bracket, the bigger the IRS's share. But if a loss is realized, the IRS is a partner in the loss *only* up to $3,000 per year. For long-term losses it takes $2 of loss to offset $1 of income. It takes $6,000 of long-term losses to offset the $3,000 deduction limit. The odds are against the investor.

But the tax situation would be different if you were to invest in a "small" company, that is, small in the tax sense that it qualifies under the IRS Code Sec. 1244. In such a case, the investor is able to get capital gains on appreciation. Also, if the stock loses value and the investor realizes a loss, he can deduct his losses dollar for dollar up to $50,000 per year—$100,000 per year on a joint return. That puts the *tax odds* in his favor.

He still has the investment and economic odds to contend with, however. To reduce the investment risk, some form of diversification would seem to be prudent, perhaps two or more other Sec. 1244 corporations whose prospects seem good.

SAVING ON SECONDARIES

Did you know that while you save a brokerage commission when you buy a secondary offering (acquiring either the company's stock or that of an important shareholder when the company's shares are already being traded), the registered representative frequently gets more than his normal compensation for selling those shares?

Case in point: 100 shares of a $9 stock would have earned a regular commission of $8; the secondary offering, selling at the same price (*lure:* no brokerage fees on top of it) was actually earning $18 for the broker for every 100-share lot.

The stories of reps and firms pushing secondary offerings for that reason alone are alarming.

WHAT'S A BLUE CHIP?

Blue-chip stocks are better collateral. Banks will lend 70% of the market value of blue chips. May allow only 50% on mutual fund shares.

What makes a stock blue chip:
- Its dividend has been raised at least five times in the past 12 years.
- It carries a Standard & Poor's quality ranking in the "A" category.
- It has at least 5 million shares outstanding.
- At least 80 institutional investors must hold the stock.
- There have been at least 25 years of uninterrupted dividends.
- Earnings have risen in at least seven of the last 12 years.

BAD ADVICE FROM A BROKER

Registered representatives' recommendations aren't *necessarily* legally binding on the brokerage house—so if you have a legal complaint and it turns out that a recommendation came from the rep and not the house, you may not be able to collect, unless the rep is rich. If it's the firm's recommendation and it proves ill-advised, you have a shot at two defendants, at least one of them (hopefully) having substantial assets. This gives you more leverage and a better chance of settlement and/or recovery, especially if the rep and the broker start fighting among themselves.

Indicated action: Find out the source of the recommendation; document it; nail it down.

Source: Gordon v. Burr, C.A. 2, CCH ¶94,874, 1974.

CHECK BROKER'S TIMING OF TRADE

Over 60% of all stockbrokers do the major portion of their business the last week of every month. Since this is not invariably the best time to buy or sell securities, the conclusion is almost inescapable that registered representatives churn accounts to generate commissions that will cover their draws.

If you use a broker with discretionary power—at the very least, check his timing.

INVESTMENT ADVISORY SERVICE NOT LIABLE FOR REPORT PROVEN FALSE

Investment advisory services that merely engage in statistical reporting are under no duty to investigate or verify the statistics of companies which they collect and publish as submitted to them. That's the essential thrust of a recent decision stemming from an investor's charge that Standard & Poor's and A.M. Best violated SEC rules by publishing encouraging reports about a life insurance company. The reports claimed that the insurance company

had "substantial overall margins for contingencies" which the investor charged the services had failed to investigate.

Comment: Most of us know by now that the recommendations of advisory services aren't guaranteed as to accuracy and aren't to be taken at face value without further investigation. This makes it official.

Source: National Life Insurance Co., U.S.D.C., S.D.N.Y., 1/14/75.

SAYING NO TO YOUR BROKER

The few words the average investor finds hardest to say to his broker are, "Thanks for calling, but no thanks." There are times when it is in your own best interest to be able to reject the broker's blandishments. *Some of those times:*

• When the broker's *hot tip* (or your barber's or tennis partner's) is that a certain stock is supposed to go up because of *impending good news.* Ask yourself: If the "news" is so super-special, how come you (and/or your broker) have been able to learn about it in the nick of time? Chances are by the time you hear the story, plenty of other people have, too. Often you can spot this because the stock has already been moving. That means that insiders have been buying long before you got the hot tip. After *you* buy, when the news does become "public," who'll be left to buy?

• When the market is sliding. When your broker asks, "How much lower can they go?" the temptation can be very great to try to snag a bargain. But before you do, consider: If the stock, at that price, is such a bargain, wouldn't some big mutual funds or pension funds be trying to buy up all they could? If that's the case, how come the stock has been going down? It's wildly speculative to buy a stock because it looks as if it has fallen "far enough." Don't try to guess the bottom. After all, the market is actually saying that the stock is weak. That is the fact, the knowable item.

• Don't fall for the notion that a stock is "averaging down." It's a mistake for the broker (or investor) to calculate that if he buys more "way down there," he can get out even. The flaws are obvious. The person who averages down is busy thinking of buying more just when he should be selling. And if a little rally does come along, he waits for his target price "to get out even"—so if the rally fades, he's stuck with his mathematical target.

Stock market professionals average *up*, not down. They buy stocks that are proving themselves strong, not ones that are clearly weak.

FIGURING OUT THE REAL COST OF LOAD FUNDS

Upper-income investors are now being bombarded with ads and offers for the new municipal bond funds. Sales charges (the "load") on some muni-funds are as high as 4.5% of the offering price. This works out to be 5.0% of the sum *actually invested*. With muni-fund yields running about 10.5% recently, the sales charge is equal to nearly half a year's interest, *with no offsetting advantages*.

Any number of studies, some fairly recent, others decades old, have shown there is no relation between mutual fund performance and the selling charge. A salesman's advice rarely helps an investor to select a better-performing fund than he can select on his own. Continuing expenses are the other major cost of a fund, and there is no relationship between a low-expense ratio and a sales charge. (There *is* a relationship between expenses and fund *size*; small funds typically have a higher expense ratio.)

MONITOR MUTUAL FUNDS TO FIND THOSE BEST SUITED TO YOUR INVESTMENT OBJECTIVES

Investors willing to assume risk sometimes seek aggressive mutual funds for rapid capital appreciation during a rising market. Other investors, to maximize safety, opt for mutual funds that show the greatest resistance to decline. And still others, who prefer to remain invested at all times, try to find mutual funds that perform better than the market averages during both up and down swings.

Douglas Duke, vice president and portfolio manager of Fundpack, a mutual fund that invests in shares of other mutual funds, suggests that there are techniques useful to investors for evaluating fund performances and finding the ones that meet the investor's investment objectives.

INVESTMENT STRATEGIES

FOR AGGRESSIVE INVESTORS. Each week that the market rises, divide the closing price of the mutual fund at the end of the week by the closing level of either the Standard & Poor's 500 Stock Index or the N.Y.S.E. Index. Plot the results on a graph for comparison. If the fund is indeed stronger than the average during a rising market, it will show up clearly, indicating that it is suitable for an aggressive investor.

Since such funds also frequently decline more sharply than the averages during falling market periods, these mutuals may be suitable vehicles only for investors with an accurate sense of market timing.

FOR SAFETY-ORIENTED INVESTORS. Each week that the market declines, divide the closing price of the mutual fund at the end of the week by the closing level of one of the averages. If your fund resists the downtrend more than the average stock during a falling market, the plotted results will show the fund's line declining less than that of the average.

Such funds *may advance less* than more aggressive funds during rising market periods.

For investors who want to try to beat the averages: At the end of each week divide the price of the mutual fund (rising or falling) by the price of one of the broad market averages, and plot the results. The result will demonstrate the relative strength curve of the fund, indicating whether it is outperforming the broad market, regardless of the price trend. *Caution:* As soon as your fund's relative strength curve begins to show weakness, consider switching your holdings into a better-performing vehicle.

ONE WAY TO PURCHASE STOCKS AT A DISCOUNT

Many savvy investors look to convertible bonds as an attractive alternative to common stock. Convertibles can be exchanged for common shares in lieu of repayment of the note signified by the bonds. They generally yield more than the underlying common and provide nearly as much upside potential as the common with less risk.

One drawback to many bonds: They sell at a premium over the dollar amount of common shares into which they may be converted (conversion value) because of the higher yields.

What to look for: Situations do occur where the common provides the higher yield and/or where the bond is selling so far above par value that its yield has become relatively insignificant. As a result, the convertible bonds may be selling *below* their actual conversion value.

Investors familiar with convertible opportunities may be able to take advantage of such situations by following the procedure below:

● Before purchasing common stock, check to see if convertibles either *at conversion value* or *below* happen to be available.

● If you can purchase convertibles *at* conversion value, you will almost certainly save on commissions, at the least.

● If you purchase convertibles below conversion value, you will save on commissions. In addition, you will have purchased the underlying common at an effective discount: The differential between the bonds' conversion value and actual price.

• If the common provides a higher yield than the convertible bonds, have your broker submit the bonds for conversion (usually takes two to three weeks). You will then be holding the higher-yielding common, purchased at a discount. *Warning:* Don't submit the bonds for conversion until immediately after the next interest payout, unless the payout has just passed. Bondholders lose accrued interest upon conversion. Most bonds pay interest semiannually.

Buying advice: Don't place "market orders" for convertibles. Bond markets are thinner than stock markets, and you can be hurt by a wide spread between bid and asked prices. Place definite limit orders.

Some examples: During one week in January, you could have purchased at a discount National Distillers & Chemicals (yield, 5.6%) via the corporation's 4⅔s 1992 convertible bonds (yield, 4.6%), Houston Oil & Minerals via its 6¼s 1995 convertible, and International Minerals & Chemicals via its 4s 1991 convertible bonds.

Source: *KV Convertible Fact Finder,* Kalb, Voorhis & Co., 27 William St., New York 10005; *Value Line Options & Convertibles,* 711 Third Ave., New York 10017.

EYE THE TERM ON CERTIFICATES

Investors with long-term savings certificates should keep posted on their maturity dates. Usually, warning notices are sent out by institutions, but it's still your responsibility to take ac-

tion when the time comes. At termination, interest on fixed-maturity instruments *stops* or the return drops to the going passbook rate. Either way, procrastination costs money.

In the case of multiple-maturity certificates, failure to act within 10 days normally triggers automatic renewal. Rollovers eliminate bother of going to the bank, but you may not want your money tied up again, and yields could have dropped in the interim. In addition, some institutions that treat renewals as original deposits impose waiting periods and minimum penalties —stiffer than federal norms—on withdrawals. Accordingly, be sure of terms *and* maturity dates before certificates are issued.

HOW TO SELECT A BOND INVESTMENT

Question: Should you buy taxable corporate bonds or tax-free municipals? That depends largely on the investor's tax bracket.

One example: If the break point between corporates and municipals is the 31% federal income tax bracket, investors in lower tax brackets will receive more after-tax interest income by buying corporates. Those in higher brackets will find tax-free municipals delivering a larger effective yield.

Further advantages to owning municipals: Most states give preferential tax treatment to their own municipal bonds. Thus, a resident who owns municipal bonds of his own state or one of its communities or authorities often need not pay state property or income tax on the interest from those municipal bonds. This lowers the tax bracket needed to benefit from municipal bonds.

PROBLEMS FOR CONVERTIBLES IN MERGERS

Mergers and tender offers generally represent good news to common stock holders of the company being approached. However, under certain conditions, holders of *convertible bonds* and *convertible preferred shares* or *warrants* can get hurt.

Here is how to protect yourself when news of the merger discussion becomes known:

• *If the convertible bond is selling at no or little premium over its actual conversion value* (that is, value if converted into common shares): Do nothing until deal is announced. *Reason:* If a tender offer is made either in cash or stock, the convertible will rise equally with the common. You will be in position to simply sell your bonds or to convert them, using the common shares received to participate in the tender offer.

• *If the bonds are selling well above conversion value:* Assess chances of tender offer being made in cash. If that happens, the bond could lose value.

Example: You own convertible bonds, priced at $500, which can at the moment be converted into $300 worth of XYZ Corp. common.

If the buyer's offer comes to $400 worth of stock per bond, the bond will, lose its convertibility into equity.

Indicated action: Consider selling the convertibles immediately.

• A more favorable situation occurs if shares are being offered. Since the tendering company is usually stronger than the takeover candidate, the convertible holder may benefit from holding bonds convertible into that company's shares.

Source: *The Value Line Options & Convertibles*, 711 Third Ave., New York 10017.

TRADING IN OPTIONS

The appearance of the Chicago Board Options Exchange (CBOE) in 1973 popularized a form of investment once reserved only for more sophisticated market traders. Although listed options offer many advantages, you can transact unlisted options through over-the-counter dealers. Both are highly speculative investments.

How options work: An investor can buy a *call*, which represents the right to buy a stipulated number (usually 100) of shares from the option writer (seller) at a specified price until a specified time.

Example: You believe that X common will rise far beyond its recent price of 93 within two months. For roughly $900 you purchase such an option. The call entitles you to purchase 100 shares of X at 90 a share (the striking price) through a certain date.

Not counting fees, you'd break even if the price rises to $99. Now suppose X rises by 20% to 111 5/8 by then. Since your option allows you to purchase the shares, resellable on the open market at 111 5/8, for 90, the option itself will be worth at least 21 5/8.

You can resell the option (which is readily possible on CBOE). Or you can exercise the option, purchase the shares at 90, sell them immediately at 111 5/8. Your $900 investment in the call option has resulted in a 21 5/8 point profit, or a gain of 140%—based on a stock that has moved up by only 20%

The buyer of the option is clearly *gambling* on a *rapid rise* in the shares. Unless the shares are priced at 90 or above at expiration (CBOE options expire on the third Saturday of the specified month), the option will expire worthless.

FOR FAVORABLE COVERED OPTION EXECUTIONS, SPECIFY A SPREAD ORDER

Investors seeking to establish *covered option positions* (the writing of call options against the holding of common shares or equivalents) frequently find themselves in the following dilemma: If they purchase the underlying common shares first and *then* attempt to write the options, they may find the price of the common has declined before the option transaction can be executed.

Result: The need to either accept a lower option premium (the price of the option is likely to decline in sympathy) or gamble the stock will soon recover so they can get the option premium originally hoped for.

Conversely, if they first sell the op-

tion and then attempt to purchase the underlying security, they may find that the underlying common has risen before the option sale.

Solution: Some brokerage firms will now accept orders stipulating that both must be executed. It's called a spread. *Example:* Suppose XYZ Corp. is selling at 15, its January 15 option at 2. An investor can enter a spread order to buy the stock and sell the option at a net cost of no more than 13 points. If he has to pay 15½ for the stock, the orders won't be executed unless he gets at least 2½ for the option. But if the stock can be bought for 14½, he may get no more than 1½ for the option.

Once the firm accepts the spread order, he is assured he will either execute both sides at the stipulated spread or he won't transact at all.

The placing of spread orders of this nature may prove particularly useful during periods of violent market movements, creating rapid-fire fluctuations.

STOCK OPTIONS: THE PROTECTED SHORT SALE

Selling short (the sale of shares borrowed from your broker with the hope of subsequent purchase at lower levels to repay the stock loan) can prove profitable during bear markets *and* bull markets. How? By timing your sales and cover points properly. Short sales are generally highly speculative. While there is a definite limit as to how *low* stocks can fall, there is no limit as to how *high* they can rise. Should your short sale run against you, you incur loss by having to pay more for the shares you sold than you received in proceeds.

Professional traders frequently protect themselves against serious loss by placing *buy stops* on shares sold short —orders to their broker to immediately *cover* the short sale should the price of the shares rise beyond a predetermined point. While this does offer some insurance, short sellers who are *stopped out* (where prices exceed buy stops) frequently find their position does subsequently decline after all— but too late to benefit.

Investors willing to sacrifice some potential profit for peace of mind might consider this strategy instead—ideally suited for periods when Chicago Board Options Exchange and American Stock Exchange option premiums are running low:

If an option exists whose striking price (exercise price) lies relatively close to the price level at which you are selling the shares short and whose cost carries a low premium over tangible value, simultaneously purchase the option when you put out the short sale. *Example:* The Brunswick April 10 option was selling in early February at 2 1/8, the shares priced at the time at 12. The call, therefore, was selling at only 1/8 point above its tangible value ($12 stock price minus $10 exercise price leaves $2).

Suppose you sold Brunswick short at 12 at the time, and the shares rose instead of falling. You simply exercise your option, purchasing the shares at 10, to cover your short sale, for which you received 12. Your only risk involved the 1/8-point premium on the option, plus the commissions.

And if the shares decline in value after all? In early February the Brunswick April 10s still had three months of life remaining—even were the stock to decline seriously, the options figured to retain some value. For example, were Brunswick to rapidly decline to, say, 8, providing a 4-point gain on the short side, we might expect the option to lose only 1½ of its 2 1/8-point value, for a loss of $150 on your offsetting long position. You would net 2½ points (less commissions) on a fully protected short sale by selling the option at 5/8 at the time you cover the short sale. Or if you anticipated a price recovery at the time, you could simply hold the option.

The Brunswick option, incidentally, represented a fine alternative to buying common stock for investors who anticipated a rapid rise in the shares. Selling at such a minimal premium, they offered limited risk, lower commissions, and virtually a dollar-for-dollar move with the common—*but the percentage returns were much greater. Example:* Were the common to rise by 16⅔%, the April 10 option figured to rise by 2 points as well, for nearly a 100% gain.

USING OPTIONS TO INCREASE DIVIDEND PAYOUTS BY 32.9%

When a sharp stock market rise trims dividend yields on common shares, income-minded investors can restore these dividends, at least in part, by purchasing deep-in-the-money calls that are now available from member firms of various exchanges including the Chicago Board Options Exchange and the Amex.

Deep-in-the-money calls are options whose striking price falls well below the current market price of the shares, options almost certain to be exercised prior to expiration.

For example, at a bear market low of 12, International Telephone's $1.52 annual dividend represented a yield of 12.7%. By February 1, the shares had risen to 19¼; the yield, as a result, declined to 7.9%. You might have sold, at the time, an October 15 call on the CBOE, priced then at 5, or $475 net to you after CBOE commissions.

Since you receive this option premium *immediately*, it can be used to offset the cost of the shares to you. Therefore, you would have had to put up only $1,450 to buy 100 shares of ITT (19¼ × 100 shares = $1,925 − $475 = $1,450). Based, then, on this cash outlay, your dividend of $1.52 amounts to a yield of 10.5% annualized.

This represents an effective increase of 32.9% in ITT's rate of dividend pay out.

Since the strike price of the call (15) was 22.4% below the actual price of 19¼, the odds appeared excellent that your shares would be called away from you and that the dividend would accrue to you at that rate. With the shares at 19¼, the option price 5, you are fully protected against loss so long as the share price doesn't decline below 14½.

The above example is given for illustration only. High-dividend paying stocks are regularly followed by traders to find deep-in-the-money call opportunities.

COMMON INVESTING PITFALLS

• *Making game plans and not sticking to them.* Example: You buy a stock with fine long-term prospects, but you lose patience and sell when the stock doesn't join in a short-term market rally. Or you buy a stock for a fast trade and fail to sell when the market turns down.

• *Selling a stock and then impulsively repurchasing it.* Example: After buying a stock at 15 and selling at 20, you watch the stock climb to 30 and then repurchase it. By then, the stock is probably overpriced. *Be optimistic:* If you sold too soon, whomever you bought from sold even sooner.

• *Listening to too many advisers.* Investment advisers are never unanimous. If you want to follow a professional adviser instead of your own system, then select and follow the adviser. *Be realistic:* No adviser is right all the time.

• *Being unwilling to admit a mistake.* The greatest pitfall of them all. *Result:* Investors allow small losses to grow into big ones. Admit your errors. Learn from them.

Source: Gerald Appel, publisher, *Systems & Forecasts*, 185 Great Neck Rd., Great Neck, NY 11021.

INVESTING IN BROADWAY

People who invest in the Broadway theater are called *angels.* Everyone, including the producers themselves, agrees that it's one of the *riskiest* investments you can make. There's an 80% chance you won't ever recoup all of your

INVESTMENT STRATEGIES

original investment and about a 50% chance that you'll lose every penny.

Should you hit it big, like those who invested in the musical *Grease*, you stand to return 10-15 times your investment.

How to get involved: Become familiar with the industry. Read trade publications like *Variety, Show Business,* or *Backstage.* Talk to CPAs or lawyers who specialize in the theater. And most important if you're new to the business, invest in a producer who has a *good track record.*

Write to blue-chip producers. *Here are some:*

Waissman & Fox, Inc., 1501 Broadway, New York 10036; Harold Prince, 1270 Ave. of the Americas, New York 10020; Morton Gottlieb, 165 W. 46 St., New York 10036; Joseph Beruh, 1650 Broadway, New York 10019, and Robert Fryer Productions, 1350 Ave. of the Americas, New York 10019.

There is no formal licensing procedure for producers. They must, however, file a prospectus for a new production with the Attorney General of New York (if it's based in New York, which it usually is) and with the SEC (if more than $1,500,000 is being raised), since it's considered a public offering.

The legal vehicle for a play or musical is almost always a limited partnership—the producer (the general partner) gets 50% of the profits (after taking his management fee). The limited partners (the investors) usually put up *all* of the money in return for the other 50% (it can be 60-40 or a 40-60 split, depending on the difficulty of raising money). We're talking about $200,000-$400,000 for a play and $500,000 to $1 million for a musical.

The capitalization is generally broken down into 50 units, so to buy one unit of a $500,000 production costs $10,000. Even then, a single unit can be split up among many investors. It's conceivable that you can invest as little as, say, $1,000. Your investment, *plus* an extra 10% or 20% if money runs short and an "overcall" clause is exercised, is the extent of your liability.

Beyond that, the producer assumes the risk. If he still runs short but has confidence in the show's eventual success, he may then lend the partnership additional money. He may, in turn, borrow money for which he gives up some of his 50% share of the profits. Lenders are the first to be paid back; then come the limited partners. Only after *both* are paid back does the profit sharing begin.

You will be asked to sign the partnership agreement between six months and a year before rehearsals begin, although you will probably have to actually put up your money only two or three months before that time. Rehearsals take about six weeks, so about five months elapse before you start receiving a return, if any.

You will know pretty quickly if you have a winner or a wipeout. If the show survives for three or four months, your investment is looking pretty good. With a big hit, you ought to recoup it all within a half year (for a play) or a year (for a musical). You have to treat the income as ordinary income on your tax return.

You will probably not be able to deduct any business expenses, such as traveling to New York to meet with your producer, since you are not involved in the actual production. The partnership's accountant will notify you as to your profit or loss each year, since what you receive as a cash distribution may differ from the profit-loss picture.

The revenue from a successful show comes from a variety of sources. Aside from the Broadway box office receipts, there are touring companies, royalties from foreign language productions, movie and television rights, record royalties, merchandise connected with the show (T-shirts, posters, etc.).

Investors may get additional royalties for the next 20 years from any sale of the production rights to stock and amateur productions. These rights, called *subsidiary rights*, belong to the authors, but they must give 40% of any royalties to the original production company. An investor in a big hit will often funnel this long-term income into a trust for his children.

What can you expect from your investment other than a financial return or a tax write-off? You get the opportunity to *buy* tickets for the show's opening night performance, and you can attend the opening night party. You have the glamour of being a Broadway angel (the bigger the hit, the greater the glamour). You can probably buy "house seats" (the best seats in a theater) for *other* shows at regular box office price by asking your producer to arrange it (producers have reciprocal arrangements). You may be solicited for an investment by other producers, as your participation is a matter of public record (the names of all investors of a limited partnership must be published in two publications, one of which is the *New York Law Journal.*)

And what not *to expect:* To attend rehearsals, watch auditions, read the script, or have any hand, creative or otherwise, in the production. Do not expect to get your nephew or girl friend a part, either.

OFFBEAT INVESTMENT: AFRICAN ART

Increasing numbers of collectors and investors are turning to African and other "primitive" type art. Opportunities for price appreciation are large—but so are the dangers of such speculation.

Irwin Hersey, one of the leading African art experts (an adviser to museums and private collectors), sees current internal conflicts in Africa and natives' growing heritage interests adding to the rarity of good art.

Most items are carvings of ancestor figures, spirit or other images, and fetishes for magical purposes. *Also big:* Masks for initiation ceremonies, etc. Few paintings.

It's not unusual for high-grade work to double or quadruple in price over a few years, Hersey says. The problem is finding objects with the highest artistic value.

Hersey, who appraises African objects for collectors and for tax-deductible gifts to museums, warns would-be collectors to exercise caution before buying an expensive object. If an investor isn't dealing with a well-known dealer, he should turn to a museum with competence in the field for expert recommendation. Occasionally, there's someone on the staff who can help; otherwise, an outside expert would be recommended.

It's possible to buy a high-grade (in terms of artistic level and investment potential) object for as little as a few hundred dollars. Top-quality objects sell for several thousand dollars. Some go into hundreds of thousands.

INVESTMENT STRATEGIES

Excellent book for African art "starters": *African Sculpture*, by William Fagg and Margaret Plass (Dutton Vista, 201 Park Ave. S., N.Y. 10016).

Tax angle: Many museums and schools are anxious to build African art collections—especially because of the growth of interest in black culture—and with African art appreciating sharply, tax-conscious art donors can leverage their investments effectively—if they concentrate in top-grade objects as gifts.

Source: Irwin Hersey, Hersey Associates, 106 W. 69 St., New York 10023.

INVESTING IN ART AND ANTIQUES

• Concentrate on quality pieces. One $5,000 antique is likely to appreciate more rapidly than ten $500 pieces.

• Avoid flawed specimens. They have little collector-investor value.

• If possible, secure matched pairs of specimens. A matched pair will be worth approximately 30% more than the total cost of the items purchased separately.

• Specialize. A general collector isn't likely to accumulate enough knowledge of any category to recognize true bargains when he sees them.

• Avoid dealers in major cities. Better prices are likely to be secured a bit off the beaten track.

• Specimens are likely to cost more near their point of origin. For example, you might be able to purchase antique furniture in England at better prices than you can secure within our shores.

California artists may sell for more within the state than elsewhere.

• For a piece to have any significant collector value, the artist or artisan must be identifiable, and the piece should represent a period of his work and the general historical climate in which it was produced. Mass-produced trays, medallions, and such don't meet these conditions.

• In general, any item that has survived two generations in excellent condition is likely to begin to increase in value.

Source: Sigmund Rothschild, New York.

TAX DISADVANTAGE OF INVESTING IN GOLD

Now that U.S. residents can legally invest in gold, it's important to consider the federal income tax impact. Except in the case of a party who is a gold *dealer*, the metal represents a capital asset to an investor. That's fine if the gold is sold at a gain, but capital losses are limited in usefulness for tax purposes.

However, it has been held in the case of investments in warehouse receipts for whiskey (where the property involved is a capital asset) that all expenses in connection with the property are capital expenditures, which must be added to the cost of the whiskey and cannot be deducted as paid out.

If the warehouse receipts are held for several years, costs of storage and insurance aren't deductible currently. But they do serve to increase the basis of the commodity when the investor ultimately sells it.

Gold isn't something that has insignificant custody and carrying problems. It's heavy, bulky, and requires storage and insurance charges. If you hold the gold for several years, you may have quite a bit of out-of-pocket expense which isn't deductible *currently*, if ever. Further, you may have to pay assay costs, which are another nondeductible item.

INVESTING IN U.S. COINS

Median wholesale value of $100 worth of uncirculated U.S. cents is $132 after one year, $199 after four years, $343 after 10 years, $821 after 15 years, $2,124 after 20 years, $4,459 after 30 years.

Other benefit: All profits are taxed as capital gains when the coins are sold. And there is little chance of losing the original investment.

How to buy them: Best source is the main office of the largest bank in your city. Some banks consider collectors a nuisance, so use your clout. Or open an account, and see the same teller frequently until you establish a relationship. An occasional gift to the teller won't hurt. Purchase coins in cartons— $25 worth of pennies, $100 worth of nickels—it's easier all around. *The best time:* Anytime after the bank's extended Christmas rush is over and there are more coins available. *Long shot:* Occasionally, the mint changes a coin slightly during the year, adding to the value of the ones issued earlier.

Selling: Check the coin publications once or twice annually for dealer asking prices for uncirculated coin rolls. To find the wholesale price, multiply the asking price for cents by 78%; nickels, 83%; dimes, 79%, and quarters and half dollars, 76%.

To sell coins, simply take them to a dealer, or get bids from several over the phone. If you want to take the trouble, you might earn more by offering your coin rolls for sale in coin publications (at a price slightly lower than the current dealer asking price).

Source: Howard E. Deutch, *High Profits Without Risk*, Jefren Publishing, 1216 Holy Cross, Monroeville, Pa. 15146.

MARKETING

THE PLAN

AVOIDING COMMON MARKETING ERRORS

To beat the odds, avoid the three most common marketing mistakes. The same principles apply whether your product is marketed nationally in mass media or locally in select media and whether the product is consumer-oriented or industrial.

Mistake No. 1: Testing the undeveloped idea. Almost everyone does it. You develop an idea for a new product and go out and test it among hundreds or thousands of people *before* you talk to small numbers of people about making it work. You guess the price, package, name, positioning. You don't explore options: Single product—or line? Economical big size—or trial size?

You test a mixture of educated guesses. Why not develop the idea first?

Start with your potential competitors. Take a sample of their ads or packages and put your name or names on them for testing purposes with a small group of consumer prospects. Then take *your* idea and do your own ads. Use an *economy* appeal. Then create a premium price approach, too. Vary the package, claims, names. Show *all* the ads to the test prospects. Ask them what they *remember*. Ask them what they *like*. Before long, your guesses will change to *informed decisions*. Then, when you test your idea

with many people, you'll test the fully developed idea—developed among consumers to maximize your chances of success.

Mistake No. 2: Overkill. Telling people more than they want to know.

You want your new product to be really different. So you show people your factory. "See for yourself how we do it. It's the greatest thing since penicillin. See! It will change your life."

That's exactly what Maxim did. They invented freeze-dried coffee and were proud of it. They took the TV viewer into their factories, showed the machinery.

Then Taster's Choice came along and concentrated on the one thing people wanted to know about their product—*How does it taste?* They were soon first in sales.

Note: The more information you ask people to absorb, the longer it takes them to absorb it.

The greater the change in habit or idea, the more reluctant people will be to change. *Example:* Baking soda was sold to freshen refrigerators—not as a revolutionary natural deodorizer, but a "a nice little secret for your refrigerator." Believable. And successful beyond belief.

Mistake No. 3: Selling for your competitor.

Maxim made another mistake. They sold the idea of freeze-dried coffee instead of selling Maxim. Why sell anything you don't exclusively own? It was all too easy for Taster's Choice to become the "tastier" freeze-dried coffee.

When the new cigarette filters were first introduced, one brand boasted "40,000 filter traps." Another brand came along and announced "100,000 filter traps" and took their edge away.

Surf detergent pioneered with new *no-rinse* Surf. Along came Tide with no-rinse Tide and outspent them many times over, capturing the market.

Ajax, on the other hand, advertised "stronger than dirt." You can't take that away from them. There is no stronger-*er* than dirt.

Preemption is more important than ever, since advertisers are now allowed to name their competitors, and it is a greater temptation to say you're better than they are—instead of convincing people that you're good. *Moral:* Never sell something you don't own.

Rolaids absorbs 87 times its weight in stomach acid. Another product could promise to absorb 187 times its weight. *But Alka-Seltzer says:* "Plop, plop. Fizz, fizz. Oh, what a relief it is." No other tablet can make that statement.

Source: Gerald Schoenfeld, Gerald Schoenfeld, Inc., 341 Madison Ave., New York 10017.

REAL MARKETING: HOW TO DO IT

Most companies think they're doing *marketing*—but all they're really doing is *sales*, and giving the function a fancy name. So says one of the leading figures in marketing, Dr. Philip Kotler, professor at the Graduate School of Management, Northwestern University, Evanston, Ill.

Marketing, he says, starts *before* there is a product. Sales is the work the company does *afterwards*— getting the product out the door and to a customer.

Why the confusion between the two? Mostly because *real* marketing is more difficult—it upsets established plans, and forces managers to overturn long-held biases and premises. People struggle against such change.

Real marketing is the analysis, planning, and control of all the market-making forces that impinge on a potential customer. Thus the activity includes, among other things, an analysis of who the potential customers are, what they need, what they want, and what the competition is doing (and may eventually be doing.)

How, then, does a company get started in the real activity of marketing—avoiding obvious traps and inefficiencies. *Kotler's formula:* Start small. Plunging into marketing too fast and too boldly is a sure way to produce disillusionment with what marketing can do for a business. Marketing requires a slow learning curve—to educate the key marketing people to the company's real needs and ability to change, and to educate the general management to new ways of looking at its business. Failure to recognize this simple advice is what frequently dooms corporate marketing efforts.

THE FIRST STEPS. Begin with an "audit." It should be done by a competent *outsider*—someone who has no vested interest in maintaining the company's status quo. A consultant would examine the product, the customers, the distribution channels, the sales and ad efforts, the goals of the company, the strategies used to achieve those goals, and the planning process. He would outline the company's shortcomings (and strong points) and could become the blueprint for a future marketing program.

AUDIT GOALS. The marketing audit should:

- Accurately analyze the competition, distributors, suppliers, customers.
- Study the objectives of the firm.
- Assess whether those strategies are meeting those objectives.
- List the essential tools (manpower, budget, time, etc.) that management will need to attain those objectives.
- Develop alternative objectives in light of what is learned about the market, the customers, and the suppliers.

FULL-TIME MARKETING. If the audit clearly indicates that marketing programs are necessary, the next question is: Who will do the job? Frequently, a company isn't fully committed to the idea or is uncertain whom to hire. *Result:* It hires outsiders—consultants, part-timers—to implement the program. That's usually a mistake. Most companies need the marketing function operating on a full-time, continuous basis.

It's best not to select a person too far away, in experience, from your business. It's best if his experience is with a firm that's a bit bigger.

Consider the consultant who did the audit. If the audit is good—and the working relationship is good, too—he would be a good candidate.

Some marketing people (maybe 50% of them) suffer from an *industry fixation.* That is, if a marketing concept worked for the one industry they have experience in, they'll try to repeat that concept in every other business—whether it applies or not. An interviewer can uncover this fixation by asking the candidate for an assessment of how to approach the company's problem. If the response is heavily biased toward that person's experience, that's a clue.

A candidate who is quick to provide *answers* to problems *without* really having the marketing facts and background can be dangerous. A prime candidate will only venture to analyze the approach to a problem after intelligent research. If his approach is tied too tightly to his past experience, it's a clue to *industry fixation.*

ORGANIZATION. Where in the corporate organization the marketing authority be placed is critical.

Best situation: Place the sales functions within the overall marketing function. Make marketing the controlling department. Let the head of marketing research (1) the customers, (2) market need, and (3) select the sales approach. Thus marketing would set company pace in new products, goals, and strategies. It leads to better corporate coordination.

Typically, *marketing* is included, improperly, under *sales*. The marketing man is hired by (or for) the sales manager. In such a setup, the marketer may do some research for the sales department, but for the most part the effort lacks equilibrium because the marketing person proves either *too useful* or *too useless.*

If he's too useful, his suggestions pit him against the traditional sales drive—urging instead, say, new products, different products, a shift from sales via salesmen to ad programs, etc. None of these steps will endear the marketing person to the sales manager. If the marketing person holds back those suggestions, then his output is useless, and he fires himself.

If the marketing director is put on a par with sales—both vice presidents, say—the equilibrium is equally unstable. Both are driving in different directions, each seeking to usurp the other's power and budget.

Dr. Kotler is author of *Marketing Management: Analysis, Planning, and Control,* 3rd edition. (Prentice-Hall, Englewood Cliffs, N.J. 07632).

'SPINNING': HOW TO BRING CREATIVE THINKING TO MARKETING

Too many managers—and marketing experts—approach the creative side of marketing in the wrong way. They try to be "logical," but creativity and logic have little to do with each other. The technique that *does* work is what I call *spinning.*

Spinning is a kind of *lateral thinking.* In spinning, one lets his mind wander—and fantasize, too—about a subject.

Where it's used: Searching for new applications and new markets for an established product.

In conventional thinking, a marketer would list all the logical possibilities, immediately rejecting anything with a flaw and only investing time to think about those with obvious potential. In spinning, don't reject any idea out-of-hand! List even the most outrageous ones; dwell on them. *The concept:* Out of the most outrageous ideas, legitimate ones will bloom, if you give them time to develop.

Important premise: A truly creative idea rarely grows out of a logical search. It comes while shaving, driving along a highway. In short, while "woolgathering" with no logic to interrupt the fantasy.

Some areas to explore: List all the "givens" about your market or service —all the traditional notions about its limits, the reasons for the limits that you know, that your salesmen know, and that your customers know. Then, for the sake of this exercise, put them aside. Now, ask yourself basic and simple questions: What do people really do with the product? What do they really like to do with it? What else could they do with it? *Ask also:* What if the reason were. . .? Then go way out on a limb with no supportable facts in your *spinning.* Follow the thinking as far as it will go. Since spinning is a *private* exercise, there's no danger of "losing face."

Spinning is *time-consuming* (also a great deal of fun), and you may discover that once you start doing it, a new range of ideas will start popping into your mind. And many of them may be golden.

Source: Dr. Ernest Dichter, Ernest Dichter Assoc., Albany Post Rd., Croton-on-Hudson, N.Y. 10520.

BACK TO THE FACTORY

Climate of long-range materials shortages moving more product decisions out of the marketing department and into the factory. Greater attention to be paid to production, purchasing and financial experts—at expense of markets. The question will no longer be, "What will the consumer buy?" but, "What is it possible to offer him?" Signposts:

• Food industry is encountering a back-to-basics movement, and that trend will accelerate. Top-of-the-line convenience foods are feeling the pinch.

• Quality cooking utensils selling well as long-term *investments* replacing less expensive items that were changed regularly with the decor of the kitchen.

• Assemble-it-yourself furniture sales are booming. *Reason:* Low cost. Look for this trend to move into other consumer products.

• Inflation is forcing families with incomes of $20,000 annually or less out of the ranks of discretionary spenders.

ON THE HORIZON. Capital shortage will erode advertising budgets, curtail allowances to retailers and wholesalers. Importance of institutional markets will grow. New taxes will be levied to *discourage* consumption. Advertising content will require new approaches, possibly an emphasis on conservation rather than consumption.

Result: Advertising allowances to retailers and wholesalers will be curtailed on some products—in response to the capital and resource shortages.

USING COMPETITOR'S VIEWPOINT

Work out a detailed *plan of attack* on your company from the viewpoint of a chief competitor. Use it to firm up company plans, strategy. *What should be in the attack plan:*

• How would a competitor go about increasing its market share?

• What new products would it come out with?

• What weak spots would it concentrate on?

• How would it try to destroy your company?

Face the situation with candor. Think of it as writing the history of the demise of your company. If this is too difficult to do, your ad agency might be able to do it. One agency, Leber Katz Partners, New York, does this for clients. Its predictions have been both accurate and very useful.

SALESPEOPLE CAN HELP MARKETING PLANS

Big missing link in most company marketing efforts: *the view of the sales force.* The people that advertising is supposed to open doors for.

How to harness some of their know-how:

• Consult with experienced sales staff on all upcoming campaigns and promotions. The sales exec who's lived in the field has a feel for specific responses and themes that produce a bust (or bonanza) that no in-house marketing expert can possibly sense.

• Don't make a secret of upcoming ad campaigns. Double effectiveness by giving every salesperson copies of every ad *before* it hits the media. He *has* to know your message and objectives beforehand, to reinforce them on his personal rounds.

- Don't sit on all that hard-won trade and business press publicity. Get reprints out to all salesmen for distribution to customers, at least half of whom will never see the story otherwise. And tap your salesmen for case histories and other publicity material.

- Let your salesmen draft or screen audiovisuals, brochures, and technical literature. They have useful information on drawings and specs that should go into an applications bulletin.

- Stop holding onto inquiries generated by direct mail, ads, and publicity pieces as proof your campaigns work. They're sales leads; get them out *fast* to someone who can close the sale.

WHAT WORKS FOR P&G DOESN'T WORK FOR YOU AND ME

The most common mistake in marketing today is copying Procter & Gamble's techniques.

P&G uses a manager for every *brand*. Few other companies have brands big enough to support a full-time manager. Result? The bored manager spends a fortune on unnecessary research and other gimmicks to justify his salary.

A bigger mistake: Copying P&G advertising techniques, *e.g.*, a slice-of-life TV—those little dramas where husband and wife, for example, have a spat over the cooking oil. P&G spends up to $20 million a shot on these tired *but tested* approaches, so they work. If

others try to get by with spending less with the same techniques, they fail.

But P&G also has the resources to develop superior products and *sample them universally*. Most other companies can't count on clear-cut superiority and don't have the resources to sample.

Smaller companies would be wise to take a clue from Colgate. It seems to recognize reality. Through the years its sex-appeal toothpastes and Irish Springs have done well in the marketplace *without* copying the techniques of Procter & Gamble.

Source: Gerald Schoenfeld.

CO-OP ADVERTISING MISTAKES

Traditional co-op programs are on the wane. *Reasons:* They present too many problems for both the manufacturer and the retailer.

What to use instead: Dealer support program. It gives both the maker and the retailer more flexibility in targeting ads and solving many of the problems inherent in traditional co-op programs.

Some of the mistakes manufacturers make, which hold down the effectiveness of co-op advertising:

- Failure to understand that national advertisers can buy large ad contracts and get low rates roughly comparable to those of local retailers.

- Failure to understand that national advertisers can buy large ad stores, the ads must reflect the unique marketing needs of that store. This effort often requires use of a special ad agency for a creative approach that different size retailers can relate to and that doesn't ignore the identities of the individual stores.

• Failure to understand that the dealer support program goes a long way in solving one critical shortcoming of the traditional co-op program. *That is:* In a regular co-op, when the ads are created by the store and often paid in part by the store, the manufacturer is at the mercy of the retailer. If the retailer isn't selling much of the product, he's not likely to want to invest even part of the cost of ads supporting the product.

Yet, that's the time when the ads are needed most. Under dealer support, the manufacturer, since *it* decides when and where its money is spent, can target the promotion when and where promotion dollars will be needed most and where experience indicates the biggest impact will be made.

Further, the manufacturer can discriminate in selecting areas. Such discrimination isn't a violation of the Robinson-Patman Act (the federal law that, among other things, regulates the spending of money in co-op ads).

Even though the law allows it—and marketing wisdom demands that marketing spending be directed at weak areas—too many manufacturers still spend their co-op ad dollars on the strongest sales areas by linking co-op spending with retailer purchases of the manufacturer's product.

• Failure to understand that manufacturers who have traditional co-op ad programs shouldn't place undue ad restrictions on the retailers. *Example:* By demanding that the retailer carry the manufacturer's logo in the local ad; some stores object to a "foreign" logo

that takes away from their image. *Another example:* Refusing to pay for some ad production costs when the major store actually incurs them and when the manufacturer knows he lacks the marketing clout needed to win the argument.

• Failure to get cooperation from the media. Since many smaller retailers don't want to bother with co-op ads, they often require the assistance of the media (radio, television, newspapers) to teach them how to use the program. Thus, a manufacturer should work closely with the media on this educational program.

• Failure to realize that an effective co-op program can be built on small budgets. Workable ones have been as small as $250,000 (nationally), with as little as $30,000 earmarked for a single target.

THREE CO-OP PROGRAMS

TRADITIONAL CO-OP PROGRAM. Manufacturer sets up an advertising allowance with the retailer based on size of the retailer's past orders. Each time the retailer runs an ad that promotes the product, he bills the manufacturer. Depending on the arrangement, the co-op portion can cover from 50% to 100% of the ad's cost. Ad cost reimbursement by manufacturer generally is made in cash.

PROMOTION ALLOWANCE PROGRAM. Common in package goods (food, etc.). Retailer features manufacturer's product in price promotion during certain prearranged period. Size of payment to retailer depends on size of order bought for that promotion. Size of ad not an issue—idea is to get the store behind the product: Off-shelf display, price promotion, stickers in store windows, etc.

DEALER SUPPORT PROGRAM. This is the big one—the technique that is growing very fast because it solves many of the problems inherent in traditional co-op. Manufacturer doesn't set allowances, nor does it receive bills for promotional dollars from store:

Instead: If the retailer orders certain minimum quantities, producer will create an ad and buy a certain amount of space or time for the retailer, in the retailer's market and in such a way that it will look like the retailer is creating the ad.

WHEN IT PAYS TO BUY A RETAILER'S INVENTORY

One way to get a product on the retail shelf: When a retailer won't buy a product because it has a heavy supply of competing brands, offer to buy out the excess inventory if the retailer will take on your product.

This is known as *stock lifting*, and the FTC now permits it. (An earlier rule prohibiting the practice of stocklifting has been withdrawn.)

Caution: Don't overdo it and violate other rules of fair competition. *Example:* Brand A salesperson offers to buy out the supplies of brands B and C if the retailer will stock brand A and agree *never to sell brands B and C again.* That would be unfair in the FTC's eyes.

BASIC CONCEPT

Top executives of consumer goods corporations should adopt a basic concept—one that may actually be quite radical. *The concept:* Meet and mingle with the public and the trade.

If concept is carried out, channels of communication would be established, enabling management to be tuned into the virtues, shortcomings, and potentials of their products to a greater degree than would otherwise be possible.

Everyone—top executives, the corporation, and the public—would benefit if the executives came out of isolation. *Additional benefit:* The top executives would be closer to *their* staff.

HOW A FUTURIST LOOKS AT TOMORROW

Manufacturers and merchants who sell to age-based markets (especially those in beverages, clothing, specialty foods, etc.) should be in touch with the ways that the aging of the population affects lifestyles and tastes. Examination of readily available figures on population by age groups may not define what a product line ought to look like on a given date, but it will indicate the need to prepare for change.

The Bureau of the Census* is the source of population figures on age distribution, size of households, geograph-

*Free sample of data: Write Census Bureau, Commerce Dept., Washington, D.C. 20233.

ic shifts.

Certain ages prove to be bellwethers of long-term trends. One such key group is women age 24-28. They can offer major indications of shifts in attitudes of their entire generation on marriage, families, work, leisure-time activities, and much more. For companies selling the whole range of consumer products and services, it's worth being in touch with the results of surveys of their tastes and interests.

Don't overreact to talk of continuing declines in birth rates, which are likely to hold at around 2.1 children per woman of child-bearing age. In other words, *total* population probably will hold at about the replacement level during the next decade.

Do focus on the *movement* of the age-group bulges, especially the post-World War II baby boom. By the end of the decade, the leading edge of this group will be well into middle age. And 25 years from now, they'll be approaching retirement age.

As this group moves up the age scale, some shortages of people, especially at the younger end of the bracket, will soon begin to affect businesses. Companies heavily dependent on low-cost teenage workers will probably find it profitable to automate many jobs now performed by this group.

Changes in telecommunication and information technology won't be as dramatic during the next decade as they have been in the recent past. As costs continue to fall, more businesses will be able to sharpen and enrich management skills.

None of these technological developments will change what makes businesses succeed or fail. What they are doing is relieving managers, especially middle managers, of the dull, tedious gathering and assembling of information, the jobs that ought to be done by machines. That will give them more opportunities to analyze, make judgments.

Smaller companies will find increasingly that they will have advantages once reserved for the giants. Communications, more sophisticated management techniques, and—maybe most important—better quality recruits. That's because the values of younger people are more in tune with the pace, the freedom, and the opportunities of smaller businesses. Successful small companies will find it much easier to attract top young people.

TRENDS

• The shopping center is shrinking in size. A sizable percentage of the smaller shopping centers will specialize in fashion inventory. The managers of this new style of shopping center will become increasingly important to marketing executives. Yet comparatively few of those executives have *accurate* records of those shopping centers (including the name of the manager and the promotion director). Even fewer have accurate, up-to-date records of inventory carried, including categories, shifts in categories carried, price lines, etc. Still fewer have developed creative programs for those centers.

• Crime and violence-ridden TV programs to disappear gradually as public pressures against them continue to mount. Sex and permissive themes next in line as a public target. *Replace-*

ment candidates: Situation comedy, quality drama drawn from history, biography. More programs like *Roots, Winds of War. Impact on advertisers:* Higher production/sponsorship costs; skyrocketing premiums for spots on action-type and sports programs, attracting an increasingly hard-to-reach young male audience.

• It is clear that government will play a growing role in the regulation of all marketing directed to children. That includes not only advertising but also packaging, labels, product demonstrations, etc. *For a peek at the future of consumer goods marketing in general,* keep tabs on marketing programs directed to kids and Uncle Sam's regulation of marketing to children.

GROWTH OF PERSONAL INCOME

Personal income in the South Atlantic states is expected to grow much faster than any other area of the country. So make sure your marketing plans are on target. Forecast of income growth in the years to 1985: South Atlantic, 138%; Pacific, 124%; Mountain, 124%; East South Central, 122%; West South Central, 121%; Northeast, 119%; Middle Atlantic, 115%; East North Central, 110%; West North Central, 108%.

RESEARCH

SIX COMMON RESEARCH MISTAKES

Research is the most misunderstood tool in marketing, and the biggest companies and agencies are often guilty of the biggest research errors. Used correctly, concept and copy research can multiply chances for success. *The most frequent errors—and how to avoid them:*

THE ONE-TIME ERROR. Showing an ad or commercial just once and testing for recall and buying persuasion. The newer the idea, the more exposure it needs. Dull, tired ideas are immediately understandable and do well on one-time showings—which explains why so many television commercials are slice-of-life playlets, featuring such traumas as the embarrassment of spotted drinking glasses. Such commercials soon peak and fade in effectiveness. *Good commercials build and build.*

Don't use any testing service, no matter how well known, which shows an ad or commercial *just once.*

BLIND PRODUCT TESTS. People don't consume products in a vacuum. When you fail to identify the qualities of the product and the reputable company behind it, the results you get are distorted. Thus, humble Schmidt's beer of

Philadelphia beats famous Coors in blind product tests and Pepsi beats Coke. Blind product tests reward mediocrity; those products that offend least tend to do best.

Products with substance and character deserve the support of product information and brand-name reputation. Never agree to test your product without brand name and brand information.

BEST-REMEMBERED TRAP. Much research works on the premise that the best ad is the one you can play back 24 hours later, and, if you show a batch of ads to consumers, the best ads will be remembered best.

The problem: Any cynical professional copywriter knows how to raise his recall score by giving his television character a foreign accent (Mrs. Olsen for Folger's Coffee), or by putting a girl in uniform (an airline stewardess), or by switching sex roles (the lady plumber).

Do such techniques make the ad better? Absolutely not. They merely raise the recall score, giving you a misleading impression on the effectiveness of the ad.

Do not use any technique that equates memorability with effectiveness.

FOCUS GROUP PANELS. Many of the focus group leaders—the moderators who show the ideas you want to test to a typical group of consumers—use outlines covering all the information they seek to discover. Such a moderator might begin: "How many of you use after shave? When do you use it? Do you use it at night as well as in the morning? How many use it before going out at night?" Such an approach precludes learning. If you already know the right questions to ask, you don't need to ask them.

Better to present the group with the stimulus of new ideas and *let them* tell *you* their ideas about usage, product qualities, etc.

Asking people for information directly is like handing them a blank piece of paper for their reactions. We all do better when we're handed a piece of paper with a point of view already on it, or better yet, five pieces of paper with five different points of view. Then we can say, "I like the third idea for after shave, but not the part about using it before going out at night. I want an after-shave lotion that's really going to wake me up in the morning."

Do not use any focus group technique that outlines the ground to be covered. Instead, show the panelists ideas and follow the discussion wherever it leads.

"DEFINITELY WOULD BUY" ERROR. A surprisingly common mistake is to ask people if they would (a) definitely buy, (b) probably buy, (c) probably not buy, etc., Then the "definitely buys" are heavily discounted. Yet many people feel the statement, "I would definitely give up," implies a change of brand—"I would definitely give up Old Spice for new "Fresh 'n Cool"—and they're reluctant to make such a commitment, saying, "I said I probably would buy, meaning I would definitely buy it once and then see how I like it before making a commitment about changing brands."

Better to eliminate "probablys" and simply say, "I would definitely *try* new Fresh 'n Cool." Number of promising products have been killed because people were asked to be definite in their opinions about a product before they tried it.

SECONDHAND RESEARCH. Most research users get their information secondhand. Yet it's easy to be there when the research is conducted to see your potential customers with your own eyes, hear their words with your own ears, get their reactions firsthand.

If it's a telephone survey, ask to listen on another phone to at least some of the interviews. In focus groups, insist on attending. In shopping center interviews, be included on one of the research teams.

There will be a double benefit. Your presence will make for better research *and* the results will have real meaning for you.

Source: Gerald Schoenfeld.

CHECKLIST: BEFORE TEST-MARKETING

- Product has been tested internally. It is thoroughly formulated, and it performs well.
- Shelf life had been determined.
- Reliability has been determined.
- Expenses and distribution costs are budgeted so that test results can be checked against targets.
- Clear goals and basic rules are established for the test, and all those involved agree to them and understand them.
- Reaction from your competition is planned for. How will your company respond if they step up advertising and promotion?

- Plan for adequate consumer research to distinguish between repeat purchases and sampling purchases if your product depends on the former.
- Make sure size and sophistication of the test are related realistically to what the product is worth to you.

GET VALID RESULTS FROM MARKET ANALYSIS

- Establish bench marks on successful products before evaluating new ones' results. How many respondents said they would buy the established item in the first 6 months? Compare that figure with the number saying they'll purchase the test item.
- Ask if you're really *testing* the product. Are you accepting people's verbal assurances that they like it, or are you asking for a deposit on the purchase or permission for a salesman to call? Do you include competitive items in purchase preference tests?
- Is the *market position* you assumed for the product the right one? Check to see if interest is coming from a segment other than the one you're targeting. If it is, *reposition*. Is the customer's primary interest in the product different from your prime selling point? Consider changing your theme.
- Are you testing specialized products only with *past users* or people *specifically interested* in the device? (Don't waste time and money surveying those who couldn't care less about the product you are researching.)
- Don't cut a test short just because

the new product looks "hot." Allow time for your staff to fully evaluate.

- Include product in budgets and long-range planning only *after* market evaluation has been completed.

Source: Robert R. Sachs, director of marketing planning, Consumer Products Div., SCM Corp.

USING FOCUS GROUPS*

- Participants are inhibited by the formal setting in which interviews are usually conducted.
- They frequently give the "correct" answer instead of saying what they really think.
- They are restricted to discussing only the questions on the interviewer's list, and may answer questions they've never even considered before—just to have something to say.

Group dynamics, on the other hand, uses a trained observer of behavior in an informal atmosphere (a home). Instead of direct questions, indirect inquiries are used to simulate discussion in small groups. *Result:*

- Participants often disclose reasons behind their answers spontaneously— without probing by the interviewer.
- Often, questions surface that would have been impossible to anticipate— and are answered.

Focus groups may not give a true reading of the consumer's feelings. *Reasons:*

- Questions that aren't important to participants can be easily passed over. (This behavior is in itself an answer.)

The moderator notes the dynamics of the group (tone of voice, gestures, etc.), describing what caused agree-

ment or disagreement. (Focus group reports only give the replies, not *how* they were made.) *Value to market researchers:* They discover what was said and *why*. Quantification indicates the results are statistically reliable when compared with straight question-and-answer surveys.

*Half a dozen or so interviewees respond to a leader's questions. Groups are frequently observed through one-way mirrors. Leader is usually fed questions through earphones.

PROBLEM RESEARCH IS USEFUL

Instead of asking consumers what they want in a product (*benefit research*), ask what problems they have with the item (*problem research*).

In 200 such studies, researchers came up with an average 156 problems per product. Key is to identify those problems which can be turned into opportunities for new product development. This can turn around the normal new product failure rate, which is currently about 75%. (Benefit research merely results in consumers telling you what they've been conditioned to want by years of advertising.)

Source: Larry Light, senior vice-president, Batten, Barton, Durstine & Osborne, Inc., 383 Madison Ave., New York 10017.

MARKET TESTS TESTED

Traditional test market and research patterns for new products are changing. Movement is toward more preliminary testing and research before test-marketing stage.

HOW TO GET FEEDBACK FROM CONSUMERS

Every time you listen to the people who buy the things you sell, you can learn something. The question is, what do you say to get them to talk?

Just asking consumers in research panels for new ideas never seems to get anywhere. That's why one of General Foods' top specialists in new products uses two key concepts with those panels: *stimulation* and *serendipity.*

By *stimulation* he means: Don't just talk, show them things: ads, packages, magazine articles (especially *Reader's Digest*). *Show* instead of tell.

By *serendipity* he means: Encourage the happy accident. Listen closely as consumers talk. When they make a mistake, don't correct them, but ask why they said what they did. Encourage confusion by showing them lots of things at once. Then ask, "What do you remember?"

This GF marketing executive finds that by giving customers lots of stimulation and listening with an open mind, you not only hear the problems but the solutions as well.

Source: Gerald Schoenfeld.

LIFESTYLE TRENDS

KEEP TABS ON UNEMPLOYMENT RATE FOR WOMEN

Sales of practically all consumer goods are now extremely sensitive to the earnings of women employees. Keep your projections finely tuned to *changes in the unemployment rate.*

The percentage of unemployed women may remain high as the economy recovers, although the total number of *employed* women continues to rise.

WHEN BLUE COLLAR WORKERS GO BACK TO WORK

Blue collar workers returning to work usually have been unemployed for a longer time than white collar counterparts. (Construction trades, which employ a large segment of blue collar workers, feel the recession first.) These blue collar workers (many of whom are *women*) have new attitudes about spending and saving because of the pinch they've been through.

What's likely to happen: Their percentage of savings will tend to rise, in part due to reducing outstanding loans. They will buy more carefully, be more determined to find better values.

Stay alert for changes:

• The wife of the blue collar worker will have a stronger voice in family buying decisions than has been the tradition.

• Teenagers in blue collar families may be faring better than teenagers generally. Many of them acquire trade skills, hold part-time jobs, and earn the privilege of making more independent buying decisions.

WOMEN QUESTIONING SOME OF THEIR NEW FREEDOMS

Fashion trends always reverse themselves. *Reason:* A reasonably prosperous and sophisticated society relishes change. *What to count on:* Women are beginning to question how some of their newly gained freedoms benefit them. Men have benefited at least as much from feminine freedom as the women.

• The warm glow of self-satisfaction that so many married women get from gainful employment has dimmed somewhat—perhaps because it has become so common.

• The husband's tendency to accept his wife's gainful employment as par for the course.

• The husband's decreasing willingness, after a time, to share household tasks.

Suggestion for adventurous marketers: Tone down marketing—especially advertising—with respect to the joys of feminine independence.

TAKE A FRESH LOOK AT THE "YOUTH" MARKET

Marketing programs aimed at the under-25s should be carefully scrutinized and revised. *Reason:* By 1985, the 25-45 age group will have increased sharply while there will be a steep downturn in the number of teenagers. Also look for gains by senior citizens. Don't neglect the older population groups in new product development. Look for ways to make existing lines appeal to those more mature groups.

TEENAGE MARKETING IS MORE THAN RECORDS AND SODA POP

Trend toward a rise in young generation wage earners as part of the family wage earners should not be ignored in your company's marketing strategy. (There is even a growing trend in the number of young members of the wage-earning family contributing to the family budget.)

Teenagers, both male and female, are fast feeding the growth of the do-it-yourself market. Manual skill among teenagers is astounding—particularly for car maintenance and repair. The paint industry would be astonished if it checked the amount of house-painting done by teenagers—who also now do a lot of wallpapering, putting down floor tiles, and installing ceiling squares. (Instructions for do-it-yourself teenagers lag behind their skills and comprehension.)

REACH THE WORKING TEENAGER

The working teenager used to contribute all, or a major share, of his (or her) earnings to the family's finances. Now the employed teenager tends to look upon a portion of earnings as "spending money" and spends it as he or she sees fit.

WILL FAMILIES GET LARGER AGAIN?

Census Bureau reports an uptrend in child adoption, primarily by young families that already have one or more children. Does this signal a return to larger families? Could be. The slice in family size over the last decade has been the sharpest in recent history. Now the Census Bureau reports that many women are having their first child at 35 to 40 years of age. If larger families are indeed on the way, most of the buying patterns predicted for the small family will now fail to put in an appearance, all of which suggests keeping in close touch with the U.S. Census Bureau. *Suggestion:* Be dubious about any life-style trend that has been strong for more than five years. It's due for a sharp change.

HUSBAND-BREAD-WINNER/WIFE-HOME-MAKER TRADITION BREAKS DOWN IN NEW WAYS

Recent studies by social scientists have uncovered fascinating—even startling—shifts in current attitudes toward traditional husband-breadwinner/wife-homemaker concepts by both husband and wife. *Example:* More men are adjusting without too much struggle to the stark fact that their wives are capable of topping the husband's earnings. And as one consequence, more husbands—with their spouse's approval, even encouragement—are taking up long-delayed projects. More husbands, when asked whether it bothers them that their wives earn more, now tend to reply, "Are you kidding?"

This may lead to new educational programs for the husband developed by his employer's personnel department. It may lead to new types of correspondence courses, more day courses. Sociologists conclude this situation encourages more divorces that are initiated by women as they achieve financial freedom.

For sure, the two-check family has yet to be adequately studied by most marketing departments. It is obviously the family that is changing its life-style to a greater degree than any other type of family. That must be reflected in consumer demand for many categories of consumer products and especially services. The change must also be reflected in advertising, particularly in media reaching segmented audiences. One conclusion that demands attention is that more men will accept a change of job more slowly because, with the wife's earnings, the wolf no longer prowls so insistently at the door.

MAJOR MARKETING TREND: SEARCH FOR ROOTS

This country has reached a critical turning point. It will affect all business, large and small, manufacturer and service organization. The change can be described simply as the end of the "plastics age" and the beginning of the age in which people search for roots—something consistent in their lives.

There are many reasons for the shift: Maturing of the youth culture, dissatisfaction over the emptiness of the so-called plastics age, the frustration of the endless (and often mindless) change for the new, the bigger—but not necessarily the better.

There is another reason, too: The "aging" of the population. The members of the baby boom are now moving into middle age and, soon, into old age. There are no new waves of babies replacing them, so our population is aging. And with more older people comes a change in what's thought to be important.

WHAT THAT MEANS. Some of the changes are apparent—and we've seen some starting:

● *Interest in nostalgia.* At its extreme, the nostalgia is for *events of 1965*! Resist laughing at such recent nostalgia. It tells much about people's need to find something more permanent than the present, which is changing and shifting so quickly. The interest in nostalgia is not a passing trend. It's a sign of permanence, something that marketers should stay tuned into for a long time.

● *Interest in restoration*—whether it's old homes or junk. Again, a search for roots, for something more permanent. Expect to see more evidence of such searches in the future. The focus will be on handmade, personal style, products with a unique quality—from arts and crafts to custom-made goods. Most will be sold through the boutique-type store. Sophisticated department stores will pick up on the trend, too.

● *Life-styles will shift.* The seminomad lives of many young people are falling out of fashion. *Of importance will be:* Steady work, sticking with one employer, a greater sense of cooperation and commitment between employee and employer. The corporation will modify its interest in growth for growth's sake.

● *Interest will grow in the concept of "struggle"*—because only through struggle can one appreciate accomplishment. An old-fashioned idea that will be rediscovered by tomorrow's youth.

● *The inner city will gain new focus.* Economic conditions permitting, watch for a revitalization of the city as a place to both live and work.

● *Growth of the older generation will*

produce profound changes in products and services—from the obvious shift in medicines and medical equipment designed for the older people, to a growing interest in travel and retirement. *This will create problems:* Will it be possible for the younger workers to produce enough to provide for the retired population without impairing their own living standards? Does this mean we'll need faster growth and more productivity than ever?

Looking back, the 1950s and '60s will be seen as a strange and brief madness in the country's history. The search for roots, through nostalgia and other interests, is thus a leading edge in an inevitable trend that will soon become relatively permanent.

Astute business will be watching these trends very carefully—to be sure they don't lose the opportunities that are presented.

Source: Dr. Theodore Levitt, *Working for Business Growth* (McGraw-Hill, 1221 Ave. of the Americas, New York 10020).

FAMILY RE-INTEGRATION A NEW TREND?

Through much of 1974 and 1975, and continuing at a somewhat slower pace in 1976, sociologists were consistently reporting a trend toward the disintegration of the traditional family structure. But starting with the first indications of economic recovery, that trend has lost some of its strength.

For marketing executives, a reversal in the weakening of the traditional

family structure would be of considerable importance.

It could, for example, apply some brakes to the current mobility of the family. It is axiomatic that the more solid the family structure, the less mobile the family tends to be.

KEEPING UP WITH THE JONESES IN LIFE STYLE TRENDS

Some life-style trends—many, in fact—become the socially correct, or "in" thing to do. Many new life-styles are a "statement"—a statement which is flashing a signal saying, "Look, we're with it."

This "keeping up with the Joneses" in life-style trends tends to be the most impermanent kind of marketing development. Like any fad, it will be short term.

The trick the marketing executive must carry off is to determine which new life-style change is a fad, and how close to leaking out the fad may be. It's a neat trick to pull off with any regularity, and most companies aren't even 80% right. But that's no reason to stop trying.

SEGMENTED LIFE-STYLE MARKETING

Individual taste, individual decisions by a more knowledgeable society constitute the basis of segmented marketing. Example of the potential scope of segmented marketing: cookware. On the one hand, the demand for *gourmet* cookware is strong. But equally strong is the *utilitarian* trend (stainless steel and cast aluminum). Then there's the *floral* look for those consumers who want a garden in the kitchen: the *coordinated* look; a market for the latest *color* fashions; the *first-set* market (budget-conscious); the *second-home* market; and the *trade-up* aluminum market. The growing popularity of Chinese and Japanese foods is helping sales of rice cookers and tempura dishes.

CAPITALIZING ON 'LEFTOVER' MARKET WITH CREATIVE ADVERTISING

A fundamental change is coming over traditionally extravagant and wasteful American families. *Result:* New market opportunities for wise advertisers.

• *Food:* American families have wasted more food when preparing meals at home than families anywhere else in the world. But the food industry is alert to consumers' need to stretch food dollars as family expenditures for food rise to higher percentages of the family's disposable income. *One idea:* Campbell Soup's advertising theme "Give me something different to do with holiday leftovers." *Subtitle:* "There's nothing like Campbell Soup for turning yesterday's meal into today's treat"—a potent appeal considering high meat prices.

• *Furniture:* "Mix-match" in home furnishings brings together odd pieces of furniture in new groupings. "Making do" becomes something to boast about in a sort of reverse snobbery. *Example:* The currently popular "platform bed."

• *Kitchenware:* Various pieces of cookware, often not color related, are brought together. Fundamentally, Americans, who are wasteful people, are tending toward less wastefulness—opening up new markets for many advertisers.

MORE PRODUCT CATEGORIES GO UNISEX

"Personal-care items" have the strongest brand loyalty, according to research by J. Walter Thompson ad agency. As men use more personal-care items (often "borrowed" from the woman's vanity), more personal-care packages will be designed for unisex appeal.

Sex distinctions are eroding even in other products. S. C. Johnson reports that more men are sharing housekeeping functions. Is your company keeping on top of sex-use changes for its product line!

HOW GROWING FAST-FOOD BUSINESS IS CHANGING MARKETS

At least 75% of away-from-home food consumption will eventually be controlled by 50 large food firms. That includes foods served in offices, plants, hospitals, schools, as well as in neighborhoods and along the highways.

These 50 giant firms will move *away* from the franchise system and become integrated food processors. Maybe even become a new kind of food wholesaler or broker.

Fast-food outlets will find new kinds of business to fill in valleys between peak food-serving times. Choice conventional locations are becoming scarce. New sites will be found along waterfronts, underground, on the upper floors of new high-rise office and apartment buildings.

HEALTH TRENDS

The decline in house calls by physicians, rising educational levels, rising medical fees, and the skyrocketing costs of a hospital stay are among the factors leading to a sharp rise in *self-medication at home*. Over-the-counter drugs are being formulated for greater potency. Barriers to over-the-counter consumer advertising are tumbling. New markets are being created for a broad range of consumer products—some of which, traditionally, had not been considered by marketing executives to qualify as *bona fide* "consumer" products.

Marketing to the booming spa chains:
More retailers and manufacturers will serve the nation's preoccupation with health and physical well-being. This is turning health and physical fitness into a growing service.

In city after city, health and beauty spas are opening up. The health and beauty spa may turn out to be one of the fastest growing businesses of the late '70s and early '80s. More retail stores will soon include spa and exercise facilities. Why not? If the store has a beauty shop, this is a logical extension.

And more manufacturers will now design and produce the equipment used by these chains—particularly the producers of home equipment.

DON'T WRITE OFF THE BABY MARKET

Even though the birth *rate* is declining, *more babies* are being born, according to the latest available figures. Even though women are having fewer children, the number of women who are in their childbearing years is growing faster than the population as a whole. This growth will continue for the next decade. *Other considerations:* With fewer children, more may be spent on each child. Women are having babies later in life, when they have more money to buy more baby products.

'GENERATION GAP' IS OLD HAT

Time to forget about a sales theme built around "the generation gap." The latest evidence is contained in a survey by *Seventeen* magazine. *Among the findings:* The man and woman that a teenage girl admires most are her father and mother. In matters concerning home life, morality, career choice, and politics, teenage girls are more *like* than unlike their parents. Very few hold radical political views; most hold views that reflect their parents' thinking.

Source: *Seventeen*, Research Dept., 850 Third Ave., New York 10022.

PRICING & PACKAGING

STRATEGIC PRICING

Key ingredients in any recession/inflation antidote are *cost calculations* and *pricing*. Typical costing pitfalls:

• Straight-line depreciation, especially in capital-intensive industries, artificially inflates profits during inflation. *Remedy:* Figure actual replacement costs for cost determination.

• Many companies base cost and profit margins on ratios calculated annually. *Danger:* Ratios are always out of date. Last year's experience generates figures that are far too low for this year's economic climate. *Remedy:* Figure costs and margins on quarterly or monthly basis (in some cases, weekly or even daily).

• Pricing is even more difficult, with many companies forced to choose between maintaining profit margins or maintaining market share. *Additional peril:* If you lower prices for competitive reasons, you may be stuck with them if price controls are revived.

Best bet: If you can do it, compete on a *nonprice* basis and hold your profit margin. If your customers have a special reason to buy from you—superior service, for example, or on-site engineering aid, or marketing assistance—don't sacrifice it to reduce prices.

• Charge separately for extras. It may forestall a rise in your basic price (a psychological advantage), and customers who don't want the extras, such as shipping, warehousing, distribution management, and the like, won't have to pay for them.

• In return for a price cut, let the buyer assume responsibility for obtaining sensitive components that could grow scarce or rise sharply in price during the life of a sales agreement.

• Keep your sales contracts short, or include provisions for escalation as your costs rise. Another possibility: Peg sales price to a widely used economic indicator of inflation ("indexing").

• Include renegotiation clause triggered by related economic indicator.

GOOD WAY TO TEST PRICING. Use direct mail for a new product. Quick way to find out what the public will really pay. Avoids problems caused by salespeople relying too much on industry tradition or competitive factors in recommending price levels.

PRODUCTS SUPERMARKETS WILL BUY TOMORROW

Supermarkets are changing their buying habits. Manufacturers should take note of the new opportunities, especially those companies that don't currently sell their products through supermarkets.

Supermarkets are actively looking for new products to sell—*other than foodstuffs. Major reason:* Nonfood items carry a higher profit margin than food, and with food-price competition as keen as it is, the smarter stores will seek to offset those narrow profits with nonfood items.

Also, supermarket managers see the discretionary dollar (the money over and above that needed for food and other essentials) getting more plentiful among the younger generation, since they are tending to have fewer children and both husband and wife are working, and supermarkets want a bigger share of that discretionary amount.

Indicated action: Reexamine your product line with the above information in mind. See if any item your company makes is a potential for a supermarket shelf.

PACKAGING. *Take a close look at your product's packaging.* You probably made sure it looks striking and attractive. But is it strong enough to withstand the rough handling it gets in the supermarket? Is it awkward to set up? Does it open too easily? Can the package be strengthened to make the supermarket *want* to stock your product?

Source: John Whitney, president, Pathmark Division, Supermarkets General Corp., at a talk given at the Sales Executive Club of New York.

FTC AND DISCOUNTS FOR INCREASED BUSINESS

One wholesaler found that neither the 4% discount it was offering for cash nor the 3% for payment within 30 days was doing the job to its complete satisfaction. They wanted to encourage customers to increase their business with the firm.

Hence, it planned to offer, in *addition* to a 3% discount for payment within 30 days, 1% if purchases for the current year exceeded those of the prior year and 2% if they exceeded those of the prior year by 50% or more.

The firm checked out its plan with the Federal Trade Commission. *Verdict:* The 1% discimininates against those who were not customers during the prior year, as well as against those who didn't increase their purchases. The 2% discriminates against customers who may have increased their purchases but not by 50%. Such discriminations might violate Sec. 2(a) of the Robinson-Patman Act, and would also be illegal if the effect was to substantially lessen competition.

Comment: Price differentials can be justified where they're geared to cost savings, or if necessary to meet competition, or if they won't result in competitive injury. The whole area is a minefield that's only to be negotiated with the aid of tested experts, who may advise you against even asking the FTC for a prior ruling.

Baumgold Bros., Inc., FTC Advisory Opinions, 5/14/74.

TRADEMARKS NEED TENDER LOVING CARE

The value of your company's trademarks may be carried as "$0" on the balance sheet, but their real value is staggering. Make sure the advertising, marketing, and sales people take very good care of that property. *Suggestions:*

• Trademarks should *always* appear in a form made distinctive by using capital letters or quotation marks.

A graphic *trademark notice* should appear immediately after the mark at least once (best after the first mention of the mark) every time the work is used in a communication. If the mark has been registered with the U.S. Patent Office, the proper notice is "®" or "Reg. U.S. Pat. Off." If the mark has not been registered, the proper notice is "TM" or an asterisk with a footnote explaining, "A trademark of [your company].

• Like any other adjective, a trademark ("X") should have a noun—in this case the generic name for the product—to refer to at least once in each communication in which the mark is mentioned ("X" sponge).

• A trademark should *never* be used in the possessive form ("X's" sponge).

• A trademark should never be used in the plural, although many marks end with an "s" (thousands of "X's").

• A trademark for a raw material should never be used to describe finished products made with the raw material ("X" mops).

• A trademark is not and should not be used as a verb ("X" your floors).

You can use an asterisk after the trademark with a footnote: "[The mark] is a registered trademark for [a generic class of products] made by [your company]."

Source: *A Guide to the Care of Trademarks,* available free from the U.S. Trademark Assn., 6 E. 45 St., New York 10017.

SIMPLY REGISTERING A TRADEMARK DOESN'T PROTECT IT

Rights in a trademark (or tradename) can be acquired only by putting it to *commercial use.* Registration, which is optional, cannot take place until *after* the required use.

Even experienced trademark lawyers may disagree with their colleagues about how to establish commercial use.

Case: On advice of counsel, one company shipped samples bearing the new trademark to its regional sales managers, who *personally* paid for them. The firm believed that would be enough to establish commercial use. But a Federal court ruled that because a trademark exists so the customer can identify a product, the mark must be exposed to the *purchasing* public to be protected.

MARKETING

Another firm attached a *new* trade name to shipments that had been ordered by customers under an old established trade name, so goods went out with both names. The court ruled that the company had failed to make *bona fide* use of the mark, considering this a bad-faith attempt to reserve it for future use.

TOO LITTLE USE. While a single use may be enough to entitle you to register a trademark, *more* is required to sustain it. And the use must be for a *bona fide* business purpose—not contrived for trademark maintenance purposes.

In a recent case, 89 sales of a trademarked perfume extending over 20 years weren't enough to protect the mark, even though all sales were at a profit.

Comment: Even though the attempt to appropriate trademark names and so exclude possible competition ultimately fails, as it did in this case, it may have the practical effect of holding off competition during the interval. However, registering of a broad range of trademarks for the purpose of appropriating the field and limiting competition, if that could be established, might possibly run into trouble as being in restraint of trade.

La Societe Anonyme des Parfumes Le Gallon v. Jean Patou, Inc., C.A. 2,495 F. 2d 1265.

PACKAGING TRENDS

Bulk products like salt and pet food, which are commonly packaged in multi-wall bags, are being switched into corrugated boxes. *Reason:* Supermarkets are demanding the switch; bags clog automated warehouse and distribution systems.

RECYCLED MATERIAL FOR PACKAGING

Recycled packaging is competitive in whiteness, brightness, and printability when it is sandwiched between surface layers of higher-quality fiber and finished with quality coatings.

If made properly, recycled board is *flatter* than virgin fiber. Machinability on packing lines is then excellent—and production costs are lower.

Contaminants are no longer a problem. Recycled packaging board meets current government health requirements. Consumer acceptance of recycled packaging is high.

Strength is somewhat less than that of virgin board, but this problem can be corrected by addition of higher-quality fiber to the mix.

PRESSURE-SENSITIVE POSSIBILITIES

Use pressure-sensitive labeling for short-term product promotions. A consumer products company used pressure-sensitive labels, applied to the caps of aerosol cans, as coupons for a free-gift-with-purchase promotion.

Labels were easily removed for

redemption. The introductory lead time was considerably less than what would have been needed to have the promotion printed on the can. *Another use:* Pressure-sensitive labels to cover a seam on an aerosol can in a foreign country accustomed to seamless cans. (That label was in that country's language, and *not* easily removed.) Pressure-sensitive labels can also be used to tell store clerks how to best display a new product.

DIRECT MARKETING

GUIDELINES

Direct marketing presents opportunities for big and small marketers. There's no guaranteed system for success, but here are guidelines recommended by Bob Stone of Rapp, Collins, Stone & Adler Advertising, Chicago:

- *Best mail order products:* Items not readily available in retail stores. Items not available by mail at a price as low as yours.
- *Recommended markup:* On a single item, sell at three to four times cost. Items sold together in catalog can be marketed profitably by selling at twice what you pay for them (preferably 2½ times).
- *How to get started:* Test items individually first. Then build catalog around those that sell best.
- *Mailing lists:* Stick to lists of people who have bought by mail. *Best prospects:* Names that appear on two or more such lists (a good list broker can be very helpful).
- *Best pages in a catalog:* Back-cover; inside front cover; pages 3, 4, 5; inside back cover; center spread; page facing order form.
- *To get bigger orders:* Accept credit cards. (Average *charge* order from a catalog is 20% larger than order requiring a check.)
- *When to use TV for mail order:* Best as support medium for saturation mailings or newspaper inserts. Small TV budget can increase response from prime medium by 25%. *Best items to sell directly via TV:* Merchandise that lends itself to visual demonstration.

PROJECTIONS FOR DIRECT MAIL

How to project the results of a direct-mail campaign before all the results are in:

Keep a *daily record* of results from each mailing to build a history to serve for the projection. If you mail to various lists, key (mark) each order card so you can identify the source.

Divide the total produced from each list by two. See how many days of response it took to reach that "half total."

That is your *doubling date.* No matter how long a period it takes for the replies to come in, half the total arrives within relatively few "mail days."

On a first-class *national* mailing, the doubling date will run about five mail days. Third class might be about 2½ times as long. Smaller envelopes will be faster than the 9x12 size. Christmas and summer responses will take longer.

HOW A SMALL PLASTICS FIRM COMPETES WITH GIANTS

Small companies and divisions of giants can be inspired by Chemplex, which chose direct mail and a limited print ad campaign in trade journals. The total market for Chemplex products is small—only about 800 customers and prospects. Direct mail is a far cheaper way to keep the company's name in front of prospects than the heavy institutional advertising of its larger competitors.

Direct mail gives the company more room to exercise ingenuity and a light touch than a print campaign would. *Example:* One of its first mailings was of a wooden egg on two legs. When the egg is pressed down, the company's name and address pop up.

Other promotions include football jerseys, crew hats, beach towels, and spill-proof cups for people who drink coffee while they drive to work, all carefully linked by accompanying copy to Chemplex's products and its ability to service customers.

Bonus: Trade magazine ads *rarely* attract *many* comments from cus-

tomers. But Chemplex salesmen are constantly getting feedback on the mailings.

CRITERIA FOR DIRECT MAIL SUCCESS

• *Choose items with care:* They should appeal to everybody (watches, radios, kitchen knives), or to everybody in a distinct market segment you can identify and segregate with precision (tools, kits for home-owners, devices and gadgets for scientists, boat owners, hobbyists).

• *Don't be guided by personal preferences:* A fake diamond, a 76-piece socket wrench set *you* wouldn't touch, can be successes with some group or a select list of way-out hobbyists.

• *Aim for uniqueness:* Build into the product if need be. Ideal mail-order items aren't readily available in retail or discount stores. Look for those that differ in design, style or material; those you can offer at a lower price. *Examples:* Unusual imports, industrial products adapted for home use, complete home movie outfits, repair kits, a full selection of prime meats or cheeses of all nations, or chrome molybdenum kitchen knives. Fight discount store competition on ordinary items (and get away with charging regular prices) by offering a unique package: Add a high-intensity lamp, radio log, distinctive cabinet, extra equipment or supplies, carrying cases, free photo enlargements, recipes, serving pieces.

• *Test your price:* Try out several price offers on a sample drawn from your selected market. *It must be right for that market's particular value perceptions:* (A $3 clothing item may be wrong for a salesman and just right for a blue-collar worker.) Low price may suggest poor quality on a high quality item. Pennies' difference in shipping and handling charges can turn off customers even if item is priced right.

• *Add incentives, guarantees:* Use installment-payment arrangements on big-ticket items. Money-back guarantees (with time limits) on products whose performance or benefits won't be obvious for a few months. Free gifts to promote purchase of run-of-the-mill items.

• *Choose the right advertising:* Print media, if full story can be told well in a page or less (or can't get a good prospect mailing list for, say, old men or tall girls). TV, if visual demonstration's the big need. Direct mail, when you really need "personal" appeal, lots of illustrations and selling copy.

Source: Bob Stone, chairman, Rapp, Collins, Stone & Adler, Chicago.

UNTAPPED DIRECT MARKETING

Business confuses the concept of a *product* and a *service.* Too often, it tries to sell me a one-time product, whereas if it could shift its perspective and sell me a continuing *service,* I'd be happier and the business would have a much better customer.

A simple, but instructive example: Let's say I smoke a pack of cigarettes a day; that's 30 packs a month. What if the manufacturer promised me he'd deliver 3 cartons of cigarettes every month? I'd *gain,* because: (1) I'd conceivably save money buying directly from the manufacturer; (2) I'd never run out of cigarettes. The manufacturer would gain, because there'd be less chance of my switching brands, since I now have the convenience of not having to shop for them and thus fewer opportunities to switch. What a difference—all because the manufacturer now sees me as a consumer of a service rather than a buyer of a box which I must decide upon each time I walk into a store.

The example points up the big benefits of direct marketing. It's a service/product that's sold on a continuing basis directly from the manufacturer. And the same simple technique can be extended to any number of types of products/services as well.

Other ideas to stimulate your thinking:

Automobiles: Instead of trying to lure me into a showroom to order those wonderful cars, why not keep track of when I pay off my auto loan, then call me up and say, "I understand you're about ready for new transportation. I've got some transportation you should like, let me bring it around so you can try it out. Drive it for a few days. If you like, you can have it for so many dollars a month."

Once again, a service—this time transportation. The same thing can be done with television sets, refrigerators, and other high-ticket items.

Important: It may cost a lot, relatively speaking, to find the unique buyer, but once you do, you make it up easily, since that buyer comes back over and over again.

Consider the laundry service: Who is better able to sell me shirts and sheets—after all, who knows better when my present ones are worn out than my laundry?

Biggest untapped potential: Industrial prospect locator. With salesmen so costly, straight prospect canvassing is just too expensive. You've got to save the salesmen for the real sale. Through direct marketing, you can find the potential customers—the people who can use your service; the high-level "hidden" people that the salesmen can't easily get to. The concept is being used effectively, for example, in selling business airplanes. But few other industries have professionally tested direct marketing methods. That's a mistake.

What you can't sell by direct mailing: Products that can't be translated easily into a service, or which have traditionally done well in specialized retail stores: most foods, some drugs, where volume and the fact that the retail outlet has been designed specifically to sell it are already successful.

Variations: Stores like J. C. Penney's have developed interesting variations of direct marketing. Customers pick out the item through ads or on display in stores, then order it directly from the Penney's warehouse. Sears does about the same, but they go through the added expense of distributing an elaborate catalog, which Penney's sidesteps.

Cost of getting in: That depends on how you want to break into direct marketing. A small test costs very little, and can be done with simple in-house facilities. But a big catalog program requires many specialties and shouldn't be attempted without careful planning.

Source: Lester Wunderman, president, Wunderman, Ricotta & Kline, New York.

MANAGEMENT ESSENTIALS FOR DIRECT MARKETING

Forget the traditional advertising concepts of cost per thousand mailing pieces. *Cost per order* is far more important. That can often be improved by *raising* the cost per thousand, not shaving it.

Also important to measure: Cost per *paid* order (some mail order respondents are deadbeats). And cost per *converted* order (the *second* order is considered the conversion; once prospect has bought twice, he's much easier to sell a third, fourth, and fifth time).

Be prepared to spend as much *after* an inquiry has been received as before.

Caution: Direct mail can unsettle company's normal procedures. Salespeople may resent or fail to put forth best effort for prospects enticed into showroom by "bribe" (free book, free package of seeds, etc.). However, some premium, or incentive (trial offer, special price for limited time, supply limited) is imperative to give prospects a reason for taking action *now*.

Be careful of "free" merchandise upfront. *Better:* Make people pay a little. Often the premium can be used as an *incentive for payment*.

Direct marketing is easiest where purchase involves *fun* or pure enjoyment (as opposed to *work*). Being first on the block to own something also has strong appeal.

Where to find help: Best bet is to check with nearest Direct Mail/Marketing Association office (main office, 1730 K Street, N.W., Washington, D.C.

20006) for the names of local specialized agencies and freelancers who have been in business for a year or more.

Expect to pay $4,000 to $5,000 for an initial campaign to develop leads. Ongoing annual programs will cost a minimum of $12,000, exclusive of production and postage. Figure a commission rate of 17.65% on production costs.

Source: Dick Benson, 30-year direct marketing veteran at Time Inc., American Heritage.

HOW TO FIGURE AN ORDER MARGIN

Here's a form to use for all marketing efforts. Helpful in knowing if the company is making money, breaking even or losing. It should be a basic tool for all marketers. It's particularly useful for those in *direct mail* marketing.

ITEMIZED EXPENSE (CREDIT)	Per Unit	Projected per 1,000
1. Cost of product or service being sold	$	$
2. Royalty, commission, etc.		
3. Ancillary services		
4. Premiums, prizes, etc.		
5. Order receipt and processing		
6. Fulfillment, labor and materials		
7. Fulfillment, postage, freight, etc.		
8. Fulfillment, other		
A. TOTAL (Items 1-8)	$	$
9. General and administrative		
10. Credit checking		
11. Billing and collection		
12. Follow-up correspondence		
13. Refunds, cancellations		
14. Returns (handling, refurbishing only)		
15. Bad debts (at selling price)		
B. TOTAL (Items 9-15)	$	$
C. TOTAL (Items 1-15)	$	$
16. Returns, inventory value	( )	( )
17. Residual value of prospect names	( )	( )
18. Ancillary sales, profits only	( )	( )
D. TOTAL (Items 16-18)	($)	($)
E. TOTAL (Items 1-18)	$	$
19. Product/service selling price*	( )	( )
20. Extra charges	( )	( )
21. Extra charges	( )	( ) F. TOTAL
F. TOTAL (Items 19-21)	($)	($)
G. GRAND TOTAL/ORDER MARGIN	$	$

*In the case of two-step selling programs (*i.e.*, leads/sales, inquiries/orders, etc.), be sure to apply appropriate *conversion factors*. For instance, if only one in ten leads results in a closed sale, then product/service selling price should be entered at only 10% of actual.

Source: Jack Oldstein, president, Dependable Lists, 257 Park Ave. South, New York 10010.

CUSTOMER SERVICE

COMMUNICATING WITH MORE SOPHISTICATED CONSUMERS

One company recently informed its managers: "Increasingly, customer inquiries require more than superficial response, because one result of consumerism has been a drastic change in both the *volume* and *nature* of such inquiries."

From the relatively simple "how," "why," and "whatever became of" letters of only a few years ago, today's queries are much more sophisticated and cover a broadening range of technical subjects.

What organizational changes has your company made to improve the deaf ear that most corporations *still* turn to the inquiring or complaining consumer?

CUTTING CUSTOMER SERVICE COSTS

Last place many companies look to cut costs is on customer service. But there's ample room for doing so—without losing what may be your only major edge over competitors. Steps to take:

• *Appraise your service.* Is it substantially better or worse than that offered by the competition? (Don't use *complaints* alone as a guideline: Many customers never complain, and some complain for no good reason.) Check for length of total order cycle, promptness of arrivals, condition of shipment, accuracy of billing, service you may give free when others charge.

• *Improve ordering practices.* If your salespeople write orders *for* the customer, see that *they* get them *right* and *you* get them *immediately.* Walking around with orders in their pockets over weekends, for example, can delay shipment a week or more. Wrong or incomplete specs can hang up the customer and your service department with costly delays, cross-queries, premium transportation charges, and a mad tangle of rush replacement orders.

Related: If the customer writes his own orders, teach him how. (And how to estimate his requirements to avoid special rush orders and bring his purchasing cycle into phase with your own order cycle.)

• *Don't let your sales force offer unnecessary service as a ploy to land orders.* Given a chance at special lead times and deluxe service, your customer will grab them. And learn to demand them. Have your staff probe for customer's *minimum* requirements; the lead times, quantities, partial shipments, and substitutes they can live with. Then try to make them happy with it.

• *Encourage:* Longer lead time. Larger orders. Order cycles that avoid peaks and valleys of warehouse activity. *Avoid:* Special orders that send your trucks out half empty (or emptier). End-of-month or end-of-quarter shipment requests from salesmen looking to commission credit for the period (forcing order and warehouse departments into costly overtime).

• *Train salesmen in basic logistics that count with customers:* Cases per standard pallet. Carton stackability limits pallet exchange and back-haul allowance, etc.

• *Charge a little for* selected services (shipping, repairs, small orders, custom engineering services). Particularly if your competitors do it.

• *Say "thank you."* It's unbelievable how few companies send a real "thank you" for the business they've spent months or years cultivating.

• *Notification of delivery:* Let the customer know by mail if possible, by phone if necessary, that the shipment is on its way (and when the carrier can be expected to deliver it).

HANDLING INQUIRIES

Cheapest way to handle product inquiries is to answer all of them. It costs less than trying to figure out which ones are genuine leads.

All inquiries, of course, don't have to be answered in the same way. An obvious prospect can get an immediate phone call, another a fully detailed catalog. Everyone should get something—a folder and a reply card, for example, or the answer to their specific question.

If your company is too busy to undertake this effort itself, there are services that will do it for you. Some will answer all queries, follow them up, keep track of results, and regularly submit a computer printout showing inquiries, replies, and sales broken down by region, product, media, and the like.

Others provide trained interviewers who telephone each inquirer by WATS line and evaluate him as a prospect.

Critical point: If too many of your inquiries aren't really prospects, evaluate your advertising and the media. You may be saying the wrong things or not talking to the right people.

HOW MANY DISSATISFIED CUSTOMERS?

Rules of thumb: Only 20% of all dissatisfied *industrial* customers actually mention it. Multiply customer complaints by 5 to get the actual total. For *consumer* products, multiply the complaints by 50. Only 2% of all dissatisfied consumers complain.

IMPROVING INSTRUCTION SHEETS

Simple note at bottom of product's instruction sheets, particularly those which tell how to assemble product, can be helpful in many ways. Note should say, "We welcome suggestions for improvement of these instructions." Customers may see things your designers have missed. Offering cash awards for suggestions should be weighed.

OFFICE MANAGEMENT

PERSONNEL

WHAT MAKES A GOOD OFFICE MANAGER

If the conduct of your office routines is often sloppy and out of hand, maybe it's time to appoint an office manager. The cost, for a small business or branch office, may be as little as giving a title and a raise to an existing employee. Or it could be the cost of a new employee. Against this must be weighed the probable increase in office efficiency and the extra time that this gives to upper management to concentrate on matters other than office procedures. However, the main advantages are dependent on having the right person for the job. General characteristics to look for are these:

• Skill as a planner, leader, teacher, and communicator.

• Knowledge of office procedures, paperwork systems, and the effects of different machines on office procedure.

• Experience with budgeting and accounting.

• Flexibility to adjust to changing requirements.

RESPONSIBILITIES

The administrative manager (or office manager) should have the authority to decide what happens in the office of a company. That authority should include the systems to be used, the machines and furniture which are necessary, administering costs of operating the office, hiring of office clerks.

Supervisors and managers who might efficiently report to the administrative manager include: Manager of the accounting department, manager of data processing, director of personnel, director of security and records, manager of the employee cafeteria, supervisor of maintenance, supervisor of microfilm department, supervisor of word-processing center, and purchasing manager.

In smaller companies, the administrative manager is likely to report directly to the president and be equal in rank to the sales director and treasurer. In larger companies, the administrative manager may be a vice-president and report to a senior (or executive) vice-president.

Most common complaints of administrative managers:

(1) Not paid enough for the amount of work they do and their responsibilities.

(2) They don't have enough time to do all the work that comes with the job.

TEMPORARY OFFICE WORKERS

To get the most out of temporary help, start by giving the service that provides temporaries accurate job descriptions. No need to pay secretarial rates for a receptionist. *Special case:* If you're ordering a temporary worker for one of the new types of word-processing machines, be *specific* about the model description of the machine and the work to be done. There are various machines, and it's easy to wind up with a worker trained for the wrong one.

Assign one regular person to supervise the temporary to avoid confusion and keep other workers from dumping work on her or him. Check upon temporary's work several times during the first day. If you're dissatisfied, call by 3 o'clock to have a replacement for the next day.

Warning: Before dealing with a temporary agency, make sure it carries adequate insurance. Have your lawyer check its workmen's compensation insurance certificate. Be absolutely certain the agency assumes liability for any risks its employees encounter while working for you.

TRAINING EXECUTIVE ASSISTANTS

A secretary can be trained to function as a real executive assistant, but only if the executive is willing to invest some time. Here's how it's done:

• *Begin by examining the frequently heard comment:* "It takes me less time to do it myself." The statement is usually wrong, because most business functions occur over and over again, so by explaining it once, an executive can benefit many times over.

• *Evaluate the general training provided:* Has the assistant been clued in to what the boss's business goals are— short-term and long-term? Has she been asked whether (and to what extent) she wants to share in the work necessary to meet those goals? The less ambitious person, given the right opportunity, will make her goals clear—at which point the boss has to determine whether he wants to hire someone else.

• The best training, often, is nothing more than an ongoing daily conversasation between executive assistant and boss on such things as: *Today's goals. Tomorrow's goals. What the assistant can do to meet those goals.* It usually takes only 10-15 minutes a day. It's got to be done every day to be useful.

• Ask the assistant, after some familiarity with the job, what function she can do which the boss now does. That question should create some irritation for some executives. Many managers use "simple" chores as a change of pace. So they may be reluctant to give them up. But those functions should be examined. Giving up some responsibilities could be as fruitful for the boss as for the assistant.

• Important to provide feedback to your assistant on results of her efforts. Some assistants need frequent (daily) feedback, others are so independent that weekly or monthly discussion is sufficient. If an executive is dealing with a sizable number of assistants, he should actually make a checklist to be sure feedback is occurring at good intervals.

• *How to build your assistant's stature in the eyes of others on your staff:* Let the assistant schedule meetings, handle follow-ups, receive status reports.

• *Another way to build an assistant's image of herself—and to provide self-*

learning: Have her do your advance reading of magazines and other material. She can alert you to important items—or where valuable, provide a summary. Steady feedback on how well she does builds both her knowledge and self-assurance. And it's very helpful to the executive.

Source: Alice van Horen, training and development consultant, 2053 Fletcher Ave., Fort Lee, N.J. 07024.

WHAT NOT TO THROW AWAY FROM FILES

Clearing out files? Have a senior executive advise everyone, particular-ly file clerks, not to destroy anything without *clearing it with the tax department* or tax advisor.*

Records necessary to support, substantiate, or document a federal income tax return must be kept readily available until the statute of limitations runs out—at least three years and often more.

This includes travel and entertainment bills, contribution write-offs, details of bad debt write-offs, and depreciation expense.

Contemporary records are the only ones the Internal Revenue Service accepts. Be sure to collect them from retirees or terminated employees.

*For details: *Records Retention* (Ellsworth Publishing, P.O. Box 3162, Evansville, Ind. 47731).

EQUIPMENT

DOING WITHOUT WORD PROCESSING EQUIPMENT

Before you're oversold on a new, centralized "word processing" system, see if you can achieve equal results (or better) simply by improving your current secretarial system.

The average secretary spends only about 20% of her time typing, less than 4% taking shorthand. She is *away from her desk more than 30% of the time* on errands, filing, duplicating documents, etc.

Checklist for your present office system:

1. Are secretaries near their principals? Is each secretary near another secretary, typist, or other aide, so that empty desks can be easily covered?

2. Has everything been done to keep high-priced secretaries at their desks, such as the use of messengers, pages, aides and the like?

3. Is your equipment compatible, so that work can be done by more than one operator?

4. Are secretaries promoted for productivity and work quality rather than

for the boss' status?

5. Have the administrative skills and judgment of each secretary been measured and used?

Source: Paul G. Truax, Truax, Smith & Assoc., Wilmington, Del., in *The Office.*

WORD PROCESSING: HOW A FIRM MADE IT WORK

Weyerhaeuser began to phase in word processing in the early 1970s. After about a year, the company moved to a new building which was about a quarter-mile long, and one big word-processing center was established at the end of one floor. It was supposed to take care of all the typing needed by the whole building.

It didn't work. Secretaries didn't cooperate because they feared loss of their jobs. Work took too long to complete. Weyerhaeuser experimented by decentralizing word processing. A *mini*center was started on one floor. Those who would use the center attended an open house to have the functions explained. They saw what it could do for them and that it wasn't going to eliminate jobs. Eventually, more minicenters were established. Word-processing personnel working in each area became familiar with that area's technical language and needs. Work was completed more quickly and done better. The central word-processing department was finally eliminated and 14 minicenters now do the work.

A word-processing system can speed up output of letters, memos, and reports, *but only if you keep down turnover of operators.* Take special care to rotate WP assignments. Some of them (transcribing from earphones) are unusually tedious. Many operators quit. *Budget salary increases* for new WP operators within six months of hiring. That is how long average training takes. (*Important:* Don't let your operators quit for better-paying jobs as soon as they become proficient.)

Uncomfortably loud clatter of word processing equipment can be muffled by *acoustical enclosures.* If you buy them, check these points: (1) Joints should be held securely by rivets and screws. (2) The enclosure should not restrict operator's performance or obscure operator's view of the equipment. (3) The enclosure should permit the circulation of cooling air. If a fan is required, make sure it doesn't make more noise than the machine.

MICROFILM SUCCESS STORY

The Gorton Group, Massachusetts frozen fish processor, had about one million hard-copy documents filed in 1,500 square feet of space. It was adding about 500,000 documents annually.

After a year-long study, they bought a Kodak Miracode II microfilm filing system, consisting of a camera, retrieval unit, film processor, and film duplicator. Each microfilm image was imprinted with a retrieval code.

Cost: $40,000. *Result:* (1) Filing space was reduced from 1,500 square feet to 400. (2) Average retrieval time was cut from 4 minutes to 30 seconds. (3) Document loss rate was reduced to zero. (4) Invoices and credits were cross-referenced in the retrieval code to facilitate quick comparison.

Planned training of clerks for retrieval of documents proved unnecessary since the system was so simple.

• The Internal Revenue Service has lengthy guidelines on the conditions under which microfilm and microfiche can be used to store corporate records. Ask your accountant to review the details of Revenue Procedure 76-43 with the people at your company involved with records storage.

WHAT TO LOOK FOR IN OFFICE FURNITURE

• *Secretarial chairs:* Should be adjustable within a range of at least 16⅔-19⅔ inches from the floor to accommodate short and tall individuals comfortably. To avoid pressure against the lower spine, an open space adjustable within a 4-6 inch range is advisable. Padding ought to be medium firm and textured to permit periodic shifts of position. For nontypists, swivel armchairs might be a better choice.

• *Desks:* Should be checked for structural strength, quality of top material and finish, and smooth drawer operation. Old-fashioned secretarial units with typewriter wells are on the way out; most clerical employees don't want to bother shutting up their machines at quitting time.

• *File cabinets:* Smooth drawer operation, structural strength, and dura-

bility are the key criteria. In vertical units, ease of adjustment of follower blocks is a consideration; laterals should be checked for stability, since some tip over when drawers are yanked.

BUSINESS INTERIOR DESIGNING

A well-designed, attractive office environment generally increases efficiency and productivity—and makes your employees feel happier, dress better, studies show.

To get the effect you want, select a designer whose work you have admired and who you feel has solved similar design problems.

Expect to pay the design firm via one of three methods: (1) By the square foot. (2) A percentage of the amount spent on base drawings and net price of furniture and construction. (*Note:* Generally, on a medium-size job, the totals for each of these methods are very close.) (3) On an hourly basis. Trade discounts should be passed on to you.

Get a breakdown of the cost for each phase: planning, work drawings, and design. (This is especially useful if the job is halted before completion— you'll know exactly what you owe.) Also, expect the designer to tell you how much any revisions in scope will cost you.

Representative costs: Design fees for a total design should be about $1.25 or $2.00 per square foot (although this figure can run as high as $6 for offices under 10,000 square feet). Construction for an average job goes from $6-$12 per square foot up to $50. Furniture usually costs $4-$10 per square foot.

Information the designer will need: What business the company is in, what work is actually done, future expansion plans, who visits, paper flow, the real budget for the job, and top management likes and dislikes. They will probably survey the employees (by written questionnaire or orally, if staff is small) to determine department size, whom it works with, work flow, visitors, etc. This should take about a week. One key executive must work closely with the designer. The designer should have a single decision-making source, so he's not getting input from the wrong people.

Expect to see two preliminary presentations before actual work begins: First: the designer tells what he'd like to do and gives you a cost estimate based on what he has learned about your company. You should be ready to indicate if the figure is reasonable or too high. Next, the designer provides more details on materials, construction, colors, etc., including samples. Expect a firm indication of cost.

Source: Neville Lewis, Neville Lewis Associates, interior designer, New York City.

SURVEY COPIER APPLICATIONS TO CUT COSTS

Use logs that don't require much time to fill out. The survey should record the employee making copies, the person the copies are made for, how many things are copied, how many copies are made of each, and the time and the day the copies are made.

What to look for: What times during the day the copier is most used. Do lines form? Do people group materials to be copied together? Are numerous trips made for small numbers of copies? Are regular forms and correspondence copied (suggesting insufficient use of carbons)? Would a collator be helpful?

PROTECT AGAINST COPIER FRAUD

Color copiers (Xerox 6500) produce such high-quality copies that counterfeiters are using them to print bogus stock certificates, and employees are using them to reproduce paychecks.

Here's how to tell a color copy:
• If rubbed with a piece of white tissue, the smudge will be a different color from the item rubbed.
• If touched with a hot iron with a plain piece of paper between the copy and the iron, the copy will stick to the paper.

MAKE FACSIMILE USAGE MORE PRODUCTIVE

Concentrate on larger volume communications to increase fax productivity. These areas include data you're now sending by messenger service, special delivery, priority air dispatch, mailgrams, telegrams, Telex, or TWX. One-of-a-kind crisis documents may be important, but are only a small part of your volume.

Typically, 60% of a company's crucial inputs go to only 15% of its addresses. Determine where priority information comes from and where it goes to. Information now sent in the mail may be better faxed.

Analyze incoming and outgoing telephone calls. Typically, you'll find 15% to 20% of the calls are strictly for passing data; 30% involve sending some sort of figures and discussion of them. This 30% can be faxed rather than phoned to make the fax more cost-effective and cut phone bills.

THE RIGHT SPOT FOR A COPIER

Put your office copying machines in central locations where they are widely visible.

Reasons:

• The copying machine is replacing the water cooler as the natural spot for casual conversations in American offices.

• Visibility discourages use for non-business purposes.

• A central location saves employee time by shortening trips to the machine and saves wasteful waiting time because employees can see whether the machine is in use without leaving their desks.

Do you have a specially marked basket next to your office copier where employees can put unsatisfactory copies? If you're paying for per-copy usage, *you can get a refund* on those unsatisfactory copies.

DICTATING MACHINES: BOOST PERSONAL EFFICIENCY

One of the worst executive time-wasters: Writing reports, letters or memos *longhand.* A faster way—which also guarantees the ability to capture fast-moving thought: *Dictating equipment.*

But most executives (about 90% by latest count) refuse to use dictating equipment, offering these excuses: *I find I can't get the words out in order. . . . I can't really review what I've said. . . . It's too hard to talk it out.*

The real reason: They're disorganized, and when they try to put their thoughts on tape, the disorganization becomes more apparent.

How to solve the problem: If the executive will just go through the small exercise of making notes about what he wants to dictate—not full sentences, just the highlights of the points he wants to make in the right order—he'll find the dictation moving along very swiftly. The combined time—note-taking and dictation—will be far less than the time spent in writing out the material longhand.

Experienced executives use this technique: If the letter or memo is simple, instruct the secretary to type it in its *final* form. You'll find you can even live with minor "errors." If the dictation is complex, instruct her to type triple-spaced with no worry about neatness. You can then edit the transcript for the final typing. (You'll find, after some practice, that you won't have to do very much editing. As you get more practice, you'll find less need to use the rough draft approach.)

EQUIPMENT: WHAT TO BUY. When buying, don't insist on a trial period. It sounds nice in theory, but doesn't work in practice. *Reason:* If you make no financial commitment to dictation equipment, you won't try very hard to make it work for you, and there's no question that the biggest obstacle is your own working habits.

Avoid the big, desk-top dictators. They're great for prestige, but the small, portable equipment serves you better. You can leave it on your desk, carry it to meetings, tote it in your briefcase, carry it around for the times you do homework, have it handy for dictation during waiting periods (between appointments, between planes, and those moments when a great idea comes to you).

WHAT SIZE TAPE. In general, avoid the early-model *mini*cassette recorders. These units provide poor fidelity. *Worse:* If you are traveling and need extras, you'll find it very hard to buy a minicassette tape in a small town. So stick to the more recent, full-size cassette units—even though they're bulkier. [The new Sony minicassette recorder, which fits in your shirt pocket, is handy, provides excellent sound. It's quite expensive—but worth it.]

Avoid cheap machines. The transcriber is going to have a very difficult time catching your words—because of bad fidelity, poor noise filtering, etc. Before buying, try out the unit for reproduction quality. *Smart move:* Invite your secretary to listen to it—and get the unit she feels most comfortable with in playback.

THE PLAYBACK UNIT. *Also important:* The transcribing unit should be of the best quality. Makes no sense to have a good-quality recorder and then ask the secretary to struggle over poor playback fidelity and other playback inconveniences. [*Editor's note:* Again, after much experimenting, we settled on Sony equipment, even though the cost was somewhat higher than some of the competing equipment we tested.]

WHAT TO AVOID. IBM desk units. They're good, *if* you limit their use to the office. In reality, that rarely happens. Once you get the hang of dictating, you'll want to use it in other places as well, and the IBM unit isn't compatible with cassettes—and thus is less flexible.

Source: Robert M. Bloomfield, president, Marshall, Roberts & Co., office procedures consultants, 2 Pennsylvania Plaza, New York 10001.

OTHER IDEAS

• Inroads being made by the Dvorak-arranged typewriter keyboard. It has letters arranged according to the frequency of usage (vowels next to each other, punctuation marks at the top rather than at the bottom of the keyboard). Machines can be ordered with that keyboard arrangement.
Source: *Word Processing World.*

• Switch on the tape recorder as you summarize a telephone agreement. Then have it transcribed as a letter of confirmation and send two copies to the other party for signature and return of one copy. This avoids later misunderstandings on points that are agreed to on the telephone.

COMMUNICATIONS

WATS LINE VS. REGULAR LONG DISTANCE CALLS

• Widely used, *Wide Area Telecommunications Service* (WATS) can save 10% to 50% on long-distance phone charges. WATS is a "wholesale" service. A company purchases 10 or 240 hours a month of talking time (or multiples of these amounts). There are no refunds if less time is used. Overtime charges are calculated in tenths of hours for talking more than the basic allowance.

• A WATS package can be purchased for either *outward* or *inward (800* numbers) telephone service. The WATS bands (geographic areas) are selected on the basis of the general distribution of a company's calls. Only one telephone call can be placed on a WATS line at a time.

How to keep WATS costs down:

• Route requests for long distance through company operator. If employees can dial a code to secure a WATS line, costs may well exceed what was formerly paid for toll calls alone. Up to 30% of WATS traffic is personal on "dial-access" systems. Employees think WATS is free.

• Make the company operator the long distance boss (users can dial local calls) to award priorities, handle emergency calls that need immediate handling. The operator should ask the caller for the number wanted and require identification of caller and organization and person called.

Calls can also be queued for the circiut. This will permit the use of the 240-hour service with its lower cost-per-minute.

Don't use 10-hour service, since no one usually uses them after 5 p.m. on Monday through Friday and at all times Saturday and Sunday. A discount of 60 percent applies on regular calls daily, from 11 p.m. to 8 a.m., all day Saturday, and until 5 p.m. Sunday. Ten-hour WATS service *always* costs more than regular long-distance service during these periods.

• Be cautious about installing inward WATS. If your company's competitor has *800* service, installation might be necessary. It's certainly less expensive if a large volume of calls are on a collect basis.

Dangers: Salespeople will use the telephone for quick answers to questions instead of using mail, Telex, or TWX. Non-urgent matters will become urgent. *800* lines will be very busy. *Telephone company regulations require buying enough service to eliminate multiple busy signals.*

• *Remedy:* Assign an identification number to each employee who uses inward WATS. Tell the operator not to accept a call without a number, and to prepare a ticket for each call. Relatives will find it more difficult to call employees long distance without an identification number. Sort tickets by cost centers and prorate cost of inward

WATS by department against the number of calls. Rely on budget-conscious managers to take steps to decrease excessive calling by the field force.

Monitor every WATS bill closely. Each WATS bill should indicate: (1) how many calls were made, and (2) how many minutes were spent on each circuit or group of circuits in the same WATS area. Divide calls into total cost for *cost per call*, and minutes into costs for *cost per minute*. Divide calls into minutes for *average call length*. Adjust call length upward to the nearest minute. Now check the cost of a call on long-distance toll facilities to the cities frequently called. Price out the same call on WATS. *Make sure that WATS is less expensive* than a long-distance toll call.

Check total hours of usage monthly. The telephone company is under no obligation to warn that its usage rate suggests a move from the 10-hour to the 240-hour rate, or vice versa. If your 10-hour circuit is being used more than 88 hours monthly, it will be less expensive to change to 240-hour service. Get figures from the telephone business office.

FIVE STEPS TO TAKE BEFORE MOVING TO WORD PROCESSING

Executives are as worried about losing their personal secretaries as the secretaries are about being absorbed into a WP team. Handle both very gently. The executive, in particular,

can kill the program.

In collecting data about secretarial services in the office, an outside WP consultant can be helpful. But the field is a new one, and any consultant needs to be carefully checked out.

Surveys often show that WP is *not* the answer for a particular firm at a particular time. That's valuable to know. In addition, they disclose flaws and duplication in the present system.

Set up a team of two executives, an administrative assistant, and a typist to develop a system and let them work out the kinks. This is the tried and tested team-of-four approach. Add more teams when necessary.

When the routing and typing chaff has been separated out of the system, it's time to activate the WP production unit.

FACSIMILE TRANSMISSION

Beating the mail by facsimile transmission is scoring a major breakthrough.

Old problem: Low speed—as much as six minutes per page—and lack of compatibility between sending and receiving units. *New solution:* Units that can "talk" to each other—as many as 78% of the models now coming into distribution—at speeds of 20 seconds to 120 seconds per page.

Save salesmen's time, cut the cost of their phone calls to the office by installing a special line to the sales manager. Limit to incoming field calls.

HOW TO CHECK PHONE BILLS

Periodically, ask the phone company for an *equipment inventory form* —which provides a complete listing of every item included in the *local service* portion of the bill. If any part of it is not clear or if any code or abbreviation isn't understandable, check with the phone company's business office. If it can't supply you with what you need, ask the phone company's *marketing department* for it.

If there are any problems in getting the inventory, tell the credit manager that no further bills will be paid until they furnish the itemization.

If an error is found, claim a *retroactive* refund. It is up to the phone company to prove the claim incorrect.

Keep careful records of the service changes that have been ordered. Also, issue *written* orders to the phone company for moves, changes, installations, and disconnects. You are entitled to *credits* for any disconnected equipment. Telephone equipment is billed in *advance*. Refunds should be made for unused service within the month when the disconnect is made.

MESSAGE UNITS. In a small office, personnel can tally every local call, providing the charge is only a single message unit for a call of any length to any place in the metropolitan area. The phone company's meters aren't infallible. If you pay only a single message unit charge for a call of any length to any point in the metropolitan area, it may be practical for employees to tally every local call dialed. If that total

count is different from the phone company's count, request a credit.

If your company has a telephone switching system (PABX), remember that it's possible to *semirestrict* employees' phones. Those phones will be able to receive incoming calls, but no outside local or long-distance calls can be dialed. Why give unlimited dialing privileges to people whose jobs require calling only within the company?

LONG-DISTANCE TOLL CHARGES AND TELEGRAMS. If you find an unverified telegram on the phone bill, call the business office for a copy of the message to substantiate the bill. Further, tell the person who signed the telegram to use Western Union's Mailgram service from now on. A 15-word *telegram*, delivered, costs $15.70, plus the 20-cent charge for the phone call to Western Union's "800" number. The Mailgram costs $6.40 for 100 words and will be delivered in the first mail the next day.

On long-distance calls, look for distant numbers which aren't familiar. Keep a log of the calls dialed. If a number is not familiar, call the phone company's business office. If you are sure the call isn't from your company, it will be *instantly* removed from the bill. The telephone company will then call that number and try to find out who made the call. If you're not sure about it, the phone company will take the number and call back in a few days, giving the name of the called organization or residence. If you're still not convinced, have them remove the charge from your bill. They will promptly bill it back if they find that one of your employees made the call.

DIRECTORY ADVERTISING. To check a

bill under this section, call the Yellow Pages number in the phone book and ask for a copy of the "directory advertising contract." Review the contract and see if any of those charges can be either eliminated or expanded. A single "boldface" listing may cost you more than $50 yearly. Is the Yellow Pages advertising that was sold years ago still correct? Yellow Pages contracts are usually automatically renewed. (You can request an annual contract that must be signed, but if someone forgets, your firm may be omitted.) You will often discover listings for branches that are no longer in existence, or which don't need a separate identification.

The company may have numerous extra listings in the white pages which are in ordinary, not boldface, type. Without a copy of the "equipment inventory form," they won't be found. Each extra line of type beyond the main number in the white pages may cost over $12 yearly (plus tax). Check the extra listings carefully, making sure that users of the white pages really need the extra listings to find another location or department. Extra listings frequently carry the same number as the main listings. If all calls are handled by the main switchboard, why use other lines of type to list departments reached by the main number?

HANDLING BUSINESS PHONE CALLS

● Answer before the third ring. Never keep the caller waiting while unfinished business is completed. Give your full attention immediately to the person on the phone.

Personalize the call. Jot down the caller's name and use it when replying to his comments. Be cheerful. If necessary, put a mirror near the phone. Smiling while you talk makes you *sound* friendly.

● Listen carefully. Show the caller you're doing this by giving specific answers (not just "uh huh") and letting him speak his piece without interruption. *Also:* Listen for the true meaning of what he's saying by being alert to changes in tone and inflection.

● Ask questions that will move from the general to the specific. Find out what he *really* wants.

● Realize that questions are a signal that he's interested. Be ready to overcome objections without antagonizing him. (Keep a list of common objections and their answers near the phone.)

● Gently nudge him toward a buying decision. Give him reassurance and a reason to buy. Offer him a choice, if necessary.

● Always thank the caller, even if the sale wasn't made.

● Review what's been said with him and make sure there are no misunderstandings. (Always talk in terms he can understand. Avoid technical jargon.) Let him hang up first.

Source: Lloyd T. Tarbutton, chairman, Econo-Travel Motor Hotel Corp., Norfolk, Va.

COST-CUTTERS

● A time-shared, computer-based system for routing telephone calls over company WATS and tie lines can reduce long-distance charges and volume by at least $10,000 a month. When a call is made, the computer chooses the cheapest route. Or if a line isn't open, it queues the call and lets the caller know when a line opens. A test by Montgomery Ward, using 500 company phones, cut long-distance expenses over 20%. *Information:* TDX Systems, Inc., 7670 Old Springhouse Rd., McLean, Va. 22101.

• Instead of having executives make phone calls from home charged to the company credit card, encourage them to use *direct dialing* instead. Reimburse them through their regular expense accounts.

DON'T OVERLOOK TELEX

It can be far cheaper than the telephone. Your company gets a printed record of every message sent or received, and employees don't have to hang around waiting for the party they're trying to reach to be at his desk.

How it works: You buy or lease a teleprinter and join a network of 125,00 terminals in the U.S., Canada, and Mexico (and 375,000 additional terminals worldwide). Simply direct-dial and exchange identifyng codes to reach your party. Anyone who can type can learn how to operate the manual keyboard in about 10 minutes, so no special personnel are required.

Typical cost: Initial purchase of equipment, $2,000; charge for installation and user training, $400; after 1-year warranty, average monthly service fee, $24. One company found combined Telex/telephone monthly cost $400; phone *alone* had been *$500.*

CONTROLLING MAIL COSTS

Keep an eye on exact mailing weights. A package weighing a *tenth of an ounce less than 12 ounces* can ship for 37¢ less than if it weighed an exact 12 ounces.

• Avoid International Air Freight where possible. Shipments sent this way must be cleared through customs by a broker. Minimum charge for the customs fee and broker-handling is $50 per shipment plus the Air Freight charge.

• Use the Air Small Packet Class instead of Air Parcel Post in mailing overseas if the package weighs two pounds or less. It's a lot cheaper.

• Be sure the volume and profits from business-reply mail are sufficient to justify the business-reply fee charged by the Postal Service (check Post Office for details). Consider letting customer affix the correct postage on reply card or envelope.

• Include "address change" forms in your mailings to winnow out the waste in *your* mailing list. (But *don't* use them when your company mails to rented lists, because that only adds to your cost.)

• See if all those separate enclosures (reminders, notices, special offers, coupons) really need to be there. Maybe fewer pieces can be used.

• Test a self-mailer. These eliminate envelopes, and they can even be designed to include return envelopes.

• Check out Nylon Trans-Sac Pouches for interoffice mail instead of using disposable envelopes.

PRACTICAL POSTAL ALTERNATIVES TO REGISTERED MAIL

Registered mail is frequently used incorrectly. The Postal Service offers four other special services that are not as costly and often serve the businessmen's purpose even better than registered mail. Registered mail costs a minimum of $3.25 per piece. The Postal Service supplies special security for this mail and includes insurance up to $100. (Higher coverage costs more.)

All costs mentioned in the alternatives below are in addition to regular postage and other fees.

• *Certificate of mailing.* For 40¢ the sender receives a document that states his letter was mailed from a particular post office on a specified date.

• *Certified mail.* The postman gets a signature so that the Postage Service has proof the mail was delivered. *Cost:* 75¢.

• *Return receipt.* The sender gets the record that the letter was delivered, with date of delivery and signature of recipient. Prepaid, this costs 60¢. The charge is 70¢ if address where delivered is also requested. (A receipt requested after mailing with just recipient and date costs an additional $3.05.)

• *Restricted delivery.* The sender pays an extra $1.00 and the mail will be delivered only to the person to whom it is addressed or to that person's legally authorized representative.

• *Special delivery* gives sender no legal protection. It just provides that mail will be delivered outside regular delivery hours. *Special handling* and *insured mail* are available for protection of first-, third-, and fourth-class mail.

SHIPPING SMALL PACKAGES

Compare costs for shipping small packages. Which way is best? Depends on how important speed is and whether you want to pay for pickup service.

FOR SPEED.

• *Emery Air Freight.* To major cities in U.S. by next business day. Door-to-door service. No limit on size or weight of package. *Cost:* Three to four times Postal Service priority mail.

• *Federal Express.* To 10,000 U.S. cities, arriving by the next business day. Door-to-door service. Package limit: 70 lbs.; 120 inches length plus girth. *Insurance:* Up to $100 free; 30¢ charge for each additional $100 up to $5,000 maximum. *Cost:* Three to four times Postal Service priority mail.

• *United Airlines Small Package Dispatch.* (Similar to services offered by most domestic airlines.) 113 cities in U.S. Shipper brings package to ticket counter 30 minutes before flight. Consignee picks up at destination airport. (Pickup and delivery available, at extra charge, in major cities.) Package limits: 50 lbs.; 90 inches length plus girth. *Insurance:* 45¢ per $100; maximum $750. *Cost.* Same for any size package, determined by destination. Examples: New York to Los Angeles: $60. Chicago to New York: $44.10.

308

SPEED PLUS ECONOMY.

- *Amtrak Package Express.* To 300 cities in 45 states. Fast as train, but depends on next train out. Shipper must bring package to station; consignee must pick it up. Package limit: 50 lbs. for a box, 75 lbs. for a foot locker. Box size must not exceed 9 cubic feet. *Cost:* Cheaper than parcel post.

- *Greyhound Package Express.* To most cities in U.S. and Canada. Fast as bus travels. (New York to California about 70 hours.) Shipper must bring package to terminal; consignee must pick it up. Pickup and delivery service avialable, at a charge, in major cities. Package limits: 10 lbs.; 161 inches length plus girth plus height; no dimension over 60 inches. *Insurance:* Up to $100 free; maximum $1,000. *Cost:* Two to three times parcel post. *Example:* 50 lbs. Atlanta-N.Y. is $36.30.

- *United Parcel Service.* Anywhere in continental U.S. in six working days (two working days if sent by air). Nearby states, usually one working day. Shipper must bring to terminal; delivery to door. Pickup service available (maximum charge: $4). Package limits: 50 lbs.; 108 inches length plus girth. *Insurance:* First $100 free; 25¢ for each additional $100. *Cost:* $1.78 to $48.00, depending on weight and distance.

SLOWEST.

Parcel Post. Anywhere in continental U.S. within ten days. Shipper brings to post office; delivery to door. Package limits: 40 lbs. in first-class post office; 70 lbs. in others. *Insurance:* Same as priority mail. *Cost:* $1.15 to $19.16 for 70 lbs. to California.

OTHER IDEAS

- Current limits on first and third-class mail went into effect April 15, 1978. *Banned altogether:* Any piece of mail less than seven thousandths of an inch thick; any envelope less than a quarter of an inch thick that is less than 3½ inches high or 5 inches long. New surcharge on mail with height-to-length ratio of more than 1:2.5 or less than 1:1.3 for all first class mail weighing an ounce or less and all single-piece third class mail weighing two ounces or less.

- Post Office refunds 90% of face value of spoiled metered mail if the total amount is $250 or less. For larger amounts, Post Office refunds 100%, but deducts $10 for each man-hour it takes to process the refund (minimum charge of $25). The spoiled tapes and envelopes can, of course, be accumulated.

- Save two cents per piece on postage with pre-sorted first-class mail. But few mailers are doing it because it seems like too much work for a modest gain. Worth a second look. Some companies sort easily with existing staffers. They're saving money and trimming a day off mail delivery times (in many cases). *Simple system:* Mail-room employees sort during spare moments and meter and bundle in the afternoon. *Don't get locked into presorting.* Be prepared to skip it for one day if things get rushed or the department is short-handed.

OPERATING
THE PLANT

IMPROVING THE EQUIPMENT

BIG SAVINGS ON MATERIAL-HANDLING EQUIPMENT

It's possible to save as much as 40% of the cost of a new system, an automated warehouse, or other material-handling system.

How: By providing the vendor with full and accurate information about the company's material-handling needs and costs. The vendor doesn't have to include the cost of that study in the cost of the job. *That's the 40% the customer can save* by providing the right information to the equipment vendor.

Questions that must be answered:
• What is the daily rate—and the peak rate—at which material is brought into (*and* shipped out of)—the warehouse?
• **What are the size and shape of the** usual *unit load* (the amount usually handled as a single unit)? This helps establish the best size of aisle width and rack opening.
• How will orders be picked? By *zone* (with an order broken up and several people picking)? Or will an entire order be picked by a single person? (This helps establish how much floor activity there will be.)
• If zone picking is used, how will orders be accumulated?
• What do the company's marketing projections say will be the average shipping and receiving requirements—

and the peaks—next year, 5 years from now, and in 10 years?
• How does the company want to stage expansion? Build space for 10 years? Buy equipment for 5 years? Or some other combination?
• Are there any special characteristics to the products handled? Fragile? Subject to pilferage?
• Does the company want to collect any special on-line information to keep control of inventory? (Too many customers decide they want this important addition in the middle of an installation. That adds greatly to the cost and delay.)
• What is the best layout for a work station?
• What is the anticipated rate of error in assembling and sorting material?

MORE IDEAS. A rack-supported warehouse has many advantages over a conventional building. Construction cost of this rack-type unit can be as much as $6 less per square foot. And there are tax savings too. A rack-supported warehouse qualifies as *equipment*, with a 5 year write-off (15 years for a conventional warehouse). Rack-supported installations also qualify for investment tax credit.

• Make sure the size of your company's shipping cartons is geared to the size of the individual packages and to warehouse pallets so that there is little or no wasted space. Consult with material-handling management *before* marketing changes a package size. Warehouse, shipping, and purchasing departments need the word quickly, so they can shift carton sizes and stacking patterns on pallets. Try to keep your pallet and warehouse rack dimensions compatible, too.

Source: John A. White, professor, Georgia Institute of Technology, Atlanta 30332.

BUILD IN
THE FACTORY

Just because your *product* is an entire factory or *some other massive item*, don't reject the concept of building it at your facility, packaging it and then shipping it—rather than handling the full assembly at the customer's site.

DuPont did just that with a chemical plant. Its engineers designed the plant to fit in four standard-size intermodal cargo containers, 8x8x20 feet, the size used for international shipping. The container actually became an integral part of the plant's floors, walls, etc.

Maker of special containers: Theurer, 225 Parkhurst St., Newark, N.J. 07114.

MORE WAREHOUSE
SPACE PRODUCED BY
NEW LIFT-TRUCKS

Storage capacity can be tripled without adding to existing space by switching to new breed of electric lift trucks. *Narrow-aisle turret trucks* can rack 1,500-pound loads up to 40-feet high in five- to six-foot-wide aisles. They're much less expensive ($31,500-$70,000, plus racks) than stacker cranes ($500,000 and up).

Other benefits: Better performance (pallets racked per hour) than sideloaders, the narrow-aisle reach trucks, and the counter-balanced lift trucks. Less rack and product damage. Direct computer interfacing possible.

Minimum conditions to justify a narrow-aisle turret truck:

Warehouse with at least 1,000-unit loads.

Activity of at least 20 unit-loads hourly or 150-250 per seven-hour shift.

Aisle length of 100-500 feet.

Manufacturers: Lansing Bagnall Canada, Ltd., 10255 Cote de Liesse Rd., Dorval, Quebec; ATM Industries Ltd., 6380 Northwest Dr., Malton, Ontario L4V 1J7, Canada; Raymond Corp., 131 Madison St., Greene, N.Y. 13778; Clark Equipment Co., 24th & Lafayette Sts., Battle Creek, Mich. 49016; Cleco-Kane, P.O. Box 699, Millville, N.J. 08332.

PALLET SAVINGS

Probably better and less costly to repair pallets instead of paying a hauler to take them away.

Rising prices, shortage of hardwood makes initial outlay for repair equipment all the more attractive.

Fact is that haulers repair discarded pallets anyway. Often get about 65% of the price of a new pallet for them.

Rule of thumb: If 400 pallets cross receiving docks a day, your company can afford a major recycling system. Also, if you're in a pool operation, you can return pallets to the pool at less cost because they will be in better condition.

BUYING SECOND-HAND MACHINERY AND EQUIPMENT

Key legal and tax factors to be considered in second-hand buying:

Warranty of title: A warranty of title is implied, unless you have a specific disclaimer. But how valuable is it if the seller is—or is about to become—insolvent, or is simply not responsible? In either case, you assume at your own risk that the seller really owns the property. It's prudent, if large sums are involved, to have your lawyer check for outstanding liens on the property. But be aware that such checking isn't foolproof. The seller may have it filed in another district. In short, to a large degree, you must rely on the seller's integrity.

Exclusion of other warranties: Used machinery and equipment is usually sold *as is* or *with all faults* or some other language which calls to the buyer's attention the exclusion of warranties, and in such a case no other warranties, express or implied, will arise. In any case, if the seller examines the machinery or equipment or is given an opportunity to examine and refuses, no warranty question will arise about defects which the examination disclosed or should have disclosed.

Investment credit: The buyer of used equipment is generally entitled to investment credit, but only up to an aggregate cost of $125,000 per year for all used property purchased through 1984, $150,000 per year thereafter.

Trade-ins: If the seller is willing to take a trade-in, bear in mind that Section 1031 of the Internal Revenue Code permits a tax-free exchange, which you will most likely want to take advantage of if the trade-in property would show a profit if sold separately. If you can show a loss on the property available for trade, you would most likely want to shape the transaction as a separate sale and purchase so as to establish your loss. You will also want to consider the impact of local sales taxes. Generally, when you trade in property, the *difference* between the value of the property acquired and that traded is subject to the sales tax.

NEW WAYS TO CUT BUILDING COSTS

When business activity picks up, many firms revive plans for plant construction and renovation. This is a good time to reexamine the way a building contractor is usually chosen. The traditional way, competitive bidding, is often not the most cost effective—it brings the contractor on board after many key decisions have been made, and so a lot of cost-cutting opportunities are missed.

Choose the contractor at the time you retain the architect. This allows the contractor to be a part of the planning team, to translate preliminary cost factors, and to recommend materials and systems for the building. This can reduce prices and speed the process. The faster a project can go from conception to occupancy, the less expensive it will be.

A good contractor has a strong knowledge of local markets and national conditions. If a hard-to-purchase component is needed, the contractor can begin the acquisition process early.

315

Usually, contractors establish a guaranteed maximum price *before* the architect's final drawings are approved. This gives the purchaser several months' lead time to arrange the best financing.

Request estimates and schedules during the design phase. Computer techniques now make it possible to generate flexible, sophisticated *Critical Path Method* (CPM) scheduling. CPM tracks the interplay of the different tasks so they are done in the proper sequence, and helps coordinate the activities of the subcontractors who do the work.

Check the contractor's experience with the type and size of the planned project. Do the same for each of the key members of the contractor's team, who include:

• Project executive, who has overall responsibility for the project and coordinates with the client company.

• Estimator, purchasing agent, project engineer. The project engineer handles administrative details, clarifies sketches with the architect, and monitors a subcontractor's procurement and fabrication of materials and components.

• Project supervisor, the onsite overseer of the day-to-day work.

MODELING FOR EFFICIENCY

High cost, low availability and lack of awareness have kept U.S. mechanical designers away from a technique that Europeans have been using for years—making models to speed design of complex mechanisms. The models have the added advantage of helping sell a concept to corporate skeptics who may have trouble visualizing a drawing. In addition, it helps reduce expensive machine shop time, since system is based on two types of framing. Models can also be used to check complex machine sequencing, confirm mechanical function, test simple processes. *Cost:* $17 to $1,000 or more.

For further details on kits, contact Herb Arum, Stock Model Parts Div. of Designatronics Inc., 54 S. Denton Ave., New Hyde Park, N.Y. 11040.

ALTERNATIVES TO EXPENSIVE WOODEN PALLETS

• Slip sheet: The simplest alternative (a corrugated, fibreboard or plastic sheet under a load).

• Carton clamps: For use in industries using strong stiff cartons or containers.

• Roll clamps: For less damaging handling of huge rolls of paper.

• Additions to fork-lift truck, such as combination carton clamp and rotating truck carriage.

ENERGY SAVING

BETTER THAN STEAM CLEANING

High-pressure hot water may be better than steam to clean machinery (or facilities). As soon as steam leaves the nozzle, it loses heat and velocity faster than water. When it actually reaches the surface to be cleaned, steam is cooler, slower, and does less work. *Additional advantage:* Additives can improve the cleaning ability of hot water.

Examples: (1) Nontoxic detergents are approved for use with hot-water systems to clean food-processing machinery. (2) Adding a water-soluble oil to water used to clean machinery can free the equipment of sludge, gum, or caked grease, and leave it with a thin film of rust-resistant oil.

WASHING AND COATING PARTS: ENERGY-SAVING IDEAS

Washing and drying:
• Some parts that are washed separately can be washed together.
• By changing detergents, some production parts can be washed in cold water.
• Parts may pick up enough heat during washing to dry out.

• Use a high-pressure blower instead of compressed air to save electricity.
• Divert hot-water overflow from rinse tank as replacement water for the wash tank.
Stripping and coating:
• Paint-stripping tanks may work as well at temperatures as low as 170°F.
• By slowing the movement of the line through a paint-drying oven, the oven temperature can be reduced.
• Consider switching to coatings that bake on at lower temperatures. Even if they cost more, saving on energy may be greater.

PLACING LIMITS ON SYSTEMS TO CONTROL ENERGY USAGE

No question about the ability of *demand-limiting systems* to cut electric power bills for heavy users. But consider these cost factors:
• Many electric motors are designed for *continuous* rather than *intermittent* operation. The increased number of starts and stops could burn them out quickly. And some motors of these types are equipped with timers that won't permit them to restart until a cool-down period expires. This could make them incompatible with your load-shedding system.
• Bearings, belts, and other mechanical equipment in systems designed for

continuous operation will not take the stress of frequent starts and stops; may have to be replaced.

• Some air compressors, chillers, and the like are already equipped with power-saving devices to reduce current consumption during periods of limited demand. These may be incompatible with a load-shedding system.

NEW LIGHTING CONCEPT

Task lighting, which concentrates light where peple need it, has these advantages over conventional *ambient lighting:*

• *Power consumption.* Task lighting usually requires about 2 watts per square foot vs. 5 watts for ambient lighting.

• *Initial cost:* Task lighting usually requires fewer fixtures and less wiring.

• *Other benefits:* Task lighting reduces glare and reflections on work surfaces. It provides a balanced brightness between the work and the surrounding area to reduce eye adaptation problems.

WAYS TO SAVE ELECTRICITY

• Install cam-operated controls in mechanical power-press dies. The controls release a short blast of compressed air to blow away dust, replacing a continuous blast of air. If proper precautions are taken, air compressors may not need to run continuously. They can be shut down during idle shifts and on weekends.

• Install timers on office air conditioning to shut down during lunch hours, shortly before closing, and on weekends.

• Reduce air-conditioning needs by installing reflective solar film on office windows that are exposed to the sun.

• Change *pulleys* on ventilation fans to reduce the speed of the fans by about 20%.

• Cut down on peak electricity demand by charging forklift truck batteries during low-demand periods.

• Turn off lights in vending machines.

• Changing from a constant to a *variable air-volume* system curbs the amount of air going to a given space. Installation of *flow valves* and *hot-water coils* in the three buildings reduced one organization's fuel consumption by 15%-20%.

• *Solar shades*, or sun screens, can reduce heat load on existing heavily glassed buildings.

• Overhead lighting fixtures can be removed (or dimmed) and reworked with *single fixtures at the work place.*

• *Infrared scanning* can help you find trouble spots.

If a new facility is in your future plans, be sure your engineer is up to date on what mechanical and design energy savers are available.

Information sources: Government agencies; seminars (American Society of Heating, Refrigerating & Air Conditioning Engineers, 345 E. 47th St., New York 10017, for instance); *Energy Opportunities Notebook*, American Institute of Architects, 1735 New York Ave. NW, Washington, D.C. 20006.

GOVERNMENT PROGRAMS FOR ENERGY SAVINGS

The federal government has many programs that provide financial and informational support for businesses and individuals to develop and use alternate energy sources and to conserve on current fuel use. Here is a description of two programs and their addresses:

1. *Energy Extension Service.* Purpose: To encourage, through formula grants, individuals and small businesses to reduce energy consumption and convert to alternate energy sources. *Eligible:* States, and via the states, small-scale energy users and groups that influence their energy consumption. *Contact:*

> Director, Energy Management & Extension
> Department of Energy
> Forrestal Building
> 1000 Independence Ave., N.W.
> Washington, DC 20585

2. *National Energy Information Center. Purpose:* To serve as the central energy office providing information and assistance. *Uses:* Comprehensive source of statistical and analytical energy data, information, and referral assistance. *Eligible:* State and local governments, nonprofit institutions, businesses, individuals. *Contact:*

> National Energy Information Center
> Office of Energy Information Service
> Department of Energy
> 1000 Independence Ave., N.W.
> Washington, DC 20585

In addition to the business opportunities suggested here, there are tax incentives to encourage saving and alternate energy source development. Check with your IRS office for current tax credits for residence and business use.

CAPACITORS CUT ENERGY COSTS

The electricity consumed in a factory can be reduced significantly through the use of *capacitors.* This is especially true if the facility uses numerous electric motors or compressors. The difference in a small plant can be 2% to 6% of the total utility bill.

Installation costs usually are repaid in less than two years. But it's rarely economical if utility bill runs under $5,000 per month.

WHAT TO DO ABOUT THE FUEL PROBLEM

We *are* running out of oil—*and* natural gas. Whether it's exactly 30 years or more makes very little difference in the long run. As we begin to drill more deeply into hard-to-reach reserves, the supply will become more spotty and more expensive. So start planning for oil-gas alternatives.

The best is coal. It's conservatively estimated that we have 300 years of coal reserves. However, the cost of mining and transporting it will grow sharply as demand builds. (Much of the coal will be difficult to reach, too.)

Should a company convert its boilers to coal-burning from oil or natural gas-burning? In many cases the answer is *yes.* But a generalization is impossible. It's easier to generalize about a *new* facility. New installations should have a boiler unit able to use oil or coal. The dual-fuel capability today adds only about 5% to the cost of the building's heating plant, so it's almost irresponsible to design new facilities without such flexibility.

In designing new facilities, don't fail to consider the cost of generating electricity, too. In a surprising number of cases (depending on the local utility's electric rates), a small generating station may be quite economical. Certainly as time goes on, the economics will become more apparent.

Conversion (rather than new installation) is more complex. The decision to take that action is more difficult to generalize on. *Critical questions to ask:*
- How much energy do you use?
- How price-critical is the fuel? (Can a competitor with lower fuel costs injure your position?)
- How close is the plant to a coal-producing region? (Transportation can be a big cost factor.)

The more price critical your business is, and the closer you are to the coalfields, the more you should lean to converting your equipment to accommodate coal, too.

SOLAR ENERGY. We're a long way from a *totally* cost-efficient solar-heating system, but if you are in a high energy cost area and have all-electric facilities, it's usually desirable to have some basic solar-heating equipment. Even if the facility is limited to heating water for washing, it's worth the investment. Conversion is more complex and rarely worth the investment—unless you are in a high energy cost and have all-electric facility.

ELECTRICITY PERSPECTIVE. Time to think about the long-range cost of electricity. Prices surely aren't going to come down. *The trends:*
- No discount for volume users. In fact, volume users may have to pay a penalty.
- Cost of peak use may also soar.
  What to do:

Begin to develop ways of cutting use of electricity. More important, consider spreading out its use. *One way:* Heavy energy use during low-demand night hours. As costs jump, such a work-turn shift may be justified.

Source: Peter Flack, partner, Flack & Kurtz, Inc., 475 5th Ave., New York 10018.

OTHER SAVERS

- *Cheapest outdoor industrial security lighting:* Low-pressure sodium lamps. Fleischmanns Distilling Corp. found 22 lamps provided the required amount of light for illuminating the outside of its facility at Dayton, N.J., for an annual operating cost of about $832. That compared to $1,358 for high-pressure sodium and $1,971 for mercury vapor units.
- Simple now to adjust home or office heating or air-conditioning thermostats at preselected times with a small gadget consisting of a heating element (placed next to the thermostat) attached to a timer (plugged into nearest wall outlet: Contact *Fuel Sentry*, 79 Putnam St., Mt. Vernon, N.Y. 10550.
- Consider work-shift changes to switch some electric usage to night-time hours. *Reason:* Utilities all over the country gradually moving to "time-of-day" rates. That means lower rates (as much as 30%-40% lower) at night, maybe also an *increase* of 30% or more for use during peak daytime hours.

SAFETY

WHY AUTOMATIC SPRINKLER SYSTEMS FAIL WHEN FIRES START

Conspicuously high failure rates for automatic sprinklers—running to 75% of major fires, in one survey—underline need for constant maintenance and supervision. And for alternative protection: Notably automatic roof venting if the sprinkler fails and rapid heat and smoke buildup threaten the entire structure.

Precautions:

• Be sure sprinkler meets current needs. Changes in building's storage content can render a system inadequate.

• Police system periodically. Usual malfunctions: Clogged heads in dirty or corrosive locations. Water valves shut when they should be open. Water-pump failure. Insufficient water supply.

Install an automatic roof vent for emergency use. By altering the airflow pattern, the vent:

• Prevents back-draft explosions by releasing gas and smoke.

• Provides better visibility to firefighters—vital in event of power failure.

• Reduces heat spread, precluding losses due to inappropriate activation of distant sprinklers (and loss of water pressure where it's needed).

• Prevents sagging joints and roof collapse due to heat spread and distortion under the roof deck.

Choosing a vendor: Consult Underwriters Laboratories (207 E. Ohio, Chicago 60611) or Factory Mutual Research Co. (1151 Providence Hwy., Norwood, Mass. 02062); look for their approved labels.

PLANT SAFETY COMMITTEE

If your plant has enough employees, select six to ten of them every month, at random, to be members of a plant safety team. *Result:* Increased safety consciousness among team members as they inspect one department at a time. Those unfamiliar with a work area are more likely to spot hazards than those who work there every day. Individual employee participation also reinforces safety-consciousness among team members back on their own jobs.

TREAD SAFELY

Poor stairway design is a major cause of accidents. Risers should be 4 to 8 inches and treads 11 to 14 inches for optimum safety and ease of climbing.

Stairs with extra-thick treads and deep overhangs (often designed for aesthetic purposes) are natural traps for the foot.

Caution: Stair materials are often slippery. Exterior concrete steps, for example, frequently lack metal nosings or tread plates and drainage for water, which makes them more slippery. Even more slippery when wet or walked upon with wet soles are marble and terrazzo.

DANGERS OF STATIC ELECTRICITY CAN BE MINIMIZED

Cold and dry weather increases prevalence of static electricity, which can cause discomfort to personnel and damage to expensive word-processing machinery and computers.

• Keep relative humidity at 48% and dry-bulb temperature at 78 degrees.

• Make sure high-speed computers have suppressors and electronic precipitators that are used with filters.

• See that installers provide for air conditioning or air distribution to reduce heat generated by minicomputers and electrical equipment.

• Don't place units of electronic equipment too close to each other.

• Put rubber mats under machines.

• Install antistatic carpeting.

HOW TO MINIMIZE FLOOD DAMAGE

Flooded basements can be "good": If flood reaches your property, water inside will equalize underground pressure outside and prevent collapse of basement walls. Don't pump out basement until flood recedes.

If you have no second floor: Remember, water inside a building often gets no higher than 2 or 3 feet. Use high shelves for valuables (including furnace motor).

Keep underground fuel tank full: Otherwise, it can buoy up to the surface, causing foundation walls to collapse. (If no fuel is available, fill tank with water.)

'THANK YOU FOR NOT SMOKING'

Nonsmokers are becoming more militant, and some implications are already evident in personnel policies.

A court in New Jersey has ordered the telephone company to forbid smoking in work areas. This ruling was based on evidence that the amount of smoke in the air sickened an employee and caused her to lose time from work. "The portion of the population which is especially sensitive to cigarette smoke is so significant that it is reasonable to expect an employer to foresee health consequences and to impose upon him a duty to abate the hazard which causes the discomfort," the court stated.

Oddly enough, New Jersey Bell already had rules against smoking in the vicinity of equipment which might malfunction—a circumstance which strengthened the case against management.

"A company which has demonstrated such concern for its mechanical components should have at least as much concern for its human beings," the judge concluded. "Plaintiff asks nothing more than to be able to breathe the air in its clear and natural state."

Schimp v. New Jersey Bell Telephone Co., N.J. Sup. Ct., 12/22/76.

INJURIES TO A SUBCONTRACTOR'S EMPLOYEES

The owner of property can be held liable for injuries to an independent contractor's employees if the work undertaken by the independent contractor is likely to be risky, unless the owner takes special precautions. The owner won't escape liability, even though the contract calls for the independent contractor to take the precautions.

This rule was applied in a case that permitted employees of the independent contractor to recover for injuries suffered when a wall, which the owner should have known was defective, collapsed.

Comment: The owner can't change the applicable rule of law in these situations, but he can insist upon a *hold harmless* agreement from the independent contractor backed by adequate contractor insurance. Naturally, he should consider getting appropriate insurance coverage on his own; the *hold harmless* agreement and the contractor's insurance would hold down the premium on his own coverage.

Hargrove v. Frommeyer & Co., Pa. Super., 323 A. 2d 300, 6/21/74.

WHAT TO DO (AND NOT TO DO) WHEN OSHA DESCENDS

Although Occupational Safety and Health Administration inspectors have virtually free access to any workplace, a company does have certain rights during the inspection. Basic points to protect company's interest and help achieve a smoother, less disruptive experience:

Check inspector's credentials. This can be done politely. His right to be there must be established. Never detain or deny access to someone with proper credentials, but others who may accompany him (*i.e.*, equipment expert) can be stopped. Ask for their business cards. Top management and/or the company's safety consultants should be alerted immediately.

Exchange information before inspection. Try to determine nature and scope of inspection. Advise inspector of work schedules. Ask permission to contact pertinent people along the route.

Go along with the inspector. (If possible, take company's safety consultant, too.)

Also note areas visited, people involved, condition of machinery, equipment or materials examined and practices observed. During and after inspection gather as much information as possible about the inspector and his reasoning.

And make detailed notes. These can be critical to company's success in dealing with any resulting citations. Jot down all relevant conversations with inspector, especially those that seem to indicate reason for inspection.

Always maintain cool, businesslike posture (carefully avoid any appearance of hostility). Try to find out why he feels condition or practice constitutes a hazard, how he rates violation.

Expect some disagreement. Stay calm. Arguing only aggravates the situation and may negatively influence company's standing with OSHA.

You can request that the area or practice in question be *avoided* until top management and/or safety consultants can be contacted in cases of dispute.

Correct imminent hazard situations quickly. Post notice. Deny entry by any person, without inspector's permission, into any area judged an imminent hazard. Area then should be entered only for the purpose of making it safe. Notify top management and safety consultants immediately.

Make post-inspection report as soon as possible. Tape record or write down details while still fresh in your mind. (*Note:* Tape recorders are *not* permitted on inspection tour itself.) And discuss thoroughly with appropriate company people.

Source: James R. Hinson, Safety and Health Consultants, 1730 South Amphlett Blvd., San Mateo, Ca. 94040.

CONTESTING OSHA CITATIONS

First citation usually costs less than compliance with the regulations. But a second or third citation for the same violation can be an extremely expensive proposition.

How to contest: First, arrange a meeting within 7 days (of receipt of the citation) with the area director to discuss its merits. If you can convince him that your procedure is safe, although not in compliance with Occupational Safety and Health Administration standards, he can amend the citation. If that fails, you still have time to file a protest. Deadline is 15 days from the day the citation was issued.

Warning: Don't ask for an interview and file a notice of intent to protest in the same letter. If you do, the director will simply turn the letter over to the solicitor's office and it will be out of his hands.

Pitfall: Having a piece of required equipment on order doesn't necessarily constitute compliance. The equipment must arrive on time. If it is delayed, you must ask for an extension; you'll get it. Be sure to give yourself sufficient time; second extensions are rarely granted, since OSHA will assume you aren't acting in good faith.

Another common hazard: If one item of equipment is cited, the citation covers all similar items. If an inspector returns to your facility and discovers that new equipment has the same violation as the old equipment, you are liable to heavy second offense penalties.

SUCCESSFUL CHALLENGES TO OSHA

Industry has become less accepting of expensive demands of the federal safety agency. And the courts are often responsive to industry's problems. If the costs of safety are way out of proportion to results, it may be profitable to challenge the ruling.

Case in point: Metal stamping presses produced loud noises. However, the company provided ear protectors for all employees working in the area. These reduced the noise level at the inner ear to an acceptable level and no employees complained of hearing problems.

But the Occupational Safety and Health Administration demanded $30,000 worth of noise control modifications. On appeal, OSHA lost. The court held that the cost was economically impractical when balanced against the benefit to employees who already had ear protectors.

Turner Co., div. of Olin Corp., v. Secy. of Labor, 561 F. 2d 82.

Another case: Part-time and transient workers handled packages averaging 10 pounds. Occasionally a worker wearing sneakers would drop a package on his toes. OSHA demanded that steel-toed shoes be provided. But the court held the cost unreasonable, especially since there was high employee turnover.

UPS v. OSHRC, 8th CCA, 2/17/78.

> *Classic case:* Occupational Safety and Health Administration required ear protection be worn when working in high noise areas. The company offered a choice of four kinds of protection. One employee refused to wear any of them. He was fired, and when he applied for unemployment compensation, the company objected. A court upheld the company and denied compensation to the ex-employee.
>
> 194 S.E. 2d 210.

SAFETY ON THE JOB

Expect more complaints, both to the company and to OSHA. One worker survey showed that 78% believe that they are exposed to safety or health hazards where they work. *Most frequently reported hazardous conditions:* Air pollution (40%), fire or shock (30%), noise (30%), and dangerous chemicals (29%). More than three-quarters of respondents expressed a strong desire to have a bigger voice in safety decisions in the plant.

Source: National survey of 1,500 workers by University of Michigan's Institute for Social Research, Ann Arbor, MI.

MORE IDEAS

Message to management: Put more emphasis on safety education of workers. The investment pays off much better than same money spent on safety equipment.

Idea to bounce off the unions: Line workers cannot move up to supervisor unless they have taken a safety course. Concept working with painters in New York.

> For information on procedures for compliance, request *OSHA Closing Conference Guide,* free from OSHA regional offices.
>
> Free booklet on managing safety and health problems: *Occupational Safety and Health Administration Handbook for Small Businesses,* NAW, 1725 K St., N.W., Washington, D.C. 20006.

PERSONAL
FINANCE

THE RIGHT PROGRAM

LIQUIDATING CAPITAL FOR RETIREMENT

Many investors are overly fearful of liquidating the principal of their retirement funds. That reduces their standard of living unnecessarily during retirement years by making use of only the interest and other income produced by funds in their estate.

Frequently, such planning is motivated by either the desire to leave an estate to children or other heirs or by anxiety concerning what could happen should assets become depleted.

withdrew only the interest, 8%, you would have to make do during your retirement with $16,000 a year. However, if each year you were to withdraw 10% of your original principal, or $20,000 a year, you can see from the table that your capital, *including interest received*, would last for 20 years or until you reached the age of 85.

You will have to make your own assessment of how much return to anticipate. Funds placed in Triple-A corporate bonds with a higher return would last 26 years (at the same percentage of liquidation).

Source: *Consensus of Insiders*, Ft. Lauderdale, Fla.

NUMBER OF YEARS YOUR MONEY WILL LAST

Annual Rate of Withdrawal	Rate of Return									
	1%	2%	3%	4%	5%	6%	7%	8%	9%	10%
10 %	10	11	12	13	14	15	17	20	26	—
9	11	12	13	14	16	18	22	28	—	—
8	13	14	15	17	20	23	30	—	—	—
7	15	16	18	21	25	33	—	—	—	—
6	18	20	23	28	36	—	—	—	—	—
5	22	25	30	41	—	—	—	—	—	—
4	28	35	46	—	—	—	—	—	—	—
3	40	55	—	—	—	—	—	—	—	—
2	69	—	—	—	—	—	—	—	—	—
1	—	—	—	—	—	—	—	—	—	—

The table above should give you some idea how long your capital would last if you withdrew interest income *and* liquidated a portion of your estate each year.

Example: Suppose your capital was placed into Treasury notes, providing 8% yield. Also, assume that you start with $200,000 in capital at age 65. If you

MISTAKES EXECUTIVES MAKE IN PERSONAL FINANCIAL PLANNING

Here are the most common errors and omissions in executives' personal financial planning:

- No "umbrella" insurance policy to cover risks excluded by or in excess of other policies.
- Executive or spouse lacks will (or the will needs updating).
- No plan for financing retirement.
- Failure to make use of short-term trust to save family taxes.
- Overconcentration in one stock (often the stock of the employer).
- Sitting on investments that no longer make sense.
- No (or insufficient) disability protection.
- Reliance on *variable* income to meet fixed expenses.
- Getting into unsuitable or unnecessary tax shelters.
- No coordination between personal financial planning and estate planning.

USE OF MUTUAL WILLS CAN FORFEIT MARITAL DEDUCTION

A husband might want to leave a big chunk of property to his wife when he dies, but he may fear that she will make no provision to bequeath any of this property to *his* relatives or friends. She may feel the same way about leaving property to him. One solution to this dilemma is to have the spouses make *mutual wills*, in which each party agrees to leave inherited property to the survivor, who, after death, will leave specified property to designated relatives or friends of both parties.

Problem: The solution may create tax problems involving marital deduc-

tion on the estate tax return. If the wife, for example, was contractually bound by a mutual will to bequeath whatever remains of her late husband's property to, say, the children, his property *has not passed on to her without strings*. The marital deduction only applies if property passes outright.

State law is important here to determine whether the property passing to her under her husband's will really was contractually subject to a condition. In a decision on this issue, the court held that under *New York* law, a state resident is bound by such a restriction and hence the property earmarked for the children upon her death didn't qualify for the marital deduction because she didn't receive this property outright and without strings.

Indicated action: Check with tax counsel for the precedent in your state.

David A. Siegel Estate, 67 T.C., No. 50, 1/12/77

HOW TO COORDINATE INSURANCE AND WILL ARRANGEMENTS

Almost everyone with an estate within range of the Federal estate tax* who also owns a significant amount of life insurance knows the one basic rule: *To keep the insurance proceeds from being taxed as part of his estate, one must get rid of ownership of the policy and all incidents of ownership.* Those "incidents" include the right to change the beneficiary or the right to borrow against the policy.

The standard solution: Transfer

the policy to the beneficiary, usually the insured's spouse.

What too many people ignore, however, is the possibility that the beneficiary may not survive the insured. *Problems:*

• If the policy winds up back under the insured's ownership, he again has the problem of keeping the assets out of his estate.

• If his spouse was the beneficiary and owner of the policy, the benefit of the marital deduction has been lost, unless he remarries.

• Any new transfer of the policy ownership runs a higher risk of being disqualified because of the estate tax rule that makes life insurance gifts made within three years of death includible in the estate of the donor.

One way to anticipate these problems: The beneficiary of the insurance prepares a will that puts the policy, along with other assets, in a trust for the benefit of the children. *Problem:* According to Internal Revenue Service rules, if the insured is named the trustee, he possesses incidents of ownership of the policy, which makes the proceeds *includible* in his estate. *Alternatives to consider when the insurance policy is purchased:*

• The beneficiary could make an *outright bequest* of the insurance policy to someone other than the insured.

• The policy could be left to a separate trust with another person as trustee.

• A single trust could be set up for both the insurance policy and other property, with someone other than the insured as trustee

The important thing is to coordinate insurance and will arrangements now to save taxes.

*Exemption covers estates up to $400,000 in 1985, rising to $600,000 by 1987. This exemption can be reduced if part of the credit was applicable to lifetime transfers that would otherwise have been subject to gift tax.

HOW TO CONTROL INVESTMENTS IN YOUR KEOGH RETIREMENT PLAN

Self-employed persons who want to save on current income taxes and provide for their retirement by putting money into a Keogh (HR-10) plan, are often discouraged to learn from the bank trustee that they won't have a say about how their money will be invested. But it is possible to invest in common stocks and take full charge of investment decisions and trading *if* the right steps are taken.

Ask your broker to recommend a few banks that will act as trustee for your plan and let you control investments. *Fees:* Minimum annual charges range from $25 to $100. Make sure the bank you pick pays interest on uninvested funds. Then trade stocks through your broker, who will probably hold shares in his firm's account.

Banks that offer this service will rarely challenge your decisions. The bank trustee will not have any liability for losses to your account. If you are an *owner-employee,* you must assume liability for losses to all *other* participants in the plan. Capital gains are taxable only when money is withdrawn at retirement.

Note: New law permits you to act as your own Keogh trustee.

INSURANCE

KEY-MAN MINIMUM-DEPOSIT INSURANCE

Young executives often require more insurance than they can afford. One way to bring required insurance within practical reach of the executive:

The company takes out a policy on the life of the executive, naming itself as beneficiary. It pays the first four annual premiums. At the end of four years it sells the policy to the executive for the then cash value. The executive then borrows against the annual increase in cash to pay future premiums.

Details:

• If the insured were to die during the first four years of the policy, the company would receive the proceeds, and it could then pay that amount to the executive's heirs as a death benefit. The company gets no tax deduction for the premiums paid but may get a deduction on the death benefit, depending on whether it's structured as compensation or gift. Up to $5,000 may be received by the executive's beneficiaries income tax-free in any event. If it's compensation above $5,000, it's taxable as ordinary income.

• The cash value of the policy at the end of four years will be less than the four annual premiums paid by the company, but the difference isn't taxable to the executive when he buys the policy.

• The executive has postponed payment of anything on the policy for four years, giving him time to accumulate money for the policy purchase. The premium rates will be based on his age when the policy was taken out four years earlier and will remain at the lower rate.

• The executive can borrow against the policy to pay premiums at the low policy rate, and will get a deduction for interest paid on the loan. After seven years he can borrow not only the annual increase in cash value but the *full* cash value of the policy, including the first four premiums, without jeopardizing his interest deduction.

• *Further benefit:* On acquiring the policy, the executive is able to take future proceeds out of his estate on his death by transferring the policy and "all incidents of ownership" (right to change the beneficiary, choose settlement options and various other policy rights) to a beneficiary other than his estate. He could, for example, transfer the policy to his wife or to an irrevocable trust for the benefit of his children.

PREMIUM SAVINGS

Ask your agent about *penalty and reward policies*. Could save you as much as 20% on premiums.

What they are: The installation of a policy usually costs the insurance company more than it receives during the first year.

If the policyholder drops out after a few years or even months, that's a loss, and it's normally chargeable to the policyholders who stick.

With penalty and reward policies, the holder is required to put up an extra sum to cover setting-up costs. If he drops out, the company keeps that amount.

If, on the other hand, the executive stays with the firm for a minimum number of years (say ten or so), he gets the sum back with interest.

BE CAREFUL WHEN YOU BORROW AGAINST LIFE INSURANCE TO INVEST

Many "smart" people are borrowing against the cash value of their life insurance (usually at rates under 5%) and then investing the proceeds in a bank time deposit (at about an 8% yield) and pocketing the profit.

Such a ploy sounds prudent, but there is this danger:

If borrower dies before repaying the loan, estate taxes could easily wipe out the investment profits.

Borrowing against a policy is considered an "incident of ownership" in the policy. That means that the full proceeds of the policy (face amount less the outstanding loan) are included in the deceased's estate.

Without the incident of ownership, a special provision of the estate tax law excludes insurance proceeds paid directly to a beneficiary other than the estate.

Investment cautions: Savings bank

time deposit (or other investments) are certainly included in your estate. Under the new tax law, though, if that investment is jointly held with a spouse, half of it is excluded from the estate. (Joint real estate investments require a special election to get this treatment.)

Remember: The Internal Revenue Service will *disallow* an interest deduction if the loan is used to buy tax-free municipal bonds.

INSURANCE: TERM VS. WHOLE LIFE

Buy term insurance, instead of whole life, invest the difference and you're better off, right? The quick answer is apt to be "yes."

The logic runs like this: With term insurance, you pay only for *pure* insurance. With whole life and other types of *cash-value* policies, you combine insurance and *savings*, but most insurance companies pay only 2⅔% to 3⅔% on the savings portion (the cash surrender value). You can do better than that with your own savings and investment program. What's more, if you die during the *term*, your beneficiaries get not only the full face amount of the policy, but your *outside* savings as well, whereas with a whole life policy they'd get only the policy proceeds.

But *what if you should live out your life expectancy*, the more likely probability, and die after the term? Then, of course, your term policy would pay nothing. Your beneficiaries would get only what's in the outside savings fund, which might not be much, depending on investment experience, and, to a degree, on the kind of term policy you had and the resulting spread between the term and the whole life premium.

Additional point: The annual increase in the cash value of a whole life policy isn't taxable to you. But your own investment income will most likely be taxable to you, unless you get into tax exempts and accept the risk of interest fluctuations affecting principal value before maturity, plus the risks of default.

How to make an evaluation: Think of insurance primarily as a substitute for missing assets on premature death; secondarily as a means of supplying liquidity to your estate. Structure your insurance program to fit your family needs, taking into account your other resources. Your wife, for example, may need protection *beyond your attaining age 65*, if your other resources prove insufficient or are illiquid. A whole life policy might be best here. But, if you have young children, a term policy might be the best way of assuring funds to rear them.

Comparison shop: Do it before buying anything, unless you have an insurance agent on whom you're willing to stake your life and your family's fortune.

When looking at whole life: Check cash values in 10 and 20 years. Check the interest factor used in computing cash values. Using this rate, figure out how much money the insurer would have to set aside each year to equal cash value. Subtract this from the premium. The rest is the cost of the pure insurance portion of the policy. You can then compare either portion (insurance or savings) of the policy to available alternatives. Can you get pure insurance at lower cost? Can you get a better after-tax return on your savings in investments with equal safety?

Generally avoid buying "extras" (waiver of premium on disability, double indemnity, insuring the lives of children), since the insurance company's profit margin is usually apt to be even higher on the extras than the rate on the basic policy.

HOW TO SPOT A BAD INSURANCE AGENT

• He advises you not to file a small loss claim under your homeowner's or auto policy; or you're turned down for policy renewal even though your claims have been infrequent and negligible in amount.

What to do: Go to the company directly, cite your loss record. Odds are your claim will be paid or your policy reinstated. And then change agents.

• He begins to churn your account, urging you to drop older policies and buy new ones.

What to do: Insist on written justification for the switch in terms of better coverage, rates or features; verify the proposal by checking it with the insurance firm. You could be a big loser, especially on straight-life policies, where shifting means higher premiums and loss of your head-start on cash value and dividend build-up.

• You take on a new policy (and perhaps drop an old one), find yourself billed for a higher premium than expected.

What to do: Fire him—and refuse

the policy. Even if he didn't anticipate the higher premium (for example, you may have been reclassified to a special or substandard group as a result of a new medical examination), it was his responsibility to tell you *before* the prior policy was canceled.

● He changes carriers frequently without telling you. If you've maintained a good claims record—and several coverages with the same company—you should stay with them, unless he's actually getting you better premium or benefits elsewhere. Insist on being consulted in advance of any change in your insurance program.

PROS AND CONS OF MUTUAL FUND-LIFE INSURANCE PACKAGES FOR IRAs

Mutual fund organizations are putting together mutual fund-life insurance packages as funding vehicles for Individual Retirement Accounts (IRAs).

While an individual can fund his IRA with an endowment policy to provide death benefits for his family in the event of his premature death, it won't give him much of a capital build-up for his own retirement.

For growth, he might turn to savings bank time deposits, which currently offer interest rates of 8% or more. But there's no guarantee that such high rates will continue until a program is completed.

If he still believes that a diversified

fund of common stock under professional management can beat the yield on time deposits, he may be a prospect for the new IRA package: Mutual funds *plus* insurance.

Before buying such a package, consider these facts:

● Each year that you make a contribution under the package program, you will have to pay substantial commissions on the life insurance portion. And if the mutual fund portion is in a load fund, the sales charge could be as high as 8.5%. It takes time for your investment to recover from these bites.

● Only that portion of the endowment policy premium attributable to savings is deductible as part of your IRA contribution. The life insurance portion comes out of *after-tax* dollars.

● As an endowment policy ages and the savings portion builds up, you have less and less pure insurance coverage.

● When you buy a mutual fund-life insurance package you are locked into the *package*. By shopping around you might do better buying each component separately. Group term (and possibly group permanent) offered by your employer or an association you may join can probably provide less expensive coverage than you're apt to get in the package.

● While it's true that there's no guarantee that savings bank time deposits are going to continue to provide high current rates of interest, you can always move into another qualified investment offering higher yields with safety. Nothing in the Internal Revenue Service rules prevents that.

IRS CAN ATTACH INSURANCE TO SATISFY A TAX LIEN

An individual owed back taxes to the Internal Revenue Service, which obtained a judgment against him. Then the IRS learned that he had transferred two policies of insurance on his life to his spouse. But he still had the right to change the beneficiary designations, thus he still had an incident of ownership—which meant he owned them for tax purposes.

How to avoid this trap: When assigning insurance policies to one's wife or other person, make sure you have retained *no significant rights* in the policy, such as the right to change beneficiary.

U.S. V. Mandel et al., D.C., S.D. Fla., 5/23/74.

ESTATE PLANNING STRATEGIES

HOW TO SAVE GIFT & ESTATE TAXES

Put simply, an individual can make gifts of up to $10,000 per year to as many different donees as he chooses without incurring any gift taxes, and the aggregate amount of those gifts can be excluded from his estate and from the federal estate tax. Tax-free gifts can now be made during the last three years of one's life. That couldn't be done before unless the executor was able to show that the gifts were not made in contemplation of death. That is very hard to do and resulted in a great deal of expensive and time-consuming litigation.

The 1981 law eliminates all controversy on whether a gift made within three years of death was or was not in contemplation of death. It abolished *subject to a few exceptions*, the rule that gifts within three years of death are includible in the donor's estate.

Lifetime giving. Grandfather, in his declining years, can siphon off a good amount of his estate without gift tax liability. Looking at his last three years alone, let's say he has four children (all married) and twelve grandchildren (four of them married). Among his four children and their spouses he has eight donees. There are another 16 among his grandchildren and their spouses, for a total of 24 donees. Thus, he can give away $240,000 per year for each of the three years preceding his death, for a total of $720,000 *without gift tax liability.* At the same time, he has removed that amount from his estate. If, during the gift-giving program, he gave securities or other property with appreciation potential, he would be excluding from his estate not only the initial $10,000 value of the gift, but the appreciation as well.

• *Higher taxes on gifts:* Under the

1976 tax law, if a gift is made *in excess of* the annual exclusion ($10,000 to each recipient per year, and double that if your spouse consents), the gift will be taxable at a higher rate than formerly. The separate gift tax rate schedule, which was only three-fourths of the estate tax rate for like amounts, is no more. Now there's a *unified* rate, generally a percentage point or two higher than the old estate tax rates. True, there is a credit which increases year by year to a top of $192,800 after 1986.

From 1987 on, one can make such gifts without paying tax up to a total of $600,000 (at which point you use up the $192,800 tax credit). But it's still desirable to avoid taxable gifts and stay within the annual exclusion limits as far as possible. *Reason:* Taxable lifetime gifts are cumulative and push the estate into higher and higher tax brackets.

If the intended gift property is worth more than the $10,000 (or $20,000) annual exclusion, it's important to explore techniques for making several annual exclusions available for the particular gift. *Some ideas:* Gifts of a part interest in the property at annual intervals. A bargain sale or installment sale of the property, taking back notes, payable at annual intervals, and canceling the notes as they fall due. Mortgaging the property and paying off the mortgage annually.

Gifts are also a way to *postpone* the payment of capital gains taxes, possibly for many years. When appreciated property is given away, that is not a taxable transfer. The recipient of the gift has the same cost basis for the asset as the giver. If the recipient keeps the asset, there's no capital gains tax until he decides to sell it, which could be many years later.

On the other hand, if the recipient sells the property immediately, it could be a way to *reduce* the capital gains tax sharply. If the original owner of the asset is in the top (50%) tax bracket, he would pay a tax of 20% of the realized profit when selling property that has been held for more than one year. But if it is given away to a family member in a much lower bracket, the tax would be his top bracket rate applied to 40% of the realized profit. For a child with no other income, it could be as low as 4.4% of the gain.

• *Gifts for a child with outside income:* Suppose your child has outside sources of income, perhaps a trust or custodial account for his benefit set up by a grandparent, or earnings from employment. In this situation, setting up a trust for him with the idea of diverting income from the parent's high tax bracket to his, that added income, if payable currently, would push him into a higher tax bracket and reduce the family tax savings.

The 1976 Tax Reform Act provides a new and effective way of dealing with such situations. *Have the trust provide for accumulation of income during the child's minority.* The income so accumulated will not be subject to tax when ultimately attributed to him, as it would have been under prior law. True, the trust will have to pay a tax on the income as earned, but since there will now be two taxable entities, the child and the trust, rate-splitting tax savings will result.

There are still smart ways of saving taxes by intrafamily gifts; some are augmented by the 1976 Act. The most advantageous implementation calls for professional guidance.

IRS APPROVES THIRD-PARTY GIFT LEASEBACKS

Gift leasebacks are a key income-shifting technique for parents who own businesses. The parent gives business property or equipment to a trust for his children, then leases the property back from the trust. The trust's income is shifted from the parent's high-tax bracket to the children's low bracket.

The IRS has been somewhat successful in attacking these transactions, primarily on the grounds that they lacked economic substance. But what if the parent does not lease the property back himself? Instead, it is leased by a third party—the parent's professional corporation, for example. In this situation the courts have sided with the taxpayer. Unfortunately, it has been necessary for taxpayers to go to court to secure the tax benefits from a gift lease-back.

IRS backs down: The IRS has now taken the position that it will no longer litigate gift-leaseback transactions where the lessee is a third party—i.e., a corporation—*unless* the third party is a partnership or an S corporation.* *Impact:* Parents who own businesses can now take advantage of properly structured third-party gift leasebacks *without* having to take the IRS to court.

Caution: As with any sophisticated family financial planning technique, third-party gift leasebacks should not be undertaken without professional advice. See your tax adviser.

Acquiescence in Hobart A. Lerner, 71 TC 290.

CLIFFORD TRUST

Clifford trusts are no longer limited to the very wealthy. Citibank, N.A. recently introduced a Clifford trust package that's well within the reach of the average family. It's called the University Trust.

It's affordable: You can start the trust with as little as $10,000. (Most other big banks won't touch a trust of under $300,000.) If you don't have the $10,000, Citibank will lend it to you.

It's simple: The bank gives you a standard, single-page, plain-English trust document in a package that has everything you need to open the turst. You and Citibank can handle it together without the help of a lawyer, although you may want to get professional advice before opening the trust.

It's inexpensive: There are no start-up fees, no closing fees and no legal fees (unless you choose to consult your own lawyer). The bank charges an annual tax-deductible administration fee of $250 or 1% of the amount in the trust, whichever is greater. For that fee, the bank manages the investments and does the trust's tax returns.

GIFTS TO CHILDREN FOR FAMILY TAX SAVINGS

Gifts of income-producing property to children are often used to move income from a high bracket family member to one in a lower tax bracket. Nothing in the Tax Reform Act of 1976 changes the basic concept. But there are some key gift-related changes which need to be noted:

338

• *Special tax on appreciated property sold by a trust:* In the past, a parent holding highly appreciated property which was ripe for sale might give it to a child, who would then sell it at a lower capital gains cost than if the parent had sold it. If the intended donee were a minor and the intended gift property was worth a good deal, the best way to handle the gift would be through a trust for the benefit of the child.

• *The 1976 Act effectively bars the use of a trust when, for investment or personal reasons, the sale should be made quickly:* It does this by providing that if the trust sells appreciated property transferred to it within two years of the transfer, the trust is subject to a special tax measured by the additional tax the donor would have had to pay if he'd sold the property when the trust did.

To get around this rule it is necessary to make an outright gift to the child. *Or,* if the property is securities, it's possible to set up a custodial account under the Uniform Gift to Minors Act of your state. The outright gift might be okay if the child were old enough and the parent had confidence about his wise use of the proceeds. Otherwise, it might be a risky business, unless a guardianship were used. A guardianship, though, would introduce red tape, inflexibility, and costs which many would prefer to avoid.

The custodial account is much simpler than a guardianship. But it has an element of inflexibility not found in a trust. That is, when the child is no longer a minor (18 to 21, depending on the particular state's law), the account must be turned over to him, whether he is "ready" or not.

SAFE DEPOSIT BOXES

It is unwise to keep anything in a safe deposit box that may be needed quickly when the owner dies. At that time, a bank normally seals the box until legal proceedings (sometimes lengthy) take place.

Don't store:

Original will, cemetery deeds or burial instructions. (Keep them in a safe place at home or in a vault belonging to your lawyer, executor or accountant.)

Large amounts of *cash.* Money in a safe deposit box is not working for you and suggests intent to evade income tax.

Unregistered property (such as jewelry or bearer bonds) belonging to *someone else.* Courts could presume these items to be your property, and proving otherwise might be difficult.

Store these:

Personal papers, such as birth and marriage certificates, military service or citizenship papers, important family records.

Jewelry, medals, rare coins, stamps, family heirlooms.

Original signed family or business documents, such as house deeds, mortgage papers, trust agreements, contracts, leases, court decrees.

Securities, registered or bearer.

Never buy and forget about a stock. Nothing is that good. Always re-examine even the best decisions in light of new market and economic conditions.

SUBSTITUTE A LIVING ESTATE FOR A DEATH ESTATE

Buying the wrong kind of life insurance is one of the major reasons people fail to become financially independent. *The other major reasons:* Investment procrastination. Lack of financial goals. Ignorance of what to do with money to accomplish those goals. Failure to apply tax laws to advantage.

LIFE INSURANCE TRAPS TO AVOID:

• *A policy that does not use a current mortality table.* Many premiums are still being paid and policies are still in force based on the American Experience Table—the death rate from the days of Abraham Lincoln. Another table, the 1941 Commissioner's Standard Ordinary (CSP) table, was devised before penicillin. The current 1958 table is out of date. If you have a policy based on an old table, you may be paying as much as *300% more* than you need to because you are on the wrong table. (Most policies are computed on the 1941 table.)

• *Cash surrender policies.* Considered by some to be one of the greatest frauds in our country. People are convinced by insurance companies that these are worthwhile because the company gives you a level premium on a whole-life policy and you can borrow your cash value. That may sound attractive, but the reality is that insurance is based on a mortality table, and all the funny banking in the world won't change that. The companies are willing to give a level premium on whole life because you are overpaying until you reach age 72. Then you can underpay when you don't need the insurance anyway. *Parallel:* Would you go to the telephone company and say, "Could I overpay my bill for each of the next 30 years for the privilege of underpaying after age 72?"

On the cash-value side, you would never go to a bank that takes away everything you deposit the first year and then charges you to deposit money in the account. And if you want to borrow, it charges you 5½% for your own money. And if you die, the insurance company can keep the money. No one would open that kind of bank account. Neither should you accept such terms from an insurance company. *Principle:* People are willing to believe you can combine a living estate and a dying estate. In reality, these are incompatible. Insurance should be bought as an umbrella in case you die before building up a life estate. Don't ever consider it a method of building up your net worth (or "living estate").

• *Dividend participating policies.* These are not really dividends. They are partial returns on an overcharge. Again, people are victims of the belief that they can combine nest eggs for life and for death. A controversial FTC report says that if you keep a policy for an average period, you would receive 1.3% on your money. That means it takes 55.4 years for $1 to become $2. *Worse:* if you hold the policy under five years, you could have as high as a *negative 18%* interest. Holding for 10 years could produce a *negative 4%*.

• *Insurance that is in your pension plan.* The incidental costs are much higher than most people are led to believe. After all, your pension plan is for living, not for dying.

BETTER METHODS OF INSURING. If you can pass a physical, you get a lower price per thousand on insurance if you switch to annual renewable term or 10-year deposit-level term.

Which to choose: If you know you are going to need insurance for the next 10 years, there is merit in the 10-year deposit-level term, since your premiums will be level for 10 years. However, realize that you are being overcharged in the beginning and undercharged at the end. But by making a deposit, you do get a discount on the rates you pay.

Best: If you believe you will soon start making enough to take care of your family out of your living estate (the money you build up over a lifetime), you will want to drop your insurance incrementally as your estate grows.

How to manage it: If you have a dependent who requires $1,000 a month if you die, then you need an estate of $200,000 (at a 6% return a year—half of that at 12%). If you have only $20,000 in your living estate, you need a $180,000 death estate (or insurance policy). As you build up your living estate, you can annually decrease your death estate. When your living estate rises to $50,000, then your death estate should go down to $150,000. Naturally you may want to adjust this in accordance with inflation. But your goal is to be self-insured, so that benefits don't hinge on death. Insurance should be viewed as a way to buy time before you build up your own fortune.

GENERATION-SKIPPING TRUSTS CAN STILL SAVE ESTATE TAXES

Generation-skipping trusts, the target of tax reformers for at least a generation, are still effective tax-savers.

The Tax Reform Act hasn't affected the most typical arrangement: Trust income is paid for life to the surviving spouse and the *principal* goes to the children when the spouse dies. The principal passes to the younger generation tax-free.

Under the new law, there's a tax when there are *two* younger generations (child and grandchild).

Exception: Each child is allowed to pass along—tax-free—a combined total of $250,000 of the trust to his children (the grandchildren of the estate-creator).

Example:

Adjusted gross estate	$1,000,000
Half goes to wife tax-free (qualifying marital deduction)	- 500,000
Estate left for two children	$ 500,000
Estate tax (assuming original settlor's unified credit of $47,000 was used **before death)**	- 108,800
Estate left to be divided between two children ($195,600 each)	$ 391,200

Unless each child's share of $195,600 appreciates to $250,000 or more when he later dies, the trust will pass to the *grandchildren* tax-free—just as it did under the prior law when there was no dollar limitation.

TAX-FAVORED WAYS OF BUILDING A COLLEGE FUND

By 1990, it's been estimated, it will cost over $100,000 to put a child through six years of any Ivy League college. Here are four tax-favored approaches that can help ease the burden. First, the *common elements:*

All approaches rely on income-splitting: Removing income from the high-bracket parent or grandparent to the low-tax bracket child or trust. The child has a personal exemption of $1,000 ($1,040 in 1985) and a $200 dividend exclusion, before he gets hit with income tax.

Trusts have lower exemptions.

While the child remains a minor (from 18 to 21, depending on the state), any income used to pay for what's considered (under state law) to be part of the parent's obligation of support will be taxable to the parent. In many states a college education may be considered a support obligation.

All approaches rely on a transfer of property for the benefit of the child—a gift—and so expose the donor to possible gift tax liability. Every donor may give up to $10,000 each year ($20,000 if spouse consents) to as many individuals as desired without gift tax liability, provided it's not some future interest (as where you provide that the child is to get the principal of a trust at, say, age 25). Gifts in excess of $10,000 per year ($20,000 from a couple) to any one recipient will use up part of the combined lifetime gift-estate tax exemption of $121,800 in 1985, $155,800 in 1986, and $192,800 in 1987 and after.

Consider the following trusts:

CUSTODIAL ACCOUNT. These are the simplest. You put securities or money in the name of your minor child. The child is taxable on the annual income. *Disadvantages:* The fund must be turned over to the child upon attainment of majority. Permissible investments are limited, varying from state to state, but generally *exclude* real estate. If you're the custodian, the pro-

perty will be included in your estate if you die during the custodianship.

SHORT-TERM TRUST. The trust must last for more than 10 years from the time of transfer. The child *receives income only*, and at the end of the trust, the principal reverts to you or to someone you've named. You will have to make a larger transfer of property than if principal could be used. There are no limitations on investments and no requirement that income be paid to the beneficiary instead of applied to the child's benefit, or attainment of majority. Distribution of income or its use for the benefit of the child will normally be **made discretionary, although it could** be made mandatory and then put into a custodial account. To the extent that distribution is discretionary, you lose the benefit of the annual gift tax exclusion because this is considered a *gift of a future interest.* Income which isn't currently distributed is taxable to the trust first and later to the child when it is distributed to him. A special formula applies for determining the child's liability, which takes into account the tax paid by the trust.

TRUST UNTIL THE CHILD ATTAINS MAJORITY. The trustee (an independent one is best) must be given broad discretion to use both income and principal for the minor without restriction. Income not applied currently but accumulated is taxable as described in the above section on short-term trusts. The principal and undistributed income remaining when the child reaches majority must be distributed at that time without strings. If these requirements are met, the annual gift tax exclusion will be available for the full value of the gift, not just the value of the right to income.

MANDATORY INCOME DISTRIBUTION TRUST. All income must be paid to the child or for his benefit at least annually until the trust ends, which can be virtually as long as you want it to last. The trustee may have discretion to pay out principal to the child or for his benefit. The annual gift tax exclusion is available, however, only as to the value of the right to income given to the child; not as to discretionary distributions before the end of the trust. There's no problem on tax treatment of accumulated income, since current distribution is mandatory. Income distributed to the child after attainment of majority may be used as the child pleases.

DEBTOR'S GIFT TO RELATIVES CAN BE SET ASIDE BY CREDITORS

The law makes it clear that a debtor can't beat his creditors by the simple device of making gifts of his property to relatives, thus making himself insolvent. Creditors can sue to have the gifts set aside as fraudulent without showing that the debtor actually intended to defraud or that the recipients knew that anything was wrong.

But obviously a creditor is in a much better position if adequate security arrangements are made at the time the loan is made.

Case in point: The debtor made gifts of stock in a closely held corporation.

What the creditor should have done: Gotten the stock to hold as collateral for the loan. If not, the creditor should have gotten a lien on it. This wouldn't have prevented the debtor from transfering property to a relative, but it would have helped the creditor to gain possession on default from the recipient or from persons to whom the recipient might have transfered the property in question.

HOW A TRUST MAY PROTECT AGAINST CREDITORS' CLAIMS

In most states you can set up a trust with a so-called *spendthrift clause.* This will protect the income beneficiary of the trust from the claims of creditors. So if the beneficiary falls upon hard times and is declared bankrupt, his interest in the trust fund won't, under ordinary circumstances, pass to his trustee in bankruptcy. He will come out of bankruptcy proceedings freed of the claims of his creditors and can go on receiving the income of the trust.

With a *spendthrift trust* the beneficiary can't anticipate income from the trust. But he may be able to borrow money from the trust as the need arises, giving the trustee unsecured notes.

That was done in a 1975 case in which the beneficiary was declared bankrupt. The question was whether the notes held by the trustee would support claims against his estate, which would share with the claims of other creditors, or whether they were to be subordinated to the claims of general creditors. A federal appeals court held that subordination wasn't required.

Comment: This device might be of use by an individual planning to set up a family member in a new business involving significant risk. Whether the device might prove equally effective in a situation where an individual undertakes to set up a trust for his *own* benefit is an open question.

The further removed the creation of the trust is from the establishment of the business, the greater the chances of its protection. If the business is to be operated in corporate form, the limited liability feature of corporate operation makes use of this device of little or no value. Of course, corporate realities are quite different, and in a start-up situation shareholders are almost invariably called upon to *personally* guarantee corporate debts.

A lender in a situation where the guarantor has trust funds beyond the reach of creditors must take this into account.

Stebbins v. Crocker Citizens National Bank, C.A. 9, 4/29/75.

TAX-SAVING WAY TO BENEFIT CHARITY AND FAMILY

Many charities, schools, and other organizations use a technique to make donations pay off handsomely for the philanthropist as well. *The technique:* Pooled income funds.

The benefits:

• Fund (a trust) pays income during the life of one or more beneficaries.

• When the beneficiaries die, the principal goes to the charity.

• Meanwhile, the donor gets a tax deduction based on (a) the present value of the principal, (b) the life expectancy of the beneficiaries, and (c) the pooled fund's rate or return. (The older the beneficiaries are, the bigger the income tax deduction will be.)

• If appreciated property is put in the fund, its higher value is used to determine the gift, but the appreciation escapes capital-gains tax.

Technical points: When the donor dies, the value of the principal is included in the estate. However, if the donor is married and makes use of the maximum marital deduction, the basis of the marital deduction will be increased for computation. Further, the estate will get a 100% offsetting charitable contribution deduction for the pooled income interest that's included in the donor's estate.

Example: A 65-year old executive contributes stock which cost him $10,000 but is now worth $100,000. The pooled income fund produces a yield of 6%. He would get a charitable contribution deduction of $51,788. Assuming he is in the 50% bracket, that would save him half in taxes, or $25,894.

Assume further that the stock transferred was ripe for sale, for investment reasons. The capital gains tax on a $90,000 gain would have a tax of $18,000. So the tax savings add up to

$43,894. That means he is really only out-of-pocket $56,106.

The anticipated yield of 6% on the $100,000 contributed translates to 10.69% return on the out-of-pocket sum. Of course, there will be nothing left on the beneficiary's death for his estate or family. This needs to be taken into account in determining the true yield. However, there are tax advantages for his estate which may help reduce the loss of capital. For example, assume he has an adjusted gross estate of $1-million. The net effect of the exclusion of the $100,000 from his estate would be a reduction in the estate tax of $18,500.

If the donor (or other beneficiary) outlives his life expectancy, further benefits will be reaped. In effect, he will make a profit. On the other hand, if he dies earlier, there will be a loss. From a purely financial point of view, the donor should shop for a pooled fund that can be expected to produce the highest yield. While higher yields reduce the income-tax charitable contribution deduction, they will more than make up for the loss by the higher income paid for life.

BOOSTING THE CHARITABLE CONTRIBUTION DEDUCTION

You may deduct your out-of-pocket costs of doing volunteer work for charity. *That includes:* Phone calls, postage, stationery, transportation, special uniforms (and the cost of maintaining and cleaning them), meals and lodging (while away from home overnight in rendering services or attending a relevant convention).

If you use your own car, you may either deduct the actual cost of gas and oil or a flat allowance of 9¢ a mile in 1984 (12¢ in 1985 and after). If you permit a charity to use your property, you can get a deduction for the fair rental value *if it's done under a lease.* You may also be able to get a deduction for the expense of maintaining a refugee in your home under an arrangement with a charity. You *may* be able to get a deduction for the expense of a baby-sitter for a refugee child if the charity knows about it, otherwise not.

PROTECTING YOUR PROPERTY FROM THE STATE

Financially strapped state governments are seizing more and more personal wealth under revised unclaimed property statutes. Unclaimed property is deemed abandoned (ownership reverts to state) if the legal owner doesn't make some overt contact with his property within a stated period of time, typically, seven years. The property can include bank accounts, contents of safe deposit vaults, insurance policies, etc.

Four basic rules to protect yourself against joining the thousands who lose valuable property every year out of sheer neglect:

• Keep a single list of all your owned

assets with value, relevant ownership information, requirements for proper care, locating, and name and address of custodian (bank, lawyer, brokerage house, insurance company, real estate manager, etc.)

• Keep the list where it will be accessible either to your next of kin or to your legal or financial agent, should anything happen to you.

• Review the list regularly (a) to bring the entries up to date, and (b) to take appropriate action on closing accounts, collecting dividends, cashing coupons, paying premiums, selling stock, etc.

• When your address changes, notify each entry on the list, noting on the list that the change has been made *after* you have evidence to that effect.

PERSONAL TAX STRATEGIES

High-income executives need *not* worry about what deductions to take until year-end. *Reason:* A deduction can be taken for payments made up until the last day of the year. A key question in taking deductions is whether to claim them in the current year or save them for the next year. That decision is best made as close to December 31 as possible.

What high-income executives should be thinking about right now:

• *Gifts.* Executives can give family members up to $10,000 a year per recipient gift-tax-free ($20,000 if the executive's spouse joins in on the gift). The sooner this is done in a tax year, the better. *Reason:* Income generated by money given early in the year will be taxed at the family member's low-bracket

rate rather than the executive's high-bracket rate.

Point: The same principle holds true for *all* transfers of wealth within the family. *Result:* Executives planning to establish Clifford trusts for their children this year should do it now, not later.

• *Tax shelters.* Shop for them at the beginning of the year rather than in the fall. *Reasons:* The sooner in a tax year a sheltered investment is obtained, the greater the losses it generates. When demand for shelters increases at year-end, quality decreases and prices rise.

• *Investment portfolios.* Executives who wait until December to sell investments at a loss to offset gains realized lose considerable room to maneuver. *Better bet:* Keep a running tab on investment gains and losses to maximize time for advantageous maneuvering.

Source: Herbert Paul, tax attorney, Herbert M. Paul, P.C., 805 Third Ave., New York 10022.

FITTING THE COMPANY'S RETIREMENT PLAN WITH AN ESTATE PLAN

The 1976 tax law made important changes in the tax treatment of qualified retirement-plan benefits paid to *beneficiaries.* A lump sum distributed to a beneficiary is includible in the decedent's estate, and he receives favorable income-tax treatment. Find out from the plan administrator the answers to the questions below. Then check the answers with your lawyer or tax advisor. Make any necessary changes in your designation of the beneficiary and form of payment.

• Does the plan provide for lump-sum distributions?

346

- Who determines whether a lump-sum or some other form of distribution is to be made? The plan administrator? Executive? Beneficiary?
- Who should make the choice?
- To whom should plan benefits be paid?
- Should a trust or an individual be named the beneficiary?
- If a trust is to be used, what form should it take?
- Which is worth more: The estate tax exclusion or the income tax savings possible with a lump-sum distribution?
- How can lump-sum treatment be avoided or nailed down?
- How does the lump-sum distribution affect: The marital deduction; the estate-tax liabilities of the surviving spouse; the interests passing to others?

LENDING MONEY TO RELATIVES

If a relative comes to you to borrow money *for use in his business*, you'll usually be better off *from a tax standpoint* to guarantee his loan from a bank or commercial lender instead of lending him the money directly.

They get a *bad business loan deduction* if the borrower is an individual who uses the borrowed funds in his business when the guarantor pays the debt and can't collect.

If you simply made a direct loan to your relative and the debt became worthless, unless you yourself had some interest in the relative's business or were yourself in the business of lending money, you'd be limited *to a non-bad business loan deduction.* Your loss would be treated as a short-term capital loss, with limited deductibility.

Short-term capital losses may be used to offset capital gains, dollar-for-dollar, but any excess is deductible against ordinary income up to $3,000 in any one year.

Alternately, as a way of cushioning your possible loss, you might try for an equity position in the business which would entitle you to a full deduction if the business turns sour. If it's a corporation, the issuance of so-called Sec. 1244 stock could accomplish this purpose (ask your tax adviser about this).

Any transaction with a relative by blood or marriage will be carefully scrutinized by IRS if and when a bad-debt deduction is claimed. IRS will want to see whether there was a debt or whether the transaction was really a gift, contribution to capital or other arrangement not resulting in a debt. Loans to children are presumed to be gifts, but the presumption may be overcome by convincing evidence.

ONE THING IS SURE. If you want to stand a chance of getting a bad-debt deduction on a loan to a relative, it must be handled from start to finish in a businesslike way. Essentially, handle it the way you would if you were dealing with a stranger, although the terms needn't be quite as tough.
- Use a formal loan agreement.
- Spell out the amount of the loan, when and in what amounts repayment is to be made, the interest rate, the notes to be given, the effect of default in the payment of installments, and the collateral security, if any, to be furnished.
- The loan agreement must be signed before any money is advanced.

But IRS won't be taken in by mere form. In order to establish that you have a valid debt and that it became worthless, you'll have to show that you followed through in enforcing the terms of the loan and trying to collect. You'll want to keep records of payments, all correspondence with the debtor (collection letters, notice of default and the like) along with a record of other steps taken to collect.

HOW TO AVOID PROBATE

Probate of a will and administration of an estate in probate court can be time-consuming and expensive. (Fees for executor, trustee, lawyer, appraiser, etc., eat up 5% to 10% of the estate.) These facts of life and death were parlayed into Norman Dacey's best-seller, *How to Avoid Probate*. Dacey, a mutual fund and life insurance salesman, advocates that you simply make a written declaration that you are holding certain property in trust for certain beneficiaries, name yourself as trustee, and provide for a successor trustee on your death who is directed to turn over the property to the beneficiaries and terminate the trust. He supplies the form for this self-declaration of trust. The result, according to Dacey, is "no lawyer's, executor's or appraiser's fee, or probate court costs."

This is *not* quite so. There will be appraiser's fees, for example, if the property involved does not have any established market value (any property other than publicly traded securities). There will most certainly be lawyer's fees for preparing an estate tax return, for filing the decedent's last income tax return, for transferring the property to the beneficiaries and for terminating the trust. There may also be much larger lawyer's fees for defend-

ing the validity of the declaration of trust if challenged by those disinherited or short-changed as they see it, including quite possibly, the Collector of Internal Revenue.

Some lawyers also suggest that if the same person is both trustee and lifetime beneficiary, his two interests merge, and there's really no trust. An independent co-trustee might solve this problem. You might also provide that if the trust is declared invalid, the property is to be held under the same terms as a testamentary trust. But the effect of this would be to make the property subject to probate.

Even assuming the self-declaration trust is valid, what real savings can be achieved, bearing in mind probate expenses are deductible against the estate tax? What assets are to be included? (Vehicles, stock in a Subchapter S corporation, an interest in a sole proprietorship, and qualified options all present problems.) What happens if the estate owner becomes incompetent?

For estate planning, seek qualified professional advice, *now more than ever*, because of the complexities, opportunities and pitfalls of the 1981 Tax Act.

HOW SWISS BANKS TREAT HEIRS

Swiss impose no inheritance taxes on nonresidents. The bank will turn an account over to an heir on presentation of probate papers or an authenticated will.

Making it simple: Write a separate will covering only Swiss assets and leave it with a Swiss lawyer.

Also simple, but risky: Give someone power of attorney for your account

—you can do it right on the bank's signature form. In Switzerland, power of attorney survives death of the grantee. Remember, the bank will give the person you grant power of attorney any funds he asks for, no questions asked—so appoint someone you can *really* trust.

Warning: Swiss bank accounts are part of your estate and subject to the same U.S. and local taxes.

EXECUTOR PROTECTION

Executors or trustees of an estate should look into an *errors-and-omissions insurance policy*. It could make a huge difference in the event of a conflict over fiduciary activities. The Internal Revenue Service allows a tax deduction on the premiums of such policies.

However, if you graciously offer to serve as an executor for a friend *without a charge*, the insurance premium could not be connected to the production of income—and the basis for a tax deduction would be lost.

EXECUTOR LIABILITY

Executor trap: One executor distributed the estate assets to beneficiaries without leaving enough money to take care of taxes. The court required that he personally pay the Federal estate tax. Then he sought to deduct that payment to the IRS as an expense in carrying on an income-producing trade or business. (He had received a fee for serving as executor.)

Ruling: *Negative.* Work as an executor or trustee was *not* part of the individual's business.

Albert J. Uhlenbrook et al, 67 T.C. No. 64, 2/17/77.

LET THE IRS KNOW WHEN YOU'RE ACTING AS A FIDUCIARY

Whenever you're called upon to act as executor or trustee for a friend or relative, be aware that you must give written notice of that fact to the IRS. Failure to do so can be expensive.

The case: An individual was institutionalized, and a fiduciary was named to look after his affairs. The IRS issued a notice of additional taxes due to the institutionalized person. This letter was sent to him at the facility where he was being cared for. But the tax was never paid. When the IRS caught up with the delinquent taxpayer after his release, he claimed he couldn't be touched because he had never properly been sent a deficiency notice.

The court didn't see it that way. His failure to get the deficiency notice was not the IRS' fault but the fault of the fiduciary, for the IRS had not been told who was representing the taxpayer or where the representative could be reached.

Comment: Predictably, a taxpayer will seek restitution from the fiduciary who failed to file the necessary notice.

U.S. v. Pugach, D.C., S.D.N.Y., 11/4/74.

TAX ANGLES

THE TAX LAW, THE ECONOMIC CLIMATE, AND TAX SHELTERS

The reduction of the top tax rate from 70% to 50% has made investors cautious about risk-taking for immediate tax gain. More than ever, investors are looking for sound long-term investments. And there are many shelters that fill the bill. *What looks good:*

OIL AND GAS. The long-term economic prospects for oil- and gas-drilling investments are more favorable than ever before. Lease and drilling costs are down. And, despite the so-called oil glut, world reserves are constantly shrinking.

There are also good opportunities in oil and gas income funds, or investments in producing properties. A large part of the income is tax free, and they're selling at lower prices now, as many companies are freeing cash by selling properties.

REAL ESTATE. The accelerated cost recovery system (ACRS) allows real property to be written off in only 18 years (15 years for low-income housing), either by the accelerated depreciation method (with higher immediate deductions) or by the straight-line method (with tax advantages on resale through capital gains treatment).

Among the better real estate deals is subsidized low-income housing. Faster depreciation, special tax breaks, and investment credits make this area even more favorable than other real estate deals. And investments are available in relatively small units.

EQUIPMENT LEASING. Fast write-offs, interest deductions, and investments make equipment-leasing deals attractive. The key is the residual value the equipment acquires after the term of the lease, so that it can be resold. The higher the residual value, the better.

CABLE TV. The fastest-growing crop of new tax shelters can be found in cable TV. Basically two types of cable TV shelters are being offered:
• Blind pools, which do not designate any locations to be developed.
• Deals, usually private offerings, involving specific locations where franchises have already been granted.

Investors should feel uncomfortable with blind pools. Without knowing which cities are involved, investors have little basis for judging market prospects or competition. On the other hand, offerings at specific locations *can* be evaluated, and many are excellent opportunities, as expansion of cable is certain to continue.

RESEARCH AND DEVELOPMENT. R&D enterprises are among the most attractive and fast-growing new tax shelter opportunities, as technology has become a sounder and sounder issue. And many corporations now use the services of R&D enterprises for risk-shifting purposes—to create and develop new products without increasing the corporation's own debt or infringing on stockholders' equity.

RESIST LUMP-SUM PAYOFF

Don't bite if the bank offers you a big saving in return for a lump-sum payoff of the old low-interest mortgage on your home. *The catch:* the discount "bonus" comes from principal—not interest—and is taxable income. You will gain a greater return on your money if you set aside the amount sought by the bank and invest it yourself.

HAVING A LAWYER PREPARE TAX RETURN IS NO ASSURANCE OF CONFIDENTIALITY

A person might prefer to have his income tax returns prepared by an attorney, rather than an accountant, bank employee, etc., thinking the IRS therefore can't compel the lawyer to divulge anything because of the time-honored lawyer-client privilege.

If that's what you have in mind, don't bother paying the higher fees for a lawyer.

Reason: The attorney-client privilege protects confidentiality of papers or communication only when the lawyer has been consulted or engaged as a lawyer. When an attorney acts as business adviser, collection agent, invest-

ment counselor or handler of financial transactions for his client, communications between him and his client aren't privileged.

In re Edwin Shapiro, D.C., N.D., Ill, 9/19/74.

INFLATED TAX SHELTERS

In many tax shelters, the promoters acquire property which they then sell to a limited partnership or to individual investors at a price substantially above cost.

A close look at an offering of a cattle breeding program disclosed this: The promoters acquired cattle at an average cost of $663 a head and were selling them to investors at $8,000 per head (with a warranty for substitution on death or theft and for additions to the herd if the annual live calf birth rate falls below 80%). The company promoting the program estimates the warranty cost at $2,040. It states that the purchase price accurately reflects fair market value, taking into account the company's "expertise and experience in selecting and breeding" cattle and the value of the warranties. In any event, the $8,000 becomes the basis for depreciation and investment credit, two key factors in the shelter. *But the IRS might challenge the $8,000 value* as one designed to inflate depreciation deductions and the amount of investment credit, which can trigger severe penalties, even if the overstatement of value is made in "good faith."

Cattle shelters appear to be especially vulnerable to price juggling. To a lesser degree, the same thing can occur in real estate or other types of shelters. Let the investor beware.

IS IT REALLY
TAX DEDUCTIBLE?

Be wary of the words "tax deductible" when someone is trying to sell you something.

Example: A catalog describes a home safe as "Tax Deductible: When Used To Store Tax Records!"

Fact: It isn't really deductible but must be recovered in the form of depreciation over a five-year period of useful life. And you may have to allocate whatever deduction you *do* get between business and non-business use if personal valuables are also cached in the safe.

Example: Tickets to charity-sponsored evenings at the theater or sports events sold as tax deductible.

Fact: Only the *excess* of what was paid over the regular box-office charge is allowable.

Example: Raffle tickets for a drawing for an automobile, with proceeds going to a religious organization.

Fact: Not really deductible, despite what's printed on the ticket because you are actually buying something—a 1 in 200,000 (or so) chance of winning the car.

Example: Cruises offered to professionals, because another professional aboard gives technical lectures in their areas of specialization.

Fact: Internal Revenue Service characterizes such cruises as personal vacation jaunts.

Example: Business diaries and credit card memberships are touted as devices to make business travel and entertainment deductible.

Fact: Sketchy records alone usually result in disallowance of the costs of serious entertainment.

GOVERNMENT SUPPORT
FOR HOBBY

Many activities individuals engage in may be looked upon as hobbies but at the same time may have some profit potential. But unless the activity is one that, in the eyes of the Internal Revenue Service, is being conducted for profit, deductions for ordinary and necessary expenses in *excess* of income *won't be allowed.*

The Internal Revenue Code creates a presumption in favor of the taxpayer. This places the burden of rebutting the presumption on the IRS.

Factors that determine whether an activity is a business:
• Complete books of account.
• Expertise of the taxpayer and his advisers in the activity.
• Time spent on the activity by the taxpayer or his employees.
• Expectation that the assets may appreciate in value.
• Taxpayer's past success in similar activities.
• Occasional substantial profit, where investment or losses are relatively small.
• Absence of substantial income or capital from other sources.
• On the other hand, factors indicating a *nonprofit* motive are:
• Losses continuing beyond the period usually necessary to bring the activity to profitable status.
• Substantial income from other

sources.

- Substantial tax benefits.
- Significant personal pleasure.
- The fact that a taxpayer enjoys the activity won't of itself indicate a non-profit motive if there are other indications of a profit motive.

Indications of IRS treatment:

Activity	Treatment
Farm	For profit*
Breeding cattle	For profit*
Horses (breeding, show)	For profit**
Race horses	Uncertain
Dogs (breeding, show)	Uncertain
Experiments by employed chemist	May be for profit

* If profitable in 2 of 5 years.
**If profitable in 2 of 7 years.

DEDUCTIBLE JOB-HUNTING EXPENSES

A corporate executive is in the business of being an executive, so he can deduct his expenses in connection with his business, including those for seeking a new job, *e.g.*, attending interviews.

Fees to executive research firms are tax deductible. The Internal Revenue Service has long held that fees paid to employment agencies *for securing employment* are deductible. But payments to executive search organizations often are paid *before* employment is obtained and regardless of whether a new job is landed. Such fees often are well in the four figures.

- The secretary-treasurer of a manu-facturing company, being dissatisfied with his prospects, went to an executive search agency. The following year the agency found him a new job. The IRS sought to disallow the expenses paid in the year before the new position was secured. In 1970, the Tax Court held that the fee was deductible as an ordinary and necessary expense in the business of being an executive. Now the IRS has agreed to accept this decision.

- The decision that the Treasury has agreed to follow has been applied where an executive decided *not* to leave his old employer, who agreed to match the salary of the new job that had been offered.

- And it has been applied to a *self-employed* person who wished to pursue his business elsewhere.

Rev. Rul. 77-16.

SELF-IMPROVEMENT IS NOT TAX DEDUCTIBLE

Ambition to better oneself is not tax deductible. Almost any business-man will benefit from a law school education, be he pharmacist, builder, credit manager or whatnot. But expenses in pursuing a program of study leading to a law degree are not deductible as business expenses *if the expenditure qualifies the payor for a new trade or profession*, such as being a lawyer.

Even if an individual testifies that he had no intention of changing to a different trade or business, his intentions could change. At the very least, he now is *qualified* to step into a different profession.

Nondeductibility extends to the taking of a bar review or CPA cram course, as well as the fee paid for the privilege of taking an examination, where a person is not required to take such an examination as a condition for keeping his *present* job.

WHAT'S DEDUCTIBLE IN MEDICAL EXPENSES?

An individual claimed $3,505 in medical expenses, although she paid no medical insurance premiums and had had no professional medical services during the year. But she argued that for medical insurance purposes, she was a *self-insurer*, and she deducted the *value* of the treatment she gave herself. Why, she demanded to know, should she be required to seek treatment from doctors or hospitals? The Internal Revenue Service, she continued, has no right to force any individual to seek treatment from "medical" practitioners as opposed to caring for one's self.

Ruling: Praise for her self-reliance was all the court would allow her. Actually, a medical expense deduction is available *even if one doesn't want to go to medical people.* Payments to Christian Science practitioners, psychologists, practical nurses, etc., may be deductible. But the claimant must show that the payments were for the alleviation or mitigation of a physical or mental condition. And the testimony of a self-healer is, at the least, self-serving.

Bessie Doody, T.C. Memo. 1973-126, 6/12/73.

LIMITS ON ESTIMATES OF EXPENSES

Business travel and entertainment expenses are deductible if they are documented at the time of expenditure. Estimates aren't acceptable. If records are lost through circumstances beyond a taxpayer's control (such as destruction by fire, flood, or earthquake), the substantiation may be reconstructed at a later date. A taxpayer claimed this privilege, as he maintained that his receipts and other records had been lost as a consequence of frequent moves. *Tax Court ruling:* Loss of records doesn't constitute a casualty beyond the taxpayer's control.

Charles P. Schafer et al., T.C. Memo. 1976-369, 12/6/76.

'TOO BUSY' IS NO EXCUSE FOR LATE FILING, SLOPPY RETURNS

Early in the year, business-people are apt to be at their busiest, what with closing the books, annual statements, financial reports, income taxes, etc. But this seasonal bunching-up of work isn't a justifiable excuse for omitting income from a return or filing belatedly. As stated by the court in an important case, the excuse "that he was too busy to give his return adequate attention" is wholly inadequate to justify a late filing.

Robert W. Rhodes et al., T.C. Memo., 1977-33, 2/7/77.

NO BUSINESS T&E DEDUCTION WITHOUT CONTEMPORARY INDICATION OF WHY

Commercial stationers are advertising their business diaries as the essential ingredient in getting a travel and entertainment expense deduction. Some ads go so far as to say that use of their diary will assure you of deductibility. Unfortunately, it is not enough to note in a diary, or other contemporary record, the *who, what, where, when,* and *how much* of each business expenditure. When taxpayers suffer T&E disallowances, most frequently it is because they have included no timely reference to *why.* The expenditure must be related to a business need or purpose. Without this, the other notations will not help you in the least.

WHEN THE IRS HAS THE BURDEN OF PROOF

The taxpayer has the burden of proof in the vast majority of tax situations. But in the following areas, the Internal Revenue Service has the burden:
• Where the IRS alleges fraud, it must establish that there has been a deliberate attempt to evade taxes known to be due.
• When a taxpayer is confronted with his own admissions and disclosures in a criminal matter (such as tax evasion), the Service must show that he had first been advised of his right to remain silent and to be represented by counsel.
• If a party is requested to pay unpaid income taxes of another person to the extent of the value of property received from the latter without consideration, the IRS must show that the transferor had been insolvent at the time of the transfer or had been made insolvent by it.
• Where more than three but less than six years have elapsed since the filing time of a tax return, the Service must show that gross income had been understated by more than 25% in order to reopen the case.
• Where the IRS would reopen a year for which a closing agreement had been signed, the Service must show that the agreement had been obtained through fraudulent misrepresentations.
• Where an individual had failed to file a tax return and later argues lack of mental capacity, the IRS can only impose a penalty by establishing sanity beyond a reasonable doubt.
• Where a bribe or kickback has been made to a nongovernmental employee, the IRS must show that the payment was illegal under Federal or state law.
• In areas of hobby-like activities, which don't appear to be totally for profit, a taxpayer is assumed to be engaged in an activity for profit in a taxable year, if in two or more years of a period of five consecutive taxable years ending with the current one the activity had been carried on at a profit (seven years, where *horses* are involved). *Significance:* These losses and expenses are then considered legally deductible.

• Where the IRS has notified a corporation of an intended accumulated earnings tax assessment, and within 30 days the corporation submits a full statement of its reasons for not paying dividends, the burden of proof shifts to the Government. This is limited to controversies in the U.S. Tax Court.

THE BASIS FOR TAX FRAUD

• A taxpayer failed to report certain income items, and the IRS added to the tax deficiency notice a penalty for fraud. Yes, the taxpayer did omit some income, agreed the court. But he also failed to take a number of perfectly proper tax deductions to which he was entitled. That indicated he was merely careless or ignorant, not a tax dodger.

Decision: There was a reasonable doubt that he had *knowingly* violated the tax laws, which is essential for a fraud penalty.
U.S. v. Celetano, D.C., S.D.N.Y., 2/19/75.

• Failure to report the *source* of income—even if the correct amount is listed—can be considered a tax fraud, a court rules. Despite a taxpayer's arguments that the only material matter was the amount, the court decided that fraud was involved. It reasoned that without truthful representation, it becomes difficult, if not impossible, for the IRS to verify items on the return.

• The Government rarely can prove that a taxpayer willfully intended to dodge taxes. The Internal Revenue Service wins by uncovering evidence of some *badge of fraud.* One such badge, declared the court in a recent case, is a taxpayer's consistent practice of placing assets in the names of other persons.
Frank Costello et al., T.C. Memo. 1976-399, 12/29/76.

• A person charged with tax evasion is entitled to counsel. It will be supplied by the court without cost to a needy taxpayer. But he must prove that he can't afford to pay for his own defense. In a United States district court, a party seeking cost-free representation must list his assets, liabilities, etc. One alleged tax dodger refused to answer questions about his resources on the ground that it would amount to testifying against himself. "No one but I see your replies," declared the judge, "and I can't supply you with free aid unless I'm satisfied you qualify." The defendant still refused to answer any personal questions, got no free counsel—and lost his case.

RECONSTRUCTED INCOME FIGURES

The bank deposit method is a procedure used by the IRS to reconstruct a taxpayer's income where regular, credible books of account are not available. Under this method, unexplained bank deposits are regarded as taxable income. The technique is usually used with persons who don't keep (or produce) records, but others can also be affected by this device.

Court's decision: Even "where records are misplaced or lost, there is considered to be an absence of records, and the [IRS] may then reconstruct the taxpayer's records." *Advice:* Photocopy important data and store it in a safe place.

Elliott E. Thomas, T.C. Memo. 1973-105, 5/7/73.

MINIMIZING CHANCES OF A FEDERAL TAX AUDIT

To be perfectly candid, there is no way of being sure that your Federal income tax return won't be audited. Even overpaying won't protect you from IRS scrutiny. Some returns are pulled out by random selection. Others are chosen by Internal Revenue Service computers which analyze returns to score the likelihood of collecting further. Computers select a return for audit if medical expenses, contributions, property or sales taxes, etc., represent an unusually high percentage of the taxpayer's income (according to nationwide experience). Returns also invite scrutiny when figures do not agree with other information received by the IRS. (A corporation reports on Form 1099 that it paid $2,000 in dividends to a taxpayer, but that taxpayer reports only $1,000.) And returns may be audited by reason of tips provided by tax informants.

But the chance of audit can be reduced greatly by following these suggestions:

• Answer *all* questions on the tax return form.

• Complete all schedules that are required. Be sure to use the words "None" or "Not applicable" where appropriate.

• Include full documentation of items which are certain to be questioned, such as large casualty losses or large moving expenses. If the IRS asks for that unsupplied substantiation, expect it, unquestionably, to come up with additional questions in other areas of the return at the same time.

• Send tax returns and other documents to the right office at the right time so that correspondence or personal contact isn't necessary. Once begun, such correspondence or contact is often difficult to end, for one thing leads to another.

• If you are uncertain about the correct year for a deduction (vacation pay, for instance), take it in full for *both years* but attach a note to the item saying that "honest uncertainty" accounts for your taking the deduction twice. The IRS will make a ruling and tell you what to pay.

• Don't deduct a type of item which had been disallowed on a previous tax return. The IRS records or computers may be programmed to remember this and look for a repeat.

• Don't use a tax preparer of dubious character. If the Service, through its investigators, finds a preparer who is grossly incompetent *or worse*, all his clients, however innocent, will have their tax returns checked by experts in this sort of thing.

• Be certain that the return has the right signatures and identifying serial numbers. If it is a corporate return, the title of the signer should be one of the officers *authorized by law* to sign.

CHOOSE YOUR TAX AUDIT SITE CAREFULLY

You can meet an IRS agent at your attorney's or accountant's office for an audit even though your report was filed from a home address. It's wise to do so if your home surroundings are luxurious. The IRS instruction book tells the examiner to use his eyes as well as his calculator to assess your tax liability.

> "Taxpayer's standard of living is subject to observation. The agent should observe the neighborhood, furnishings, automobiles, etc. The quality of clothing worn by taxpayer and family, as well as their shopping places and methods, should be noted. Their travel, entertainment and recreation styles are good barometers. The schools attended by the children afford another good guide. The observant agent can draw a very good picture of taxpayer's income by evaluating these signs of taxpayer's standard of living."

Technique Handbook for In-Depth Audit Investigations, IR Manual MT 4235-1 (12-13-7), Section 642.4.

DISCONTINUANCE OF A TAX AUDIT CAN BE COSTLY

If a tax examiner abruptly discontinues an audit, celebration on your part may be premature. This doesn't imply that the examiner feels further digging is a waste of time or that you've been forgotten. "The Internal Revenue Manual requires that a revenue agent immediately suspend his investigation, without disclosing to the taxpayer or his representative the reason for his action, when he discovers what he believes to be an indication of fraud."

So what the absent examiner may be doing is turning over his suspicions (and workpapers) to the Intelligence Division. *What to do:* Discuss the matter with an experienced lawyer if the agent suddenly disappears.

Internal Revenue Service Audit Technique Handbook, Section 10.19.

UNFAVORABLE TAX RULING BECOMES PART OF TAX FILE

A taxpayer requests a tax ruling from the Internal Revenue Service in Washington, D.C. Then he has second thoughts, realizing that a negative ruling will certainly come to the attention of the *district* office auditing the tax return. Before the ruling can be issued, the request is withdrawn. Is the taxpayer safe? *Not at all.* The National Office of the IRS may provide its views on the matter to the office making the audit, anyway.

Regulations Section 601.201(j)

'EXPENDITURES METHOD' CAN BE USED TO LEVY TAX

Where an individual appears to be living on a far grander scale than the income on his tax return would justify, the IRS can use the "expenditures method," which focuses on a taxpayer's expenditures during a certain period as proof of income received.

That is what happened in a recent case, where an individual, while filing *no tax returns for several years*, had expenditures of more than $67,000 during that period. There was no evidence that the money he spent had come from nontaxable sources. He had received no gifts, inheritances or loans. Although no mention was made of the fact, presumably the taxpayer couldn't show that he owned any tax-exempt municipal bonds.

WHEN THE CONSTITUTION STOPS PROTECTING YOUR TAX RECORDS FROM THE IRS

If you are involved in a tax case with the Internal Revenue Service, there are times when you don't have the right, under the Fifth Amendment to the Constitution, to refuse to testify against yourself. So when a corporate executive learned that his Federal income tax return was being reviewed by the Internal Revenue Service, he requested the accounting firm that had prepared it to deliver to him all records and documents which related to his business affairs and tax returns. He then refused to let the IRS see this material on the ground that disclosing the data amounted to testifying against himself. Not so, ruled the court. The accountant's workpapers weren't the taxpayer's personal papers, even though they were in his possession,

hence they weren't protected by his Constitutional privilege. What he originally prepared and sent to his accountant ceased at that moment to be his "private papers." Getting the material back didn't again make them private.

U.S. et al. v. Case, D.C., S.D. Ill., 12/15/76.

DONATING LAND TO PROTECT AGAINST DEVELOPERS

If you want to dispose of real estate but keep it out of the hands of developers, donate it to a conservationist trust like Girard Bank's Natural Land Trust in Philadelphia or the Fund for Preservation of Wildlife and Natural Areas, administered by the Boston Co. *Advantages:* (1) The tax break. (2) Keeping the acres around your home beautiful and clutter-free. If the market value is greater than 30% of your income, you can take deductions over a period of years. If it's less, you can write off the fair value in a single year.

KEEP TAX DATA PERSONAL

When personal records or company books are turned over to the accountant to prepare income tax returns, chances are he'll develop work papers that he will return when he's completed the job. If the tax return is later audited, the Internal Revenue Service will want to see those papers and, under the law, can demand them.

But you may have turned them over to your attorney to assist him in preparing for the audit.

The U.S. Supreme Court has ruled that those papers aren't protected by the attorney-client privilege or by the privilege against self-incrimination; that an attorney must produce an accountant's papers in response to an IRS subpoena.

Indicated action: Avoid possession (or attorney's possession) of papers prepared by an accountant that might be useful to the IRS. Keep the books and records in their original form. As *your* statements, not someone else's about your operations, they will be protected by the privilege against self-incrimination and also the attorney-client privilege (if they're found in his hands). Fischer, 76 S. Ct. 1569.

IMPERSONAL DEPLETION

Depletion or depreciation doesn't extend to a businessman's *body* and *skill*, even though these represent wasting assets with a shortening productive life. One's body and skill, says the court, are not among the "natural deposits" to which the depletion deduction applies.

● An engineer wasn't permitted to depreciate the cost of his professional education, because no one knew how long he would use it in his business. Even though at his particular age he had a life expectancy of x years, it was unpredictable how long his desire, health and bank account would keep him in the practice of engineering.

● A professional baseball player might be said to have an average productive business life of y years, but Satchel Paige showed how meaningless the term "useful life" is when applied to a ball player.

● But the holder of a Pontiac agency was permitted to write off the cost of his General Motors franchise over his remaining life expectancy, for GM could cancel the franchise upon his death.

● A physician who paid a flat-sum for lifetime hospital privileges could spread his cost as a tax deduction over the predictable life of the hospital, which was shorter than his own life expectancy.

OTHER IDEAS

● Various publishers of tax services compile tables that show the average deductions taken by individual taxpayers in various income ranges for contributions, medical expenses, state and local taxes, and the like. If the deductions you took were *less than the average* claimed by taxpayers in your income bracket, is your return less likely to escape further IRS scrutiny? If you take a bigger-than-average deduction, that may raise a warning flag at the IRS. But taking less-than-average doesn't guarantee escape from audit.

● Don't abbreviate the name of the Internal Revenue Service on checks. A large number of checks for tax payments are made out to *IRS*. That makes it too easy for a check thief having minimal skill with a pen or typewriter to change *IRS* to *MRS* (and then fill in a name).

• According to a report issued by the Comptroller General of the United States, *How the Internal Revenue Service Selects Individual Income Tax Returns for Audit* (GGD-76-55), persons who overpay their Federal income tax returns are not as likely to be audited as persons who underpay.

PRODUCTIVITY

STRATEGIES

TEN CAMPAIGNS THAT FAIL

Most common frustration in increasing productivity: Short burst of improvement followed by fade-out. *Chief reason for failure:* Tunnel vision. Managers fix on a single factor, ignoring interrelations. *Solution:* In-depth productivity planning.

Ten examples of tunnel vision:

• *Productivity is limited to manufacturing.*

Illusion: Manufacturing is where results show up, so that's where the problem is. *Reality:* Manufacturing is seldom the sole cause. Look for productivity problems in poor coordination and scheduling, faulty product specifications, badly engineered processes, insensitive wage and incentive systems.

• *Across-the-board cost cut.*

Illusion: Cost-control data is adequate. *Reality:* Cost-cutting should be fine-tuned. A 10% cost cut could weaken one department or just scrape the surface of inefficiency in another. *Trap:* Managers will postpone spending during the campaign and incur costs later. Cost-saving measures that require investment up front will be ignored.

• *Direct incentives for production workers.*

Illusion: Only direct labor is productive. *Reality:* Workers on incentive "go into business for themselves,"

hoard tools, materials and knowledge, play games to increase their own income while overall productivity suffers.

• *Problem-of-the-month campaign.*

Illusion: Motivation can be manipulated with pep talks and posters. *Reality:* After a campaign, bad habits revive. This approach concentrates on symptoms rather than causes.

• *Crackdown on absenteeism and turnover.*

Illusion: The cause of these problems lies in the work force. *Reality:* Harsher discipline combined with rewards for longevity will yield only temporary results. Long-term improvement depends on correcting underlying problems—weak supervision, disorganized management, bad scheduling, frustrating working conditions.

• *First-line supervisory training.*

Illusion: If foremen take the right course, their crews will perform better. *Reality:* Few packaged courses change supervisory behavior. Foremen usually find them interesting but irrelevant to their day-to-day needs.

• *Suggestion box.*

Illusion: Good ideas arise spontaneously. *Reality:* First-line supervisors feel bypassed. A common result of bitterness about fairness of awards.

• *Operator training.*

Illusion: Skill is the only factor in operator performance. *Reality:* Operators gear performance to "signals" they get from management about what will be rewarded.

• *Competition.*

Illusion: Stimulus provided by competition between employees, shifts, or departments will benefit the company. *Reality:* Except in the case of autonomous employees—such as outside salesmen—this approach is usually counterproductive. It damages cooperation between interdependent groups. (*Example:* Day shift postpones maintenance, exhausts supplies to increase its own output at the expense of the next shift.)

- *Self-improvement.*

Illusion: Each functional department can set its own goals and meet them in its own way. *Reality:* Some departments will overreact, increase costs and create expensive conflicts with others; opportunities for coordination between departments are hindered.

RECOMMENDATIONS. Each of these illusions contains an element of truth. What makes them dangerous is that managers tend to focus too heavily on one or two—ignoring the fact that all productivity problems contain many elements. Problems must be attacked on many fronts simultaneously.

Source: The Berwick Group, Locust Park, Belmont, Mass. 02178.

EFFICIENCY BOOSTERS

No productivity program can succeed without top management involvement.

Those words have become such a cliche that most managers don't hear them any more. Yet that's the single most important insight into productivity. In spite of this, most productivity projects are relegated to some relatively powerless subordinate, who lacks the overview, the muscle, and often the desire to get a productivity-improvement program under way.

BETTER INVENTORY. Typically, a company takes a facility-wide physical inventory at least once a year. Usually, the facility is closed—a big investment in time and effort.

Better way: Break down total inventory into groups according to value. The priorities are determined by a cost-usage factor (unit cost multiplied by the frequency of usage). If a company lists its inventory in descending order according to cost-usage, it will usually find that 15%-20% of the parts account for 80% of the annual inventory cost.

It's obvious, then, that it pays to concentrate attention on those high-priority items.

Next step: The A (high-priority) items should be counted most frequently, the B items less frequently, etc.

The technique, called *cycle counting,* can completely eliminate the regular, once-a-year inventory.

Other payoffs: It'll give the production manager an opportunity to fine-tune inventory needs on his high-priority, high-cost items—which will sharply improve cash flow. Material shortages can be reduced and customer service improved as well.

FOREMEN AND PAPERWORK. In most companies, foremen are misused. And that's a big loss of productivity opportunity. No matter how smart the management, or how efficient the manufacturing process or the purchasing techniques, the biggest potential waste usually occurs right on the production floor. *The foreman holds the key to it all.*

For a foreman to be effective, he has to play two roles: (1) production scheduler and (2) overseer. The *overseer* role is complex. He must not only stay in frequent contact with each production-line person, but he must monitor each machine to anticipate bottlenecks.

Yet the average foreman lacks the time to handle all these assignments. He is usually so bogged down with paperwork (time sheets, work schedules, etc.) that he ignores the area that appears *to him* least important: His role as overseer.

Result: Production-line workers feel ignored, absenteeism increases, and so do various forms of sabotage. *Worse:* Ideas for productivity improvements, the best of which should come from the line workers themselves, never get communicated to the foreman.

Simple solution: Give foremen techniques and qualified aides to eliminate the tedious paperwork, so they can handle the primary job.

ABSENTEEISM. That's a problem faced by most companies (even during a recession). There have been many suggestions over the years, and none is really effective.

An unusual solution: Instruct the line manager to approach every first offender without a legitimate excuse with a statement like this: "Joe, we missed you yesterday. We got backed up because Ed and Sam couldn't handle the extra load, etc." Such a statement makes it clear that he was missed, that he is important to the company, and that his fellow workers were hurt. Frequently, that technique works.

If it fails, and the absences persist, the best thing for the company to do is to fire the employee rather than continue to try to rehabilitate him.

Source: R. Michael Donovan, president of the consulting firm Productivity Resources, Inc., 209 W. Central St., Natick, Mass. 01760.

EFFECTIVE TRAINING

WHAT NOT TO DO IN A TRAINING PROGRAM

Wade right in, show the employee, in detail, how to perform the job. Usual result: He's overwhelmed by detail and confused.

Instead: Find out what he already knows about the subject, the job, and the operation. Then supply an overview or fill in the gaps on function, methods of approach, the way the job fits into the company's overall operations. Don't supply detailed instructions or information until he "knows where he's at" and can absorb them. Or let *him* ask for details.

• Rely on the "watch and learn" technique.

Solution: Since people learn by doing, not just watching, provide descriptions, explanations, whys and wherefores of procedures and operations, and demonstrate. Then let the employee take over while you do the watching.

• Emphasize the negative—what not to do.

Prescription: No harm in pointing out hazards, but put your emphasis on the positive—on instilling the right approach and method.

• Leave training to your most efficient employees or supervisors.

Advice: Only if they have the patience and teaching ability essential to training. Your most efficient employees often work by reflex, have forgotten the steps and details the novice has to learn and master, lack patience and ability to communicate. Worse yet, they may have grown a little careless themselves.

SOLVING PROBLEM OF LAST HIRED, FIRST FIRED

Put an end to:

• Craft or departmental seniority that limits mobility of workers and keeps them from bidding for jobs which might still be operating elsewhere in the company.

• Written tests that have never been validated for their ability to project competence on the job.

• Requirement of high school diplomas for jobs that involve little intellectual effort.

• Rules that one must have been on his present job for, say, a year before he can move up.

• Obsolete standards which might make it possible to retain some new employees who might otherwise have to be laid off.

HOW TO BE SURE EMPLOYEES REMEMBER WHAT THEY LEARN

Here's how to prevent an employee from forgetting all he has learned from a job-related training course:

• Put him on jobs that will use the new knowledge and stretch his abilities.

• Have the employee instruct another person in the methods he has learned. Help and enthusiastic support will be necessary to do this effectively.

• Three months to a year after the training course, follow it up with another short course that concentrates on any of the weaknesses that may have developed since the first training course was taken.

AUTOMATIC INCREASES

Make sure the union contract clauses calling for automatic raises for employees who attain required skill and performance levels offer you an out in cases where poor work attitudes, persistent absenteeism, or other factors would ordinarily disqualify the individual for advancement. Lacking stipulations consistent with those ordinarily required for merit increases, you may be forced to promote unreliable, undeserving workers who have demonstrated the ability—though not the will—to perform consistently at the higher expected level.

A COSTLY MISTAKE

Personnel managers usually seek the best-qualified person to fill a job—irrespective of how low level and dull that job is. They prefer workers they can train easily. The result is an excessive raising of hiring standards for no better reason than that the supply of better-educated people has become more abundant. This has led to wholesale *under*utilization of talent.

The performance problems of barely capable workers can be solved (by more and better training). But problems with the overly capable worker yield to no known motivational method.

Source: Saul W. Gellerman, Saul Gellerman/ Consulting, Inc., 991 E. Saddle River Rd., Ho-Ho-Kus, N.J. 07423.

FIRST LINE SUPERVISORS

FORGOTTEN SUPERVISORS

Up-from-the-ranks supervisors may be the forgotten people of manufacturing concerns.

Though corporate results depend heavily on the competence and skill of foremen, *only 20%* receive *any* formal management training after promotion.

At over 60% of the companies checked, they take home less salary than their highest paid subordinates do in wages.

Incidence of incentive plans is only 16%, though over 40% of companies have programs for hourly workers.

Among other findings, it was determined that less than 25% of respondent concerns surveyed line supervisors to determine whether their sympathies are with management.

Patton Consultants (2200 E. Devon Ave., Des Plaines, Ill. 60018), the firm which compiled the data, didn't set out to diagnose rights or wrongs; their researchers simply aimed at defining the role of foremen in the industrial sector. But their findings add up to an indictment of a generally slipshod system.

SELECTING AND TRAINING FOREMEN

Best person for the foreman's job is usually *not* the diligent, punctual, efficient "company man" you're apt to pick. *Better:* The knowledgeable, sociable union-organizer type with leadership qualities and the ability to create and lead a team, if you want real dividends in productivity.

Foremen play a major role in reducing absenteeism and turnover, waste and spoilage, customer returns, accidents, strikes that happen because management ignores the need to communicate or waits until a plant gets organized before trying.

- Ability to listen, sympathize, detect underlying causes of job dissatisfaction, take a genuine interest in workers' on-the-job problems.
- Willingness and ability to go to bat for them—against you, if need be—for better equipment, ventilation, repairs, safety equipment, even minor gripes (tasteless cafeteria or vending machine food or muddy parking lots).
- Solid, technical job knowledge that helps workers reach quota, maximize incentive earnings. This means really knowing what to do when the machine needs adjusting, the forklift gears stick, or the electric ovens overheat.

Training: Deemphasize routine courses on cost analysis, work planning and scheduling, and writing effective reports. *More important:* Leadership training in motivating employees. If you can't get such a program, create your own or get together with your trade association to create one jointly with other companies in your industry.

Source: A. A. Imberman, president, Imberman & DeForest, Chicago.

TRAINING BASICS FOR FOREMEN

To be successful, even a modest-sized training program for foremen should:

- Interview the foremen and their superiors for a thorough understanding of *their* work goals and abilities.
- Use in-plant materials and situations as much as possible. "Canned" training has less impact.
- Measure progress before and after training by specific bench marks—absenteeism, turnover, unit labor cost, percent on-time deliveries, percentage of rejects, accident records.
- Tailor class and homework assignments to individual motivation.
- Get higher managers to participate in some sessions to endorse the program. If they can't be bothered, the training is wasted.

Warning: About 30% of the foremen will turn out to be untrainable, no matter what the instructor does. *Promote them sideways*, to jobs where they are responsible for *things* rather than *people*.

Bright side: About 10% will show a sufficient managerial aptitude to merit a promotion to the executive ranks, as positions open up.

Source: Imberman & DeForest.

Secrets of Japan's success in producing high technology products on production lines, says Akio Morita, chairman of Sony Corp., is the first-line supervisor. At Sony that person is a graduate engineer, trained to make changes on the line even *after* production is under way—without wasting time by notifying engineering department first.

RULES
FOR SELECTING
A GOOD FOREMAN

Best sources: Experienced workers. Former union officials and shop stewards with good records. Choose a hard worker who *also* has a good temperament.

Qualities in a foreman that will bring out the best in workers:
- Ability to argue well but not hold grudges.
- Forthrightness and honesty.
- Ability to consider past record before imposing penalties.
- Willingness to let workers work.
- Good communications skills.
- Trustfulness and tolerance.
- Compassion and empathy.
- Thoughtfulness.
- Tenacity.
- Readiness to pitch in when needed.
- Impatience with shirkers.

Steps to take to bring out the best in foremen.
- Pay at least 10% more than his highest paid workers.
- Emphasize work accomplished.
- Provide channels for handling complaints.
- Encourage feedback.
- Let him "fight" when he thinks he's right.
- Seek worker input for his performance evaluation.
- Minimize paperwork.

PROBLEM SOLVING

GETTING MONEY'S WORTH
FROM OFFICE TEMPS

Departments staffed to meet *peak* load requirement often operate at as little as 55% efficiency—since few operations *always* function at peak levels. Employees may average as little as 20 hours of actual work in a 37½-hour week. Allowing for fringe benefits and nonproductive time, $9,000-a-year clerical worker in a department staffed for peak loads may cost $14,000 to $21,000 a year. *Solution:* Reduce your staff through normal attrition. Then meet *peak* workloads with *permanent* or *temporary* part-time help.

Some precautions:
- *Recruitment.* Be wary about using temporaries from agencies that supply personnel on an as-needed basis for one, two, or three days, weeks, or months. There are benefits—and pitfalls. *Plus:* Your company will save money even at the high hourly rates temporary agencies charge for their recruiting services (and their fringe benefits costs that you'd otherwise be liable for). *Minus:* Your chances of getting someone who knows your operation—or of getting the same person twice in a row, once you've trained them, are just about zero. *Better:* Per-

manent, part-time retirees, house-wives, others who can be available at the hours and times of the month or year that you need them.

• Be specific about job requirements. If you need a typist, not a secretary, make that clear.

• Analyze peak load needs so you can realistically indicate exactly how often, and how long, you need an individual. Otherwise your temporary or perma-nent part-timer may be reassigned elsewhere, or be tied up with other commitments.

• Preplan temporary's work at all times. Be sure the supervisor or an-other employee is on hand to answer questions, explain office rules and poli-cies, provide needed supplies, check on work performed. Remember, an unin-structed outsider can mess up your fil-ing system quickly.

If you use a temporary agency regu-larly, be sure to check into:

• Testing procedures, screening me-thods used in selecting personnel.

• Workmen's compensation cover-age, health and medical benefits. If the agency doesn't protect its employees, you could be liable in the event of acci-dent or job-related illness.

• Insurance coverage—including fi-delity bonds, public liability, or proper-ty damage coverage in the event the employee damages equipment, causes a fire, etc.

• Financial responsibility, ability to meet payrolls, withholding taxes, etc.

A "work effort scale" of energy ex-pended at the job shows female em-ployees' effort is 112% that of males. Single women, *part-timers*, union members, professionals rank highest. Source: Institute for Social Research.

GETTING MONEY'S WORTH FROM RESEARCH AND DEVELOPMENT

• Have R&D personnel been selected more for technical knowledge than for creative talent?

• Is R&D too inbred? Have most of the researchers spent too much time on a limited line of products?

• Is R&D initiative being smothered by too much control from upper man-agement, the legal department, sales?

• Is there an incentive program for R&D?

• Is R&D isolated from the ultimate consumer, receiving all its information only after it has filtered through other departments?

• How swift is top management's feedback to R&D projects?

• Has top management tried to spur R&D projects by keeping the depart-ment up to date on competitors' activi-ties? *Caution:* Too much emphasis on "meeting the competition" will give you imitations rather than innovations.

MEASURE-UP ENGINEERS

Have industrial engineers direct their work measurement activities at *themselves* from time to time. *Some possible results:* (1) Improved analyti-cal methods. (2) Better performance and a better understanding of the limi-tations of their work. (3) A good example for other groups scheduled for measurement. (4) Extension of work measurement to yet other white collar groups within the organization.

BETTER THAN CAR POOLS

Less tardiness and fewer one-day absences are just two of the benefits of company-run van pools—like car pools, only using the larger-capacity vans. The company usually provides the van. It's driven by an employee who rides free in exchange for driving, and may use the van on weekends.

Other advantages: Less company parking space required, gasoline savings, less traffic. A 12-passenger van can break even with 9 passengers paying about $60 a month each for a daily 100-mile round trip.

Drawback: High liability insurance. (This problem may be solved by new plan being developed by some insurance firms.)

LUNCHTIME MORALE BOOSTER

Voluntary lunch-hour company programs sound like a low-cost way to acquaint employees with the company, its objectives, and how it functions. *But* the idea involves some hazards.

First, voluntary programs that employees attend on their own time tend to draw persons who are already highly

motivated and probably have found out what you want to tell them already.

Second, the program will give malcontents good target for criticism.

Remedy: Build attendance by mixing information about the company with films and video tapes on subjects of general interest, such as gardening, carpentry, or other hobbies. Find out what your employees want to know and give it to them, even if you have to make the video tape yourself. Cost of a 30-minute tape program starts at about $300.

ANTIABSENTEEISM LOTTERY

One way to cut absenteeism: Run a lottery aimed at the employee *and* spouse. Employees get a card bearing name and work identification number each month; those with perfect attendance turn them in at month's end for drawings and one of the prizes. Be sure prizes include items that appeal to spouses. Three months' perfect attendance nets any employee a special prize. Implementation of this plan should result in a 10% decline in absenteeism.

WHEN TO RETURN TO WORK

The final determination as to whether an employee is in condition to return to work following an injury or protracted illness should be made by management, based on the opinion of doctors of management's choosing.

That's the gist of a recent arbitrator's ruling holding that the company was within its rights in refusing to reinstate an employee even though his personal physician insisted he was able to resume his previous duties. *Reason:* Company's doctor is usually more familiar with the strains imposed by any given job. It's the company that has final responsibility for safety, as well as legal liability if the worker's ailment recurs.

USEFUL IDEAS

FOUR-DAY WEEK FOR SMALL FIRMS

Smaller companies are finding the four-day workweek an appealing working condition that brings in many outstanding recruits who otherwise would go to work for bigger companies paying higher wages. It's a real drawing card for younger workers with off-the-job interests. Few workers try to work two jobs with this schedule. Most take the three days for leisure activities.

Five-day coverage isn't a problem. Handle it with two shifts. The shifts rotate so everyone gets an opportunity to get off the three days that include the highly desired Saturday and Sunday.

Problem: Productivity. No firm should expect to get the same production per hour on a 10-hour day as it gets during an 8-hour day. Employees just pace themselves to put forth as much effort in 10 hours as they would have in 8. (Industrial engineers have long noted that overtime—and that's what's involved in 10-hour days—takes a heavy toll in both fatigue and boredom.)

Good compromise: 35-hour week with $8\frac{2}{3}$-hour days. But if you end up paying for 40 hours of work, the trade-off may not be very attractive, unless there is no other way to attract the right worker.

HOW TO IMPROVE COMMUNICATION WITH EMPLOYEES

Two methods of management-employee interaction:

• *Treat workers like stockholders.* One company prints a special annual report for employees outlining trends in benefits, pay, sales efforts, foreign operations, etc. Tied to this is a yearly jobholders' meeting (held on a divisional level, if big enough). After a short report from management, question-and-answer session permits discussion of any topic—except personalities.

• *Regularly held forum for exchange*

of ideas and problems. A monthly council meeting between management and employee reps on various organizational levels encourages two-way communication that can nip budding troubles.

Aim: Higher productivity, less turnover, fewer absences. *Drawback:* Executives must be able to devote a large amount of time to these efforts.

LESSONS FROM JAPAN

The legendary dedication of workers that have contributed so much to giant Japanese productivity gains didn't just happen. Big factor was Oriental-style management philosophy, employing elements in tune with progressive U.S. concepts.

Examples:

• Value systems that place individual human dignity first—even at the *temporary* expense of the bottom line.

• Determination to use human resources wisely and imaginatively. Continuous training for personal growth throughout a worker's career. Foremen and managers dedicated to teaching and counseling, not just supervising. Flexibility in utilizing workers, less rigid confinement to narrow niches, dead-end jobs.

• Total communications—making workers privy to sales, profits, costs, and other "secret" company information; aware of personal, company, and national stake in technological change and innovation.

• Teamwork—a consistent search for common goals and ground for cooperation among government-labor-business.

• Willingness to listen and act on advice of personnel and industrial relations experts.

Result: Workers who really feel like insiders, part of the company team.

WHEN CONFRONTATION WORKS

Productivity doubled in one year at Pullman Inc.'s Chicago plant. *Reason:* Confrontation meetings between production control, quality control, material control, and purchasing departments have replaced "poison-pen" memo-writing.

HOW TO START IT WORKING.

• Plant manager schedules special Saturday meeting of all production managers and foremen.

• Small groups (no more than eight people) are organized, with representatives of different departments in each group. Each group is told no holds barred. Lay everything on the table. Make a list of work problems by lunch-time.

• Collect the list during the lunch break. Consolidate and put list of problems on the blackboard.

• Identify common problems. (At Pullman, crane service turned out to be one major problem causing conflicts.)

• After lunch, rearrange groups *by department*. Each group picks a couple of problems listed on the board and spends the afternoon working out proposed solutions.

• At the end of the session, each group is told to return to the plant, put the solution into action, and report to management on results. (Crane service problems were solved in a couple of hours by a system of setting priorities.)

WHAT TO EXPECT.
- Much more activity back at the plant.
- Increased worker enthusiasm generated by front-line foremen.

Next step: Same kind of meeting with other departments. Right away.

Result: Managers get into the habit of picking up the phone and solving conflicts *at the outset.*

Should your company use this technique? Ask two departments that are in conflict to prepare a list of what is wrong *with the other department.* Then try a limited confrontation meeting with a few members of each department.

JOB SHARING

A shared job is an arrangement in which two people hold responsibility for one full-time job that was once held by one individual. Full-time salary and fringe benefits are divided in proportion to the time worked by each.

Job sharing began as an isolated experiment in the 1960s. It has since grown because of these advantages:
- Greater flexibility in apportioning work hours during peak periods of the day.
- Absenteeism and turnover are lowered.
- Productivity rises because fatigue factor due to long hours is reduced.
- Affirmative action requirements

are met more easily.
- Older workers who wish to retire early—but not into total idleness—can be accommodated.

Most people either don't want part-time work or can't afford the reduction in salary. For those who desire it, though, this opportunity may make business sense as well as social sense.

RAISES THAT INCREASE PRODUCTIVITY

It's possible to let workers decide when and what kind of "raise" to get without its costing the company any more. In fact, productivity may go up. One method is the "cafeteria" approach to fringes. The employees select those they want instead of being told what they'll receive. *Another idea:* Plant workers get the opportunity to improve their pay scale by learning other jobs.

How it works: Employees move from the starting pay rate to the next level when they have mastered five jobs in a plant. Each employee is on a work team and the members of that team determine when a job has been learned. The top rate is reached when all jobs have been mastered.

Results: (1) Better training; (2) flexible work force (each worker knows several, if not all, jobs); (3) increased job satisfaction; (4) lower absenteeism and turnover; (5) greater cooperation among team members in assisting one another to learn jobs.

Source: Edward Lawler, professor of psychology and program director, Institute for Social Research, University of Michigan, Ann Arbor.

BREAKING IT OFF

A simple, inoffensive—but very effective—way for the boss to break up chitchats at the water cooler: He walks up, greets everybody warmly. No hint of the irritation prompted by the time-wasting. Tells a brief anecdote, and breezily says, "Well, it's time to get back to the old grind." The message is that the break is over and he's not really angry, since it was short.

PERFORMANCE APPRAISALS TOO OFTEN INACCURATE

They also lend themselves to abuses, put subordinates in fear and make fair-minded superiors ill at ease. *Solution:* Distribute funds budgeted for raises equally among a unit regardless of individual performance. Restrict ratings to satisfactory or unsatisfactory and use them as a basis for counseling, job enrichment, transfer training or other developmental programs.

*An additional rating—*promotability*—could maintain motivation.*

If an employee failed to improve an unsatisfactory rating after repeated attempts, he would be terminated. *Results:* Supervisors would find it easier to take decisions about performance. Workers would be given an opportunity to improve in a supportive environment.

Source: Richard A. Morano, manager, management development, Xerox Corp.

PRODUCTIVITY RULES

The first rule in a management attempt to improve productivity: *Set a good example. Reason:* No one will take the manager seriously if he takes two hours for lunch and tells everyone else to take one hour.

The second rule is consider setting *negative* productivity incentives that take away from employee who performs below standards. *Reason:* The worker who already is performing at peak productivity can't do better, no matter what incentives are offered.

> Substitute relaxation periods for traditional coffee breaks to improve employee health, productivity. Teach employees simple relaxation response during two 15-minute breaks a day. Set aside a Quiet Room. Companies report greater output, lower blood pressure, fewer headaches, less sleep problems from employees who chose the quiet alternative.

EMPLOYEES' RIGHT TO PRIVACY

Employees' right to privacy and individuality becoming a big issue, notably where standards of appearance interfere with personal lifestyle or where surveillance is involved. Recent examples you should be aware of:

• *Surveillance.* Unions are jittery about TV cameras being installed for process and equipment monitoring purposes. Some groups have sought contract clauses barring their use.

In a recent case, employees filed grievances charging invasion of privacy. The arbitrator ruled the camera permissible, but for security purposes only. Warned it could *not* be used to discipline workers caught goldbricking.

• *Lifestyle.* California arbitrator ordered reinstatement of a Ford dealer employee fired for driving his new Rambler to work, holding there's no "law of the shop" requiring workers to like (or drive) the cars they work with.

• *Office rights.* (1) Vacationing executive sued because the company president opened his locked desk in pursuit of desperately needed papers. The court sustained the company, but warned that outright fishing expeditions are illegal. (2) Postal authorities ruled a company could open mail addressed to a former employee before forwarding it—on the presumption that the correspondence might involve company business and providing the person opening it is "someone in authority."

WHITE-COLLAR OVERTIME EXEMPTIONS

Job descriptions, although not required by law, are a prudent investment in time. They can protect you against heavy back wage settlements that would be incurred if federal inspectors rule against your white-collar exemptions to overtime provisions of the wage and hour regulations.

Keep the description detailed. The best are sequential—what the employee does daily, weekly and monthly. It should also answer specific questions, *e.g.*, is he in charge of a department, does he supervise, how often does he do the same kind of work as the employees he supervises, what kind of decisions does he make.

Danger area: Employees tend to stress the important side of their jobs and omit trivial duties. Have them include all. If an *inspector* finds employee's *lesser tasks take more than 20% of his time*, you may be in for trouble.

How to manage it: Assign one person to familiarize himself with the exemption requirements and give him final authority to determine whether an employee is exempt.

Hour Rules, Research Institute of America, Inc., Mount Kisco, N.Y. 10549.

HELPFUL HINTS

PRODUCTIVITY AND WORKERS. Most productivity programs fail, and they fail for basically the same reason—they're based on a naive assumption: If the company pays a premium to a worker to produce more, he *will* produce more and the company *will* profit somewhat from the higher productivity. But other, more serious problems will develop. The error is to confuse *produce* with *productivity*.

Example: Most workers know how to step up output. They tailor their work pace to generate the most dollars for themselves with the least effort. That pacing and work style may not be the most efficient for the company. That's especially so if the incentive formula is based on *units produced per hour*. With such a formula, the worker isn't inspired to work *well*, just *quickly*.

Result: Errors and material waste—with high output. Often workers will ignore cooperation with fellow workers if that slows down output. So the incentive program usually produces inefficiency, angry workers (victims of the lack of cooperation), and makes cheating "acceptable."

The "units-produced-per-hour" formula demoralizes everybody. Workers don't like to cheat or be uncooperative, but they do it because the "System" rewards them for it.

PARTICIPATORY MANAGEMENT. What's the alternative? It's basically the adoption of more *participatory management.* The employees are encouraged to get more involved in the business. That can't be done with more money alone. The problem to overcome is the suspicion among workers that they are being tricked into working harder.

There's no easy way to achieve this, he says. It usually involves calling in an expert for guidance. Essentially it means paying attention to the human dimension. That's not in terms of what the psychologists call motivation (which is a very mechanical thing). It has more to do with management caring what the workers think, and management's wanting to know about new ideas. Without mutual trust, incentive plans can't work (long-term).

An effective incentive plan is really a cost-saving and -sharing plan. The worker and the company share the fruits of higher efficiency. The plan can't come down from on high. It has to be developed by labor and management working together.

Side benefit: To devise a saving plan, workers have to learn about costs and how the business operates. They then become more valuable as workers.

Always ask these questions about any incentive plan:
- What kind of worker traits are being strengthened: Speed, competition, cheating, waste? Or is it really cost savings?
- Can one worker "profit" by fouling up another worker or another department?

- POWER OF DELEGATION. *Example:* A manager called in his staff and said:

"I plan to offer a formal class after hours here at the plant. The subject: How to do *my* job. Anyone interested in learning that is welcome to attend."

The manager invested much time in the classes—preparing course material, reading lists, etc.

Result: Most of the staff took the course, and after a few months many of them had actually picked up portions of his job. Within a short time, he found that he was "managing" and not running around doing errands, as he had before.

By giving away "power," that executive had actually gained an enormous amount of power: His staff trusted him (and he trusted them), so he could give them more responsible work to do—freeing him to undertake new, more difficult projects. The staff wasn't trying to hold them back, so they worked harder at everything they did. Motivation became automatic. The concept can work practically anywhere in a company.

Side benefit: Courses give more staff overview of company.

Source: Michael Maccoby, author of the best-seller, *The Gamesman.*

PRODUCTS
& PROMOTION

PRODUCT DEVELOPMENT

HOW TO TREAT OLD PRODUCTS LIKE NEW

Several years ago, when Bristol-Myers introduced a slew of new products, it ignored names it already owned and spent millions introducing products called *Resolve* and *Vote*. Vote was a toothpaste, and about the time it was introduced, Bristol-Myers actually sold, for a nominal sum, the name *Ipana*, which they owned.

Today, few of us remember Vote and Resolve, while most of us still recall tried-and-true Bristol-Myers products, such as *Four-Way, Bromo Quinine, Minit-Rub*, and Ipana. Little wonder. These old names have been buttressed by hundreds of millions of advertising impressions.

Successful examples:

• *Vaseline*, with the credentials of a century of use, introduced a new line of skin products under the name *Vaseline Intensive Care*.

• *Arm and Hammer*, which has introduced a successful laundry detergent and oven cleaner, in addition to increasing baking soda sales many times over.

Smart marketers know that one answer to consumer skepticism is a name you can trust and a product or service that lives up to it.

How can you tell if the name of a product, service, or company packs credibility with consumers?

Try attaching the name to a broad range of products or services. Rough out ads for any product or service even remotely connected with the business, and use the name in the ads. Be sure to range far and wide from the company's present business so you can test "how high is up." Have competent market research people show the ads to consumers. Find out what they remember. More can be learned about the strengths and weaknesses of the name in one day of actual exposure than in a full year of speculative thought.

Some years ago, Scott Paper did exactly such a test when it was considering whether to drop the *Cut-Rite* brand name altogether. The result astonished them, for it indicated that for disposable items, Cut-Rite was a better name than Scott. In fact, one of the people interviewed suggested that Cut-Rite could make an excellent disposable diaper: semiwaterproof and economical.

Scott decided to keep their wax paper as is, but introduced Scott plastic wrap (instead of Cut-Rite) and Scott disposable diapers. Both failed. While Scott is a quality name, research indicated that it was the wrong name for some disposable items. Just because a name's been around a long time doesn't mean it is automatically a winner on *any* new product.

Chesebrough-Ponds, the owners of the *Vaseline* name, knew that Vaseline was a trusted name and would provide valuable credentials for skin care.

But they coupled it with the *Intensive Care* name to show that their *new* product combined the best of the old and the new.

Many options are open to marketers if they will "pretend" that their old product is *just coming on the market.* (With old products, everything is taken for granted. A million dos and don'ts have arisen. Perhaps it's time to ignore them.)

What's the right price? Is the size unit the one most customers want? Does the product have a competitive edge? Can we give it one? Should we package it like this? Should we advertise it as we have been doing? Can we combine that advertising with something new, something people don't know about the product?

Before ignoring an old product or company name, find out what it means to customers now. It could be made to mean more tomorrow.

Source: Gerald Schoenfeld, Gerald Schoenfeld, Inc., 341 Madison Ave., New York 10017.

NEW PRODUCT BASICS

• If you're going to have competitors, make sure you're stronger than they are.

• Only work on ideas that will *significantly* boost profits.

• If you must pioneer, consider making a licensing arrangement with a major (potential) competitor so you can survive imitations from other big firms seeking to enter the marketplace.

• Be sure your *basic* product remains competitive while you're working on the new one.

LIES ABOUT LIFE CYCLES

The oldest Procter & Gamble brand is Ivory—and it's still going strong. P&G doesn't believe in "life cycles" for brands. Five brands account for the lion's share of P&G's huge volume—Tide, Ivory, Crest, Crisco, and Pampers. Pampers is the youngest (it was born in the late '50s). Tide has gone through about 40 formula changes in its long history—and the veteran product was reformulated again early in 1977.

CHECK BEFORE WEEDING OUT PRODUCT LINE

"Unprofitable" items are often necessary to round out your product line. Small steps that could make them winners:

• Review cost analysis for overallocation of warehouse, sales, and other costs to apparent losers.

• Find out why they're on the loser list. Big pilferage losses? Too many returns? Maybe a simple change will help, like offering fewer sizes, colors, or shapes. Or consider making the item part of a combination deal that will yield a better return on the total package.

• Raise your markup, or establish minimum order or service charge. (If you're suffering losses, odds are your competition is too, so it's likely they'll follow suit.)

• If all else fails and you're still losing money, stop promoting the item: No ads, no sales effort. Then let the customers who really need it twist your arm to get it. And you can tie shipment in with orders of more profitable products.

OPPORTUNITIES IN NARROWER LINES

To cut costs, many manufacturers—from clothing to hardware—are narrowing product lines.

To the clothing buyer, that may mean fewer odd sizes. To the hardware buyer, it may mean less choice, especially on bottom-of-the-line items. The logic is obvious: Produce for the biggest share of the market, because it's much more profitable.

With many manufacturers narrowing product lines, suddenly there are new opportunities for small firms to fill the gaps. Resurgence possibilities for specialty products, custom-made goods, and semicustom-made goods. Opens new doors for old products, too.

LIABILITY PROTECTION

To avoid product liability suits, take steps long before the product is sold. Company policy should ensure that products are designed, manufactured, assembled, and installed properly.

Designers must know the requirements the product has to meet. Prepare specifications from legal, manufacturing, purchasing, and marketing departments.

Marketing must identify ultimate consumer's needs, reasonable expectations, and possible misuses of the product.

Law department must identify legislation and regulations which might affect product design, as well as pending and enacted legislation.

HOW ONE HEAD OF A BUYING COMMITTEE EVALUATES A NEW PRODUCT

• What additional costs will we incur if we add this new item or line?
• What about quality standards? Will the customer get a good value?
• Will we get an exclusive? Do we want an exclusive? If so, what kind? For how long?
• Can we be assured of adequate inventory? How about reorders?
• What are the terms? Discounts? Mark-up? Other details?
• What special deal, if any, is involved?
• Is it strongly presold? If not, what will the supplier do to presell it?
• What are the details of the advertising program?
• What kind of retail promotional program will be carried out?
• Is cooperative advertising offered? Any other allowance?
• Does it fill a genuine need? Is it truly superior in a demonstrable way?
• Does the suggested retail price of-

fer better value?
- How good is the package?
- Will fixtures be provided?
- Are the requirements on the initial order economically sound from our viewpoint?
- In how many of our stores should we put it initially? Does the supplier have a specific testing program? Are we in a position to work intelligently with that testing program? If the test fails, to what extent will we be involved?
- Will "sticky" inventory be returnable?
- What are the new profit potentials?
- Can we be sure of the integrity of the supplier? What have been our past experiences with this company?
- Will the new item simply switch volume from a present inventory or will it, in whole or in part, represent additional volume?
- Does it fit in with our trading-up program?
- Are the new virtues of the item easily recognized by the shopper—or does it require demonstration?
- What is our inventory of similar or competitive items?
- Are we getting in on this too early? Too late? Should we wait for "calls" for the new item?
- Will we have to throw out any part of present inventory to make room for the new item?
- Are there any case histories on what the new item or line has done in a few other outlets?
- What economies are offered in handling, transport, warehousing, etc.?
- Could the new item take us out of a bad price-cutting situation?
- What rate of inventory turnover can we expect per store?

TRENDS WORTH WATCHING

- A whole new category of appliances, major appliances and small, will now be marketed to solve the problem of deteriorating drinking water. Sunbeam's purchase of the Illinois Water Treatment Co. suggests the trend.
- Private- and store-label products are gaining now against nationally advertised brands as consumers grow more price-conscious. Private labels, for example, now hold 50% of the facial tissue market, could get 75% within the next few years.

Other areas where private labels are thriving: canned and frozen foods, grooming aids and detergents.

Counterattack: National brand marketers are increasing their budgets for coupons and cooperative promotions, particularly in newspapers, where the cost per thousand exposures is far less than for direct mail.
- Cable TV had reached *30%* of the homes by 1981. Good for medium-budget advertisers, because cable TV will carry low rates for the next several years. *Important:* Cable TV will include *two-way* communication. That makes it attractive to direct marketers.
- *Source for almost any product sample:* FIND/SVP, 500 Fifth Ave., New York 10036. Cost will vary, according to the type of product or service requested.
- *The catered meal delivered to the home,* ranging from a single item to a multicourse dinner, is being given a shot in the arm by the young "singles" and working wives. More catered meals will be delivered to the home

and served—that's dinner, lunch, brunch, breakfast, and late supper and snacks.

The caterers will supply linens, silverware, table decor—and some may even provide entertainment. A few luxury high-rise apartment houses are already making moves in this direction.

• *Some surprises in appliance sales:* Notably the number of male-only buyers, suggests some reorientation of advertising appeals. Examples:

Dishwashers: 49% of all retail purchases are made by husbands and wives together—but twice as many portable as built-ins are bought by *husbands* shopping on their own. Another unexpected fact: 28% of all owners have *no* children.

Food waste disposer: 45% of those purchased at retail are bought by the *husband.*

Trash compactors: Half the buyers are men.

Home freezers: Although promoted as an aid to the big family, there's only one child in more than half of all freezer-owning homes. Wives do the buying on their own in 25% of cases, husbands in another 25%; couples shop together for balance.

Room air-conditioners: 71% of purchases are made by men. Also, second-time buyers almost always choose a larger unit.

• *How a company took an old-fashioned product, hung a new name on it, and revitalized it for today's buyers:*

The traditional cedar chest (often called the "hope" chest) was falling out of favor with young brides. So the Lane Company called its products *love chests.* Lane positioned itself as the company that makes *furniture for lovers.*

An object lesson in the genteel art of keeping long-established lines abreast of new life styles.

• *Major source for new-product or diversification ideas:* Customer inquiries. These should be carefully monitored to generate new ideas and identify target markets.

• More retailers will promote home goods rentals—including *completely furnished* rental homes and apartments. Especially second homes.

TEN WAYS TO AVOID A NEW PRODUCT FAILURE

• Don't place blind faith in consumer research. Make sure there's a discount built into your figures to compensate for the large number of consumers who may say, just to be nice and not offend, that they like the product.

• Be prudent in projections of the market results. Test market promotions will be hard to duplicate on a broad basis. If test market promotion can't be duplicated nationally, scale down expectations.

• Even if the product is very good, the market may not be ready for it.

• Make sure the package functions. It should preserve the product in a way that's convenient to the consumer, *and* it should also function as a selling tool.

• Make sure the package and carton are easy to stack without being damaged.

• Be assured of several sources of raw materials and packaging, so that one supplier can't knock the whole marketing plan off schedule.

• Look for help in other divisions of the company. Some key problems may already have been solved by someone else. Even where inter-office secrecy prevails, a little quiet sleuthing can bring rewards.

• Be open with the advertising agency. Give them every detail, and ask questions. If something seems amiss, speak up early.

• Keep in mind that the sales force probably *can't* handle the introduction when scheduled. The task will pull salesmen away from other work, throw off sales call cycles, and can cause other sales to slip. Plan the introduction carefully and well ahead of time. Consider employing a consultant to set up a specialized, temporary sales force. It will work under the company's direction, *without* the costs of fringe benefits, office space, compensation bookkeeping, and the like.

• Don't ease up and celebrate when a major chain buys the product. *The hardest part is ahead:* Generating sufficient consumer interest to pull through the checkout counter.

CURRENT APPEAL OF SOMETHING FOR NOTHING

• Billions of "cents-off" coupons now flooding the market. (A.C. Nielsen Co. reported that in 1977 about $300-million was returned to customers who redeemed coupons.)

Signs of the "something for nothing" trend in marketing:

• Accelerating use of sales premiums.

• Wider use of sweepstakes promotions.

HOW TO ENCOURAGE AND SCREEN NEW PRODUCT IDEAS

Goals: Keep up the flow of new product ideas. Give ideas the best chance to flourish. Screen out the bad ones.

How to do it:

• *Keeping up the flow.* Most new product ideas come from a zealous advocate, an individual who has an idea and promotes it himself. Encourage these individuals by eliminating fear of embarrassment or failure. Employees should be encouraged to feel that ideas are welcome. *Caution:* Make sure that expectations about rewards are realistic. Recognition, not necessarily money, can be the reward for a successful idea.

• *Giving an idea the best chance.* Let the idea-advocate pursue the idea *himself* by consulting and working with others before it is turned over to a special development group.

• *Separating out the good from the bad.* Isolate the *screening function* from *idea generation.* Realize that they require contradictory approaches— tight control vs. open encouragement. Be sure that the screening aims at turning up the *real* risks and uncertainties.

Continuously challenge programs that are already under development. At each step, ask if it's still a good idea. *Stop the project,* firmly and dictatorially, if necessary, when it becomes clear it's not going to make it. Make clear *who* makes this decision. (It's necessary to convince the advocate.)

Put the tightest screening controls where the big money is spent: Development and commercialization phases. Too much *initial* screening can stop the flow of new ideas.

Common traps:

• Turning to new ideas/products for the wrong reasons. (*Example:* to fill idle capacity.)

• Building on a company weakness instead of on a strength.

• Using new product development to solve corporate problems. (Strong firms have more success in launching new ideas than weak ones.)

Tip to top management: Don't get so involved in trying to generate ideas that you forget about the rest of the process. The value of *ideas* in product development is overrated. The actual steps to commercialization are probably more important, and deserve more top management attention.

Source: Paul I. Brown, president, Foster D. Snell, Inc. (Subsidiary of Booz, Allen & Hamilton, Inc., New York.)

PROMOTION STRATEGY

HOW TO RUN A COUPON PROMOTION

With the cost of TV and radio time escalating, many marketing managers are dusting off cooperative merchandising plans, particularly coupon promotions.

A cooperative plan has the advantages of encouraging retailers to stock up on the product and of requiring the retailer to pay some part of the cost of the promotion. Studies indicate that retailers often participate but then don't bother to claim the reimbursement to which they are entitled.

A coupon promotion has the additional advantage that only a fraction of the coupons issued are ever redeemed.

Marketers using coupons enclosed in consumer packages ought to review their procedures against the Federal Trade Commission enforcement policies:

• Coupons enclosed in consumer products must contain no expiration date.

• If an expiration date is deemed necessary, it must allow purchasers of the product at least six months for redemption.

• Manufacturers who choose to state on labels or in advertising that a coupon is enclosed in the consumer product, must clearly disclose on the label (or in the ad) all the material terms, conditions, and limitations of the coupon. *Some examples:* Coupon is valuable only in obtaining a reduction on the next purchase of the same item, or on the purchase of a different size of that same product, or on the purchase of a different product altogether. The FTC has indicated that it is no defense to a breach of these guides that competitors are engaged in similar activities.

CHEATING. Coupon promotions do, however, run the risk of misredemptions—coupons supposedly redeemed by retailers for which no consumer purchases were in fact made. Some estimates run as high as 30%. A few cities have such bad misredemption histories that some manufacturers simply won't run coupon promotions there.

Various ways to meet this threat:

• Spot check retail outlets to make sure that orders and inventories of the product are consistent with the number of coupons being turned in.

• One big company has recently distributed stickers to be put on registers reminding the cashier to compare coupons with product purchases.

• Giving each coupon its own number could eliminate the practice of simply duplicating coupons, but the procedure is too expensive unless the coupons are very valuable.

• When the coupon is run in a paper or magazine (rather than enclosed in the product package), the media will be willing to use *their* sales force to check newsstands to make sure that the coupons haven't been torn out of the papers or magazines on sale. They can also police the return or destruction of stale copies.

DON'T PLAY FOLLOW THE LEADER

Rule: Don't copy your competitor's sales promotions. Those who have done so get the expected bad results. Recently, three competing drug firms offered a cash refund to cold sufferers who used their product. *Result:* Poor response to all three.

What to do: Check retailers constantly to uncover the promotions they are being offered. One marketing executive has arranged to have some retailers save all the promotional announcements they get from their suppliers to keep him abreast of competition.

STIMULATING SALES WITH SAMPLES

Sampling is a sophisticated way to boost sales, learn more about product reaction. But if done badly, it's a huge waste of money. Significant points to remember:

• Sampling is only good for new or little-known products; or if the product has just undergone a major change in design, formula.

• Don't rush the product into the sample stage until some preliminary advertising has been performed, or the public will be completely ignorant of it. Advertising enhances its value.

• Include a cents-off coupon with sample to promote subsequent purchase of product.

• Be sure retail outlets have sufficient stocks at time sample offer is made, or customers won't be able to follow up after sample.

• Quantity of sample should be sufficient to provide *adequate* trial.

• To enhance visual impression, try to make sample package a miniature of full-size product. Mark product "Sample," or retailer may try to sell it.

• Total promotion campaign should be ready to roll after sampling test suc-

cess.
- Tying in your ad campaign with in-store promotion is valuable.
- Test the various sample techniques: free, paid (at cost), mail, in-store, house-to-house, tie-in with other products, etc. It's worth the investment.

RENT A CELEBRITY AT BARGAIN PRICE

If you've always thought big names commanded six-figure fees for appearing in advertising, you're in for a surprise. You stand a good chance of getting a famous personality for *four* figures. Providing:
- Your project doesn't cut him out of an important national advertising category.
- It isn't on network TV.
- He needn't work more than a half-day.

For $1,000-$2,000 you could buy a star for your trade magazine ad that could turn *your product* into a star. The smaller your name is, the more good a famous personality's recognition can do for you. But you will never know unless you ask.

Getting in touch with big names: The two biggest theatrical agencies in the country are William Morris Agency, 1350 6th Ave., New York 10020 (7 offices in the U.S. and overseas) and International Creative Management, 6th Ave., New York 10020 (6 offices in the U.S. and overseas). Or subscribe to *Celebrity Service*, 171 W. 57 St., New York 10019, if you're interested on a continuing basis.

Promotion dollars spent first year a product is introduced usually will be much more than is spent in later years. Use money to launch a *line*, not a single product.

TESTING PREMIUMS

One way to test premiums before making a marketing decision: Submit all premiums to a cross section of your company's employees. Using controlled conditions, have the employees vote on the ones most attractive to them. Test a group roughly similar to your company's target market.

BOOSTING RETURNS FROM TRADE SHOW INVESTMENTS

- Research a show. Seek facts from the show's management. Attend the show to assess the kind of audience before renting space. Contact some show registrants and ask them for their frank opinions.
- Space costs are usually the smallest portion of the total cost for trade show exhibits. Rent enough to avoid an overcrowded booth.
- Before designing the booth, *define* your exhibit objectives in detail. Many firms fall down in this area, leaving the booth designer with no direction. Objectives are essential if you want to measure a show's success.
- Keep exhibit contents simple. You

needn't show every product your firm makes. Select the most important ones that meet your objective. New products are great, but also think of *new* uses for old products, and remember an "old" product to you may be "new" to many visitors.

• Allow at least 90 days to design and build the exhibit. Once you accept the design, avoid changes. They're expensive and *usually* add little to the overall end results.

• Staffing: Use only your best people (sales trainees should *only* observe). If specialized engineers or technicians are required, get them there. They might make the difference on a sale.

• Promote your exhibit before the show with trade ads, releases and mailings. Remember not to tell your whole story—leave enough untold to entice visitors to see you at the show.

• Carefully record comments from visitors. Make sure requests for literatue, samples, or simply more facts are *promptly* followed up after the show. Don't forget to send a letter to all your show visitors to thank them for their visit to your booth.

Source: Raymond R. Ramelay, manager, advertising and sales promotion, American Can Company.

STAFFING TRADE SHOWS

Use nonsales personnel on the team that staffs your company's trade show exhibit. *Company secretaries* can handle brochure order processing and appointment scheduling more efficiently than a temporary worker who's not familiar with the firm and its people. *Corporate executives* are a good lure for their decision-making peers at other companies. *Technical experts* can field difficult questions.

TRADE SHOW SPACE CONSIDERATIONS

• *Storage:* Some back-to-back booths have storage space created by columns; others don't. If you need storage, make sure it's nearby, if not in the booth itself.

• Booths near a freight entrance may have to be set up late and dismantled early.

• *Water and gas:* If you need these utilities, make sure they're available. If they are available and you *don't* need them, make sure your space won't be reassigned at the last minute to a company that does.

• *Obstructions:* Check plans for columns, changes in ceiling height (usually indicated by dotted lines), changes in floor level shown by ramps or stairs, utility control boxes that must not be covered by an exhibit.

• *Layout:* On most diagrams, heavy lines indicate back walls of exhibits, light lines are space limits.

• *Traffic pattern* is important in picking a trade show booth location.

When people have a choice, they tend to *turn right* as they enter an exhibit hall.

Pick a spot that maximizes the booth's visibility to a visitor walking in this counterclockwise pattern.

• *Best corner:* One that permits the

visitor to see your booth *before he turns.*

• *Setting up a trade show booth:* Do not crowd it with equipment. Space is needed for demonstrations, ashtrays, wastebaskets, and for your salesmen to mingle with prospects. Prospects are reluctant to stop if they feel they will be crowded.

LIMITS TO DEALING

When deals account for up to 70% of a manufacturer's annual volume (and this is no longer extraordinary), how much more potential for *deal* growth exists?

The *consumer deal*, in particular, has reached the point of stalemate. Nielsen Research has been pointing out for years that most consumer deals fail to provide a lasting sales increase. Now economics of this merchandising procedure are more disturbing than ever. With few exceptions:

• Competitive consumer deals tend to balance each other out. At times, in major outlets, as many as five or six competitive deals are currently displayed.

• Consumer deals are so numerous in some stores that the shopper is confused. It isn't unusual to find a brand simultaneously displayed both at regular and at deal price. Occasionally, two different deals for the same brand are displaying simultaneously in the same outlet.

• Consumer deals no longer serve as effective sampling techniques (one of the original objectives) for at least two reasons:

1. Shoppers are so thoroughly conditioned to expect price concessions that brand loyalty is too weak to overcome the thrift appeal of competing deals.

2. There's so little difference between many competing brands that the shopper has little reason to resist picking the "best bargain." Not only is competing merchandise much the same, consumer deals also tend to be very much alike.

• Consumer deals tend to increase brand disloyalty.

• Consumer deals work at cross-purposes to the great objective of modern advertising—the creation of a brand "image." In the very merchandise classifications where brand image is most talked about, there exist the most consumer deals.

WHAT TO BE WARY OF IN BASIC PROMOTION TECHNIQUES

Knowing the basic strengths and weaknesses of the dozen basic promotion techniques is essential if your company is going to pick the right one—or the right combination. Here they are:

• *Samples.* To reach new customers. To introduce a new or improved product. To break into a new market. Costly and imprecise.

• *Coupons.* For almost any type of promotion. Usage increasing. Works better with older, better educated, married urban consumers than with young, single, or less educated consumers. Results, costs, hard to predict.

• *Trade coupons* (coupons the stores run in their ads). To boost distribution, get better floor displays. Lots of false redemptions make it difficult to predict costs. Some big companies simply have a coupon allowance and tell store what they will pay before coupon runs.

• *Trade allowances.* For new products. To boost distribution. Frequently abused. Savings frequently don't get to consumers.

• *Deals.* To boost sales, force savings through to consumers. Will not generate new loyal customers.

• *Reusable containers, premiums in boxes.* Attached premiums help product image, give customer good value. A bad one can actually *cut* sales.

• *Free, mailed premiums.* Not measurable. Won't get new customers if more than one label or proof-of-purchase is required.

• *Self-liquidating premiums* (ones that pay for themselves). Can boost brand image and increase ad readership. Won't get new customers.

• *Contests and sweepstakes.* Good for increasing ad readership, boosting brand image, getting on-floor displays, getting some new users. Costly. Won't produce many new users.

• *Refund offers.* Generate interest, boost brand loyalty. Won't produce new customers. Slow and not easily measured.

• *Bonus packs.* Generate interest on the shelf. Get people who've tried the product to become repeat buyers. Won't get totally new customers. Won't help the image of the product.

• *Stamp plans or continuity premiums.* Get regular repeat customers and create a difference between essentially identical products. Limited appeal, but they won't get the retailer to do anything to increase sales.

Source: William A. Robinson in *Advertising Age.*

TURN CASE HISTORIES INTO SELLING TOOLS

Illuminating case histories are too rarely used by marketing men as a selling tool. Ways to get something out of them:

• Trade magazine articles.
• Reprints for a salesperson to use.
• Promotion brochures for use in direct-mail programs.
• Use in sales training programs.
• Place in employee publications and in customer publications.
• Make them into films or slides for various presentations or into exhibits for trade shows.
• Try to use in local newspapers for publicity.

SECRET OF PREMIUM SUCCESS: SEE THE RIGHT SPECIALIST

Good premium programs often succeed when tools like couponing and trade allowances fail. A good premium sets your product apart on the shelf with its eye-catching offer. It gives your salesmen an excuse to go to the dealer with a new program—and push for a new commitment.

A bad premium is a bottomless pit.

Here's what Bernie Rosten and Danny Leonard (Allied Premium Company, 175 Fifth Ave., New York 10010) have learned after creating premium programs for such sophisticated users as Nabisco, Lever Brothers, Scott Paper, and Red Rose Tea.

• Work with a premium specialist. Most companies call a manufacturer and end up working with an ordinary sales representative whose experience is in selling to wholesalers or *retailers*, not *premium* users.

• Different standards apply to premiums than to retail items, since your customers don't get to actually see the premium before they order it. That's why it's especially important for your representative to know the track record of an item *as a premium*. (Most good premiums have been used before; they're good, and that is why they are used again.)

What's more, an ordinary representative isn't prepared to learn your business and tailor your premium program to your needs. To locate a good premium specialist, talk to anyone who buys premiums for a major company, or call the Premium Merchandising Club (1605 Vauxhall Rd., Union, N.J. 07083). Ask for an independent premium representative who works only in premium promotion; that experience is vital.

• Talk to a few premium specialists. Ask them what companies they've worked for and what they have done in the last few months.

• Ask if they deal directly with factories or if they're jobbers (*i.e.*, middle men who will cost you more).

• They should represent at least 10 lines covering different categories and different price levels. (With two or three lines, it's too easy to end up with a premium that isn't exactly appropriate for the need.)

• *Tell them your objectives:* Introduce a new product, increase sales of an old product, provide incentives for salesmen, distributors, etc.

• *Danger signals:* If they don't probe into the "nuts and bolts" of your business or if they make recommendations before they hear your story, they'll probably come up with some pet project (that means extra profit for them, but not necessarily for you). When they do come back with recommendations, beware of items right off the drawing board with no track record. Better to let somebody else pay for testing a new product.

• A good premium specialist will do more than show recommended premiums. He'll show you exactly what the premium will look like in an ad and on a package. He'll recommend couponing, in-store display, on-package offers, or some other promotional technique. He'll give you complete background: Who has used this kind of premium? With what kind of success?

• *Important:* A good premium man will give *projected prices* along with current prices. What will the premium cost be six months from now? All too often, premiums are sold to users at one price, then as the program develops, costs rise dramatically, leaving you locked into that higher-priced item.

The right premium isn't only priced right for its market, but is shipped well and inexpensively (in line with whatever the value of the item may be.)

Objective: A premium program providing a change of pace from couponing and other basic tools. One that gives your salespeople something to talk to the trade about. (The free premium sample you give the dealer returns many times its cost to your company.)

GIFT-GIVING TOO OFTEN FORGOTTEN

It's certainly a rarity among marketers of big-ticket items. Making the purchase of such items as autos and refrigerators into a gift-giving occasion is a fresh idea. Rolls-Royce, for example, offers gift-givers a handsome, hand-lettered calligraphy document to accompany the gift.

Even a simple gift wrap elevates the purchase into something much more exciting—even for mundane products.

GOOD INFORMATION

Press kits, the nifty information packets your public relations people hand out to the media, may be one of the most underutilized marketing tools you have.

More value: Provide your salesmen and distributors with kits, too. Encourage their disbursement along with business cards. *Pointers:* Make sure the words "Press Kit" appear on the cover so the recipient knows what to do with the information. Good idea to include a covering letter, too. Make sure you date the information and keep it updated at least every six months. Im-

portant that the kit contains *genuine* news material and intelligent background info. Most importantly, it should have *users'* interests in mind.
Source: Richard Conarroe, president, Walden Public Relations.

THE PRIVATE SALE

A first-rate private sale is one of the best promotional investments you can make to bring old customers back, gain new ones, reinforce customer loyalty and develop your reputation as a leader. Key elements that bring people in:

• The flattery of being remembered and invited or specially selected as a potential customer.

• Convenience and exclusivity of special sale hours (usually a series of half-day events, or convenient evening or Sunday hours).

• The chance to grab bargains or pick up hot new items without fighting the crowds. (Note *deep* price cuts aren't necessary major motivators. *Example:* Successful appliance industry private sales often shave only 3%-5% off list except for samples or damaged merchandise.)

Preselect your targets (old customers, marginal ones, prospective new ones from special interest or income groups). Invest in a *good* mailing list aimed at prime prospects. And make it a *big* list. (1½% to 2% attendance constitutes an excellent response to an invitational mailing.)

Go all-out for invitations that emphasize the theme, value, exclusivity and short duration of the event. Invest in first-class mailing; time arrival for four or five days before the sale begins. You'll probably save money by farming the job out to a mailing house.

Make your sale an *event*: Aim to build prestige, regardless of purpose (unloading merchandise, promoting new lines).

Needed: Special sales tags for sales items. A hostess to collect invitations, offer refreshments. Cash register clerks so salespeople give customers undivided attention. A comfortable waiting area if you draw an overflow crowd.

Display, model or demonstrate *new* lines even if your drawing card is sale merchandise. Consider having a name personality on hand as greeter or consultant, if your image or prospect list merits or demands it.

The payoff's augmented by immediate returns: 75% to 80% of persons attending buy—and most of them purchase bigger-ticket items.

SWEEPSTAKES

Basically, sweepstakes promotions are lotteries. To play, the consumer either returns a proof of purchase or facsimile or a card or envelope indicating whether or not he wishes to make a purchase.

Critical element is the prize. It's got to be big enough—about $50,000 for adults, $15,000 for adolescents—to make a significant difference in the winner's life.

Specific prizes—houses, super vacations, and such—generally draw larger responses than straight cash, although usually when the winner collects he'll ask for the cash equivalent rather than the actual prize. The prize also determines the demographic appeal of the promotion—houses for adults with children, for example, vacations for a somewhat younger group.

The mailing piece itself should be designed so the respondent doesn't have to pick up a pencil—if he does, responses will drop about 20%. Use action devices—peel-off symbols to be transferred or "yes" and "no" envelopes to be chosen with tabs that can be torn off and placed in the envelopes.

OTHER IDEAS

● More than 75% of all public relations statements—including new product releases—sent to trade publications are discarded. *Reason:* They make no mention that the product or idea is really new or why and how it's useful.

● Federal Trade Commission ruling that an offered premium must be delivered in 30 days means the premium promoter must place larger orders and place them farther in advance. *Just as important:* Give premiums (and the details of the premium offer) more sophisticated testing.

● *How much do promotional T-shirts cost?* You can get 10 dozen white cotton medium-weight shirts with a single impression for $2.37 each. Buy a thousand dozen and the unit cost drops to $1.45. For additional colors, add two cents per shirt per color. The price doesn't include the cost of preparing art and film for reproduction.

PURCHASING

TACTICS

SMART BUYING TACTICS

Most managers don't realize it, but the true cost of inventory is between 24% and 36% a year *over and above* the cost of the stockpiled material. *Sources of expense:* Cost of borrowing money, lost opportunity with that money, warehousing, spoilage, insurance, theft, damage, need for warehousing manpower, obsolescense, etc.

So, with all those cost factors on top of the actual cost of merchandise, the reasons for building inventories must be well justified.

HOW TO AVOID STOCKPILING. It is almost always more economical than buying on an as-needed basis. But there are traps, the worst of which is growing too dependent on one supplier. So, though there is loss of price leverage, it's safer to use more than one source.

Also important: Although it is time-consuming, check out each long-term contract supplier not only *before* but also *periodically* thereafter. Regularly demand from the supplier a report on how he'll be able to supply your company in the months ahead—especially if the quantity, quality, or delivery schedule will be changing.

If the supplier is vital to your materials pipeline, keep up contacts with various executive levels of that firm—from president down to the sales-man. And don't ignore that firm's purchasing department. Buyers there keep you tuned into *its* supply of raw materials. Might also be wise to check on the *vendors'* suppliers. That depends on the importance of your company's dependence.

As volume from a supplier rises, there tends to be a drop-off in quality. *How to avoid that:* Instead of doing your quality inspections of deliveries on *your* loading dock, send your people into the vendor's facility to do the checking. If they don't like that, consider a new supplier. It's good protection for your company. And you must "buy" peace of mind as well as good materials.

Caution: Even when long-term contracts for suppliers are signed, keep doors to future orders open with other suppliers. *Reason:* Impossible to tell when new designs come along—and your company shouldn't be the last to know. *Strategy:* Reserve a fair portion of your business for these other suppliers. Be sure they are aware of your long-term contract—and your interest in new ideas, which could influence a shift to them in the future.

Instruct your purchasing people to maintain close contacts with the suppliers' purchasing departments. Let them trade marketing information to keep abreast of your needs. *Side Benefit:* Your company's buyers will learn of any bottlenecks at the supplier's end of the pipeline. Require that your purchasing people regularly report the fruits of their investigation. Make it clear to them that their job isn't just buying items at the best price, but also reducing bottleneck and quality risks. *In short:* No surprises.

Source: John O'Connor, editor of *Purchasing World.*

CREATIVE BUYING RULES

• Rather than *ask* vendors about their products, *tell* them about your needs. The products you get will be better for your purposes and your company will benefit from the vendor's expertise.

• Let your vendors know about your budget restrictions and cost comparisons. They'll respond with better prices and show you how to save money.

• Buying is 70% learning, 20% negotiating, and only 10% deciding. Ask questions. Read available literature. Keep abreast of developments. Study samples and specs.

MANAGEMENT BY OBJECTIVES FOR PURCHASING EXECUTIVES

Management should develop some short-term projects for each purchasing agent. These can be set when the standard objectives and longer goals are worked out. *Purpose:* To set specific goals and tie rewards into the achievement of those goals. The long-range (and usually more abstract) objectives usually include some specific improvement in supplier performance indexes or in value analysis participation.

Spicing annual goals with projects that can be completed within a few months (or less) gives purchasing people a chance to earn a sense of achievement quickly—and to do so several times a year.

Best short-term projects are those that result in a tangible result: Preparation of useful charts, written reports, a welcome booklet for new suppliers, or guidelines for suppliers on packing, labeling, testing, or quality requirements. Other ideas:

• Visit and report on a new supplier's plant.

• Find some new suppliers for an item that is currently being single-sourced.

• Make/buy study on an item not previously analyzed.

• Comparison of benefits of single contract vs. blanket order.

CALCULATING REAL COST

Focus on total cost: Purchase order *price* is only part of the story. It actually tells less than the complete cost. Knowing what item sells for is only one piece of cost information.

Other factors: Cost of delivery, inventory, transportation, warehousing, payment terms, discounts, lead times, etc. Unusually high price for any one of these can offset original price savings.

Indicated action: Add up all factors leading to a buying decision; calculate how much each costs.

Typical hidden cost: Product must be bought in lots of 1,000 (six-month supply). Figure cost of unproductive capital for six months.

Buyer can negotiate on each such point. But he must have the relative value of each one in hand.

Problem: Probably, the accounting system can't easily isolate this information. It's going to require accounting changes so all real costs can be assembled—from marketing, manufacturing, finance, legal, etc.

Technique to explore: Find out from supplier at what volume it produces most efficiently. If possible, have it produce at that volume. But request to be billed only when your firm actually consumes that product. Naturally, it must have an accurate picture of your firm's future buying plans.

Then negotiate to *share* in the savings. Since the manufacturer is producing at economical production runs, it may be willing to slow up billing. Cash flow between buyer and seller can be major area of negotiation.

Aim: Avoid short-term buying and move toward long-term buying.

How to gain leverage: Centralize/coordinate as much purchasing as possible. One team should do all long-term negotiating for all real costs of item. Local delivery schedules and other details can be worked out by branches and plants as their needs arise. Central office, for example, should figure whether it's cheaper to buy on 60-day consignment or push for a 5% price cut.

Source: John J. Davin, GTE Products Corp., Stamford, Conn.

BOTTOM LINE REASONS

Neat and realistic way to stimulate the same profit results you'd get from a 6% to 8% increase in sales is to have your purchasing department save 1% of the cost of purchased goods and services. Every dollar you save in purchasing goes to the bottom line of the profit-and-loss statement.

AIM TO SUBSTITUTE

In these volatile and uncertain markets, you must be ready to substitute for many of your raw materials and components. Planning ahead pays dividends:
• High-priced items, where even a small percentage cut can yield a large saving.
• Items with a history of price increases.
• High-volume items where a tiny reduction will mount up.
• Long lead-time items.
• Items that are on allocation—or are in potentially short supply.
• Items that are produced by only one supplier.
• Nonstandard items similar to standard items or items bought in a variety of types where one type may do—with *some* redesign.
• Items whose suppliers are uncooperative about prices, delivery schedules, etc.

Management problem: You may have to exert some leadership to keep substitution from turning into a confrontation between the people who do the buying and your production and design staff. That "war" could be expensive; a joint effort will save you money.

Typical substitutions that work:

Plastics: high-impact styrene for ABS; polypropylene sheet for PVC; Teflon coating for solid Teflon.

Chemicals: lime for caustic soda; hot-melt for solvent-based adhesive.

Metals: low-alloy steel for drawing steel. Cl1L14 cold-drawn rounds for Mil-S-43 heat-treated rounds; bar stock for forging; brass for phosphor bronze strip; hard-rolled spring wire for oil-tempered spring steel; unplated bright wire for galvanized or copperized; A.R. steel for C-1045; zinc coated or "dipped" steel for galvanized; stainless steel for the brass/chrome-plated material; aluminum screw machine parts for steel plated; hard-coat anodized aluminum for stainless steel; flame-cut parts for steel castings.

Wood products: West Coast veneer for custom-cut plywood; chipboard for black glazed pressboard; poly bags for chipboard cartons.

CALCULATING LEAD TIME

Total lead time must be considered when purchasing. It's the combination of vendor lead time and internal lead time. *Internal lead time* covers time consumed in requisition forms, order processing, transit from vendor to buyer, receiving and inspection of the order.

Vendor lead time may be three weeks, but internal lead time may add an additional three weeks. Thus, purchasing should make all departments aware that it may be as long as six weeks before the item would be available for production.

LEASE OR PURCHASE?

The current wide swings in the cost of funds plus the desire to reduce financial risk make a lease/purchase decision difficult.

Here is a method that will make it easier to choose between the two alternatives:

First, identify the cash flows (cash *in* minus cash *out*, without regard to depreciation and other non-outlay charges) created by the choices, and determine the present value (what you would have to pay now to get each dollar at some future date and interest rate) of those flows at various interest rates. Then, plot them on a graph.

As an illustration, assume the following alternatives for a piece of machinery:

Purchase:
  Cost: $100,000
  Useful life: 5 years
  Corporate tax rate: 46%
  Salvage value: $10,000
Lease:
  Rental: $2,000 per month
  Term: 60 months
  Residual value: None

To evaluate the purchase option, it is necessary to identify the cash flow from the purchase.

• Cash outlflow at the present time of

$100,000 to purchase the machine.
- Cash inflow in years 1 to 5 from the tax saving due to depreciation expense.
- Cash inflow at the end of the machine's useful life of $10,000 in salvage value.

When these inflows are calculated on the present value basis over an interest range from 6% to 12%, the following present values of the cash flows are obtained:

6%	$(54,902)
8%	(56,095)
10%	(57,204)
12%	(58,294)

Applying the same technique to the lease option, we find that the only cash flow is the rental payments net of taxes. *On a present value basis, these are:*

6%	$(58,904)
8%	(56,864)
10%	(55,024)
12%	(53,238)

Plot these results on a graph.

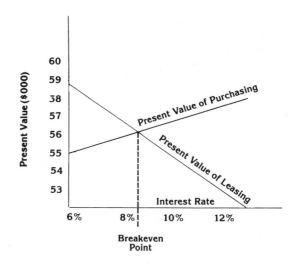

The graph shows management that, at a cost of funds of approximately 8.5%, leasing or purchasing have an equal financial cost. However, as the interest rate rises, leasing becomes less expensive—since the funds used for leasing are future dollars, which in the context of present value analysis are always worth less than current dollars.

SIMPLIFIERS

WAYS TO CUT DOWN

- Systems contracts: Rather than your company maintaining inventory, let the supplier maintain the inventory for you. Calculate needs and let the supplier *automatically* fill them. Give the vendor the responsibility of checking and maintaining deliveries on time.

Run regular spot checks on his accuracy.
- List each of your product's components—down to the smallest item. Assign a priority to each. Ask whether it's possible to do without any item or whether a substitute is readily available. Take nothing for granted. Insist that purchasing department regularly investigate the availability of each item and report any kind of shortages to upper management.

PURCHASING

● Reduce paperwork by applying the "blank check" concept used by some purchasing operations to pay freight bills. *How it works:* In purchasing, the vendor receives a blank check attached to a purchase order. He fills in the amount the buyer owes and deposits the check. (Limit is printed on check.) Buyer saves the expenses of billing and paperwork. In shipping, a blank bill of lading draft is used with the same results.

SOME
TIME SAVERS

● *Traveling requisition.* Use it for frequently ordered items. It works like an ordinary requisition form, but has permanent requisition data for a single item written in space at top, room for a series of requisitions at the bottom. Requisitioner fills it out, sends it to purchasing, which places the order. When order is received, purchasing sends the form back to the requisitioner for use when he needs additional supplies.

● *Requisition forms designed so the requisitioner (not purchaser) does most of the work.* One part of the snap-out form is the requisition. Another part becomes the purchase order when purchasing adds information and confirms it. Other parts go to accounting, inventory, etc. There could be parts that can serve as requests for quotes. The purchasing agent simply mails them to suitable vendors. When the requests for quotes are returned, one of them becomes a purchase order.

● *Self-ordering:* For some frequently used expendables, let the salesmen check inventory and order what is needed. The salesmen would fill out the order form, too.

WAYS TO AVOID
LATE DELIVERY

● *Determine the possible cost of a supply interruption.* Is it worth it to buy from a less expensive, but not necessarily reliable, supplier? Or does it pay to buy from a supplier who is very reliable but whose prices may be slightly higher?

● *Don't "create" emergencies for suppliers when none really exists.* Be honest. Then, when a real emergency occurs, the supplier will be likely to help out.

● *Check out suppliers.* Are their claims for inventory size, production capacity, etc., backed up by what can be seen?

● *Simplify components.* See if parts of components of products can be redesigned so that more commonly available parts can be used, and purchased from several suppliers.

● *Have a friend at the top.* Gain clout with a supplier by dealing with a person in that organization who can really be helpful. Develop your own contacts high enough up the management line to have access to the supplier's top executives when needed.

● *Keep track.* Ask suppliers for regular progress reports on the status of order fulfillment, but be sure to keep the demands for such data simple.

PITFALLS

STRENGTHEN ORDERS

A purchase order by itself *isn't* a binding contract. It won't give your company an enforceable claim against a supplier. But there's a way you can turn the purchase order into a *contract that's enforceable* if you're a merchant and your supplier is also a merchant (almost always applicable).

• Orally agree with the supplier over the phone or otherwise about all the terms of your contract: items to be purchased, quantity, price and delivery details.

• Then send him a signed order form which conspicuously refers to the oral contract made in your conversation.

• As an added precaution, send a memorandum with the order which refers to the oral contract and sets out its basic terms, including when and how they were agreed on.

LAW ON PHONE BIDS & ORDERS

• When a general contractor or a manufacturer has to get bids from various subcontractors or suppliers before submitting a bid, he may rely on oral bids made over the phone, forgetting that any contract for the sale of goods for $500 or more must be in writing in order to be enforceable. One way to nail down the sub-bidders is to send a written confirmation of the phone contract; if there's no objection to the confirmation, there's an enforceable contract. The better way is to insist on a "firm offer." The Uniform Commercial Code makes a written offer irrevocable for up to 90 days if it's made in writing and recites that its irrevocable for a specified period of up to 90 days.

• Follow up a telephone order for goods worth $500 or more with a written confirmation. A sale involving goods worth $500 or more will not be enforceable, unless written confirmation of an oral order is received by the buyer and not objected to by him in writing within ten days of receipt of the original, written confirmation.

SYSTEMATIC COST-CUTTING

Trim manufacturing costs with a *systematic appraisal of purchases and labor.*

Begin by setting up a list of *every* purchased item used in the end product. Then:

• Find out unit costs.

• Multiply unit costs by quantity of each item used in end product to get the *total cost* of each purchased item in the final product.

• Consider shipping products unassembled. It's frequently cheaper. Assemble the items at a company location nearest the final destination.

• Similarly, check transportation tariff rates for assembled and unassembled items. The unassembled rate may be higher. *Note:* Tariffs may vary considerably, depending on what the final product is. Thus, it may be cheaper to attach a motor (for instance) to one item and pay the duty on the whole assembly, but in another case, leave it unassembled.

• Focus on cost-consciousness by stressing price-per-pound. The figure is usually more dramatic than cost per shipment or per hundred-weight.

• Build customer goodwill and trim loading time by posting photos of customer receiving docks where shipping personnel can note special loading requirements.

Source: *Purchasing* magazine.

SAVINGS IN STANDARDIZATION OF FREQUENTLY PURCHASED SUPPLIES

There are ways to boost purchasing efficiency by ordering less frequently and in larger quantities. A successful program requires concerted effort on two fronts:

1. *Discourage the use of non-stock items.* Big companies have computers programmed to classify order specifications and flag those that can be filled by stock items. Small companies can obtain similar results by listing all stock items and then requiring an explanation on the requisition when a listed item won't do.

2. *Persuading different departments to coordinate their needs.* This involves: (a) Asking suppliers to propose ways of filling diverse requirements with the same product, and (b) conducting interdepartmental meetings, at which department heads are asked to negotiate on their specifications (and cut them down).

How to keep it working: Make sure that departments that change specifications to ease purchasing are *credited* with cost savings.

HANDLING LOW-VALUE ITEMS

Check purchasing operations for niggling procedures that eat dollars, yield pennies. Two ideas:

1. Use a blanket order number that covers all suppliers for low-cost, one-shot purchases. Accounting doesn't check invoices that bear the identifying number.

Possibility for abuse: Limited.

Savings in administrative costs: High.

2. Nuts and bolts and similar low-value items are dispensed cafeteria style. Workers simply take what they need.

Result: Some pilferage occurs, but the cost is minimal compared with the expense of writing, handling, and storing thousands of withdrawal slips a year.

REJECTING FAULTY GOODS

If a supplier ships you faulty supplies, components or merchandise, there are six prescribed steps to avoid being forced into legally accepting them.

1. Formally inform the supplier of the problem.
2. Be prompt—usually that means within 30 days of receipt.
3. Make the rejection report specific, indicating exactly what's wrong, if it can be repaired, and how much of the load is defective.
4. When goods are on your property, don't let them be used at all, or supplier could prove you've actually accepted them.
5. Simply treat the goods with reasonable care long enough for him to pick them up and dispose of them.
6. If you're a merchant specializing in the sale of such goods, you may be required under the Uniform Commercial Code either to try to sell them, collecting any expenses from the seller, or to follow any other reasonable supplier instructions on what to do with them.

BRIBE, KICKBACK SIGNALS

• The purchasing agent takes no vacations.
• The list of suppliers and vendors never changes. (Most firms change 20%-25% of their suppliers every year.)
• The lifestyle of the purchasing agent is better than what would be expected from his salary.
• Only one person decides what to purchase; little or no assistance is given by technical staff people.
• Large purchases are "chopped up" into small and misleading elements (such as add-ons and changes) instead of being taken care of by one single order.
• The scales on the company loading dock are never working properly.
• The cost of supplies has increased faster than inflation in the supplier's industry.
• Vendors complain to top management that they can't get an appointment with the purchasing agent.

Some ways to prevent bribes of purchasing agents:
• Rotate agents to different areas regularly.
• Make it clear that purchasing isn't a dead-end job.
• Pay purchasing agents better. Encourage them with incentives and bonuses based on performance.

The contract calls for the delivery of goods by the seller at a specified time and price. If the seller fails to deliver, the Uniform Commercial Code gives the buyer the right to *cover*. That is, the buyer has the right to buy goods of the kind contracted for from others.

If the buyer *covers* promptly, he may recover from the seller the excess cost over contract price he's required to pay.

NEGOTIATING

TIPS FROM SUPPLIERS

Unlock a flow of cost-cutting ideas from your suppliers by *sharing* the savings with them. *One way to do it:* Include incentive clauses in their contracts. The clauses should spell out a definite split between you and the vendor, indicating a lump sum for an immediate saving, a royalty for a continuing reduction.

Caution: Make sure the provisions set limits on the amount of time for which royalties will be paid, and that they give you sole right to decide when and if cost-cutting proposals from vendors should be implemented.

MAKE SUPPLIERS RESPONSIBLE FOR OSHA STANDARDS

When your company leases or buys equipment, ask your lawyer to get you as much protection as possible—on performance, patent infringement, and liabilities—under OSHA (Occupational Safety and Health Act).

Getting the supplier's assurance that the equipment complies can be a troublesome point. And he may take the reasonable position that he will only be responsible for OSHA liabilities if his company installs the equipment in your plant and that, if you make any change in that installation, it is relieved of such liabilities.

Your lawyer may suggest that you try to get something along the lines of the following in the contract of sale or the equipment lease:

"Lessor (Seller) agrees to comply with the standards of the Occupational Safety and Health Act of 1970 and the regulations issued thereunder. Lessor (Seller) warrants that all items furnished and all work performed hereunder will comply with said standards and regulations.

"Lessor (Seller) agrees to indemnify and hold Lessee harmless for any loss, damages, fine, penalty, or any expense whatsoever as a result of Lessor's (Seller's) failure to comply with the Act and any standards or regulations issued thereunder.

All defects in the equipment shall be repaired at Lessor's (Seller's) sole cost and expense."

You will wish to have adequate opportunity to inspect the equipment. If it is the supplier's obligation to install the equipment for you, the time for inspection should commence from the time at which the equipment has been installed and is in operation, not from the time you first receive the equipment.

Watch out, especially if the lease or bill of sale has been drafted by the supplier. It may contain language which would require you to hold the supplier harmless from all liability in connection with the equipment. That would conflict with any warranties, both express and implied, agreed to by the supplier.

In the case of a lease, especially, watch out for any clause that permits the lessor to assign its rights under the lease to a third party and upon such assignment the lessor is relieved from all further responsibility under the lease. If the assignee should turn out to be a shell, you would then have no real recourse against anybody with respect to the warranties on which you rely.

BEFORE, DURING, AFTER A NEGOTIATION

BEFORE.
• Is there time enough to negotiate thoroughly, or is it best to spot-buy for the time being?

• Does my negotiating team include representatives from all departments interested in the product?

• Do I know as much as possible about the supplier's position in his industry, how his other customers are faring and how much they are paying?

• How much real authority does the vendor's representative have?

• What are my high, medium and low goals? What tradeoffs am I willing to make?

• Do I need competitive bids?

• What are the possibilities of lowering *total cost* vs. *initial price*?

DURING.
• Remember to negotiate *with* the supplier, not against him.

• Lead off with your company's optimum goal, and wait for his reaction.

• Don't hesitate to ask for a cost/ price analysis and point out "learning curve" economies (as the supplier produces more it learns how to be more efficient and less costly).

• Indicate that you're aware of his competitors.

• Maintain an appearance of strength, but show why the deal is important to *both* firms.

• Use visual aids, ask leading questions, and don't let the conversation digress.

• Call recesses only when the recesses won't tip your hand.

• Take notes.

AFTER.
When an agreement has been reached, be sure everyone understands it. Get it in writing, including reasons for tradeoffs. Critique the session with your team and *keep track of results* to prepare for next round.

WAYS TO STRENGTHEN POSITION IN MAJOR SUPPLIER NEGOTIATIONS

1. Talk to competitors.
2. Let salespeople wait in the reception room while their competitors are waiting too.
3. Request new quotes.
4. Show that your boss is angry about delay.
5. Go over your supplier's salesperson's head.

6. Reject a shipment while the talks are on.

7. Demonstrate a new product design that could eliminate need for the supplier's product.

8. Let the seller know you may make the product yourself.

9. Create surprises of any kind.

Source: Dr. Chester L. Karrass, director of the Center for Effective Negotiating.

NEGOTIATING LONG-TERM OR SINGLE-SOURCE CONTRACTS

With shortages for the most part a thing of the past, many firms are looking once again at single-source contracting. *Advantages:* Uninterrupted supply flow. Pared inventories. Reduces need for double-ordering as insurance. Also a hedge against price increases, by outright forward purchasing of goods stored for you at the supplier's distribution facilities.

Elements to include in a long-term (three-to-five-year) single-source contract or letter of intent:

• *Supplier obligation to:* stock raw materials and finished inventory adequate to meet your forecast requirements; adhere to pre-agreed price schedules; or explicit formulas for renegotiation to take account of increasing (decreasing) costs.

• *Your obligation to:* provide forecasts of requirements, indemnify supplier for obsolete inventories carried for your account.

• Provision for accommodating increased or decreased requirements due to changes in market demand.

• Specification of engineering and technological service and information to be sure you'll be kept abreast of new technologies and new products.

• Provision for termination of contract for nonperformance (usually 30 days). Assurance you won't cancel based on price renegotiations you initiate.

Important: If the supplier maintains forward stocks you've paid for and have title to, be sure to insist on (1) vendor's *written* representation that he carries adequate insurance—plus certificate of insurance from his carrier, (2) contract clauses permitting your carrier to take possession of stocks to which you've taken title in event of insolvency, bankruptcy, litigations, dissolution, etc.

DON'T NEGOTIATE ON PRINCIPLES

First principle of negotiation is that you *can't negotiate on principle.* If you do, the result is almost always a stalemate.

When something is of crucial significance to the other party and represents (in his eyes) all he stands for and believes in, it's just non-negotiable. To try is to create dispute.

How, then, are emotion-laden symbolic issues dealt with in negotiations?

First, *identify them.* That's easy: The other party gets tense or flustered, pontificates, is absolutely unyielding, and the intensity of emotion seems to far outweigh any objective measure of the "value" of the issue.

Example: When asking vendors for a change in their product line, to them it actually means you don't accept (or understand) their approach to design or manufacturing.

How to cope:

• If a sensitive issue has to be negotiated, save it for last, after some successful resolution of other issues.

• If possible, avoid negotiating that issue at all. To get around it, gloss over differences by indicating your basic belief in the symbol: "Of course, we accept the principle that you shouldn't be at risk in this deal, and it's our basic responsibility . . . ." Then seek to bypass the symbolic level and arrange to get down to a level which *is* really negotiable.

DANGER IN CONDITIONAL ACCEPTANCE OF A CONTRACT

The Uniform Commercial Code liberalized the old contract rule which required that an acceptance conform exactly to the offer if a contract was to be reached. If it varied, it amounted to a counter-offer, and only exact acceptance of the counter-offer could be relied on to create a contract.

Under the UCC, varying the terms of offer and acceptance won't necessarily bar the formation of a contract, but this doesn't mean that we can abandon the old notion that an acceptance varying the terms of an offer may, indeed, amount to a counter-offer and wipe out everything that's gone before.

Classic case: A orders equipment from *B. B* accepts on condition that a warranty which *B* writes out be substituted and that the terms of payment be changed. *A* asks for a change in the terms of payment (which *B* agrees to in writing), but says nothing about *B's* warranty. When the equipment proves defective, *A* sues *B* not on the *express warranty* but on *implied warranty*, which would have been read into the sales contract if there'd been no *express warranty.*

Court's ruling: B's acceptance amounted to a counter-offer. The *express warranty* excluded the *implied warranties* that might otherwise have been read in. *A* loses, *B* wins.

A, who had relied on the UCC rule that offer and acceptance needn't exactly match, was, in effect, hoisted by his own petard, when the counter-offer, *although not accepted in precisely the same terms*, was effective to form a contract.

MORE EFFICIENT BUYING FROM SERVICE CENTERS

Companies that regularly purchase small quantities of aluminum and steel from service centers can get better service and lower prices in three ways:

• Standardize requirements. Aim toward eliminating small differences in size, which require individual orders.

• Allow plenty of time when ordering. The service center may then process similar orders together, cutting costs.

• Consolidate orders for same specifications from different units.

SECURITY

EMPLOYEE THEFT: 20 SIGNALS YOU CAN UNCOVER IN YOUR RECORDS

1. Inventory records and physical counts don't match.
2. Control documents missing or out of sequence.
3. Excessive voided forms.
4. Decline in employee purchases.
5. Discrepancies in cash funds.
6. More units received or manufactured than shipped.
7. Daily bank deposit doesn't correspond with receipts.
8. Bad checks frequently accepted or approved by one employee.
9. Tools or equipment replaced more than normal wear would require.
10. Unusual rise in consumption of supply items.
11. Merchandise or supplies frequently paid for on the basis of vendor's proof of delivery rather than normal receiving documents.
12. Cost of materials per unit rises above average.
13. Unexplained drop in gross profit percentage.
14. Unusually high percentage of refunds or credits.
15. Different figures on original and carbon copy of the same form.
16. Erasures, changes, pencil entries on forms that are not supposed to be altered.
17. Unexplained alterations of inventory records.
18. Documents not signed or countersigned.
19. Substitute documents used excessively to replace "lost" records.
20. Employment record cannot be checked.

MERCHANDISE THEFT: 15 SIGNALS

1. Merchandise or material missing from boxes or containers.
2. Merchandise or material in an unusual place; typically, in a corner, in the washroom, on top of a telephone booth.
3. Merchandise wrapped in a bag or package for no good reason.
4. Merchandise in wrong box.
5. Merchandise among trash.
6. Partially empty cartons where only full cartons are stored.
7. Ladders, fixtures, or piled boxes located to give access to windows.
8. Tools that can be used for burglary—crowbars and the like—left lying about where they aren't ordinarily used.
9. Something moved out of position between night and morning.
10. Extra merchandise in receiving or shipping area.
11. Wrappings, labels, critical documents in rest room, locker room, or trash bins.
12. Packing or wrapping materials out of place.
13. Files or documents missing or out of place.
14. Frequent damage to containers of expensive merchandise.
15. Documents and authorization stamps in possession of employees who don't need them for their work.

FOLLOWING THE LAW ON EMPLOYEE THEFT

Theft by employees is a serious matter, not only in terms of the direct financial loss suffered by the employer, but also in terms of civil, and possible criminal, liability in trying to deal with it.

Probably the simplest way of dealing with it is to fire the proven or suspected thief and let it go at that. But if he's protected by a union contract, the matter should be handled with the same care that must be used in initiating criminal proceedings.

If you nail him with the goods, you can make a "citizen's arrest." The following procedures should be observed:

• Advise the employee that he's being arrested.

• Inform him of his constitutional rights, *i.e.*, his right to remain silent and right to counsel and that anything he says may be used against him, even though this may not be necessary in the case of a citizen's arrest.

• Notify the police immediately of the arrest. Avoid detention for more than one hour.

• If you question him, again inform him of his constitutional rights, and keep a tape recording of the interrogation.

• If the questioning produces a confession, have it typed and signed by the thief and witnessed by another employee.

• Get an acknowledgment by the thief at the time of signing the confession that he was not coerced in any way and was not promised anything in return. This, too, should be witnessed by another employee.

It is extremely hazardous to make a citizen's arrest on the basis of suspicion. In such a case, if the suspicion appears to be well founded and the loss is serious, contact your local law enforcement agency for advice on how to proceed. Don't ever threaten the suspected employee with criminal prosecution. Initiate the prosecution, but say nothing to him about it.

SHOULD A CORPORATION 'FORGET' ABOUT EMPLOYEE DISHONESTY?

If an employee is discovered to have embezzled company funds or otherwise engaged in a criminal act against the corporation, there is a strong temptation to fire him and then not press charges. That causes no waves, such as poor public or employee relations, or a slander suit based on what's said about the offender. *But* there are two tax traps:

1. A corporation won't be able to deduct a theft loss if the matter isn't reported to the police.

2. If an employee is discharged for cause, his subsequent claim for state unemployment insurance benefits should be resisted by the injured corporation. In most states, a corporation's unemployment insurance tax rate can be affected adversely by the size of allowable claims made by former employees now out of work.

TEMPORARY WORKERS CAN RUIN THE BEST SECURITY SYSTEM

Don't use a temporary worker without *at least* some verification of identity, such as a driver's license or mail that has been delivered at home. If important, check each temporary out as you would a new hire. *Other measures:*

• Bar temporaries from areas where there are high-value items, either stock or equipment.

• Use a buddy system, with each temporary working with a dependable regular employee.

• Keep temporaries away from keys or other security equipment. They could be casing your warehouse, looking for an opportunity to leave a door or window unlocked for a later burglary.

• Don't count on the presence of cartons on the shelves to show whether the merchandise is actually there. The cartons may be empty, with their contents smuggled out.

• Make sure temporaries actually leave the premises at the end of each working day.

REDUCE MERCHANDISE THEFT FROM LOADED TRUCKS

• Always make two people separately responsible for what is loaded on the truck. Neither should be the driver.

• If the loaded truck stands unattended, be certain the truck is locked, ignition keys removed, and the vehicle parked in a locked garage or securely fenced yard.

• If loaded trucks are regularly parked *overnight*, the garage or yard should have a watchman.

• Truck keys should be kept in a secure place, not given to drivers or others when not in use. Minimize opportunities for making duplicates.

• Parked trailers should be protected by a kingpin lock to prevent hookup to an unauthorized tractor.

• Paint the company name in large letters on the roof of the truck or trailer to assist spotting from police aircraft should the vehicle be stolen.

Source: Charles F. Hemphill, Jr., in *Security World*.

BUSINESS ESPIONAGE

How business uses dirty tricks to get competitors' secrets:

Interviewing competitors' employees about a job opening that doesn't exist.

Negotiating with a competitor for license, with no intention of taking it.

Bribing competitors' suppliers.

Planting employee on competitor's payroll.

Using private investigators.

A survey found only 5% of business managers willing to admit that they *knowingly* used unethical tactics. But *70% admitted winking at dirty tricks* carried out by subordinates.

One said, "If he's a good marketing research man, ethics won't stop his research for vital info on a competitor."

CONFIDENTIALITY AND THE SEC

You'll want a lot of the information which the Securities and Exchange Commission acquires about your company to be kept confidential. You'll also want many of the things which the SEC tells you viewed as confidential. But there's often a fine line between the requirements of confidentiality and the requirements of the Freedom of Information Act.

Here's how the SEC walks that line: Some types of information will automatically be kept confidential, *e.g.*, trade secrets and information submitted for limited purposes, such as preliminary proxy statements and information gathered as a result of inspection of your books and records.

Other information will be kept confidential only on written request showing the need and period of confidentiality requested.

Important: If you receive no response from the SEC on your request for confidentiality within 20 days, you must promptly write back and ask for its return.

CRACK DOWN ON JOB-SITE THEFT

An identification system, tighter control of tools, equipment, and materials, and going all out to trace stolen goods and prosecute thieves may be **your answer to job-site pilferage.**

What tough-minded companies, notably contractors, are doing:

• Identifying and recording every valuable tool and piece of equipment in the shop—and those assigned to outside job sites: Item, location, person responsible for it, identification marks or serial numbers.

• Employing records and controls clerks at outside job sites (and inside ones where suitable) to check tools and equipment in and out. (And, incidentally, to see to proper maintenance, repair, replacement, and to keep duplicates of essential tools on hand in event of loss or breakage.)

• Marking all tools, equipment, and materials with distinctive identifying colors, symbols, or serial numbers. This prevents employees from getting past guard inspection by claiming items as their own. It also makes valuable equipment hard to fence and easier for police and owners to identify if it turns up in scrap-dealer hands, second-hand shops, and the like.

• Making cooperative arrangements with local contractors or other local firms utilizing similar tools and equipment. *Objective:* Coordinating marking systems that avoid duplication, permit easy identification locally and/or nationally. Permit all potential buyers of stolen goods to identify them.

SECURITY FOR TRADE SHOWS

Never leave an exhibit unguarded. At closing time each evening, transfer valuable items to a security room which should be provided by every show manager.

Most vulnerable time: Moving out. Make sure someone from your staff is on the spot, even if it means forgoing post-show camaraderie in the bar.

Watch for these signs of a well-managed show security program:

• Nothing is *allowed* to leave the hall during *moving-in* time.

• At other times, nothing leaves the hall without a pass-out slip signed by the show manager and initialed by the exhibitor.

• Workers are checked in and out of a single door, with permanent employees wearing photo ID badges and temporaries wearing color-coded badges.

• Cleanup crews work in groups, aisle by aisle, under the eye of a security guard.

For more information: Burns Security Institute, Briarcliff Manor, N.Y. 10510, for their *National Survey on Exhibition Hall Security.*

EMBEZZLEMENT PRECAUTIONS

As difficult as warehouse or shop losses are to detect, *embezzlement* is even harder. The obvious and not-so-obvious reminders:

• Have mail containing checks under the supervision of a responsible officer rather than a cashier or bookkeeper.

• Have bank statements reconciled by someone other than the person in charge of your receipts and disbursements.

• Examine all canceled checks for proper endorsements and possible alterations.

• Maintain control over confirmation letters in verifying outstanding accounts.

• Make all disbursements by check except those from the petty cash fund. Checks should be written on a check-writing machine or in permanent ink. Disbursements from the petty cash fund *must* always be supported by vouchers.

• Prenumber requisitions and issue in triplicate. Block out the quantity of goods ordered on the receiving clerk's copy. Let the clerk fill in that number, based on the pieces actually received.

• Checks issued in payment of goods should be attached to invoice and initialed by the person signing the checks. The drawn check should never go back to the bookkeeping department, but should be sent immediately to the mailing department.

• Issue *employee* checks in different colors to effect tighter control.

• Make up a checklist of all areas to be audited. Make sure your employees know when or how it works.

• Insist that all employees take a vacation. It's nearly impossible to be a successful embezzler and take a vacation.

CROSS-BILLING RIP-OFF

Rip-off to watch for—cross-billing: Commission driver delivers order to small-quantity cash buyer, credits sale to *high-discount* buyer, and pockets difference.

How to spot it: Look out for unexplained increases in *small* orders from *high-discount* customers.

FRAUD DANGERS IN SALES

Incentive programs to move built-up inventories are vulnerable to fraud.

How the fraud works: In general, a company promises its salesmen or distributors a substantial cash or gift incentive to move certain products or a certain volume of products. The salesman starts looking for ways to boost volume—sometimes illegally. At the same time, corporate executives may be in collusion with the salesman—or even directly with the customer.

A typical situation—although the variations are endless: Product is offered to customer with the understanding that the incentive (meant for the salesman) will be shared by the salesman and the customer. The customer (usually the corporation purchasing agent) pockets the money instead of passing it to the firm as a price reduction.

Another possibility: By prior arrangement, the goods are ordered, the award split, and later the goods are returned as unacceptable on some made-up excuse. Upshot, of course, is that the supplier is out in two ways: He has his goods back and he's paid the incentive payment.

Use of incentives: This *isn't* to imply that incentive programs should be scrapped. They are valuable sales tools —if used with the proper auditing. Without careful auditing, not only are they ineffective, but the incentive program will probably cost you (in gifts alone) much more than you had budgeted.

FRAUD DURING SHORTAGES. Another kind of fraud develops when there are shortages. *Example:* A top sales executive of a supplier approaches a small customer who's been allocated much less than he'd like to keep his production lines full. *The deal:* The supplier will sell him all he needs—in exchange for stock in the little company. The stock, of course, goes to trusted family or friends of the sales executive.

Then, in order to set aside sufficient supplies for the new customer, the sales representative drains off shipments to regular customers—many of which have long-term contracts. In fact, in order to siphon off enough supplies, he frequently has to break supply contracts with these established firms (using some pretext, like the supplies were damaged en route, etc.) which may cost the supplier *penalties*.

SALES AGENCY FRAUD. In very large firms, where the accounting departments for sales and manufacturing are separate, the following is a common rip-off. It requires the culpability of top sales executives of the supplier and buying agents of customers.

A product—usually some capital goods item rather than a nationwide branded product—is contracted for. The buyer and seller agree on a price— and then a false sales agency is created, which adds another 20% or so on top of the price. The buyer's employer writes a check for the full price (including the "commission"). The supplier's sales division receives the check, sends the manufacturing arm its share of the money, and headquarters gets its share —leaving 20% to be split between the deal-makers.

This is one of the most widespread rip-offs in industry, particularly in international commerce. The bigger the corporation, the easier it is to get away with, and the bigger the stakes.

How to stop the fraud: More accounting controls, real auditing of results, and spreading the monitoring functions as broadly as possible. *Reason:* The broader the controls, the less profitable the fraud, because too many people have to be paid off.

Source: Norman Jaspan, president, Norman Jaspan Associates, New York.

A BURGLAR'S VIEW OF BURGLAR ALARMS

SYSTEMS TO AVOID.

Door and window alarms. They are usually turned on by key when the last employee leaves the premises, monitoring all the doors and windows. If anyone tries to open them, an alarm sounds.

These systems are an invitation to a potential burglar.

Reason: They are visible (tape on windows and contact points around doors), so the burglar knows what he has to deal with. He enters through a roof vent or uses a jumper wire.

Electronic eye alarms. These rate no better. They operate like automatic supermarket doors. When an invisible beam is broken, a silent alarm is tripped. Since the eye can be moved and aimed easily, it can be shifted to cover doors, windows, walls, or a safe. Like door and window alarms, these systems are easy to breach using optical equipment to discover their position from a

safe vantage place. Once the burglar spots them, he just works around them.

EFFECTIVE ALARMS.

Proximity alarms. Usually, they are activated by noise. Microphones are placed throughout an area and are activated when the premises are empty. They are sensitive to any noise they are programmed to register.

Generally very effective. *One weakness:* The last person to leave activates the system. If anyone wishes to return, he must telephone the monitor, giving a code number and the length of time he expects to be in. If a burglar spots this kind of activity, he may (among other things) place a miniature recorder near the phone and learn the code.

Solution: Code numbers, security information, and schedules must be protected and changed frequently.

Tip: If you're shopping for an alarm, check out systems used by drugstores in your area. Generally the best.

Source: Michael Weaver, Walla Walla prison.

A GUARD SERVICE FOR COMPANY NEEDS

Before signing a contract for guard service, be aware of the following:

If the service charges $5.00 or so an hour, chances are the guards are receiving no more than minimum wage. This may be okay if the guards are only responsible for reporting fires, say, but can be no bargain if more is required.

An agency fee of $7.50-$9 an hour usually ensures a salary of no less than $6 and means personnel with a high school education, some special training.

and means personnel with a high school education, some special training.

The guard service should provide a background investigation of the employees assigned to your company *in writing.* A minimum should include five years of previous employer experience (longer on contracts requiring high levels of security); residence verification for five years, and criminal record check (when permitted).

When possible, a pre-employment polygraph test helps screen out potential criminals or damage-suit risks. Beware of the short 15- to 20-minute exam; *more* time is required for useful testing.

PERILS OF HANDLING SUSPECTED SHOPLIFTERS

Detention of a person suspected of shoplifting may expose the shop owner to a suit for false imprisonment under state law.

It may also give the suspect the right to sue the owner under the *federal* Civil Rights Act if he *appears* to be acting under state law.

This was found to be the situation in a recent case in which the owner was shown to have a prearranged plan with the local police department to come and assist him when he needed help, particularly when he was holding a suspected shoplifter.

The care with which suspected shoplifters must be handled is reflected in the view expressed by the trial court in this case, in which a woman had

placed a jar of cold cream in her purse. The court said that while her deposit of the jar in her bag during shopping created some cause for suspicion, this fact didn't create reasonable grounds to detain the woman as a shoplifter before she had been given an opportunity to pay for the item.

Comment: Laws against shoplifting wouldn't be apt to have much deterrent effect if the view expressed by the court were to become widely publicized. A more practical approach would be to let the shoplifter pay for the goods. It's certainly better than suffering a $12,000 judgment, as resulted in this case. In addition, consider the time lost and the expense of being a defendant.

Smith and McClure v. Brookshire Bros., Inc., C.A. 5, 9/15/75.

PINKERTON'S ADVICE ON PROTECTION

PERSONNEL DEPARTMENT. The personnel department should be checking the applications of all job applicants. Do they call the former employer to establish the reason the person left the old job? Do they double-check to be sure that major periods of the applicant's work career are accurately accounted for?

This is elementary, and the most effective way to filter out potential trouble.

Rule of thumb: Some checking of *all* employees is justified.

KEY CONTROL. As vulnerable as they are, keys are the most *cost*-effective security device. There are ways to make them much more secure:

• Make one person totally responsible for issuance of keys—and for their retrieval. That person will know, instantly, who has which keys for each facility.

• Stamp "Do Not Duplicate" on keys. It's not foolproof, but it helps to hinder unauthorized key copying.

• Use locks that require very-hard-to-get key blanks. Some blanks are "secure," that is, licensed key makers don't stock the blanks; they must be acquired from the lock maker.

• Consider putting a little bend in the bow of the key—it won't stop it from opening a lock, but will make duplication a bit difficult.

MAGNETIC KEYS. An increasing number of businesses are trying magnetic "keys," which resemble a credit card. Implanted inside the card is a magnetic code; when the card is inserted in a special lock, it will open only those locks with matching magnetic codes.

Problem: A malfunctioning lock may respond to *any* plastic credit card —with or without magnetic codes.

PARKING LOT. The most obvious "error" is situating the employee parking lot too close to storage or shipping areas. Such proximity is an invitation to internal theft: Sneaking tools or parts out the door to a close-parked car.

SECURITY GUARD. The mere placement of a security guard at the employee entrance is often effective in stopping internal theft. (Be sure the guard runs spot inspections every day, and that everyone *knows* about those in-

spections.)

COMBINATION LOCKS. Many lock combinations (those which can be adjusted) are set to the user's birthday, Social Security number, phone number, or some other obvious set of digits. And crooks know that. In "casing" a potential burglary site, sophisticated thieves gather all the obvious numbers—and usually open the safe quite easily.

If none of the numbers works, the burglar looks at the "obvious" places for hiding the number: In the executive's diary or calendar, under the desk pad, on the sliding desk arm, etc.

Recommendation: Don't use a related number. Memorize the digits and don't put them in "safe" places.

WEAPONS. Don't leave a pistol in a desk. If you have a real need for a gun (and you have a license), certainly do carry it. But don't leave it in the desk. *Problem:* An unarmed burglar may discover it and could become quite dangerous to any security force he may suddenly meet.

Avoid having guards use a *trick* device—tear gas, electric shock, etc. *Reason:* The burglar may not recognize it and may respond dangerously to the guards' approach. If clearly necessary, arm the guard with a gun—which the burglar can quickly recognize.

GUARD DOGS. Dogs taught to attack present more danger than security loss. *Instead:* Use watchdogs, which growl but don't bite. *Worse danger:* Use of attack dogs on the premises *unattended.*

Source: John R. Hitt, Pinkerton's top security executive.

SECURITY

EMPLOYEE THEFT TIPOFFS FROM CUSTOMERS AND OUTSIDERS

Outside signals that your employees are stealing:
- Frequent complaints of shortages or substitutions in shipments.
- Unusually large or frequent credits to a customer.
- Unusually friendly relationship among employees and outsiders (such as truckmen, repairmen, trash collectors).
- Customers refusing to deal with any but a single, favored employee.
- Your merchandise on sale in outlets that never buy from your company.
- Gifts or favors to accounts payable employee from suppliers—or to accounts receivable employee from customers.
- Reduced purchase by customers who deal closely with warehouse or shipping personnel.
- Presence of outsiders—repairmen, customers, salesmen—in areas where they have no business.

WHEN BANK IS— OR ISN'T LIABLE FOR CHECK FORGERIES

Problem: An employee forges authorized signatures on corporate checks or substitutes his own name for that of the payee on others.

Question: Is the bank liable?

Answer (according to recent decision): Yes or no, depending on how quickly the company uncovers the forgeries and what it does about them.
- The bank *is* liable if the company *promptly* examines its canceled checks and notifies the bank of the forgeries and alterations.
- The bank is *not* liable if the company does *not* examine the checks promptly, *unless* it is able to prove that the bank exercised less than ordinary care in cashing them, *i.e.*, the forgeries or alterations were blatant and easily apparent.
- The bank is certainly *not* liable if the company fails to report a forgery or alteration within a year from the time it receives the bank statement, *even if* the bank was careless about detecting the forgeries (as happened in a recent case).

Comment:
- Keep blank checks locked up.
- In reviewing bank statements, don't simply compare amounts on checks with bank statements. Compare payee and amount with check stub.
- Look for insurance or adopt some form of self-insurance against such employee crime.
- Consider limiting maximum amount of certain checks by printing limitation on check and embossing the amount.

SAFETY WHEN FACING THIEVES

Every office should be ready for a robbery. *Instructions to give all em-*

ployees: As difficult as it seems, it's crucial that everyone remain calm. The robber may be more frightened than the victim. An unexpected shout or move could result in injury. Be as cooperative as possible. Let the thief get out the door (with his loot) so that no one is harmed. Make a point of designating some people in the office as *identifiers*—they should make a note of the thief's hair and eye color, height, weight, complexion, etc.

• Office equipment is always a target of thieves. Often the theft occurs during working hours. In a typical case, the thieves monitor the janitorial services (schedules, clothing, equipment) and then plan their operation slightly ahead of the usual schedule. They'll wheel, say, a large trash container through a building and pick up typewriters, dictating machines, adding machines—stashing them in the trash container.

What to do: Maintenance people should always display distinctive identification badges. Limit them to one elevator or staircase. Designate one person (and a backup person) in the office to monitor the comings and goings of the maintenance staff.

Important: Avoid direct confrontation. If something is suspicious, a supervisor should call police.

Repairmen: Bogus repairmen can pull a similar ploy. Require that all repairmen check in with a supervisor, who will then monitor their comings and goings.

• Many managers set the safe on a so-called "day lock." That is, they complete the first two numbers in the combination so only the last number must be dialed to complete the combination. Because of this, sophisticated teams of thieves travel around looking for such safes. A team usually has three people. One is often a female (to distract store personnel near the safe). When the safe watchers are distracted, the second member of the team signals that it's clear for the third person to approach the safe. Since the safe is "day locked," it can be opened quickly. The second person is the security person, or "muscle." He will intercede if the situation should "sour." This person may be armed.

Prevention is simple: Don't use "day locks."

Some managers suppose they are protected by stashing the operating cash in file cabinets during business hours. The teams are aware of this and learn the location when they "case" the store.

HOW TO STOP THEFT FROM THE LOADING PLATFORM

The shipping and receiving dock is one of the most vulnerable areas for theft. *Best protection:* Good paperwork on materials shipped and received. It's got to be well monitored. Beware of lost copies, erasures, errors or changes in quantities. All are signs of theft.

Other loading platform activities to watch:

• Products or partial loads separated from shipments. This is the first stage of inventory loss. *Also:* Check the disposition of returned, canceled, or delayed orders that have occurred for *legitimate* reasons. These goods are often handled outside normal operational channels and become especially vulnerable to theft.

• Some schemes make storage of stolen inventory necessary until it can be removed from the premises. Check unused storage areas. At the same time, check main inventory in storage, and be sure main warehouse isn't being used to hide previously diverted material.

• Monitor traffic in and around the loading area. Question presence of any vehicle that doesn't appear to belong there.

• Delegate someone to note outside calls to and from your shipping department. This sort of theft often requires such last-minute contact from the *outside* thieves.

• Be alert for extra containers on the dock or in the staging area.

Warning: Remember, in dealing with possible criminal activity there is potential danger, so approach the situation cautiously *and with help*.

SOME WAYS TO SPOT THE INSIDE THIEF.

• Periodically check whether the employee has changed a usual pattern: Avoided intercompany transfer or promotion, improved lifestyle to a notable degree, stopped activity with a credit union (doesn't need it any more), failed to show interest in pay raise.

• What does the employee do during lunch and coffee breaks? Is he visible? These times provide opportunity for theft.

• Has any employee been seen talking with noncompany persons during working hours? Often this sort of theft involves an *inside* and *outside* man. The

outside person will proceed with his vehicle to the dock on signal, frequently during lunch or coffee break. However, it isn't unusual for these people to coordinate large rip-offs during the scheduled shipping and receiving activity.

• Do *not* broadcast suspicions or defensive measures. When culprit is suspected, go slowly. Observe, record evidence. Where possible, use cameras, and seek witnesses in order to keep legal footing solid. This approach will aid in the return of previously stolen goods. When the thief is confronted with ample proof, he is more likely to aid in recovery.

A CONVICTED THIEF TELLS HOW TO RECOVER STOLEN MERCHANDISE

Michael Weaver is serving time (20 years) for armed robbery. He also has experience as a burglar and forger. Here's his "inside" story on how to recover stolen goods, which may be more important to your company than arresting the crooks.

Don't close your eyes to the importance of getting back stolen property.

It sounds crass, but management must make a realistic appraisal of the loss and decide whether its need to meet production schedules and/or orders make it worth paying for return of the merchandise.

Remember: Just because your company places top priority on recovery of the goods is no reason to think that arrest of the crooks won't follow. In fact, the recovery may be a major step toward finding the thieves and gathering evidence to convict them.

Realize, too, that the police will understand your problem and will usually cooperate in helping you make contact with the thieves.

First step: Decide who should attempt the contact. It usually should be a third party—like an insurance rep. In most cases the company has to tell the third party of its interest. It's not often that the police or the insurance company will make the suggestion. So if return of merchandise is important, bring up the question with them.

• *The insurance rep:* Most agents will understand your priority. If yours doesn't, point out that an arrest usually results in the evidence (the merchandise) being tied up for long periods of time. Once the rep gets involved (and he will because it may mean much less payout on the insurance claim), you've got a third party to use as a contact.

• *Local newspaper:* Try to get a line into the *first* newspaper report of the crime (which thieves often read), indicating the possibility of a deal. *Signal:* A reward is offered and information is confidential; include a telephone number. (Your insurance agent might help get this in the paper if he's called immediately.)

• *Police:* Make them aware of the importance of return of merchandise. Detectives seldom *suggest* this possibility, even when they honestly consider it to be the best alternative. (They fear misunderstanding.) But most police departments have experienced personnel in this area.

• *Advertise:* If news of the robbery and reward didn't make the newspaper *immediately*, chances are the criminals

won't catch it there later. Try advertising on the most popular "hip" FM rock music radio stations in your area. Station personnel can be temperamental. When you call, tell them you were ripped off and would like them to word an ad for you. The station may become your contact. *Possibility:* Underground newspapers (only if they are close to the ad deadline).

Have the word spread in hangouts, cafes, streets in the vicinity of the loss that the company is interested in a quiet recovery.

Don't set the price. The thieves will always set it lower. The person who handles the transactions should suggest that the goods aren't really important and that the company is simply concerned about future insurance rates, etc.

Warning: Business "on the street" is a matter for experienced people. Use them. Don't think you are "slick" enough. You will waste time and money. And people who commit felonies are *dangerous!*

PROTECTING TRADE SECRETS

DEFINITION. A trade secret is "any formula, pattern, device, or compilation of information which is used in one's business, and which provides an opportunity to get an advantage over competitors who don't know it or use it." *Vital element:* In order for it to be considered a trade secret, the company *must treat it* as a secret and must make its secret status known to employees and others in the industry.

SELLING

SALES MANAGEMENT

HOW TO MONITOR MARKETING

Product profitability report. Helps management set priorities for product sales efforts. Compares products and product variations (size, capacity, features, etc.). Triggers elimination — or increase — of product categories.

Sales representative profitability report. Compares a salesperson's profit performance across accounts. Indicates the best areas for sales concentration.

Account profitability report (dealers, distributors). Lists, by account, the products purchased, price paid, gross margins realized, selling expenses and commissions allocated.

Market summary report. Usually assembled according to sales regions (or by market). Monitors trends, areas worthy of concentration.

UNDERSTANDING SALESPEOPLE

What salespeople like:
• Being treated as entrepreneurs with full knowledge of the financial aspects of their work: overhead expenses, manufacturing costs, etc.
• Being consulted by marketing people and helping to shape marketing strategies.

• Participating in setting objectives with their managers and *meeting* those objectives.
• Being given more—or tougher—territory.

What salespeople don't like:
• Laying the groundwork for a sale and then yielding the close to a sales manager or vice president.
• Authority and knowledge held back from them so that they cannot make decisions quickly in the field about adjustments or payment deadlines.
• Petty rules. Filing meaningless reports filled with data that they never hear about again.
• Having their territory cut, especially when they were responsible for developing the territory.
• Being pushed by senior management about *what* to sell.
• Having special promotions dumped on them without consulting them.
• Sales contests. They regard them as childish and irritating.

Source: Survey of 1,761 salesmen in various industries by Roy W. Walters & Assoc., P.O. Box 1001, Glen Rock, N.J. 07452.

SALES SUPERVISOR CHECKLIST

• Avoid the temptation to select a star salesperson to be a first-line supervisor. He has all the wrong credentials.

He's independent—and the job requires the *ability to work with other salespeople.*

He's impatient to close a sale—and the job requires that he *help a salesperson learn from his own mistakes.*

He has the entrepreneur's instincts —and he has to repress his aggressiveness to *give his salespeople room to develop.*

He's sales oriented—and the job requires that he *concentrate on setting goals, benchmarks, mapping strategies (for others).*

He's concentrating on being the perfect salesperson—and the job requires that he *devote a great deal of time to seeking out new salesmen and teaching them the fundamentals of the product, the customer, and the sales mechanics.*

- The type of person who would make a *good* first-line sales supervisor:

A steady performer. Able to sell reasonably well (even in bad times), but not the best salesperson.

Highly efficient. Understands the need for paperwork, keeps good records, and plans wisely.

Leader. Not so overwhelming that the other salespeople are stifled by his personality.

Flexible yet firm with people, so that he is able to teach an inexperienced salesperson and keep a star performer in line.

Frequent errors of sales supervisors:

Don't devote enough time to reviewing *time-management* with their staff. *Example:* Salespeople usually have to be taught how to allocate *less* time to low-level prospects and customers and *more* time to the high potentials. Salesmen tend to invest too much time in good, steady customers, not enough time in the substantial but hard customer who has to be developed.

- *What to do with the star salesman if it's not wise to promote him to sales manager:* Give him a special job, a special title, a better compensation arrangement. But *don't* let him manage other salesmen.
- *Where to get specialized sales training:* It's a hard job for the smaller firm, because of the manpower investment. But some industries are discovering that they can pool their resources.

Source: Steward Washburn, certified management consultant, Porter Henry & Co., 370 Lexington Ave., New York 10017.

USING MARKET RESEARCH FOR SALES

If sales vary excessively from territory to territory, market research can pinpoint the problems. Telephone interviews work well as a practical compromise between the cost of personal calls and inflexibility of mail. Purchase business lists of names for each area, instead of just using your company's customers and prospects. Results will be more accurate, plus there will be a clearer picture of what the competition is doing. (Be sure any list includes those considered to be important buying influences.) A sample of 100 respondents for each group is usually sufficient. Break the questions down into these categories:

- Respondent qualification. Does his firm use the product, and does he get involved in its purchase or use?
- What does he know about your com-

pany and competition?
- Which ones call on him personally?
- Does he (did he) buy from any of them?
- Criteria for product selection and their importance. (First, list representative criteria for use as aided recall for this segment. Be sure to include those factors that you feel are of significance to your company.)

Be sure to compare the analysis of your company (awareness of, sales calls, etc.) with those of your competitors to focus on strengths *and weaknesses.*

Source: George A. Young, Business Marketing Services, Bronxville, N.Y.

MAKE IT EASY TO DO BUSINESS WITH YOUR COMPANY

Is your company losing sales because it's unnecessarily difficult for customers and potential customers to buy your products? Make it as easy as possible.

Be sure the company's listing can easily be found in other directories besides the phone directory. (And have *full listings* in all directories.)

Does the company's advertising ask prospects to do something specific, like contact a particular person or use a toll-free phone number? Is someone's name mentioned for them to contact? Is that person a good telephone salesperson?

When someone calls, will he be directed to the proper person?

Do your salespeople know what your advertising says? Are they supplied with lots of good, informative literature?

Do you know whether or not the salespeople are doing what they are supposed to do? What about the distributors?

SIGNS OF SALES-PEOPLE WHO SHOULD BE IN ANOTHER JOB

- Too enthusiastic. Get excited about all sales prospects equally. Don't differentiate between good and bad leads.
- Don't get down to the nitty-gritty of the job. Present all the facts about the product, but don't get the sale.
- Regularly ask for the manager's assistance on what they think might be a sale.
- Overwhelmed by complaints. Each complaint is considered a major event.
- Can't move a prospect to make a decision. Those who do buy from this type of salesman were probably already sold on the product.

What to do if you have someone like this on your salesforce: Transfer him to telephone sales or elsewhere in the organization.

BOOST SALES PERFORMANCE

To raise a salesperson's performance, combine each individual's performance evaluation with a plan for improvement. Begin by measuring the individual by using these monthly figures:

- Amount of gross profit dollars contributed.
- Sales volume in dollars.
- Sales volume in units.
- Sales expenses compared with volume.

Compare results monthly with those of the previous month and with the same month last year to date. Set goals in the four areas for the next month. Continue to monitor the results and consult with the salesperson.

RECEIVING AGENT AN AID TO FOREIGN SALES

Key person in arranging a meeting overseas is the contractor, known as the *receiving agent*, who supplies local sightseeing, entertainment, events for spouses, almost anything a tour group does once it arrives. Either the corporate meeting manager or travel agent will be dealing with him. In either case, you should follow these guidelines in selecting:

- Check with colleagues who have held meetings in the same area. Get a list of all *receiving agents* from the local tourism office. Write to each, asking for meeting suggestions, available facilities, special needs. The answers will tell a lot about the agents.
- Ask candidates for lists of other associations or corporations they have dealt with.
- Don't judge by size. You may get more personalized service from a small-

er company.
- Make sure the agent speaks your language. Some specialize in groups from different countries and yours may not be one of them.
- Interview some of the "little people" who actually do the work—bell captains, taxi drivers, head waiters. When the agent is respected by people he depends on, things get accomplished more efficiently.
- If your group is large, insist that the receiving agent not accept another major group during your meeting. With their small full-time staffs, it's too easy for them to get spread too thin for efficiency.
- Don't give too much weight to the number of buses and limousines actually *owned* by the agent. It has no relationship to efficiency or ability to supply local transportation.
- Having a permanent service desk in your hotel isn't that important. Other agents may be more suitable to your needs. Usually they can set up a temporary desk. Find out.
- Ask prospective agents to offer innovative suggestions for your meeting with a local flavor.
- Don't rely solely on hotel recommendations. For any number of reasons, a hotel may omit capable agents. *Best procedure:* To make your own selection first, and then check with the hotel.

ALLOCATING SALES TIME

Here's a good rule for salespeople to remember in setting up their schedules for repeat calls: Ranked by volume, profits, or units, the top 15% of your customers will provide 65% of your business, the next 20% will provide 20%, and the rest (65%) will account for only 15%.

Work out the ratio of monthly sales expenses to sales volume. *Goal:* Maintain expenses with a certain percentage gain in volume. This ratio grows larger at the beginning of a big push for more sales, but it should come back down again after the sales start coming in.

The average salesperson has slightly more than a third of his time to spend actually selling person-to-person, and can't waste any of it. Good salespeople record *all* their activities for a one-month period, then focus on which were productive—and which weren't. Determine which can be cut out. Reduce the time spent on smaller accounts to as little as a periodic phone call or a constructive note.

HANDLING TOP SALESPEOPLE

Do you give your *top* salespeople too much autonomy? It's true that they like to be left alone to do their work. But they also need to feel that they belong to the organization, and that top management knows what they are doing. *Ask yourself these questions:*

Are top salespeople required to go to sales meetings? Do you go on sales calls with them once in a while? Do you send them information on a regular basis? Do you criticize their reports when necessary? Do you make them cooperate when you need them? Do you ever talk about opportunities for promotions with them? Do you ever discuss personal problems that they may be facing? Do you agree too quickly to requests they make which should be refused? Do you help them with their weak areas of selling? Do you automatically expect them to deal with slowdowns or dry periods by themselves?

If most of your responses are "No," you are not making enough contact with your top salespeople. Change, or they will feel they are totally alone out there, become dissatisfied, and may quit.

Source: *Marketing for Sales Executives*, Research Institute, 589 Fifth Ave., New York 10017.

SALES BY OBJECTIVES

Tired of setting sales goals for your people, then watching half of them lag behind quota while the other half carry the ball? Consider *sales by objectives*—letting salespeople set their *own* goals (and compensating them accordingly).

Ask them to set down *their* objectives in four major categories:
- *Routine.* The amount of business each salesman expects he'll do just by holding on to regular accounts.
- *Problem-solving.* Business he thinks he can supplement by going after lost accounts or those serviced chiefly by competitors.
- *Innovative.* New business he thinks he can generate with missionary work.
- *Personal.* Courses, reading, other job-related self-improvement.

Salary increases are made in accordance with goal achievement, taking into account just how much *effort* was made to *try* to achieve each goal, what *was* achieved, and how *hard* each goal was to achieve.

HOW TO MAKE SALES MEETINGS MORE EFFECTIVE

Before each meeting, the Westvaco Corp. mails each salesperson a form to rate planned meeting topics for their importance to him. The salespeople complete the forms and return them before the meeting.

After the meeting, the forms are returned to the salespeople, who use them to score each topic in terms of whether their needs were fulfilled.

On the back of the form is a questionnaire with seven sentences to be completed:

1. For me, the best idea to come out of the meeting was...

2. Here's how I can use this idea in my work...

3. By using this idea, here's how I hope to achieve these results...

4. Some things in my job situation may hinder my use of this idea. They are...

5. Some things will facilitate my use of this idea. They are...

6. Here's my plan for limiting the negatives and accentuating the positives (questions #4 and #5)...

7. What I need from my sales manager is...

The questionnaire works in two ways. First, it helps management conduct meetings that actually help salesmen sell. Second, it prepares the salesman himself for a meeting at which improved performance is more important than entertainment.

Source: *Sales & Marketing Management.*

HOW TO CUT SALES TERRITORIES WITH LESS RESISTANCE

Be sure the salesperson knows where sales are coming from to maintain his income level. Consider new products sold to existing accounts as new accounts for commission purposes (if sales commissions are weighted to favor establishing new accounts). It helps overcome resistance to a territory cut.

Ask the salesperson's opinion. If you think an area would benefit from more intense coverage, talk to the salesperson about it, carefully going over what prospects there are, and what can be done in that area, and how it would benefit from more attention.

If there is mutual respect and trust between the sales force and the managers, all should understand that they're working toward common objectives, and therefore understand that cutting territories is obviously not done by the manager to cut the personal income of the salesperson.

Source: *Research Institute Marketing for Sales Executives*, The Research Institute of America, Inc., 589 Fifth Ave., N.Y. 10017.

SALES INFORMATION SYSTEM

One way to keep sales efforts channeled: Put each account on an index card. Sort accounts according to potential. (*Example:* No. 1 buys $100,000 or more, No. 2 buys $50,000 to $100,000, and so on.) Use the same system to rate potential customers.

Have two sections in the index file, one for months, the other for days during the month. Use the daily section for regular appointments. The monthly section is for accounts to be called on in the future. File all No. 1 accounts first, No. 2 accounts second, and so on.

How the system operates: In the morning, a salesman takes out account cards for the day, makes his phone calls, plans his sales calls.

When a customer makes a purchase, record it on the card. After each call, the next target date is recorded and the card is then filed appropriately.

This type of system brings organization and control to a sales territory and to the salesman himself.

WHEN A SUPER SALES-PERSON COMES ALONG

Superior salespeople are so scarce that it pays to *make* an opening rather than pass one up because your roster is full. *Four ways to do it:*

1. Create a new territory.
2. Replace a salesperson. Establish performance standards and let your staff know that those who fail to meet them will be replaced when a suitable candidate is found.

3. Refer the candidate to the manager of another region or division.

4. Find a job for the candidate to do while he or she waits for a territory. *Examples:* Sales correspondent or helping other salespeople and replacing them during illness or vacations.

Alternatives: Keep his or her file active. Explain that while there is no current opening, you'd like him or her to go through the hiring procedure anyway. This will create a pool of qualified applicants that you can draw from later. *Tip:* Invite the candidate to check with you from time to time. This will let you gauge his or her interest.

Source: *Marketing for Sales Executives*, Research Institute of America, Inc., 589 Fifth Ave., New York 10017.

MONITOR THESE AREAS

Four areas should be regularly checked, both for short-term results (one year or less) and longer-term results (over a year or a year and a half):

Sales volume vs. plan: This includes checking sales of each product line, each area or territory, each distribution channel (if more than one is used), and sales for the industry. Results along with your questions and comments should be forwarded to the responsible salesperson, and performance should then improve. You should get this necessary information, but if you are instead getting meaningless data, find out why and do something about it.

Sales costs: Both big and little expenses should be checked. But the most important influence in the control of sales costs is probably the boss.

Market share vs. competition: It is essential to know whether your company is gaining or losing share of market. Information on *total market* can come from a variety of sources—trade associations, annual and 10K reports, paid researchers, trade gossip. Sales and marketing plans must be geared to constantly increase your share of the market.

Development of salespeople: This should be part of the corporate sales plan. Should be administered, if it's possible, by a training director outside of the personnel department. As part of training, subscribe to relevant periodicals for the sales staff. Have training sessions run by staff and/or outside consultants. The sales force should be continually developing and improving. *Management must work at that.*

Source: James P. Mannelly, vice president-sales manager, Tennant Company, Minneapolis.

HOW TO RECRUIT GOOD SALESPEOPLE

Ten ways to find salesperson prospects:

1. *Junior colleges:* Most companies recruit at four-year institutions, although few sales jobs require much of an education.

2. *Customers and suppliers:* Ask them to alert you to good salespeople.

3. *Present employees:* There may be overlooked talent in your office.

4. *Your own salespeople:* Their colleagues outside the company.

5. *Trade advertisements:* They can attract more of the right people than the standard newspaper help wanted columns.

6. *Minorities:* Many young men and women with talent and drive.

7. *Women:* Another group with a surplus of talent waiting to be tapped. Best prospects are women over 40.

8. *Veterans:* Contact nearby military posts and let placement officers know your needs. (*Also helpful:* Employment Clearing House of the Retired Officers Association, 201 N. Washington, Alexandria, Va. 22314.)

9. *Evening schools:* Especially those that offer courses in sales and management. Let the instructors know you're looking for job candidates. They'll probably be glad to refer their better students. Also, let your banker, civic groups, clergymen, politicians know your needs.

10. *Dropouts:* Lots of men and women with modest educational drives make good sales people. Let them know they're welcome in your recruiting ads. Also, if you recruit at colleges, you might tell placement officials that you're interested in people in the lower half of their class.

Source: Edgar M. Ellman, Ellman & Associates, Chicago, in *Industrial Distribution.*

RECRUITING SALESPEOPLE FROM WITHIN: PROS AND CONS

Advantages:
• More is known about their ability, character, and loyalty than can be

known about an outsider.

• Increased opportunity to change jobs within the company improves morale.

• Insiders know more about the company and its product line.

Disadvantages:

• Some supervisors may feel that their operations are being "raided" by the sales department.

• Disappointed candidates for sales jobs may return to their old spots with morale problems.

• It may be easier to teach an experienced salesperson about the company and its product line than it is to teach an insider how to sell.

QUESTIONS FOR SALES MANAGERS TO ASK THEMSELVES WHEN HIRING

• How directly does the list of job qualifications relate to the actual job involved?

• Is a college degree really that important for selling?

• Is previous experience absolutely essential?

• Is too much consideration being given to the possibility of eventual promotion? Some who are very good at selling don't want to be promoted.

• Are the qualifications for the job relatively general or quite precise? Distinctions should be made between weaknesses which can be overcome through training or on-the-job experience and weaknesses which nothing

can be done about. Applicants who could learn should be considered.

MORE WOMEN SALES REPS THAN EVER

With women now attending West Point and functioning as linemen for AT&T, it was inevitable that they would eventually be employed to sell industrial and related equipment to industry. It should come as no surprise, therefore, that increasing numbers of women are now calling on the industrial purchasing agent. Pitney Bowes has doubled the number of women in its sales force over the last two years. IBM, which had 400 female sales reps in 1973, at the end of 1982 had 1,689, or about 20%. At Xerox the percentage of women in the salesforce was only 1.7% in 1971. By 1973 they rose to 15% and by 1983 approximately 40% of all Xerox sales representatives were women. National Cash Register Company is increasing its number of women sales representatives. Producers of *industrial* equipment are moving in the same direction.

ADD AUTHORITY TO SALES FORCE

Have a salesperson spend all his time on one or a few industries. Then the industry will view your specialist salesperson as a person with authority. Also makes it easier to sell total systems.

COMPENSATION

CAN A WEAK SALESPERSON BE TURNED INTO A GOOD ONE?

Sales representatives who perform poorly can develop the skills they need, if their difficulties are in the areas of time management, telephone sales, or in knowing how to host a business luncheon, says Barbara Pletcher, executive director of the National Association for Professional Saleswomen. These skills can be taught fairly easily. But the odds for improvement are *very poor* if the person lacks even one of the basic attributes of a good salesperson: self-confidence, sensitivity to what customers want, and creativity in trying new sales approaches.

NEW INCENTIVES

Fascinating prizes produce fabulous results for very little cost. A Philadelphia savings and loan association offered belly-dancing lessons, golf with a pro, batting lessons from a Big Leaguer, or a night in a haunted house for a new account. The $25,000 campaign ($5,000 in prize costs) brought over $13 million in deposits.

The idea can be used in many businesses. Course instructors charge little or nothing, since they get publicity that they could never afford.

HOW TO MOTIVATE YOUR SALESPEOPLE TO SPEND MORE TIME ACTUALLY SELLING

Show them how much they make per hour of actual selling. If they spend 15 hours a week actually selling, face-to-face, that adds up to about 750 hours a year, minus about 150 hours for time lost when they can't get to see anybody, around Christmas time, for example. That leaves about 600 hours a year actually selling. It costs the company about $150 to $200 for each of those 600 hours spent selling. (*Total:* $90,000 to $120,000.)

If the sales force doesn't believe those costs, point out that they include all support facilities, office space, telephones, overhead, parking, etc., in addition to the regular expenses of car and sales commissions. Then divide their annual income by that 600 to show them how much *they actually make* per hour of selling. If a salesperson makes $20,000 a year, he or she earns $33 an hour for every hour of actual selling time. Point out that it may take several hours to take a customer to lunch, so that time might be better spent elsewhere, unless the customer is truly an outstanding source of business. If your salespeople can see how much they make per hour of actual selling they may waste less time and become more productive.

KEEP SALES FORCE OUT OF CREDIT MANAGEMENT

Reasons: A big potential sale can have very biasing effect on credit judgment. Sales stars are not usually financial specialists. May avoid potentially good customers because of mistaken fears about credit-worthiness.

REIMBURSEMENT POLICY

If your company's policy for reimbursing salesmen for their expenses is less generous than what your competition offers, expect to lose customers *and* good sales personnel to the competition.

A majority of firms recently surveyed will "normally" pay for: Coach air transportation; excess baggage charges; cocktails and dinner with a customer; taxis and local transportation; gratuities; postage, telephone calls, and telegrams to home; valet or laundry service while traveling.

A majority will "never" pay for: Travel insurance; cocktails for the salesmen only; personal entertainment; doctor or dentist while traveling; barber, manicurist, or bootblack; theft,

loss, or damage to personal property while traveling; movies; hunting and fishing trips; certain kinds of entertainment especially for customers, such as club dues.

Also: A majority of firms provide salesmen with an advance and with credit cards, mainly for air and auto travel and telephone/Telex use.

THE RIGHT EMPHASIS

Base salespeople's personal calls on an account's *profit potential*, not on order size. (A big order sold at a discount may be less profitable than a smaller, more frequent one.) Offer free delivery or discounts only on bulk orders. Use reply coupons to check effectiveness of ads. (Will smaller ads work as well?) Trim packaging and wrapping excess.

● Want your customers to listen more closely to a sales presentation? Bring along a letter which recaps the sales presentation. As soon as your prospect starts taking notes, tell him you'll give him all the pertinent information in letter form. The customer will be able to give his full attention to what's being said. He'll also be impressed with your foresight. *What to include in the letter:* A brief restatement of the most attractive benefits of the product or service, showing how the benefits are based on verifiable facts. Answer questions which are likely to arise when your customer talks about your product with others involved with the decision in his company.

PROSPECTS

WHERE THE PROSPECTS ARE

• *Customer lists*. Tabulate company customers by type of business and size —the number of employees might be a guide. Then establish an average volume of sales for each product to each company by size.

• *Look for exceptions*. Find out why some companies are buying less (or more) of your product than expected. The answers can lead to new sales or prevent the loss of existing sales. You can use the same method to separate profitable customers from marginal ones.

• *Business and trade publications*. Review them for news of contracts or purchases in your field, especially those that point to new kinds of users for your product.

FIVE GOOD QUESTIONS TO ASK SALES PROSPECTS

1. What benefits in this product might influence your decision to buy?

2. How do you rate quality vs. price?

3. I can appreciate your satisfaction with your present supplier, but would your decision to buy from me be a question of what more we can offer to meet your needs?

4. Can the benefit I just described help your operation?

5. If you were to order, what kind of delivery would you expect?

SELLING TO TOP EXECUTIVES

If your company is making a major marketing change which requires that the salespeople see higher-level executives than previously, here's how to get them in:

Your top-level executives should warm up the prospect first. Have them send personal letters with information about your company. Letters should include information on what your company has sold the prospect up till now. *Also:* What the new product is *and* why they should be interested in it. Mention how well they have been handled in the past with service or allocation problems. Or, if the record is bad, go over the new changes that will prevent or avoid past problems or mistakes. *Point:* Your management won't be happy unless *they* are.

Use the best salespeople—those who know all about your company. They should have several years' experience, should be comfortable and equipped to deal with top executives. *Possibility:* Send a note ahead of the salesman, telling the prospect who the salesman is, what his credentials are, and that he will be calling a certain week for an appointment.

For repeat business, credibility must be maintained. Salespeople should be able to recognize needed service after the big sale and follow through. Your top-level executives should continue to update customers on the developments.

Source: Research Institute's *Marketing for Sales Executives*, 589 Fifth Ave., New York 10017.

RECAPTURING OLD CUSTOMERS

Some methods that have been used to turn them on again:
- Send a special discount coupon that must be redeemed by a specific date.
- Mail a blank bill or statement printed with the words: "We miss you!" (And include a promotion for some very attractive items.)
- Offer a special catalog (usually sent only to best customers), showing how important you think they are.

WHY SALES FOLLOW-UPS PAY

Recent marketing research indicates that consumers are particularly happy when they're anticipating a purchase, opening it, using it for the first time—even reading the instructions. *But:* In a few days, the buyer begins to wonder if he made a wise choice—and this doubt is associated with the *un*happiest moments of a purchase.

Smart manufacturers and retailers look for ways to prolong the happiest experience with a product. *Reassure the customer.* Have a salesman call or send a thank-you card or letter a few days after delivery. Let the customer know what a good choice he made and that the company is interested in him.

SECRETS OF INDUSTRIAL SELLING

Here's some good advice from an award-winning industrial salesman that should be passed on to your salespeople:
- Keep building your mailing list. Send new product brochures to all the potential customers you can't get to see. When something interests them, *they'll* call *you.*
- Sell lines, special services—not products. Use every inquiry as an opportunity to tell the caller what else you can do for him.
- Keep an eye out for customers' special needs. If you establish a reputation for solving tough operating problems and meeting tough specs, your clients will cut their searching of competitors' catalogs.
- Aim for the customers that are the most demanding and hardest to see. They're the easiest targets: Their attitude usually discourages your competitors from even trying.

MOBILE SALES ROOM

Consider a demonstration van to boost your salesman's impact. They're great for instructional seminars, new product introductions, and the like.

Among the advantages: Getting the prospects *away from their phones* and other office distractions into a relaxed atmosphere that's conducive to negotiations. Motor homes whose interiors can be converted with modular display storage units are ideal for the purpose. (General Motors Corp. will now take orders for stripped-out units that can be custom-designed from scratch.) Equipped with movie projectors and screens, the vans can handle audiences of up to nine persons. *Early report:* They pay off handsomely.

GOOD INFORMATION

Press kits, the nifty information packets your public relations people hand out to the media, may be one of the most underutilized marketing tools you have.

More value: Provide your salesmen and distributors with kits, too. Encourage their disbursement along with business cards. *Pointers:* Make sure the words "Press Kit" appear on the cover so the recipient knows what to do with the information. Good idea to include a covering letter, too. Make sure you date the information and keep it updated at least every six months. It's important that the kit contain *genuine* news material and intelligent background info. Most important, it should have *users'* interests in mind.

Source: Richard Conarroe, president, Walden Public Relations, Inc., 246 E. State, Westport, Conn.

NAILING DOWN AN ORDER

An order for a truck, equipment, or supplies does not necessarily *make a contract.* The seller's order form often states, "This order is not valid unless signed here as accepted by the sales manager or officer of the company," or similar words. This gives the seller an opportunity to renegotiate the deal if he thinks he can up the ante. Similarly, the buyer can withdraw his order (which amounts to an offer) any time before acceptance by the seller. When the buyer wants to know the price and delivery date are firm, he should write on the order form that the offer will automatically terminate unless he *receives* written notice of acceptance by the person designated on the order by a certain date.

Great value in a personal follow-up note to prospects whose first meeting didn't result in a sale. (Certainly send a thank-you if it did.) One salesman writes personal same-date note on postcards printed with his photograph, thanking prospect for time, mentioning his product again, and inviting himself back for another meeting.

TERMS

HOW TO SELL GOODS "AS IS"

If it's important that you sell on an "as is" basis without having to worry about claims that the goods were defective, do this: Use a sales slip or contract with the words "Sold as is" displayed *conspicuously*. Even better, use a special "Sold as is" stamp, with letters larger and bolder than the lettering on the sales paper. As you stamp the paper, tell the buyer what you're doing. You can't rely solely on an oral warning, fine print on the sales slip, or an "As is" tag attached to the merchandise.

BEWARE OF GIVING OR RECEIVING CUMULATIVE VOLUME DISCOUNTS

Special discounts can bring a company into conflict with provisions of the Robinson-Patman Act that prohibit discriminatory pricing.

Generally, it's safe if it can be shown that the volume generated by the cumulative discount actually reduced the supplier's costs in manufacturing, shipping, billing, and the like.

Cooperative buying arrangements are risky unless all the merchandise is shipped to a single point and redistributed to members. If each member receives his merchandise directly and is billed separately, the co-op will run afoul of the Robinson-Patman Act.

Warning: Legally, when enforcing the act, the FTC is supposed to consider whether or not a pricing policy is actually harmful to competition. In practice, the FTC will act in either case, leaving your company with a long, costly legal effort to prove that competition hasn't been harmed. And even then, the ruling might go against your company.

WHEN A PRICE QUOTATION IS MORE THAN A PRICE QUOTATION

A *contract* requires an offer *and* acceptance. That's basic. However, a *price quotation* by itself isn't an offer and can't form the basis of a contract based on offer and acceptance. Still, if what is said to be a price quotation (and is labeled as such) has detailed terms similar to a contract or an offer of a contract, it may be construed as an offer rather than a mere price quotation.

If a buyer asks for a quote and receives such a form and responds with a purchase order, he runs the risk of having his purchase order construed as an acceptance binding him to all the terms of the seller's form. *Exception:* He must make it clear that his purchase order is merely an offer to purchase. This has to be done by a conspicuously placed notice on the face of the order in *larger than usual* letters to the effect that "This is an offer to purchase on our terms and conditions, and your acceptance must exactly conform to our terms and conditions." (Each company's counsel may have preference on exact wording.)

LETTER OF CREDIT MAY MAKE A SALE (OR PURCHASE) POSSIBLE

Where a buyer is reluctant to pay in advance of shipment and a seller is reluctant to ship in advance of payment, a letter of credit may make the deal possible. The buyer asks his bank to issue a letter that promises to make payment to the seller (or to accept his drafts on the bank) provided the seller complies with the terms and conditions spelled out in the letter: Price of the goods; time allowed for shipping; the shipping documents, or other documents, *i.e.*, bill of lading or warehouse receipt, that the bank or buyer want to receive.

If the seller meets the conditions, he's sure of payment. *Caution:* The buyer is assured only that the documents presented for payment appear to be genuine, not that they are or that the goods are as described. In this perspective it's the seller who fares best.

REBATES

Rebates are becoming a fixed part of the *new* marketing. Benefits to manufacturers beyond increased sales: Price structures are undisturbed (important if the government imposes a freeze). Overall consumer attitudes improve as rebates coax disposable income out of hiding.

How to use rebating successfully:
• Have a reduction large enough to attract the consumer's interest.
• Establish the idea of *value* before a rebate is offered. Buyers lured into the auto market by rebates soon discovered that many foreign models were better buys, even without the rebates.
• Be prepared to launch your rebate program quickly, to gain a head start on competitors.

Look for *new forms* of rebating as the idea becomes common—offers of products instead of cash, for example.

INFLATION SELLING

Strategies to consider to hedge against rising costs:

Cut out free services where they can be eliminated without losing customer good will. (Special packaging, free delivery, free warehousing.) Bill customers for the service instead.

Drop prices from catalogs and other sales literature. Insert inexpensive price sheets instead, which can be changed quickly, cheaply.

DISTRIBUTION

BEST SALES REP FIRMS ARE THE TOUGHEST TO LIVE WITH

One way of appraising a manufacturer's sales agency is by its demands on the supplier companies. The most effective reps are the most demanding. And they're worth it. A top sales agent will require (and should get):

• Guaranteed prompt, accurate shipments.

• Assurance that commissions will be paid on time.

• A contract that spells out the selling relationship clearly—with a protective termination clause.

• Evidence of the supplier company's financial stability, reliability, and good reputation.

• Information on product growth rate, new products, research and development.

• A history of past sales in the rep's territory with sound predictions of future sales.

• Instructions on whom to contact, how to get questions answered, and how to straighten out problems quickly.

• Supplier aid in sales programs and promotion campaigns, with adequate supplies of promotion material.

• Knowledge of the company's overall policy, particularly regarding sales, deliveries, credit, complaints, advertising, and relations with suppliers and agents. (A policy manual is helpful.)

• A willingness on the part of the company to consult its sales agents before it makes decisions that affect them.

• Consideration for the agency's independence and right to operate without interference. (Supplier executives should respect the reps' schedules. Avoid unannounced visits.)

PERFORMANCE CHECKLIST

Big distributor complaint: Factory representatives who don't measure up to the job or the technical complexities of their products. What distributors would like to see:

1. Top-notch people with top-notch technical training and on-the-spot know-how, not vague promises and delays while they check with the home office for answers to questions.

2. Ability to train *distributor* sales force (distributors are upgrading staffs).

3. Regular visits by your people instead of having to ask the factory to have a salesman call. No sudden drop-ins when it's convenient *for the salesman*. Two or three weeks' advance notice allows firms to plan to make the most of such visits.

4. Time—lots of it. Up to a whole day with a single distributor salesman calling on accounts, helping resolve cus-

tomer hang-ups and complaints, introducing new products, promoting the items their customers don't buy. Up to a week at a time in sessions with sales staff when it's needed.

GETTING MORE FROM FACTORY REPS

Problem: A distributor found that when his sales force met with representatives of his suppliers, the meetings dragged and the factory reps droned through memorized talks. The salesmen were embarrassed to bring up problems in public.

Solution: A few weeks before a factory rep is scheduled to call, his name and company are labeled on a box. Members of the distributor's sales force think of questions, write them on slips of paper and drop them in the box.

Later, the rep picks up the questions and uses them to prepare for the meeting.

Result: Lively meetings with a flow of useful, relevant information to the distributor's sales force.

RATING COMPANY'S SALESFORCE AGAINST MANUFACTURERS REPS

Usually a salesman is more expensive but can sell more than a manufacturer's representative. Expect a rep to sell *and* cost less.

When few sales are expected, an agent is more profitable than a salesman. As sales increase, the profitability of a salesman gradually approaches, then exceeds, that of an agent. The problem is to find the *crossover quantity*. This is the number of sales that will be equally profitable whether sold by a salesman or an agent. If expected sales are above this point, a salesman will be more profitable.

You can use this formula to determine that critical quantity:

$$Q = \frac{F}{CM_s - r(CM_a)}$$

F = salesman's budgeted cost for a decision period, such as salary and benefits plus travel expenses.

CM_s = contribution margin per unit sold by the salesman, *price minus variable costs.*

r = ratio of expected sales by the agent during the decision period to expected sales by the salesman. (If the agent can sell 45% of what the salesman can sell, $r = .45$.)

CM_a = contribution margin per unit sold by agent, again *price minus variable costs.*

Example: A unit is sold for $640, manufacturing cost is $535 and the company also incurs a delivery cost of $42. A salesman's budgeted costs for month total $1,100 in salary and benefits and $1,400 for travel. He also received $15 commission per unit sold. An agent for the same territory receives a straight 8% commission and can be expected to sell only 45% of what a salesman could sell. To use the formula:

$F = \$2,500(\$1,100 + \$1,400)$
$CM_s = \$640 - \$535 - \$42 - \$15 = \$48$
$r = .45$
$CM_a = \$640 - \$535 - \$42 - (.08 \times \$640) = \$11.80$

Simply solve the following equation for Q:

$Q = \$2,500/(\$48 - [.45 \times \$11.80]) = 58.56$

Result: The crossover quantity is 59 units. If a salesman will sell fewer than that, use an agent. If he will sell more, use a salesman.

DISTRIBUTOR TRENDS

• The high cost of keeping salesmen in circulation is moving many manufacturers to switch to distributors. If your company goes this route, expect complaints from some customers. *Standard gripe:* Distributors don't stock enough of what they need. Ingersoll-Rand met this problem by giving distributors an extra 10% discount if they agree to stock a third of the amount sold the previous year. The deal (10% on top of regular 20% to 30% discounts) was picked up by the majority of its distributors.

• Manufacturers can cut their distributors' costs with only a nominal expenditure of their own. They can extend product liability insurance to cover distributors. A provision in most policies allows them to do this at nominal cost, since distributors almost never make any changes or alterations in most products. Coverage includes only the manufacturer's line and doesn't extend to other lines carried by the distributor.

• Typical industrial marketing failure: Company wins acceptance for its products among end producers, but sales fail to increase. *Problem:* The distributor has been left out of the marketing plan. He finds it more advantageous to steer customers to other brands whenever possible. *Solution:* Make sure your product is competitive among distributors as well as ultimate consumers in terms of profit, service, and even contest prizes, etc.

TELEPHONE TECHNIQUES

TELEPHONE SELLING

Telephone selling is growing quickly —and for a very good reason: It works!

With the cost of an average in-person industrial sales call running at least $80, the cost advantages of telephone selling become very important.

There's little doubt that most products and services *can* be sold by phone. *The real question:* Is it cost effective? There's only one way to find out—by testing.

General rule: Low-priced items (under $5) often aren't cost effective in phone selling. But there are exceptions. Higher-priced goods or services usually work out better.

Misconception: Many firms believe that complex products or services can't be sold by phone. That is usually not true. The programs have been working in almost every instance.

How to test telephone selling for your company:

• Reuben H. Donnelley Corp., one of the nation's leading telephone-selling organizations, has inaugurated a program to teach other companies to sell by phone.

• Donnelley can recommend a telephone-selling specialist to run the test.

• Donnelley has prepared a self-learning course that takes from 1⅔ to 3 days to develop sufficient selling skills. The course—recorded instructions and workbooks—provides the basics of telephone selling, leaving the job of integrating the product or service into the sales presentation to the customer.

• Donnelley will also provide one of its instructors (at $300 a day plus expenses) to train the staff at your company.

• For special situations for which the "universal" program isn't adequate, Donnelley tailor-designs sales programs for customers. *Typical cost range:* $5,000 to $10,000.

Some of the extras that phone selling can provide, often making marginal sales very profitable:

• Follow-up on direct leads generated by ads.

• Opening of old, inactive accounts.

• Canvassing to "qualify" sales prospects for later direct selling.

• Reaching busy people who are hard to meet.

Telephone salespeople needn't be on your premises to do the actual selling. They could be situated in field offices or in their own homes.

What makes a good telephone salesperson? The quality is hard to define. It's easy to find out how good someone is by letting the person try it. *What to look for:* A voice with a "smile" and a person who *sounds* intelligent.

Expect high turnover if your operation requires salespeople to make a certain number of calls per hour or for *scripted* or *semiscripted* situations where every call is the same.

Build motivation into your program via incentives (both specialized and those for your regular sales force). *Also:* Local contests offering modest prizes, like a great dinner for two or theater tickets, are very effective with people who are locked into an office day after day. When phone personnel are situated in a general office with other employees, don't isolate them; include them in meetings and other activities.

What about phone equipment? Let employees choose the sets they like. (You'll never find one that pleases everyone.) Be sure to analyze phone requirements to see whether WATS line or direct-distance dialing is needed. Set up a norm so you and your salespeople know where you stand: How many calls per hour (or day, etc.); how many conversations to telephone orders; dollar figures, etc.

Source: Irwin C. Slater, director of training, Reuben H. Donnelley Corp., 825 Third Ave., New York 10022.

TELEPHONE SALES A GOOD WAY TO HANDLE MARGINAL ACCOUNTS

When credit is tight, companies tend away from marginal accounts. But marginal accounts should not be overlooked. They are important for their growth potential, and can be handled profitably by phone. (The average cost of a phone sales call is $10.)

Salespeople should be chosen, at least in part, on the basis of telephone interviews. Often, members of a firm's customer-service staff make good telephone salespeople. They know the company's products, deal regularly with customers over the phone, and are often motivated by the chance for a more financially rewarding job.

A person's telephone personality depends on his working conditions, so make sure to:

• Put a working supervisor in charge, someone who does more than simply watch others.

• Provide adequate back-up materials (catalogs, price lists).

Don't make telephone selling a dead-end job. Move some of the most successful telephone salespeople out into the field.

Measure the results by recording:

• New accounts added by telephone sales calls.

• Before-and-after sales volume in marginal accounts served by phone.

• Before-and-after profitability of marginal accounts.

HIRING AND TRAINING A TELEPHONE SALES STAFF

Permanent telephone staffs—employed to dig up leads, promote new products, handle routine orders, and save field personnel time and travel costs—can pay big dividends, providing you invest in a *quality staff.*

• Hire the *right* people for the job. Personality is vital: a telephone solicitor must make a big impression in the *first 30 seconds*. A badly handled telephone call is an intrusion and offensive to the customer. *Best producers:* Those who rank *themselves* high on the scale for creativity and leadership qualities, such as self-expression, drive, adaptability, interest in people, ability to motivate others and clarify ideas for them.

• Use some imagination in recruiting. Supplement newspaper ads with contacts to college placement agencies and those that have access to retirees and the handicapped. *Women* often make outstanding solicitors, even where technical products are involved. *Older persons* produce significantly better quality leads than younger ones.

• Train them well. Solicitors must know and understand your product, talk your customer's language, and field questions or meet objections as effectively as your top field men. Invest in an operations manual and a top-notch training course.

• Keep them by making the job pay. If you treat them like second-class employees, your department will operate like a revolving door. Pay a decent salary, with a generous fee or percentage per closing made or lead produced. (You should be increasing sales and cutting field costs enough to afford it.)

• Weed them out. Most solicitors reach peak production after 6 to 10 weeks. Single out poor performers for retraining. Fire if they don't pick up.

• Save money using split shifts, part-time people. Part-time solicitors perform significantly better (full-timers tend to burn out from too many long days on the phone). Monitor production records to determine your best lead-procurement or sales hours. Set up a split shift that cuts costs and accommodates part-time people perfectly.

RETAILING

RETAIL PROMOTION IDEAS

In order to get customer traffic into the *rear* of the store, a drugstore installed a telephone in the back *that customers could use free. One result:* Many customers used the phone to call home to find out what items needed to be purchased at the drugstore.

• A furniture store had a photographer take photos of each of 500 homes in a recently developed area, keying each photo to its proper address. The owners of the homes were sent postcards on which was mounted a tiny photo of their home. They could get a free enlargement at the furniture store. 440 of the 500 showed up for the free enlargement and almost all purchased something. The whole promotion cost the store $225.

Source: *Brainstorms*, 1280 Saw Mill River Rd., Yonkers, N.Y. 10710.

EMPLOYEE DISCOUNTS

How retail-store employee discounts work:

Discounts range from cost to 5%-20% off the ticket price. Payment method varies. Some stores require employees to pay in cash, others allow them to charge merchandise and deduct sums owed from paychecks.

Employee discounts, once initiated to discourage pilferage, have become a traditional part of the retail compensation package. Many retailers record employee purchases, on the theory that employees who *don't* make them are probably pilfering.

Security: In most stores, only managers or assistant managers are allowed to write up employee sales—to prevent collusion between employees. But in others, a manager designates an individual in each department to write them up.

Put a mirror in the store window. Few people can resist the temptation of a passing glance. Most will linger longer to look at rest of the display. *Hint:* Order mirrors that reflect a slimmer view of the customer.

IS CHRISTMAS ALL THAT PROFITABLE?

Christmas profit for retailers is an

institution never—but never—doubted, questioned, or debated. Would sophisticated analysis of the retail Christmas season come up with profit ratios *substantially lower* than the figures customarily posted? *Mass retailers really don't know.* They have rarely, if ever, put the Christmas season under modern cost analysis. Yet every instinct, every bit of logic indicates that retailers' Christmas profits are generally vastly overstated.

• Substantial costs for Christmas promotion are incurred throughout the year—and, in some instances, costs are incurred as far back as two years. These costs include administration, planning, buying, financing, transportation, warehousing, receiving, and marketing. They are rarely properly isolated and charged to the Christmas program. Yet the total sum involved would surely take an enormous bite out of the presumably lush December profits.

• No effort has ever been made to determine what part of December volume represents deferred purchases of gifts that otherwise would have been made in November or January as non-gift, own-use purchases.

• How much of the money deposited in Christmas savings accounts represents deferred purchases that otherwise would have been made in other months?

• What about the shocking total of inventory shrinkage during the Christmas season—much of it not even audited until long after Christmas?

• Extra costs are inherent in extra personnel hired and trained in November.

• Display costs are accumulated months before Christmas—and also are incurred in January as store displays return to normal.

• Costs are incurred over several months for shifting departments, expanding departments, contracting departments. Restoring departments represents still another Christmas cost.

• Extra costs are involved in moving inventory into warehouses—into the stores—back to the warehouse.

• Clerical errors multiply during the Christmas season, but the costs inherent in these errors usually appear in January and even February statements, not December.

• The cost inherent in wear and tear on the various levels of executives during Christmas is difficult to measure, of course, but still demands measurement.

• Extra housekeeping costs are inevitable.

WHY SHOPPERS SWITCH STORES

Minneapolis-St. Paul is a major market testing area, so reasons why 19% of the shoppers there switched supermarkets last year can be useful elsewhere in the country. *Lower prices* lured away 33% of the switchers. *Other causes:* Better quality meat, 21%. More convenient location, 19%. Better fruits, vegetables, 19%. Faster checkout service, 16%. More helpful employees, 11%. New store in the area, 10%. Average shopper buys at 3.2 different supermarkets regularly.

Source: Minneapolis Star and Tribune Marketing Research Dept.

SYSTEMS FOR MANAGEMENT

STRATEGIES

UNDER PRESSURE, LOOK FOR DECISIONS WITH LEVERAGE

Fear may prompt management to overreact in the wrong areas. *Advice:* Focus on strategies with much more leverage than simple cost cutting. Seek benefits for the long run as well as for a period of slump.

Suggestions you may have heard before but worth heeding:

DON'T FIRE PEOPLE RECKLESSLY. Usually one of the most costly ways to retrench. Hewlett-Packard needed to cut overhead in a business downturn and could easily have cut the work force. It cut back the *workweek* instead. After business snapped back, the full workweek was restored. *Result:* Immense benefits from heightened employee goodwill, preservation of the investment in indoctrination and training, and lower recruitment costs.

RESIST LOWERING PRICES. The rush to cut prices may be understandable, but it is unjustified. Price is the point-of-profit leverage and should be reduced only when cutting it has been proved to be a profit-effective strategy. Most price cutting serves neither *profitability* nor *survival.* And when the cost of everything else declines (materials, labor, money, etc.), it is likely to be poor strategy to hold the line on prices.

SHIFT GEARS IN MARKETING. As purchasing power or markets shrink, firms should move from emphasizing *volume* to emphasizing *profitability,* from emphasizing *sales* dollars to emphasizing *marginal income* related to investment. Sales increases shouldn't be obtained at the expense of future requirements, especially working capital. Many companies grow to their deaths.

RIDE THE EDP INVESTMENT HARDER. Cut the EDP bill up to 40% by stripping the glamour away from computers and treating them as another business resource. Look outside for solutions to data processing problems. Investigate acquiring software packages as alternatives to internal development. Fight the "it wasn't built here" syndrome, which has cost many companies a lot of money. Be willing to change internal procedures to conform to the package, rather than changing the package to conform to internal procedures.

Look for ways to use the computer to "make" rather than save money. One firm we know has each item in its enormous inventory costed out to four decimal places—but knows nothing about the productivity of the workers.

CHANGE THE BASIS OF COMPENSATION. In times of stress, companies often ignore opportunities for improving performance by revising their compensation plans. (It is strange how companies go rigid when times get tough.) Take compensation out of fixed overhead as far as possible and make it a direct cost (administration, production, selling, etc.). Convert as much of compensation as possible to incentives. Remember, you can give anything as long as it brings you more. Don't be cheap with incentives.

MAINTAIN LIQUIDITY. Put as little money as possible into fixed investment. Lease or use installment purchases. Renegotiate long-term liabilities to reduce current cash needs. It usually makes sense to reduce current cash outflows even if you have to increase the total debt balance. Strengthening present liquidity, making use of cash now, and taking advantage of inflation all work for you.

Source: J. K. Lasser & Co.'s Management Services staff.

SELF-PROTECTION CHECKLIST

• Guard against impulse buying. Include in corporate bylaws a stipulation that all purchase decisions over a certain amount are contingent upon approval by a third party. Could be the board of directors, a partner, a departmental head, etc. (If the business is a proprietorship, there is some built-in protection: Individuals have a three-day period to rescind any purchase.)
• During negotiations, don't hesitate to be unreasonable—especially in the beginning. You may have to compromise in the end, but more often than not, the compromise will be closer to the "unreasonable" position than if you had been reasonable from the beginning. But great care must be taken,

including concessions on minor points, to remain courteous and allow the other fellow to save face.
• Have the *outside accountant* compute: (1) Return on investment, (2) accounts receivable turnover, (3) inventory turnover. The in-house accountant generally reflects management's thinking and produces information to support it.
• Set up an *advisory* board of directors. Most people are honored to be asked to serve. Their expert advice can be invaluable.
• Use the credit bank is offering, even if it's not needed. This will produce interest expense, but it can also ensure quick money availability when most needed.
• Join local and national trade associations. They offer a wealth of information on competitors, aggregate sales figures, new products and services, and trends.
• Have your spouse work in the business for at least three or four weeks a year. This provides for a stand-in if something takes you out of commission for a while.

HOW TO RESOLVE A DIFFICULT ORGANIZATIONAL CONFLICT

If there's a conflict within your organization between two departments, for example, and it hasn't been resolved through regular channels, try this procedure:

Set up a meeting between major

participants in the two conflicting groups, ideally in a neutral location. Limit the groups to no more than a dozen from each side. The meeting should be conducted by an outside consultant or by another manager not tied to either group. Each group meets by itself first and draws up a list of five complaints about what the other does that results in conflict.

The complaints must meet two requirements: (1) One side cannot tell the other side what they should do or how they should be running things— only what they are doing that causes conflict. (2) The complaints shouldn't be a recital of past history or future speculation, but should relate to what is happening right now.

Each group numbers the five complaints in order of importance. Each group chooses one person to speak for it and another to check that the other side keeps to the rules. After each draws up its list, it should also list the other group's possible complaints.

Then the two sides come together to discuss their complaints. Probably each will have the same complaints about the other and will guess accurately what the other will complain about. Both may be trying to deal with the same things.

After discussion, the groups meet individually again to write down how and when they will alter what they did that caused the conflict or why certain things cannot be changed.

Next, another joint meeting to (1) Agree on these changes and (2) set up further meetings to discuss the progress of the changes.

Source: Donald G. Livingston, Electronic Associates, Inc., West Long Branch, N.J., in *Personnel Magazine.*

MATRIX MANAGEMENT— WHEN IT WORKS

Now may be the time to switch from a traditional pyramidal table of organization to a matrix management system, in which employees report both to a functional manager and to one or more project managers.

The switch might help you cope with a recession, but even if it can't, changeovers are easier when business is slow, and it could make your company a stronger and more flexible contender.

How do you know you need it? Look for these signs:
• You are satisfied with technical skills, but projects are still far short of time, cost, or other goals.
• Projects are accomplished on time, but quality of performance is irregular.
• Talented specialists feel exploited or misused.
• Squabbling occurs frequently among technical groups over failures to meet specifications or deadlines.

Will it work? Historically, matrix management is successful when an organization's output comprises primarily complex, short-run products; when speed is required to complete an innovative design; when a variety of sophisticated skills are required for a product; when the market place or a single customer demands rapid major changes in design.

Setting it up: First, diagnose the problem with formal questionnaires, group discussions, and individual interviews with key personnel. Later, hold a broad one- or two-day meeting with everyone involved, and, if suitable, seek a commitment to the new concept from them.

If the commitment is made, use the information you gathered during the diagnosis phase to spell out roles and responsibilities.

For more information: *Managing Large Systems: Organization for the Future*, by Sayles and Chandler, Harper & Row, 10 E. 53 St., New York 10022.

MATRIX MANAGEMENT— HOW IT WORKS

The term *matrix management*, unlike many of the buzz words that represent temporary fads or exaggerated gimmicks, has real substance and potential for long-run change in nearly every manager's job.

Put simply, matrix management is an organizational setup in which many employees have more than one boss. They'll have to respond to purposefully *conflicting* demands from at least two kinds of managers. Traditional management thinking associates more-than-one-boss organizations with inept organizational design or just stupidity. However, more and more companies are now recognizing that their business requires multiple bosses and legitimately conflicting objectives on the part of their managers.

In the simple world in which most management theorists grew up, managers were a nice, small, unified group sharing a single goal or two. In the modern organization, diversification and specialization introduce a number of quite self-contained departments, each of which sees the world through its own biased experiences.

In almost every organization I know, the completion of work—whether it's a special project, a production flow, or some service for a client—requires the collaboration and coordination of a number of separate departments. These are typically staffed with some type of functional expert, even professionals, say, in marketing or assembly or computer processing. These same functional groups process work for a number of different internal "users." For example, a market research department will be working on studies for literally dozens of new and existing products.

NEED FOR CONFLICT. Inevitably (and this is where many managers are unrealistic) there *will* be conflicts between the technical standards and work routine needs of each functional group and the needs of the larger work-flow system. Thus, in a consumer goods company getting out new products, the product manager concerned with all the functions associated with the introduction of this new product—research and development, market analysis, production, sales, advertising, pricing—will come up against some work methods and routines in each of those departments he needs that are contrary to the needs of his total program. Thus, continuing our example, market research may have developed consumer-evaluation procedures that require at least six weeks of field testing. Given the competitive situation—or other problems—the product manager responsible for the overall job of getting this new product out and onto the store shelves may not have six weeks to give them for their part of the work.

This is where the conflict comes in —and rightly so.

The group of market researchers assigned to this particular new product start insisting that *their* technical experience tells them that nothing short of six weeks provides valid data, and the product manager says he can only give it four weeks. Good modern management practice says that these negotiations aren't only inevitable but wholesome because top management wants only carefully thought-through— even argued-through—trade-offs between technical excellence and the need for overall effectiveness in moving work along through all the stages involved in completing a total product or project.

In traditional management thinking, there was no need for such trade-offs. Top management could plan everything in advance and make all the technical decisions so work could progress smoothly.

Now, however, there are so many technical and specialized groups involved in the delivery of any product or service (each with its own legitimate voice and viewpoint) that no one manager can make all the coordinating decisions —several must get involved in the decisions.

Further, what one group does impacts every other group. Therefore, the organization introduces total work-flow managers — called project or product or program managers — who crosscut all the specialized groups. That's where the *matrix* comes in. These total work-flow managers have to negotiate among and between and go back and forth to keep the demands of each contributing "expert"

department consistent with the needs of the total product or project.

EFFICIENCY VS. EFFECTIVENESS. In part, this is also the inevitable conflict between efficiency and effectiveness. Every manager has experienced the process by which each group or department evolves a way of doing things that meets its "professional" standards of what's right and its management standards of what's efficient. (These are the routines and practices that are always so hard for the outsider to change or penetrate.) Only through such routinization is it possible for the group to develop reasonable internal solidarity and efficiency.

But this *efficiency* for the small group may not be—and, in fact, usually isn't—consistent with the overall organization's need for total effectiveness. Matrix management is simply recognition that modern organizations require a constant working between groups seeking to maintain their efficiency and sense of professional expertise and the needs of the larger institution for systems effectiveness.

Employees have to get used to being exposed to these conflicting tugs-of-war between their technical boss and the work-flow boss. Managers have to get used to coping with bargaining and trade-offs.

In the modern organization there is no simple, single best way to do anything, no simple plan that is going to work as it has been written down. Instead, there is the need for constant readjustment, trade-off, and negotiation. Matrix management legitimizes what most companies have become and alerts managers to their very new and challenging responsibilities—to keep making trade-offs between efficiency and effectiveness.

Source: Leonard R. Sayles, professor, Columbia Graduate School of Business.

Further reading on matrix management: *Managing Large Systems: Organizations for the Future*, by Sayles and Chandler (Harper & Row, 10 E. 53 St., New York 10022).

ORIGINS OF MOTIVATION

Managers tested in a recent study proved to be motivated by either *affiliation* or *power*. (All managers tested were men; women's characteristics are somewhat different.)

Power managers have the *best* records. But their success varies, depending on whether they're driven by *personal* or *institutionalized* needs.

The *personal-power* manager wants to dominate, is impulsive, sometimes rude, and rejects institutional restraints. Can become a great (and inspirational) leader, but subordinates' loyalty is to him, not the company. If he leaves, the group falls apart.

The *institutionalized-power* manager is a "company man" and excels in creating a good work climate. He is mature, less defensive, and sticks to the rules (making sure his people do the same). Excellent type to lead morale- and productivity-raising activities. *Drawback:* He's the most likely to develop high blood pressure or heart problems.

Affiliative managers need fellowship and make the worst bosses. *Reasons:* They make poor and inconsistent decisions because in their desire to be liked by subordinates, they put individuals' needs ahead of the group's well-being.

Result: Subordinates become confused; feel their behavior won't necessarily control their future.

Source: Dr. David C. McClelland, Harvard University; David H. Burnham, McBer & Co., Boston, in *Psychology Today*.

READING CRITICAL SIGNS

All companies have warning signs: Critical ratios should signal management to step in and reassess policy.

Example: Most firms have a reserve for bad debts; it may be fixed at 2% of gross sales—a number determined by historical experience. But what happens to the ratio when the price of a commodity suddenly surges? Now the historical connection between volume and bad debts breaks down.

Practical problem: In an inflationary economy, what happens to *overhead*, the administrative cost of doing business, which management ties to each department's costs? Management overhead may rise much more *slowly* than production costs and raw material prices. Yet, management's budgeting of overhead—tied as it is to surging outside costs—will soar also.

Impact: The danger is that overhead expenses will balloon to accommodate the higher prices—even though the extra spending isn't necessary to operate the business.

Key error: Assuming that inflation, or recession proportionately falls on all things. It doesn't.

This type problem isn't limited to overhead costs. It frequently impacts research and development, warehousing, product and raw materials inspection, etc.—all situations in which funds are allocated proportionately, measuring total volume of the business or the costs of purchasing raw materials.

Warning: A typical large company has literally hundreds of such critical signals, and managers are trained to react only when one of the signals deviates from its standard—a level set by historical experience. But under the current business environment, those standards are no longer valid because the connection between the signals and the outside world has been severed.

What to do first: Pick out the handful that have the biggest impact on business, and correct them.

Remember: It may not be practical to correct all the outmoded ratios now being used.

Source: Roger Mesznik, professor, Baruch College, City University of New York.

WHAT CORPORATE PLANNING SHOULD DO

- Help the chief executive formulate strategies and chart the basic course of the business and its separate divisions.
- Determine and analyze new possibilities for the company.
- Check on and analyze the use of capital.
- Recommend how capital should be allocated.
- Assist top management in analyzing the effect of corporate research and development and the costs involved.
- Check on and analyze the fore-

casting at the divisional level, and furnish assistance and guides to divisional planners.
- Produce vital information on the fundamental external changes and impending trends which the company must react to.

Source: Donald R. Schoen, Philip Medical Systems, Inc.

PLANNING FOR OPPORTUNITIES

While major corporations spend millions on economic and social trend analysis to spot future threats and opportunities for long-range planning, another approach that can be useful to smaller companies is a one-day meeting of key people. How it's done:

PHASE ONE. Get participants to talk freely and develop a list of possible developments over the next 10 years that could affect the business: Legal, legislative, technological, economic, political, social, demographic—anything that can increase or decrease sales and earnings. *Icebreaker:* Have a professional futurist (or a business university marketing professor) speak for the first hour. Good chance he won't say anything *directly* useful, but he will unlock imaginations and start ideas flowing.

PHASE TWO. Write down all the possible developments suggested in the brainstorming session, discard those that don't fall into one of the following categories:
- Near-term developments that can

increase or decrease sales or earnings 10% or more within the next full fiscal year.

- Midterm developments that could change earnings at least 50% within five years.

- Long-term events that could eliminate a major market or at least triple earnings within 10 years.

PHASE THREE. Assess the near-term threats and opportunities. If the development has less than 10% probability of occurring, discard it or postpone considering it until next year. If probability is from 10% to 33%, after seeking further information to confirm the probability estimate, assign someone to develop a contingency plan. (Once you have approved the plan, have him monitor the situation and signal you when he thinks it is time to activate the plan.) Events with probability higher than 33% are handled in the same way, but as probability rises, you reach a point (no higher than 66%) when you must assume the event will occur. In such a situation it is best to begin at once your defense against the threat or exploitation of the opportunity.

PHASE FOUR. Assess the midterm developments—those which could expand or shrink earnings 50% within five years. Estimate the earliest possible time each development could begin to affect your business. Then figure the time needed to respond. If the response time is less than the time it will take for the development to have an effect, postpone consideration for the following year. For developments that could occur within response time, calculate the "50/50" year (the year when the event is beyond your response time); put consideration off until the following year. If the 50/50 year falls within response time, assign an executive to develop a response.

PHASE FIVE. Long-term threats and opportunities which could eliminate a major market or triple earnings within 10 years are too critical to ignore. If the development's 50/50 year occurs beyond your response time, assign someone to develop a tentative plan. If the 50/50 year falls within your response time, get an appropriate plan operative on a crash basis. The risk involved means so much to your company that you have to act as if the forecast is a certainty.

Source: Merritt L. Kasten, *Long-Range Planning for Your Business* (Amacom, American Management Assns., 135 W. 50 St., New York 10020).

LINEAR THINKING TRAPS

A common mistake in business and economic forecasting: Linear thinking. Forecasts which project current trends to forecast future developments fail because they don't include the additional unanticipated events which intervene to alter the linear progression of the trend. *Example:* The widely forecast capital shortage for 1978 and 1979, which did not occur because that forecast failed to take into account slower economic growth rates—among other factors. Better forecasting should concentrate on taking all factors into account to try to predict turning points in trends instead of where a linear progression leads.

THERE ARE TIMES TO USE UNORTHODOX MANAGERS

He may be the kind of dynamo your company needs right now. The main question is whether the company can afford to settle for just a good executive or whether it's at a stage of growth where it should have a *great* executive. The trouble with that special person is that he or she is frequently unorthodox and rebellious. But this type of person has a wealth of ideas, a passion for improvement, fearlessness in implementing ideas and programs, and a willingness to take risks. If the company is still in an embryonic stage, it may need this kind of thinking. In fact, if the company is mature, it may need invigoration.

HOW TO END ISOLATION AT THE TOP

The life of an *isolated* executive can be full of surprises—none of them pleasant. Here's how to prevent problems from building up unknown to you until they explode:
- Cultivate the will to hear bad news without losing your temper or behaving punitively. Every subordinate should be able to make an occasional mistake without drawing an *unreasonable* reaction from his superior. Recognize this, and you'll hear about problems while they're still manageable. Fail, and bad news will be secret until too late.

- Leave your office to spend time talking with first-line management and *non*management people. Budget a fixed weekly or monthly amount of time for this. But pick your spots and the timing of your visits at random to get a valid sample.
- Pick a group of people, go to their part of the operation, and conduct a review. You might follow an order through the production cycle and out the door, for example, looking for bottlenecks and problems that your managers may be unaware of. Or concentrate on some aspect of their operation, such as housekeeping or safety. The point is *contact*.
- Meet periodically with groups of your people to discuss operations or problems, looking not for decisions but to get to know people and let them get to know you.

CHECKLIST: MAKE OR BUY OR START?

Questions the company should answer before starting a new operation, buying an existing one, or considering whether to make or buy components:
- Is the fun of growing important to us?
- Could we gain a psychological lift by doing something new?
- Are we well organized?
- Do our managers have real authority and responsibility?
- Are our present operations going well?
- Are we highly profitable?
- Do we have a good information system and controls?

- Do we have budgets—good ones?
- Do we do long-range planning on a regular, organized basis?
- Have we been able to make major decisions without heartache or excess time?
- Has our record on major decisions been good?
- Do our key people have time to devote to new projects?
- Do we have real strength in every area of our business?
- Are the owners willing to risk part of what they now have for growth?
- Do we have funds which can be used without jeopardizing the present business?
- Are our people adaptable enough to be able to work with a new group?
- Are we free from overcentralized departments which have become empires, making cooperation difficult?
- Do we have available skills in research, in investigating other properties, and in negotiating?
- Do we have excess managerial manpower?
- When we try something, do we see it through?
- Do we get rid of proven losers?
- Are we able to plan and organize a project from scratch?
- Do we have available a manager with an entrepreneurial approach?
- Do we also have available a manager who can continue operations once the launch has been made?
- Do we have available skilled manpower in areas where it will be needed?
- Do we know how to test and research a new idea?
- Can we get information about the areas of business we don't know?

Source: James Kobak, *Folio Magazine*, 37 W. 57 St., New York 10019.

HOW DOES YOUR COMPANY MEASURE UP?

Top managers tend to think their company's strength is in its organization. Middle and lower managers more often see the strength coming from a particular function, say marketing, finance, technical skills.

But both groups measure their company's *strengths* by its *past* experience. They measure *weaknesses* by what they read about other companies and what consultants tell them.

What's too often missing?

Measuring the company *against the competition's performance.*

The correct question to ask: *Is our company stronger or weaker than our opponent?*

Source: Howard H. Stevenson, associate professor, Harvard University Graduate School of Business, in *Sloan Management Review.*

MORALE

Employers are building morale by arranging with suppliers to allow discounts on purchases made by employees.

These bargain prices affect goods and services outside the company's own product line. Most popular products are household goods, furnishings, appliances, and hobby crafts.

While this plan enables employees to meet rising living costs, in effect it is a means of increasing wages without tax. It costs nothing for the company to operate, and cooperating suppliers benefit from a major increase in customers.

WHEN NOT TO USE CONSULTANTS

Hidden motives that make the hiring of a consultant wasteful:

Serving as a scapegoat for unpopular or unfruitful decisions.

"Shaking things up," even if he doesn't accomplish anything substantial.

Counterbalancing deficiencies of management on a long-term basis.

Lending outside weight to a management decision that's already been made.

Helping to enhance the company's image.

Source: *May Trends*, George S. May International Co., 111 S. Washington St., Park Ridge, Ill. 60068.

THINK SESSIONS

Pick members for *expertise*, not necessarily creativity. Feel free to select members beyond their usual work areas.

Before the meeting: Distribute written ground rules, including the problem, exemplary solutions, and the like. Encourage members to discuss them with others.

When to meet: In the morning. Never on Friday or Monday. Choose a room unfamiliar to group members. It should be no larger than necessary to accommodate the group comfortably. Team spirit tends to dissipate in a large room.

The leader should create a relaxed, uncritical mood where zany ideas can surface without drawing ego-bruising comment. And he should make sure the quieter members get a chance to talk.

Follow-up: Don't evaluate anything until a few days after the meeting. Then review the notes; pick out the most promising ideas. Appoint a *new* committee—with *new* people—to evaluate them.

NEW FACES FOR FREE ENTERPRISE

We are witnessing the emergence of a new corporate philosophy, a philosophy based on the acceptance of these rather startling premises:

• Any corporation of size is no longer private business—certainly not in the traditional sense.

• The larger the share of market controlled by a corporation, the smaller its status as a private enterprise.

• A corporation's responsibilities to its employees and to its stockholders are best met by catering to the public's rising tide of expectations, rather than by resisting this irreversible trend.

• The free enterprise philosophy no longer serves business as an iron curtain.

• Just as the public's own right to privacy has regularly been diminished, so will the corporate right to privacy continue to diminish.

• Business is a means to an end for society and *not* an end in itself. Therefore, private business must act in concert with the broad public interest and serve the objectives of society, or *it probably won't survive.*

HOW TO SELECT THE RIGHT RISK

The broad outlook: Management must decide boundaries for growth. How big are the rewards wanted from investing company resources? What kinds of businesses can produce these rewards for the company?

The close-up look: Does the new venture fit in with the company's marketing experience, philosophy, and capabilities? Does the venture base itself on the existing technical capabilities of the company? Does it meet the company's financial goals?

Most important: The facts of the venture itself.

Source: Mark Hanan, *Venture Marketing* (McGraw-Hill 1221 Ave. of the Americas, New York 10020).

WHY EMPLOYEES RESIST CHANGE

First step in a smooth transition to a new way of doing things is to get the support of employees involved in the change. Employees not convinced of need for change will be skeptical

of *any* proposed move. They'll often try to sabotage it—probably subconsciously.

Convince them that there is a problem and it affects their own individual services or performance. *Example:* A system that makes extra paperwork or slows delivery of paychecks.

Show employees personal advantages they will gain if the current way of operating is changed and improved.

INCREASED EMPLOYEE ROLE IN DECISION-MAKING CAN GO SOUR

If the shift from hard-line order giving to increased employee participation in decision making is instituted too abruptly, or if decision sharing doesn't suit the employees, there can be *real* problems.

Before shifting the decision-making process, management should ask these four questions about employees—as a group and individually:

• *How will they react to independence?* Some employees want direction, are uncomfortable without management confirmation of their plans. Others are too impulsive and need restraint.

• *Are they psychologically mature enough for added responsibility?* Some see it as a recognition of their ability. Others will resent it as a management effort to "pass the buck."

• *Can they tolerate ambiguity?* Some workers become anxious unless they receive concrete, detailed orders. Even clear guidelines aren't enough.

• *Do they understand and endorse*

the goals of the company? (Profits, costs, customer relations and the like.) Without that decision-sharing will fail.

THE OPEN DOOR

Open-door policies may be good for bosses of small companies, but it just doesn't work for top management of larger firms. *Reasons:* Employees are reluctant to impose on the boss. Policy implies the boss is an open and jovial guy. If the boss is not, in fact, an easygoing fellow, the contradiction only creates resentment among employees. Also, nobody wishes to be the bearer of bad news, especially to the boss. *Result:* The chief executive who thinks open door works is only going to hear what his employees think he wants to hear.

In fact, the policy often embarrasses employees who think they should drop in on the boss and be sociable with him. They will therefore often avoid going by the boss' door altogether, taking alternative routes to other parts of the office.

Source: Ari Kiev, psychiatrist, Cornell University.

MANAGING CREATIVE PEOPLE

- Be generous with personal recognition.
- Set deadlines to overcome inertia, but don't do it arbitrarily. Work out a schedule with the employee.
- Maintain contact, and let artists, writers, and the like know how they are doing. It's difficult to create anything without feedback.
- Don't panic when creative people don't seem to be working. Creativity often occurs in bursts between bouts of idleness.
- Be flexible about office rules and tardiness, even if it means defending your creative staff against attacks from other quarters of the company.
- Listen sympathetically, and speak frankly about the work. Creative people are often at their best when their creativity is challenged, rather than their economic security or their egos.
- Tolerate failure. Nothing works every time. If you don't include margin for error, you will stifle initiative. Leave room in your schedule for regrouping after a creative failure or two.

EMPLOYMENT CONTRACT: A TWO-WAY STREET

A typical employment contract defines the job, the terms and conditions of employment, and provides that when employment is terminated, the employee will not compete with the employer within a designated territory and period of time.

If the employer changes the working conditions and the employee leaves, the employer is *not* going to be able to enforce the non-compete covenant. That was the ruling in a recent case in which the employer reduced the agreed commission rates, took away a credit card used for customer entertainment expenses, cut the gasoline allowance, and began charging the employee with customers' bad debts and the cost of sales materials.

LETTING SUBORDINATES RATE THE MANAGER

Consider having your subordinates rate your performance. It may be less painful than you think, and you'll probably learn some things about yourself as a manager that would improve your career.

Here's how it's done at RCA's Missile & Surface Radar Division:

The manager, accompanied by a training officer, meets with his subordinates and explains that he wants their opinion of his performance. Key issues to be stressed: (1) The program is voluntary; if some people object, it won't be carried out. (2) The staff is guaranteed complete anonymity; no opportunity for reprisals for poor ratings.

Next, the training officer mails each subordinate a questionnaire in which he rates the manager on a series of characteristics on a scale from 1 to 10.

Later, the training officer reviews each questionnaire with the subordinate who filled it out, makes a series of notes of his impressions, and gives the notes to the subordinate to study and approve. Purpose—to eliminate snap judgments or errors of communication.

Meanwhile, the training officer spends as much time with the manager as possible, accompanying him to meetings, for example, as an observer. *Purpose:* To clarify in his own mind what he has heard from the subordinates.

When all the ratings are in, the trainer summarizes them and discusses them with the manager. They are weighted to reflect the number of persons who concurred in each opinion. After talking things over, the manager decides which negative factors he wants to change and which aren't worth bothering with. (One, for example, was found to be lacking in innovation. He decided he simply wasn't an innovative person and his subordinates would have to live with it.)

Final step: The manager meets with subordinates again, reviews the ratings, and discusses which can be improved and which can't.

HOW TO GET THE MOST FROM CONSULTANTS

Don't hire a management consultant unless:

Clear-cut objectives are agreed upon. (*Best method:* Set up specific questions to be answered.)

The objectives include short-range as well as long-range goals. That tests the consultant's performance early.

You are reasonably certain the consultant's recommendations can be acted upon.

The consultant has been made aware, as explicitly as possible, of what internal resistance can be expected. (And both company and consultant agree on how to handle it.)

The consultant shows respect for the talent and know-how of corporate personnel. (*Aim:* Collaboration, not competition.)

The consultant agrees to suggest methods of implementation *as well as* ultimate goals.

The consultant is used as a counselor, not a surrogate manager. (The consultant can help managers do their jobs better, but he can't do their jobs for them.)

Source: Robert H. Schaffer, Robert H. Schaffer & Assoc., in *S.A.M. Advanced Management Journal.*

TRAPS TO AVOID IN USING CONSULTANTS

THE GO-GO SYNDROME. A company has a new-business idea (acquisition, new product, or service) and wants an impartial outsider to analyze the venture. The client uses the word *impartial*—but the message conveyed is usually quite different: *There's nothing we want more than to get into this business.* It takes an unusual consultant to tell a client what he doesn't want to hear, especially if the consultant's future business relationship depends on his saying "yes." So he fudges the risk analysis, picks the rosiest-looking market potential, and estimates low on expenses and capital needs.

THE GURU SYNDROME. The company seeks out the best consultant for a particular problem. He's internationally known. Once hired, the manager

who brought him in feels relieved and contentedly leaves the problem in the hands of the expert.

At the extreme, the manager's critical thinking becomes paralyzed—*after all, who can question the top person in the field?* In most cases, the manager's reaction is something less than that, but there's still a drop-off in judgment.

THE JET AGE SYNDROME. Top management feels that the company is lagging behind the rest of the business world in applying *sophisticated* business techniques and equipment.

The most common: Computer services contracted before a hard-nosed benefits analysis.

THE SOFTWARE PACKAGE SYNDROME. The manager determines that he has a "problem." Actually, he does not know what the real problem is—he's nearly always getting "problem" confused with "symptom." He finds a consultant who specializes in that "problem." And before the initial interview is over, the consultant whips out a complete solution (which, he contends, has worked marvelously for scores of other clients).

The logic of using this prepackaged solution is hard to refute: After all, why reinvent the wheel?

The truth, however, is that rarely are corporate problems so similar that prepackaged solutions work. The *symptoms* may be similar, but not the *causes.*

THE BROAD VIEW SYNDROME. This disorder is perhaps the most damaging. It often occurs when a well-known consultant is hired—but it can happen even with lesser lights. In this case, only upper management people are consulted during the problem-definition (diagnosis) stage of the assignment. This is done intentionally by the client in order to avoid bogging the expensive consultant down in a mass of extraneous data, data that the lower-level staff might thrust on him.

Result: The consultant will have serious trouble finding the real problem—and may actually believe that the problem as interpreted by top management is the one that needs treatment. A self-fulfilling prophecy.

HOW TO AVOID THE TRAPS. When a consultant is being considered for an assignment, conduct a detailed interview. If the consultant seems rigid (he has the answer before he has the problem), it's a good clue to keep looking. Some consultants ask to be paid for these interviews. There is no fixed rule on such payments. It depends on how hungry the consultant is or how much potential he sees in your company's business.

• If the consultant wants a contract that ties together both the *diagnosis* and the *solution*, be wary. By linking the two, you guarantee that his bias will guide him into finding a particular problem (which he believes he can solve). It's better to insist that he be paid a fixed hourly fee for the diagnosis. On the average, a good diagnosis for a company that is physically situated in one location and in which everyone is accessible takes about two weeks.

• Require progress reports—not to "look over his shoulder" and second-guess him, but to be ready to offer any extra assistance or information that he may need.

• Make it easy for the consultant to learn as much as possible about the company. The more he knows, the better the chance of a workable solution to the problem.

• If the consultant's report isn't clear, get an explanation. All too often, consultants couch their comments in jargon (to protect themselves, since the jargon is just a way of saying nothing specific). Insist that the report be in clear, everyday business language and that it can be easily understood.

Source: James Moore, internal consultant on the staff of Gulf & Western.

The wise executive never fails to ask questions just because he's afraid of seeming ignorant. Answers often provide *nuances* that are more important than facts.

BUSINESS MANAGER AND HIS ESSENTIAL ADVISERS

Every effective manager should have a solid backstop of professionals with whom he can consult regularly on business problems and strategy. *Who they might be:* A lawyer familiar with business practice. An accountant from a firm that handles businesses of comparable size. A bank officer from the bank where the business has most of its deposits, gets most of its loans. An insurance agent who is a chartered property and casualty underwriter. A consultant who specializes in personnel practices could also be useful.

Source: Leon A. Danco, president, University Services Institute, Cincinnati.

COST CONTROL

HOW TO CUT STAFF AND INCREASE BUSINESS

Top management of Norske Folke, a Norwegian insurance company, was committed to an internal organization-wide effort to change. Prior to the big three-year push, an atmosphere was created to get employees to view change positively, as an opportunity to learn and get a more satisfying job, not negatively as something to be avoided. Management promised that no one would lose his job as a result of changes. Staff reductions were to be achieved through normal attrition.

The big change over the three-year period was based on three simple principles:

1. All the work done should be handled as simply as possible, should be sensible and useful.

2. Superfluous or wasted work is not worthwhile.

3. Individuals are responsible for their own work.

Ten percent of the workers were trained in administrative change techniques. About 25% of the departmental heads were released from normal tasks for one year to work on implementation of the program.

Wall charts coded for tasks were used to describe the flow of paper work through the company. All were encouraged to participate and ask questions in work analysis meetings: Why is this done? Is this a waste of time? Can this process be speeded up? Do we need all these data? The wall charts allowed everyone to participate. By seeing how one's job fit into the total picture, individuals were stimulated to think creatively about their jobs and suggest improvements.

Suggestions were classified for immediate action or further discussion. Immediate changes were incorporated into the wall chart, forms were changed and redesigned, data flow was redirected, tasks were redelegated, and everyone was involved.

Source: *International Management.*

HOW TO CUT STAFF

Two alternative approaches to bringing overstaffing in line as painlessly as possible:

1. *Reduction by attrition:* In a union shop faced with the prospect of forced layoffs, no union leader will block the offer of using attrition to cut back on payroll. Management frequently doesn't bring it up because it expects that unions will fight to protect their membership. The fear is unfounded—most unions understand the choice and accept the less painful one. But don't expect attrition to be as effective in a recession as in boom times, when job switching is more frequent.

2. *Voluntary layoffs:* Call in department heads. Ask them to survey their

staffs to find out which workers would accept layoffs (in effect, exchange paychecks for unemployment insurance). Surprising number of workers (especially low-pay staffers and women) will jump at the chance. Low-pay people and married women (with no deductions) may do almost as well with unemployment checks.

Source: Mitchell Fein, labor consultant.

HOW TO CUT THE COST OF COMPANY CARS

• *Use smaller cars:* Based on 10,000 miles a year, a compact car costs about 10% less per mile to run than a full-size car and about 7% less per mile than an intermediate.

• *The more a car is used, the less it costs:* An intermediate driven 15,000 miles per year costs 7% less per mile than one driven only 10,000 miles a year. Driven 25,000 miles, it costs about 12% less per mile than the 10,000-mile car.

CHECKLIST FOR COST-CUTTING

Measure your company's cost-cutting program against this checklist:

• Does your company have an inventory control system?

• Has it been reviewed or altered to reflect changes in costs of money and materials?

• Do you know your current order costs, carrying costs, shortage costs?

• Have you reviewed your space layout in the last two years?

• Do you know what proportion of total space is used for production, administration, aisles and hallways, active storage, dead storage?

• Is nonproduction space fully used?

• Could you reorganize your use of space to allow some area of your business to be sublet or otherwise used in a profitable way?

• Are any office tasks performed manually that could be automated?

• If you use computers, do you know at what point it's cheaper to use a service organization than to have your own machine?

Source: J. K. Lasser & Co., CPAs.

PRODUCTION COST CUTTING

Trim manufacturing costs with a *systematic appraisal of purchases and labor.*

Begin by setting up a list of *every* purchased item used in the end product. Then:

• Find out unit costs.

• Multiply unit costs by quantity of each item used in end product to get the *total cost* of each purchased item in the final product.

• Compile list of all purchased items in descending order of cost.

You'll probably find up to 85% of overall purchase cost is contained within first 5% to 10% of items on your list. Seeking lower-priced equivalents for *these* items (which may include some very low-priced items used in great quantity) will have greatest impact on cost reduction.

Apply same formula to labor performed in each step of manufacturing cycle for a complete cost-reduction program.

NO-LONGER-FREE SERVICES

Many companies have begun charging for previously free services such as after-hours or weekend assistance, engineering, special deliveries. (Other companies are cutting out the special services wherever possible.)

Key in deciding whether or not to charge: Customer's past history. 54% of *distributors* recently surveyed said some customers abused 24-hour or emergency services. It's those who can probably expect to pay the next time around, while "good" customers won't have to.

Innovative approach by one distributor may discourage abuses without losing business. Cunningham Bearing Corp., Houston, prepares a *value-added invoice.* It lists major services rendered, plus an estimated price for each, along with a total. At the bottom of the invoice is printed "No Charge."

LITTLE SAVINGS

Walk-through inspection of your plant can save dollars. Look for little things. Are small parts, like washers or bolts, lying around? How come? What about cleanup rags? Too many in sight could mean they're used carelessly. Check the scrap heap for salvageable parts or excess spoilage. What about leaky taps and hoses? Drips of fuel or solvent or whatever cost money—in various ways.

Even if you find very little, the fact that someone was looking establishes management's views on waste among employees.

• *Employment agency fee refunds:* Do you have a system to identify terminated new hires so the fee you paid the employment agency to find them can be refunded? If your turnover is high, unpaid refunds can add up.

• Are dividends or interest payments you receive from invested funds posted *immediately* by your bank? Some banks have been known to delay posting for up to 30 days.

• *Unbilled orders:* Check your invoice logs to make certain that every order generates an invoice. Slipups can be costly.

WHEN A CONSULTANT SAVES MONEY

• Company needs competence in a particular area, but cannot justify taking on a full-time staffer with the needed knowledge.

• Management must get a job done quickly. A consultant can supply leadership and staff temporarily without diluting existing company efforts.

• Company is fighting for survival. A consultant can save critical time in identifying opportunities, rebuilding competitive position.

ANNUAL MEETINGS

MAKING YOUR ANNUAL MEETING PAY OFF

Most annual meetings are counterproductive—a chore for management and a bore for shareholders. That's shortsighted. Annual meetings are marketing tools—if used correctly.

Positive results that a well-planned annual meeting can yield: Improved stockholder loyalty. Receptivity to any future financing. Strengthened defense against corporate raiders. New customers for company products or services. Voter support against government encroachment.

Nine ways to make your next annual meeting more productive:

1. Use personal letter from the chairman or president to solicit proxy votes.

2. Invite press coverage. Provide special accommodations for the media, and schedule a press conference or interviews with top officers.

3. Give away samples of company products or suitable accessories.

4. Cultivate community relations in a small- to medium-size city by holding your meeting on a weekday evening or Saturday morning. Open it up to company employees and the general public as well as to stockholders.

5. If your company is a sprawling giant, schedule regional meetings—semi-annually or quarterly—in addition to the mandatory annual blowout.

6. Develop an active, interesting meeting agenda.

7. Put your question-and-answer program on TV. If you're a big employer in a small town, the local TV outlet may be willing to broadcast the Q&A as a public service. And if you're a major firm with holders all over the country, consider a closed-circuit showing at satellite locations.

8. Have a lunch or reception following the meeting.

9. Parlay tangible benefits and incremental goodwill by distributing a *post-meeting report* along with your first-quarter financial results and a succinct statement of management's outlook for the rest of the year.

LET THE CPA ANSWER THE STOCKHOLDERS

A dangerous gray area is developing in the relationship between a company's management, the board, minority shareholders, and the firm's accountants. The problem involves the treatment of expenses, fringe benefits, and possible dubious payments. It isn't uncommon for management, especially in smaller companies, to run the firm without much real involvement of the board. Yet, such matters are the board's ultimate responsibility. And, if the trend in CPA accountability continues, they will be the legal watchdogs.

Advice: Invite your CPAs to annual

meetings, and let them discuss informally anything that's making the shareholders uncomfortable. It is better than preparing a formal management report.

ANSWER THESE QUESTIONS BEFORE THE ANNUAL MEETING

Challenges to corporate policy from individual stockholders, institutional investors, consumer groups getting more common and sharper. Now SEC is opening the way for more disclosure in proxy statements, even more questions in the future. Management should prepare itself to face informed questioning at annual meetings.

LIQUIDITY. Does the company have enough cash or readily obtainable credit to operate normally during the coming year? Is dividend coverage adequate, and do you expect to comply with debt covenants? Will the company be sufficiently liquid to take advantage of prompt-payment incentives? How will money market conditions impact planned debt, equity offerings, or other financial alternatives? Also, will you be able to stick with commitments for capital expenditures or replacement programs?

INFLATION. How will profit margins and overall profitability be affected by inflation? If the company has long-term sales contracts or private-label agreements, how will these be affected by continued inflation? What will be the impact of labor settlements and other cost-modifying considerations on operating results? If inventories are significant, why was (or wasn't) another accounting method adopted?

RECESSION. What is your analysis of the impact of the recession on anticipated sales and profits? How does your company stack up against others in the industry in terms of key indicators? Are you planning to cut back staff or discontinue any operations? If so, how will these impact financial results and future operational efficiency? Is your backlog real? Have orders subject to cancellation been confirmed? What's the financial condition of single-source suppliers and major customers? Have you lowered credit standards for potential customers or had to add incentives to maintain collections from present customers?

FINANCIAL DISCLOSURE. Are your interim financial reports consistent with the annual report? Has the company consulted with independent auditors during the year about the impact of new accounting rules and disclosure requirements, and have the auditors reviewed quarterly financial statements prior to issuance? Do you plan to publish earnings forecasts this year?

STEWARDSHIP OF CORPORATE ASSETS. How well-qualified is the audit committee? Does it meet regularly with the independent auditors, and do they otherwise have direct access to each other? What measures have been taken to guarantee that all business dealings conducted with outside directors are kept at arm's length and that officials have no conflicting outside interests?

TROUBLE SHOOTING

CONFLICT OF INTEREST

According to one survey, 11% of companies had conflict-of-interest problems, but *purchasing* personnel involved in only *one out of six* cases.

Big offenders: Management. Operating departments (especially engineering and their sole-source requirements).

Protection: Competitive bidding. Internal audits. External audits.

IRS AND ARM'S-LENGTH DEALINGS

If two corporations that are under common control deal at less than arm's length, the Internal Revenue Service may reallocate any item of income or expense between them.

Two electrical contracting corporations were engaged in the same type of business, but in different geographical areas. When one corporation needed money, the other lent it *without* charging interest. The IRS said it would increase the lending company's income by interest at the going rate. The companies argued that the rule for reallocating less-than-arm's-length income didn't apply, since they were *not* under common control. Nobody

owned more than 39% of the stock of either company. None of the stockholders were related to each other.

"Control," for most tax purposes, means more than 50% of the stock. But according to the IRS, for the purpose of arm's-length transactions, control doesn't mean any particular percentage. It doesn't refer to stock ownership at all. *The only test:* Are two or more corporations in effect under common control for management purposes? Here, two individuals made all decisions for both of the companies on a continuing basis. Minority shareholders took no part in the running of the corporations. In every practical sense of the word, the two dominant shareholders had 100% control over both corporations. *Ruling:* The IRS could set up an appropriate interest rate and add this amount to the lending corporation's taxable income.

Source: Collins Electrical Co., Inc., 67 T.C., No. 75, 3/9/77.

PENALTY FOR SEIZING CORPORATE OPPORTUNITIES

A director or officer can't seize for himself a business opportunity that belongs to his company or which should have been offered to the company. The law on the subject varies from state to state, but the majority view is that each case is to be decided on its own with a view to determining what protection of the corporation is called for in the particular situation.

The vagueness of this and other judicial standards makes it imperative that an officer or director proceed carefully whenever he has a mind to seize anything resembling a corporate opportunity.

A recent case in which directors beat the rap: Their corporation, which owned a golf course, considered buying some land next to the course, but decided against it. A year later, the directors bought it on their own, resold it (making a handsome profit), and were sued by a minority shareholder, who claimed that the profits belonged to the corporation.

In deciding in favor of the directors the court held that the corporation had turned down the opportunity, that there was no corporate opportunity at the time of their later purchase, and that the company was in the business of operating a golf course, not buying real estate.

AVOID THE RISK.
• Make full disclosure of the intended action (in writing) to the board of directors after weighing the possibility that the board may feel pressured to seize an opportunity for the corporation or otherwise open the matter to a shareholder.
• Show company's inability (financial or legal) to capitalize on the opportunity.
• The board might formulate policies inconsistent with the opportunity.
• Negotiate and set up the deal outside the office—and not on company time.

• In a small corporation it may be possible to get an agreement with all shareholders which, if made with full disclosure, will prevent them from later changing their minds and attacking the seizure.

Source: Farber v. Servan Land Co., U.S.D.C.S.D. Fla., 393 F. Supp. 633, 1975.

PRIORITIES IN TOP-LEVEL BUDGET CUTS

When operating results start looking sour, budget cuts are inevitable in the executive suite. More often than not, though, the first cut is made in executive development programs—subsidized education programs, in-house management programs, etc. These cuts are made long before the perquisites are cut: Country club dues, executive dining rooms, etc. *That's a serious mistake*—because it's cutting into programs that affect the long-range continuity of the corporation. A different priority should be assigned to programs by the chief operating officer.

The easiest way is to swap—one fringe benefit for a less expensive one. This won't eliminate the pain, but it'll make it more palatable. *Example:* An executive may lose company payment of country club dues, but you replace that with, say, *extra medical insurance*, adding little to the premium, but maybe equally attractive to the executive in terms of *potential* benefit.

The areas most hurt by recession: Stock options, profit-sharing plans, etc. If it's necessary to keep such inducements to avoid losing your top people, consider a complete revamp of your compensation packages. Move to outright stock-purchase plans (subsidized by the company) and performance share plans (where you give stock as an incentive for achieving goals). They'll cost you no immediate dollars, only long-run dollars in terms of stock dilution and dividends.

Source: William H. Cash, principal, Cresap, McCormick & Paget, management consultants, 245 Park Ave., New York 10017.

CUTTING BACK SUCCESSFULLY

Top management has experience in *building* business—but not in *cutting back* to alleviate the problems of recession. There are no MBA courses in *undoing* to manage the crisis of a sharp decline in business activity.

Impact: Too many managers panic and violate the cardinal rules: *They try to cut across the board and fail to audit results.* As a result, they too frequently *fail* to trim back sufficient fat from *overhead* and *payroll* and fail to improve *productivity. Worse:* They inadvertently chop programs that shouldn't be reduced or eliminated.

What to do: Start by assigning a task force of operating and staff people —from production, finance, and marketing—to assess the situation. Provide them with guides on how much of a *net* improvement is needed.

Don't tell them to cut production's payroll by X%, or some such costsaving by fiat. Give them a chance to determine *where* and *how* they can cut, how much—in each situation—is necessary to cut, how much can be saved by

improvements.

Procedure: Group the ad hoc task force in their own work area. Make it clear they must act as a team—that only by teamwork and prudence can they achieve the short-range goal of cutting losses and the long-range goal of establishing a healthy-enough business to be able to spring back when the economy begins to grow again.

Where to trim: Don't be quick to just cut overhead—like public relations. When you total the dollar savings, you'll probably realize the net savings are relatively small. *General rule:* Even a small percentage cut in production cost will produce a big dollar difference; whereas a big percentage cut in administration will produce only a small overall reduction.

LAYOFFS. Prepare a quick audit on the real cost of firing. Not only must you assess contractual obligations (severance pay) but include the hidden costs (such as higher unemployment insurance) and the morale consequences. Balance that against the cost when you'll probably have to hire the staff back. In fact, determine if certain skills will be available at all.

When cutting people, keep an accurate head count—company-wide. *Reason:* People selected for layoff have a way of turning up in other departments, so that the net impact on the staff reduction isn't what you anticipated.

General rule: Audit the cutbacks and improvements to be sure that what you called for was actually done. Cutbacks are hard; expect managers to seek loopholes to save friends.

TAKE INVENTORY. Be sure to check

your backlog of orders — especially if your lead time is long. How much of the business on the books is *real* — not double- or triple-orders by customers uncertain of delivery times? Check the health and credit-worthiness of each customer. A big order from a near-bankrupt customer is much worse than no order at all. Be alert to salesman's natural proclivity to inflate his customer's credit-worthiness. Set stiff credit standards — and require salesmen to double-check each customer. *Better:* Develop backup checking system.

Reassess inventory levels: Can they be adjusted downward? Readjust buying levels and turnover rates.

CASH MANAGEMENT. In a recession, cash is the name of the game. Do everything prudent to keep your balance sheet healthy. Keep cash moving and working. Idle money is costly.

Aim: Slow payouts, and speed pay-ups. Don't bother to establish a bank account in Montana to take advantage of the "float" for payment of an invoice in New York. Saving is there, but it's minimal compared with headaches and other costs — such as need to leave extra cash in that Montana account.

Two general rules:

1. Take advantage of all deadlines on bill payments. Get off the once-a-month or twice-a-month payment schedule, and pay at the deadline.

2. Get *your* invoices out on time. Unbelievable number of firms wait weeks, because of slow billing procedures, to get invoices out after shipment. *Aim:* Same-day billing. Cash flow improvement is sizable.

Tighten, if competitively possible, the deadlines on receivables. Add late charges (1.5% a month is common), but be sure that charge is clearly shown on *original* order.

Overall advice: Don't panic; don't slash budgets indiscriminately. This is the time for prudent actions.

Source: J. Thomas Presby, partner, Touche Ross & Co., 1633 Broadway, New York 10019.

ALTERNATIVE TO CUTTING BACK ON R&D

Alternative to cutting back on R&D: Consider joint research program with a company in the same or related field. If your lawyer has doubts about legality of joint program, ask him to get a business review letter from Antitrust Division.

As a practical matter, the only companies that get into trouble with the trustbusters are the very big companies with substantial market power — and only when they try to prevent each other from getting an innovative edge or to protect themselves against an outsider getting a foothold.

If your lawyer has any doubts about the legality of a joint R&D program, ask him to get a business review letter from the Antitrust Division in Washington.

LONG-TERM TAKEOVER DEFENSE

When common-share prices sag below book value, attractive companies are especially vulnerable to takeovers.

Managements hope that in a pinch they can count on a few friends among major holders.

But the chairman of a very attractive Midwest company has no fears on that score. He relies on this preventive defense: Instead of studiously ignoring important shareholders to discourage any interference in the running of the business—a common management hang-up—this chief executive keeps a personal address-and-phone file of about 300 VIPs (1,000 shares or more). He phones or writes them several times a year on an essentially social basis.

Though VIP stockholders receive the same financial reports as other shareowners, their proxy materials always come with a return envelope marked to the attention of the chairman (instead of the secretary). *Result:* He has a better chance of support against outside challengers.

It may take years to cultivate this kind of personal, nonbusiness relationship, *but it's never too late to start!*

DEFENDING AGAINST TAKEOVERS DURING DOWNTURNS

Recessions and bear markets make many companies vulnerable to takeover bids via tender offers. The company whose stock price is way down, whether its earnings are down or not, may be an especially good target. Its unhappy shareholders aren't likely to stick with management.

Sec. 13(d) of the Securities Exchange Act provides that, within 10 days after a person acquires more than 5% of a company's stock, he must file a schedule 13D with the company, the SEC, and the stock exchanges where the stock is traded. This calls for detailed information about the person filing the schedule, the source of funds, the purpose of acquisition, interest in the company, and other matters.

Often, before a tender offer is made, the intending offerer will go about acquiring up to 4.9% of the stock of the target company. Once this is done, he will ready himself to launch the tender offer the instant his acquisitions pass the 5% limit. In this way, it is hoped, the battle will be over and the war won before the target company knows what hit it.

HEED EARLY WARNINGS. To defend against such a blitzkrieg, an early-warning system should be developed. This involves a careful watch by all management for signs of unusual, unexplained stock activity, along with a daily review of transfer sheets and the list of shareholders.

At the same time, a plan for immediate communication with shareholders should be worked out that can go right into action when needed.

LONG-TERM DEFENSE. Best defense against such a blitzkrieg involves long-term defense measures designed to make the company an unlikely target for attack, no matter how attractive the price of its stock may be at any point in time.

Some prime possibilities:
• Change certificate of incorporation to provide for cumulative voting for directors, classifying directors (each class of stock to have its own direc-

tors).
- Stagger the election of directors.
- Limit the persons entitled to call a special meeting of shareholders.
- Require high voting percentages to effect a merger.

Other long-term defensive moves:
- Long-term employment contracts with management.
- Negotiating loan agreements that permit the lender to call the loan on a change of management.
- Cultivating better shareholder relations through better communications and techniques, such as offers of company products on more favorable terms than available to the general public.

WHEN UNDER FIRE. Once an attack is under way, other types of defenses may be employed. Common technique: *Cry antitrust.* Maintaining that Schedule D should have disclosed that the acquisition might involve a possible antitrust violation. If this technique is to succeed and result in a preliminary injunction against the tender offer, it must be rooted in economic and legal reality.

CHECKLIST FOR THE DEFENSE.
- Target company's repurchase of its own securities in an attempt to nullify the premium being offered.
- Issuance of additional shares through private placements.
- Declaring a substantial stock dividend to all shareholders of record a few days after the expiration of the tender offer.
- Arrange a friendly merger, usually prearranged.
- Prearranged acquisition that is incompatible with the offerer's operation.

PROTECTING TRADE SECRETS

Key points to remember when setting up procedures with employees in protecting your trade secrets:

Definitions: A trade secret is "any formula, pattern, device, or compilation of information which is used in one's business, and which provides an opportunity to get an advantage over competitors who don't know it or use it." *Vital element:* In order for it to be considered a trade secret, the company *must treat it* as a secret and must make its secret status known to employees and others in the industry.

Employment contract: Obviously desirable to have a contract with anyone who could have knowledge of trade secrets, to the effect that use of these secrets or their disclosure outside the company is forbidden.

Restrictive covenants: For key people, use covenants reasonably restricting competition on termination of employment. Their enforceability—and what may be considered "reasonable" —may vary from one state to another. Strive for an element of mutual fairness to minimize the risk of having the covenant declared invalid and unenforceable as "unreasonable." The *not-too-restrictive* restrictions are tricky. *One possibility:* A provision which would allow the former employee some income while limiting—but not eliminating—his competitive activities. Another approach would provide for release from the covenant if the competing new employer gives assurance he won't use this material.

Dealing with outsiders: In dealing with independent contractors and other outsiders who may have access to secrets, seek a contractual agreement against use and disclosure.

This is critically important when dealing with prospective licensees of the secret or purchasers of the business. Spell out the rights and duties of the parties before providing access. Bear in mind the possibility that sometimes access to secrets may have antitrust ramifications. Access may be considered equivalent to acquisition.

Hiring and firing: Familiarize employees with their trade secret obligations when they're hired. Be especially wary when hiring ex-employees of a competitor. *Reason:* If that employee possesses the competitor's secrets, *your* company may be liable for *wrongful appropriation.*

When an employee leaves, make him aware of his legal obligation not to disclose trade secrets he's acquired in the course of employment with you.

USE INDEXING FOR CONTRACTS

Indexing has been proposed as a *government* technique for dealing with inflation. While the idea is being mulled for *national* use, managers should consider it for *their own use.*

Example: You have a long-term contract to supply a component—but the prices of many of its inputs (raw materials) are changing dramatically. Inflation is driving up some costs, and recession may be trimming others.

What to do: Develop an indicator or a series of indicators that closely reflect these changes. It could be the Labor Department's wholesale price index, or it could be the actual posted price of one or a series of key commodities.

The *buyer* of the product, naturally, has a different problem: He must assess not only the cost changes of your raw materials but also his future sales of a product that contains the component. He's looking for some yardstick to measure the impact of recession, say.

Merging the two needs (between buyer and seller) may take some negotiation in developing a useful index, but it's frequently worth the trouble because it reduces the uncertainty on prices.

What to do: If you agree on a single indicator, the next step is simple—use the indicator to "index" your price either up or down. Thus, if the selected index moves up from 100 to 120, your price increases by 1.2. If, on the other hand, more than one indicator is used, each one has to be weighted by how it impacts the total cost of the component, and the price will be proportionately indexed by all.

DEALING WITH CONTRACTS DURING PERIODS OF SHARP COST INCREASES

Many businessmen with firm contracts with suppliers agree to contract-breaking price *increases.* They do so for practical business reasons, waiving what they've regarded as their legal right to insist on performance of the contract to the letter.

It may be that in many instances the supposed firm contract wasn't that firm, and their right to insist on the contracted price was far from absolute. The Uniform Commercial Code (Sec. 2-615) provides that a seller may be *excused* from his contractual obligations under a sales contract if performance "has been made impracticable by the occurrence of a contingency, the non-occurrence of which was a basic assumption on which the contract was made" unless he has "assumed a greater obligation."

EXTREME AND UNFORESEEN. So far, courts have given this provision a restricted interpretation, but it is clear that, when drafted, a more liberal construction was intended. To excuse contract performance, the cost increase must be "extreme" and "unforeseen." There is little doubt that some cost increases have been extreme, but there's question whether they were unforeseen.

There may be situations which, while not so serious as to excuse performance entirely, may require price adjustments in good faith. That many businessmen have been agreeing to price adjustments may be taken as evidence of a "commercial standard" calling for them, at least in cases where the cost increases have been "extreme" (probably 100% or more).

Recommendation: From the seller's standpoint, the prudent course would be:

• Try for a price escalator clause geared to specific cost increases affecting the product sold.

• To negate any express or implied obligation to deliver if costs exceed a fixed or determinable level.

The buyer, on the other hand, if he really wants to count on a fixed price over the long term, without any "equitable" adjustments, must get the seller to expressly agree to deliver regardless of cost increases. However, unless there is some reasonable ceiling on the seller's obligation, even that might not do the trick.

GETTING OUT OF A LEASE

It may be necessary to get out of a lease when space projections turn out to be more optimistic than actual needs. *Some ways to get out:*

The sublet: This is the cleanest method — that is, to rent the space to another tenant. To do this requires some smart negotiating when the primary lease is drawn up.

Key point: Every lease should contain carefully formulated sublet provisions. Rarely will the landlord resist that. But he will insist on the right to screen the prospective tenant. Be sure the provision to screen contains a section that says any rejection be based on "reasonable" grounds. The word "reasonable" is purposely vague.

Typical situation: If the landlord gets sticky about what is reasonable, the leverage is on the side of the tenant. He can claim the landlord is acting in an arbitrary way and, as a result, refuse to pay rent for "just" cause. He can then move — inviting the landlord to sue if he wishes. Usually, the landlord accepts the sublet tenant at that point and the primary tenant wins by default.

If landlord wishes to push the suit, the tenant's greatest potential loss is the payment of rental dollars during the disputed period. Courts generally don't saddle the tenant with the landlord's legal expenses for the suit.

Important phrase: Landlord must decide on suitability of the tenant *without unreasonable delay.* Rarely is this provision in a sublet section. It is a good idea to include it.

The cancellation clause: Many landlords will accept a tenant cancellation clause at specific periods in the lease. Say you take a 10-year lease. You could negotiate to have the right to cancel any time after the third year by paying some pre-arranged penalty, which usually gets smaller each year. That clause should be used in conjunction with the sublet clause, since if you are able to sublet the space you should not have to pay the cancellation penalty.

Walking away: If the space is rented for a business operation that is physically separate from the main office (in another city or another part of town), set up a subsidiary to rent the space. Retail chains do this all the time.

In general, if the space is rented by a *new* company (even though it's owned by a well-known parent), the landlord will request that a security deposit accompany the lease. The size of that security will depend in part on the amount of site preparation needed for the new tenant.

Should the tenant have to withdraw early, all he has to do is move and leave the security deposit behind. The ethics of such a move are in the gray area, and few major corporations would want to use this device, but it's something that one should be aware of.

Leveraged ploy: If a landlord becomes unreasonable, a smart tenant brings in any subtenant, even a less than desirable one. If the landlord rejects the subtenant, the *primary* tenant cries "foul," and uses that as justification for claiming the lease has been breached by the landlord. He refuses to pay rent and notifies the landlord of plans to move out.

Once the landlord realizes this ploy is being used, he may back down and try to bring in a more acceptable tenant or let the primary tenant bring in someone else. Timing and bluff are critical elements of this ploy.

Another trap: Be sure the original lease states the type of business to be conducted in the space in the most *general* way. *Reason:* If the statement is too specific, the landlord may use that as a way of rejecting a subtenant.

THE ALTERATION CLAUSE. Be sure this clause is flexible. If not, the landlord may bar even minor redecorating for the new tenant.

AIR CONDITIONING. Decide on your needs before going into lease negotiations. *Reason:* If you close a deal and then seek to amend it on extended hours for air conditioning, you'll often find it difficult to get a fair arrangement.

INSTITUTIONAL OWNERS. Frequently, when a building is owned by an institution (bank or insurance company) the lease is very tough and inflexible. *But don't be put off by that.* The institutional landlord seldom enforces any of those harsh provisions. In fact, in practice, institutions are the best, most flexible landlords. *There are no guarantees:* Some institutional owners may enforce the lease strictly and you always have the risk of the building being sold to a new, tough landlord. If you go into an institutional building with such a tough lease, be sure that at least you have the right to make some modification in the event the building is sold.

LAWYERS AND NEGOTIATIONS. Be wary of letting your lawyer handle the financial provisions of the lease. Even those with good real estate knowledge may not understand the intricate cost calculations such as escalation. In addition, they are rarely familiar with specific market conditions. In this area, be guided by a good real estate broker.

BROKER VS. CONSULTANT. A delicate and difficult area. Remember, by definition, even if you seek out a broker to find a rental space for you, his allegiances are mixed: Between his economic gain (he gets paid only when a deal is consummated), the landlord (his client), and you (his customer).

A better way: Select a broker as a consultant. Offer to pay him a fee—closed deal or not—based on hours worked.

Some consultants use this ploy with a landlord to save the client money: A consultant retained on a fee basis, upon becoming entitled to a brokerage commission from the landlord by written agreement, may then disclose his consulting relationship to the landlord. He then insists that, as a condition of the deal, the commission be put back into the deal. And that it be done by cutting the rental cost or by using it to pay for part of the construction.

NEGOTIATING FEES WITH YOUR LAWYER

Resist demand for a fixed rate per hour for the time worked by the law firm. Different tasks should be priced differently. Reviewing a file should cost less per hour than going to court. Handling an emergency that entails rearranging a lawyer's schedule should be more expensive than doing research that's not time-pressured.

Important: Lawyer should be paid for every hour worked—even when he gives a quick decision on the phone. But the rate should depend on the task. *Also:* Ask that bills be accompanied by a complete breakdown of work accomplished. Don't be satisfied with a slip of paper that says, "For services rendered in March."

MINIMUM WAGES

Many businesses can get around the minimum wage law. Students can work at part-time jobs and earn 85% of the minimum wage ($3.35/hr.), and as much as 40 hours a week during vacation periods. A one-page form must be submitted to the government for the exemption and it must be shown that older workers won't be eliminated.

Details are available from *local* Labor Department offices or Wage & Hour Division, Labor Dept., 200 Constitution Ave., N.W., Washington, D.C. 20210.

UNIONS

MANAGEMENT STRATEGIES

LANGUAGE DURING A UNION DRIVE

A union begins signing up your employees, and you'd like to tell them they're better off as they are. How far can you go?

To begin with, the Taft-Hartley Act specifically protects your right to free speech in a labor organizing situation, as long as you don't threaten reprisals, promise benefits for shunning the union, or coerce anyone.

But the National Labor Relations Board and the courts are less indulgent with employers who speak out after an NLRB election has been ordered. Many seemingly harmless statements of fact may then sound like self-fulfilling prophecies.

• It may be all right to say unions have driven business away from an area, but the same statement made during a campaign may sound like a threat to move if the union is certified. To predict something will happen, when you have the power to make it happen, is always risky.

• If you want to make the point that strikes seldom recover for workers what they lose, be careful not to hint that you will not grant increases to compensate for lost time or for union dues.

If a union comes knocking at your door, you will obviously need a lawyer who knows his way around the maze of rules and regulations. Meanwhile, it will be a good idea to caution supervisors against making remarks that will result in an overturned election even if the majority of the employees vote "no union."

DON'T EXAMINE UNION ORGANIZING CARDS

What to do when a union organizer shows up with a fistful of cards, allegedly signed by your employees, and asks for recognition: Don't examine them, and don't engage in preliminary bargaining over a contract, *unless* you intend to recognize the union. *Request a supervised secret ballot election instead.*

The National Labor Relations Board recently ruled that a company committed itself to recognition of the union by manager's actions alone.

When the boss was shown membership cards, he riffled through them briefly, and then casually asked what sort of contract the union might want. Discussion ensued. Then the employer said he would not recognize the union on the mere showing of cards.

The union filed an unfair labor practice charge with the NLRB, and won. *Reason:* The Board was convinced that refusal to bargain was based not upon genuine doubt that the union represented a majority of employees, but rather a reluctance to yield to economic demands.

FIGHTING UNIONIZATION

Unions are losing ground in National Labor Relations Board elections. They won only 50% in 1979 compared with 62% a decade earlier. Encouraged by the success of Eastman Kodak, IBM, and Texas Instruments in keeping unions at bay, many companies are now hiring consultants to teach their plant managers what to do and what not to do when a union comes knocking at the door. *What to do:*

• Never let pay become an issue. Respectable raises are less expensive than unionization, which can add 20% to operating costs.

• Beat union organizers to the punch. Make sure grievance procedures work the way they're supposed to. *Example:* Prod the insurance company if employee benefit claims aren't being processed promptly.

• Tell employees point blank not to sign union recognition cards. This tactic is surprisingly successful. Many people sign the cards without knowing what they are.

• Emphasize that a union is a business like any other, looking for a place to invest its organizing money.

• Show workers that the company can do as much for them as any labor union, *without collecting dues.* (Whatever the company has to do will cost it less than unionization.)

STATE COURTS CAN BE USED TO CONTROL UNION ORGANIZERS

Federal law controls most labor disputes and state courts can't interfere.

But two exceptions exist: (1) Activity that is peripheral to the concerns of federal law; and (2) conduct that is deeply rooted in local feeling and responsibility and not expressly covered by federal law.

A recent case held that a state's law of trespass falls into both of these exceptions. *Non*employee union organizers were enjoined from trespassing on the employer's premises in an attempt to sign up employees. The ruling stood, even though one of the union's claims of unfair labor relations was pending before the National Labor Relations Board.

Comment: This decision quite clearly offers the employer a useful weapon in resisting union organization in situations where victory by the union isn't inevitable.

May Department Stores Co. v. Teamsters Union Local No. 743, Ill. Sup. Ct., 9/20/76.

RESTRICTIONS ON OVERTIME

A worker's physician told him to accept no overtime work because of his heart condition. But the company continued to assign overtime to him, and he willingly accepted it. However, a new manager, in going through the worker's file, noticed the health restriction, and ordered the overtime assignments stopped. Ultimately, the worker was laid off because there were no jobs available that did not *require* overtime. *Union protest:* The worker was really laid off because he had filed safety complaints against the company. The health restriction was merely a pretext. *Arbi-*

trator's decision: The company had acted properly.
Simplex Industries, Inc., and UPIU Local 1008.

Maternity leaves must be treated just like any other temporary disability leaves. One employer violated the Civil Rights Act by requiring employees returning from maternity leave — but not others — to accept demotions if their jobs had been filled.

WORKING WITH A UNION

UNIONS AND WHAT TO DO ABOUT THEM

DO NOT:
- Make a threat *of any kind* based on the employees' interest or activity in the union, or in reprisal against union success or showing.
- Promise any benefit *of any kind* related to employees' union activities, or to the outcome of the union's success or failure.
- Discriminate against any employee based on union membership or interest.
- Ask employees about their interest in union membership.
- Spy on employees or on union meetings.
- Impose work rules which prohibit union solicitation before or after work, or in any free periods (lunch or coffee breaks).
- Impose work rules which operate unequally in regard to union solicita-

tion as opposed to other forms of solicitation (charity, social, etc.).
- Bar union solicitors from company property where the plant is isolated and there is no other reasonable means of access.
- Falsify, overstate, or understate *factual* matters: wages, working conditions, fringe benefits, said to prevail internally or elsewhere.
- Distribute or exhibit inflammatory material.
- Engage individual employees or groups in union discussions, particularly in "places of authority" (official's offices, etc.).
- Address employees on company time and company property one minute beyond the start of a 24-hour period before the representation election is held.
- Accept an invitation to count a packet of cards delivered by a union delegation which purports to show that a majority of your employees favors the union. Insist on an *election*. This helps employees who may have had second

thoughts, or have been coerced. *Other advantages:* You can challenge votes and question improper ballots. And in the preelection period, you can electioneer, persuade, and combat false propaganda. *Remember:* The only elections the NLRB is legally obliged to recognize are those conducted under its own auspices.

YOU CAN:

• Communicate to employees by letter or speech, if you prefer, on company time and on company property. Just be sure to finish speeches a full 24 hours before the polls open. The 24-hour rule does *not* apply to: (1) letters, leaflets or other written material, and (2) speeches on other than company property where no compensation is given for attendance and attendance is purely voluntary.

• Express your personal views concerning unions, and state your opinions concerning individuals connected with the union (but *not* any of your own employees).

• Compare the advantages your employees enjoy with those of employees in union shops.

• Scotch the lie about the union's promise of job security. Point out that no union can compel you to continue obsolete or uneconomical jobs, that the union has no way of perpetuating unnecessary personnel, that the union's claim is a deliberate deceit.

• Show (if you can) how your fringe benefits exceed those enjoyed by union members in other plants or, if not, that you put the cost of such plans into take-home pay (if it is the case).

• Refer to employees who have had bad union experience, and suggest that other employees talk to them directly.

• Discuss the union's dues, initiation fees, assessments—and ask them to figure what they're getting for their money.

• Tell employees that they are free under the law. They are free to join a union—and free to have nothing to do with it.

• Discuss the "union security" clause in every union contract. It *doesn't* mean "job security." It *can* mean compulsory union membership, with dues, assessments.

• Tell employees that employers may not disturb contract wage scales by raises or bonuses for good performance, without union permission.

• Explain to employees that you have no way of telling whether union restrictions will put you out of business.

• Tell them that the union itself neither *gives* nor promises the members anything; it simply tries to compel the employer to do so.

• Tell them that employees have a right to strike, but employers have the right to continue to operate, and, under some circumstances, to *hire* permanent replacements for strikers. The union cannot, by law, force those replacements to be fired.

Source: *Labor Unions,* by I. Herbert Rothenberg and Steven Silverman (Management Relations, Inc., Executive Plaza, Elkins Park, Pa. 19117).

When *past practice* may bind a company, even though the right is not written into a contract:

• Past practice is clear and consistent. (Occasional lapses won't count if they can be explained.)

• Practice is known *generally* to management and union.

• Practice is in effect long enough to create expectation it will continue.

SUBCONTRACTING AND THE UNION

Whether a company can move to "the outside" without violating a union contract is questionable. Most labor contracts are silent on this question, and that is because the differences in attitude are so enormous that no contract would be concluded if management and labor tried to get agreement in writing. And so it's left for arbitrators to rule on specific subcontracting issues.

Here are the rules a leading arbitrator promulgated after studying every decision on record:

Under a contract which neither expressly permits nor forbids subcontracting, an employer will be permitted (by arbitrators) to buy components rather than make them if:

• The action wasn't intended to, nor did it in fact, deprive a substantial part of the bargaining unit of jobs.

Example: A company that used to make its own wooden skids in the shipping department decided to buy metal-reinforced skids from a company specializing in that product. Only a few employees were affected, none was laid off.

• The company has subcontracted in the past without objection by the union.

Example: A newly elected local union administration decided to challenge the company's practice of subcontracting. Past practice clearly favored management, but the union argued that it couldn't be bound by what a previous administration had wrongfully

tolerated. Past practice prevailed.

• The motive is purely economic, not affected by an intention to damage the union's standing or deprive employees of the benefits due them according to the contract.

Example of a case in which this wasn't so—and management lost: After agreeing to a higher premium rate for weekend work, management decided to avoid most of the weekend assignments by hiring an outside firm for certain maintenance and policing activities which bargaining unit employees had done.

PRODUCTION WORK BY FOREMEN

Union contracts usually bar foremen and supervisors from doing ordinary production work, except in the case of emergencies or for instruction. Most of the time, the restriction is easy for management to live with, because the employer, too, wants foremen to supervise, not spend their time at menial tasks.

But during slack periods, it often happens that a piece of work comes along requiring the skill of a person who isn't immediately available. It seems to make sense for the foreman to do the work himself.

If the union files a grievance, the remedy may be four hours of pay to the worker who should have been called in, unless the employer can get away with the argument that the amount of work involved was *de minimis*—too trifling to be concerned about.

497

The trouble with the *de minimis* argument is that unions are very sensitive to losing work to foremen, especially when members are on the lay off list. Arbitrators share their sensitivity. This is particularly true where foremen cross the barrier repeatedly. Arbitrators are then inclined to fashion the most costly remedy they can, hoping to deter erosion of bargaining units and job security.

In any event, there is no profit, even in a management victory, when costs of arbitration are taken.

UNION RESIGNATION GUIDELINES

Management can help workers who have lost faith in their unions to resign. It's against the law for a company to solicit union resignations, but the National Labor Relations Board has recently spelled out just how far management can go without crossing the line into illegality.

The technique is to provide all members of management—particularly the *lowest* level—with information on just how workers can quit their unions. Management can give that advice *only if asked*. Then the employee can be advised to simply write a letter of resignation to the union.

Don't let management mail the resignation letters for the workers or provide stamps or stationery. Workers are most likely to *want out* during a long strike but worry about being fined by the union. If they resign *first*, the fines can't stick.

WAGE RATES AFTER A TAKEOVER

No second thoughts about maintaining wages and hours after taking over a business after the new management has gone along for several weeks without a change. A unilateral reduction after such a period amounts to an unfair labor practice.

It's a different story if the reduction is made simultaneously with the takeover.

Comment: The concept involved here appears to be somewhat like the so-called doctrine of *estoppel*, which is frequently evoked in many different kinds of transactions. *The basic idea:* If you misrepresent or conceal material facts by acts, words, or silence—knowing that the party you're dealing with will rely on what you've said or done—and he does so rely, you will be barred from adopting a different course.

Zims Foodlines, Inc. v. NLRB, C.A. 7, 495 F. 2d, 1131, 1974.

If a newly hired worker isn't working out, don't let him stay beyond the probationary period (usually 30 days) unless you and the union understand that you are *extending the trial period*, not conferring job security. Don't go into too many details about dismissal. It usually isn't subject to arbitration unless facts are alleged that are questionable.

BARGAINING EFFECTIVELY

BARGAINING TO WIN

Major reasons managers often come off second-best at the union bargaining table: Lack of negotiating know-how, lack of preparation, and underestimating union strength.

Just boning up on bargaining table strategies and tactics can help you avoid disasters.

• Approach each issue and situation as if it had never come up before. In essence, it hasn't—simply because conditions change, and approaches have to, too.

• Aim for the forest, not a single tree; for a settlement within a *predetermined range*, not for one that pins the union to the wall. If you corner your opponent, you're probably in for a fight. Give the union a chance to negotiate within a range, so you both have a chance to win.

• Keep company demands realistic. But *always* ask for more than you expect to get. You may get more than you expected.

• Introduce several issues at a time. This gives you a chance to make gains on one in return for concessions on another.

• Don't press demands that aren't important to the company. The union may only accede to extract some big concessions from you.

• Don't make hasty, ill-considered, last-minute concessions you'll regret later. The union may be looking to get its foot in the door in a small way to press for a bigger concession on that issue next time.

• Be credible. Admitting to an outright error, giving up a weak position, can disarm your opponents, make it easier for them to admit when *they're* wrong. And don't say *never* to a demand when you really mean *not now*. If you have to give in later, you'll look pretty foolish.

• Don't rely on interpreting "body language" (blinking, shuffling papers, other alleged giveaway indications of mood and feeling). Their importance has been highly overrated, and the opposition may even use them to put you on.

• Keep your cool. Explode on issues if you have to. Don't let differences degenerate into open personality conflicts.

• Press for prompt rank-and-file ratification (preferably within 2-3 days), just as soon as you've reached a settlement.

LIMITS TO 'INTEREST ARBITRATION'

When either management or a union wants to negotiate a clause in one contract that binds the other party to submit certain terms of the *next* contract to arbitration (known as "interest arbitration"), that isn't a mandatory subject of bargaining.

Briefly stated, a mandatory subject of collective bargaining under the labor laws is one over which parties must attempt to reach an agreement—usually by making some concessions. On nonmandatory subjects, either party can just say: "No, I won't talk about it," and that's that.

An ingenious union argued that it needed the "peace of mind" of an interest arbitration guarantee in order to bargain effectively for wages, hours, and other conditions of employment—which *are* mandatory subjects of bargaining.

But the National Labor Relations Board said "no" to what amounts to perpetual arbitration of contract terms—and, now, so has an appeals court.

Advice: Management can't demand that the union submit further wage issues—or anything else—to interest arbitration, either.

'SURFACE BARGAINING' PENALTY

According to the Taft-Hartley law, employers are supposed to bargain in "good faith" with unions. Anything short of that is called "surface bargaining" —an evasion of law and an unfair labor practice. Some companies (and unions) have indulged in this forbidden tactic in the hope of exhausting the union's (or company's) treasury and dissipating support through futile "negotiations." The National Labor Relations Board has looked at ways of making the terms

of the law stricter, so that the intent to bargain in good faith can be established more clearly.

In one memorandum, the NLRB's general counsel suggested to the agency's regional directors that it may be appropriate, in such instances, to require the offending party to pay the other's bargaining expenses, which might include salaries and expenses of representatives who wasted time in fruitless sessions.

Acknowledging that the basis for this novel and harsh remedy is "not clearly established in present NLRB law," regional directors were advised to clear it with Washington before acting on the proposal.

Important: The obligation to bargain in good faith doesn't mean you are required to accept particular terms, or even to achieve an agreement. You must bargain to an impasse. That means you must listen to offers, make counteroffers, and *try* to find common ground. That you are still too far apart after your best, honest efforts to conclude a contract isn't, of itself, evidence of "surface bargaining."

Union locals sometimes include on their panel of contract negotiators representatives of *other* locals. Management can *refuse* to bargain with such a panel if there are plans to discuss business strategies that should be kept secret from a competitor (whose workers the outsider represents). That has been the position of the National Labor Relations Board, upheld by the courts (Electrical Workers v. NLRB, USCA, 2nd Cir., 7/11/77).

DISPUTES

FAST ARBITRATION IS LESS COSTLY

Expedited arbitration is coming into vogue in union-management relations. *Aim:* To reduce the costs (a typical "simple" grievance may cost each party over $200, under conventional procedures, not counting time) and to get quicker decisions.

Chief characteristics of *expedited arbitration:*

• A rotating panel of arbitrators is agreed upon in advance. Eliminates the bickering of selecting an arbitrator on a case-by-case basis after a grievance arises.

• Arbitrators agree not to write any opinions, or if one seems necessary, to keep it very brief. Cuts down "study time" for which an arbitrator charges his normal per-diem rate.

• Parties agree in advance to use lesser-known arbitrators. Under standard procedures, they usually want one of the nationally known arbitrators (who are busy and command top fees). Their expertise isn't really needed in run-of-the-mill grievances.

• No transcripts of hearings are permitted. Court reporters are expensive and time-consuming.

The negative side: Some arbitrators feel it is unfair to ask them to hand down decisions without explaining their reasons. Moreover, they say, if no reasons are given, a decision in one case doesn't help parties settle future issues of the same kind without incurring the expense of arbitration.

INTEGRITY OF GRIEVANCE PROCEDURE UPHELD

Management and labor alike can breathe a sigh of relief over a U.S. Supreme Court decision *(Emporium Capwell Co. v. Western Addition Community Organization).* The Court ruled, in effect, that employees who resort to "self-help" instead of the union contract's grievance and arbitration procedure can be discharged. They lose the protection of the Taft-Hartley Act even though, as was the case here, they claim to be trying to vindicate statutory rights as minority employees to nondiscriminatory employment.

The case: Two black employees had complained that their employer was improperly refusing to grant them promotions. The union pressed the case to arbitration, and a first hearing was actually held. But the employees, supported by an outside group, wanted the union to make a "class action" out of their case. When the union chose not to fight along that line, the two picketed the employer. They were warned to desist, and when they refused, discharge followed.

National Labor Relations Board

ruling: Since the union had acted in good faith, the dissidents had to stay within contractual grievance procedure or lose the protection of law. The Supreme Court sustained that ruling.

But note: The decision apparently leaves untouched previous law (the leading case: *Vaca v. Sipes*), which holds that an employee can proceed immediately if the union representing him isn't acting in *good faith*. The union may even show bad judgment in processing, or not processing, a case to arbitration. But it can't act for a discriminatory reason.

OBEY FIRST, GRIEVE LATER

It has become virtually a cliche of labor relations that an employee who thinks a work order is unjust must obey first and file a grievance about it later. The worker who disobeys this rule risks discipline. Even if he should ultimately be found correct, he may be cutting himself off from a remedy.

But there are exceptions. The most obvious is where the worker genuinely believes a safety hazard to exist. Another exception is a case where the worker would suffer severe hardship that cannot be recovered.

Recent case: A union steward obtained permission four days in advance to leave work two hours early to prepare for an election of union officers. On the morning of election day, however, management found it inconvenient to let him go. There were many absentees, and there was no one to take

over his machine. A supervisor therefore told him the permission to leave early was rescinded. The man left early anyway. He was given a five-day suspension, but an arbitrator later reversed the discipline.

Recommendation: Work orders must be reasonable. If there is some way to compensate the worker who was compelled to obey an unjust order, the "work now, file a grievance later" rule can be easily applied. If obedience involves a greater inconvenience to the employee than to the company, expect disobedience to be ruled *justified.*

WILDCAT STRIKE STRATEGY

Most union contracts contain provisions barring strikes over matters that can be settled by grievance procedure. And even where a contract lacks specific language to that effect, a prohibition of work stoppages has often been inferred from the very existence of machinery for settling grievances.

But what are the remedies for the employer when employees nonetheless break the contract by stopping production?

No answer is fully satisfactory. Discipline, including discharge, is, of course, one way of dealing with the situation. But it is seldom possible to fire the entire work force. To pick out the "ringleaders" is risky when one deals with sophisticated union stewards who know how to signal a walkout without incriminating themselves.

Some employers have sought to hit the union with monetary damages, with mixed results. The trouble is that in most instances it is impossible to prove damages; production lost during one week may be made up the next, perhaps with some overtime. A few notable exceptions are on record. One involved The *New York Times*, where the pressmen's union was required by an arbitrator to reimburse the compay for lost newsstand sales. In this instance it was easy to demonstrate that what was lost one day could never be recovered later.

Some comfort in a new decision: There has recently been published an arbitration award in which the employer won not only remedial and punitive damages, but attorney fees as well.

The circumstances were instructive. Employees had walked off the job over a grievance, and the union official, upon arriving at the scene, merely told them they were violating the contract. This, he thought, satisfied his obligations under the agreement. The employer had urged the union official to walk through the picket line as a demonstration of good faith, and as an example for others to follow. He refused. Management pointed chiefly to this when its demand for compensation came before an arbitrator.

The union's defense was that it couldn't be held financially responsible for what wildcat strikers had done, because the stoppage had not been "authorized" by a responsible union leader.

The arbitrator's reply: "A union breaches its contractual duty to undertake every reasonable means to end such a strike where it utilizes only the politics of persuasion to get employees to return to work and cease such strike activities but does not use more forceful measures, such as threats or fines or suspension."

Employers who have encountered difficulties with illegal walkouts (which the union claims it lacks the power to control) might consider demanding contract clauses which spell out exactly what the union must do if it wants to escape liability.

Hint: Checkoff of union dues is very precious to unions. Without it, they incur heavy collection expenses and loss of revenue. A contract clause that discontinues the dues checkoff if the union can't stop rank and file walkouts and disruptions might give union officers the incentive they need to keep their members in line.

MANAGEMENT STRIKE WEAPON

If management expects a strike, it can quite legally train supervisory (and other nonbargaining-unit) employees for emergency assignments without telling the union about its plans.

In a recent case, the union found out about management's action and demanded the names and addresses of the trainees. Management refused to comply and the court and the National Labor Relations Board supported its refusal.

Deciding point: Were the trainees in the bargaining unit? If not, then the union had no right to demand the information.

American Newspaper Guild, Local 95 v. NLRB.

SUBJECT INDEX

SUBJECT INDEX

SUBJECT INDEX

SUBJECT INDEX

SUBJECT INDEX

SUBJECT INDEX

SUBJECT INDEX

SOURCE INDEX

SOURCE INDEX